Computer Crime

International Library of Criminology, Criminal Justice and Penology - Second Series
Series Editors: Gerald Mars and David Nelken

Titles in the Series:

Gender and Prisons
Dana M. Britton

Quantitative Methods in Criminology
Shawn Bushway and David Weisburd

Computer Crime
Indira Carr

Insurgent Terrorism
Gerald Cromer

Criminal Courts
*Jo Dixon, Aaron Kupchik and
Joachim J. Savelsberg*

Crime and Immigration
Joshua D. Freilich and Graeme R. Newman

Crime and Security
Benjamin Goold and Lucia Zedner

Crime and Regulation
Fiona Haines

Recent Developments in Criminological Theory
Stuart Henry and Scott A. Lukas

Gun Crime
Rob Hornsby and Dick Hobbs

The Criminology of War
Ruth Jamieson

**The Impact of HIV/AIDS on Criminology and
Criminal Justice**
Mark M. Lanier

Burglary
R.I. Mawby

Domestic Violence
Mangai Natarajan

Women Police
Mangai Natarajan

Crime and Globalization
David Nelken and Suzanne Karstedt

Surveillance, Crime and Social Control
Clive Norris and Dean Wilson

Crime and Social Institutions
Richard Rosenfeld

The Death Penalty, Volumes I and II
Austin Sarat

Gangs
Jacqueline Schneider and Nick Tilley

Corporate Crime
Sally Simpson and Carole Gibbs

Green Criminology
Nigel South and Piers Beirne

Crime, Criminal Justice and Masculinities
Stephen Tomsen

Crime and Deviance in Cyberspace
David S. Wall

Computer Crime

Edited by

Indira Carr
University of Surrey, UK

ASHGATE

Wherever possible, these reprints are made from a copy of the original printing, but these can themselves be of very variable quality. Whilst the publisher has made every effort to ensure the quality of the reprint, some variability may inevitably remain.

Published by
Ashgate Publishing Limited
Wey Court East
Union Road
Farnham
Surerey GU9 7PT
England

Ashgate Publishing Company
Suite 420
101 Cherry Street
Burlington, VT 05401-4405
USA

Ashgate website: http://www.ashgate.com

British Library Cataloguing in Publication Data
Computer crime. – (International library of criminology,
  criminal justice and penology. Second series)
  1. Computer crimes 2. Compter crimes – Prevention
  I. Carr, Indira
  364.1'68

Library of Congress Cataloging-in-Publication Data
Computer crime / edited by Indira Carr.
    p. cm. – (International library of criminology, criminal justice & penology. Second series)
  Includes index.
  1. Computer crimes – United States. 2. Computer networks–Law and legislation–United States–
Criminal provisions. 3. Data protection–Law and legislation–United States. 4. Computer crimes–
Europe. 5. Computer networks–Law and legislation–Europe–Criminal provisions. 6. Data protection–
Law and legislation–Europe. I. Carr, Indira.
  KF9350.C645 2009
  345.73'0268–dc22

                                                                                        2008030280

ISBN: 978-0-7546-2835-4

Mixed Sources
Product group from well-managed
forests and other controlled sources
www.fsc.org Cert no. SGS-COC-2482
© 1996 Forest Stewardship Council
FSC

Printed and bound in Great Britain by
TJ International Ltd, Padstow, Cornwall

Contents

PART III   INVESTIGATION, JURISDICTION AND SENTENCING ISSUES

PART IV   CYBER SECURITY

Acknowledgements

The editor and publishers wish to thank the following for permission to use copyright material.

Copyright Clearance Center for the essay: Richard W. Downing (2005), 'Shoring Up the Weakest Link: What Lawmakers Around the World Need to Consider in Developing Comprehensive Laws to Combat Cyber Crime', *Columbia Journal of Transnational Law*, **43**, pp. 707–62. Copyright © 2005 Columbia Journal of Transnational Law.

Emory International Law Review for the essay: Lauren L. Sullins (2006), '"Phishing" for a Solution: Domestic and International Approaches to Decreasing Online Identity Theft', *Emory International Law Review*, **20**, pp. 397–433.

Fordham Intellectual Property, Media and Entertainment Law Journal for the essay: Jessica Habib (2004), 'Cyber Crime and Punishment: Filtering Out Internet Felons', *Fordham Intellectual Property, Media and Entertainment Law Journal*, **14**, pp. 1051–92. Copyright © 2004 Fordham Intellectual Property, Media and Entertainment Law Journal and Jessica Habib.

George Mason School of Law for the essays: Christopher J. Coyne and Peter T. Leeson (2005), 'Who's to Protect Cyberspace?', *Journal of Law, Economics and Policy*, **1**, pp. 473–95; Bruce P. Smith (2005), 'Hacking, Poaching, and Counterattacking: Digital Counterstrikes and the Contours of Self-Help', *Journal of Law, Economics and Policy*, **1**, pp. 171–95; Orin S. Kerr (2005), 'Virtual Crime, Virtual Deterrence: A Skeptical View of Self-Help, Architecture, and Civil Liability', *Journal of Law, Economics and Policy*, **1**, pp. 197–214.

John Marshall Journal of Computer and Information Law for the essay: Miriam F. Miquelon-Weismann (2005), 'The Convention on Cybercrime: A Harmonized Implementation of International Penal Law: What Prospects for Procedural Due Process?', *John Marshall Journal of Computer and Information Law*, **23**, pp. 329–61. Copyright © 2005 John Marshall Journal of Computer and Information Law.

John Marshall Law School for the essay: Adrienne N. Kitchen (2002), 'Go to Jail – Do Not Pass Go, Do Not Pay Civil Damages: The United States' Hesitation Towards the International Convention on Cybercrime's Copyright Provisions', *John Marshall Review of Intellectual Property Law*, **1**, pp. 364–82. Copyright © 2002 John Marshall Law School.

Mary Ann Liebert, Inc. for the essay: John McMullan and Aunshul Rege (2007), 'Cyberextortion at Online Gambling Sites: Criminal Organization and Legal Challenges', *Gaming Law Review*, **11**, pp. 648–65. Copyright © 2007 Mary Ann Liebert, Inc.

Preface to the Second Series

The first series of the International Library of Criminology, Criminal Justice and Penology has established itself as a major research resource by bringing together the most significant journal essays in contemporary criminology, criminal justice and penology. The series made available to researchers, teachers and students an extensive range of essays which are indispensable for obtaining an overview of the latest theories and findings in this fast-changing subject. Indeed the rapid growth of interesting scholarly work in the field has created a demand for a second series which, like the first, consists of volumes dealing with criminological schools and theories as well as with approaches to particular areas of crime criminal justice and penology. Each volume is edited by a recognized authority who has selected twenty or so of the best journal essays in the field of their special competence and provided an informative introduction giving a summary of the field and the relevance of the essays chosen. The original pagination is retained for ease of reference.

The difficulties of keeping on top of the steadily growing literature in criminology are complicated by the many disciplines from which its theories and findings are drawn (sociology, law, sociology of law, psychology, psychiatry, philosophy and economics are the most obvious). The development of new specialisms with their own journals (policing, victimology, mediation) as well as the debates between rival schools of thought (feminist criminology, left realism, critical criminology, abolitionism etc.) make it necessary to provide overviews that offer syntheses of the state of the art.

GERALD MARS
Honorary Professor of Anthropology, University College, London, UK

DAVID NELKEN
Distinguished Professor of Sociology, University of Macerata, Italy
Distinguished Research Professor of Law, University of Cardiff, Wales
Honorary Visiting Professor of Law, LSE, London, UK

Introduction

The information technology (IT) revolution in the form of the Internet,[1] a communication medium enabling rapid dissemination of and access to information stored on servers using a computer, a modem, an Internet service provider (ISP) and the World Wide Web, needs no special introduction. It has now become a vital tool for conducting everyday human affairs in many countries, developing and developed. However, major technological innovations always raise important issues: among them the economic, moral and social impact of the technology and the legal framework to establish the rights and liabilities of the various actors involved in the use of that technology. The extent to which a state should intervene in the affairs of those affected by the technology is dependent on a number of factors: the level of the perceived risk, both in the short and in the long term, to a given society by the various actors, including the criminal elements, interests and individuals within that society; the flexibility of the existing legal framework to cope with legal issues that arise in the context of the new technology and its use; the abilities of those within a given society to regulate their affairs in a manner that ensures that legal rights of individuals (or, for that matter, the moral fabric of that society) are not undermined; and the nature of the actors involved in the use of the technology. Policy-makers, legislators and other stakeholders such as non-governmental entities face tough choices. Among the questions they need to address are the following:

- Does the Internet pose problems that are unique to that medium?
- Does it pose special security risks?
- To what extent should the authorities regulate this medium? What form should this regulation take?[2]
- To what extent should dissemination of information using the Internet be monitored?
- Would self-regulation be an adequate means of protecting the vulnerable against exploitation?

On the plus side, the Internet provides a global reach such that people regardless of their geographical location can acquire as well as distribute information as long as they have the necessary tools. It has the advantage of being cheap. Its global reach means new opportunities for growth for the commercial sector. Sellers can advertise their wares and services globally,

---

[1] The Internet is a vast collection of interconnected computer networks that use a protocol known as TCP/IP. The Internet evolved from ARPANET (Advanced Research Projects Network) established by the US Department of Defense. It is a wide area networking system that will survive nuclear attacks. See http://1001.resources.com for further definitions. The World Wide Web is not the same as the Internet. Using a language called HTTP protocol it is a means of disseminating information over the Internet. The Web is also used for various purposes such as e-mail and instant messaging. For further on this, see http://www.webopedia.com.

[2] See Geist (2003) for a review of the different approaches to regulating the Internet, including through code proposed by Lawrence Lessig and Joel Reidenberg.

and buyers, businesses and consumers alike have access to products at competitive prices. Sellers can provide product information, prices and delivery terms, and interested parties can negotiate terms and conclude contracts electronically. Direct access to a potentially large customer base means that sellers do not have to opt for the traditional methods for selling their products – for example, the use of agents to market their products in distant lands. Equally, buyers do not have to go through agents to find suitable manufacturers of the products they require. The IT revolution has created a new means of conducting business electronically, namely e-commerce. The financial and entertainment sectors have also realized the potential of the Internet to provide services such as online banking and online gambling that are instant and uncurtailed by geographical location or time (see, for example, Field, 1997).

On the minus side the Internet is an open network lacking security and so it is open to a variety of abuses. In the 1990s unauthorized access of computers, and the non-availability of computer systems through the introduction of viruses, worms and denial of service attacks[3] were seen to undermine computer security, thus raising the need for criminal law to make the network a safe place to conduct everyday human affairs. Since the 1990s computer crimes have become more sophisticated partly as a result of the realization of the potential of the Internet by criminals for conducting activities ranging from fraud, extortion and blackmail to dissemination of offensive and illegal information. In recent years, we have witnessed, for instance, the growth of identity theft through 'phishing' attacks where users are tricked into divulging details of bank accounts and other personal information for the purposes of fraud; extortion via threats to bring down websites through distributed denial of service attacks; software piracy; and terrorists exploiting the opportunities that the Internet creates for funding their activities (see, for example, Hinnen, 2004).

Securing computer networks from the threat of criminal activity became one of the top priorities of governments in the mid-1990s and remains so to this day. The literature on national laws on computer crime and emerging trends of criminal activity on the Internet has grown steadily over the last twenty years. There are well over three thousand articles on the subject written in the English language and published in national and international academic journals. The task of adhering to the page limit imposed by the publishers made the choice of essays for inclusion in this volume an extremely difficult task and necessitated a selective choice. The selection is intended to give the reader an appreciation of the legal framework for countering cyber crime,[4] the move towards harmonization of the laws on computer crime through an international legal instrument, the issues in respect of investigation and jurisdiction of computer crimes that transcend borders, and non-legal means of countering cyber crime. Since it was not possible to include in this volume all the essays chosen in the initial shortlist, this Introduction concludes with a list of references and further reading for the interested reader to follow up. The extensive references of the essays selected for the volume will also prove a rich source for delving further into the subject matter.

The book is organized into four parts: Part I focuses on the definition of computer crime and emerging criminal activities on the Internet; Part II examines the only international convention aiming to harmonize the laws on computer crime, the Council of Europe Convention on

---

[3]   See Kroczynski (2008) for definition of terms such as viruses and worms.

[4]   'Computer crime' and 'cyber crime' are used interchangeably here.

Cybercrime; Part III highlights issues surrounding investigation, jurisdiction and sentencing; and Part IV looks at ways in which cyber security could be improved.

The Parameters of Computer Crime

Computer crime (also known as cyber crime or net crime) has been variously defined but as yet there is no consensus on its definition. The interpretation of computer crime extends from situations where the computer is the target of the crime (such as in hacking and the spreading of the viruses) to situations where the computer is used as a tool to commit other offences found in traditional criminal law (such as blackmail, fraud and extortion), computer-related economic crime (such as software piracy) and computer-related infringements of privacy (see Sieber, 1998). While it would have been desirable to include essays on all types of computer crime the limited choice in this section was driven by page length.[5]

Richard Downing's essay (Chapter 1) provides a comprehensive legal framework to address computer crime and in this process deals with the issue of definition of terms such as computer crime and network crime. Downing's essay includes substantive and procedural laws in building the framework and also draws the attention of the reader to the Council of Europe Convention on Cybercrime. Chapters 2–4 deal with hacking, phishing and extortion.[6]

In Chapter 2 Brian Hoffstadt, who bases his analysis on US law, is of the view that the law is haphazard when it comes to dealing with the hacker who, for instance, obtains information on a real-time basis through wireless access points.[7] He proposes that a response to protecting against the threats posed by what he terms the 'voyeuristic hacker' needs to be informed by two questions, namely 'what information is worthy of criminal protection and what conduct should be made criminal' (p. 69). Lauren Sullins, in Chapter 3, focuses on the ever-increasing threat of identity theft using phishing attacks and puts forward suggestions that would bring both the private sector and consumers within the fold in the fight against identity theft. She sees co-operation between the private sector and the enforcement authorities, and consumer awareness as vital tools in combating phishing (see also Lynch, 2005). John McMullan and Aunshul Rege's essay (Chapter 4) highlights the challenges and possible solutions for the governance of the online gambling sector by focusing on an emerging threat on the Internet – cyberextortion of online gambling sites where cyber intrusion, destruction and modification of data, and fear are used for the purposes of financial gain.

Harmonization of Computer Crime Laws – The Council of Europe Convention on Cybercrime and the Additional Protocol to the Council of Europe Convention

Many jurisdictions since the 1990s have passed legislation to address computer crime. The problem, however, is that there is no uniformity in the legislation adopted across jurisdictions

---

[5]   For an interesting essay on virtual crimes in virtual worlds, see Lastowka and Hunter (2004–2005).

[6]   Some of the traditional forms of criminal activities now found on the Internet such as child pornography and hate speech are dealt with in Part II on the Council of Europe Convention on Cybercrime.

[7]   For more on wi-fi and wireless hackers (whackers), see Kern (2004).

and this can pose problems when it comes to prosecution because of the borderless character of computer crime. For instance, State X could have made unauthorized access of computers an offence while State Y may not have. An individual located in State Y could access a computer located in State X without authorization. While this access under State X's law is a criminal offence, prosecuting the individual is likely to be difficult since he is located in State Y. It is possible for a state to include an extraterritorial component in its computer crime legislation, as has been done by a number of states such as Singapore and the US (see, for example, Geist 2003). This, however, does not provide a satisfactory solution since cross-border investigation and extradition may be problematic. Against this context it makes sense to harmonize the substantive law across jurisdictions through an international convention which also provides for cross-border investigation and co-operation and extradition.

The Council of Europe responded to this need with its Convention on Cybercrime (COE Convention). The work commenced in 1997 and the final draft was adopted on 23 November 2001. It is the only international treaty on the subject of computer crime and came into force on 1 July 2004.[8] From the beginning, observer nations such as Canada, Japan, South Africa and most importantly the US have participated fully in the negotiations and this inevitably has had marked effects on the shape of the final document. It is also seen as an instrument for global adoption.

As for the historical background, the Council of Europe started work on computer-related crime in the late 1980s and in 1989 published its Recommendation R89(9) on Computer-Related Crime (R89(9)).[9] R89(9) suggested that eight specific types of conduct should be incorporated into the criminal laws of member states: computer-related fraud, computer forgery, damage to computer data or programs, computer sabotage, unauthorized access, unauthorized interception of data transmissions, unauthorized reproduction of a protected computer program, and unauthorized reproduction of a topography. It also suggested four other activities that should be discouraged: alteration of computer data or computer programs, computer espionage, unauthorized use of a computer and unauthorized use of a protected computer program. Since investigation of crime involving information technology poses special problems for enforcement authorities, the Council of Europe started work on this aspect in the early 1990s culminating in Recommendation 95(13) on the Harmonisation of Criminal Procedural Laws Relating to Information Technology (R95(13)).[10] This recommendation includes provisions not only on search, seizure, surveillance and cryptography but also on other aspects such as collection of statistics, training of personnel and co-operation between enforcement authorities.

Casting its net wide, the COE Convention requires signatory states to criminalize a host of activities that, in one way or another, are connected to a computer, computer material, computer operation or a computer system. Offences are categorized into four groups:

---

[8]   CETS No. 185. Text of the convention is available at http://www.coe.int. Ratifications have been received from Albania, Armenia, Bosnia and Herzegovina, Bulgaria, Croatia, Cyprus, Denmark, Estonia, Finland, France, Germany, Hungary, Iceland, Italy, Latvia, Lithuania, Netherlands, Norway, Romania, Serbia, Slovakia, Slovenia, the former Yugoslav Republic of Macedonia, Ukraine and the United States of America.

[9]   1989, Strasbourg, Council of Europe.

[10]   1995, Strasbourg: Council of Europe. The text of this document is also available at http://www.coe.int.

Group 1: Offences against confidentiality, integrity and availability of computer systems (to include unauthorized illegal access to a computer system, illegal interception encompassing eavesdropping, blocking or interfering with the use of a system, import, sale or distribution of devices capable of commission of the offences against the confidentiality or integrity of a computer system or data)

Group 2: Computer-related offences (computer forgery and computer fraud)

Group 3: Content-related offences (offences related to child pornography through the medium of a computer)

Group 4: Copyright-related offences (infringement of copyright as defined in the Berne Convention for the Protection of Literary and Artistic Works 1886, the WIPO Copyright Treaty 1996 and the 1993 TRIPS Agreement involving a computer system).

Offences listed in Groups 1, 2 and 4 are to be found in Recommendation R89(9) on Computer-Related Crime. Group 3 is an important development in the light of the use of the Internet for distribution of offensive material and aims to uphold human dignity by focusing on child pornography. Equally the drafters of the COE Convention seem to have taken R95(13) fully on board, while expecting parties to ensure that in the implementation and application of the COE Convention there will be safeguards in place for the adequate protection of human rights and liberties (Art 15). The COE Convention imparts enforcement authorities to search computer systems and seize information (Art 19); to order service providers (within its jurisdiction) to provide information in respect of the subscriber, such as identity, postal address, billing and payment information (Art 18); to collect traffic data in real time and ask others such as service providers to assist in its collection (Art 20); and to intercept content data (Art 21).

An area that was the subject of much discussion during the drafting of the COE Convention was the provision on criminalizing hate speech on the Internet. Largely due to resistance from the US which does not have laws criminalizing or prohibiting hate speech the relevant provisions were omitted in the adopted text. The Council of Europe drafted the Additional Protocol to the Convention on Cybercrime, Concerning the Criminalisation of Acts of a Racist and Xenophobic Nature Committed through Computer Systems, which was adopted on 28 January 2003 and came into force on 1 March 2006.[11]

Part II begins with Mike Keyser's essay (Chapter 5) which provides an article by article analysis of the COE Convention. It also highlights some of the deficiencies of the procedural provisions – for instance, the extensive powers imparted to the investigating authorities that call into question the protection of human rights and the right to privacy. Carr and Williams (1998, pp. 475–79) in an essay on R95(13) raise their concerns about both the wide powers conferred on investigating authorities requiring the co-operation of those investigated and possible breaches of human rights – for instance, under Arts 6(1) and (2) of the European Convention of Human Rights. Since many of the recommendations made in R95(13) have been adopted by the COE Convention the issues raised in relation to R95(13) resurface. In Chapter 6

---

[11]   CETS No. 189. Text of the protocol is available at http://www.coe.int. Ratifications were received from Albania, Armenia, Bosnia and Herzegovina, Croatia, Cyprus, Denmark, France, Latvia, Lithuania, Norway, Serbia, Slovenia, the former Yugoslav Republic of Macedonia and Ukraine.

Miriam Miquelon-Weismann considers the procedural provisions of the COE Convention and examines the model for due process in that Convention. She finds the model wanting since no minimal standard for due process is provided and the excuse of 'cultural differences' given by the Council of Europe in its Explanatory Memorandum to the Convention for the absence of providing such a standard unjustifiable. In Chapter 7 D.C. Kennedy, after examining the increased police powers imparted by the COE Convention and the privacy issues, argues that the increase in police powers necessitates an offsetting in privacy protection for individuals and that suitable provision for this should have been made in the Convention.

On the substantive side, the two most important departures in the COE Convention from the list of offences found in most national computer crime legislation are offences in respect of copyright and child pornography. The inclusion of the copyright offence within the COE Convention has come under constant criticism since the purpose of copyright protection is largely seen as protecting creativity, and infringements are normally addressed using civil law. In a thoughtful essay Adrienne Kitchen (Chapter 8) raises the issue of whether the creation of the criminal offence in respect of copyright infringement involving a computer system will make serious inroads into deterring such activities since it does not address issues of enforcement. She suggests that the inclusion of issues and consequences of copyright infringement which are largely economic would have more impact if included in the context of a free trade agreement since it would provide a 'practical forum through which laws may be created and effectively enforced in the marketplace' (p. 281). The US-Jordan Free Trade Agreement is provided as a model of how intellectual property rights could be protected. An alternative suggestion put forward is for the drafting of an international convention for copyright infringement in the digital environment.

Chapter 9, by Dina Oddis, examines the COE Convention's provisions on computerized child pornography, the procedural law and the safeguards to protect individual human rights. In a tightly argued section Oddis concludes that, despite criticisms that the COE Convention has not 'adequately attended' to the protection of human rights, the Convention is firmly embedded in the fundamental freedoms and human rights enshrined in the European Convention on Human Rights.

Chapter 10 focuses on the important issue of hate speech. While providing an analysis of the hate speech provisions in the COE Cybercrime Protocol Christopher van Blarcum considers the impact of the Protocol on the US and whether it will have the effect of making the US a safe haven for Internet hate speech. In examining ways to mitigate the US as a safe haven, he suggests, among other solutions, that 'if hate speech becomes a debilitating social problem in the US, a "Constitutional moment" could occur' (p. 374) that may result in a reassessment of the First Amendment which protects free speech.

Investigation, Jurisdiction and Sentencing Issues

Since the Internet is borderless, the enforcement of computer crime laws poses special problems. Investigation across borders is a major issue and so also is the issue of jurisdiction. And where these difficulties have been surmounted and the offender has been apprehended and successfully prosecuted, questions arise in respect of sentencing.

In Chapter 11 Michael Sussman highlights the challenges that computer crimes pose to enforcement authorities – from sufficient laws to punish computer crimes, personnel and resources, locating and identifying criminals, preservation of data and means of obtaining evidence from other jurisdictions,[12] to preservation of evidence and extradition. He also considers the various international organizations working towards finding solutions to these issues. Reference is also made to the COE Convention on Cybercrime, which has extensive provisions on questions such as preservation of data and trans-border searches.

In Chapter 12 the issue of international criminal and civil jurisdiction in cyberspace is explored by Ray August, using examples. He concludes that in respect of international criminal jurisdiction the nexuses of territoriality, nationality, protection and universality used traditionally by courts will apply equally in cyberspace. Since there is a high risk of multiple and conflicting jurisdictional claims in applying the nexuses his view is that there is a strong need to harmonize international criminal jurisdiction in cyberspace through an international convention. Jessica Habib's essay (Chapter 13) focuses on the issue of sentencing computer criminals. Some jurisdictions have indeed taken a tough stance[13] while others have given rather light sentences in the form of community services orders.[14] Habib raises the interesting question of denying computer criminals access to the Internet. Using developments in respect of such bans in the US courts she argues that given the central role of the Internet as a communication medium in modern society the courts need to balance the question of banning Internet use against how the Internet use related to the criminal act committed by the offender.

Cyber Security

Given the threats to the computer environment the question of how this space should be protected remains. Christopher Coyner and Peter Leeson's thoughtful essay (Chapter 14) strongly suggests that an analysis of cyber security requires the inclusion of economic considerations. They make a number of interesting suggestions for increasing cyber security through, for instance, cyber insurance and extending liability to software authors and system operators.

Much has been written about the ineffectiveness of criminal legislation to control criminal activity on the Internet. Besides problems such as low reporting of breaches of computer security by corporations and cross-border issues in respect of investigation, there is also a lack of adequate enforcement personnel. In these circumstances, use of technological means to protect computer systems seems attractive. Firewalls and anti-virus programs are the widely used means for protecting computers and computer networks. However, in March 2004 Symbiot Inc. announced the development of a product that that could not only repel hostile attacks but counter-attack the originators of the hostile attack. In Chapter 15 Bruce Smith examines both the physical and the legal pitfalls of the counterstrike technologies, especially whether such technologies would violate laws on computer crime. Relying on an analogy of the use of spring guns to combat illegal poaching in nineteenth-century England for his analysis, he concludes that unlike the spring guns that proved to be "'remorseless engines,

---

[12]   On trans-border searches see Seitz (2004–2005).

[13]   For instance, Singapore (see Carr and Williams, 2000).

[14]   See, for instance, the following cases in England: *R* v. *Mark Hopkins*, Westminster Magistrates Court (9/8/2007); *R* v. *Joseph McElroy*, Southwark Crown Court (3/2/2005).

[that] sacrificed every thing within their range," twenty-first century digital counterstrike technologies at least hold out the prospect of counterattacks that are clear-sighted, calculating, discriminating, and – if not remorseful – at least compensable' (p. 555). Finally, Orin Kerr's essay (Chapter 16), which questions securing the Internet through self-help, redesigning the architecture of cyberspace and civil liability, provides much food for thought.

Conclusions

There is no doubt that computer crime, be it defined narrowly or broadly, causes both untold human misery and economic harm to organizations. For organizations it can cause reputational loss alongside the financial cost of putting things right when computer systems have been subject to computer attacks. In the event of identity theft it causes individual loss and misery. And through dissemination of illicit images it greatly undermines human dignity and decency and questions basic human values. Computer attacks have the potential to lower the security of a state thus putting lives at danger. In these circumstances it is clear that the question of who is to ensure that the Internet is a safe environment in which to carry on legitimate activities is an important one.

Should it be left to criminal law and governments to bear the burden of making the Internet a safe place? Criminalization of itself is insufficient to increase the safety of the Internet since it is dependent on detection, investigation and successful prosecution. There is only a certain amount a government can do in enforcing its laws due to its myriad of national commitments ranging from education, health and safety to infrastructural support. Other means of protecting this space, ranging from self-help, setting minimum levels of security against cyber attacks for software and hardware manufacturers to setting minimum standards of security to be met by the users, are equally important. As for the dissemination of illegal materials through the Internet, more could be required of the ISP on whose servers racist and child pornography websites are located. It may also be worth thinking further about setting up an international organization to regulate Internet content, a solution put forward by Paul Przybylski (2000). Inevitably all this will raise the cost of using the Internet. Ultimately it is a policy decision, a matter of balancing safety against cost.

References and Further Reading

Barnes, Douglas A. (2004), 'Deworming the Internet', *Texas Law Review*, **83**, pp. 279–329.

Baron, Ryan M.F. (2002), 'A Critique of the International Cybercrime Treaty', *CommLaw Conspectus*, **10**, pp. 263–78.

Bellia, Paula M. (2004), 'Defending Cyber Property', *New York University Law Review*, **79**, pp. 2164–273.

Benoliel, Daniel (2005), 'Law, Geography and Cyberspace: The Case of On-Line Territorial Privacy', *Cardozo Arts and Entertainment Law Journal*, **23**, pp. 125–96.

Brenner, Susan W. (2003), 'Complicit Publication: When Should the Dissemination of Ideas and Data be Criminalized?', *Albany Journal of Science and Technology*, **13**, pp. 273–429.

Brenner, Susan W. (2007), '"At Light Speed": Attribution and Response to Cybercrime/Terrorism/Warfare', *Journal of Criminal Law and Criminology*, **97**, pp. 379–476.

Brenner, Susan W., Carrier, Brian and Henninger, Jef (2004), 'The Trojan Horse Defense in Cybercrime Cases', *Santa Clara Computer and High Technology Law Journal*, **21**, pp. 1–54.

Brenner, Susan W. and Scherwa IV, Joseph J. (2002), 'Transnational Evidence Gathering and Local Prosecution of International Cybercrime', *John Marshall Journal of Computer and Information Law*, **20**, pp. 347–96.

Carr, I. and Williams, K.S. (1998), 'Council of Europe on the Harmonisation of Criminal Procedural Laws Relating to Information Technology (Recommendation No. R 95(13)) – Some Comments', *Journal of Business Law*, pp. 468–84.

Carr, I.M. and Williams, K.S. (2000), 'A Step too Far in Controlling Computers? The Singapore Computer Misuse (Amendment) Act 1998', *International Journal of Law and Information Technology*, **8**, pp. 48–64.

Corbett, Patrick E. (2004), 'Anatomy of a Computer Crime: Awareness of the Problem may Provide a Remedy', *Thomas M. Cooley Journal of Clinical and Practical Law*, **7**, pp. 149–73.

Field, Richard L. (1997), '1996: Survey of the Year's Developments in Electronic Cash Law and the Laws Affecting Electronic Banking in the United States', *American University Law Review*, **46**, pp. 967–1025.

Geist, Michael (2003), 'Cyber Law 2.0', *Boston College Law Review*, **44**, pp. 323–58.

Goodno, Naomi Harlin (2007), 'Cyberstalking, a New Crime: Evaluating the Effectiveness of Current State and Federal Laws', *Missouri Law Review*, **72**, pp. 125–97.

Heller, Ian (2007), 'How the Internet has Expanded the Threat of Financial Identity Theft, and What Congress can do to Fix the Problem', *Kansas Journal of Law and Public Policy*, **17**, pp. 83–107.

Hinnen, Todd M. (2004), 'The Cyber-front in the War on Terrorism: Curbing Terrorist Use of the Internet', *Columbia Science & Technology Law Review*, **5**, available at: http://www.stlr.org/cite.cgi?volume=5&article=5.

Howell, Beryl A. (2004–2005), 'Real World Problems of Virtual Crime', *Yale Journal of Law and Technology*, **7**, pp. 103–22.

Katyal, Neal Kumar (2001), 'Criminal Law in Cyberspace', *University of Pennsylvania Law Review*, **149**, pp. 1003–114.

Katyal, Neal Kumar (2005), 'Community Self-Help', *Journal of Law, Economics and Policy*, **1**, pp. 33–67.

Kenneally, Erin E. (2005), 'Confluence of Digital Evidence and the Law: On the Forensic Soundness of Live-Remote Digital Evidence Collection', *UCLA Journal of Law and Technology*, **1**, pp. 5–40.

Kern, Benjamin D. (2004), 'Whacking, Joyriding and War-Driving: Roaming Use of Wi-Fi and the Law', *Santa Clara Computer and High Technology Law Journal*, **21**, pp. 101–63.

Kroczynski, Robert J. (2008), 'Are the Current Computer Crime Laws Sufficient or Should the Writing of the Virus Code be Prohibited?', *Fordham Intellectual Property, Media and Entertainment Law Journal*, **18**, pp. 817–65.

Lastowka, F. Gregory and Hunter, Dan (2004–2005), 'Virtual Crimes', *New York Law School Review*, **49**, pp. 293–316.

Leeson, Peter T. and Coyne, Christopher J. (2005), 'The Economics of Computer Hacking', *Journal of Law, Economics and Policy*, **1**, pp. 511–32.

Lynch, Jennifer (2005), 'Identity Theft in Cyberspace: Crime Control Methods and Their Effectiveness in Combating Phishing Attacks', *Berkeley Technology Law Journal*, **20**, pp. 259–300.

Marler, Sara L. (2002), 'The Convention on Cyber-Crime: Should the United States Ratify?', *New England Law Review*, **37**, pp. 183–219.

Preston, Cheryl B. (2007), 'WIFI in Utah: Legal and Social Issues', *Utah Law Journal*, **20**, pp. 29–37.

Przybylski, Paul (2000), 'A Common Tool for Individual Solutions: Why Countries Should Establish an International Organization to Regulate Internet Content', *Vanderbilt Journal of Entertainment and Technology Law*, **9**, pp. 927–56.

Roche, Edward M. (2007), 'Internet and Computer Related Crime: Economic and Other Harms to Organizational Entities', *Mississippi Law Journal*, **76**, pp. 639–64.

Seitz, Nicolai (2004–2005), 'Transborder Search: A New Perspective in Law Enforcement?', *Yale Journal of Law and Technology*, **7**, pp. 23–50.

Sieber, U. (1998), *Legal Aspects of Computer-related Crime in the Information Society – COMCRIME-Study*, Prepared for the European Commission (Legal Advisory Board). Available at: www. archividelnovecento.it.

Williams, Katherine S. and Carr, Indira (2002), 'Crime, Risk and Computers', *Electronic Communication Law Review*, **9**, pp. 23–53.

Yang, Debra Wong and Hoffstadt, Brian (2006), 'Countering the Cyber Crime Threat', *American Criminal Law Review*, **43**, pp. 201–16.

Xiaomin Huang, Radkowski III, Peter and Roman, Peter (2007), 'Computer Crimes', *American Criminal Law Review*, **44**, pp. 285–335.

Part I
The Parameters of
Computer Crime

[1]

Shoring Up the Weakest Link: What Lawmakers Around the World Need to Consider in Developing Comprehensive Laws to Combat Cybercrime

RICHARD W. DOWNING*

While many countries have modernized their laws to take into account law enforcement needs to counter the threat of cybercrime, many others are in the process of doing so or have yet to begin. Drawing from the laws of a number of countries and from the provisions of the Convention on Cybercrime (2001), this Article discusses the policy choices lawmakers must make in developing appropriate substantive and procedural laws to combat cybercrime.

* Richard Downing is Senior Counsel at the Computer Crime and Intellectual Property Section, United States Department of Justice, where he participated in the drafting and negotiation of significant revisions to the computer crime laws of the United States in 2001 and 2002. Through a project in the e-Security Task Group of the Asia-Pacific Economic Cooperation (APEC), Mr. Downing has provided assistance to policy-makers considering cybercrime legislation in a number of Asian countries. He also served as the Deputy Chair of the APEC e-Security Task Group from 2003 to 2004. Mr. Downing received a B.A. in Political Science from Yale University and a J.D. from Stanford Law School. Earlier drafts of portions of this Article were presented at a workshop titled, "Legal Frameworks for Combating Cybercrime," in Moscow, August 17–18, 2002, in connection with the 26th meeting of the APEC Telecommunications and Information Working Group. The author would like to recognize Miriam Smolen, then Assistant United States Attorney for the District of Columbia, for her work in developing Part III. In addition, the author would like to thank Aubrey Rupinta for her research and editing assistance.

INTRODUCTION

Today, the exploding use of information systems and networks has caused countries to become increasingly interconnected. In developed countries, computer networks play a major role in how companies do business, how governments provide services to citizens and enterprises, and how people communicate and exchange information. They support critical infrastructures such as electricity and gas, transportation, and banking and finance. By providing easy access to information and benefits, "e-government" improves services to citizens and reduces bureaucratic inefficiencies. The number and type of information technologies have multiplied and will continue to grow, and so have the nature, volume, and sensitivity of information that is moving from place to place.

As in more developed countries, computer networks hold the potential for economic growth and prosperity in developing countries as well. E-commerce increases productivity and allows access to markets in other countries like never before. Small- and medium-sized enterprises in particular benefit from development of this type. Secure computer networks can improve infrastructure reliability, such as by enhancing transportation services and improving the consistent delivery of electricity and natural gas. Moreover, secure networks and favorable laws attract foreign investment in such industries as information processing and software development.

Further, the Internet also holds out the promise of benefits that particularly may assist developing economies. "Telemedicine" may allow doctors to treat patients in remote or rural areas that do not already have access to modern medical care. Similarly, providing educational services over the Internet may allow many to receive training and college degrees who would previously have been unable to obtain them. In sum, providing the right environment for the development of secure computer networks can provide numerous benefits to both developed and developing societies.

Yet with this blossoming potential come new dangers. Criminals and terrorists have recognized the potential of the Internet and have exploited it. Hackers have broken into bank computers, transferred funds to their own accounts, and extorted the banks; criminals use computers and computer networks to make child pornography cheaply and easily and to distribute it over the Internet to pedophiles they may never meet in person; and terrorists and drug dealers use encrypted electronic communications to evade government surveillance. Indeed, even improvements of critical infrastructures through computerization have a dark side: insecure information networks make infrastructures vulnerable to the attacks of hackers and "malicious code" such as viruses and worms. For example, in 1997, one hacker recklessly damaged a telecommunications switch that interrupted service at a regional airport in Massachusetts,[1] and malicious code has caused disruptions

---

1. Press Release. U.S. Dep't of Justice, *Juvenile Computer Hacker Cuts Off FAA Tower at Regional Airport—First Federal Charges Brought Against a Juvenile for Computer*

in train traffic, automated teller machines, and police emergency phone lines.[2]

The threat caused by these crimes is not limited, however, to the direct harms of the crimes themselves: all of the benefits of information networks are at risk if the networks are not safe and secure. If users become unwilling to send their personal and credit card information over the Internet, e-commerce will not flourish. Similarly, citizens will not file their tax returns, bid on government contracts, or use other e-government services if they are afraid to use the networks. Moreover, if a particular country gets a reputation as a haven for Internet crime, consumers and businesses will refrain from interacting with it. For example, the prevalence of fraud by criminals located in Indonesia has caused many online retailers to block Internet Protocol (IP) addresses that originate in Indonesia, affecting online transactions both to and from the country.[3]

So how should a country respond to the threat of cybercrime? To begin with, national governments can promote better network security practices by government agencies, businesses, and the general public.[4] Governments can also promote the sharing of information regarding new security flaws and vulnerabilities so that experts can develop "patches" to counter them and users of all kinds can protect their computers. They can also promote security consciousness among software creators as well as promote the development of security technologies that can detect or prevent criminal misuse of networks. Yet when crime occurs—and it will— law enforcement must have the ability to respond to deter and punish it.

Law enforcement, however, faces a number of challenges in its efforts to respond to these new crimes. The first is a *technical* challenge: computer networks often do not allow for access to the electronic evidence needed to detect and identify criminals. The

Crime (Mar. 18, 1998), *available at* http://www.cybercrime.gov/juvenilepld.htm.

2. *See* Jonathan Adams & Fred Guterl, *Bringing Down the Internet*, NEWSWEEK, Oct. 28, 2003, *available at* http://msnbc.msn.com/id/3339638/; *'Slammer' Worm Could Pick Up Steam Monday*, CNN.COM, Jan. 27, 2003, *at* http://www.cnn.com/2003/TECH/internet/01/26/internet.attack/; Press Release, U.S. Dep't of Justice, *Louisiana Man Arrested for Releasing 911 Worm to WebTV Users* (Feb. 19, 2004), *available at* http://www.cybercrime.gov/jeansonneArrest.htm.

3. *Indonesia Hotbed of Cyber Terror*, THE JAKARTA POST, July 23, 2003, at 13.

4. *See* ORGANIZATION FOR ECONOMIC CO-OPERATION AND DEVELOPMENT, OECD GUIDELINES FOR THE SECURITY OF INFORMATION SYSTEMS AND NETWORKS: TOWARDS A CULTURE OF SECURITY (2002), *available at* http://www.ftc.gov/bcp/conline/edcams/infosecurity/popups/OECD_guidelines.pdf.

second is an *operational* one: law enforcement agencies often do not have the training and equipment needed to collect the evidence that the networks do make available. The third is a *legal* challenge: many national laws neither empower law enforcement to collect electronic evidence nor provide for effective punishment for criminal misuse of computer networks. The attempt to craft a solution to this third challenge is the subject of this Article.

A comprehensive legal structure to combat cybercrime contains several important components. First, it must specify appropriate substantive crimes; that is, it must create penalties for various types of harmful conduct that affect the functioning and integrity of computer networks. A substantive law provision might look like the following: "Anyone who accesses a computer without authorization will be punished with a fine and imprisonment for a maximum of ten years." Second, the legal framework must grant law enforcement authorities the power to collect electronic evidence to solve the crimes. Without this authority, the substantive laws will go unenforced. The following is an example of what a procedural provision might look like: "If a law enforcement officer provides a judge with specific evidence to show that a crime has been committed, the court shall issue an order compelling the disclosure of electronic mail relating to that crime stored by an Internet service provider." Finally, because crimes involving the Internet invariably cross national boundaries, a comprehensive law must allow law enforcement agencies located in one country to participate in international investigations and to collect and share evidence located within the country's borders with law enforcement agencies in other countries.

This Article seeks to detail the components necessary to create effective substantive and procedural laws in order to deter and punish attacks on computer networks and information. It uses the laws of many different countries to illustrate concepts.[5] Where relevant, this Article also presents articles from the 2001 Convention on Cybercrime,[6] because many countries have agreed that the Convention provides the necessary standards for an effective legal

---

5. Although the United States has one of the oldest and most frequently amended computer crime laws, it contains certain flaws and historical anomalies and therefore in many respects does not provide an ideal model for direct duplication. Instead, in drafting computer crime laws, lawmakers should consider the efforts of a wide range of legislatures.

6. *See* Council of Europe, Convention on Cybercrime, *opened for signature* Nov. 23, 2001, E.T.S. No. 185, *available at* http://conventions.coe.int/Treaty/en/Treaties/Html/185.htm [hereinafter Convention on Cybercrime].

framework.[7] The Convention took four years to negotiate and entered into force on July 1, 2004.[8] Its text reveals an enormous amount of discussion and debate from experts from around the world (many of the drafters came from countries outside of Europe, including Japan, Canada, the United States, and South Africa). The Convention achieves three important goals: (1) it sets a baseline standard for the kinds of criminal laws relating to attacks on computer networks that all countries must enact to assure that countries can cooperate in cybercrime investigations; (2) it describes the legal capabilities that law enforcement investigators need in order to gather electronic evidence to enforce these laws; and (3) it creates improved mechanisms for cooperation in international investigations. Thus, the Convention provides an important benchmark for any country in the process of evaluating the completeness of its domestic laws, whether that country signs the Convention or not. Of course, countries can decide to develop legal frameworks that go beyond the Convention on Cybercrime to provide more comprehensive protection against attacks on computer networks and information.

I.   TERMS AND DEFINITIONS

A.   *What Is Cybercrime?*

Terms such as "cybercrime," "computer crime," and "network crime" have no universally accepted definitions. Part of the confusion arising from their use comes from the fact that criminals now use computers in the course of committing almost any crime. The computer's role in an offense, however, can be characterized in one of three ways: as a tool, as a storage device, or as a victim.

1.   Computer As a Tool

First, a computer can be used as a tool for committing criminal activity.   This   category   includes   those   crimes   that   criminals

---

7. *See* Convention on Cybercrime, CETS No. 185, Status, *at* http://conventions.coe.int/Treaty/Commun/ChercheSig.asp?NT=185&CM=8&DF=28/02/05 &CL=ENG (as of February 28, 2005, thirty-two countries had signed the Convention and nine countries had ratified it).

8. Convention on Cybercrime, Summary of the Treaty, *at* http://conventions.coe.int/Treaty/en/Summaries/Html/185.htm.

traditionally have committed in the physical world but that are now occurring with increasing frequency on the Internet as the primary means of completing the crime, such as online auction fraud, the distribution of child pornography and copyrighted software, and money laundering. Criminals also use the Internet in the furtherance of a broad range of traditional crimes that continue to take place in the "real world." Email and chat sessions, for example, can be used to plan or coordinate almost any type of unlawful act, such as the sale of drugs or the commission of a murder, and they have even been used to communicate extortion demands following a kidnapping. For the most part, existing "physical world" laws already govern these kinds of unlawful conduct. But because criminals may use computer networks to commit traditional crimes in new ways, lawmakers should review existing criminal laws to ensure that what is prohibited in the physical world likewise is prohibited in the virtual world.

2.   Computer As a Storage Device

Criminals, like businesses, governments, and individuals, take advantage of the ability of computers to store large amounts of information. Criminals store information when committing a wide variety of traditional crimes, and that information becomes electronic evidence relevant to the investigation of the crime.[9] For example, a drug dealer may store his customer list on his cell phone or laptop computer. Similarly, a kidnapper may type a ransom note on her computer, potentially allowing investigators to link her to the crime. In addition, information stored on a computer may be relevant to solving a crime even where the criminal did not create that information. For example, a fraud investigation into the submission of false invoices for goods or services may depend on the contents of an electronic database maintained by a victim corporation that contains the firm's bills and payments. Use of computers as storage

---

9. Electronic evidence is information that is relevant to a criminal investigation and that is created or stored in digital form. Electronic evidence may be created when, for example, a person types an email or enters data into a database. In addition, computers themselves may generate electronic evidence. This occurs when computer programs create stored logs or files in response to some other activity. Examples of this type of evidence include: bank statements where the software used by the bank calculates sums; phone logs recording phone numbers called or received; and the address logs for electronic communications. In addition, electronic evidence may be the contraband itself, such as images of child pornography or illegally copied software. Electronic evidence can be easily destroyed, deleted, or modified. For example, digital photographs can be altered in ways that may prove difficult to detect. As a result, law enforcement officials must be cognizant of how to gather, preserve, and authenticate electronic evidence.

devices generally does not require the creation of new substantive laws, but the need for electronic evidence may require a country to consider amendments to its laws that regulate law enforcement access to such evidence. Part IV examines such procedural laws in more detail.

3. Computer As a Victim

A computer can also be the target of criminal activity. Commonly called "network crime," this activity involves attacks on the confidentiality, integrity, or availability of computer systems or information.[10] Criminals undertake these attacks to acquire information stored on the victim computer, to control the victim computer without authorization or payment, to intercept communications, to delete or modify data, or to interfere with the availability of a computer or the information it contains. These attacks often result in the theft of information and monetary loss to the owner of the victim computer. Criminal activities included in this category are unauthorized access to a computer, the release of viruses and other malicious code, website defacements, and denial-of-service attacks that impair the availability of computer systems or data. Part III will explore the legal framework necessary to address situations in which the computer is the target of the crime.

B. Definitions of Some Common Terms

The Convention on Cybercrime provides some commonly-accepted definitions of a number of key terms. The following definitions from the Convention on Cybercrime apply to the discussion that follows:

> *computer data* means "any representation of facts, information or concepts in a form suitable for processing in a computer system, including a program suitable to cause a computer system to perform a function."[11]

---

10. A network is any collection of connected computers. A network may be as simple as two computers joined on a local area network (LAN) or may have hundreds or thousands of computers connected by common servers and routers. The Internet is an interconnected network of millions of computers.

11. Convention on Cybercrime, *supra* note 6, art. 1(b).

714   *COLUMBIA JOURNAL OF TRANSNATIONAL LAW*   [43:705

computer system means "any device or a group of inter-connected or related devices, one or more of which, pursuant to a program, performs automatic processing of data."[12]

service provider means "i. any public or private entity that provides to users of its service the ability to communicate by means of a computer system, and ii. any other entity that processes or stores computer data on behalf of such communication service or users of such service."[13]

traffic data means "any computer data relating to a communication by means of a computer system, generated by a computer system that formed a part in the chain of communication, indicating the communication's origin, destination, route, time, date, size, duration, or type of underlying service."[14]

subscriber information means:

any information contained in the form of computer data or any other form that is held by a service provider, relating to subscribers of its services other than traffic or content data and by which can be established:

> a. the type of communication service used, the technical provisions taken thereto and the period of service;
>
> b. the subscriber's identity, postal or geographic address, telephone and other access number, billing and payment information, available on the basis of the service agreement or arrangement;
>
> c. any other information on the site of the installation of communication equipment, available on the basis of the service agreement or arrangement.[15]

In addition, although not explicitly defined in the Convention

---

12.   *Id.* art. 1(a).

13.   *Id.* art. 1(c).

14.   *Id.* art. 1(d).

15.   *Id.* art. 18(3).

on Cybercrime, this Article will use the following definitions:

- *content* means any information concerning the substance, purport, or meaning of a communication.

- *interception* means the acquisition of the content of a communication; it does not imply that the communication is prevented from reaching its destination.

II. GENERAL PRINCIPLES FOR DRAFTING CYBERCRIME LAWS

Computer network technology can change the manner in which individuals commit crimes and the types of evidence that are needed to investigate those crimes. Many judicial systems have discovered that laws created decades ago do not clearly apply to new types of criminality. Moreover, as technological change continues, lawmakers must consider ways in which to draft laws flexible enough to remain effective without the need for further amendments. The following general principles have proven effective in promoting the longevity of statutes and in assisting lawmakers with amending laws to take into account technological change. These principles apply not only to laws criminalizing attacks on computer networks, but also to the wide number of laws that define traditional crimes that computer networks now facilitate.

A. Consistency Between the Physical World and the Virtual World

As a general matter, laws should criminalize a type of conduct uniformly, whether or not a computer network facilitates it. For example, laws should punish with the same penalty a fraud scheme carried out using a letter, a newspaper advertisement, a telephone call—or an email. Similarly, if it is illegal to distribute child pornography through the mail, it should be equally illegal to distribute it over a computer network. If a law criminalizes the theft of trade secrets in the form of paper documents, that law should also cover the theft of trade secrets by unauthorized access to a computer system and the downloading of the information. Indeed, prudent lawmakers should conduct a thorough review of their nation's criminal code to assure that criminal laws drafted before the rise of computer networks cover that same conduct when mediated by a computer network.

A corollary to this rule, however, involves assuring that new modes of criminal activity that did not exist before the rise of the Internet are criminalized by the most analogous traditional law.[16] For example, traditional criminal codes often provide penalties for "stalking"—a course of conduct intended to harass an individual—such as following the person in public, making intimidating or repeated telephone calls, or sending threatening letters. The Internet, however, has created new ways for an abuser to harass and abuse a person with little or no direct contact with the victim. An abuser can create websites or post messages on newsgroups that defame the individual and stimulate others to send harassing or threatening communications to the victim. Similarly, an abuser can sign up to hundreds of email lists in the victim's name, causing the victim to receive thousands of unwanted emails every day and making it difficult to use a particular email account. Most troubling, an abuser can easily post messages pretending to be the victim. One particularly egregious case of this ruse in California involved a forged message posted on a public bulletin board in which the victim appeared to state that it was her fantasy to be raped. The abuser in that case was prosecuted successfully for solicitation to commit rape, but not before several men had attempted to respond to the posting and come to the victim's home to help her fulfill her "fantasy."[17] Lawmakers should thus confirm that existing criminal laws adequately cover these new methods of stalking.

B.   Technological Neutrality

One powerful way for lawmakers to assure that laws treat online and offline conduct uniformly is to draft laws that do not refer to any particular technology. If a legislature decided to ban a particular sort of activity when committed using a home computer hooked up to the Internet, a "technology neutral" strategy would dictate making that same conduct criminal if achieved using a hand-held "personal digital assistant," a cellular phone, or the next generation of electronic gadgets. Similarly, lawmakers should avoid referring to particular sorts of attacks or particular categories of

---

16. One whole category of crimes that did not exist before the rise of computer networks involves attacks on computers themselves. Part III discusses this class of crimes in detail.

17. Greg Miller, *Man Pleads Guilty to Using Net to Solicit Rape of Woman*, L.A. TIMES, Apr. 29, 1999, at C1.

software, such as "viruses" or "worms." Instead, laws describing the conduct that results in a particular harm—in this case making computer data and networks unavailable—will remain efficacious even when five years later, criminals develop a new sort of malicious code that has the same effect.

This drafting strategy applies equally to procedural laws that govern law enforcement's access to electronic evidence. The United States has had to repeatedly amend its laws because legislators had one particular sort of technology in mind when they drafted statutes in the mid-1980s. In 1986, the United States passed a law that allowed law enforcement investigators to gather the source or destination of a communication as it was occurring.[18] However, the lawmakers drafted the law with one particular technology in mind: the telephone. Thus, parts of the statute referred to "attach[ing]" a "device" to a telephone line, and the information to be gathered included the "numbers dialed" by an identified telephone.[19] As time passed, however, collection of this sort of information about cellular phones no longer involved attaching a piece of hardware to a copper wire. Moreover, with the rise of crime on the Internet and the need to gather the non-content portion of electronic communications, courts began to grant orders under this statute to collect the "to" and "from" information in an email header.[20] Yet litigants began to challenge this position,[21] and Congress amended the statute in 2001 to clarify that

---

18. 18 U.S.C. § 3123 (1986), *amended by* USA PATRIOT Act, Pub. L. No. 107-56, § 216, 115 Stat. 272, 288 (2001). This and other U.S. statutes cited below are available at http://www.cybercrime.gov/cclaws.html.

19. 18 U.S.C. § 3123(b)(1)(A); 18 U.S.C. § 3127 (3) (1986), *amended by* USA PATRIOT Act, § 216, 115 Stat. 272, 290 (2001).

20. In a 2000 hearing before the U.S. House Subcommittee on the Constitution regarding, in part, proposed amendments to the Electronic Communications Privacy Act, Deputy Assistant Attorney General Kevin DiGregory stated:

> Law enforcement investigators use such orders [pursuant to 18 U.S.C. §3123 for electronic mail] to collect the "to" and "from" information associated with communications from a particular e-mail account. For example, when a criminal uses e-mail to send a kidnaping demand, to buy and sell narcotics, or to lure children for sex, law enforcement needs to know to whom he is sending messages and from whom he receives them. Current law requires the applying government attorney to certify that the information likely to be obtained through the Order is relevant to an ongoing criminal investigation.

Electronic Communications Privacy Act of 2000, Digital Privacy Act of 2000, and Notice of Electronic Monitoring Act: Hearing on H.R. 5018, H.R. 4987 and H.R. 4908 Before the House Subcomm. on the Constitution, House Comm. on the Judiciary, 106th Cong. (2000) (statement of Kevin V. DiGregory, Deputy Assistant Attorney General, U.S. Dep't of Justice).

21. *See* In re United States of America, Cr. No. 99-2713M (C.D. Cal. Feb. 4, 2000) (McMahon, Mag. J.) (unpublished opinion) (on file with author). *See also* Orin S. Kerr, *Internet Surveillance Law After the USA PATRIOT Act: The Big Brother That Isn't,* 97 Nw.

718   *COLUMBIA JOURNAL OF TRANSNATIONAL LAW*   [43:705

the statute covered the non-content portion of all sorts of communications.[22]

The convergence of technology created a similar problem with respect to cable television providers. In 1984, Congress passed a law that created substantial hurdles for law enforcement to access records and information held by cable television providers.[23] A decade later, cable companies began to offer many other services, such as Internet access and telephone service. When law enforcement investigators served certain cable companies with the same legal process that they traditionally had used for Internet service providers, the cable companies balked.[24] In one case, citing the Cable Act, a cable company refused to disclose the identity of an active child molester despite receiving a search warrant issued by a federal court. Fortunately, investigators were able to use other means to identify the perpetrator, but the delay allowed him to remain at large for a week and exposed the children living nearby to unnecessary danger.[25] Congress has since corrected this lack of technological neutrality by clarifying that all providers must comply with a single set of statutory rules, whether they provide telephone or Internet service over copper telephone wires or coaxial cable.[26]

U.L. REV. 607, 613 (2003).

22. USA PATRIOT Act, Pub. L. No. 107-56, § 216, 115 Stat. 272, 288–89 (2001).

23. The Cable Act sets out an extremely restrictive system of rules governing law enforcement access to a cable company's records. 47 U.S.C. § 551 (2000), *amended by* USA PATRIOT Act, § 211, 115 Stat. 272, 283 (2001). Congress apparently intended to protect the privacy of television viewers and their viewing choices. For example, the Act does not allow the use of subpoenas or search warrants to obtain such records. Instead, the government must provide prior notice to the customer (even if he or she is the target of the investigation), allow the customer to appear in court with an attorney, and then justify to the court the investigative need to obtain the records. The court may order disclosure of the records only if it finds by "clear and convincing evidence"—a standard greater than probable cause or even a preponderance of the evidence—that the subscriber is "reasonably suspected" of engaging in criminal activity. This procedure is completely unworkable for virtually any criminal investigation.

24. *See, e.g.*, In re Application of United States, 36 F. Supp. 2d, 430, 433 (D. Mass. 1999) (noting apparent statutory conflict and ultimately granting application for order under 18 U.S.C. 2703(d) for records from cable company providing Internet service).

25. Telephone Interview with Assistant United States Attorney, Central District of California (Sept. 2001).

26. Section 211 of the USA PATRIOT Act amended 47 U.S.C. § 551(c)(2) by inserting a new subsection to confirm that cable companies, like other providers, remain subject to the Electronic Communications Privacy Act (ECPA), the wiretap statute, and the trap and trace statute with respect to the provision of communication services—such as telephone and Internet services—notwithstanding section 551(c)(1). The law now provides: "A cable operator may disclose such information if the disclosure is . . . to a government entity as authorized under chapters 119, 121, or 206 of title 18, United States Code, except that such disclosure shall not include records revealing cable subscriber selection of video

Of course, it is not always easy to draft laws in such a way that they will not become outdated over time, but pursuing this strategy will promote their longevity. Where reference to particular technologies is required to make meanings clear, some lawmakers successfully have used non-exclusive lists. For example, one possible way to address the problem with the U.S. Cable Act described above might be to include a provision stating: "These procedural rules apply to providers of communications service by any medium, *including but not limited to* telephone lines, cable lines, satellite communications, wireless towers, *and any similar medium.*"

C. Jurisdiction

With the advent of global communications, more and more crime is being committed across national boundaries. Simply stated, the Internet ignores borders. Yet the ease with which criminals can harm victims in other countries must not bar an appropriate law enforcement response. To meet this need, substantive laws must allow for prosecution of offenders in several jurisdictions.

Moreover, if domestic jurisdictional rules do not allow for prosecution of a domestic person for harm to foreign victims, the legal system must at a minimum allow for extradition of all such criminals (even nationals of the country) to the countries where the harms of the crime occurred. If neither domestic prosecution nor extradition is possible, the country becomes a safe haven for criminal conduct.

In a similar way, a country also will provide a safe haven for criminals if its procedural rules do not allow domestic law enforcement to gather electronic evidence at the request of foreign law enforcement authorities. Without this ability, domestic law enforcement officials will not be able to assist their foreign counterparts, and crimes originating from—or passing through—their territory will go unsolved.[27] Jurisdictional issues are discussed in

---

programming from a cable operator." 47 U.S.C. § 551(c)(2). As the text indicates, the amendment preserves the Cable Act's primacy with respect to records revealing what ordinary cable television programming a customer chooses to purchase, such as particular premium channels or "pay per view" shows. Thus, in a case where a customer receives both Internet access and conventional cable television service from a single cable provider, a government entity can use legal process under ECPA to compel the provider to disclose only those customer records relating to Internet service.

27. For example, hackers commonly use computers in foreign countries as a launch point or "pass through" for attacks on other computers. In seeking to identify the source of a hacker's communications, investigators in the victim country will need to ask for the

720   *COLUMBIA JOURNAL OF TRANSNATIONAL LAW*   [43:705

more detail in Part III.F.

D.   *Considering Other Societal Concerns*

In formulating criminal substantive and procedural laws, lawmakers should consider not only the needs of investigating and prosecuting crime, but also a number of related issues. For example, how will a proposed procedural rule affect the privacy of citizens? Who will bear the cost of complying with law enforcement's requests for electronic evidence? How will e-commerce be affected by the public's perception of the safety of using the Internet? Policy-makers need to listen to a wide variety of societal stakeholders in order to develop balanced cybercrime laws.

E.   *Inchoate Crimes*

As with traditional criminal statutes, it is appropriate to criminalize inchoate crimes such as "attempt" and "aiding and abetting." In this case, the "aid" may take the form of providing computer software or informing others of computer security vulnerabilities with the intent that they be used criminally.[28]

III.   SUBSTANTIVE LAWS CRIMINALIZING ATTACKS ON COMPUTERS AND INFORMATION NETWORKS

A.   *Computer Intrusions*

1.   "Unauthorized Access" or "Exceeding Authorized Access"

A computer intrusion, also called a "hack," occurs when an

---

assistance of law enforcement investigators in the "pass through" country. Without this assistance, the trail stops, even if the ultimate source of the attack lies in the victim country itself.

28. *See, e.g.*, *Master Hacker 'Analyzer' Held in Israel*, CNN.COM, Mar. 18, 1998, *at* http://www.cnn.com/TECH/computing/9803/18/analyzer/ (describing investigation and prosecution of Israeli hacker for counseling California teenagers about how to hack into U.S. military computers).

individual trespasses into a computer or part of a computer system to which that person is not entitled to have access. Such intruders may be divided into two categories: persons who attack from outside the network and wrongfully access a computer "without authorization," and persons who are insiders and thus have authorization to access specific portions of the network but intrude into other parts of it by "exceeding authorized access." Prohibiting computer intrusions is the heart of any network crimes law.

Although hackers have developed thousands of ways to gain access to a computer system "without authorization," a typical attack by an outsider might occur in the following way: (1) a hacker locates a victim computer system by scanning the Internet and finding a hole in the security of a computer; (2) the hacker runs a specialized software program, also known as an "exploit," tricking the computer into giving him access to it as if he were an authorized user; (3) the hacker runs a second specialized program and gains "root level" access, also known as "superuser" status, giving him complete control over the computer; (4) the hacker reads email or other files, deletes files, causes the system to crash, stores his own files on the system, or uses it as the launching point for further hacking activities; (5) the hacker may then alter logging or accounting systems to make it appear that he has not used the system, and he may change these monitoring programs so that they do not record his presence if he uses the computer in the future; and (6) the hacker installs a "back door" or a specialized program that will allow him quick, root level access if he returns, even if the computer's owner patches the security vulnerability that he initially exploited.

Obtaining access to a computer by "exceeding authorized access," on the other hand, refers to the activities of "insiders"— persons who, by employment or some other relationship, have authority to access certain areas of a network, but who then use that authorized access to obtain privileges beyond those to which they are entitled. Like outsiders, such users might then access stored files that they would not normally be able to access, intercept communications of other users, delete or modify files, or cause the system to crash. Recent studies in the United States have revealed that a large number of reported intrusions actually originate from authorized users who exceed their authorized access. In fact, a 2004 study by the Computer Security Institute and the U.S. Federal Bureau of Investigation revealed that the source of unauthorized access was fairly evenly split between insiders and outsiders.[29] Lawmakers should thus craft laws

---

29. LAWRENCE A. GORDON ET AL., COMPUTER SECURITY INSTITUTE, 2004 CSI/FBI

722   *COLUMBIA JOURNAL OF TRANSNATIONAL LAW*   [43:705

to deter and punish the activities both of outside hackers and of insiders who exceed authorized access.

A network crimes statute may use the phrases "accessing a computer without authorization" and "exceeding authorized access" to treat insiders and outsiders differently. Some network crimes laws do not make this distinction, however, and treat all hackers the same. Some of the other phrases commonly used to describe a hacker's lack of authority to have access to a computer include: "illegal access," "access without right," "access without color of law," "fraudulently obtaining or maintaining access," and "unlawfully intruding into a computer."[30] Determining which of these formulations is appropriate for a particular legal system may depend on the meaning of these words in related laws, how the network crimes law defines them, and the way in which a court of that country is likely to interpret them. Framing the element of the crime in terms of "authorization," however, may provide the clearest definition and create the least risk of error in interpretation.

Many countries criminalize the act of gaining unauthorized access or exceeding authorized access to a computer, even if the individual does nothing more.[31] Other countries either require proof that the hacker took some additional action or impose some other limitation such as requiring that the affected computer be part of a computer network. Japanese law, for example, does not criminalize unauthorized access to a computer unless the intruder has circumvented a security measure.[32] By limiting the scope of the

---

COMPUTER CRIME AND SECURITY SURVEY 8–9 (2004), *available at* http://i.cmpnet.com/gocsi/db_area/pdfs/fbi/FBI2004.pdf (for companies that experienced between one and five unauthorized uses of their computers, 52% of the incidents originated from inside the network).

30. *See, e.g.*, Act on Promotion of Information and Communication Network Utilization and Data Protection, art. 48(i) (2000) (S. Korea) ("Any person shall be prohibited from infiltrating into information and communications networks without any justifiable access right or beyond his permitted access right"); Criminal Code, R.S.C., ch. C-46, § 342.1(1) (1985) (Can.), *available at* http://laws.justice.gc.ca/en/C-46/index.html ("Every one who, fraudulently and without colour of right . . . obtains, directly or indirectly, any computer service . . . is guilty of an indictable offence . . ."); THE DUTCH PENAL CODE, art. 138a (Louise Rayar & Stafford Wadsworth trans., 1997) ("A person who intentionally unlawfully intrudes into a computerized device or system . . . is guilty of computer intrusion . . .").

31. *See, e.g.*, THE FRENCH PENAL CODE OF 1994 (as amended Jan. 1, 1999), art. 323-1 (Edward A. Tomlinson trans., 1999) ("Fraudulently obtaining or maintaining access to the whole or part of a system for automated data processing is punishable by [imprisonment and a fine].").

32. *See* Unauthorized Computer Access Law (provisional translation), Law No. 128 of 1999, art. 3 (Jap.), *available at* http://www.cybercrimelaw.net/countries/japan.html (providing that "[n]o person shall conduct an act of unauthorized computer access" where such an act involves "making available a specific use which is restricted by an access control

statute in this way, however, the law may allow a hacker who causes severe damage to a computer system to escape punishment where the owner of the system—perhaps through inexperience or ignorance—failed to secure it.[33]

Article 2 of the Convention on Cybercrime addresses this criminal activity, explicitly stating that signatory countries must criminalize not only the intentional access to a computer system without authorization, but also access to "any part" of such a system.[34] This language provides an important standard by which to measure the comprehensiveness of a country's basic hacking statute.

2.   "Unauthorized Access" or "Exceeding Authorized Access" and Obtaining Information

Criminal laws should prohibit individuals from using unauthorized access or exceeding authorized access to obtain information.   By obtaining information, a hacker violates the confidentiality of the information stored on the computer.   This invasion of privacy can take the form of the theft of: (1) financial information, such as credit card or bank account numbers; (2) medical information, such as the treatment received by a celebrity; (3) government or national security information, such as military plans or troop movements; or (4) trade secrets or proprietary business information, such as confidential customer lists or industrial formulae.

In this context, the concept of "obtaining" or "stealing" data includes the act of merely viewing the data, regardless of whether an intruder copies or downloads a file to a permanent storage device. Indeed, by merely "viewing" data, a copy of it is transferred to the

---

function . . . through inputting . . . another person's identification code" or other information "that can evade the restrictions.").

33. Although lawmakers should probably avoid narrowing the coverage of unauthorized access in these ways, the Convention on Cybercrime permits signatories to adopt laws that contain them. With respect to unauthorized access, Article 2 states, "A Party may require that the offence be committed by infringing security measures, with the intent of obtaining computer data or other dishonest intent, or in relation to a computer system that is connected to another computer system." Convention on Cybercrime, *supra* note 6, art. 2. This provision was added to the Convention to satisfy the requests of several of the negotiating parties. *See* Council of Europe, Convention on Cybercrime, Explanatory Report paras.   49–50   (Nov.   8,   2001),   *available   at* http://conventions.coe.int/Treaty/en/Reports/Html/185.htm [hereinafter Explanatory Report].

34. Convention on Cybercrime, *supra* note 6, art. 2 ("Each Party shall adopt such legislative and other measures as may be necessary to establish as criminal offences under its domestic law, when committed intentionally, the access to the whole or any part of a computer system without right.").

hacker's computer screen where it can be "cut" and "pasted" into another file. This act alone invades the privacy of the data owner.

Many statutes that criminalize unauthorized access to data do not distinguish between different types of data stored in a computer. Some statutory schemes, however, distinguish between types of stolen data for purposes of severity of punishment. For a more detailed discussion of this idea, see Part III.G.

Countries have used varying language to criminalize obtaining data through computer hacking. Singapore, for example, has made it a crime to "cause[] a computer to perform any function" that allows the individual to "access without authority . . . any program or data" stored on a computer.[35] This wording applies both to those who access the computer without authority and to insiders who exceed their authorization. The United States has a similar provision that makes it an offense to "intentionally access[] a computer without authorization or exceed[] authorized access, and thereby obtain[]" information.[36] This statute does not require that the hacker download a complete file to some permanent medium; "obtaining information" includes merely viewing it on the screen of a remote computer.[37] The Netherlands has enacted a two-tiered system whereby accessing a computer without authority carries a maximum sentence of six months' imprisonment, while accessing a computer and copying or recording data carries a maximum sentence of four years.[38]

---

35. Computer Misuse Act, pt. II, § 3 (1998) (Sing.), *available at* http://agcvldb4.agc.gov.sg/.

36. 18 U.S.C. § 1030(a)(2) (2000).

37. When 18 U.S.C. § 1030 was amended in 1996, the Senate Judiciary Committee emphasized this point:

> "Information" as used in this subsection includes information stored in intangible form. Moreover, the term "obtaining information" includes merely reading it. There is no requirement that the information be copied or transported. This is critically important because, in an electronic environment, information can be "stolen" without asportation, and the original usually remains intact. This interpretation of "obtaining information" is consistent with congressional intent expressed as follows in connection with 1986 amendments to the Computer Fraud and Abuse statute: Because the premise of this subsection is privacy protection, the Committee wishes to make clear that "obtaining information" in this context includes mere observation of the data. Actual asportation, in the sense of physically removing the data from its original location or transcribing the data, need not be proved in order to establish a violation of this subsection.

S. REP. NO. 104-357, at 7 (1996) (citing S. REP. NO. 99-432, at 6–7 (1986)).

38. *See* THE DUTCH PENAL CODE, art. 138a (Louise Rayar & Stafford Wadsworth trans., 1997).

3.   "Unauthorized Access" or "Exceeding Authorized Access"
         and Facilitation of Another Crime

In many situations, intrusions occur not as an end in themselves but as part of a larger criminal scheme. Criminals may, for example, hack into a computer in order to obtain information that they can use to commit some other crime, such as obtaining credit card or bank account numbers in order to make fraudulent purchases or to transfer funds fraudulently.[39] Alternatively, they may use the computer's functions to further the offense, such as using a hacked computer as a storage site for images of child pornography.

Some countries have created special statutes to criminalize computer intrusions where the hacker breaks into the computer to further a particular crime. The United States has taken this approach by criminalizing the act of accessing a computer without authorization, or exceeding authorization, in furtherance of a crime of fraud.[40] A network crimes statute need not focus on particular crimes,

---

39. The Convention on Cybercrime addresses computer related forgery and fraud, although these provisions do not necessarily require unauthorized access. Instead, Articles 7 and 8 deal with any sort of fraud crime that the actor uses a computer to perpetrate. The Convention provides:

Article 7 – Computer-related forgery

Each Party shall adopt such legislative and other measures as may be necessary to establish as criminal offences under its domestic law, when committed intentionally and without right, the input, alteration, deletion, or suppression of computer data, resulting in inauthentic data with the intent that it be considered or acted upon for legal purposes as if it were authentic, regardless whether or not the data is directly readable and intelligible. A Party may require an intent to defraud, or similar dishonest intent, before criminal liability attaches.

Article 8 – Computer-related fraud

Each Party shall adopt such legislative and other measures as may be necessary to establish as criminal offences under its domestic law, when committed intentionally and without right, the causing of a loss of property to another by:

a. any input, alteration, deletion or suppression of computer data;

b. any interference with the functioning of a computer system,
with fraudulent or dishonest intent of procuring, without right, an economic benefit for oneself or for another.

Convention on Cybercrime, *supra* note 6, arts. 7–8. A party need not adopt a "computer crime" law to cover these sorts of offenses if its traditional fraud law contains a sufficiently broad definition to encompass them. For example, U.S. courts have routinely applied the U.S. statute prohibiting "wire fraud," 18 U.S.C. § 1343, written originally to address fraud committed using a telephone, to crimes committed using computers and the Internet. *See, e.g.*, United States v. Lee, 296 F.3d 792 (9th Cir. 2002) (wire fraud conviction for sales from fraudulent website); United States v. Gajdik, 292 F.3d 555 (7th Cir. 2002) (wire fraud conviction for fraud scheme over eBay, an Internet auction site); United States v. Pirello, 255 F.3d 728 (9th Cir. 2001) (wire fraud conviction for posting Internet advertisements soliciting money for products defendant had no intention of providing).

40. *See* 18 U.S.C. § 1030(a)(4) (2000). This section allows punishment of a fine or imprisonment for anyone who

726   *COLUMBIA JOURNAL OF TRANSNATIONAL LAW*   [43:705

however, but rather can criminalize conduct where an unauthorized access was undertaken with the object of facilitating any crime or any of a broad class of crimes. For example, Australia has made it a crime to access a computer without authorization with the intent to commit a "serious offense" (one with a penalty of five or more years' imprisonment).[41]

B.   Damaging Computers or Information Stored on Computers

An effective network crimes law must also prohibit conduct that causes a computer system to fail to operate as it should. Often called "damaging" computers, such conduct can have far-reaching effects. For example, a business may not be able to operate if its computer system stops functioning, or it may lose sales if it cannot retrieve the data in a database containing customer information. Similarly, disrupting a computer that operates the phone system used by police and fire fighters could cripple emergency services and result in injuries or deaths. Such damage can occur following a successful intrusion, but an individual can also disrupt a computer without ever gaining access to it.

A network crimes law should take into account two sets of concepts: on the one hand, the concepts of integrity and availability; on the other hand, the concepts of information and computer systems. First, the law should cover not just an attack on the proper functioning of a computer system, but also attacks on *information* stored on such a system. Even if a computer continues to be capable of storing or manipulating data, the system is rendered effectively inoperable if the data itself is corrupted or deleted. Conversely, data stored on the system may remain intact, but the system's integrity may be breached. Second, the law should apply to acts that, without changing or deleting data, simply make the data unavailable. The value of a computer to an individual or a business is harmed if the user cannot access the relevant information, even if in a technical sense the data has not been changed. Similarly, hackers can cause a whole computer system to become unavailable.

---

knowingly and with intent to defraud, accesses a protected computer without authorization, or exceeds authorized access, and by means of such conduct furthers the intended fraud and obtains anything of value, unless the object of the fraud and the thing obtained consists only of the use of the computer and the value of such use is not more than $5,000 in any 1-year period.

41. Criminal Code Act, 1995, pt. 10.7, div. 477.1 (Austl.), *available at* http://scaleplus.law.gov.au/cgi-bin/download.pl?/scale/data/pasteact/1/686.

Harm to the integrity or availability of information or a computer system might occur, for example, where a disgruntled employee of a company sabotages a computer. She could: (1) harm the integrity of data by accessing a database and inserting false entries so as to disrupt business operations; (2) harm the availability of data by moving it to another computer; (3) harm the integrity of a computer system by deleting particular programs that the computer generally runs, such as programs that authenticate and monitor users; or (4) harm the availability of a computer system by causing the whole system to crash. A comprehensive law should criminalize each of these acts and, since it can be accomplished by an "insider," not require that access to the computer be unauthorized.[42]

An "outsider" could also accomplish these same sorts of harms. If a company fires an employee, and that employee hacks back into the firm's network, he could similarly delete data or cause the system to crash. Outsiders can also send out viruses[43] and worms[44] that gain unauthorized access to systems in an automated way. Such software programs commonly damage systems and information and use up communications resources, making data unavailable.

In addition, a person can cause damage to a computer system from the outside without first gaining access at all by sending certain

---

42. *See, e.g.*, Press Release, U.S. Dep't of Justice, *Disgruntled UBS Paine Webber Employee Charged with Allegedly Unleashing "Logic Bomb" on Company Computers* (Dec. 17, 2002), *available at* http://www.cybercrime.gov/duronioIndict.htm (a disgruntled computer systems administrator was charged with using a "logic bomb" to cause more than $3 million in damage to his company's computer network).

43. Viruses are computer programs that reside in or "infect" some other file or program. If a user gives an infected program to another user—as an attachment to an email, for example—the virus can enter the second user's computer. Once activated, the virus can do any number of things, such as delete files or cause the computer to malfunction. Various companies sell programs that check files for viruses by looking for the "signatures" of known viruses. The effectiveness of such programs depends, however, on the user constantly updating the software so that it will recognize the signatures of new viruses. Even then, some viruses can change their appearance each time they infect a new computer system. These so-called "polymorphic viruses" make it very difficult for anti-virus programmers to create a single signature to detect them.

44. The distinguishing characteristic of a worm is that it multiplies across networked systems without the need for human action. Unlike a virus, a worm does not rely on being carried by other files or programs. Rather, it exists as a free-standing program, designed to copy itself onto as many systems as it can. Like a virus, a worm may be able to perform a myriad of tasks. The first worm to become famous was the Morris worm in 1988, which crashed thousands of computers by simply replicating itself with exponential growth. More recent examples of worms include the Microsoft Blaster (or "LovSan") worm in 2003 and Code Red in 2001. *See* Byron Acohido & Matt Krantz, *Worm Squirms into Thousands of PCs; People All Over the World Hit by LovSan*, USA TODAY, Aug. 13, 2003, at B1; *Code Red Worms into 150,000 Computers*, USA TODAY, Aug. 2, 2001, at B3.

specialized communications or programs to it. For example, a malicious user can flood a particular computer with so much information that it cannot process data in the way that it normally should, rendering it effectively inoperable. Commonly called a "denial of service attack,"[45] this activity has caused large monetary losses over the past several years.[46] Thus, an effective network crimes law should prohibit the transmission of a program, information, code, or command that causes harm whether or not the person first gained unauthorized access to a computer or computer network.

The Convention on Cybercrime helps to clarify these distinctions by addressing damage to data and damage to the functioning of computer systems in separate articles.[47] The drafters of the Convention focused on penalizing "serious" data and system interferences.[48] According to the Explanatory Report on the Convention:

> Each Party shall determine for itself what criteria must

---

45. Denial of service attacks can take a number of forms. Some attacks work by consuming scarce, limited, or non-renewable resources such as disk space, network bandwidth, or processor time, so that none of these resources is available to the legitimate users. Other attacks destroy or alter configuration information to make it impossible for legitimate users to access it. A third form of denial of service attack sends special data to a computer that causes it to crash because of a flaw in its programming.

46. *See, e.g.*, Press Release, Dep't of Justice, *Background on Operation Web Snare Examples of Prosecutions* (Aug. 27, 2004), *available at*
http://www.usdoj.gov/criminal/fraud/websnare.pdf (describing, among other cases, the indictment of Jay R. Echouafni for hiring computer hackers to launch distributed denial of service attacks against several websites. The attacks "caused the victims to lose over $2 million in revenue and costs associated with responding to the attacks."). Computer criminals can also combine attacks modes, such as by using a virus that first infects many computers and then uses them to launch a denial of service attack against a particular computer. *See* Press Release, Dep't of Justice, *Juvenile Sentenced for Releasing Worm that Attacked Microsoft Web Site* (Feb. 11, 2005), *available at*
http://www.usdoj.gov/criminal/cybercrime/juvenileSent.htm (the juvenile was sentenced for releasing a computer worm that directed infected computers to launch a distributed denial of service attack against Microsoft's website, rendering the site inoperable to the public for approximately four hours).

47. Article 4 of the Convention addresses "data interference" and provides that a party "shall adopt such legislative and other measures as may be necessary to establish as criminal offences under its domestic law, when committed intentionally, the damaging, deletion, deterioration, alteration or suppression of computer data without right." Convention on Cybercrime, *supra* note 6, art. 4. Article 5 addresses "system interference" and provides that a party "shall adopt such legislative and other measures as may be necessary to establish as criminal offences under its domestic law, when committed intentionally, the serious hindering without right of the functioning of a computer system by inputting, transmitting, damaging, deleting, deteriorating, altering or suppressing computer data." *Id.* art. 5.

48. Article 5 provides for criminalizing only "*serious* hindering" of a computer system, while Article 4 provides that parties "may reserve the right to require that [data interference] result in *serious* harm" before it is considered a criminal offense. *Id.* arts. 4–5 (emphasis added).

be fulfilled in order for the hindering to be considered "serious." For example, a Party may require a minimum amount of damage to be caused in order for the hindering to be considered serious. The drafters considered as "serious" the sending of data to a particular system in such a form, size or frequency that it has a significant detrimental effect on the ability of the owner or operator to use the system, or to communicate with other systems (e.g., by means of programs that generate "denial of service" attacks, malicious codes such as viruses that prevent or substantially slow the operation of the system, or programs that send huge quantities of electronic mail to a recipient in order to block the communications functions of the system).[49]

The Convention thus aims to avoid criminalizing the situation where a person uses a computer without permission to run a relatively innocuous program (such as an employee's using his company's Internet connection to play multi-player games during work hours, explicitly against corporate rules). Although such activity might slow down the corporate network slightly, it would be inappropriate to criminalize it unless it "seriously hinders" the functioning of the network and prevents other employees from doing their jobs.

Countries have taken different approaches to drafting statutory text to criminalize the act of causing damage to information or computers. Some countries simply prohibit causing "damage" generally, where damage is defined as harming the integrity or availability of information or a computer system.[50] Other countries have attempted to define the prohibited conduct with greater specificity, using terms such as: "the deletion, addition, modification, alteration, suppression, or deterioration of data;" "rendering data unusable;" or "the obstruction, interference with, or denial of access to data."[51]

---

49. Explanatory Report, *supra* note 33, para. 67.

50. The United States has taken this approach. *See* 18 U.S.C. § 1030(a)(5)(A)(i) (2000) ("Whoever . . . knowingly causes the transmission of a program, information, code, or command, and as a result of such conduct causes damage without authorization to a computer [commits a crime]"); § 1030 (e)(8) ("The term 'damage' means any impairment to the integrity or availability of data, a program, a system, or information . . . .").

51. For example, the Canadian penal code contains the following provision:

Every one commits mischief who willfully

(a) destroys or alters data;

(b) renders data meaningless, useless or ineffective;

730   *COLUMBIA JOURNAL OF TRANSNATIONAL LAW*   [43:705

If the latter approach is adopted, lawmakers should ensure that the language used is technology-neutral. For example, the law should avoid defining crimes using the names of technology-specific attacks such as "virus" and "worm." Hackers will continue to create new types of attacks, and lawmakers should strive to draft statutory language broad enough to apply to future technologies. Moreover, the statute should make clear that whatever list of terms it provides is not exclusive.[52] Finally, lawmakers should make sure that the same terminology is used in each relevant portion of the law. Using a different definition of "damage" in the context of damage to information than the one used in the context of damage to computer systems, for example, may lead to confusion in application and gaps in the law's coverage.

C.   *Interception of Data in Transmission*

Network crimes laws should also criminalize the interception of data and communications in transmission where it is done without the knowledge or permission of the people communicating. As with the interception of a telephone call, a significant privacy invasion occurs when a person captures the content of an individual's email, the information downloaded by another from a website, or the content of other electronic communications.

> (c) obstructs, interrupts or interferes with the lawful use of data; or
>
> (d) obstructs, interrupts or interferes with any person in the lawful use of data or denies access to data to any person who is entitled to access thereto.

Criminal Code, R.S.C., ch. C-46, § 430(1.1) (1985) (Can.), *available at* http://laws.justice.gc.ca/en/C-46/index.html. Note that this portion of the statute applies to causing damage to information but not to computer systems themselves. Articles 4 and 5 of the Convention on Cybercrime also use long lists of verbs to cover the range of methods by which offenders can cause this sort of harm. *See* Convention on Cybercrime, *supra* note 6, arts. 4–5. Moreover, the Explanatory Report of the Convention further defines a number of these terms:

> In paragraph 1 [of Article 4], 'damaging' and 'deteriorating' as overlapping acts relate in particular to a negative alteration of the integrity or of information content of data and programmes. 'Deletion' of data is the equivalent of the destruction of a corporeal thing. It destroys them and makes them unrecognisable. Suppressing of computer data means any action that prevents or terminates the availability of the data to the person who has access to the computer or the data carrier on which it was stored. The term 'alteration' means the modification of existing data. The input of malicious codes, such as viruses and Trojan horses is, therefore, covered under this paragraph, as is the resulting modification of the data.

Explanatory Report, *supra* note 33, para. 61.

52. Of course, legislative text must still provide sufficient notice about what conduct falls within the definition in order to avoid challenges that the statute is overly vague.

This type of activity may take place inside a computer system following a successful intrusion. Indeed, hackers commonly install "sniffer" programs to read the content of communications on a network, such as users' passwords. A law criminalizing such interceptions should not require unauthorized access to a computer system by an outsider, however, because individuals who have authorization to use the network may also impermissibly invade the privacy of users' communications. For example, a system administrator may have authorization to access emails on a corporate computer network in order to make sure that it is operating correctly and to prevent it from being misused. It should be a crime, however, if that administrator improperly reads the email belonging to the corporation's board of directors in order to use that information, for example, to buy or sell shares of the corporation's stock.

The definition of the crime of unlawful interception of communications must, however, exclude certain types of conduct. One such exception should be made in certain circumstances where there is a reduced expectation of privacy. For example, many countries have decided not to prohibit interception and recording of communications where one of the parties to the communication consents (e.g., where two people are communicating using text messaging and one of them stores a communication for later review).[53] In addition, there should be an exception to the general prohibition on interception for system owners or system administrators who must be able to intercept the system for performance and security purposes.[54]

Article 3 of the Convention on Cybercrime, which requires signatories to adopt laws banning surreptitious interception of

---

53. *See, e.g.*, Criminal Code, R.S.C, ch. C-46, § 184(1)–(2)(a) (1985) (Can.), *available at* http://laws.justice.gc.ca/en/C-46/42095.html (providing an exception to a general prohibition on intercepting private electronic communications where one party has given his or her "express or implied" consent); 18 U.S.C. § 2511(2)(c), (d) (2000) (similar exception where one party has given "prior consent" to interception).

54. U.S. law contains such an exception:

> It shall not be unlawful under this chapter for an operator of a switchboard, or an officer, employee, or agent of a provider of wire or electronic communication service, whose facilities are used in the transmission of a wire or electronic communication, to intercept, disclose, or use that communication in the normal course of his employment while engaged in any activity which is a necessary incident to the rendition of his service or to the protection of the rights or property of the provider of that service.

18 U.S.C. § 2511(2)(a)(i). In 2004, Canada added a similar provision to its criminal code. *See* Criminal Code, R.S.C., ch. C-46, § 184(2)(e) (1985) (amended 2004) (Can.), *available at* http://laws.justice.gc.ca/en/C-46/index.html.

communications, implicitly takes into account these considerations.[55] By only requiring signatories to criminalize interceptions that occur "without right" or with "dishonest intent," it allows countries to make appropriate exceptions to their criminal statutes, such as allowing system administrators to intercept communications in order to catch hackers.[56]

Article 3 of the Convention contains two other interesting details. First, it applies only to interceptions accomplished by "technical means."[57] It would not include obtaining a communication by direct observation, such as by standing behind a person who is typing an email and reading or photographing the screen. Second, it does cover "electromagnetic emissions" from a computer system, presumably to take into account some high-tech snooping devices that can detect the radiation released by traditional computer monitors and decipher the text that appears on the screen.[58]

---

55. Article 3 states in full:

> Each Party shall adopt such legislative and other measures as may be necessary to establish as criminal offences under its domestic law, when committed intentionally, the interception without right, made by technical means, of non-public transmissions of computer data to, from or within a computer system, including electromagnetic emissions from a computer system carrying such computer data. A Party may require that the offence be committed with dishonest intent, or in relation to a computer system that is connected to another computer system.

Convention on Cybercrime, *supra* note 6, art. 3.

56. According to the Explanatory Report:

> The act is justified, for example, if the intercepting person . . . acts on the instructions or by authorisation of the participants of the transmission (including authorised testing or protection activities agreed to by the participants), or if surveillance is lawfully authorised in the interests of national security or the detection of offences by investigating authorities.

Explanatory Report, *supra* note 33, para. 58.

57. *See id.* para. 53 ("Technical means includes technical devices fixed to transmission lines as well as devices to collect and record wireless communications. They may include the use of software, passwords and codes. The requirement of using technical means is a restrictive qualification to avoid over-criminalisation.").

58. The Explanatory Report notes:

> The creation of an offence in relation to 'electromagnetic emissions' will ensure a more comprehensive scope. Electromagnetic emissions may be emitted by a computer during its operation. Such emissions are not considered as 'data' according to the definition provided in Article 1. However, data can be reconstructed from such emissions. Therefore, the interception of data from electromagnetic emissions from a computer system is included as an offence under this provision.

See id. para. 57. This sort of interception featured centrally in the plot of a recent novel. *See* NEAL STEPHENSON, CRYPTONOMICON (1999).

D. Trafficking in Passwords and Other Access Devices

If a criminal possesses the password to an account on a computer, or similar information, commonly known as an "access device," he can readily gain unauthorized access to that computer. Just as some states and nations have adopted criminal prohibitions on tools used to commit crimes in the physical world, such as burglary tools and unlicensed handguns,[59] a comprehensive computer network law, in order to address the underlying problem of computer hacking, should prohibit the unauthorized transfer of access devices or their possession with the intent to employ them criminally.

The phrase "access device" is in some ways a misnomer; such "devices" are generally not physical things but rather passwords, codes, account numbers, and other information that allow access to a computer or computer network. Laws should define "access device" broadly enough to cover all the means for obtaining unauthorized access. Indeed, it should even cover information about a system's vulnerabilities that, if used, allows the user to find an unauthorized "back door" into a system. Moreover, in prohibiting the unauthorized transfer of access devices, lawmakers should not require that a "sale" occur. Hackers commonly trade access devices without any exchange of money.

Countries have implemented a prohibition on access devices in a number of ways. Canada, for example, prohibits the possession, use, or distribution of a "password" with the intent to commit a computer hacking offense.[60] The law, however, provides an

---

59. *See, e.g.,* Criminal Code, R.S.C., ch. C-46, § 91(1)–(2) (1985) (Can.), *available at* http://laws.justice.gc.ca/en/C-46/index.html (criminalizing the unauthorized possession of a firearm and the unauthorized possession of a prohibited or restricted weapon); Criminal Code Act, 1995, pt. 9.4, § 360.1 (Austl.), *available at* http://scaleplus.law.gov.au/cgi-bin/download.pl?/scale/data/pasteact/1/686 (relating to prohibitions on "dangerous weapons" including firearms). Several U.S. states have also adopted criminal prohibitions on certain weapons and tools that are commonly used to commit crimes in the physical world. Pennsylvania law, for example, provides that "[a] person commits a misdemeanor of the first degree if he possesses any instrument of crime with intent to employ it criminally." 18 PA. CONS. STAT. ANN. § 907(a) (1998). The statute defines "instrument of crime," in part, as "[a]nything specially made or specially adapted for criminal use." 18 PA. CONS. STAT. ANN. § 907(d)(1) (1998). Virginia law contains a similar prohibition:

> If any person have in his possession any tools, implements or outfit, with intent to commit burglary, robbery or larceny, upon conviction thereof he shall be guilty of a . . . felony. The possession of such burglarious tools, implements or outfit by any person other than a licensed dealer, shall be prima facie evidence of an intent to commit burglary, robbery or larceny.

VA. CODE ANN. § 18.2-94 (Michie 2003).

60. Criminal Code, R.S.C., ch. C-46, § 342.1(1) (1985) (Can.), *available at* http://laws.justice.gc.ca/en/C-46/index.html.

expansive definition of the term "computer password" to include "any data by which a computer service or computer system is capable of being obtained or used."[61]

The Convention on Cybercrime contains a provision that covers not only passwords and access devices but also any other information or computer program useful for violating any of the Convention's provisions that pertain to crimes against computers or computer data.[62] This provision thus applies to such programs as a virus that penetrates computer security and steals information, a program that can cause a denial of service attack, or a program that can surreptitiously intercept communications.[63] The broad coverage of this provision shows considerable insight into the ways in which such crimes are perpetrated, and it does so in an admirably technology-neutral manner. Moreover, this provision takes into account the fact that computer security professionals need to utilize some of these programs to test the security of the networks they are trying to defend. Because Article 6 applies only to the production, sale, procurement, importation, and distribution of such devices when it is done "without right," it allows domestic lawmakers to write laws that do not criminalize these acts when done with legitimate intent.[64]

---

61. *Id.* § 342.1(2).

62. Article 6 of the Convention states:

1. Each Party shall adopt such legislative and other measures as may be necessary to establish as criminal offences under its domestic law, when committed intentionally and without right:

a.the production, sale, procurement for use, import, distribution or otherwise making available of:

i.a device, including a computer program, designed or adapted primarily for the purpose of committing any of the [hacking offences described in the earlier articles];

ii.a computer password, access code, or similar data by which the whole or any part of a computer system is capable of being accessed with intent that it be used for the purpose of committing any of the [hacking offences]; and

b.the possession of an item referred to in [earlier] paragraphs, with intent that it be used for the purpose of committing any of the [hacking offenses]. A Party may require by law that a number of such items be possessed before criminal liability attaches.

Convention on Cybercrime, *supra* note 6, art. 6(1).

63. *See* Explanatory Report, *supra* note 33, para. 72 ("The inclusion of a 'computer program' refers to programs that are for example designed to alter or even destroy data or interfere with the operation of systems, such as virus programs, or programs designed or adapted to gain access to computer systems.").

64. *See id.* para. 77 (noting that, "[f]or example, test-devices ('cracking-devices') and network analysis devices designed by industry to control the reliability of their information technology products or to test system security are produced for legitimate purposes, and would be considered to be 'with right.'").

E. Mental State Required for the Commission of the Crime

In drafting network crime laws, lawmakers can require proof of a particular mental state for each element of an offense. For example, a law could require proof that the actor *intentionally* transmitted a command and that the actor thereby *recklessly* caused damage to information or a computer system. Different legal systems use different mental states, although they generally fall into three major categories: "intentionally,"[65] "recklessly,"[66] or with no required mental state.[67] Lawmakers should consider their legal system's historic use of the various mental states when deciding which are most appropriate in defining network crimes.

In certain circumstances, it can be difficult to prove the defendant's mental state at the time that the activity occurred. Where a statute requires that a defendant have acted intentionally, the intent requirement should be limited to showing that the defendant intended to do the actions that he did, rather than proving that he intended to cause some particular monetary loss or consequential harm. For example, a law could require proof that a criminal intended to cause damage—meaning the interference with or deletion of data or the shutting down of a computer system—but not that she intended to cause a specific amount of monetary harm.

---

65. Intentional acts are those where it can be said that a person had the purpose to do a thing. He acted, or failed to act, consciously and voluntarily, and not inadvertently or accidentally. For example, the U.S. Model Penal Code provides that "'intentionally' or 'with intent' means purposely." MODEL PENAL CODE § 1.13 (12) (1962). The Model Penal Code further defines "purposely":

> A person acts purposely with respect to a material element of an offense when:
> (i) if the element involves the nature of his conduct or a result thereof, it is his conscious object to engage in conduct of that nature or to cause such a result;
> (ii) if the element involves the attendant circumstances, he is aware of the existence of such circumstances or he believes or hopes that they exist.

Id. § 2.02(2)(a).

66. Reckless acts are those taken carelessly and in willful disregard of the rights or safety of others, or without regard to the impact of those actions. For example, the U.S. Model Penal Code provides that "[a] person acts recklessly with respect to a material element of an offense when he consciously disregards a substantial and unjustifiable risk that the material element exists or will result from his conduct." *Id.* § 2.02(2)(c).

67. Statutes that criminalize actions without regard to mental state do not require that there be a showing that a person knew the result of his actions; merely that he takes those actions and a result occurs.

736   *COLUMBIA JOURNAL OF TRANSNATIONAL LAW*   [43:705

F.   Jurisdictional Issues

The borderless nature of global networks means that a single criminal act using a computer may affect several countries.   In addition, hackers increasingly attack computers located in countries other than the ones in which they reside.   Indeed, even when their ultimate goal is to gain unauthorized access to a computer located within their home nations, they commonly will first hack into computers located in foreign countries and then use those computers as intermediate computers or staging grounds from which to attack their ultimate targets.   This process, sometimes referred to as "looping," allows them to hide their identities.   Although it is almost trivially easy for the hacker to accomplish, it creates a tremendous burden on international law enforcement cooperation.

The increased incidence of transborder hacking, as well as hackers' use of looping to hide their identities, have forced legal systems to adapt in creative ways.   For example, legislatures have reexamined policies and legal rules relating to extradition to assure that no country will provide a safe haven for hackers.   In addition, if a hacker in one country breaks into bank computers in five other countries, it may make more sense to have the hacker's home country vindicate the rights of the victims worldwide by prosecuting the hacker for all of these crimes at one time, rather than have the hacker undergo a separate trial in each jurisdiction.   For example, although the Nimda worm damaged computers in probably every country in the world,[68] it would make little sense for the person who released it to undergo repetitive trials and punishments.

At the very least, each country should have the maximum flexibility to prosecute hackers located both inside and outside of its borders. First, domestic laws should criminalize attacks on computers inside a country's borders regardless of whether the criminal is located inside or outside of the country. Second, each country's laws should allow for prosecution of domestic offenders who attack computers located in other countries. If such a domestic prosecution is unavailable, the law and treaties of that country must allow for extradition of such individuals to the country in which the victim is located. Moreover, each country's procedural laws must be capable of supporting the investigation and prosecution of individuals in foreign countries, by collecting and sharing evidence of the crime

---

68.   Jaikumar Vijayan, *Nimda Worm Biggest Driver of Security Over Past Year,* COMPUTERWORLD, Sept. 16, 2002, *available at* http://www.computerworld.com/securitytopics/security/story/0,10801,74284,00.html.

with foreign law enforcement agencies and prosecutors.

Australia's computer network crimes law provides an example of the first of these concepts as it gives Australian authorities the jurisdiction to prosecute a criminal who attacks computers located in Australia from anywhere in the world.[69] Similarly, the United States recently amended its law to confirm that U.S. prosecutors can bring criminal charges against foreigners who attack computers in the United States, as well as against any U.S. hacker who attacks computers in other countries.[70] This statute has the additional benefit of granting U.S. authorities jurisdiction to investigate intrusions in which a foreign-based hacker uses computers in the U.S. to attack computers in a foreign country. Although such crimes may eventually be prosecuted in a foreign court, U.S. investigators can open an investigation, obtain evidence, and share it more rapidly than if they had to wait for a formal request for assistance from the foreign country.

The Convention on Cybercrime requires signatories to criminalize computer offenses when the victim resides within the nation's borders, as well as acts committed on ships and aircraft registered under its laws.[71] In addition, it seeks to eliminate safe havens by requiring that if a signatory will not extradite an offender because of his nationality, it must have jurisdiction to prosecute the

---

69. *See* Criminal Code Act, 1995, pt. 10.7, § 476.3 (Austl.), *available at*

http://scaleplus.law.gov.au/cgi-bin/download.pl?/scale/data/pasteact/1/686 (citing section 15.1 of the Act and providing for jurisdiction over computer offences where the criminal conduct occurs "wholly or partly in Australia" or where the conduct occurs wholly outside of Australia, but "a result" of that conduct occurs "wholly or partly in Australia").

70. The U.S. computer hacking statute, which criminalizes attacks on "protected computer[s]," defines a protected computer in part as one "which is used in interstate or foreign commerce or communication, including a computer located outside the United States that is used in a manner that affects interstate or foreign commerce or communication of the United States." 18 U.S.C. § 1030(e)(2) (2000).

71. Article 22 of the Convention on Cybercrime states

1. Each Party shall adopt such legislative and other measures as may be necessary to establish jurisdiction over any offence . . . when the offence is committed:

  a. in its territory; or

  b. on board a ship flying the flag of that Party; or

  c. on board an aircraft registered under the laws of that Party; or

  d. by one of its nationals, if the offence is punishable under criminal law where it was committed or if the offence is committed outside the territorial jurisdiction of any State. . . .

Convention on Cybercrime, *supra* note 6, art. 22. *See also* Explanatory Report, *supra* note 33, paras. 232–39.

offender domestically.[72]

G.   *Determining the Appropriate Punishment*

There are as many different frameworks for the punishment of network crime offenses as there are countries with network crime laws. While there is no single correct answer to the question of how severe punishment should be for the various network crime offenses, lawmakers should at a minimum create penalties severe enough to punish the invasions of privacy, thefts of information, and monetary and other harms that result from this misconduct. In addition, because it is quite difficult to detect and apprehend computer hackers, lawmakers should set appropriately severe penalties in order to deter the conduct. This deterrence and punishment ought to include meaningful periods of incarceration as well as fines and restitution to victims. As the Convention on Cybercrime succinctly states, national laws should create "effective, proportionate and dissuasive sanctions, which include deprivation of liberty."[73]

1.   Monetary Harms

One important criterion in determining the severity of punishment for a particular crime is the monetary harm or "loss" it has caused. In many computer intrusions, a major harm caused by the crime is the disruption in the use of the computer and the expense incurred in getting the computer running correctly again. This harm is multiplied exponentially when a virus or worm is involved because it can affect so many computers in a short period of time. Thus, even where there is no "permanent" damage, laws should define "loss" to include all of the costs associated with discovering the intrusion and determining its scope, and with the time and resources spent restoring the computer and data to their state prior to the offense. This figure should include the hourly wage of employees who repair a computer system, as well as the decline in business productivity or lost profits associated with an inoperable computer.

For example, where an intruder breaks into a computer network, deletes records in a database, and causes the system to crash,

---

72. Convention on Cybercrime, *supra* note 6, art. 22 (each signatory's computer crime jurisdiction must cover "cases where an alleged offender is present in its territory and it does not extradite him/her to another Party, solely on the basis of his/her nationality").

73. Convention on Cybercrime, *supra* note 6, art. 13.

the monetary loss might include: (1) the cost of detecting and investigating the intrusion; (2) the cost of determining what data the intruder corrupted; (3) the cost of restoring the data from a saved back-up; (4) the cost of re-creating data that was lost permanently; (5) the lost sales associated with the computer outage; (6) the loss in productivity resulting from employees unable to do their work; and (7) the cost of checking to make sure that the intruder has not left a "back door" to regain unauthorized access to the system. Where an expert can estimate monetary harms resulting from a drop in reputation or customer good will, they should be included as well. The United States recently amended its law to include such a broad definition of "loss."[74]

Depending on the type of activity during an intrusion, the crime may cause other quantifiable monetary harms. For example, where a hacker breaks into a computer in order to use the computer itself—such as where an intruder hacks into a super-computer to use its computing power to run his own programs—the monetary harm would include the value of the computer time used in addition to any investigation and repair costs.

Similarly, if an intruder steals information, the value of that information should be included in the total loss amount. At times, a court can determine the value of the information quite easily, such as where the information is itself for sale. Where the information is of a proprietary nature, however, such as certain manufacturing formulae, a court may need to attempt to determine the value of the information to the business. Figuring out the value of the information also may be possible by examining what benefit, economic or otherwise, the intruder gained. For example, if an intruder obtains data about a secret production process and sells that information to a competitor for $100,000, a court could fairly use this figure as the actual value of the information.[75]

For a number of reasons, these methods of calculating the monetary loss associated with a crime may not adequately account for the severity of the offense. First, the actual effects of a network

---

74. *See* 18 U.S.C. § 1030(e)(11) (2000) (defining loss as "any reasonable cost to any victim, including the cost of responding to an offense, conducting a damage assessment, and restoring the data, program, system, or information to its condition prior to the offense, and any revenue lost, cost incurred, or other consequential damages incurred because of interruption of service").

75. The fact that a defendant did not personally benefit, however, should not prevent effective punishment. Many hackers have intruded successfully into computer networks simply to prove that they could do it or to raise their personal reputations, rather than to obtain a financial benefit. These acts should still be punished appropriately.

intrusion may reach far beyond the network itself and cause monetary harms that cannot reliably be determined. More importantly, many of the harms resulting from network crimes cause other kinds of societal harms that simply cannot be quantified in monetary terms. The following sections explore some of these non-monetary harms.

2.   Physical Harm to Individuals, Threats to Public Safety, and Damage to Critical National Infrastructures

Lawmakers should consider raising penalties for network crimes where the conduct causes, or threatens to cause, physical harm to an individual or a threat to public safety. A network intrusion could cause physical harm, for example, where a hacker breaks into a hospital computer and alters medical records or simply prevents doctors from being able to access their patients' treatment records. Similarly, a threat to public safety might occur when a hacker breaks into a computer that controls air traffic at an airport. Although shutting down such a computer may cause little quantifiable monetary harm if detected quickly, even a short outage may have an enormous impact on air safety or flight schedules. As computers continue to take on more important roles, they increase the ways in which an unauthorized user could cause harm to a person or threaten public safety. The law should recognize such threats and provide for commensurate penalties.

In addition, many countries have recognized that their critical infrastructures increasingly rely on computer networks. "Critical infrastructures" are those physical and electronic systems that support the basic functioning of an economy, such as telecommunications, banking and finance, electricity and energy distribution, transportation, water and food distribution, emergency services, and medical care. Damage to these infrastructures can have far-reaching consequences to an economy in addition to threatening public safety. Because of the increased role of computers in maintaining them, critical infrastructures are vulnerable to cyber attack in new and serious ways.[76] Network crimes laws should severely punish conduct that threatens to disrupt critical infrastructures even when such harms

---

76. Protecting critical national infrastructures is imperative. Yet it is difficult for a host of reasons, including: the number of different computer systems involved, the interdependency of these systems, the varied nature of the threats (physical and cyber, military, espionage, criminal, and natural), and the fact that in many countries these infrastructures are maintained primarily by the commercial sector. Addressing cyber-threats to infrastructure is particularly difficult because of the need to balance interests relating to privacy, economic competitiveness, commercial risk, national security, and law enforcement.

cannot be easily translated into monetary terms.

3. Nature of the Victim

Many countries' network crimes laws do not separate victims into categories. Instead, they simply use the term "any computer" to identify the victim of specified offenses. However, some legal systems use the identity of the victim to alter the severity of the punishment.[77] Lawmakers may decide, for example, that certain computers are simply more sensitive, necessitating increased penalties for crimes affecting them.

This differentiation appears particularly important where a particular category of victims is generally associated with significant non-monetary harms. For example, the disruption of a military logistics computer may not cause any loss in business revenue, and the agency owning the computer may incur a relatively small cost to restore service, but even the temporary unavailability of such a computer could cause grave harm to the country's security or prevent the military from fulfilling an important mission. Similarly, lawmakers may choose to heighten penalties for attacks on critical infrastructure computers because of their extreme sensitivity, whether or not it can later be determined that the crime actually threatened to disrupt the provision of basic goods and services.

4. Invasions of Privacy and Stolen Data

Network intrusions that involve access to confidential information can have a severe impact on privacy that may not be easy to quantify in monetary terms. For example, in one case in the United States, a hacker broke into a health care provider's database, stole personal medical information about a celebrity, and sold the information to a tabloid newspaper.[78] Although this kind of invasion of personal privacy may cause little or no financial loss, lawmakers developing penalties for the obtaining of information during a computer intrusion must still recognize and work to deter this type of

---

77. *See, e.g.,* Computer Misuse Act, pt. II, § 9 (2003) (Sing.), *available at* http://agcvldb4.agc.gov.sg (providing for enhanced penalties where the victim computer is involved in national security, public safety, law enforcement, or a critical infrastructure).

78. *Selling Singer's Files Gets Man 6 Months,* HOUSTON CHRONICLE, Dec. 2, 2000, at A2. *See also Paris' Pals Besieged with Calls After Her Cell Phone is Hacked,* CHICAGO SUN TIMES, Feb. 23, 2005, at 52 (hackers gained access to celebrity Paris Hilton's cell phone and posted phone numbers from the phone on the Internet).

harm.

In addition, lawmakers may consider the special sensitivity of certain kinds of information and assign greater corresponding penalties. For example, the theft of certain government records or national security information may pose such a danger that it should be punished more severely, regardless of whether the information has monetary value.

In a similar way, lawmakers might determine that their country faces a particular crime problem and choose to punish more severely the theft of information that contributes to that problem. For example, many nations have begun to experience the problem of "identity theft"—the unauthorized appropriation of the identity of another person in order to obtain a loan fraudulently or withdraw money from the person's bank account without permission. In this environment, lawmakers might create special penalties for network intrusions that involve the theft of financial or personal information such as banking records, credit card numbers, credit reports, and uniquely identifying personal information.

5. Mental State of the Actor

Certain countries have chosen to make penalties more or less severe depending on the mental state of the actor. A hacker who intentionally breaks into a computer system and inadvertently shuts it down probably should be treated less severely than one who intentionally causes the same damage. The provision of the U.S. law pertaining to damage to computers provides an example of this kind of scheme. The law creates a maximum penalty of ten years' imprisonment where a person intentionally causes damage to a computer, five years' imprisonment if the person recklessly causes damage, but only one year imprisonment if the person hacks into a computer and damages it, but did not intend to cause any damage.[79]

IV. PROCEDURAL LAWS EMPOWERING LAW ENFORCEMENT AUTHORITIES TO GATHER ELECTRONIC EVIDENCE

A. Considering Privacy and the Need for Law Enforcement

---

79. *See* 18 U.S.C. § 1030(c).

Authorities

A country planning to enact laws governing law enforcement access to electronic evidence must consider the importance of privacy. Privacy is critical to the functioning of a democratic society and a healthy economy. For example, it promotes the freedom of individual thought and expression, as well as the right to free association, upon which democratic societies rely. In addition, competitive markets and economic development also rely on privacy. Businesses cannot compete successfully without the ability to discuss and make decisions in private. Moreover, privacy is critical to the governmental deliberative process. Having every decision made in the public spotlight cripples the ability of government officials to carefully consider problems and develop appropriate solutions through discussion and debate.

These basic notions of privacy fully apply to communications and actions in the electronic environment. Individuals, businesses, and governments are increasingly using electronic means to communicate. More and more, sensitive personal information, proprietary corporate information, and confidential government documents are stored in electronic form. Thus, if a society is to develop appropriate protections for privacy, it cannot ignore the need to protect privacy in the online world as well.

While providing appropriate protections for privacy is important, countries also must supply law enforcement with the tools that it needs to protect public safety. Computers and the Internet have provided terrorists and criminals with a valuable tool with which to communicate and to actually commit crimes. In order to deter and punish the wide range of crimes facilitated by the Internet, law enforcement investigators must have the ability to investigate the crimes and punish the criminals. For example, if terrorists are using the Internet to communicate and coordinate attacks, law enforcement investigators must have the ability to collect those communications in order to stop the violence. Similarly, attacks on the computer networks themselves, such as the "I Love You" virus, have caused billions of dollars worth of damage worldwide.[80] In order to investigate and punish those who cause such grave harms, law enforcement must have the ability to gather electronic evidence. Indeed, in order to investigate invasions of privacy—such as when a hacker breaks into a financial institution in order to steal financial

---

80. *See* Ariana Eunjung Cha & Dana Hedgpeth, *Back to Business After 'Love' Bite; Damage Figure Reduced to $8.7 Billion*, WASH. POST, May 10, 2000, at A24.

data and credit card numbers—law enforcement investigators need the authority to gain access to electronic records and communications.

As this last example demonstrates, protecting privacy and law enforcement authority are not diametrically opposed; in other words, a reduction in one does not necessarily cause a commensurate increase in the other. In fact, three main groups in a society have the potential to invade the privacy of individuals. First, industry has the ability to invade the privacy of computer users. By tracking computer use and compiling huge databases of private information, businesses can infringe on individual privacy. Such activities generally are regulated by civil laws and regulatory practices and are beyond the scope of this paper.

Second, the government can intrude on individual privacy. When exerting their authority to investigate crime, terrorism, and foreign espionage, governments collect information about citizens, organizations, and businesses. These laws serve a critical function in society by promoting justice, enhancing the economy, and protecting national security. Even though governments enact such laws for the public good, corrupt or overzealous officials can abuse these authorities to the detriment of individual privacy.

Third, criminals can invade individual privacy. By stealing government or corporate secrets, by obtaining financial information from a financial institution, or by accessing the private files stored on an individual's home computer, criminals commit grave privacy violations. Obviously, in order to deter such crimes, law enforcement must have the procedural tools to investigate them. Thus, limiting government investigative authorities in an effort to reduce the *government's* ability to invade individual privacy will invariably, all else being equal, increase *criminals'* ability to invade privacy.

There is no easy way to balance these competing concerns. Each political body must make choices about this issue, taking into consideration the scope of the country's crime and terrorism problems, existing legal structures, and the methods historically used by the country to protect human rights. Moreover, since the Internet has established unprecedented connections between countries, these decisions must also take into account the need to assist other countries in their fight against crime, terrorism, and privacy invasions.

B.   *One Model for Thinking About Procedural Laws*

In considering how to weigh various concerns in the drafting of procedural authorities for law enforcement, lawmakers should consider the following rule of thumb: the more intrusive into individual privacy a particular authority is, the greater the need for safeguards to ensure that the authority is not abused. Figure one illustrates this model.

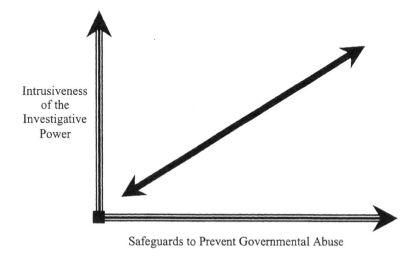

Figure 1: Graphic Depiction of the Relationship between Government Authorities and Safeguards

The laws of many countries incorporate this basic notion. Thus, for instance, the legal protections associated with the authority to obtain the content of a communication generally exceed those associated with the authority to obtain non-content traffic data related to that same communication. Similarly, legal systems often provide greater limitations on the authority to intercept a message passing over a computer network than on the authority to access the content of a file that an individual has chosen to store somewhere on a computer network. Lawmakers should decide how intrusive a particular authority is in the context of their society's privacy expectations. Following this basic decision, they can choose from a long list of possible restrictions on the use of this authority.

The restrictions that countries have placed on the use of government investigative authorities include:

- Laws that require that investigators only use the authority during the investigation of one of a class of crimes or a list of particular offenses. For example, some countries' laws permit law enforcement officials to intercept the content of messages only during the investigation of the most serious crimes.[81]

- Laws that limit the physical scope of a search for stored data or other computer hardware. For example, investigators may have to identify the item or information for which they are searching and then may be permitted to search only in places in which that item could be hidden.[82]

- Laws that limit the temporal scope of a search for data or other computer information. For example, where investigators intend to intercept communications over a period of weeks or months, laws can limit the activity to a specified period of time.[83]

- Laws that require investigators to develop predicate facts before they are entitled to exercise the authority. For example, certain laws require investigators to possess "reasonable grounds" to believe that the computer has been used to commit a crime and that electronic evidence of a crime will be found on a particular computer storage device.[84]

- Laws that require that an independent fact-finder, such as a judge, review such predicate facts before the investigators can exercise the authority. Countries commonly require a warrant or court order prior to the search of a home or office or before investigators can intercept private

---

81. *See, e.g.,* 18 U.S.C. §§ 2516(1)(a), 2516(3) (2000) (electronic interception warrant allowed only for crimes with a maximum penalty of over one year); Telecommunications (Interception) Act 1979, §§ 45–46 (Austl.), *available at* http://www.austlii.edu.au/au/legis/cth/consol_act/ta1979350/ (electronic interception warrant allowed for crimes with a maximum penalty of over seven years).

82. *See, e.g.,* FED. R. CRIM. P. 41(e)(2); *see generally* Coolidge v. New Hampshire, 403 U.S. 443, 467 (1971) (holding that the particularity requirement of the Fourth Amendment of the U.S. Constitution prevents law enforcement from executing "general warrants" that permit "exploratory rummaging" through a person's belongings).

83. *See, e.g.,* 18 U.S.C. § 2518(5) (2000) (court can authorize interception for a maximum of thirty days); Telecommunications (Interception) Act, § 49(3) (court can authorize interception for ninety days).

84. *See, e.g.,* 18 U.S.C. § 2703(d) (2000) (requiring law enforcement officer to submit "specific and articulable facts" in application for court order); Telecommunications (Interception) Act, § 45(c) (requiring law enforcement officer seeking interception authority to provide court "reasonable grounds for suspecting that a particular person is using, or is likely to use" a telecommunications service).

communications.[85]

- Laws that require that investigators only use the authority as a "last resort," i.e., when other investigative alternatives have failed or are too dangerous to try.[86]

- Laws that establish penalties for law enforcement officials who fail to comply with the rules. Such penalties could include, for example, administrative discipline, prohibitions on the use of evidence obtained in violation of the rules, and civil and criminal liability.[87]

- Laws that prohibit the disclosure of evidence gained through the use of such an authority where such disclosure occurs for any reason other than the official purpose. For example, laws can sanction officials administratively or even criminally if they leak evidence to the press or use it for financial advantage.[88]

- Laws that require the approval of a senior or politically-accountable government official before investigators can use the authority.[89] This requirement can provide a level of "quality control," restrict the number of times that an authority will be used, and reduce the danger of errors or overreaching by overzealous investigators.

- Laws that require that collected evidence be stored in certain ways, allow independent inspectors to review that stored evidence, and require investigators to destroy the evidence once the official purpose, such as a criminal prosecution, has been accomplished.[90]

- Finally, laws that require that investigators make notifications to various parties, creating greater oversight of the use of that authority. For example, laws can require investigators to notify: (1) an independent authority such as a court; or (2) the individual whose information or communications was obtained.[91] Such notification could

---

85. *See, e.g.*, FED. R. CRIM. P. 41(d); Telecommunications (Interception) Act, §§ 45–46.

86. *See, e.g.*, 18 U.S.C. § 2518(3)(c); Telecommunications (Interception) Act, § 45(e).

87. *See, e.g.*, 18 U.S.C. §§ 2707, 2712(c), 3121 (2000).

88. *See, e.g.*, 18 U.S.C. § 2707(g); Telecommunications (Interception) Act, § 63.

89. *See, e.g.*, 18 U.S.C. §§ 2516(1), 3125(a) (2000).

90. *See, e.g.*, Telecommunications (Interception) Act, § 83 (requiring, among other things, that an ombudsman inspect an Australian law enforcement agency's records at specific intervals).

91. *See, e.g.*, FED. R. CRIM. P. 41(f); 18 U.S.C. §§ 3125, 2703(b) (2000).

be required at a set point in time, or the law could allow the government to delay notification during the course of an investigation if the investigators can show that notifying the individual whose information they obtained would interfere with the investigation.[92]

Lawmakers can decide to enact these restrictions on the use of investigative authorities in any of a myriad of combinations depending on the authority and the particular cultural and legal history of the country. The remainder of this Article discusses the various authorities for obtaining electronic evidence as well as the ways in which certain countries have chosen to restrict their use.

C.   Interception of the Content of Communications on Computer Networks While the Communications Are Occurring

Technically trained experts, using computer software, hardware, or a combination of both, can intercept communications on computer networks while they are occurring.   For example, investigators can intercept emails sent from one terrorist to another, or they can intercept the commands sent by a hacker to a victim computer in order to steal corporate information.   This kind of interception is similar in many ways to the interception of telephone calls.   Both techniques allow investigators to obtain the content of communications while the communication is being transmitted. Moreover, like traditional telephone interceptions, electronic interceptions generally require the assistance of the telecommunications provider that is carrying the communication. Indeed, at times, the provider can complete the interception on behalf of law enforcement. Because of these similarities, many countries use laws to intercept electronic communications that are the same or very similar to older laws that govern the interception of telephone calls. Law enforcement needs this authority, with appropriate safeguards, to address the threats posed by cyber-criminals.

1.   Law Enforcement Needs and Privacy Considerations

Law enforcement needs computer-oriented interception authority for the same reasons that it needs the authority to intercept telephone conversations: terrorists and criminals increasingly are

---

92. *See, e.g.*, 18 U.S.C. §§ 2703(b), 2705 (2000).

using electronic communications to plan and execute conspiracies and other serious crimes. In addition, many crimes are now committed solely using computer networks such as the Internet. For example, every day, pedophiles distribute thousands of images of child pornography using the Internet, and domestic and international criminals use the Internet to commit fraud by sending communications that dupe unsuspecting individuals into parting with their money. This kind of fraud costs victims millions of dollars every year and is increasing. In addition, hackers constantly probe computers for vulnerabilities and break in to steal sensitive information. These criminals rely on the apparent anonymity provided by the Internet. Only by equipping law enforcement officers with the appropriate investigative authorities can these criminals be deterred and punished.

The Cybercrime Convention recognizes this reality and rightly requires parties to have laws that allow the interception of communications.[93] Article 21 recognizes that different legal systems may implement such laws in different ways. Moreover, it requires that parties give law enforcement officials the authority to compel providers to provide the content of particular communications, as well as the authority to collect such communications directly.[94] In many

---

93. Article 21 of the Convention provides:

Interception of content data

1. Each Party shall adopt such legislative and other measures as may be necessary, in relation to a range of serious offences to be determined by domestic law, to empower its competent authorities to:

    a. collect or record through application of technical means on the territory of that Party, and

    b. compel a service provider, within its existing technical capability, to:

        i. collect or record through application of technical means on the territory of that Party, or

        ii. co-operate and assist the competent authorities in the collection or recording of, content data, in real-time, of specified communications in its territory transmitted by means of a computer system.

Convention on Cybercrime, *supra* note 6, art. 21(1).

94. *Id.* Indeed, the Explanatory Report states

In general, the two possibilities for collecting traffic data in paragraph 1(a) and (b) [of Article 21] are not alternatives. Except as provided in paragraph 2, a Party must ensure that both measures can be carried out. This is necessary because if a service provider does not have the technical ability to assume the collection or recording of traffic data (1(b)), then a Party must have the possibility for its law enforcement authorities to undertake themselves the task (1(a)). Likewise, an obligation under paragraph 1(b)(ii) to co-operate and assist the competent authorities in the collection or recording of traffic data is senseless if the competent authorities are not empowered to collect or record themselves the traffic data. Additionally, in the situation of some local area

cases, having the provider collect the material and deliver it to law enforcement officials (perhaps in response to a court order) is favorable because it is cheaper and less likely to disrupt the provider's business. But in those situations where the provider is unable to intercept the required communications, or where interceptions occurs at a place other than the provider's system,[95] law enforcement must have the legal authority to complete the interceptions itself.

While this authority is critical to law enforcement efforts to fight terrorism and crime on computer networks, lawmakers should consider carefully the reasons for placing restrictions on its use. Interception of communications generally is regarded as an intrusive investigative technique. Unrestricted interception can constitute a grave privacy violation as it allows access to the most private communications and has the potential to inhibit freedom of speech and association. Moreover, fear of overly intrusive government interception of communications can stifle competitive markets, economic development, and the confidence in a country's legal system that underlies foreign investment. Thus, lawmakers should craft laws that take into account the intrusive nature of full-content, real-time interception.

2.   Examples of Restrictions on Interception Authorities

Various countries have chosen different approaches to restricting the interception of electronic communications. Australia's laws illustrate several types of restrictions that lawmakers can choose.

Australian law contains the following provisions in this area: (1) investigators must obtain a warrant from an independent judge by showing that the information gained will assist in the investigation of a serious crime (generally those with a maximum sentence of seven years' imprisonment or greater); (2) the judge must balance a number of factors, including the value of the information, the gravity of the conduct, the privacy invasion, and whether other investigative techniques would be just as effective; (3) certain disclosure

---

networks (LANs), where no service provider may be involved, the only way for collection or recording to be carried out would be for the investigating authorities to do it themselves. Both measures in paragraphs 1 (a) and (b) do not have to be used each time, but the availability of both methods is required by the article.

Explanatory Report, *supra* note 33, para. 223.

95. For example, in certain cases it may be advantageous for law enforcement to intercept communications of two wireless users by placing a wireless antenna nearby and intercepting the communications from the air.

restrictions apply to any information gained during the interception; (4) any evidence intercepted in violation of the law cannot be offered in a court proceeding; (5) investigators must store the evidence for review by independent inspectors and destroy it once the official purpose, such as a criminal prosecution, has been accomplished; and (6) the interception can occur for only ninety days, but the court may renew the order for additional ninety day periods.[96]

When a nation's laws create a very restrictive process for obtaining court authority to intercept communications, the laws also commonly contain many exceptions, as described below, that permit the interception of communications in particular situations.

3.   Exceptions Where Interception Is Less Intrusive

Even where their laws generally would require a warrant for the interception of the content of communications, various countries, including the United States, have created exceptions to this rule. These exceptions apply generally where participants in the communication have reduced privacy interests or where some other overriding need justifies the interception. Lawmakers might consider reducing the restrictions on law enforcement interception in the following circumstances:

- The communications system is intended to be accessible to the public. In such cases, the need for law enforcement access to such information outweighs any possible privacy interest because *no* privacy is promised by the system. In the context of computer networks, this principle might apply to "chat rooms" or "chat channels" that are open to the public.[97]

- One of the parties to the communication has consented to the recording of the communication. In the computer context, such consent might be obtained at the time the user logs onto the service (through a so-called "logon banner").[98]

---

96. *See* Telecommunications (Interception) Act 1979, pt. VI (Austl.), *available at* http://www.austlii.edu.au/au/legis/cth/consol_act/ta1979350/.

97. For example, U.S. law does not prohibit interception of an electronic communication "made through an electronic communication system that is configured so that [it] is readily available to the general public." 18 U.S.C. § 2511(2)(g) (2000).

98. For example, in the United States, interception is lawful "where [a] person is a party to the communication or where one of the parties to the communication has given prior consent to such interception." 18 U.S.C. § 2511(2)(c), (d).

- The interception is done by the provider of the computing service in the course of providing that service or ensuring that the service is not being misused. Without this kind of exception, owners of computer systems may encounter substantial difficulties in securing their systems against unauthorized users.[99]

- The interception is done by law enforcement in order to monitor the activities of unauthorized users (i.e., trespassers on the computer system). Plainly, those who are using a computer system without authority cannot reasonably expect their communications to remain private.[100]

Lawmakers should also consider situations where information intercepted by private persons may be turned over to law enforcement. For example, the United States has enacted a law that allows information lawfully intercepted by a private person (under, for example, one of the exceptions to the prohibition on interception listed above) to be disclosed in appropriate circumstances.[101] At the same time, U.S. law does not allow illegally intercepted material to be disclosed to anyone, nor used in any court proceeding.[102]

D.   *Collection of Traffic Data While the Communication Is Occurring*

Another important law enforcement authority allows the collection of non-content, traffic information. Like the interception of the content of electronic communications, this collection occurs while the communications are occurring. Investigators use software, hardware, or a combination of the two to collect the information. Indeed, in many instances, the very same software program can collect either content or non-content information depending on how investigators configure it. The difference between this form of monitoring and full-content monitoring lies in the information

---

99. Under U.S. law, for example, it is not unlawful for a provider of electronic communication service to intercept communications "while engaged in any activity which is a necessary incident to the rendition of . . . service or to the protection of the rights or property of the provider of that service." 18 U.S.C. § 2511(2)(a)(i).

100. *See* 18 U.S.C. § 2511(2)(i).

101. *See* 18 U.S.C. § 2517(3) (2000); United States v. Harvey, 540 F.2d 1345, 1352 (8th Cir. 1976) (communications intercepted by a provider in the course of protecting its rights and property may be turned over to law enforcement).

102. *See* 18 U.S.C. § 2511(1)(c), 2515 (2000).

obtained. Instead of obtaining the content of an email message, this authority would allow only the collection of such information as the source and destination of an email and the date and time it was sent. Similarly, instead of obtaining the actual commands that a hacker sends to a victim computer and the content of the files that she steals, investigators using this authority could obtain only the source and destination IP address, the date and time of the intrusion, and the size of the downloaded files.

1.   Examples of Laws

Various countries have enacted laws that impose some restrictions on the real-time collection of non-content information. The United Kingdom, for example, requires that such authority be exercised only where: (1) the collected information will be "necessary" for the investigation of crime, protection of public safety, or a similar goal; (2) a high-level government official has approved it; (3) the collection is "proportionate to what is sought to be achieved"; and (4) the collection is limited to a period of thirty days.[103]   The United States has similar rules, requiring that: (1) the collected information is "relevant" to an ongoing criminal investigation;[104] (2) a judicial officer issues a court order based upon the certification of a government attorney;[105] and (3) the collection is limited to sixty days (with the possibility of extension).[106]   These statutory schemes provide some safeguards against official misuse, but they are not so restrictive that they prevent law enforcement investigators from using the authority in a wide range of investigations and at relatively early stages in an investigation.

Finally, lawmakers should consider easing restrictions on investigations when privacy interests are less significant. Such situations might arise when one of the parties to the communication consents to the collection of the information, as well as where the provider of the communications service needs to collect the information for billing or security reasons.[107]

---

103. *See* Regulation of Investigatory Powers Act, 2000, pt. I, c. II (Eng.), *available at* http://www.hmso.gov.uk/acts/acts2000/20000023.htm.

104. 18 U.S.C. § 3123(a)(1)–(2) (2000).

105. 18 U.S.C. § 3123(a)(1).

106. 18 U.S.C. § 3123(c)(1)–(2).

107. *See, e.g.,* 18 U.S.C. § 3121(b)(1) (2000) (providing exception for collecting traffic data "relating to the operation, maintenance, and testing of a wire or electronic communication service"); § 3121(b)(3) (providing an exception for collecting traffic data

754   *COLUMBIA JOURNAL OF TRANSNATIONAL LAW*   [43:705

E.   Law Enforcement Access to Content Stored on a Network

Modern computer networks commonly allow for the storage of large amounts of data in locations distant from the computer of any given user. Law enforcement needs the authority to obtain such data or to compel the network provider to disclose that information during a criminal investigation. Such data may, for example, consist of email in the possession of an Internet service provider that has been sent to one of its customers, or the storage of a user's files in a central high-capacity server.

The laws governing access to stored information may be similar to those governing the·search or seizure of information from a person's house, but they need not be identical. Indeed, because of several considerations, many legal systems place fewer restrictions on the disclosure of information stored by a third-party than on the search of physical spaces. First, the individual or institution that stores and can access the data generally is a neutral third-party, such as a legitimate corporation or service provider. In these circumstances, the physical coerciveness of traditional legal processes, such as the authority to· enter private property forcibly without permission, do not apply. Moreover, when individuals choose to store their data with a third-party, rather than in their homes or on their persons, they generally expect to have less of a right to privacy.

1.   Law Enforcement Needs and Privacy Considerations

Law enforcement authority to access information stored on a computer network is critical to the investigation of cybercrime. For example, very often such information constitutes the "crime scene" from which investigators find clues about what was stolen, how it was accomplished, and who the perpetrator might be. Just as law enforcement needs the power to obtain evidence and to compel individuals and companies to provide evidence in more traditional investigations, they must have the corresponding power when the evidence is electronic.

Article 18 of the Convention on Cybercrime requires parties to grant law enforcement access to the content of information stored on computer networks.[108] This provision applies not only to content but

with the consent of the user).

    108.   A party to the Convention must:

also to non-content data such as log files and customer identification information, as discussed below.

Yet even if individuals may not have as significant a privacy interest in data stored remotely, they may nevertheless retain a substantial expectation of privacy of that information. Businesses, governments, and individuals store more and more sensitive data in electronic form on remote servers. Thus, lawmakers should consider reasonable restrictions on law enforcement authority to access such information, bearing in mind that investigators' access to such information also enhances privacy when used to investigate or prosecute the criminals who invade privacy by stealing that very information.

2.   Example of Laws

The United States grants the greatest level of protection to email that is stored incident to transmission; that is, email stored by the provider that is en route to its destination and about which the receiver may have no knowledge. For this category of stored information, the law requires a search warrant issued by a neutral magistrate and supported by "probable cause," the same type of legal process used to search an individual's home.[109] In addition, the law provides for administrative discipline for investigators who abuse this authority, civil suits against the government for any violation in the procedure, and disclosure restrictions on any information gained using this authority.[110]

Lawmakers should also consider, however, whether all categories of stored content deserve the same kinds of protections. For example, perhaps information that a user chooses to store at the remote location on the network may receive less protection than email en route to the user about which he has no knowledge. The U.S. Code makes exactly this kind of distinction.[111] For example, if a user

---

adopt such legislative and other measures ... to empower its competent authorities to order:

(a) a person in its territory to submit specified computer data in that person's possession or control ... and

(b) a service provider offering its services in the territory of the Party to submit subscriber information relating to such services in that service provider's possession or control ...

Convention on Cybercrime, *supra* note 6, art. 18(1).

109.   18 U.S.C. § 2703(a) (2000).

110.   18 U.S.C. §§ 2707, 2712 (2000).

111.   *Compare* 18 U.S.C. § 2703(a) (requiring a search warrant based upon probable

chooses to place picture files on a remote server such as a Yahoo! "briefcase," investigators may obtain it with a grand jury subpoena or a court order based on "specific and articulable facts" rather than with a full search warrant requiring "probable cause."[112]

Finally, lawmakers should consider the circumstances under which providers can voluntarily turn information over to law enforcement authorities. On the one hand, unrestricted disclosures by providers might unacceptably infringe on personal privacy, especially where law enforcement officials can exert unofficial pressure on service providers. On the other hand, under certain circumstances, allowing providers to make voluntary disclosures makes sense. For example, information relating to a threat to public health or safety should justify voluntary disclosure, as should information turned over to law enforcement in order to report an attack on a provider's network.

F.   Law Enforcement Access to Non-Content Information Stored on a Network

Computer networks generally create many records that show who is using the network, to whom they are sending communications, from whom they are receiving communications, and what actions they have taken with respect to computer programs and information stored on the network. Although these records are often critical to solving a crime facilitated by the network, access to these records generally raises fewer privacy concerns than access to the actual content of the related communications. For this reason, laws generally create fewer safeguards and limitations on law enforcement's authority to compel disclosure of non-content data.

Law enforcement investigators need access to these records primarily to identify the perpetrator of a crime. For example, in order for investigators to determine, some time after an email is sent, who sent it to a known terrorist organization, investigators must rely on stored traffic information. Similarly, if investigators have identified an account at an Internet service provider that is being used to distribute images of child pornography, they need to seek disclosure of logs that show what telephone number was used to access the

---

cause to obtain email that has not yet been accessed by the user) *with* 18 U.S.C. § 2703(b) (allowing law enforcement to compel disclosure of all other kinds of content stored by a provider using a subpoena based on relevance).

    112.   18 U.S.C. § 2703(a)–(b), (d).

account in order to identify the person responsible.

1.   Examples of Laws

Although laws could treat all kinds of traffic data equally, they need not do so; some kinds of non-content data raise fewer privacy concerns than others. For example, laws could differentiate basic information about the customer of an Internet service provider—such as the customer's name, home address, and the means used to pay for the account—from records that show all of that individual's activities in using the account—such as to whom she sent emails and from whom she received them. Indeed, the United States makes exactly this distinction.[113] Investigators can obtain information identifying the subscriber with legal process that requires only that the information be "relevant" to the investigation, but must justify to a court on the basis of "specific and articulable facts" the need for records that show all of an individual's activities in using an account.[114]

2.   Preservation of Stored Records and Information

One final consideration involves the preservation of records. Electronic evidence in general, and log records containing traffic information in particular, are ephemeral. Providers often do not want to bear the expense of storing such records, and some do not even keep records at all. Providers easily can delete these records in the ordinary course of business (quite apart from criminals who delete the logs with ill intent), and it is not unusual for providers to retain them only for a matter of days or weeks absent a law that compels them to do otherwise. Considering that investigators do not always know that a crime has been committed until some time has passed, it is all too common that the provider has deleted the records the investigators need to trace the communications and identify the criminal. Moreover, the legal procedures for obtaining these records often remain quite slow.

One legal tool that eases these investigative burdens is the

---

113. *Compare* 18 U.S.C. § 2703(c)(1)(B) (obtaining most kinds of logging information requires a court order based upon "specific and articulable facts") *with* 18 U.S.C. § 2703(c)(2) (allowing law enforcement to compel disclosure of the name and address of the account holder, and other information, using an administrative subpoena based on relevance).

114. *Id.*

power to compel a provider to preserve—but not yet disclose—records and other information that pertain to a criminal investigation. Because the evidence can be destroyed so quickly, law enforcement officials must be able to exercise the preservation authority very rapidly. Consequently, it must not require prior court approval if such an authority is to have any meaningful effect. Approval of an independent magistrate is unnecessary, in any event, since the privacy concerns relating to preservation are quite minimal: the provider will not disclose any information until the law enforcement officer obtains authority through the regular legal process. The request for preservation simply freezes the evidence so that it will not disappear while the investigators complete the necessary legal procedures. If they cannot later justify their need for the information or meet whatever legal restrictions apply in order to compel disclosure, then the provider never discloses the evidence to the law enforcement officer and the customer's privacy is not impaired.[115]

U.S. law provides an example of this sort of provision. By merely making a written or oral request, a U.S. law enforcement investigator can require a provider to "take all necessary steps to preserve records and other evidence in its possession pending the issuance of a court order or other process."[116] Such a preservation request freezes the information for ninety days, and the preservation request can be renewed.[117] Article 16 of the Convention on Cybercrime provides for a similar law enforcement tool.[118]

G.   Compelling Disclosure of Electronic Evidence in the Possession of the Target

As a general matter, most countries have laws that allow for

---

115.   This kind of preservation should be distinguished from laws or policies that require providers to retain a category of data regarding all users for a certain period of time. Certain jurisdictions, such as the European Union and Australia, have created rules that require providers to retain traffic data for one year. Such "data retention" rules undoubtedly increase public safety by helping law enforcement to investigate and deter crime.

116.   18 U.S.C. § 2703(f)(1) (2000).

117.   18 U.S.C. § 2703(f)(2).

118.   The Convention requires that each party adopt laws allowing authorities "to order or similarly obtain the expeditious preservation of specified computer data, including traffic data, that has been stored by means of a computer system, in particular where there are grounds to believe that the computer data is particularly vulnerable to loss or modification." Convention on Cybercrime, *supra* note 6, art. 16(1). Parties to the Convention must also adopt legal measures to ensure that service providers "maintain the integrity" of the data as long as necessary (up to a maximum of ninety days) and not disclose the fact of the preservation of data. *Id.* art. 16(2)–(3).

the search and seizure of physical objects and documents that provide evidence of the commission of a crime. Lawmakers need to consider, however, how well these existing laws apply to the seizure of intangible evidence, such as information stored on a computer hard drive.

Law enforcement plainly needs the authority to search for or seize computers and electronic evidence in the hands of criminals. In crimes facilitated by the Internet, for example, investigators generally need to trace electronic communications back to their origin. Once they have identified the home or business computer that sent the communications, they generally need to seize it in order to confirm the clues they previously have gathered and identify the individual who used the computer. Thus, if a bank computer is penetrated and money is stolen, investigators need to examine the bank computer's log records, trace the communications back to an Internet service provider, and finally identify the particular location from which the hacker committed the crime. As the final step in such an investigation, investigators generally will search that location, seize the computer or its electronic information, and arrest the perpetrator.

1. Seizing Computer Hardware vs. Seizing Electronic Data

Often, investigators need to seize the computer hardware itself. They may need to do this, for example, so that they can have it examined in a computer forensics lab or because it contains contraband, such as child pornography. In such cases, the computer should be treated like any other physical object, and the traditional rules for seizure of physical evidence should apply.

If, on the other hand, investigators do not need to seize the hardware itself but instead merely need to copy files on the computer or even make an exact copy of the entire electronic storage device, the question becomes less clear. In this scenario, the investigators do not remove any physical thing from the premises, nor do they deprive the owner of the use of that information. On the surface, it may appear that these considerations make such an action less invasive or less detrimental to the rights of the computer owner. Yet data stored in a home or business can be very sensitive and include items such as diaries, wills, and financial or proprietary information. A good argument can be made that such information should be treated the same way, regardless of whether it is stored on paper or in an electronic form.

Thus, lawmakers should strongly consider making the rules

for copying electronic data equivalent to those for seizing the computer hardware that contains that electronic data. Using accepted rules and procedures provides balance and certainty to the investigatory process and makes it easier for officers, prosecutors, and judges to learn and to apply the rules. Of course, if investigators meet whatever legal requirements apply, copying of information in lieu of seizing the computer hardware should be a permissible search and seizure method. Moreover, to the extent that the law recognizes exceptions to the traditional search and seizure rules, such as in cases in which law enforcement officers have the consent of the property owner or where there is an emergency threatening public health or safety, these exceptions should also apply to the copying of data or the seizure of computer hardware.

The Convention on Cybercrime recognizes these varied approaches to searching for or seizing computers and computer data in the possession of the suspect of an investigation.[119] It clearly requires that these rules apply not only to computers themselves, but also to any other digital storage medium. Moreover, it requires signatories to pass laws that empower law enforcement not only to seize computer hardware and to copy computer data, but also to "maintain the integrity" of computer data and to render it inaccessible if the situation requires it. This last authority might include, for example, the power to shut down a website that distributes child pornography or other contraband material.[120]

---

119. Article 19 – Search and seizure of stored computer data:

1. Each Party shall adopt such legislative and other measures as may be necessary to empower its competent authorities to search or similarly access:

a. a computer system or part of it and computer data stored therein; and

b. a computer-data storage medium in which computer data may be stored in its territory.

. . .

3. Each Party shall adopt such legislative and other measures as may be necessary to empower its competent authorities to seize or similarly secure computer data accessed according to paragraphs 1 or 2. These measures shall include the power to:

a. seize or similarly secure a computer system or part of it or a computer-data storage medium;

b. make and retain a copy of those computer data;

c. maintain the integrity of the relevant stored computer data; and

d. render inaccessible or remove those computer data in the accessed computer system.

Convention on Cybercrime, *supra* note 6, art. 19(1), (3).

120. The Explanatory Report states:

The rendering inaccessible of data can include encrypting the data or otherwise technologically denying anyone access to that data. This measure could

CONCLUSION

As we move forward into the Information Age, it has become increasingly clear that every nation must have a comprehensive legal framework to combat cybercrime. One important tool in achieving this goal is the Convention on Cybercrime as it provides an important benchmark for any country in the process of evaluating the completeness of its domestic laws, whether that country signs the Convention or not.

In addition, the Convention will provide important additional value to nations that sign and ratify it. For example, it acts as a "mutual legal assistance treaty" (MLAT) between two signatories if they do not have an existing treaty.[121] The existence of an MLAT helps to reduce the bureaucratic frictions that surround requests for law enforcement assistance and reduce the often lengthy delays. Moreover, countries that become part of the Convention commit to making their domestic investigatory powers available to foreign cybercrime investigations (with appropriate safeguards for national interests), as well as to expediting requests for assistance in computer crime cases.[122]

The benefits of ratifying the Convention will very likely become available to all nations. The Convention contains a provision that allows the Council of Europe to open the Convention for much broader membership.[123] Although it remains unclear exactly when and how other countries will be invited to join, it is quite possible that the Convention will become a global treaty.

Unfortunately, individuals within the United Nations and in certain nations have proposed developing a UN convention similar to the Convention on Cybercrime.[124] It would be far preferable for the

---

usefully be applied in situations where danger or social harm is involved, such as virus programs or instructions on how to make viruses or bombs, or where the data or their content are illegal, such as child pornography.

Explanatory Report, *supra* note 33, para. 198.

121. Convention on Cybercrime, *supra* note 6, art. 27.

122. *Id.* arts. 25, 29–35.

123. *Id.* art. 37.

124. *See. e.g., Effective Measures to Prevent and Control Computer-Related Crime,* Commission on Crime Prevention and Criminal Justice, 11th Sess., Agenda Item 5, at 6, E/CN.15/2002/8 (2002), *available at* http://www.unodc.org/pdf/crime/commissions/11comm/8e.pdf. Speakers at other international forums have also begun to raise the idea of a UN cybercrime convention. *See* Asia-Pacific Economic Cooperation Telecommunications & Information Working Group, *Conference Report, Cybercrime Legislation and Enforcement Capacity Building Project* (Aug. 25–27, 2004), at 5, *available at* http://www.apectelwg.org:8080/e-

762   *COLUMBIA JOURNAL OF TRANSNATIONAL LAW*   [43:705

Convention to become widely accepted around the world than for a new convention to be drafted by a multilateral organization such as the United Nations. The sheer magnitude of the task of negotiating a new instrument is daunting. The Convention took four years of steady work to negotiate.[125] Because of the number of delegates that would be required, a UN process undoubtedly would take longer. Moreover, it might prove difficult for many countries to provide an expert, as few individuals have experience in dealing with the complex issues implicated by cybercrime investigations. Initiating a UN process also poses the grave danger that the drafting committee will become distracted by other concerns or end up with an ineffective, watered-down draft in an effort to cater to the needs of such a large number of countries.

In addition, the process of negotiating a new convention over six to eight years would require a substantial commitment of resources by the drafting countries and the United Nations. Yet it is unclear how such a process could develop a treaty any better than the Convention on Cybercrime. If the two treaties conflicted, how would the conflict be resolved? Moreover, it would be a tremendous waste of time for countries to wait years for the completion of a UN treaty only to revamp their domestic laws in the same basic ways that the Convention already recommends. Cybercrime and cybercriminals will not wait while the United Nations starts the process over from the beginning. While the Convention is almost surely not the last international word on the question, it is the best, even essential, first word, and countries who delay recognizing this fact do so at their own—and the global community's—peril.

---

securityTG/Hanoi%20Conference%20Report%201.5%20submitted.wpd.doc.

125.   *See supra* note 8.

[2]

The Voyeuristic Hacker

By Brian M. Hoffstadt

We unquestionably live in the Information Age, a time when information is a key commodity that, whether traded domestically or in foreign markets, represents an ever-increasing portion of our national economy.[1] This evolution in our economy was ushered in by the advent of, and continues to be fueled by, the computer. Computers enable us to collect and to store vastly greater quantities of information than ever before: Data aggregators (such as ChoicePoint), banks, and credit bureaus amass detailed profiles on the financial histories of individuals; businesses rely on mainframe computers to store terabytes of data, which may contain their trade secrets, business strategies, or personnel records; and Americans each store gigabytes of information on their home computers ranging from tax filings to address books to diaries.[2] The Internet has connected computers, and the immense quanta of data they store, into a largely seamless network, enabling businesses and individuals to share information almost instantaneously, whether over email or over instant messaging services. This proliferation of Internet users, now estimated at some 211 million in the United States and 1.1 billion worldwide, has only served to increase the net societal value of the Internet.[3] Of course, the interconnectivity that gives the Internet its value also renders connected computers vulnerable to attack.

For many years, malicious hackers seemed primarily interested in *harming* the computers they accessed or using those computers as a platform for launching attacks on still other computers.[4] In recent years, however, hackers have shifted their behavior as they, too, have come to recognize the value of the information stored in electronic form on computers connected to the Internet.[5] These individuals hack not to harm the computers, but solely to view, and thereby obtain, the information stored on them.[6] These so-called voyeuristic hackers act out of many motives: Some are merely curious; others seek to provide a public service of sorts by probing weaknesses in a computer network to obtain information on the network's vulnerabilities in order to report them to the operators; and yet others have far more nefarious aspirations and seek to use the acquired information to commit various other crimes, including identity theft, corporate espionage, or extortion.[7]

Congress has already made some types of voyeuristic hacking a crime and is considering legislation to expand that universe of crimes.[8] But now is the time to develop a forward-looking approach to dealing with the threat

Continued on page 13

Brian M. Hoffstadt is a Partner, Issues & Appeals, Jones Day. Prior to joining Jones Day, he was an Assistant US Attorney, Central District of California from 2000 to 2007, Cyber & Intellectual Property Crimes Section from 2004 to 2007. Mr. Hoffstadt is an Adjunct Professor of Law, University of Southern California Gould School of Law. The views expressed in this article are the author's alone, and do not necessarily reflect the views of Jones Day, the Justice Department, or the USC School of Law. Mr. Hoffstadt thanks Brian Hershman, Rasha Gerges, Jolene Mate, and Erik Silber for their insightful comments and suggestions.

The Voyeuristic Hacker
Continued from page 1

posed by this growing wave of voyeuristic hacks. In this article, I first provide a descriptive overview of the dangers posed by this new breed of hacker and the tools that Congress has made available for federal law enforcement to prosecute these individuals. The balance of the article is devoted to examining the normative question of how to respond to this threat. Toward that end, I propose an analytical framework to be used in answering the two questions critical to formulating any comprehensive law enforcement policy regarding voyeuristic hacks: What types of information should be protected by the criminal law, and which acts with respect to the protected information should be made criminal? I suggest several approaches that Congress might consider as it addresses this issue in the coming years.

ANATOMY OF A VOYEURISTIC HACK

The primary conduit for hacking activity is the Internet.[9] Until recently, most hackers would unlawfully attack a computer using whatever landline cable appended the target computer to the Internet, whether it be cable wire, telephone wire, or a DSL line. A landline hacker obtains information in one of two ways. He can install monitoring software, usually a program that logs every keystroke entered on the computer, or a spyware program that records the user's browsing habits on the Internet, both of which can provide real-time data to the hacker.[10] Again, neither of these real-time hacks is inherently malicious, as Internet service providers are specifically authorized to maintain transaction data involving their customers (but may not disclose it except in narrow circumstances).[11] Alternatively, the hacker can aim his attacks at information that is electronically stored on the computer.

The explosion of wireless Internet technology has completely transmogrified the nature of Internet use and the threats posed by voyeuristic hackers. Internet enthusiasts and local policy makers have made great strides in blanketing pockets of several cities in wireless access points or hotspots. These initiatives are aimed at allowing anyone to access the Internet, often for free, as a means of broadening access to the wealth of information that it contains.[12] This ubiquitous coverage, however, makes it possible for many hackers to pluck information literally right out of the air, without any need to hack a computer at all.[13] Typically, wireless hacking behavior falls into three categories. First, individuals may engage in wardriving,

which is the largely non-intrusive act of searching for available wireless access points to the Internet and making note of where they exist. A wardriver typically does not attempt to *access* the Internet using that point, however.[14] Second, hackers may joyride, which refers to the act of using someone else's wireless access point, which may be harder or easier depending on whether the access point is encrypted.[15] Amazingly, most manufacturers of wireless access devices continue to program the default setting on those devices to provide an unencrypted access point that can be accessed by anyone walking or driving by.[16] Third, hackers have recently started to set up Internet access points that resemble legitimate publicly accessible access points, but are in actuality controlled by the hacker who collects any data typed by the unwitting victim.[17] As with landline hacks, the last two types of wireless hacks may obtain information on a real-time basis or gather information stored on the computer.

CURRENT FEDERAL EFFORTS TO COMBAT VOYEURISTIC HACKS

At this time, Congress has yet to enact a comprehensive package of federal crimes aimed at voyeuristic hacking.[18] Instead, this conduct is proscribed, if at all, by a patchwork of statutes aimed at other criminal conduct that incidentally happens to reach voyeuristic hacks. The conduct covered by these statutes falls into two categories: (1) the precursor act of obtaining information from a computer and (2) the subsequent act of using that information.

The statutes making it a crime to obtain information vary, depending on whether the information is obtained on a real-time basis or is retrieved from a computer's storage. Because a hacker who obtains information on a real-time basis is usually intercepting transmissions, his conduct is likely barred by Title III of the Omnibus Crime Control Act of 1968 (otherwise known as the Wiretap Act).[19] The Wiretap Act makes it a crime to intercept communications, as well as to use or disclose the contents of those communications.[20] These prohibitions do not apply when one party consents to the monitoring, and the Wiretap Act permits Internet service providers (ISPs) to monitor Internet traffic (but not content) and law enforcement to monitor the activities of a computer trespasser on a compromised system.[21]

When a hacker obtains information already stored on a computer—whether from a computer owned or controlled by the individual or business victim or from a computer operated by the victim's ISP—the Computer Fraud and Abuse Act and the Stored Communications

Act govern.[22] The hacker commits a felony if he, without authorized access or in excess of his authorized access, obtains (and does not immediately divest himself of) information involving either national defense or foreign relations.[23] For less sensitive types of information, Congress has erected a two-tiered scheme employing felonies and misdemeanors. A hacker commits a misdemeanor if he accesses a computer without authorization or otherwise exceeds his authorization and thereby (1) obtains financial or credit card information stored in the files of financial institutions or consumer reporting agencies; (2) obtains information from any government agency or department; or (3) obtains information from any "protected computer" connected with the Internet *but only if an interstate communication was used* to obtain information in this last category.[24] Any of these misdemeanors is elevated to a felony if (1) the hacker committed the crime "for purposes of commercial advantage or financial gain"; (2) the hacker committed the crime in furtherance of another federal crime or tort; or (3) the value of the information obtained exceeded $5,000.[25]

The statutes currently governing subsequent use of acquired information are neutral with respect to *how* the information was obtained, but necessarily encompass cases in which the information is obtained from a computer. The most applicable of these information-use statutes are the ones that prohibit trafficking in computer passwords;[26] possessing a "means of identification," that is, "any name or number that may be used . . . to identify a specific individual," including one's name, Social Security number, date of birth, passport number, biometric data, or unique address or routing code, with the intent to commit, or aid and abet, "any unlawful activity" that violates federal law or is a felony under state or local law;[27] trafficking, using, or possessing with intent to traffic or use unauthorized or fraudulent "access devices," which include any card, code, account number, or personal identification number;[28] and disclosing or possessing trade secrets with intent to harm their owner.[29]

Although this panoply of statutes does create *some* protection against voyeuristic hacks, it is anything but complete and creates unintended, illogical inconsistencies. For example, it is a crime to obtain information from any "protected computer" (that is, nearly any computer connected to the Internet) but only if the hack involved an "interstate or foreign communication."[30] This distinction is undoubtedly grounded in Congress' concern to confine federal jurisdiction to crimes with an interstate aspect, but that concern is largely misplaced given the interstate nature of the Internet itself and the fact that whether a particular hack involves an interstate communication may turn on the fortuity of how that communication is

routed, which is often beyond the hacker's control.[31] Thus, the applicability of the statute that arguably provides the broadest basis for prosecuting voyeuristic hackers turns on a distinction that is not controlled by the hacker and is unnecessary to support federal intervention. In a similar vein, the current statutory framework makes it a crime to obtain a victim's financial information from a financial institution's computers, but it is not necessarily a crime to obtain the same information when it is stored on the victim's computer (unless the hack happens to involve an interstate communication).[32] The laws also currently make no provision for specific types of spyware, that is, intrusions that plant a computer program on the victim's computer that collects and thereafter on occasion transmits information (though usually not on a real-time basis) regarding where the victim navigates over the Internet.[33]

To be sure, Congress is aware of some of these shortcomings and is considering legislation that would cure some of these deficiencies. The Cyber-Security Enhancement and Consumer Data Protection Act of 2007 would eliminate the first deficiency described above, the requirement that information obtained from a "protected computer" involve an "interstate or foreign communication."[34] It would also make it a crime to obtain a "means of identification" from any protected computer.[35] The I-SPY Act of 2007 would make it a federal crime, not to obtain personal information, but for the predicate act of installing a program on a person's computer that gathers personal information (defined to include one's name, address, email address, phone number, Social Security number, or other financial data) with the intent to use that information.[36] The SPY-Act would grant the Federal Trade Commission civil and quasi-criminal regulatory authority over several acts implicating the security of information on computers, including the collection of personally identifiable information through keystroke loggers and spyware.[37]

These alterations to the fabric of federal criminal law reaching voyeuristic hackers, while improving the fabric, do not alter its crazy-quilt nature. But whether Congress chooses to enact a complete overhaul or to make piecemeal amendments, it may be helpful to have a comprehensive design toward which Congress may devote its efforts. In the next part, I propose an analytical framework for fashioning this blueprint and offer some suggestions on how policymakers might proceed.

A POLICY FOR RESPONDING TO THE VOYEURISTIC HACKER

As noted already, any cogent policy response to the threat posed by voyeuristic hackers and how to respond to that threat using the criminal law requires policymakers to answer two normative questions. First, what information is to be protected by the criminal law? Second, what conduct with respect to protected information is to be criminal? Ideally, the answers to these questions will not only flow from a logical public policy analysis but also will yield a series of federal criminal statutes that closely hews to that analysis. In other words, public policy theory and the practical implementation of that theory should go hand in hand.[38]

In answering the public policy questions, policymakers should factor several considerations into their analysis. First, and as a useful starting point, it is important to consider the manner in which the criminal law has historically protected information apart from computers. If the criminal law grants demonstrably more or less protection to information stored electronically on a computer vis-à-vis information stored elsewhere, people will likely avail themselves of whichever media provides greater protection. Policymakers should be aware of the importance of this symmetry and how it may alter incentives. Second, policymakers must be cognizant that information protection involves several actors—the voyeuristic hacker who obtains information, the victim who owns the information, and the hardware or software manufacturer that provided the platform for storing the information—and recognize that the scope of criminal law may influence the behavior of all three actors.[39] For instance, a statute that makes it a crime to obtain information only when it is encrypted will likely prompt victims to encrypt their information and may encourage manufacturers to change the default settings on wireless access products to ensure encryption. A statute with no encryption prerequisite would unlikely have these collateral incentive effects. This is not a novel concept, as Congress has placed this onus on information owners in other contexts, requiring that they take reasonable steps to secure their property before its theft will be cognizable under federal law.[40] Third, policymakers should be aware that they are legislating against the backdrop of the well-established debate between privacy (usually of a non-constitutional dimension) and liberty that, to this day, continues to influence the expansion and architecture of the Internet. Those favoring liberty on the Internet seek a freedom of action and expression; those favoring privacy seek greater restrictions on Internet usage to protect information.[41] Finally, the traditional policies underlying criminal law, such as deterrence, the protection of victims, and the adequacy of non-criminal remedies, also come into play when fashioning criminal remedies.[42]

If all goes well, this analytical framework will yield a cogent policy respecting the contours of federal criminal jurisdiction over the theft of information in the cyberworld. Translating this policy into a set of workable criminal statutes is the next step. It is at this point that the fit between theory and practice becomes critical. Although, for example, public policy analysis might support an approach with fine nuances, such subtleties may be too impractical for courts and juries to interpret and too imprecise for persons wishing not to violate the law to understand. When the fit is imperfect, policymakers should be attentive to the quantity and character of any false positives (cases in which public policy does not specify that the behavior should be criminal, but the statutes nevertheless reach it)[43] and any false negatives (cases in which public policy supports criminality, but the statutes do not reach it).[44] Fortunately, neither type of imperfect fit is necessarily fatal. Where a criminal statute is over-inclusive and thereby creates false positives, prosecutorial discretion (and finite resources) may mitigate the overbreadth because prosecutors may choose not to prosecute persons who commit acts of only marginal criminality; of course, policymakers may disagree over the faith that they place in prosecutorial judgment. Conversely, when a criminal statute is under-inclusive and creates a false negative, prosecutors will have to rely upon general purpose federal criminal statutes (for example, wire fraud) or the residual police power of the states. Policymakers are likely to be wary of any glaring gaps in coverage.

WHAT INFORMATION SHOULD BE PROTECTED?

As an initial matter, it is helpful to classify the types of information that voyeuristic hackers may seek to obtain. For these purposes, information can be categorized along two different axes. The first axis hinges on whether the information is intercepted on a real-time basis or whether it is retrieved from a computer's electronic storage some time after it was input. Because this distinction deals with *how* the information is collected rather than *what* information is collected, it is of little help in defining the universe of information to be accorded protection. The second and more directly relevant distinction is the longstanding distinction between *content* information and *transactional* data.[45] With respect to telephone calls, "transactional" data refers to the numbers dialed and the duration of the call, while "content" refers to what was said during the conversation.[46] With respect to Internet communications, "transactional" data refers to the routing and header information for an email or the logs recording which Web sites on the Internet a user visited, while "content" refers to the body of the email or the information transmitted to and received from the Web sites visited.[47] Historically, content has been granted far greater protection than transactional data, largely because transactional data is usually perceived as being less private due to the fact that it is typically collected by third parties or is subject to being observed by others.

Not only has transactional data been accorded second-class status vis-à-vis content, the criminal law has similarly refused to treat all forms of content equally. Looking to how the criminal law treats information theft both outside and inside the cyber-world, Congress has generally extended federal criminal jurisdiction to reach two broad categories of content. First, Congress has made it a crime to acquire content that is particularly harmful when disclosed or used. This explains why Congress has made it a crime to steal trade secrets that underlie corporate espionage, financial data necessary for identity theft, and restricted data essential to national security.[48] Second, Congress has protected content, no matter how stored, when the protection of that content is deemed important as an economic incentive to stimulate its creation. This rationale explains why three of the four types of federally recognized intellectual property—copyrights, trademarks, and trade secrets—are protected in some fashion by federal criminal law.[49] All other forms of information either have no federal criminal protection or are protected intermittently (for example, when an interstate or foreign communication happens to be involved).

Against this backdrop, policymakers should probably not extend any protection to transactional data. In terms of symmetry, this type of information has rarely been protected by the criminal law in any context. Nor does the interest in privacy appear to warrant protecting transactional data. In this regard, it is important to distinguish between privacy as a matter of policy and privacy as a matter of practicality. For instance, a person's shopping habits at a local mall are not private, as that person could be followed from store to store and observed; they are private only because the effort of surveillance is not usually worth the information. In the online world, however, this type of transactional data is easily collected but this ease of collection does not make the data collected any more private than its off-line equivalent. Moreover, many legitimate businesses employ adware that gathers online transactional data on past and potential customers, which is then used to tailor Internet-based ads to those individuals who may appreciate the marketing guidance. Thus, the acquisition or use of transactional data should probably not be criminal.

Defining the contours of content protection may be trickier. On the one hand, privacy interests apply across the board to content: A person's diary may be as worthy of protection as her credit card number, tax return, or trade secret. On the other hand, the policy interest in maintaining symmetry between online and offline information theft would appear to support a policy of protecting certain forms of content, namely, content that is particularly harmful if disclosed or used and so-called "intellectual property" content, but not extending that protection to other forms of content. A law covering *any* information stored on a computer would grant protection to diary entries and other types of personal journals that, while undoubtedly personal and private, did not previously enjoy any special protection. Granting broader protection to content simply because it happens to be stored on a computer would create a disparity in the criminal law that would prompt rational actors to place that information on computers (which, consequently, would enlarge the universe of information available for voyeuristic hackers to reach).

On balance, Congress could logically conclude that the negative incentives created by any asymmetry outweigh the threat to privacy and accordingly restrict the universe of information protected on computers to the same subset of content protected apart from the cyber world, that is, content that is especially harmful when disclosed or used and content that Congress seeks to encourage through the use of economic incentives (*i.e.*, intellectual property).

WHAT CONDUCT SHOULD BE CRIMINAL?

The starting point for determining *which acts* of the voyeuristic hacker should be considered criminal is to examine which acts committed by information thieves are already criminalized. Not all acts involved in the theft of information are criminal. In fact, federal law typically makes only the following two acts a crime: (1) the initial act of obtaining the information; and (2) the consequential actual or potential use of the information. Outside the context of the Internet, a thief obtains information either by stealing the container in which the information is stored (for example, stealing the locked briefcase containing state secrets) or by breaking into the location where the information is stored. In either case, the thief has usually committed an independent criminal act (in the examples, theft or burglary) that is actionable apart from the theft of the information itself.[50] Similarly, Congress has often made it a crime either to actually use improperly obtained information or to possess the information with the intent to use it improperly.[51] Mere possession of improperly obtained information is rarely ever a crime. This is likely because possession of information by itself is generally a morally neutral event. In addition, the illicit possession of information, unlike the illicit possession of tangible items, does not ever dispossess the information's owner of the information; the theft of information occurs merely by looking at it and the owner still retains it.[52] Thus, possession of information inflicts a lesser harm than the theft of a tangible object. Information is also a public good that often gains value from being shared. A rule that prohibited mere possession would risk chilling the dissemination of information, and societal discourse would be less robust for the absence of that information.[53]

The policy interest in symmetry counsels in favor of prohibiting the same two acts—invasion and subsequent use—with respect to the theft of information from computers. Use crimes easily translate into the cyber realm: Use of information may be prohibited regardless of *how* the information was initially obtained. Invasion crimes, however, are not easily transferred to the context of Internet-based information theft. Even when a hacker accesses a person's computer over landline conduits, the hacker does so *remotely* and does not physically intrude on the information owner's property or otherwise dispossess the owner of the information stolen. The lack of *physicality* makes analogies to theft and burglary difficult to apply.[54] The difficulties grow exponentially when wireless Internet access is considered. In that case, there is literally no invasion at all when the hacker intercepts the radio waves that are being broadcast in the area surrounding the wireless access point.

Because the concept of invasion is so ill-suited to the cyber context, policymakers could elect not to criminalize the initial invasion and focus solely on the crimes of consequential use or intended use of information. This narrow approach to criminalizing voyeuristic hacks has the benefit of side-stepping the nettlesome problem of finding a way to translate the act of invasion into the cyber context. It would also not leave *all* invasions unprotected. Real-time interceptions would remain criminal, as they ostensibly inflict a special type of harm because they not only obtain information but also do so by tapping the conduit of the Internet itself, and federal law has long recognized that interference with the channels of interstate commerce themselves is an independent basis for federal regulation (and, hence, federal protection).[55] So, too, would the theft of information obtained by false pretenses, such as when a person unknowingly and unwittingly provides information to a thief.[56] But this narrow approach of barring only consequential use would treat information theft from computers differently than an identical theft from offline sources (where use *and* the initial invasion are barred) and thus may discourage computer use. More to the point, this approach would ostensibly disserve the interests underlying the criminal law because it would leave federal prosecutors powerless to intervene (except where a hacker made his nefarious intentions clear from the outset) until *after* the voyeuristic hacker had inflicted

harm by actually using the information.[57] In other words, this approach would effectively leave the actual theft of information immune from criminal consequence. In light of these consequences, it is not surprising that the scattered statutes that currently criminalize information theft from computers nevertheless still make some attempt to prohibit the act of acquiring information.[58]

Should policymakers nevertheless attempt to construct a crime to penalize the act of obtaining information in the first place, they would be taking a course of action that furthers the interest in symmetry as well as the interests underlying the criminal law. In selecting among various alternatives, policymakers should be mindful of how the resulting crime alters the incentives of the entities affected by the crime and how it balances privacy and liberty concerns. As one might expect, there is no single approach that addresses all of these concerns in a satisfactory manner, and thus policymakers will necessarily be forced to engage in a line-drawing exercise. The consequences of this line drawing are more vividly illustrated by considering the following series of hypothetical situations:

- *Situation 1.* A State Department employee hides sensitive government files from her employer in a safe in her locked home. (The files are a form of content protected by the criminal law.)
- *Situation 2.* The employee does not hide the files in a safe, but still places them in her home and locks all the doors.
- *Situation 3.* The employee places the files in her home on an inside ledge beside a window but does not lock the back door to her home.
- *Situation 4.* The employee places the files in her home, and locks the doors, but allows a house-keeper to clean her home.
- *Situation 5.* The employee places the files in a manila folder on the front porch of her home, which is open to the public street.
- *Situation 6.* The employee places the files in the safe of an old friend, who assures her that the safe is well guarded (but in fact, the friend is an operative for a foreign nation).
- *Situation 7.* The employee, who lives in a Washington, DC-suburb, stands on her front lawn and reads the documents in the files aloud through a bullhorn, but does so in French.
- *Situation 8.* The employee reads the files over the bullhorn in English.

These hypotheticals take place apart from computers, but they are helpful because their familiarity evokes visceral, common-sense reactions. Situations 1 through 6 may be directly analogized to intrusions into a landline computer, with 4 and 6 involving deception as a means of obtaining the information, and 5 representing a computer user who places information in a peer-to-peer network where it is on her computer but nevertheless freely available to others willing to walk over her front lawn to reach the porch. Situations 7 and 8 are analogous to the theft of information from a wireless network.

With these analogies in mind, it is useful to examine how the various interests animating the analytical framework play out and dictate differing outcomes for the different situations. The policies underlying criminal law would, for the most part, support an intrusion-based crime in all but situations 7 and 8. As one moves from the first to the last hypothetical, the victim is taking fewer precautions to protect her information, and concomitantly, it becomes easier for the thief seeking to steal that information. In situations 1, 2, and 3, the thief must either commit a burglary or at least break and enter in order to obtain the trade secret; in situations 4 and 6, the thief must commit some sort of fraud to obtain the information; in situation 5, the thief must trespass onto the victim's property (though not into her home). In each of these cases, the thief has taken at least some morally culpable step to obtain the information. This dimension of culpability is absent from the last two situations, when the thief either happens to understand French or, most fortuitously, happens to be standing nearby when the victim reads the files in English. Because the thief in these two situations has neither undertaken any morally culpable behavior nor taken any actions to be deterred, nothing is to be gained by making either of the last two situations a crime.

The public policy interest in placing burdens of information security on the proper parties as a means of encouraging socially beneficial behavior also does not favor criminal liability in all of these situations. In fact, it is only in situations 1, 2, and 3 that the owner clearly took any precautions to protect her information; in situations 4 and 6, it is unclear whether the owner conducted sufficient due diligence before entrusting access to the information to another person; in situations 5, 7, and 8, the owner affirmatively placed the information in jeopardy. Making it a crime to steal the information in the examples in which the owner took no precautions would provide little incentive for the owner to secure her information. To the extent that policymakers believe that the information owners are in the best position to guard their own information, they should refuse to criminalize information theft in situations 5, 7, and 8 and potentially in situations 4 and 6. The criminal law already draws some distinction along these lines, refusing to extend criminal liability for the interception of satellite transmissions unless they are encrypted or for the theft of trade secrets unless the owner "has taken reasonable measures to keep such information secret."[59] In the cyber context, a statute designed to stimulate users to protect their data would make it a crime to acquire information only from a landline system or an encrypted wireless system. The owner of an unencrypted wireless system would have no criminal remedy but would not be solely without civil recourse against the thief or perhaps against the hardware manufacturer that set the default configuration of its wireless access devices for unencrypted transmission.[60] Of course, many computer users are not technologically savvy, and a refusal to protect all but specially protected (for instance, encrypted) information might discourage such users from using the Internet, thereby reducing the vibrancy of the resultant Internet community. By the same token, to the extent that policymakers are comfortable with trusting in prosecutorial discretion, extending criminal liability to theft of data acquired from unencrypted wireless systems would enable the criminal law to reach the cases in which the user's failure to protect himself is excusable rather than grossly negligent.

The policy concern with protecting privacy counsels in favor of criminalizing the invasions in all but situations 5, 7, and 8, which are the only situations in which the owner has exposed the information to the public. In the remaining situations, the owner either kept the information within her control or entrusted it to a limited number of persons with whom she has some special relationship.

As this brief discussion indicates, the policy considerations implicit in the analytical framework proposed in this article point in different directions with respect to many of the situations and, thus, with respect to many of the situations likely to be encountered in the cyber context. In defining the types of intrusive conduct that should constitute a crime attendant to information theft over the Internet, it is important to work from a cogent analytical model. Thus far, Congress has relied upon one model, namely, a consent model. I have identified three other models—an interference model, a trespass model, and a privacy model—only the last of which may provide a satisfactory alternative to the consent model currently employed in federal criminal statutes:

The consent model. Using this model, an unlawful intrusion occurs whenever a hacker accesses a computer "without access" or otherwise "exceeds [his] authorized access." This is the model used by the Computer Fraud and Abuse Act and the Stored Communications Act.[61] This approach is not without its shortcomings. The primary deficiency with relying on a consent paradigm is the difficulty of determining *when* a particular hack is undertaken without "authorization." Congress has provided only minimal guidance,[62] and not surprisingly, the federal courts have splintered badly on this issue.[63] The greatest dangers posed by the consent model are its nascent and elastic boundaries. Advocates seeking broad application of criminal statutes have used it to argue that violation of any contractual term "exceeds authorization" and thus supports criminal liability.[64] At the same time, advocates seeking narrow application use it to argue that courts should *imply* consent from the failure to take precautions (such as failing to encrypt a wireless access point), thereby shrinking the reach of criminal statutes.[65] For example, the consent model could be used to justify either criminal liability or lack of liability in situation 3, depending on whether the unlocked backdoor is construed as an implied consent to entry. Moreover, how this implied consent question is resolved will influence the precautions that information owners will take to ensure that backdoors are, in fact, locked.[66] Thus, while legislators and judges have some familiarity with the consent model, its shortcomings leave it vulnerable to replacement if a better model is developed.

The trespass model. Taking its cue from the concept of trespass in real property law, the trespass model would label any invasion into a computer user's system to be an actionable invasion. Although this model would in theory seem to be the perfect source for determining when an invasion occurs, it is very difficult to import into the cyber context, and especially the wireless Internet context, where boundaries are notoriously difficult to define. Indeed, commentators continue to debate whether the common law action of trespass against chattels has any applicability to a joyriding hacker.[67] In the end, this model does little more than re-phrase the question of what is meant by an "invasion" without providing much of a cogent basis for answering it.

The interference model. A close cousin to the trespass model, this model would criminalize any access that interferes with the information owner's use of his computer system (but, unlike the trespass model, would not require any simultaneous invasion of the system). Although this approach provides some basis for defining what constitutes an invasion, it is of limited use because, due to ever-increasing bandwidth, very few hacking intrusions burden the owner's access to a degree that is either noticeable to the owner or non-negligible.[68]

The privacy model. The privacy model would borrow from Fourth Amendment jurisprudence and would justify a criminal statute that penalizes the act of invading any location where information is stored and in which the owner has an objectively reasonable expectation of privacy.[69] Because it is based on a privacy paradigm, it certainly would accord with the public policy interest in the protection of private information. In addition, it is flexible enough to reward those persons who take precautions to keep their information secret; those efforts would go a long way toward fostering a legitimately cognizable expectation of privacy. For example, a person who fails to encrypt his wireless signal (the equivalent of situation 8) is unlikely to be protected under this scenario, but information protected by an encrypted signal (potentially situation 7) or landline access point (the situations occurring inside the home) are likely to be covered by any criminal statute defined by this model. This model benefits from a wealth of case law interpreting this concept for purposes of the Fourth Amendment. Doubtless, the privacy model is likely in many cases to yield the same policy outcomes as the consent model, as courts are likely to imply consent when a person has discarded his expectations of privacy (as in, for instance, situation 8 and potentially situation 7). But these two models involve different analyses. The consent model focuses solely on the victim's acts in giving or withholding consent, while the privacy model and its inquiry into legitimate expectations of privacy look to both the victim's conduct and the actions of the hacker (including the invasiveness of his conduct).[70] As noted, the privacy model also has the benefit of granting legislators and judges greater flexibility to adapt to changing technology and policy conditions, just as the expectations of privacy test has evolved over time. However, this model is not without its flaws. There are inherent limitations in defining a criminal statute on the basis of the objective legitimacy of the victim's expectations of privacy, most notably that such a requirement, though flexible, may not provide the requisite certainty to pass muster under Due Process case law or public policy notions of equity, fairness, and predictability. On balance, however, the privacy model may nonetheless be worthy of further exploration and study.

CONCLUSION

As the number of Internet users increases, those users will store more and more information in electronic format, where it will be available for perusal or theft by a new breed of criminals engaged in voyeuristic hacking behavior. Congress has yet to address this threat directly, and the panoply of federal criminal statutes that prohibit this behavior do so only tangentially and thus haphazardly. What is needed is a cogent policy approach to responding to voyeuristic hackers. In this article, I have proposed an analytical framework for undertaking this policy inquiry, namely, by looking to the twin questions of what information is worthy of criminal protection and what conduct should be made criminal. In answering these questions, it is helpful to consider how criminal protections against voyeuristic hacks mirror those for the theft of information occurring in the non-cyber content, how any new criminal statutes will influence the behavior of victims and criminals, how these statutes affect informational privacy, and whether the statutes accord with the public policy considerations typically associated with the criminal law. Although a full exploration of these issues is beyond the scope of this article, I have suggested that Congress may not wish to extend criminal protections to *all* content; that a criminal's subsequent use of acquired information be criminalized; and that, should Congress also wish to make the act of initially obtaining the information criminal, it might use one of a handful of policy models in defining which acts of "invasion" are to be branded illegal. This brief synopsis of possible issues will hopefully inform a more fulsome debate about how best to address this new and unique danger to the sanctity and security of one of our greatest assets in this Information Age.

NOTES

1. *See, e.g.*, Raymond T. Nimmer, "Licensing in the Contemporary Information Economy," 8 *Wash. U. J. L. & Pol'y* 99, 103 (2002) ("Transactions in information account for a large portion of the gross national product."); Sean F. Cotty, Note, "The How and Why of Shrinkwrap License Validation Under the Uniform Computer Information Transactions Act," 33 *Rutgers L.J.* 745, 746 (2002) ("It is undisputed that information technology is now a significant part of the national economy"); *see generally* Statement of Phillip J. Bond, Under Secretary For Technology, United States Department of Commerce, Before the Subcommittee on Environment, Technology, and Standards of the House Science Committee (Mar. 14, 2002), available at *www.technology.gov/Testimony/PJB-020314_Tech.htm* (last viewed Apr. 24, 2007).

2. "Computers gather, store, and offer instant retrieval of huge quantities of information about us." Clifford S. Fishman, "Technology & the Internet: The Impending Destruction of Privacy by Betrayers, Grudgers, Snoops, Spammers, Corps & The Media," 72 *Geo. Wash. L. Rev.* 1503, 1510 (2004); *see also* Summary of Report of the Judicial Conference on Rules of Practice and Procedure 22-23 (Sept. 2005), available at *www.uscourts.gov/rules/Reports/ST09-2005.pdf* (last viewed Apr. 23, 2007) (noting how businesses store terabytes of information, each of which equates to 500 million typewritten pages of plain text).

3. This flows from Metcalf's Law, which holds that "[t]he value of a network rises in proportion to the power of all the machines attached to it." George Gilder, Telecosm: How Infinite Bandwidth Will Revolutionize Our World 73 (2000); *accord* Ned Snow, "Accessing the Internet Through the Neighbor's Wireless Internet Connection: Physical Trespass in Virtual Reality," 84 *Neb. L. Rev.* 1226, 1229 (2006) ("The Internet is a public good, and the law should support any means of allowing as many persons to access it."); Matthew Bierken, "Policing the Wireless World: Access Liability in the Open Wi-Fi Era," 67 *Ohio State L.J.* 1123, 1126 (2006) ("The value of Internet content and the efficiency of the Internet's functioning directly relate to the number of its users."); Benjamin D. Kern, "Whackers, Joyriding & War-Driving: Roaming Use of Wi-Fi & The Law," 21 *Santa Clara Computer & High-Tech L.J.* 101, 108 (2005).

4. The first group often includes ex-employees or complete strangers who hack into a system and damage the system or the data contained on it. *See, e.g.*, United States v. Shea (N.D. Cal.), *reported in* "Federal Jury Convicts Former Technology Manager of Computer Hacking Offense" (Sept. 8,

2005), available at *www.cybercrime.gov/sheaConvict.htm* (last viewed Apr. 21, 2007); United States v. Jacobson (C.D. Cal.), *reported in* "Computer Hacker Who Victimized T-Mobile Pleads Guilty in Los Angeles Federal Court" (Feb. 15, 2005), available at *www.cybercrime.gov/jacobsenPlea.htm* (last viewed Apr. 21, 2007). The latter group hacks into one or more computers, and uses control over those computers to launch attacks on specific computers on the Internet (in what is called a distributed denial of service or DDOS attack) or to send unsolicited commerce email or spam messages. *See, e.g.*, United States v. Clark (Criminal Division), *reported in* "Man Pleads Guilty to Infecting Thousands of Computers Using Worm Program then launching them in Denial of Service Attacks" (Dec. 28, 2005), available at *www.cybercrime.gov/clarkPlea.htm* (last viewed Apr. 21, 2007); United States v. Ancheta (C.D. Cal.), *reported in* "Computer Virus Broker Arrested for Selling Armies of Infected Computer to Hackers and Spammers" (Nov. 3, 2005), available at *www.usdoj.gov/usao/cac/pr2005/149.html* (last viewed Apr. 21, 2007).

5. *See, e.g.*, Patrick S. Ryan, "War, Peace, or Stalemate: Wargames, Warchalking, Wardriving & the Emerging Market for Hacker Ethics," 9 *Va. J. L. & Tech.* 7, 16 (2004) ("it is the widespread availability of information that is new, making the crimes of theft and fraud easier to commit"); Orin S. Kerr, "Cybercrime's Scope: Interpreting "Access" and "Authorization" In Computer Misuse Statutes," 78 *N.Y.U. L. Rev.* 1596, 1604-1605 (2003) ("The more that individuals store their private information in electronic form, the greater the possible invasion of privacy if others obtain access to their private information without the owner's permission.").

6. *See, e.g.*, United States v. Kwak (Criminal Division), *reported in* "Former Federal Computer Security Specialist Sentenced for Hacking Department of Education Computers" (May 12, 2006), available at *www.cybercrime.gov/kwakSent.htm* (last viewed Apr. 23, 2007) (viewed emails); United States v. Levine (Criminal Division), *reported in* "Former Officer of Internet Company Sentenced in Case of Massive Identity Theft from Axicom Corp." (Feb. 22, 2006), available at *www.cybercrime.gov/levine-Sent.htm* (last viewed Apr. 23, 2007) (theft of personal information of consumers). Because of its intangible nature, viewing information is the same as acquiring it. *See* Beryl A. Howell,"Real World Problems of Virtual Crimes," 7 *Yale J. L. & Tech.* 103, 111 (2005) ("The conduct covered by the term 'obtaining information' has been consistently interpreted to include 'mere observation' of the data. Actual asportation . . . need not be proved . . .").

7. All three types of activity fall under the umbrella of hacking, a term that is morally neutral. What separates the first two from the latter are the ethics of the hacker. Ryan, *supra* n.5, at 56 ("There is a distinct difference between those who wish to expose vulnerabilities and those who wish to exploit them."); Shon Harris, et al., Gray Hat Hacking: The Ethical Hacker's Handbook 12 (2006) (discussing the "dual nature" of hacking tools, insofar as they are ethically "good" or "bad" depending on how they are ultimately used). Some hacking, particularly the type that locates and reports vulnerabilities, is actually beneficial.

8. *See, e.g.*, 18 U.S.C. §§ 1030, 2511; *see also* text accompanying *infra* nn.19-29 for a fuller discussion of these statutes. *See* text accompanying *infra* nn.34-37 for a treatment of legislation currently pending before Congress.

9. Although hacks over a local area network do occur, they constitute a small portion of the universe of malicious hacks because they lack the greater anonymity attached to remote hacks over the Internet.

10. *See, e.g.*, United States v. Perez-Melara (S.D. Cal.), *reported in* "Creator and Four Users of Loverspy Software Program Indicted" (Aug. 26, 2005), available at *www.cybercrime.gov/perezIndict.htm* (last viewed Apr. 23, 2007) (program intercepted all activity on computer); *see also* Kevin Poulson, "Judge Dismisses Keylogger Case," *Security Focus* (Nov. 19, 2004), available at *www.securityfocus.com/news/9978* (last viewed Apr. 23, 2007) (discussing first federal case bought against employee who installed a logger device that recorded every keystroke).

11. *See* 18 U.S.C. § 2511(1)(h)(ii) (authorizing an Internet service provider to monitor traffic on its network on a real-time basis without violating federal law).

12. Kern, *supra* n.3, at 101-102 ("Use of open Wi-Fi [short for Wireless Fidelity] connections to enable access to the Internet should be encouraged because this use will contribute to the continued expansion, flexibility and the 'footprint' of the Internet, as well as the development of new networking technologies."). Thus far, Philadelphia and San Francisco have undertaken affirmative steps to offer free wireless Internet access. *See, e.g.*, Richard Siklos, "What We Have Here Is a Failure to Communicate," *N.Y.*

Times (Oct. 30, 2005) (discussing Philadelphia); Ryan Kim, "Wireless System is Closer: S.F. Officials Ready to Request Proposal from 26 Vendors," *S.F. Chronicle*, at D3 (Nov. 9, 2005) (discussing San Francisco). For information regarding municipal wireless projects, *see generally www. muniwireless.com* (last viewed Apr. 22, 2007).

13. Tara McGraw Swaminath, "The Fourth Amendment Unplugged: Electronic Evidence Issues & Wireless Defenses," 7 *Yale J. L. & Tech.* 51, 52 (2005) ("As wireless Internet connectivity burgeons throughout the world, unsecured connections will likely become a haven for illegal activity."); Fishman, *supra* n.2, at 1520-1521 ("[W]ireless access to the Internet . . . provides the considerable convenience of permitting a computer user to log on without having to plug in physically; it may also leave the user extremely vulnerable to someone who wants to access the Internet on Wi-Fi user's account or to someone seeking to steal data, introduce viruses, launch spam or attack other computers."); Bierken, *supra* n.3, at 1124 ("Wireless networking expands the reach and function of the Internet by breaking through physical boundaries; users no longer must physically connect to a network, but may gain access via radio frequencies.").

14. Ryan, *supra* n.5, at 3 (defining "wardriving" as "identifying open wireless nodes and then marking the location of the open nodes on the side of a building with chalk or publishing the location on the Internet"); Kern, *supra* n.3, at 101 (defining "war-drivers" as persons who "scan, locate and map Wi-Fi access points").

15. Kern, *supra* n.3, at 101 ("'joyriders' . . . use an open Wi-Fi connection to access the Internet").

16. Bierken, *supra* n.3, at 1126 ("Typically, hardware providers ship wireless access points with a default setting disabling security."); Swaminath, *supra* n.13, at 73 ("Wireless Internet appliances are inherently unsecure if installed with default, out-of-the-box configurations.").

17. Tami Abdollah, "Ensnared on the Wireless Web," *LA Times*, at B1 (Mar. 16, 2007) ("People who think they are signing on to the Internet through a wireless hotspot might actually be connecting to a look-alike network, created by a malicious user who can steal sensitive information . . .").

18. This article focuses on federal criminal remedies, but some federal civil remedies exist, *see* 18 U.S.C. § 1030(g), as does the possibility of criminal prosecution by state authorities. *See, e.g.*, N.Y. Penal Code § 156.05 (2007).

19. *See* 18 U.S.C. § 2511(1)(a) (making it a crime to "intentionally intercept . . . any wire, oral or electronic communication"); *id.* § 2510(4) (defining "intercept" as "acquisition of the contents of any wire, electronic or oral communication through the use of any electronic, mechanical, or other device"); *id.* § 2510(12) (defining "electronic communication" as "any transfer of signs, signals, writing, images, sounds, data, or intelligence of any nature transmitted in whole or in part by a wire, radio, electromagnetic, photoelectric or photooptical system that affects interstate or foreign commerce" but excludes, among other things, tracking devices).

20. 18 U.S.C. § 2511(1)(a) (making it a crime to "intercept"); *id.* § 2511(1)(b) (making it a crime to "use, endeavor[] to use, or procure[] any other person to use or endeavor to use" intercepted content); *id.* § 2511(1)(c) (making it a crime to "intentionally disclose[], or endeavor[] to disclose" intercepted content).

21 *See id.* 2511(1)(d) (carving out exception to liability "for a person . . . to intercept a . . . communication where such person is a party to the communication or where one of the parties to the communication has given prior consent to such interception . . ."); *id.* § 2511(h)(ii) (carving out exception "for a provider of electronic communications service to record the fact that a wire or electronic communication was initiated or completed in order to protect such provider . . ."); *id.* § 2511(i) (carving out exception "for a person acting under color of state law to intercept the wire or electronic communications of a computer trespasser transmitted to, through, or from a protected computer" under certain conditions).

22. The Computer Fraud and Abuse Act, now codified at 18 U.S.C. § 1030(a), was first enacted in 1984, and has been amended several times. *See* Pub. L. No. 98-473, Title II, § 2102(a), 98 Stat. 2190 (Oct. 12, 1984); *see also* George Roach & William J. Michiels, "Damages Is the Gatekeeper Issue for Federal Computer Fraud," 8 *Tul. J. Tech. & Intell. Prop.* 61, 62 n.4 (2006) (detailing amendments to the Act); Ryan, *supra* n.5, at 27 n.87 (same). The Stored Communications Act, now codified at 18 U.S.C. §§ 2701-2712, was first enacted in 1986. *See* Pub. L. No. 99-508, Title II, § 201, 100 Stat. 1860 (Oct. 21, 1986).

23. *See* 18 U.S.C. § 1030(a)(1) ("Whoever . . . having knowingly accessed a computer without authorization or exceeding authorized access, and by means of such conduct having obtained information that has been determined by the United States Government pursuant to an Executive order or statute to require protection against unauthorized disclosure for reasons of national defense or foreign relations, or any restricted data, . . . with reason to believe that such information so obtained could be used to the injury of the United States, or to the advantage of any foreign nation . . . willfully retains the same and fails to deliver it to the officer or employee of the United States entitled to receive it" [is guilty of a crime]).

24. 18 U.S.C. § 1030(a)(2) (detailing criminal conduct); *id.* § 1030(b)(2)(A) (detailing misdemeanor penalty provision for this conduct). Section 1030(a)(2)(C), which arguably provides the broadest basis for liability, reaches "protected computers," which are defined, among other ways, as any computer "which is used in interstate or foreign commerce or communication." *Id.* §§ 1030(a)(2)(C), 1030(e)(2)(B).

25. *See* 18 U.S.C. § 1030(c)(2)(B). The Stored Communications Act penalties for hacking into an ISP's database largely parallel this two-tiered system. In particular, the Act makes it a crime to obtain unauthorized access to a "facility through which an electronic communication service is provided" (that is, an ISP), and to thereby obtain access to communications stored by the ISP. 18 U.S.C. § 2701(a). The crime is a misdemeanor unless the offense is committed (1) for purposes of commercial advantage, malicious destruction or damage, or private commercial gain; or (2) in furtherance of another federal crime or tort. 18 U.S.C. § 2701(b)(1) (2007). Section 1030(a)(4) contains an independent basis for criminal liability when any "thing of value" (which ostensibly includes information) is acquired as part of an ongoing fraud. 18 U.S.C. § 1030(a)(4). While violation of this statute is always a felony, *see id.* § 1030(c)(3)(A), it requires additional proof of intent to defraud and involvement in a larger scheme to defraud.

26. 18 U.S.C. § 1030(a)(6) (proscribing "knowingly and with intent to defraud traffic[king] . . . in any password or similar information through which a computer may be accessed without authorization" if the trafficking affects interstate commerce or the computer is used by the federal government).

27. *Id.* § 1028(a)(7) (creating criminal liability if a person "knowingly transfers, possesses, or uses, without lawful authority, a means of identification of another person with" the requisite intent); *id.* § 1028(d)(7) (defining "means of identification").

28. *Id.* § 1029(a)(2) (prohibiting trafficking or use of unauthorized access devices with intent to defraud if $1,000 or more is obtained during a one-year period); *id.* § 1029(a)(3) (prohibiting knowing possession of 15 or more counterfeit or unauthorized access devices with intent to defraud); *id.* § 1029(a)(5) (prohibiting effecting transactions with intent to defraud and receiving more than $1,000 in goods within a one-year period); *id.* § 1028(e)(1) (defining "access device").

29. Trade secrets have been protected by federal criminal law since 1996. *See* Economic Espionage Act of 1996, Pub. L. No. 194-294 , 110 Stat. 3488 (1996); *see also* 18 U.S.C. § 1831 (prohibiting stealing, possessing, receiving, duplicating, transmitting, or sending a trade secret with the intent or knowledge that the offense will "benefit any foreign government, foreign instrumentality, or foreign agent"); *id.* § 1832 (prohibiting same conduct when done "with intent to convert a trade secret . . . related to or included in a product that is produced for or placed in interstate or foreign commerce . . . to the economic benefit of anyone other than the owner thereof, and intending or knowing that the offense will injure any owner of that trade secret").

30. *See* 18 U.S.C. § 1030(a)(2)(C).

31. United States v. Trotter, 478 F.3d 918, 921 (8th Cir. 2007) ("The Internet is an instrumentality and a channel of interstate commerce."); United States v. MacEwan, 445 F.3d 237, 245 (3d Cir. 2006) (same); United States v. Hernandez, 312 F.3d 1306, 1311 (11th Cir. 2004) (same).

32. *Compare* 18 U.S.C. § 1030(a)(2)(A) *with id.* § 1030(a)(2)(C).

33. *See* Daniel B. Garrie, Alan F. Blakely & Matthew J. Armstrong, "The Legal Statutes of Spyware," 59 *Fed. Comm. L.J.* 157, 159 (2006) ("Today, federal law enables spyware [and] adware . . . to mine consumer data with impunity."). Although spyware may "damage" a computer by altering data, the damage is unlikely to meet the requisite $5,000 threshold necessary for federal criminal jurisdiction. *See* 18 U.S.C. § 1030(a)(5).

34. *See* § 3, H.R. 386, 110th Cong., 1st Sess. (2007).

35 *Id.* § 2.

36. H.R. 1525, 110th Cong., 1st Sess. (2007).

37. H.R. 964, 110th Cong., 1st Sess. (2007).

38. The Supreme Court just recently reaffirmed the importance of the sister concerns of theory and practice. *See* Weyerhaeuser Co. v. Ross-Simmons Hardwood Lumber, 127 S. Ct. 1069, 1078 (2007).

39. *See* Debra Wong Yang & Brian M. Hoffstadt, "Countering the Cyber-Crime Threat," 43 *Amer. Crim. L. Rev.* 201, 207-212 (2006) (discussing how the burden of combating cyber-crime might be allocated to victim-businesses, software and hardware manufacturers, or government agencies); Ryan, *supra* n.5, at 36 ("An important question remains: *Who* should take responsibility for security: users, manufacturers, or both?") (Emphasis in original).

40. *See, e.g.,* 18 U.S.C. §§ 1831, 1832 (making it a crime to steal a "trade secret"); *see also* id. § 1839(3) (defining "trade secret" as information that, among other things, "the owner thereof has taken reasonable measures to keep . . . secret").

41. *Accord* Kerr, *supra* n.5, at 1649-1650 (citing the "competing concerns" of broad use of the Internet and privacy and security of Internet uses and data accessible from the Internet). This privacy interest is grounded in public policy not the Fourth Amendment. The Supreme Court has firmly established that there is no reasonable expectation of privacy in what a person exposes to another. *See, e.g.,* United States v. Knotts, 460 U.S. 276, 281 (1983) ("A person traveling in an automobile on public thoroughfares has no reasonable expectation of privacy in his movements from one place to another."); Smith v. Maryland, 442 U.S. 735, 742 (1979) (numbers dialed on telephone, which are exposed to telephone company, are not protected by the Fourth Amendment); Miller v. United States, 425 U.S. 435, 442-443 (1976) (banking records, which are "voluntarily conveyed" to financial institutions, are not protected by the Fourth Amendment); *cf.* United States v. Karo, 468 U.S. 507, 717-718 (1984) (government may not monitor movement of a beeper within a private residence); Kyllo v. United States, 533 U.S. 27, 34-35 (2001) (government may not use sense-enhancing technology to probe activities within a private residence).

42. 18 U.S.C. § 3553(a) (2007) (enumerating the policy goals underlying federal criminal sentencing); *see also* Kerr, *supra* n.5, at 1606 ("In the context of computer crimes, the most important of these utilitarian goals is deterrence.").

43. *See, e.g.,* Kern, *supra* n.3, at 115 ("Use of WiFi connectors for criminal purposes, like the use of the Internet for such purposes, should be addressed by targeting the underlying criminal behavior, rather than by restricting the otherwise valuable means by which the crime was accomplished.").

44. *See, e.g.,* Christopher R. Leslie, "The Anticompetitive Effects of Unenforced Invalid Patents," 91 *Minn. L. Rev.* 101, 179 (2006) ("The law should be as concerned with these false negatives as it is with false positives."); David L. Franklin, "Facial Challenges, Legislative Purpose & the Commerce Clause," 92 *Iowa L. Rev.* 41, 97 (2006) (discussing how a purpose-based test is ill suited to judicial application because it results in too many false positives and false negatives).

45. It is not always easy to distinguish these two types of information. For instance, a hacker may invade a computer system and observe the architecture of the network. What he learns is not transactional data, but is also not "content" in the sense that it is data electronically stored on the system. Ostensibly, information about the architecture of a website would be considered "content," but this conclusion is not immune from debate.

46. *Compare* 18 U.S.C. §§ 3121-3127 (rules governing pen registers and trap-and-trace devices which, respectively, capture all outgoing and incoming telephone numbers) *with* 18 U.S.C. §§ 2510-2518 (rules governing interception of content). These statutes set forth the requirements that the government must satisfy before obtaining either transactional data with respect to telephone calls or content. The former may be obtained by a certification to a judge that "the information likely to be obtained . . . is relevant to an ongoing criminal investigation"; content, on the other hand, may be collected only where a judge finds that there is probable cause and necessity and where government agents agree to minimize the intrusion. Of course, when obtaining content from a telephone conversation that is ephemeral, there is no stored content and real-time collection, with its attendant higher standard, is the only available avenue of collecting content.

47. The Stored Communications Act and Title III interact together to erect a similar distinction when the government seeks to obtain information from ISPs. Where the government seeks subscriber information, connection information or temporarily assigned network addresses for an ISP's customer, it may obtain that information with a grand jury subpoena, which requires no showing of cause. *See* 18 U.S.C. § 2703(c)(2). Transactional

data other than subscriber information may be obtained only with a court order issued upon a showing of "specific and articulable facts showing that there are reasonable grounds to believe that . . . the records or other information sought . . . are relevant and material to an ongoing criminal investigation." *Id.* § 2703(d). Where the government seeks stored content, it must obtain a warrant if the content is less than 180 days old; for older content, a grand jury subpoena or court order is sufficient with notice to the customer. *Id.* §§ 2703(a), (b). Intercepting an online chat or email in transit requires compliance with Title III and a showing of probable cause and necessity. *Id.* §§ 2511(a), 2518 (establishing procedures for issuance of a Title III warrant).

48. *See* 18 U.S.C. §§ 1831, 1832 (trade secrets); id. § 1030(a)(2)(A) (financial data from financial institutions); id. §§ 1030(a)(1), 1030(a)(2)(B) (national security information or information stored on government agency computers).

49. *See* Brian M. Hoffstadt, "Dispossession, Intellectual Property & The Sin of Theoretical Homogeneity," 80 *S. Cal. L. Rev.,* at 31-32 (forthcoming summer 2007) (on file with author) (discussing incentives); *accord* Michael A. Carrier, "Cabining Intellectual Property Through a Property Paradigm," 54 *Duke L.J.* 1, 82 (2004) ("Providing incentives for development is the primary goal of intellectual property [law] . . ."). *See also* 18 U.S.C. § 2320(a) (trademark theft); id. §§ 1831, 1832 (trade secrets theft); id. § 2319, 17 U.S.C. § 506 (misuse of copyrighted material). At this point in time, patents are protected solely by civil law. *See* United States v. Dowling, 473 U.S. 207, 227 (1985) ("Despite its undoubted power to do so . . . Congress has not provided criminal penalties for distribution of goods infringing valid patents.").

50. *See, e.g.,* 18 U.S.C. § 1153 (burglary on Indian land); id. § 2117 (breaking or entering a carrier facility); id. § 2118 (burglary of certain locations containing controlled substances).

51. *See, e.g.,* 18 U.S.C. § 1028(a)(7) (creating felony crime for knowingly transferring or using a "means of identification of another person with intent to commit" another federal crime); id. § 1029(a)(2) (making it a crime to traffic in one or more unauthorized access devices); id. § 1029(a)(3) (making it a crime to possess 15 or more counterfeit or unauthorized access devices "with intent to defraud"); id. § 1029(a)(5) (making it a crime to use access devices issued to another to "effect[] transactions" with "intent to defraud"); id. § 1832 (making it a crime to possess or transfer a trade secret "with intent to convert a trade secret . . . to the economic benefit of anyone other than the owner thereof, and intending or knowing that the offense will . . . injure the owner of that trade secret").

52. *Dowling,* 473 U.S. at 247 (noting that theft of hard copies of copyrighted works did not "wholly deprive its owner of its use"); J.E. Penner, "The 'Bundle of Rights' Picture of Property," 43 *UCLA L. Rev.* 711, 808 (1996) ("An owner cannot be dispossessed of his copyright or patent . . ."); Hoffstadt, *supra* n.49, at 55-56.

53. "Once created, intellectual property is a public good capable of enjoyment by millions without incurring significant costs." Stuart Stark, "Rhetoric & Reality in Copyright Law," 94 *Mich. L. Rev.* 1197, 1236 (1996); *accord* Lanier Saperstein, "Copyrights, Criminal Sanctions & Economic Rent: Applying the rent-Seeking Model to the Criminal Law Formulation Process," 87 *J. Crim. L. & Criminology* 1470, 1494 (1997) ("A distinguishing feature of intellectual property is its nature as a public good.").

54. *Accord* Kerr, *supra* n.5, at 1607-1611 (eschewing reliance on analogies to burglary and trespass in the computer context, as they are more concerned with the physical entry than the property trespassed, and on analogies to theft because theft is "too result oriented").

55. *See* Lopez v. United States, 514 U.S. 549, 558 (1995) (enumerating the three bases for Commerce Clause jurisdiction, which is itself the basis for much of the federal criminal law, and reaffirming that crimes affecting the "channels of interstate commerce" are an independent basis for that jurisdiction); Morrison v. United States, 529 U.S. 598, 608-609 (2000) (same); Gonzalez v. Raich, 545 U.S. 1, 17 (2005) (same).

56. This applies when a person logs in to a false wireless Internet node and is closely related to phishing crimes in which victims who are duped into providing financial information to a thief they erroneously believe is a financial institution who contacted them to update their account information. *See* United States v. Goodin (C.D. Cal.), *reported in* "'Phisher' Guilty of Posing As AOL Billing Department and Obtaining Personal and Credit Card Information," (Jan. 16, 2007), available at *www.usdoj.gov/usado/cac/news/pr2007/004.html* (last viewed Apr. 23, 2007). *See also* 18 U.S.C. §§ 1341 (mail fraud), 1343 (wire fraud).

57. This may also raise tricky statute of limitations issues, depending on whether the limitations period is triggered by the use of the information or its prior, initial theft. *See* 18 U.S.C. § 3282 (2007) (setting five-year statute of limitations period that generally governs federal crimes).

58. As discussed more fully below, these statutes require that the criminal obtain the information "without authorization" or that he "exceed[] authorized access." *See, e.g.*, 18 U.S.C. § 1030(a)(1), § 1030(a)(2).

59. *See* 18 U.S.C. § 2511(4)(b); *cf. id.* § 2511(g)(1). *See also* 18 U.S.C. § 1839(3)(A) (defining "trade secrets").

60. Indeed, some commentators have advocated civil liability against hardware and software manufacturers that fail to provide secure networks that are subsequently exploited by hackers. *See* Michael L. Rustad & Thomas H. Koeing, "The Tort of Negligent Enablement of Cyber-Crime," 20 *Berkeley Tech. L.J.* 1553, 1555, 1567 (2005).

61. *See, e.g.*, 18 U.S.C. §§ 1030(a)(1), (a)(2), (a)(4); *id.* § 2701(a).

62. Congress has not defined the terms "access" or "without authorization." *Accord* Howell, *supra* n.6, at 107 ("'Unauthorized access' is not defined in the law . . ."). The statutes do define the term "exceeds authorized access," but the definition provides no further insight on the concept of authorization. *See* 18 U.S.C. § 1030(e)(6) (defining "exceeds authorized access" as "access[ing] a computer with authorization and . . . us[ing] such access to obtain or alter information in the computer that the accesser is not entitled so to obtain or alter").

63. Some courts have held that a hacker acts "without authorization" whenever he accesses a computer for other than its intended function, *see* United States v. Morris, 928 F.3d 504 (2d Cir. 1991); others have looked to the hacker's motive, *see* Shurgood Storage Centers, Inc. v. Safeguard Self Storage, Inc., 119 F. Supp. 2d 1121 (W.D. Wash. 2000); and others have examined whether the access violated the terms of any contract delimiting the parameters of authorized access, *see* EF Cultural Travel BV v. Explorica, 274 F.3d 577, 583 (1st Cir. 2001).

64. *See* Kerr, *supra* n.5, at 1598 (arguing that cases such as *EF Cultural* "suggest that unauthorized access statutes broadly criminalize the law of contract involving the use of computers"). Professor Kerr argues for a standard that requires subversion of a "code-based" restriction before access may

be deemed "unauthorized" for purposes of federal criminal statutes. *Id.* at 1643-1658.

65. "Lack of log-in procedures, encryption, or other forms of security may create a privilege in the would-be trespassers of apparent consent to use another's Wi-Fi network." Robert V. Hale, II, "Wi-Fi Liability: Potential Legal Risks in Accessing and Operating Wireless Internet," 21 *Santa Clara Comp. & High-Tech L.J.* 543, 555 (2005). *But see* Snow, *supra* n.3, at 1257 ("that a password denotes absence of consent does not imply that an absence of a password denotes consent.").

66. *See* Kern, *supra* n.3, at 102 (arguing that "unauthorized access" exists "only if the network operator has taken affirmative steps to prevent access" because this rule "provides clarity to Wi-Fi users, . . . encourages responsible security practices, and simplifies enforcement of unauthorized computer crime statutes").

67. *See, e.g.*, Snow, *supra* n.3, at 1227 (arguing in favor of such civil liability).

68. Kern, *supra* n.3, at 109 ("The marginal cost of the bandwidth used by a roaming Wi-Fi user to the business or individual operator of the Wi-Fi network is typically negligible."). *But see* Snow, *supra* n.3, at 1244 (arguing that joyriding may cause "decreas[ed] router performance for the Wi-Fi operator").

69. *See* Katz v. United States, 389 U.S. 347, 361 (1967) (Harlan, J., concurring) (arguing that a Fourth Amendment interest is invaded only when government actors intrude upon a person's subjective and objective expectations of privacy). Indeed, the Fourth Amendment was once predicated on a prior trespass, *see* Olmstead v. United States, 277 U.S. 438 (1928); Silverman v. United States, 365 U.S. 505 (1961), a view that was ultimately rejected in *Katz* in favor of a privacy-based approach.

70. *See, e.g.*, Kyllo v. United States, 533 U.S. 27, 31-40 (2001) (determining that homeowners possessed a legitimate expectation of privacy in their homes vis-à-vis police use of sense-enhancing technology that was not in general use); *cf.* Florida v. Riley, 488 U.S. 455, 488-452 (1989) (plurality) (finding that homeowner did not have a legitimate expectation of privacy in portions of backyard exposed to public view by a police officer flying overhead).

[3]

"PHISHING" FOR A SOLUTION:
DOMESTIC AND INTERNATIONAL APPROACHES TO
DECREASING ONLINE IDENTITY THEFT

LAUREN L. SULLINS

INTRODUCTION

In less than five minutes, Jane Smith will give criminals throughout the world the ability to gain complete control of her identity and savings. Unfortunately, as she logs on to check her e-mail, she has no idea that this is about to happen. As Jane skims her inbox, she sees an e-mail with the subject "Important Security Alert for All EasyBank Users"; the sender address reads "EasyBank." As one of EasyBank's millions of customers, Jane opens the e-mail to read the important news.

When she opens the e-mail, it contains EasyBank's famous logo and a message. The message informs her that the company is initiating a new security system to protect against fraudulent activity. The message states that she must click on the following link to confirm her online banking details. If she does not do so, the message states that her account will be cancelled. Wanting to protect herself from attacks on her account and also believing that she is required to do so to keep her account, Jane clicks on the link.

After clicking on the link, Jane is taken to a website that appears official. It is identical to the site that she normally visits to conduct her online banking. Jane logs in, as she normally does, entering her customer identification number and password. She is taken to an additional page where she enters her social security number, address, mother's maiden name, and other personal information. After she provides all of the requested information, the website displays a message that thanks her for her time. Jane turns off her computer and continues her day, believing that her account is now well-protected. She has no idea that the e-mail and website were scams and that, only moments later, a criminal will empty all of the funds from her account and sell her personal information on the black market.

Jane is the victim of a "phishing" attack—a form of online identity theft that uses fraudulent e-mails to trick recipients into divulging personal financial

398   EMORY INTERNATIONAL LAW REVIEW   [Vol. 20

information on fraudulent, imitation websites.[1] These attacks not only impact consumers and corporations—they also threaten to destroy Internet commerce as a whole by destroying consumer trust in online transactions.[2] Gartner Research estimates that in 2003, in the United States alone, over 57 million people received a phishing attack e-mail and almost 5% of the recipients responded with personal information.[3] These attacks cost U.S. banks and credit card issuers more than $1.2 billion per year, and the losses continue to grow.[4] Worldwide, the annual damage from phishing attacks has reached $5 billion, and the number of attacks is steadily increasing.[5] Every day new scammers appear. Many actually learn how to conduct these scams from websites that offer do-it-yourself kits on how to build fake websites for phishing scams.[6] The Anti-Phishing Working Group received reports of 15,820 new phishing e-mails in October 2005, compared to 6,957 reports in October 2004.[7] As staggering as these figures are, the number of phishing incidents and the associated losses are actually underreported.[8]

Phishing scams do not only affect the finances of the victims and targeted companies in the short term—the attacks also have long-term effects on the growth of Internet-related transactions.[9] Individual targets of phishing scams are likely to lose confidence in the online marketplace and may not trust their ability to distinguish legitimate sites from scams.[10] If consumers do not have confidence in the authenticity of e-mails, it could lead to destruction of consumer trust in the Internet as a whole and an erosion of e-commerce growth.[11] The U.S. Department of Justice (DOJ) stresses the importance of decreasing Internet crimes as follows: "In short, if left unchallenged, computer

---

[1] *See* Press Release, Gartner Research, Phishing Attack Victims Likely Targets for Identity Theft 2 (Mar. 4, 2004), http://www4.gartner.com/resources/120800/120804/phishing_attack.pdf.

[2] *Id.*

[3] *Id.*

[4] *Id.*

[5] Jennifer Barrett, *'Phishing' for Dollars*, NEWSWEEK, Jan. 28, 2004, http://www.msnbc.msn.com/id/4079364.

[6] *See* Michael Cohn, *Phishing Attacks Linked to Organized Crime*, SECURITY PIPELINE, July 7, 2004, http://www.securitypipeline.com/22104197.

[7] ANTI-PHISHING WORKING GROUP, PHISHING ATTACK TRENDS REPORT (2005), http://antiphishing.org/apwg_phishing_activity_report_oct_05.pdf [hereinafter APWG OCT. TRENDS].

[8] *Banks Warned to Formulate Defenses Against Sophisticated 'Phishing' Scams*, 9 Elec. Com. & L. Rep. (BNA) 671, 671 (Aug. 8, 2004).

[9] *See* Press Release, Gartner Research, *supra* note 1.

[10] Dennis McCafferty, *Organized Cyber-Crime*, WEB HOST INDUSTRY REV., July/Aug. 2004, at 30, 31; Dar Haddix, *National Anti-Phishing Campaign Kicks Off*, UNITED PRESS INT'L, June 17, 2004, http://washingtontimes.com/upi-breaking/20040617-062002-9621r.htm.

[11] *See* Press Release, Gartner Research, *supra* note 1.

crime . . . may stifle the Internet's power as a tool to communicate, engage in commerce, and expand people's educational opportunities around the globe."[12]

Phishers do not limit their attacks to the United States—the culprits, victims, and effects are international. The Anti-Phishing Working Group estimates that foreign countries host over 70% of phishing websites.[13] China now hosts 9.96% of the worldwide phishing-based websites, and an Anti-Phishing Working Group report states that countries such as the Republic of Korea and Germany host many of the remaining sites.[14] Organized crime rings run many of these foreign websites.[15] The groups use individuals in their networks to carry out the entire scam, from sending the initial e-mail to committing identity theft.[16]

Phishers are now targeting consumers and companies all over the world. The United Kingdom's Association for Payment Clearing Services (APACS),[17] estimates that there are over two thousand victims of phishing scams in the United Kingdom alone, resulting in losses of £4.5 million.[18] Although, in the past, most criminals only aimed their attacks at consumers in English-speaking countries, phishers have also launched attacks against citizens of Germany and Brazil.[19] The attacks in Germany on Postbank AG and Deutsche Bank AG originated from crime rings in Russia and Asia, and it is possible that German companies will become the focus of more international phishing rings.[20]

The alarming increase in the number of phishing scams and the substantial amount of damage they have inflicted on companies and individuals worldwide demonstrate the need for an international solution to the problem. This Comment shows that phishing is a non-traditional crime that requires a non-traditional solution and asserts that this solution lies in one word:

---

[12] Dep't of Justice, Frequently Asked Questions and Answers About the Council of Europe Convention on Cybercrime, http://www.usdoj.gov/criminal/cybercrime/COEFAQs.htm (last visited Feb. 9, 2006) [hereinafter DOJ FAQs].

[13] APWG OCT. TRENDS, *supra* note 7.

[14] *Id.*

[15] *See* McCafferty, *supra* note 10, at 31. *See* discussion *infra* Part II.B.2.a.

[16] *See* McCafferty, *supra* note 10, at 31.

[17] For more information on the APACS, see Association for Payment Clearing Services, http://www.apacs.org.uk (last visited Feb. 29, 2006).

[18] John Leyden, *Four Charged in Landmark UK Phishing Case*, REGISTER (U.K.), Oct. 15, 2004, http://www.theregister.co.uk/2004/10/15/phishing_charges.

[19] John Blau, *Big German Banks Hit by Phishing Attacks*, COMPUTERWORLD, Aug. 23, 2004, http://www.computerworld.com/softwaretopics/software/groupware/story/0,10801,95429,00.html.

[20] *Id.*

400   EMORY INTERNATIONAL LAW REVIEW   [Vol. 20

cooperation. The fight against phishing is dependent upon cooperation in the following three areas: joint operations among law enforcement agencies, domestic and international legislation, and among the private companies and consumers that are the victims of these attacks.[21] Cooperation within each area alone is not enough—the groups must act together to combat each other's weaknesses and grow stronger as an integrated unit.[22]

Part I is divided into three sections. Section A gives a general overview of phishing and its history. Section B explains phishing's effects on consumers, companies, and the future of Internet commerce. Section C discusses the unique aspects of phishing that make the crime attractive to criminals and cause serious problems for those trying to stop the scams. Part II of this Comment focuses on the need for cooperation between law enforcement agencies, legislators, and the private sector. Finally, this Comment proposes that the solution to phishing depends on cooperation between all three groups.

I. BACKGROUND

A. An Overview of Phishing

Phishing is an Internet scam in which criminals design e-mails and websites that appear to originate from a legitimate business, government agency, or financial institution and then use this false identity to deceive Internet users into disclosing personal financial information.[23] First, the phisher sends an e-mail that appears to be sent from a trusted source, like SunTrust or Citibank, so that the user does not initially regard the e-mail as suspicious.[24] The e-mail informs the recipient that there is a problem with his account and instructs him to click on a link to update or validate his account

---

[21] *See* discussion *infra* Parts II–III.

[22] FIN. SERVS. TECH. CONSORTIUM, PROJECT PROPOSAL—FSTC COUNTER-PHISHING INITIATIVE 5 (2004), *available at* http://www.fstc.org/projects/FSTC_Phishing_Prospectus_Final.pdf (stating that "[n]o single solution is possible . . . coordination is essential") [hereinafter FSTC PROPOSAL].

[23] DEP'T OF JUSTICE, SPECIAL REPORT ON PHISHING, *available at* http://www.usdoj.gov/criminal/fraud/ Phishing.pdf (last visited Feb. 9, 2006) [hereinafter DOJ PHISHING REPORT].

[24] *See* McCafferty, *supra* note 10, at 31 (quoting Clarence Briggs, who states that phishing scams are effective because they play on the "trust factor"). To elicit trust, the criminal may forge the sender address listed on the e-mail so that it appears that the sender is Citibank Customer Service. Also, the criminal usually inserts the companies' trademarked images so that the e-mail looks official. *See* TRENT YOUL, FRAUDWATCH INT'L, PHISHING SCAMS: UNDERSTANDING THE LATEST TRENDS 2 (2004), *available at* http:// www.fraudwatchinternational.com/internet/phishing/report.pdf.

information.[25] The e-mail usually threatens suspension of the account or some other undesirable consequence if the user does not act quickly.[26] The victim is not aware that the sender probably used a "spamming"[27] technique to send the e-mail and that possibly thousands of people received this same e-mail.[28] Users mistakenly believe that they are acting responsibly when they click on the link and respond.[29]

Once the user clicks on the link, he is taken to a phony website that mimics the appearance of the official website of the organization mentioned in the e-mail.[30] The phisher covers the website with trademarks and copyrighted images so that the site appears to be authentic.[31] The website then prompts the user to disclose credit card numbers, passwords, and other confidential information.[32] Once the victim believes that the website is legitimate, he inputs his information and leaves the site without knowing that he has been scammed.[33] Phishers then take this information and use it to commit identity theft and fraud.[34]

Although phishing incidencts have increased recently, the practice has been in existence for many years. The word "phishing" originates from the analogy that criminals use e-mails as lures to "fish" for information from the sea of Internet users.[35] Phishing is spelled with a "ph" instead of an "f" because of its historical ties to "phone phreaking," a 1970s scam that involved hacking into phone switches to make calls for free or bill them to someone else.[36] In 1996, criminals began to use the term "phishing" to describe the process of getting unsuspecting America Online (AOL) users to reveal their passwords to criminals so that they could steal the AOL dial-up accounts. The hacked

---

[25] Anita Ramasastry, *The Anti-Phishing Act of 2004: A Useful Tool Against Identity Theft,* MOD. PRAC., Sept. 2004, http://practice.findlaw.com/cyberlaw-0904.html.

[26] *Id.*

[27] "Spamming" refers to the technique culprits use to send unsolicited bulk e-mail over the Internet. David E. Sorkin, *Technical and Legal Approaches to Unsolicited Electronic Mail,* 35 U.S.F. L. REV. 325, 328 (2001).

[28] DOJ PHISHING REPORT, *supra* note 23.

[29] Barrett, *supra* note 5.

[30] Ramasastry, *supra* note 25.

[31] YOUL, *supra* note 24, at 2.

[32] Ramasastry, *supra* note 25.

[33] Barrett, *supra* note 5.

[34] DOJ PHISHING REPORT, *supra* note 23.

[35] Anti-Phishing Working Group, Origins of the Word Phishing, http://www.antiphishing.org/word_phish.html (last visited Feb. 9, 2006).

[36] *Id.*

402   EMORY INTERNATIONAL LAW REVIEW   [Vol. 20

accounts were called "phish."[37] The trend was so popular that criminals even began to use the AOL "phish" as a form of currency to trade for other hacking software.[38] Unfortunately, phishing did not remain relegated to this one small area for long.   When hackers realized the profit-making possibilities of phishing, the attacks expanded into a full-blown criminal enterprise that targeted a wide range of users and significantly impacted individuals and the economy worldwide.[39]

B. *The Harmful Effects of Phishing*

Phishing scams jeopardize the security of individuals, companies, and the Internet. Individual victims of phishing scams are vulnerable to many forms of violation, but the damages usually occur in one of the following three ways. First, criminals can use the stolen data to purchase items or withdraw money from the victims' existing accounts.[40] Many times, consumers are unaware that these transactions have occurred until they receive their statements, and they often do not realize that criminals hijacked their information through a phishing scam.[41] Second, phishers can also "use the data to open new bank or credit card accounts in the victims' names."[42] The phishers may either use the information themselves or sell it on the black market to other criminals.[43] Third, recent phishing scams have used the fraudulent e-mails as a method of spreading computer viruses that send out phishing e-mails to even more people.[44]

Companies, not individuals, end up bearing most of the direct financial loss from phishing attacks.[45] Regulations from the Federal Deposit Insurance Corporation (FDIC) state that consumers are not liable beyond a maximum

---

[37] *Id.*

[38] *Id.*

[39] Ramasastry, *supra* note 25.

[40] DOJ PHISHING REPORT, *supra* note 23.

[41] Barrett, *supra* note 5.

[42] DOJ PHISHING REPORT, *supra* note 23. If criminals do not use the victims' addresses when opening new accounts, it is likely that users may not realize that they have been victimized until much later when they are notified by creditors. *Id.*

[43] Brian Krebs, *Technology Fueling Wave of Phishing Scams*, WASHINGTONPOST.COM, Jan. 18, 2005, http://www.washingtonpost.com/wp-dyn/articles/A17680-2005Jan18.html (discussing the existence of chat rooms where thieves trade their victim's financial information); *see also* AARON EMIGH, RADIX LABS ONLINE IDENTITY THEFT: PHISHING TECHNOLOGY, CHOKEPOINTS, AND COUNTERMEASURES 7 (2005), *available at* http://www.antiphishing.org/Phishing-dhs-report.pdf.

[44] DOJ PHISHING REPORT, *supra* note 23.

[45] Stratton Shartel, *E-Commerce Sites Forced to Fight Phishing with Low-Tech Tools: Education, Police Work,* 9 Elec. Com. & L. Rep. (BNA) 523, 523 (June 9, 2004).

payment of fifty dollars for unauthorized transactions in their bank or credit card accounts.[46] As a result, the targeted institution ends up absorbing most of the financial loss.[47] Worldwide, companies have lost $5 billion annually in customer and productivity losses, repair efforts, and business interruptions from these attacks.[48] To avoid these losses, lawyers for banks and e-commerce companies, like eBay and PayPal, are dedicating increased resources to attack the phishing problem.[49]

The companies that criminals target in phishing attacks also suffer harm to their goodwill.[50] Phishers use the reputation of legitimate companies to elicit the trust of their victims by copying the names, images, and websites of these institutions to make the consumer believe that the e-mail and website are legitimate.[51] The criminals' abuse of the brand's reputation has immeasurable effects on marketing campaigns and customer confidence.[52] The phishers' use of the targeted companies' trademarked images and good names can also cause residual problems for consumers who may continue to associate the negative effects of the scam with the company.[53] Victims may lose confidence in the company and wish to discontinue doing business there—a situation analogous to a reluctance to keep putting money in a bank that is continually robbed.[54]

Phishing's effects on consumer confidence may also decrease confidence in the Internet as a whole.[55] Individual targets of phishing scams are likely to lose confidence in the online marketplace and may not trust their ability to distinguish legitimate sites from scams.[56] In addition, the high incidence of

---

[46] *Id.*

[47] *Id.*

[48] Barrett, *supra* note 5.

[49] Shartel, *supra* note 45, at 523–24. *See also* discussion *infra* Part II.C.

[50] *See* Haddix, *supra* note 10.

[51] *See id.*; YOUL, *supra* note 24, at 5.

[52] FSTC PROPOSAL, *supra* note 22, at 3.

[53] *See* Declan McCullagh, *Season Over for 'Phishing'?*, CNET NEWS.COM, July 15, 2004, http://news.com.com/2100-1028_3-5270077.html.

[54] Pat Hurst, *Millions at Risk from Cyber 'Phishing' Gangs*, COMPUTER CRIME RESEARCH CTR., Feb. 29, 2004, http://www.crime-research.org/news/29.02.2004/95.

[55] McCullagh, *supra* note 53.

[56] McCafferty, *supra* note 10, at 31; Haddix, *supra* note 10.

cybercrime distracts from the positive aspects of the Internet[57] and undermines the basic trust that individuals have in the economy.[58]

C. Why Phishing Is Attractive to Criminals

The Internet has given identity thieves the ability to reach thousands of victims in only moments while simultaneously reducing many of the risks associated with identity theft in the physical world.[59] Phishers have become the "street muggers of the digital age, using computers instead of weapons to steal financial information and identities from innocent people."[60]

Criminals choose phishing over traditional identity theft because the speed and anonymity of the Internet make it very unlikely that the perpetrators will be caught. [61] Although there are laws against phishing,[62] law enforcement agents are not usually able to locate the perpetrators because the criminals conduct these scams so quickly.[63] Phishers can start receiving victims' credit card information only minutes after sending out the fraudulent e-mail and, as a result, the sites do not need to be around for long periods of time to do damage.[64] To avoid capture and the risk of leaving evidence, phishers constantly move the phony websites from one server to another, including servers in different parts of the world.[65] The average phishing site is only online for approximately 5.5 days.[66] By the time most victims realize that

---

[57] *See Fed Nabs 125 in Global Cybercrime Sweep*, CNN.COM, Nov. 21, 2003, http://www.cnn.com/ 2003/TECH/internet/11/21/crackdown.cybercrime.reut (quoting U.S. Att'y Gen. John Ashcroft as stating, "The Information Superhighway should be a conduit for communication, information and commerce, not an expressway to crime.").

[58] McCullagh, *supra* note 53.

[59] *See* COUNCIL OF EUR., SUMMARY OF THE ORGANIZED CRIME SITUATION REPORT (PROVISIONAL) 7 (Sept. 6, 2004) [hereinafter COE CRIME SUMMARY]; *see also* David E. Reynolds, *Industry Tackles Online Phishing Schools*, WASH. TIMES, June 23, 2004, http://www.washtimes.com/upi-breaking/20040623-045201-9488r.htm ("More criminals are turning to identity theft because there's more profit with less risk than with other types of crime. . . . There's more money in identity theft than in armed robbery.").

[60] Press Release, Microsoft, Industry, Law Enforcement Team to Launch Digital PhishNet (Dec. 8, 2004), http://www.microsoft.com/presspass/press/2004/dec04/12-08DigPhishNetPR.mspx.

[61] *See* Ramasastry, *supra* note 25.

[62] *See* discussion *infra* Part II.B.

[63] Ramasastry, *supra* note 25.

[64] Thomas Claburn, *Saving E-Mail*, INFORMATIONWEEK, June 28, 2004, http://www.informationweek. com/shared/printableArticle.jhtml?articleID=22102305.

[65] Ramasastry, *supra* note 25.

[66] APWG OCT. TRENDS, *supra* note 7.

phishers have defrauded them, the phishers have either removed the site, replaced it with a legitimate site, or have moved to another server.[67]

The anonymity of cyberspace is an additional incentive to phish.[68] In phishing scams, the criminal can separate himself from the risks of the physical world and fade into the invisibility of cyberspace.[69] The anonymity of the Internet is central to the execution of phishing attacks because the scammer will only be successful if he hides his true identity with forged e-mail headers and deceptive websites.[70] Also, the criminal's ability to hide his identity on the Internet allows the criminal to separate himself from the norms of society and act in a socially unacceptable way.[71] Because most Internet crimes take place in private, there are also fewer opportunities for deterrents such as public risk and shame to come into play.

II. THE CALL FOR COOPERATION

Phishing is a crime that can only be solved by a comprehensive effort on all fronts. The task requires cooperation in the three following areas: law enforcement, legislation, and the private sector. This Comment examines these areas individually, including current cooperative efforts between different sectors. Additionally, it explores the weakness in each sector and explains why cooperation with the other areas is necessary to fill the void. Section A of this Part analyzes the weaknesses in traditional law enforcement strategies and current efforts to correct these problems. Section B focuses on domestic and international phishing legislation. Finally, Section C describes strategies that private companies and consumers are developing to combat phishing.

A. Cooperation Between Law Enforcement Agencies

To effectively fight phishing, law enforcement agents must apply new methods of enforcement and must also collaborate domestically and

---

[67] Internet Crime Complaint Center, Intelligence Note: "Spoofed" E-mails & Web Sites, June 30, 2003, http://www.ic3.gov/media/2003/030630.htm [hereinafter ICCC Note] (stressing that "time is of the essence" in these investigations).

[68] Susan W. Brenner, *Toward a Criminal Law for Cyberspace: A New Model of Law Enforcement?*, 30 RUTGERS COMPUTER & TECH. L.J. 1, 31 (2004).

[69] *See* Neal Kumar Katyal, *Criminal Law in Cyberspace*, 149 U. PA. L. REV. 1003, 1039 (2001).

[70] *See* YOUL, *supra* note 24, at 4–5.

[71] *See* Katyal, *supra* note 69, at 1008.

internationally.[72] If agents fail to make these changes, phishers will continue to take advantage of law enforcement agents' lack of technical knowledge and exploit the difficulties that arise from law enforcement departments' lack of cooperation.[73]

1. The Need for a New Model of Law Enforcement to Combat Phishing

Phishing scams and other cybercrimes give rise to many unique problems that make traditional methods of dealing with crime ineffective.[74] A significant problem is law enforcement agents' lack of technical knowledge and training.[75] Although cybercrimes contain elements rooted in traditional crimes,[76] the technology that criminals use to commit these acts requires officials to fight them in a non-traditional way. Unfortunately, many of the individuals involved in the investigation and prosecution of these cases do not have the technical savvy to understand the complex nature of cybercrimes.[77] In some prosecutions, the *judges* themselves have never even used the Internet.[78] Although it is not necessary for law enforcement officials to be technological experts, they should at least be able to understand the terminology used by the criminals and victims, be able to use the information to gather and preserve evidence, and have the ability to present the case in terms that the court can understand.[79]

Increasing the technological knowledge of members of law enforcement agencies is not an easy task. Keeping agents aware of new technologies and

---

[72] *See* Susan W. Brenner & Joseph J. Schwerha IV, *Transnational Evidence Gathering and Local Prosecution of International Cybercrime*, 20 J. MARSHALL J. COMPUTER & INFO. L. 347, 375–78 (2002).

[73] *Id.*

[74] *See* Brenner, *supra* note 68, at 1.

[75] *See* Brenner & Schwerha, *supra* note 72, at 375–76.

[76] *See* Viktor Mayer-Schonberger, *The Shape of Governance: Analyzing the World of Internet Regulation*, 43 VA. J. INT'L L. 605, 608 (2003). For example, phishing is essentially identity theft, but the crime is conducted in a new way. In traditional identity theft cases, the criminal often gets the victim's information from receipts or solicits the information in letters. In phishing scams, the criminal seeks the same information, but solicits it through electronic means rather than through traditional methods. However, some critics, like Judge Easterbrook, believe that crimes should not be confined to the new field of cyberlaw simply because they happen on the Internet. *Id.* at 607–08 (citing Frank H. Easterbrook, *Cyberspace and the Law of the Horse*, 1996 U. CHI. LEGAL F. 207 (1996)).

[77] *See Transnational Evidence*, *supra* note 72, at 375–77.

[78] Bernhard Warner, *Europe's War on E-Mail Spam Claims First Scalps*, FORBES, Apr. 6, 2004, http://www.forbes.com/home_europe/newswire/2004/04/06/rtr1324342.html.

[79] Scott Charney, Combating Cybercrime: A Public-Private Strategy in the Digital Environment 5-6 (Mar. 31, 2005), http://www.nwacc.org/programs/conf05/UNCrimeCongressPaper.doc.

the ways that criminals are using them is a costly process.[80] To effectively train their investigators, agencies must continuously spend time and money on the training. Agencies are reluctant to invest money to train these agents because it is difficult to retain them—technically skilled investigators can receive much higher salaries in private sector jobs than they do in government agencies.[81] In addition, many law enforcement officials do not place cybercrime at the top of their priority list and feel that it is not worth their time and effort to develop these skills.[82] However, the U.S. Federal Bureau of Investigation (FBI) recently sent a strong message to these local law enforcement agencies about the importance of cybercrime investigations. The FBI announced that it was making cybercrime one of its top law enforcement priorities.[83]

Law enforcement agents also experience jurisdictional difficulties when they attempt to investigate and prosecute cybercrimes because many criminals send phishing e-mails from overseas.[84] The Internet cannot be limited to a single geographic area, and, as a result, agents cannot easily divide the Internet into legal precincts.[85] Because the Internet defies local and national jurisdiction, agents must often cooperate with foreign countries to investigate and prosecute cybercrimes.[86]

Traditionalists believe that the "cross-jurisdictional" activity involved in cybercrime is not a difficult issue.[87] They argue that conflict of laws principles adequately address the problems of international cybercrime because the same jurisdictional rules apply regardless of whether the crime occurred in cyberspace or in the physical world.[88] The concern, however, is not that the

---

[80] U.N. Econ. & Soc. Council [ECOSOC], *Effective Measures to Prevent and Control Computer-Related Crime*, ¶ 7, U.N. Doc. E/CN.15/2002/8 (Jan. 29, 2002) [hereinafter *U.N. Effective Measures*].

[81] *Id.*

[82] *See* Brenner & Schwerha, *supra* note 72, at 377.

[83] John Ashcroft, U.S. Att'y Gen., Prepared Remarks of Attorney General John Ashcroft at the High Technology Crime Investigation Association 2004 International Training Conference (Sept. 13, 2004), http://www.usdoj.gov/criminal/cybercrime/ashcroftRemarks091304.htm [hereinafter Ashcroft Remarks].

[84] *See* APWG OCT. TRENDS, *supra* note 7; Ray August, *International Cyber-Jurisdiction: A Comparative Analysis*, 39 AM. BUS. L.J. 531, 532 (2002).

[85] *See* August, *supra* note 84, at 532.

[86] *See generally id.* (discussing examples of cooperation between countries).

[87] Mayer-Schonberger, *supra* note 76, at 613–14.

[88] *Id.*; August, *supra* note 84, at 534. For a national court to have jurisdiction over an international crime, there must be some reasonable connection, or nexus, between the country and the crime or criminal. *Id.* The following four nexuses are invoked by courts to permit the exercise of jurisdiction. *Id.* First, under the territoriality nexus, there is jurisdiction if an offense is committed in whole or in part in that country. *Id.* Jurisdiction can exist wherever "any essential element of the crime is accomplished" within the forum's

rules for cybercrime vary drastically with those of traditional crimes, but rather that many local law enforcement agents are unfamiliar with international jurisdictional and criminal procedures.[89] For example, many local prosecutors do not know how to obtain evidence from other countries for their investigations and have never had contact with the Office of International Affairs.[90] The government must increase training to deal with these issues. Local prosecutors must be aware of the skills that they need to deal with cybercrime *before* the crime actually occurs; waiting until after the crime has already happened may be too late because the criminals quickly disappear into cyberspace.[91]

In addition, data protection laws frustrate law enforcement agents' ability to access information for identity theft investigations.[92] Data protection laws, such as the Gramm-Leach-Bliley Act, prevent banks and other institutions from disclosing certain data to law enforcement investigators.[93] The Anti-Phishing Working Group suggests that the Federal Trade Commission (FTC) can help reduce this problem and facilitate information gathering by creating a "central clearinghouse of information"[94] where officials could determine when it is appropriate to release financial information about victims.[95] Until governmental agencies make changes in the information gathering process, law enforcement agents will continue to struggle with their investigations.

2. *Joint Operations in Law Enforcement*

Law enforcement agencies throughout the world are realizing that interdepartmental cooperation is vital to the fight against phishing. Catching phishers is very difficult when law enforcement agents do not share skills and information.[96] In his remarks to the High Technology Crime Association, former U.S. Attorney General John Ashcroft stressed that the unique nature of

---

territory, including planning of the crime or the final effect of the crime. *Id.* at 534, 536. Next, the nationality nexus establishes jurisdiction based on the nationality or national character of the offender. *Id.* at 534. Third, the protective nexus permits jurisdiction when the offender's actions injure the national or international interests of the forum. *Id.* Finally, the universality nexus gives the court jurisdiction over crimes that are recognized by the international community as being of universal concern (such as piracy and genocide). *Id.*

[89] *See* Brenner & Schwerha, *supra* note 72, at 376.

[90] *Id.*

[91] *Id.*

[92] Shartel, *supra* note 45, at 524.

[93] *Id.*

[94] *Id.*

[95] *Id.*

[96] *See* discussion *supra* Part II.A.1.

cybercrimes requires a new approach from law enforcement agencies—namely, more emphasis on cooperation.[97]   Ashcroft suggested, "Just as computer networks offer cyber criminals opportunities to coordinate and clone each other's work, cyber crime demands that law enforcement share information, techniques, and resources to anticipate, outthink, and stop such crime."[98]

In response to the call for cooperation, U.S. law enforcement agencies have formed alliances to facilitate information sharing and to increase the number of arrests of cybercriminals.[99]   One example of this type of collaboration is the Internet Crime Complaint Center (IC3), a partnership between the FBI and the National White Collar Crime Center.[100]   The purpose of the IC3 is to provide a central referral base for complaints in order to assist law enforcement and regulatory agencies.[101]   In addition, the DOJ has established over fifty other task forces consisting of federal, state, and local agencies working together.[102]

One strong example of interagency cooperation is the DOJ's Operation Web Snare, which ran from June 1 to August 26, 2004.[103]   The DOJ considered the operation to be the "largest and most successful collaborative law enforcement operation ever conducted"[104] to fight cybercrime.[105]   The operation consisted of more than 160 investigations and resulted in 150 arrests and convictions.[106]   The initiative involved coordination between U.S. Attorney offices, the DOJ, the Postal Inspection Service, the FBI, the FTC, and a variety of other domestic and foreign law enforcement agencies.[107]   The crimes targeted in the operation included criminal spam, phishing, identity theft, spoofed or hijacked accounts, and credit card fraud.[108]   The initiative also focused on the international aspects of cybercrime.   In its executive summary

---

[97] Ashcroft Remarks, *supra* note 83.

[98] *Id.*

[99] Press Release, Dep't of Justice, Justice Department Announces Operation Web Snare Targeting Online Fraud and Crime (Aug. 26, 2004), http://www.usdoj.gov/opa/pr/2004/August/04_crm_583.htm [hereinafter Web Snare Press Release].

[100] Internet Crime Complaint Center, http://www.ic3.gov (last visited Feb. 27, 2006).

[101] *Id.*

[102] U.S. DEP'T OF JUSTICE, OPERATION WEB SNARE: A JOINT LAW ENFORCEMENT INITIATIVE 2 (2004), *available at* http://www.ic3.gov/media/initiatives/websnare.pdf [hereinafter OPERATION WEB SNARE].

[103] *Id.*

[104] Ashcroft Remarks, *supra* note 83.

[105] *Id.*

[106] Web Snare Press Release, *supra* note 99.

[107] *Id.*

[108] *Id.*

of Operation Web Snare, the DOJ stated that "[f]ocused efforts to pursue [c]yber criminals internationally has led to the development of enhanced proactive capabilities in several countries, and numerous investigative successes highlighted within this initiative."[109]

The latest of these cooperative initiatives is Digital PhishNet.[110] Unlike other efforts, this operation focuses solely on phishing scams.[111] The central idea of Digital PhishNet is that cooperation is the key to combating the phishing problem and the weaknesses in the existing law enforcement system.[112] The organization's website states that it is a "collaborative enforcement operation to unite industry leaders in technology, banking, financial services and online auctioneering with law enforcement to combat 'phishing.'"[113]

The FBI formed the organization in 2005.[114] Digital PhishNet's other members include law enforcement agencies such as the U.S. Secret Service and FTC, the National Cyber-Forensics and Training Alliance, nine of the top ten banks and financial service providers, major technology and e-commerce companies such as Microsoft, and top Internet service providers such as AOL and Earthlink.[115] The organization also has international partners in Nigeria and Hungary, and the FBI expects that more countries will join soon.[116]

The increasing sophistication of phishing demands a "multifaceted approach"[117]—Digital PhishNet is an example of the type of integration that the industry and law enforcement communities need.[118] The members of Digital PhishNet form an alliance of federal, state, and local agencies that work to increase the possibility of catching these criminals before they disappear into the "anonymity of cyberspace."[119] This comprehensive effort establishes a "single, unified line of communication between industry and law enforcement, so critical data to fight phishing can be compiled and provided to law

---

[109] OPERATION WEB SNARE, *supra* note 102, at 2.

[110] Digital PhishNet, http://www.digitalphishnet.org (last visited Feb. 27, 2006).

[111] *See id.*

[112] *Id.*

[113] *Id.*

[114] Federal Bureau of Investigation, An Unprecedented Cyber Partnership (Jan. 24, 2005), http://www.fbi.gov/page2/jan05/cyber012405.htm [hereinafter FBI Partnership].

[115] *Id.*

[116] *Id.*

[117] *See* Press Release, Microsoft, *supra* note 60.

[118] *Id.*

[119] *Id.*

enforcement in real time."[120] When a member becomes aware of a scam, the member forwards the information to the Digital PhishNet team so that the team can assess the scam.[121] The team prioritizes the threat, develops a strategy, and hands the case over to the appropriate law enforcement agency.[122]

In addition to increasing cooperation within domestic operations, the DOJ is working to increase worldwide cooperation in the fight against cybercrime. For example, the DOJ is working with the G8[123] to ensure that these eight major industrial economies are equipped with effective strategies and policies to fight cybercrime.[124] To facilitate information sharing, the G8's Subgroup on High-Tech Crime developed a network of law enforcement agencies from forty different countries to offer around-the-clock responses to urgent Internet crimes.[125] DOJ personnel also educated foreign law enforcement agents on investigative techniques.[126] The DOJ hopes that the successes of these international cooperative efforts show how "extensive and dedicated the law enforcement community is in the effort to combat Internet crime around the world."[127]

Many intelligence agencies throughout the world are also forming alliances to fight the threat of phishing attacks.[128] For example, the United Kingdom's National Hi-Tech Crime Unit (NHTCU) is working with the FBI and U.S. Secret Service to investigate phishing attacks in the United Kingdom.[129] The International Criminal Police Organization ("Interpol") also facilitates cooperation between national law enforcement agencies as they investigate multinational online crime.[130] To improve technical knowledge among law

---

[120] *Id.*

[121] FBI Partnership, *supra* note 114.

[122] *Id.*

[123] The G8 is a group of countries that meet to discuss major international political, economic, and social issues. *See* G8, Background to the G8 (2003), http://www.g8.fr/evian/extras/147.pdf. The G8 countries are Canada, France, Germany, Italy, Japan, Russia, the United Kingdom, and the United States. *Id.* at 1, 3.

[124] Ashcroft Remarks, *supra* note 83.

[125] *Id.*

[126] *Id.*

[127] *Id.*

[128] Vladimir Golubev, *Computer Crime and Organized Crime*, COMPUTER CRIME RESEARCH CTR., Mar. 7, 2004, http://www.crime-research.org/news/07.03.2004/120. *See also* discussion on organized crime *infra* Part II.B.2.a.

[129] Dinah Greek, *Police Net 12 Phishing Suspects*, VNUNET.COM, May 5, 2004, http://www.pcw.co.uk/news/1154938. The NHTCU, established in April of 2001, is focused on combating national and transnational organized hi-tech crime impacting the United Kingdom. National Hi-Tech Crime Unit, About NHTCU, http://www.nhtcu.org/nqcontent.cfm?a_id=12340&tt=nhtcu (last visited Feb. 22, 2006).

[130] *U.N. Effective Measures, supra* note 80, ¶ 7.

enforcement officials, Interpol produces a handbook that agencies use to train investigators in the best practices and techniques for dealing with information technology crime.[131] Interpol also helps to increase the flow of communication between countries by developing websites and contact directories for investigators.[132] Interpol hopes that its approach will enable law enforcement agencies to work more efficiently without duplicating one another's efforts.[133]

Because cybercrime is constantly evolving, the strategies that law enforcement agencies use should evolve as well. Cooperation between agencies, both domestically and internationally, is an important aspect of this evolution. The Internet has given criminals the ability to cooperate with a wide array of fellow criminals, and fighting these criminal alliances requires law enforcement agencies to form alliances of their own.[134] Without these kinds of joint efforts, phishers can easily exploit the educational and informational weaknesses in the traditional system.[135] By joining together, however, these agencies are not only able to compensate for one another's weaknesses, but they can also grow stronger by establishing strategies for future attacks.

Even though these combined initiatives are helpful, joint law enforcement operations alone are not the solution to ending phishing scams. Joint law enforcement operations are a strong step in the right direction, but an end to phishing also depends on cooperation from the private sector and legislators. Law enforcement agencies need the cooperation of industry leaders so that they can conduct thorough investigations and form joint strategies. These operations also depend on informed consumers who can alert the agencies about possible scams. In addition, legislators must support these operations with consistent laws and strong penalties.

B. Legislation

To effectively combat phishing, governments must create legislation that is effective across local, national, and international boundaries.[136] Below, subsection 1 examines U.S. approaches to combating phishing through

---

[131]   *Id.*

[132]   *Id.*

[133]   *Id.*

[134]   *See* Ashcroft Remarks, *supra* note 83.

[135]   *See* Brenner & Schwerha, *supra* note 72, at 375–77. For more on the weaknesses in the traditional law enforcement system, see discussion *supra* Part II.A.1.

[136]   August, *supra* note 84, at 532.

legislation. The discussion includes an evaluation of the Identity Theft Penalty Enhancement Act and the proposed Anti-Phishing Act of 2005. Subsection 2 then discusses international legislation that targets cybercrime. Specifically, subsection 2 includes a discussion of the role of organized crime in phishing attacks and the possible application of the U.N. Convention Against Transnational Organized Crime to combat the problem. This subsection also examines the strengths and weakness of the Council of Europe Convention on Cybercrime, which the United States has refused to ratify.

1. *Domestic Legislation Against Phishing*

The U.S. government is experimenting with many different legislative approaches to fight phishing. Currently, there is no specific law against phishing, but the government can prosecute criminals under existing federal laws that target identity theft, wire fraud, computer fraud, bank fraud, credit card fraud, or violations of the CAN-SPAM Act.[137] Although prosecutors can use these existing federal laws against phishers, there have been very few prosecutions, and the punishments have been light.[138] New federal legislation attempts to correct these problems by increasing punishments and specifically criminalizing phishing.

a. *The Identity Theft Penalty Enhancement Act*

The Identity Theft Penalty Enhancement Act (ITPEA)[139] increases punishments for identity thieves and is likely to increase the length of the sentences of those who are convicted of conducting phishing scams.[140] The ITPEA amends current federal law and creates a new crime of "aggravated

---

[137] DOJ PHISHING REPORT, *supra* note 23. The Controlling the Assault of Non-Solicited Pornography and Marketing Act of 2003 (or CAN-SPAM Act) was the first U.S. federal law that placed restrictions on the use of unsolicited commercial e-mail. 18 U.S.C.A. § 1037 (West 2003); Jeffrey D. Sullivan & Michael B. de Leeuw, *Spam After CAN-SPAM: How Inconsistent Thinking Has Made a Hash Out of Unsolicited Commercial E-Mail Policy*, 20 SANTA CLARA COMPUTER & HIGH TECH. L.J. 887, 887 (2004).

[138] The first lawsuit against phishing was brought in July 2003 by the FTC against an individual who sent e-mails pretending to be from America Online. Because no specific law existed against phishing, charges were brought under the FTC Act, which bars deceptive and unfair practices, and the Gramm-Leach-Bliley Act, which makes it illegal to use fabricated or false statements to obtain another's financial information. Matthew Moynahan, *Three Ways to Fight Back Against Phishing*, COMPUTERWORLD.COM, Jan. 6, 2005, http://computerworld.com/securitytopics/security/story/0,10801,98701p3,00.html.

[139] 18 U.S.C.A. § 1028A (West 2005). The Act was signed into legislation by President Bush on July 15, 2004. *Bush Signs Legislation Subjecting Identity Thieves to Tougher Penalties*, 9 Elec. Com. & L. Rep. (BNA) 636, 636 (July 21, 2004) [hereinafter *Bush Signs Legislation*].

[140] *See* Tim Lemke, *Penalties Stiffened for Identity Theft*, WASH. TIMES, July 16, 2004, at C11.

identity theft," which occurs when a criminal uses a stolen identity to commit other crimes.[141]   Under the ITPEA, those who commit identity theft will receive an additional two years of prison time in addition to whatever sentences they receive for the underlying fraud crimes they commit with the stolen identity (with a minimum sentence of five years).[142]   President George W. Bush signed the Act to ensure that the sentences for these crimes reflect the damage that was done to the victim.[143]   He stressed, "Too often, those convicted have been sentenced to little or no time in prison. This changes today."[144]

One aspect of the ITPEA that causes some concern is the fact that it imposes mandatory prison terms.[145]   By imposing these terms, some critics believe that Congress is overstepping the Constitution's separation of powers by invading the judicial branch's ability to determine the sentence; critics argue that a judge who has heard the evidence in a case is in a much better position to determine the punishment than Congress.[146]   However, there are also positive aspects of the legislation.   The ITPEA will improve state agencies' inadequate enforcement of identity theft crimes by putting the crime in federal hands.[147]   The Electronic Privacy Information Center (EPIC) believes that federal enforcement will increase victim protection because state police may have shuffled the victims around to avoid dealing with the crime.[148] In addition, EPIC hopes that the ITPEA will encourage prosecutors to bring more identity fraud cases.[149]

---

[141]   18 U.S.C.A. § 1028A.

[142]   McCullagh, *supra* note 53. *See, e.g., Bush Signs Legislation, supra* note 139, at 636. "If the phishing results in someone taking identity information, this law will allow them to be prosecuted for possessing that information with criminal intent . . . . If the phisher uses the information to commit mail fraud, for example, that phisher will get an extra two years in jail because he used stolen identity information." *Id.* (quoting U.S. Deputy Att'y Gen. James Comey).

[143]   *Bush Signs Legislation, supra* note 139, at 636.

[144]   *Id.*

[145]   McCullagh, *supra* note 53.

[146]   *Id.* Although there is some theoretical tension regarding mandatory prison terms and separation of powers, the Supreme Court has held that "Congress has the power to define criminal punishments without giving the courts any sentencing discretion." Chapman v. United States, 500 U.S. 453, 467 (1991).

[147]   McCullagh, *supra* note 53.

[148]   *Id.*

[149]   *Id.*

b. The Anti-Phishing Act of 2005

Senator Patrick Leahy believes that current laws, such as wire fraud and identity theft statutes, do not adequately cover the unique problems of phishing attacks and that a new law is necessary.[150] To combat this weakness, Senator Leahy proposed the Anti-Phishing Act of 2005.[151] Under current law, if the recipient of a phishing e-mail realizes that the e-mail is a scam and forwards the information to a law enforcement agency, the agency is not able to prosecute unless the recipient actually suffers harm by disclosing his information.[152] If Congress passes Leahy's Anti-Phishing Act, law enforcement officials could prosecute phishing scams before the culprit actually receives the financial information.[153] The Act "criminalizes the bait," not just successful phishing.[154]

The Anti-Phishing Act of 2005 establishes two new crimes. First, it would be illegal to create or procure a website that presents itself as a legitimate business if the culprit attempts to induce the victim to share personal information and if the culprit has the intent to commit fraud or identity theft.[155] Second, the Act "prohibits the creation or procurement of an email" for the same purposes and with the same intent as above.[156] Each act of the scam would be illegal, from sending the e-mail to using a fraudulent website, even if the recipient does not ultimately provide the information.[157] If the legislature enacts this bill, then each element of the scam would subject the culprit to five years in prison and a possible fine of up to $250,000.[158]

---

[150] Press Release, Senator Patrick Leahy, Speech on the Senate Floor on the Introduction of the "Anti-Phishing Act of 2005" (Feb. 28, 2005), http://www.leahy.senate.gov/press/200503/030105.html [hereinafter Leahy Speech].

[151] S. 472, 109th Cong. (2005) [hereinafter Anti-Phishing Act]. The 2005 Act is virtually identical to the 2004 version of the Act. All statements that analyze, support, or criticize one version can be assumed to apply to the other version as well.

[152] Ramasastry, *supra* note 25.

[153] Leahy Speech, *supra* note 150.

[154] *Id.*

[155] *Id.*

[156] *Id.*

[157] Moynahan, *supra* note 138. The Act protects First Amendment speech, like parodies and political speech, by only punishing acts that are done knowingly and with intent to commit identity theft. Leahy Speech, *supra* note 150; Anti-Phishing Act, *supra* note 151.

[158] Ramasastry, *supra* note 25.

Critics, however, believe that the ITPEA and the Anti-Phishing Act of 2005 are too late to stop the rampant spread of phishing.[159] They pessimistically compare the legislation to the recently enacted "spam" laws, which have had little effect on the amount of "spam" sent out.[160] Critics propose that improved technology and consumer awareness are more likely to stop phishing.[161]

All Internet offenses present the same three hurdles: (1) finding the perpetrator of the crime, (2) obtaining personal jurisdiction, and (3) collecting the judgment.[162] Unless law enforcement can overcome these inherent difficulties, the impact of domestic and international legislation will be limited.[163] Even with its weaknesses, however, domestic legislation is still a crucial component in the fight against phishing. These new laws give law enforcement agencies and private industries more options to catch and prosecute phishers. In addition, they also send a message to criminals, companies, and consumers that phishing is a top priority and that culprits will be dealt with harshly. Domestic legislation, however, is limited by the global nature of the Internet and international measures must be taken to deal with this problem.

2. International Legislation

Phishing is a worldwide phenomenon that has victims, culprits, and effects that reach across borders. For example, a Russian phisher could send a fake e-mail that uses an American company's name to target an English individual. If the victim responds, the criminal can quickly spread this sensitive information worldwide via the Internet.[164] The borderless nature of phishing results in jurisdictional issues that make it difficult for local legislators to fight the problem on their own.[165] To combat the problems that result from the international aspects of phishing, legislators must cooperate internationally. One of the most important steps that the government can take to secure the

---

[159] Jack M. Germain, *Will Antiphishing Legislation Be Effective?*, E-COMMERCE TIMES, Nov. 13, 2004, http://www.ecommercetimes.com/story/38006.html.

[160] *Id.* The Anti-Phishing Act of 2005 is closely tied to the CAN-SPAM Act and even uses many of the CAN-SPAM definitions. *See* 18 U.S.C. § 1037 (2003). For a more thorough discussion on the ineffectiveness of the CAN-SPAM Act, see Sullivan & de Leeuw, *supra* note 137.

[161] Germain, *supra* note 159.

[162] Robert Louis B. Stevenson, *Plugging the "Phishing" Hole: Legislation Versus Technology*, DUKE L. & TECH. REV., Mar. 24, 2005, at 5, http://www.law.duke.edu/journals/dltr/articles/PDF/2005DLTR0006.pdf.

[163] *Id.*

[164] Cohn, *supra* note 6.

[165] *See* discussion *supra* Part II.A.1.

Internet is to "enact and vigorously enforce well-conceived laws against online crimes, including against criminals that reside in other countries."[166]

a. Organized Crime Legislation

One possible mechanism to control international phishing attacks is to apply already existing organized crime legislation, such as the U.N. Convention Against Transnational Organized Crime ("Organized Crime Convention").[167] Although the prototypical hacker works alone, much of the increased activity, including activity in Eastern Europe, stems from organized groups.[168] As the Internet grows, so do the possibilities for making large amounts of money through cybercrime—this makes phishing a very attractive prospect for organized groups.[169] Organized crime has been linked to the increase in the volume and sophistication of phishing attacks.[170] Timothy Keanini, chief technology officer of nCircle, stated, "We are seeing more and more organized threats. The code, tactics and frameworks look like some of the best software designers' work, but it's actually the bad guys. It is all more efficient and has much more reuse."[171]

---

[166] Charney, *supra* note 79, at 4–5.

[167] Convention Against Transnational Organized Crime, G.A. Res. 55/25, U.N. Doc. A/RES/55/25 (Jan. 8, 2001), *available at* http://www.unodc.org/pdf/crime/a_res_55/res5525e.pdf [hereinafter Organized Crime Convention].

[168] Cohn, *supra* note 6. For example, a recent phishing attack in Russia, targeting CityBank customers, resulted in the arrests of Estonian, Russian, Latvian, and Ukrainian individuals who were all being used as "mules" by a Russian organized crime gang to move the money out of the country. The NHTCU believes that this gang is also responsible for attacks against U.K. banks that scammed individuals out of hundreds of thousands of pounds. Dmitri Kramarenko, *Russia: Citybank Clients Scammed*, COMPUTER CRIME RESEARCH CTR., May 20, 2004, http://www.crime-research.org/news/20.05.2004/281. The U.S. Secret Service and the United Nations' involvement in many of these investigations demonstrate the severity of these offenses. Elizabeth Milard, *Hackers Gone Phishing—Again*, TECHNEWSWORLD, Dec. 29, 2003, http://www.technewsworld.com/story/32486.html.

[169] McCafferty, *supra* note 10, at 31. This sentiment is echoed by Rick Quaresima, chief of the criminal liaison unit in the Federal Trade Commission's Bureau of Consumer Production, who states, "It's like anything else: If there's money to be made, organized groups of criminals will go to it." Cohn, *supra* note 6 (quoting Quaresima).

[170] Cohn, *supra* note 6. Some critics, however, believe that there is not enough information to concretely establish a link between phishing fraud and organized crime, but this is a minority view. *See* Paul Gosling, *Crooks Gang Up to Beat Banks*, INFOSECURITY, Jan./Feb. 2004, http://www.infosecurity-magazine.com/features/janfeb04/crooks_janfeb.html.

[171] Kate Stoodly, *In 2005, Organized Crime Will Back Phishers*, DATAMATION, Dec. 23, 2004, http://itmanagement.earthweb.com/secu/article.php/3451501.

The Internet has also changed the way organized criminals work together—now they can commit crimes without formal organization.[172] Cybercrimes require less personal contact than crimes in the physical world because criminals do not need to exercise control over a geographic area.[173] In addition, criminals can organize these groups easily because many groups consist of as few as three people.[174] The groups usually include a "spammer" who sends the e-mails, someone who designs the website, and another person who moves and launders the money.[175] Many times these groups form purely over the Internet, where the criminals brainstorm their plans in chat rooms, and then agree to split the profits.[176]

Organized crime rings are drawn to phishing for the same reasons as individuals—the scams are lucrative, and the speed of the scam and the anonymity of the Internet make it less likely that they will be caught.[177] Committing crimes online provides a "virtually invisible channel" for the illegal activity, and criminals are able to avoid authorities.[178] A research reporter for Gartner explains the allure of phishing in the following way: "There are no blood and guts to deal with. All they have to do is hire the people with the necessary expertise . . . and they're ready to go."[179]

Organized cybercrime is a serious international problem that requires international legislation. Although roughly half of the organized phishing attacks originate in the United States, other activity stems from groups in Eastern Europe, China, Korea, and Russia.[180] The worldwide reach of these scams can make it difficult to prosecute offenders.[181] The Organized Crime Convention could be an effective tool to fight these problems.[182] The Organized Crime Convention is a legally binding instrument that requires ratifying States to take steps to prevent transnational organized crime.[183] The goal of the Organized Crime Convention is to make it more difficult for groups

---

[172] COE CRIME SUMMARY, *supra* note 59, at 9.
[173] *Id.*
[174] McCafferty, *supra* note 10, at 32.
[175] *Id.*
[176] *Id.*
[177] COE CRIME SUMMARY, *supra* note 59, at 8. *See* discussion *supra* Part I.C.
[178] Milard, *supra* note 168.
[179] McCafferty, *supra* note 10, at 32 (quoting Avivah Litan).
[180] *Id.* at 32; Barrett, *supra* note 5.
[181] Brenner, *supra* note 68, at 25–26.
[182] *See generally* Organized Crime Convention, *supra* note 167. The resolution was adopted by the General Assembly on November 15, 2000 and entered into force on September 29, 2003. *Id.*
[183] *Id.*

to take advantage of the jurisdictional problems, differences in national law, and information gaps that often accompany transnational crime.[184]

The Organized Crime Convention enacts creative new frameworks for mutual legal assistance, law enforcement cooperation, and technical training across participating countries.[185] The United Nations is assisting with this task by gathering international data that individual countries can use to promote international cooperation in organized crime investigations.[186] The information includes legislation that involves the procedures that individual countries should follow when investigating international organized crime, extradition details, and a list of government agencies that can serve as contacts when dealing with organized crime.[187] In addition, the United Nations, under the provisions of the Organized Crime Convention, has initiated a global multimedia training program aimed at law enforcement personnel to prevent organized crime and encourage anti-organized crime legislation.[188] The seminar examines the best practices that countries can use to deal with international organized crime and targets a wide range of groups, including police investigators, intelligence analysts, prosecutors, judges, and customs officials.[189] The United Nations has held these seminars in Romania, Nigeria, Mexico, and various other countries.[190]

Although the United Nations did not form the Organized Crime Convention to deal solely with cybercrime, its principles apply to the international problems that stem from phishing. The Organized Crime Convention calls for increases in legal assistance and law enforcement cooperation. This framework gives ratifying States the capability to work together to determine the scope of phishing scams and assist each other in investigations. By forming an international alliance against organized crime, the Organized Crime Convention enables countries to rely on one another so that they can share information and stop organized phishing attacks.

---

[184] *Id.*

[185] *Id.*

[186] *See* United Nations Office on Drugs and Crime, Organized Crime, http://www.unodc.org/unodc/ organized_crime.html (last visited Mar. 9, 2005) [hereinafter U.N. Organized Crime].

[187] *Id.*

[188] *Id.*

[189] *Id.*

[190] *Id.*

b.   Council of Europe Convention on Cybercrime

The Council of Europe Convention on Cybercrime (COE Convention)[191] is the first international treaty to deal explicitly with Internet-based crime.[192] The main purpose of the COE Convention is to "pursue a common criminal policy aimed at the protection of society against cybercrime, especially by adopting appropriate legislation and fostering international co-operation."[193] As the explanatory report accompanying the Convention states, the Convention evolved from the Council of Europe's ("Council") belief that the only way to effectively fight cybercrime was by forming a binding international instrument.[194] In 1997, the Council formed a Committee of Experts on Crime in Cyberspace (PC-CY) to draft a binding instrument that would aid in the international prosecution of computer crimes.[195] The document eventually evolved into the COE Convention.[196]

Supporters of the COE Convention believe that it will commit ratifying nations to prosecute computer-related crimes more vigorously.[197] However, critics argue that the countries that participated in the COE Convention are not the countries where enforcement is most needed.[198] Although thirty countries initially signed the document in 2001,[199] it took more than two years for the treaty to be ratified by enough countries to enter into force.[200] After the participating countries completed the document, countries that had participated in the drafting process but were not members of the Council—such as the

---

[191]   Convention on Cybercrime, Council of Europe, Nov. 23, 2001, Europ. T.S. No. 185, *available at* http://conventions.coe.int/Treaty/en/treaties/word/185.doc [hereinafter COE Convention].

[192]   Council of Europe, Summary of the Convention on Cybercrime, http://conventions.coe.int/Treaty/en/Summaries/Html/185.htm (last visited Feb. 2, 2006) [hereinafter COE Convention Summary]. The Council of Europe was established in 1949 as a forum to promote law, democracy, and human rights throughout Europe. The Council consists of forty-four States, including all of the members of the European Union. DOJ FAQs, *supra* note 12. For more information on the Council of Europe, see http://www.coe.int (last visited Feb. 2, 2006).

[193]   COE Convention Summary, *supra* note 192.

[194]   *See* COUNCIL OF EUROPE, CONVENTION ON CYBERCRIME EXPLANATORY REPORT ¶ 9 (2001), http://conventions.coe.int/Treaty/en/Reports/Html/185.htm [hereinafter EXPLANATORY REPORT].

[195]   DOJ FAQs, *supra* note 12.

[196]   *Id.*

[197]   KRISTIN ARCHICK, CONGRESSIONAL RES. SERV., CYBERCRIME: THE COUNCIL OF EUROPE CONVENTION 3 (Apr. 26, 2002), *available at* http://www.fas.org/irp/crs/RS21208.pdf.

[198]   *Id.* For example, Yemen, North Korea, and Philippines are not included. *Id.*

[199]   DOJ FAQs, *supra* note 12.

[200]   *See* COE Convention Summary, *supra* note 192. The Convention can only be entered into force once it has been ratified by five countries, at least three of which must be members of the COE. COE Convention, *supra* note 191, art. 36.

United States, Canada, and Japan—had the right to become Parties to the agreement.[201] Although all of the non-member countries signed the agreement, none ratified it.[202] President George W. Bush submitted the COE Convention for ratification to the U.S. Senate on November 17, 2003, but the Senate has not yet reached a decision on the Convention.[203]

Members of the Council hope that the COE Convention will allow ratifying parties to minimize the jurisdictional and procedural challenges that arise from cybercrimes. The COE Convention attempts to accomplish this goal by:

> (1) harmonising the domestic criminal substantive law elements of offences and connected provisions in the area of cyber-crime[,] (2) providing for domestic criminal procedural law powers necessary for the investigation and prosecution of such offences as well as other offences committed by means of a computer system or evidence in relation to which is in electronic form[, and] (3) setting up a fast and effective regime of international co-operation.[204]

First, the COE Convention requires all ratifying countries to criminalize certain computer-related crimes, if they have not already made these crimes illegal.[205] The computer-related crimes include gaining illegal access to computer systems and data, illegal interception of data, and computer-related fraud.[206] The COE Convention attempts to prevent criminals from shifting their criminal activities to other countries to take advantage of lower legal standards by requiring parties to adopt common definitions of these cybercrimes.[207] Parties to the COE Convention hope that this will also lead to the international exchange of "useful common experiences" in these areas of law.[208]

Second, the COE Convention requires ratifying countries to have the procedural capabilities necessary to investigate and prosecute the crimes.[209] The COE Convention requires each party to adopt legislation that confers

---

[201] DOJ FAQs, *supra* note 12.

[202] *Id.*; Convention on Cybercrime Chart of Signatures and Ratifications, http://conventions.coe.int/ Treaty/Commun/ChercheSig.asp?NT=185&CM=1&DF=3/10/05&CL=ENG (last visited Feb. 2, 2006).

[203] *See* President's Message to the Senate Transmitting the Council of Europe Convention on Cybercrime, 39 WEEKLY COMP. PRES. DOC. 1643 (Nov. 17, 2003) [hereinafter Bush Message].

[204] *See* EXPLANATORY REPORT, *supra* 194, ¶ 16.

[205] COE Convention, *supra* note 191, arts. 2-8.

[206] *Id.*

[207] *See* EXPLANATORY REPORT, *supra* 194, ¶ 33.

[208] *Id.*

[209] COE Convention, *supra* note 191, art. 14.

jurisdiction on these cases in any instance where the offense is committed in its territory or "by one of its nationals, if the offence is punishable under criminal law where it was committed or if the offence is committed outside the territorial jurisdiction of any State."[210] In addition, Parties must have laws in place that allow them to collect informational data that agents can use in investigations and prosecutions.[211] This provision includes laws that permit the government to search and seize e-mail and computer records as well as perform Internet surveillance.[212]

The COE Convention has the potential to conflict with citizens' privacy rights because it requires ratifying Parties to enact information-gathering laws that give government the power to collect computer data. The COE Convention does not contain any specific provisions to protect citizens' privacy. Although the word "privacy" is used once in the preamble of the COE Convention, it does not appear in any of the COE Convention's articles.[213]

Third, Chapter III of the COE Convention requires Parties to cooperate with each other by sharing electronic information across borders. Articles 23 and 25 both broadly state that the Parties must assist each other in the "collection of evidence in electronic form."[214] As a result, virtually any crime could fall under the COE Convention, including a robbery where the criminals

---

[210] *Id.* art. 22.

[211] *Id.* art. 14. The COE Convention requires all Internet service providers, phone companies, and other businesses with access to computer data to cooperate with the information gathering. *See id.* arts. 16-21. Service providers worry that they will have to pay for the costs associated with these investigations. Mike Godwin, *Watch Out: An International Treaty on Cybercrime Sounds Like a Great Idea, Until You Read the Fine Print*, IP WORLDWIDE, Apr. 2001, http://www.cryptome.org/cycrime-godwin.htm. The DOJ, however, believes that this should not be a problem. It stated that a reimbursement obligation was not included in the treaty because it was "unworkable" for small countries but that "the current U.S. law and practice of providing reimbursement in many instances would not be affected." DOJ FAQs, *supra* note 12. This language, however, is very vague, and it appears that the U.S. government would have fairly broad discretion about whether it will give reimbursement in a given circumstance.

[212] *See* COE Convention, *supra* note 191, art. 14; *see also* Kevin Poulsen, *U.S. Defends Cybercrime Treaty*, SECURITYFOCUS, Apr. 23, 2004, http://www.securityfocus.com/news/8529.

[213] Press Release, American Civil Liberties Union, The Seven Reasons Why the Senate Should Reject the International Cybercrime Treaty (Dec. 18, 2003), http://www.aclu.org/news/NewsPrint.cfm?ID=13475&c=131 [hereinafter ACLU Press Release]. James X. Dempsey, senior staff counsel of the Center for Democracy and Technology stresses, "Consumers and businesses should be worried because the treaty promotes wiretapping and e-mail interception without strong privacy protections." Thomas Claburn, *Fear of a Hacked Planet*, ZIFF DAVIS SMART BUS., May 2001, at 39, *available at* http://www.findarticles.com/p/articles/mi_zdzsb/is_200105/ai_ziff8268 (quoting Dempsey).

[214] COE Convention, *supra* note 191, arts. 23, 25.

used a wireless e-mail device to communicate with each other.[215] It also includes any crime where the evidence could be in computerized form.[216] Chapter III of the COE Convention is so broad that States could apply it to numerous areas that are only remotely related to cybercrime.

Another concern is Article 25 of the COE Convention, which requires ratifying Parties to provide "mutual assistance to the widest extent possible" to other signatory countries that are conducting cross-border investigations.[217] One of the main problems with the "mutual assistance" requirement is that the COE Convention does not contain a "dual criminality" provision, under which an activity must be deemed a crime in *both* countries before one nation can demand assistance from another.[218] Without this provision, the COE Convention would require U.S. authorities to cooperate with foreign police, even if they are investigating an activity which is legal in the United States.[219] For example, Germany and France have laws that prohibit the discussion of Nazi philosophy or advertisements for the sale of Nazi memorabilia, but the U.S. Constitution protects these rights under the First Amendment.[220] Under the COE Convention, if these countries requested assistance, U.S. law enforcement agencies could be required to assist in the prosecution of individuals who simply engaged in constitutionally protected speech.[221]

The COE Convention's "mutual assistance" requirement could also invoke human rights concerns if countries that have a history of human rights violations ask for assistance.[222] Several signatories to the treaty have a history of using their police powers to suppress free speech and fair elections, discriminate against minorities, and harass citizens.[223] The American Civil Liberties Union (ACLU) argues that these nations could ratify the treaty and then demand assistance from the United States to prosecute these

---

[215] ACLU Press Release, *supra* note 213.

[216] *Id.*

[217] COE Convention, *supra* note 191, art. 25.

[218] Electronic Privacy Information Center, The Council of Europe's Convention on Cybercrime, http://www.epic.org/privacy/intl/ccc.html (last visited Jan. 30, 2006) [hereinafter EPIC]; Letter from ACLU to the Senate Foreign Relations Committee on the Council of Europe Convention on Cybercrime (June 16, 2004), http://www.aclu.org/privacy/gen/15748leg20040616.html [hereinafter ACLU Letter].

[219] EPIC, *supra* note 218; ACLU Letter, *supra* note 218.

[220] ACLU Letter, *supra* note 218.

[221] *Id.*

[222] *Id.*

[223] *Id.*

individuals.[224] Although Article 27(4)(a) states that the requested Party may refuse assistance if the conduct is viewed as a "political offence,"[225] the ACLU points out that this term is never defined in the treaty and the exemption only applies to parts of the COE Convention.[226] For example, the requirement of real time data monitoring does not have an exception for political offenses.[227] As a result, the FBI could be required to order Internet providers to spy on a foreign political dissenter.[228] Barry Steinhardt of the ACLU stated, "This is a bad treaty that not only threatens core liberties, but will obligate the United States to use extraordinary powers to do the dirty work of other nations."[229]

On November 17, 2003, over two years after its initial signing, President George W. Bush asked the Senate to ratify the COE Convention.[230] The ACLU subsequently voiced its concerns about the COE Convention in a letter to the Senate Foreign Relations Committee on the Council of Europe Convention on Cybercrime.[231] The letter urged the Committee not to rush its recommendation to the Senate but, instead, to conduct full hearings to explore the complexity of the agreement.[232] The letter stated, "Regardless of one's ultimate view of the merits of the Convention one thing is clear: the treaty is the result of a process that began more than 8 years ago, it should not be rushed through the Senate without a full and complete evaluation of its merits and drawbacks."[233]

The President's motives for suddenly pushing for ratification years after the treaty had been effectively abandoned by the United States are unclear.[234] Barry Steinhardt of the ACLU believes that the push was related to the

---

[224] *Id.* (stating that many of these countries received a poor ranking in *Country Reports on Human Rights Practices*).

[225] COE Convention, *supra* note 191, art. 27.

[226] ACLU Letter, *supra* note 218; COE Convention, *supra* note 191, art. 27.

[227] Barry Steinhardt & Christopher Calabrese, American Civil Liberties Union, ACLU Memo on the Council of Europe Convention on Cybercrime, June 16, 2004, http://www.aclu.org/privacy/gen/15746leg20040616.html.

[228] *See id.*

[229] Source Watch, Council of Europe Convention on Cybercrime, http://www.sourcewatch.org/wiki.phtml?title=Council_of_Europe_Convention_on_Cybercrime (last visited Jan. 30, 2006) [hereinafter Source Watch]. Cedric Laurent, a senior policy fellow at the Electronic Privacy Information Center, says that EPIC is also opposed to the treaty. *Id.*

[230] Bush Message, *supra* note 203.

[231] ACLU Letter, *supra* note 218.

[232] *Id.*

[233] *Id.*

[234] Source Watch, *supra* note 229.

September 11, 2001 attacks and the recently passed Patriot Act.[235] The September 11, 2001 attacks led to an increased government awareness of the possibility that terrorists may be using the Internet and computers to communicate, recruit, and raise money.[236] As a result, Congress passed the Patriot Act, which allows law enforcement agencies to use surveillance devices to collect information on Internet addresses and traffic.[237] The ACLU argues that ratification of the COE Convention would take the Patriot Act even further and would allow government officials to examine the actual content of Internet interactions.[238] Civil liberties groups claim that the government is simply using the COE Convention to attempt to gain even more power than the Patriot Act granted.[239] The groups believe that the COE Convention favors the interests of the federal government over those of the citizens because the cybercrime treaty "was written by government bureaucrats for government bureaucrats."[240]

Although an international treaty to deal with cybercrime is a valid idea, the COE Convention does not appear to be an optimal treaty for the United States. The positive aspects of the COE Convention, such as providing uniform definitions of offenses and increasing information sharing across borders, are overshadowed by the lack of human rights and privacy protections. The absence of a dual criminality provision in the existing treaty is also a significant problem that should not be underestimated. Instead of signing this Convention, it would be in the United States' best interest to wait until a treaty is developed that is more consistent with U.S. rights. Perhaps the United States could work with the United Nations to develop a treaty that will fulfill these ideals. In 2005, the United Nations held a workshop and discussed the international difficulties for combating cybercrime, but no specific legislation was proposed.[241] Until a proper international instrument is introduced,

---

[235] *Id.*

[236] ARCHICK, *supra* note 197.

[237] Source Watch, *supra* note 229; EPIC, *supra* note 218.

[238] ACLU Press Release, *supra* note 213.

[239] EPIC, *supra* note 218; ARCHICK, *supra* note 197.

[240] Godwin, *supra* note 211 (quoting Stewart Baker).

[241] Press Release, U.N. 11th Cong., Sub-Comm. on Crime Prevention & Criminal Justice, Criminalization of Computer Wrongdoing Prerequisite for Combatting Cybercrime, Workshop Told, U.N. Doc. BKK/CP/19 (Apr. 22, 2005), *available at* http://www.un.org/events/11thcongress/docs/bkkcp19e.pdf. The workshop included, among others, panelists from Interpol, the Ukraine, United Kingdom, Romania, and the United States. The panelists voiced concerns about jurisdiction and stressed the need for cooperation among international governments and the private sector. Recommendations included the statement that "[g]overnments, the private sector and non-governmental organizations should work together to bridge the

domestic legislators, law enforcement agents, and members of the private sector must increase their efforts in the fight against cybercrime.

C. Private Sector Cooperation

To compensate for the weaknesses in law enforcement and legislation, targeted companies and consumers themselves must engage in the battle against phishing. The corporate victims of these attacks must cooperate, not only with the government and outside sources, but also with each other—a concept that the FTC calls "coopertition."[242] Companies must form alliances to increase information sharing and to establish common strategies. In addition, it is important that companies educate consumers about these scams so that they can help prevent the attacks. If consumers are able to detect these scams, they cannot only protect themselves, but they can also act as informants to the companies and law enforcement officials.[243]

1. Corporate Responsibility

Recently, companies have realized that their cooperation is vital in decreasing phishing attacks. They are now taking a more public role in the fight against phishing. In the past, many corporations were reluctant to become public warriors against phishing because they feared negative publicity.[244] Companies believed that releasing information on actual and possible security breaches would cause more indirect financial losses and public relations problems than the actual attacks.[245] However, the rapid increase in phishing attacks has forced companies to publicly confront the harm and directly address the problem with their customers.[246]

Members of private industries, most notably those of the financial services industry, are realizing that they must cooperate with each other in the fight against phishing. Phishers mostly target financial services like banking and

---

digital divide, raise public awareness about computer-related crime and to enhance the capacity of criminal justice professionals." *Id.* at 4.

[242] Wendy Leibowitz, *FTC Commissioners Say More E-Mail Laws Likely If Authentication Issue Goes Unsolved,* 9 Elec. Com. & L. Rep. (BNA) 932, 932 (Nov. 17, 2004).

[243] Federal Trade Commission, Take Charge: Fighting Back Against Identity Theft (June 2005), *available at* http://www.ftc.gov/bcp/conline/pubs/credit/idtheft.pdf [hereinafter FTC Recommendations].

[244] FED. DEPOSIT INS. CORP., PUTTING AN END TO ACCOUNT-HIJACKING IDENTITY THEFT 14 (2004), *available at* http://www.fdic.gov/consumers/consumer/idtheftstudy/identity_theft.pdf [hereinafter FDIC REPORT].

[245] *Id.*

[246] *Id.*

credit card companies, which represent 86.9% of all hijacked brands in phishing scams.[247] Because customers expect these financial institutions to ensure that their financial transactions will be safe and secure,[248] companies throughout the financial world are forming alliances to provide this security. One example is the Trusted Electronic Communications Forum, which consists of international banks that are working together to research the best practices and technical standards for fighting phishing attacks.[249]

Other companies have teamed up with outside fraud detection companies to combat phishing attacks more aggressively.[250] The Financial Services Technology Consortium consists of eleven financial services firms and seventeen technology companies that are working together to compose a complete inventory of existing threats and responses to phishing scams.[251] The purpose of the initiative is to form a solid strategy for dealing with future attacks by building partnerships between its members.[252] In addition, companies like eBay have joined with the Information Technology Association of American (ITAA) to form the Anti-Online Identity Theft Coalition.[253] The purpose of the coalition is to share information, develop technology to deal with the threats, and collaborate with law enforcement to identify and prosecute the phishers.[254] Other alliances include the Anti-Phishing Working Group and the National Cyber Security Alliance.[255]

MasterCard has established a partnership with the technology security company NameProtect.[256] The members of the partnership cooperate with law

---

[247] APWG Oct. Trends, *supra* note 7.

[248] FDIC Report, *supra* note 244, at 6.

[249] FinExtra.com, *Phishing Alliance Formed as Gartner Study Unearths Big Losses*, June 16, 2004, http://www.finextra.com/fullstory.asp?id=12016. The founding members of this alliance include ABN Amro, E*Trade Financial, Fidelity, Fleet Boston, HSBC, National City Bank, Royal Bank of Scotland, and Schwab.

[250] *See* Press Release, MasterCard International, MasterCard, NameProtect Unite to Close Down Phishing Sites, Online 'Payment Card Black Markets' (June 21, 2004), http://www.mastercardintl.com/cgi-bin/newsroom.cgi?id=892&.

[251] *Financial Consortium, Technology Firms Gird for Battle Against Phishing Scams*, 9 Elec. Com. & L. Rep. (BNA) 842, 842 (Oct. 13, 2004) [hereinafter *Gird for Battle*]. *See generally* FSTC Proposal, *supra* note 22. Members include Bank of America, Citygroup, BankOne, Goldman Sachs, Fidelity Investments, JP Morgan Chase, Wachovia, and Wells Fargo. Technology partners include Symantec, Entrust, and IBM. *Gird for Battle, supra* at 842.

[252] FSTC Proposal, *supra* note 22, at 7.

[253] Howard A. Schmidt, Testimony Before the Government Reform Subcommittee on Technology, Information Policy, Intergovernmental Relations and the Census of the U.S. House of Representatives 5, Sept. 22, 2004, *available at* http://reform.house.gov/UploadedFiles/Schmidt1.pdf [hereinafter Schmidt Testimony].

[254] *Id.*

[255] *Id.*

[256] Press Release, MasterCard International, *supra* note 250.

enforcement agencies to dismantle the thieves' ability to use online tools and venues so that the agencies can stop phishing attacks before the victims' accounts are actually compromised.[257]   NameProtect continuously monitors domain names, online discussions, spam e-mails, and webpages to identify online trading rings and provide real-time reports to MasterCard.[258] MasterCard then provides this information to the proper authorities as well as its member financial institutions. [259]   This partnership exemplifies how industry and law enforcement agencies can successfully work together to prevent phishing scams.

For the first time, companies are also attempting to demonstrate a united front by filing joint suits against phishers.[260]   On September 27, 2004, Amazon.com and Microsoft Corporation filed suit against a Canadian company and its owners alleging that the defendant conducted phishing scams.[261]   The complaint included Amazon.com's allegations of trademark infringement and cyberpiracy, as well as Microsoft's claim that the defendants illegally used Microsoft's computer systems to send spam e-mails.[262] Microsoft hopes that this joint action will be a "wake-up call for spammers and phishers that the industry is teaming up, pooling resources, and sharing investigative information to put them out of business."[263]   This suit is an example of the power of proper legislation and cooperation—especially when companies cooperate with one another *and* law enforcement.

These private industry alliances demonstrate that companies view cooperation as a vital part of the strategy to defeat phishing. The Financial Services Technology Consortium (FSTC) stressed that joint efforts are not only recommended but necessary because independent approaches could send a confusing message to consumers.[264]   Consistent policies and open communication between companies are crucial to forming an industry-wide approach to preventing phishing scams. [265]

---

[257]   *Id.*

[258]   *Id.*

[259]   *Id.*

[260]   *Microsoft, Amazon.com File Joint Complaint Alleging Canadian Firm Engaged in Spoofing,* 9 Elec. Com. & L. Rep. (BNA) 829, 829 (Oct. 6, 2004) [hereinafter *Joint Complaint*].

[261]   *Id.* at 829.

[262]   *Id.* at 830.

[263]   *Id.* at 830 (quoting Brad Smith, Microsoft general counsel).

[264]   FSTC PROPOSAL, *supra* note 22, at 6.

[265]   *Id.*

However, there are limitations on what the private sector can do—they do not have the authority to create or enforce laws.[266] To succeed in their battle against phishing, these companies need assistance from law enforcement agencies and the backing of strong legislation. First, legislators must enact laws that make each step in the phishing attack a crime, as well as strong penalties for violations of these laws. In addition, law enforcement agencies in the United States and throughout the world must be willing and able to work together to provide the support needed to capture these criminals once they have been discovered by industry officials. The companies cannot fight this battle on their own. The private sector must join with the government so that each can take an active role to decrease phishing and support each other's actions.[267]

2. *Consumer Education*

Educated consumers also play a crucial role in the fight against phishing—consumers must have the necessary knowledge and tools to protect themselves from cybercrime.[268] First, educated consumers can decrease the success rate of these scams by refusing to respond to the e-mails and thus not become victims.[269] The easiest way to prevent a successful phishing scam is for the consumer not to reply to the e-mail or click on the link in the e-mail.[270] Companies, governments, and law enforcement agencies must make consumers aware of these scams so that the consumers are skeptical of these e-mails and know not to respond to them.[271]

FraudWatch International and the Anti-Phishing Working Group are examples of nonprofit organizations that focus on educating consumers about the dangers of online fraud.[272] Both sites offer resources to those who are already victims of phishing attacks.[273] The sites also try to prevent future attacks by educating consumers on the types of scams that criminals use to

---

[266] Charney, *supra* note 79, at 3.
[267] *Id.*
[268] *Id.* at 8.
[269] Moynahan, *supra* note 138.
[270] *Id.*
[271] Germain, *supra* note 159, YOUL, *supra* note 24, at 13.
[272] *See, e.g.*, Anti-Phishing Working Group, http://antiphishing.org (last visited Mar. 1, 2006); FraudWatch International, http://www.fraudwatchinternational.com (last visited Mar. 1, 2006); *see also* YOUL, *supra* note 24, at 2 (stressing that "consumer education is the key to the reduction").
[273] *See* FraudWatch International, *supra* note 272; Anti-Phishing Working Group, *supra* note 272.

victimize them and by informing consumers of ways to protect themselves.[274] To ensure that consumers are aware of the newest frauds and scams, FraudWatch International sends out frequent fraud alerts and newsletters to its members.[275]

Companies are also using their websites as a vehicle to increase consumer awareness of phishing.[276] For example, SunTrust's homepage has a link that customers can visit to learn about online fraud.[277] The page includes a statement that informs customers of SunTrust's policy to never ask for personal information over e-mail.[278] The company hopes that if consumers are aware of this policy, they will automatically view e-mails that ask for this information with suspicion. The site also instructs customers on how to identify phishing e-mails, protect themselves from attacks, and report the scams.[279] Other companies, like Amazon.com and eBay, have similar educational sites for their customers.[280] EBay's and SunTrust's sites include actual examples of the fake websites and fraudulent e-mails.[281] In addition, Amazon.com's site includes information on current and past litigation against phishers.[282] In the United Kingdom, banking institutions have also joined together to launch a website designed to warn consumers of phishing attacks.[283]

Government agencies are also doing their part to inform consumers about the risks of phishing. The DOJ's *Special Report on Phishing* includes a list of current scams and gives consumers a three-part strategy for dealing with e-mails or websites that they believe may be part of a phishing scheme.[284] Additionally, the FTC's website includes articles that educate consumers on general identity theft, including one that specifically discusses phishing.[285]

---

[274] *See* FraudWatch International, *supra* note 272; Anti-Phishing Working Group, *supra* note 272.

[275] *See* YOUL, *supra* note 24, at 14.

[276] *See* FraudWatch International, *supra* note 272.

[277] SunTrust, Fraud, http://www.suntrust.com/alert/index.asp (last visited Mar. 2, 2006).

[278] *Id.*

[279] *Id.* The site also provides a comprehensive "Online Fraud and Identity Theft Guide." SunTrust, Online Fraud and Identity Theft Guide, http://www.suntrust.com/docs/pdf/Online_Fraud_and_Identity_Theft_Guide.pdf (last visited Jan. 21, 2006).

[280] *See* EBay, Spoof Email Tutorial, http://pages.ebay.com/education/spooftutorial (last visited Jan. 21, 2006); Amazon.com, Efforts to Stop Spoofing, http://www.amazon.com/exec/obidos/tg/browse/-/4060771/102-5099503-5490532 (last visited Jan. 21, 2006).

[281] Ebay, *supra* note 280; SunTrust, *supra* note 279.

[282] Amazon.com, *supra* note 280.

[283] Leyden, *supra* note 18.

[284] DOJ PHISHING REPORT, *supra* note 23 (stating that the three steps are to stop, look, and call).

[285] *Id.*

The site advises consumers to check their bank and credit card statements often to make sure that there are no fraudulent charges and also provides consumers with contact information for reporting scams.[286]

Nevertheless, the informational sites are not always helpful because many consumers never read the material.[287]   To combat this problem, some companies are attempting a more direct method of informing consumers about these scams. For example, SunTrust now includes warnings about fraudulent e-mails on the screens of its ATM machines.[288]   In addition, consumer awareness of the scams will increase if victims continue to speak out and media coverage remains prevalent.[289]

If consumers are aware of the tricks that phishers use, they will be less likely to become victims. For example, if consumers are aware that their bank has a policy to never ask for personal information in an e-mail, they will automatically view an e-mail that asks for this information with suspicion. Also, when companies provide their consumers with examples of the phishing e-mails, consumers learn not to trust sites just because they appear to be legitimate. Education can encourage consumers to take personal responsibility and, as a result, decrease the number of successful attacks.

Second, educated consumers can serve as informants to help make agencies and companies aware of existing attacks.[290]   One of the biggest problems that law enforcement agencies face is that phishing scams occur quickly; if law enforcement agents are not quickly made aware of the scams, the criminals are already gone.[291]   Increased consumer education helps reduce this problem by speeding up communication. Educated consumers can increase the efficiency of investigations as well as increase the number of arrests by informing law enforcement agencies and companies when they encounter a scam.[292]   If consumers report these scams as soon as they see them, instead of not realizing that they have been victimized until weeks later when they receive their statements, consumers can decrease the lag time that allows the criminals to disappear.[293]

---

[286] FTC Recommendations, *supra* note 243.
[287] Shartel, *supra* note 45, at 524.
[288] Personally witnessed by the author.
[289] Shartel, *supra* note 45, at 524.
[290] FTC Recommendations, *supra* note 243.
[291] ICCC Note, *supra* note 67.
[292] FTC Recommendations, *supra* note 243.
[293] ICCC Note, *supra* note 67.

Each week FraudWatch International receives hundreds of complaints from consumers and uses these tips to work with authorities to shut down scams and prosecute scammers.[294] The FTC also forwards the information that it gets from consumers about phishing scams to law enforcement officials and the targeted companies.[295] These are examples of the type of multi-level cooperation and information sharing necessary to fight phishing. By informing consumers of the steps that they should take to inform authorities when they encounter a phishing scam, companies and agencies increase the possibility that the criminals will be caught before they disappear into cyberspace.

Although consumer education is very likely to decrease the number of phishing attacks, it cannot solve the problem on its own.[296] Phishing scams are becoming more advanced and harder to detect—it is practically impossible for all consumers to be educated enough to detect certain scams.[297] Many times there is no way to verify if the e-mail is legitimate unless the user calls the company. It is likely that most consumers would not be willing to take this step to authenticate an e-mail.[298] The House of Representatives stated that although there is no "silver bullet" to end phishing, consumer education will play a large role in decreasing these practices.[299] Consumer responsibility, however, must be supplemented with consistent law enforcement, strong legislation, and support from the targeted industries.

SUMMARY

Worldwide cooperation between law enforcement, legislation, and the private sector is the key to preventing phishing scams. The phishing problem cannot be solved by advances in just one area—each has too many internal weaknesses. Each group must come together to combat the problem. President George W. Bush stressed the importance of cooperation in preventing these crimes when he stated, "Securing cyberspace is an extraordinarily difficult strategic challenge that requires a coordinated and focused effort from our entire society—the federal government, state and local

---

[294] FraudWatch International, *supra* note 272.
[295] FTC Recommendations, *supra* note 243.
[296] Ramasastry, *supra* note 25.
[297] *Id.*
[298] *Id.*
[299] Stevenson, *supra* note 162, at 10.

governments, the private sector, and the American people."[300]   Phishing is a complicated crime which must be dealt with in a comprehensive manner.

This Comment examined the steps that law enforcement agencies, legislators, and the private sector are taking to combat phishing. In examining these efforts, it is clear that the most successful of these initiatives have all involved collaboration, not only within that individual group, but across all fronts. It is almost impossible for these groups to significantly decrease the number of scams unless they are cooperating with individuals in the other sectors. Although it is important for there to be cooperation *within* each of the groups explored in this Comment, all three of these groups must also cooperate *together* to successfully combat phishing. As Scott Charney, Vice President of Trustworthy Computing at Microsoft stated, "[G]overnment and the private sector . . . should work together to ensure the development of strong criminal laws and the capability to enforce them, to share information that will enhance security, and to support the security education and training of citizens."[301]

In conclusion, the unique nature of the Internet sets phishing apart from traditional crimes and requires a new approach. The only way to fight phishers is to reach across borders, departments, countries, and companies. By working together, international law enforcement officials, legislators, companies, and consumers can form a powerful alliance that will decrease phishing and establish a strong and secure Internet.

---

[300] Press Release, George W. Bush, U.S. President, *reprinted in* THE NATIONAL STRATEGY TO SECURE CYBERSPACE (2003), at iii, http://www.whitehouse.gov/pcipb/cyberspace_strategy.pdf.

[301] Charney, *supra* note 79, at 1.

[*] J.D. candidate, Emory University School of Law (2006); B.A., Agnes Scott College (2001). I would like to extend my gratitude to Professor Mel Gutterman for being my advisor on this project. Special thanks to my family for their love and support.

[4]

Cyberextortion at Online Gambling Sites: Criminal Organization and Legal Challenges

JOHN McMULLAN AND AUNSHUL REGE

COMPUTERS, information technologies, and high-speed telecommunication systems have created a new form of space that is borderless and disembodied. Cybernetic communities, e-shopping malls, digital courtrooms, virtual health clinics, e-love networks, online banking services, and gambling Web sites now permit people to accomplish conventional tasks with few spatial-temporal limits. People increasingly interact without regard to physical location in a seemingly endless web of parallel cyber networks, spaces and institutions.[1] Gambling and gamblers are now disappearing into simulated betting shops, poker rooms, casinos, and lottery sites where betting—anytime, anyplace—is the norm, and where making a bet, losing a hand, or winning a jackpot is an anonymous, digital experience to be lamented or enjoyed from the privacy of one's home, office, or automobile, or from public spaces like trains, school yards, and shopping malls.

Internet gambling may be defined as the provision of opportunities to play games of chance or obtain access to sports or race bookmaking via computer networks. Over the past decade, it has grown to the point that it now generates revenues between $10 billion and $15 billion,[2] with U.S. bettors providing about half of that amount. It is expected to continue expanding, and the projected revenues are $20 billion by the end of this decade. The current basic market segments are sports betting (35 percent), casino games (25 percent), poker (20 percent), and lotteries (17 percent), although the mix will likely change going forward. About 85 jurisdictions now offer online gambling at approximately 2,500 sites, most operated by privately held purveyors in jurisdictions such as Antigua, Costa Rica, Curacao, Belize, the Kahnawá:ke Mohawk Nation in Canada, the United Kingdom, and Gibraltar.[3]

Not only has cyberspace transformed gambling offering players new types of wagering on an easily accessible basis, it has also reconfigured the everyday world of criminal organization. The new technologies and the speed at which they operate have opened up a virtual world for crime where computers are either the new tools or the new objects of criminal conduct.[4] This has fostered new crimes

John McMullan, Ph.D., is a professor of sociology at Saint Mary's University in Halifax, Nova Scotia, Canada. Professor McMullan is the author of seven books, five government reports, and over fifty academic articles on business crime, criminal organization, law enforcement, and regulation, media, crime and justice, and gambling and social policy. He is a commissioner of the Law Reform Commission of Nova Scotia. Aunshul Rege is a graduate student at Saint Mary's University, who is currently working on a thesis about cybercrime and online gambling. ©2007 by the authors.

An early version of this paper was presented at the second annual Responsible Gambling Conference, Oct. 2–3, 2006, in Halifax. The authors thank the organizers of this conference for inspiring this publication.

[1] D. LYON, SURVEILLANCE SOCIETY (Buckingham: Open University Press) (2001); R. WHITAKER, THE END OF PRIVACY: HOW TOTAL SURVEILLANCE IS BECOMING A REALITY (New York: The New Press) (1999).
[2] All currency specifications are in U.S. dollars.
[3] American Gaming Association, An Analysis of Internet Gambling and its Policy Implications 2–4 (White Paper Series 2006).
[4] J.L. McMullan & D.C. Perrier, Technologies of Crime: The Cyber-Attacks on Electronic Gambling Machines, 45 CANADIAN J. CRIMINOLOGY & CRIM. JUST. 159–186 (2003); J.L. McMullan & D.C. Perrier, The Security of Gambling and Gambling with Security: Hacking, law Enforcement, and Public Policy, 7 Intv'l J. GAMBLING STUD. 43–58 (2007) [hereinafter McMullan & Perrier, Security].

such as hacking, cracking, phishing, and software piracy, created a parallel space where conventional crimes such as stalking, embezzlement, and theft now occur in their many cyber forms, and fostered new and different modes of organization that are project based, transient, and lateral rather than hierarchical in nature.[5] Nowhere are these changed criminal relations more obvious than in their interactions with the world of online gambling where fear and trembling about cyberextortion, money laundering, Web site cloning, identity theft, and fraud is prevalent.

Online gambling has been driven by new information communication technologies, targeted marketing, the Web's global reach, and the technical ability of operators to simulate and organize the desire to play and wager anytime, anywhere. Cyberpayment instruments involving e-cash or Internet banking have provided the players' stakes for initiating gambling and established remittances of winnings via the same rapid-paced Internet mechanisms. All a player needs is an Internet connection or a telephone and they are ready to gamble. But many e-gambling venues are located in lightly regulated jurisdictions with poor third-party monitoring of gambling transactions and records and limited law enforcement reach. Site servers are middle range in size or are located where the power grid cannot install up-to-date defensive infrastructure capable of filtering large volumes of data traffic, even though these e-gambling businesses have a high volume continual Web presence.[6] Not surprisingly, gambling Web sites are attractive targets for motivated offenders. According to government and industry sources, criminals have hit every major Internet betting site from the Caribbean to Australia and taken down hundreds of online casinos and payment processing companies.[7]

This paper examines cyberextortion at online gambling sites between 2000 and 2005. We define cyberextortion as real or threatening actions combining computer intrusion, theft, destruction and modification of data, social engineering, and fear for purposes of unlawful economic gain. The main elements explaining it are therefore found within the illegal activity, the digital environment and the sociolegal

problems confronted therein.[8] This approach asks: What types of technical problems had to be solved for successful cyberextortion of sports betting sites and casinos to occur? What division of labor emerged to handle problems of planning, detection, and safety? How were cyberextortion enterprises organized? How secure were digital gambling environments? How effective was law enforcement in detecting, apprehending, and sanctioning cyberex-

[5] W.G. STAPLES, EVERYDAY SURVEILLANCE: VIGILANCE AND VISIBILITY IN POSTMODERN LIFE (New York: Rowman and Littlefield) (2000); P.A. WILSON & R.C. MOLANDER, EXPLORING MONEY LAUNDERING VULNERABILITIES THROUGH EMERGING CYBERSPACE TECHNOLOGIES: A CARRIBBEAN-BASED EXERCISE (Washington: Rand Monograph Report) (1998); S.W. Brenner, *Organized Cybercrime? How Cyberspace may affect the structure of criminal relationships*, 4 N.C. J. LAW & TECH. 1–50 (2002); P. Williams, *Organized Crime and Cybercrime: Synergies, Trends, and Responses* (2002), <http://crime-research.org/library/Cybercrime.htm>; COUNCIL OF EUROPE, SUMMARY OF THE ORGANIZED CRIME SITUATION REPORT 2004: FOCUS ON THE THREAT OF CYBER-CRIME (2004), <http://www.coe.int/T/E/Legal_affairs/Legal-cooperation/Combating_economics_crime/Organised_crime/Documents/OrgCrimeRep2004Summm.pdf>.

[6] R. Gareiss & J. Soat, *Let It Ride*, INFO. WK., July 8, 2002, at 3–42, *available a*. <www.informationweek.com/story>; E. RATLIFF, THE ZOMBIE HUNTERS: ON THE TRAIL OF CYBEREXTORTIONISTS (2005), <http://www.newyorker.com/printables/fact/05101fa_fact>; R.A. Paulson & J. Weber, *Cyberextortion: An overview of Distributed Denial of Service Attacks Against Online Gaming Companies*, VII ISSUES INFO. SYS. 52–56 (2006).

[7] G. Bednarski, *Enumerating and Reducing the Threat of Transnational Cyber Extortion against Small and Medium Size Organizations 1* (2004), available at <http://www.andrew.cum.edu/user/gbednars/InformationWeek-CMU_Cyber_Extortion_Study.pdf>; B. Cullingworth, *Distributed Denial of Service Attacks No Joke*, WINNERONLINE.COM Apr. 15, 2004. <http://www.winneronline.com/articles/april2004/distributed-denial-of-service-attacks-no-joke.htm>; J.M. Germain, *Global Extortion: Online Gambling and Organized Crime: The Inside Story*, MAC NEWS WORLD (2004), <http://macnewswworld.com/story/31679.html>; A. Karshmer, *Virtual Villains: Global Gangsters are extorting money from online casinos with a novel threat: we'll spam you to death*, MSN.com (2005), <http://www.msn.com/id/5505593/site/newsweek/>; S. Baker, *Gambling Sites, This is a Holdup*, BUS. WK., Aug. 9, 2004, <wwwbusinessweek.com/magazine/content>; I. Thompson, *Extortion racket cripples gambling sites*, IT WK., Nov. 12, 2003, available at www.itweek.CO.UK/newsThompson.

[8] H. ABADINSKY, ORGANIZED CRIME (Chicago: Nelson-Hall Inc.) (1990); M. LYMAN & POTTER, ORGANIZED CRIME (N.J.: Prentice-Hall Inc.) (1997); M. McINTOSH, THE ORGANIZATION OF CRIME (London: MacMillan) (1975); A.A. BLOCK & W. CHAMBLES, ORGANIZING CRIME (Amsterdam: Elsevier) (1981).

tortion? What sociolegal policy challenges exist for the future governance of online gambling sites?

METHODOLOGY ISSUES

The World Wide Web is akin to a massive library. Yet, despite the staggering volume of material contained on it and despite its enormous popularity, the Web has received only cursory attention from researchers interested in studying both criminal activity and gambling. Typical of the research work to date have been studies of hacking satellite services, telemarketing fraud, software piracy, pedophilia and pornography, and problem gambling.[9] Research has tended to focus on readily available newsgroup sources and sites and ignored other areas of the Internet. We decided to be more systematic and engaged a wide assortment of materials in our study: media stories, online interviews, "how to do it" manuals, technical security reports, and police and legal documents. We used the Google search engine to retrieve much of our data. It coded more pages, created the largest index, and presented the most up-to-date data when compared to other search engines (i.e. Yahoo or Alta Vista). We coded for relevance by developing 32 combinations of keywords such as "cyberextortion and organized crime", "Ddos attacks and gambling", "betting sites and cyberextortion". The collected data was sorted around four intersecting themes: 1.) online gambling, 2.) hacking techniques and patterns, 3.) the organization of cyberextortion practices, and 4.) cybersecurity, law, and social control. Not surprisingly, the combination of keywords produced enormous quantities of page rankings. We used a 10-page, 100-article return process as a cutoff to obtain sample materials for each searched keyword. This criterion was a consistent means of retrieving data and it ensured that each category was given equal weight and consideration. Altogether we examined 3,200 Internet documents, but the number of articles for each keyword was often repetitive after the first five pages, thus narrowing our document base to about 1800 items.

Because data about cyberattacks at Web sites was not readily available from caselaw or field studies, we relied on document analysis as our research method. Document analysis may be defined as a way of analyzing texts in a systematic, objective, and qualitative manner for purposes of exploring the classic questions of who said what, to whom, why, how, and with what effects.[10] While Internet documents were easy to access, use, and link, and were presented in dynamic ways through video clips, sound bites, and animations, there were problems with quality control, accuracy of discovery, and consistency of documents over time. We dealt with these issues by relying primarily on authenticated Web sites such as news sites (e.g. MSNBC), security sites (e.g. McAfee) and law enforcement sites (e.g. FBI), indexing every relevant article's uniform resource locator (URL) and creating a registry of all sources, and triangulating multiple sources to cross-check information and to look for missing data.[11] Our analysis identifies the basic features of cyberextortion networks, their modus operandi, and their modus vivendi with the rule of law over a five-year period.

THE ACT OF CYBEREXTORTION

The extortion of gambling sites usually commenced with computer viruses that were installed on personal computers without the owner's knowledge. These viruses, in turn, permitted other secret programs to run automatically and be placed on the same computers. Eventually, "bot networks" or "zombie armies" in the thousands or tens of thousands of ma-

[9] D. Mann & M. Sutton, *Netcrime: More Change in the Organization of Thieving*, 38 Brit. J. Criminology 201–28 (1998); N. Shover, G.S. Coffey & D. Hobbs, *Crime on the Line: Telemarketing and the Changing Nature of Professional Crime*, 43 Brit. J. Criminology 489–506 (2003); M. Taylor, G. Holland & E. Quayle, *Typology of Paedophile Picture Collections*, 74 Police J. 97–107 (2001); P. Goodson, D. McCormick & A. Evans, *Searching for Sexually Explicit Materials on the Internet: An Exploration of College Student-Behaviour and Attitudes*, 30 Archives Sexual Behav. 104–118 (2001).
[10] M.G. Maxfield & E. Babbie, Research Methods for Criminal Justice and Criminology 329 (Belmont, Cal.: Wadsworth). (2001); J. Mason, Qualitative Researching 73 (London: Sage Publications Inc.) (1996).
[11] L. Neuman, Social Research Methods: Qualitative and Quantitative Approaches 115 (Mass.: Allyn and Bacon) (2003).

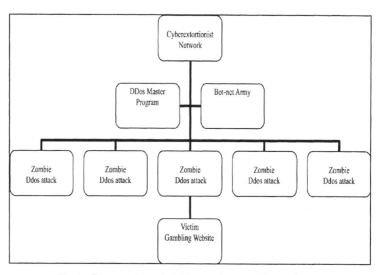

Fig. 1. Diagram of a typical ddos attack on gambling Web sites.

chines were "herded" by hackers to attack gambling venues. The objective was to deny players access to the computer system by consuming all disk space or CPU time, or by disrupting traffic band width capability or physical network components, resulting in Distributed Denial of Service (Ddos) outcomes.[12] (See fig. 1.)

Ddos attacks

Ddos attacks had several variants. SYN attacks directed so much data traffic to a gambling site that it had to cease operations. The gambling sites typically acknowledged the end senders of messages, but the latter refused to respond back. This created numerous "bogus connection results" that could not be distinguished from legitimate traffic requests, thereby permitting fake traffic to swamp the Web site at the expense of bona fide customers who could not log on. Smurf attacks used the gambling Web sites against themselves. Cyberextortionists sent "IP ping packets" or "echo my messages back to me" requests to Web sites. The return addresses in the packet were the targeted betting or casino sites and not the cyberextortionists' real address sites. When several ping packets were "herded" to the sites,

gambling and wagering shut down. UDP flood attacks or "fraggles" were more sophisticated strategies involving forged UDP echo and character generators that were then used to connect the echo service of one computer to the character generator of another machine. Once connected, these two machines relayed messages back and forth consuming the entire communication bandwidth and eventually slowing the Web site to a crawl. Legitimate players received the Internet equivalent of a busy signal indicating that the company's servers were not responding. Finally, Trinoo attacks initiated a domino effect on targeted Web sites. A master program controlled by cybercriminals launched the first set of attacks. The program then automatically and simultaneously sent corresponding orders through data packets to a waiting bot-net army who, in turn, launched an accompanying zombie-based UDP attack on a betting site causing gambling businesses to

---

[12] McAfee, McAfee Virtual Criminology Report: North American Study into Organized Crime and the Internet. (2005), <http://www.mcafee.com/us/local_content/misc/>; Thompson, *supra* note 7; M. Myser, *Gambling sites hedging bets*, Wired, Jan. 24, 2005, <http://www.wired.com/news/infostructure/0,1377,66358,00.html>.

deny play to gamblers.[13] As one security engineer observed, "When the monitors' graphs begin to spike indicating that an attack is under way", she said, "it's like looking at the ocean and seeing a wall of water three hundred feet high coming toward you[.]"[14]

The cases of BetCris, a Costa Rican-based gambling site, Multibet.com, an Australian company, and Grafix Softech, an Internet service provider, are illustrative. An extortion network demanded $40,000 dollars from BetCris in the fall of 2003. Their e-mail said, "if you choose not to pay for our help, then you will probably not be in business much longer, as you will be under attack each weekend for the next 20 weeks, or until you close your doors[.]" The general manager of BetCris was confident that he had configured a data filtering system able to withstand the attacks. When the attacks came, it took less than 20 minutes to take down both the gambling site and its service provider.[15]

Multibet.com, based in Australia, received similar digital threats in 2004. The CEO also refused to pay. His company was attacked four times and his business was interrupted for 20 days until he wired the protection money to an East European bank account.[16]

In February 2003, a Russian-based extortion network shut down Grafix Softech, which hosted 120 gambling sites worldwide. According to the vice-president of the company, the payoff to restore service was insignificant when compared to the loss of revenues and operational records. It was akin to "hacking into the Pentagon", he told police investigators.[17]

Digital shakedowns

Ddos attacks were sometimes preceded by warnings but they were always succeeded by e-mail threats demanding money in return for protection from further attacks. "Dear WWTS, as you can see your site is under attack. We have found a problem with your network" stated one e-mail. The attackers then insisted that the gambling site send $40,000 to them. "You will lose more than $40,000 in the next couple of hours if you do not resolve this problem", they warned.[18] If companies refused to pay, the attacks continued for days and weeks,

resulting in substantial monetary losses and countless customer defections. One site owner who had been extorted several times and refused to pay the ransom received an e-mail: "You are a moron . . . I figure by now you have lost 5 times what we asked [$40,000]" wrote the attacker after three weeks; "by the end of the year," he declared, "your decision will cost you more than 20 times what we asked[.]"[19] Some extortion demands were timed to occur with large sporting events such as the Super Bowl, the World Cup, the Wimbledon Tennis Tournament, and the Grand National, when wagering was high and potential lost revenue was great.[20] One network, for example, inflicted over $70 million of overall damages to British bookmakers alone in 2004.[21]

---

[13] J. Panesar. & G. Goutas, *Denial of Service Attacks – Are You Vulnerable?*, TST.com, Dec. 2, 2005, <http://www.TST.com>; CISCO, Distributed Denial of Service Threats: Risks, Mitigation, and Best Practices (2004), <http://www.cisco.com/en/US/netsol/ns480/networking_solutions_white_paper0900aecd8032499e.shtml>; A. Murphy, A. Pender, L. Reilly & S. Connel, *Denial of Service and Countermeasures*, 4BA2 – Technology Survey, 2005, <http://ntrg.cs.tcd.ie/undergrad/4ba2.05/group2/>; Vladimir Golubev, *Dos attacks: crimes without penalty*, Computer Crime Research Center, Mar. 16, 2005, <http://www.crime-research.org/articles/1049/>; Paulson & Weber, *supra* note 6.
[14] Ratliff, *supra* note 6.
[15] *Id.*
[16] Anonymous, *More on Gold Coast Phishing, Gambling Extortion*, Loose Wire blog, Sept. 24, 2004, <www.loosewire.typepad.com/blog>.
[17] C. Walker, *Russian Mafia Extorts Gambling Websites*, Rick Porrello's AmericanMafia.com, June 2004, <http://www.americanmafia.com/Feature_Articles_270.html>.
[18] Karshmer, *supra* note 7.
[19] Ratliff, *supra* note 6.
[20] B. Warner, *Hackers Heaven: Online Gambling*, CBSNews.com, 2001, <http://cbsnews.com/stories/2001/09/10/tech/main310567.shtml>; R. Miller, *UK Betting Sites Hit by Outages as Super Bowl Nears*, Netcraft, Feb. 5, 2005, <www.//news.netcraft.com/archives>; B. Vallerius, *Gaming operator Gives Amount of Ddos attack*, IGamingNews.com, Dec. 4, 2003, <http://www.lgamingnews.com/index.cfm.artlisting>.
[21] C. Biever, How zombie networks fuel cybercrime, NewScientist.com, 2004, <http://www.newscientist.com/channel/info-tech/electrontric-threats/dn6616>; C. Nuttall, *Hackers blackmail Internet bookies: Criminals believed to be targeting Grand National*, Fin. Times 2004, <http://toplayer.com/pdf/Financial%20Times_230204.pdf>; K. Smith, *Extortionists Target Online Gambling Site*, Interactive Gaming News, 2004 available at <http://www.riverhead.com/re/extortionists.htm>.

Nor have these ransom demands stopped. It is estimated that crime networks have collected "protection money from 10% to 15% of the companies they have threatened[.]"[22] The managing director of Gambling Consulting based in the UK put it this way, "despite the hush hush attitude of casino and gambling Web site operators, extortion attacks happen often[.]"[23] Prolexic Technologies, a U.S.-based Internet security company, defends about 80 gambling Web sites and thwarts at least three Ddos attacks each week.[24] Indeed, the level of intensity, the frequency, and the sophistication of these attacks is higher than ever before and now involves non-gambling venues including foreign currency exchanges, financial service companies, and online payment firms.[25]

There was, of course, variation in the size of the ransoms. Some were as low as $3,000 per gambling Web site and worked on the principle of fiddling small amounts from many targets. But most cyberextortion demands were priced between $20,000 and $60,000 per Web site. These were not thought to be exorbitant ransoms when compared to potential losses for noncompliance.[26] For example, the British site Betfair.com made $160 million per week while the Antigua based Bet WWTS.com generated $5 million per weekend. Both wired ransoms to keep their operations on line; it was the cost of doing business.[27] Numerous British gambling sites, including Canbet, Harrods Casino, Inter Bingo, Inter Casino Poker, Totalbet, VIP Casino, William Hill, Paddy Power, Corals and Blue Square, to name just one sector in the online industry, also paid millions of dollars in protection money in 2003. Similarly, Bluegrassports, Betcasade, Pinnaclesports, Caribsports, Bodog, Sportsbook and Casino, World Wide Telesports, Vipsports, and Betgameday faced heavy Ddos attacks in 2004 and lost millions in ransoms within hours.[28] One cybersecurity officer explains the modus operandi of the digital shakedown: "they got their money sent in multiple broken Western Union payments and then hired hookers to go pick them up. They got the money back together again, and then deposited it into an account where it can be wired around the world. It bounced around and eventually became impossible to trace[.]"[29]

The Hawallah banking network, which is controlled by bankers in Pakistan, the United Arab Emirates, and Egypt and which operates in 150 countries, was active in moving extortion money. Ransoms were hidden in a maze of shell transactions involving bogus receipts that complicated any paper trail. Web sites were directed to wire funds to specific banks. Money movers operating with extortion networks were then given duplicate receipts with the originals forwarded to overseas Hawallah bankers. The money movers then presented their receipts in the target countries, received the extortion monies, avoided the exportation of funds abroad and the accompanying record audit, and stayed under the radar of legal detection by appearing to follow the banking rules. Other financial networks composed of Swiss and Cayman banks were also used to transfer funds in and out of foreign accounts, making it exceedingly difficult to follow the

---

[22] Cullingworth, *supra* note 7.
[23] Walker, *supra* note 17.
[24] Myser, *supra* note 12.
[25] Reuters News Service, *Hackers attack William Hill after $10,000 blackmail threat*, 2004, *available at* <http://networks.silicon.com/webwatch/0,39024667,39119262,00.htm>; Paulson & Weber, *supra* note 6.
[26] Karshmer, *supra* note 7; Paulson & Weber, *supra* note 6, at 53–55.
[27] G. Morgan, *Locked Out: A growing band of extortionists, political activists and malevolent hackers are using denial of service attacks to overwhelm and close down online businesses and public sector web sites*, INFOCONOMY 2 2005, <http://www.infoconomy.com/pages/recent-management-articles/group107079.adp>; Karshmer, *supra* note 7.
[28] Biever, *supra* note 21; D. Kramerenko, *Russian Hacker Blackmailed Gambling Companies*, COMPUTER CRIME RESEARCH CENTER, July 29, 2004, <http://www.crime-research.org/news>; H. Eriksson, *Russian Hackers Nearly Ruined British Bookmakers*, GAMBLINGGATES.COM, Apr. 6, 2005, <http://gamblinggates.com/News/Wagering/russia-hackers-uk-bookies86081.html>; Golubev, *supra* note 13; Germain, *supra* note 7; Nuttall, *supra* note 21; Paul Roberts, *Online Extortion Ring Broken Up*, IDG NEWS SERVICES, July 21,2004, <http://www.PCWorld.com/news/articles>; J. Swartz, *Crooks slither into Net's shady nooks and crannies*, USA TODAY, Oct. 20, 2004, *available at* <http://www.USAtoday.com/tech/news>; C. Walker, *Russian Organize Crime Target NFL Superbowl in Multi-Billion Dollar Gambling Scheme*, RICK PORRELLO'S AMERICANMAFIA.COM, Jan. 2005, <http://www.americanmafia.com/feature_293.html>.
[29] Liane Cassavoy, *Web of crime: Internet gangs go global*, PC WORLD, Aug. 24, 2005, *available at* <http://www.PCWorld.com/news/article>.

money and exceedingly easy for hackers to obtain their "takes" without detection or apprehension.[30] Like the exploitation of cyber-payment systems for money laundering, extortionists deployed high-value money transfers through network-based computer systems that scrambled, consolidated, and reintegrated digital ransom funds using anonymous remailers that concealed deposit points at Internet banks in foreign countries.[31] Finally, fake gambling sites were also created and used to temporarily store, conceal, and launder ransom monies to offshore accounts or to cash out and reinvest capital elsewhere. The deputy head of the British National Hi Tech Crime Unit put it bluntly, "they have companies registered all over the place passing money through them and we can't track them[.]"[32]

Once ransoms were paid, the attacks stopped—but only for six months or less. Like conventional extortion, it was common for online gambling sites to receive further e-ransom demands. "We had to pay it," stated the manager of eHorse, an operation that wired $30,000 to extortionists on several occasions. Each site, he explained, has a high period of vulnerability that extortion networks exploit. "You can't afford to be offline at peak times . . . so you pay to play[.]"[33] The CEO of World Wide Telesports, which was temporarily shut down in 2004, estimated that thousands of customers were impacted costing the company $5 million in wagering action.[34] An outage for hours is very costly: "that's $500,000 to $1 million of action wiped out in one shot," estimated Jeff Weber, a sports book expert.[35]

EXTORTION NETWORKS.COM

Ddos attacks were deliberately coordinated techniques that struck their victims from all directions, using sustainable pulsing forces that were both proximate and distant. Akin to "swarming" in military exercises in cyber warfare, Ddos attacks deployed automatic nonlinear information technologies to extort monies from gambling Web sites in a widely distributed field of activity.[36] These technologies were embedded in several networks functioning in China, Korea, South America, the Caribbean,

Russia, Eastern Europe, and North America.[37] While the exact number of extortion networks is unknown, their organization typically involved a broad mix of people who handled the financing, created the malware, executed the cyberattacks, and arranged the payouts and pick-ups.

Division of labor

The extortion enterprises almost always involved a division of labor containing organizers, extenders, and executors.[38] Their automated techniques and predatory conduct, rather than manufacturing or wholesaling illegal goods or services, however, dictated that there was little need for advanced organizational structures with highly developed permanent staff. Strength was in software, not in numbers of individuals. The size of the networks varied. Some were mobile working teams of two or three persons but the information on those groups that have been intercepted suggests that their size ranged from six to eight members.[39]

Organizers were at the core of the networks. They made the plans to be carried out by other subnetworks in the enterprise. They were of two types. "Hired" organizers were individuals who arranged technical online attacks at the behest of existing international crime syndicates that included the Mafia, Latin American, Middle Eastern, Eastern European, and Asian crime groups.[40] The latter groups provided the

---

[30] Denise Pappalardo & Ellen Messmer, *Extortion via DdoS on the rise.* Networkworld, May 16, 2005, <http://www.networkworld.com/news/2005/051605-ddos-extortion.html>; Germain, *supra* note 7.
[31] R.C. Molander, B.D. Mussington & P.A. Wilson, Cyber Payments and Money Laundering Problems and Promise 16–22 (Washington: Rand Monograph Report) (1998).
[32] Ratliff, *supra* note 6.
[33] Walker, *supra* note 28.
[34] Swartz, *supra* note 28.
[35] Morgan, *supra* note 27, at 2; Karshmer, *supra* note 7; Warner, *supra* note 20.
[36] Brenner, *supra* note 5.
[37] Baker, *supra* note 7.
[38] Vincent Lemieux, Criminal Networks 12–14, Mar. 2003, <http://rcmp.ca/ccaps/reports/criminal_net_e.pdf>.
[39] Roberts, *supra* note 28.
[40] Germain, *supra* note 7; Williams, *supra* note 5.

capital to finance the extortion process. For example, computer hackers associated with the Russian mafia shut down Worldplay System, six other online payment systems, and hundreds of casino sites until their ransoms of $50,000 per site were met.[41] "Hybrid" organizers came from either licit businesses or transferred their skills from other hacking backgrounds (e.g. for excitement, revenge) to exploit the new economic opportunities in the global online gambling marketplace.[42] Indeed, the mastermind in one cyberextortion ring was a 21-year-old Russian mechanical engineering student who studied computer programming and Web site design before hacking gambling venues for a living.[43] We call Russia the "hack zone", a self-described organizer from Moscow stated; "hacking is one of the few good jobs left[.]"[44]

Organizers usually worked with extenders who recruited members, increased and calibrated the skill mix in the networks, and socialized new members. One network recruited college-educated hackers and used "Internet advertisements" to obtain and convey the latest skills. Another ran crack sites that schooled recruits on "150 ways to break into Web sites and technology systems".[45] As the director of a cybersecurity firm put it, the innovative exploration involving malicious code, "rigged" chips, and Ddos attacks is conducted "by skilled people in the hacking underground" not by institutions charged with the duty of providing security for these vulnerabilities.[46]

The executors were often the hackers hired by the extenders. They possessed knowledge of the inner workings of computers and network systems, algorithmic computing, reverse engineering, program codes, virus installation, and bot-net systems. Some cracked casino servers and altered the computer programming code to change payouts and random number generator designs. Some specialized in virus modifications and installations and used them to infect PCs to launch Ddos attacks. Others formed partnerships with other hackers and code writers to execute increasingly synchronized Ddos attacks involving as many as 80,000 zombie computers targeting multiple victims at once in a series of simultaneous digital shakedowns. Still others monitored the gambling industry's

reactions and remedies to attacks so as to adapt the next version of their malware for future swarmings and extortions on numerous victims.[47]

The cybercrime networks, however, did not have formal roles for insulators or guardians who typically protect the internal structure and external order of extortion networks from exposures, defections, and betrayals. Nor was there much evidence of formal positions for communicators or monitors who manage information flows between members or subnetworks within the enterprises and who handle problems of internal network security and of external law enforcement. These roles were either performed by existing organizers or extenders or were absent because they were not needed because stable long-term criminal memberships were rare and there were no easily identified and easily tracked methods to pursue these "mafias of the moment".[48]

Most networks, as noted, did have roles for money movers who laundered profits from ransom victims and crossovers who offered insider information to the network. (See fig. 2.) One online casino employee sold company secrets, to hackers, including a sophisticated algorithmic program for deciphering random number generators. The network then cracked an online casino corrupting the play of craps and slots so that consumers could not lose.

---

[41] Walker, *supra* note 17.
[42] Patrick Gray, *Hackers: The Winds of Change*, IBM INTERNET SECURITY SYSTEMS, Mar. 2005, <http://www.iss.net/newsletters/secured/mar2005/winds_of_change.php>.
[43] McConnell International LLC, *Cybercrime . . . and Punishment? Archaic Laws Threaten Global Information* 1–2 (Report, Dec. 12, 2000), <http://www.iwar.org.uk/law/resources/cybercrime/mcconnell/CyberCrime.pdf>; COMPUTER CRIME RESEARCH CENTER, U.S. CYBER-CRIME UNIT FOCUSES ON RUSSIAN HACKERS, May 11, 2005, <http://crime-research.org/analytics/1226>.
[44] Walker, *supra* note 17.
[45] *Id.*
[46] Patrick Gray, *Hackers: The Winds of Change*, IBM INTERNET SECURITY SYSTEMS, Mar. 2005, <http://www.iss.net/newsletters/secured/mar2005/winds_of_change.php>.
[47] Reuters News Service, *Hackers Win High Stakes at Gambling Sites*, Sept. 10, 2001, *available at* <http://www.CNETnews.com>; Warner, *supra* note 20; Swartz, *supra* note 28.
[48] Brenner, *supra* note 5, at 50; Lemieux, *supra* note 38, at 14.

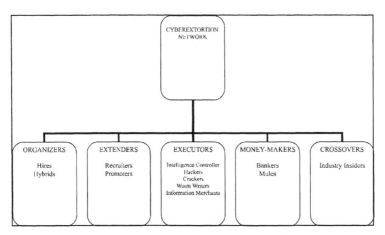

Fig. 2   Diagram of a cyberextortion network.

Every spin on the virtual games generated a perfect match, and, in a matter of a few hours, 140 customers acquired $1.9 million in winnings.[49]

Motivations, associations, and subnetworks

Even though hacking was sometimes an exercise in showboating for fun and status capital accumulation, not revenge, notoriety or politics was the primary rationale behind cyberextortion of gambling sites.[50] In the words of one hacker, cyberextortion "was a godsend"; taking from the rich and training others to hack was his "donation to society," a way for him and others "to climb the ladder of social mobility" in times of economic crisis.[51] Like online telemarketing fraud, it was a way of earning a good income without working too hard or subordinating oneself to others.[52] It was also a way to signify power and impose one's will upon others as evinced in the e-mails that frequently demeaned Web site owners by calling them down and boasting that hackers were smarter than gambling operators. The extortionists derived an odd moral virtue from the fact that their crimes could not succeed without the acquiescence of their victims and that the latter deserved what befell them because they were "greedy" or "idiots".[53]

Most extortion networks required moderate expenditures to accomplish their tasks. Items

such as computers, hardware, software, and communication devices were their major expenses. But unlike hackers of brick-and-mortar gambling sites, who operated locally and did not tap economies of scale,[54] online extortion networks developed persistent partnerships for accumulating profit, obtained external funding for some of their ventures, and announced their services to victims and competitors through chat rooms, IRC channels, online recruitment schemes, and direct e-mail threats. One network advertised that it could protect "their" customers from other hacking competitors by blocking the others' attacks. Another announced an underground cyberstore for the rental and sale of bot-net armies (i.e. zombie

---

[49] Reuters, *supra* note 47.
[50] McAfee, *supra* note 12; Cullingworth, *supra* note 7.; Australian Institute of Criminology, *Hacking Motives*, (Project no. 0074, 2005), <http://aic.gov.au/publications/htcb/htcb006.pdf>; Myser, *supra* note 12; Walker, *supra* note 28.
[51] Walker, *supra* note 17.; Eriksson, *supra* note 28.
[52] Shover, Coffey & Hobbs, *supra* note 9, at 495.
[53] Walker, *supra* note 28; Ratliff, *supra* note 6.
[54] McMullan & Perrier, *Security*, *supra* note 4; K.D. MITNICK & W.L. SIMON, THE ART OF INTRUSION: THE REAL STORIES BEHIND THE EXPLOITS OF HACKERS, INTRUDERS AND DECEIVERS (New York: Wiley) (2005).; J.H. SKOLNICK, HOUSE OF CARDS: LEGALIZATION AND CONTROL OF CASINO GAMBLING (Boston: Little, Brown) (1980); D. Crenshaw, *Slot machine Cheat Bilked Casinos with Ingenious Gadgets*, U.S.A. TODAY, Aug. 11, 2003.

machines rented for $40 a device), a third actively supplied do-it-yourself phishing kits for $300 and, and a fourth ran an Internet café where recruits learned how to create and install viruses and generate "zombies" from computer discs such as Hacker's Toolkit, All You Need to Start Hacking, and Hack the World, which sold for around three dollars a disc.[55] Cyberextortion was not circumscribed in its operations or in its membership by territorial boundaries or local cultural constraints. To the contrary, its perpetrators shared a hacking culture that transcended national borders and contexts. Geography was no barrier, explained a manager of a security company; "they find a specific type of company like online gambling . . . and they work their way around the world, picking people off quite happily[.]"[56]

While some types of criminal organization have formal vertical hierarchical structures, centralized concentrations of power, monopoly markets, and strong kinship bonds based on ethnic or cultural values,[57] cyberextortion operations were loosely aligned, collaborative patron-client, business-related partnerships.[58] Associations between network members were not personal, family-based or ethnic derived. Team members typically met each other in virtual spaces or were recruited through acquaintances and formed what Lemieux[59] calls "common association ties" based on supplier-customer relations, except that neither party knew the real-world identity of those with whom they interacted. Instead, technical cues and symbolic tokens determined people's expertise and established trustworthiness.

Not surprisingly, the structure of the networks was primarily horizontal rather than vertical, and the organization was remotely controlled rather than directly locally managed. Nodal subnetworks coexisted in a dispersed lateral field of global collaboration.[60] Power did not usually flow to a central command and control apex. Nor was physical violence used to police network members or extort victims, although a type of automatic force was needed to swarm the Web site's electronic defenses to appropriate monies and intimidate victims.

Compartmentalization from the top down ensured that no subnetwork of organizers, executors, or extenders was more prominent than others. The extortion scene was always seeking and upgrading the skills of designers, engineers, routers, scanners, and couriers. Once they developed reputations, they often freelanced as independent contractors to the highest bidders or to trusted organizers and extenders on a need-to-know basis. There was competition for labor supply, mostly young males in their twenties, and between rival networks for control over bot-net armies. For example, one virus that removed its competitors from zombies as it loaded itself was created by one network leaving virus writers in other crime networks scrambling to develop new advanced malware to stay competitive.[61]

There was also competition for and between Web site designers who created fake phish sites that served as fronts for money movers to hide extorted funds before forwarding them overseas for a fee.[62] No single network appeared to achieve a monopoly over supply of services, and few Web rings could really protect the victims of their rackets from others in the marketplace.

Each node was crucial to the overall success of cyberextortions because the networks themselves were not elaborate enough to be protected by separate insulators or guardians. If a successful series of Ddos attacks was compromised by a bungled ransom scheme, then the

---

[55] Eriksson, *supra* note 28; Ratliff, *supra* note 6; Smith, *supra* note 21; Cassavoy, *supra* note 29; McAfee, *supra* note 12; Associated Press, *20 year old hacker rented out attack network*, 2006, *available at* <http://www.msnbc.com>.
[56] Walker, *supra* note 28.
[57] D. Cressey, Criminal Organizations: Its Elementary Forms (London: Heinemann) (1972); A.J. Ianni, A Family Business Kinship and Social Control in Organized Crime (New York: Mentor) (1973); Abadinsky, *supra* note 8; Lyman & Potter, *supra* note 8.
[58] J. Albini, The American Mafia: Genesis of a Legend (New York: Appleton Crofts) (1971); D.C. Smith, *Paragons, Pariahs and Pirates: A Spectrum Based Theory of Enterprise*, 26 Crime & Delinq. 358–86 (1980).
[59] Lemieux, *supra* note 38.
[60] McAfee, *supra* note 12; P. Reuter & J. Rubinstein, Illegal Gambling in New York: A Case Study of the Operation, Structure and Operation of an Illegal Market (Washington, D.C.: U.S. Government) (1982).
[61] McAfee, *supra* note 12.
[62] Ryan Naraine, *'Money Mules': The Hidden Side of Phishing*, eWeek.com, Oct. 16, 2006, <http://www.eweek.com/article2/0,1759,2029953,00.asp>.

overall extortion failed and the network was open to exposure. For example, in a rare "sting" operation, British police arrested 10 suspects and charged them with collecting extortion payments from gambling sites.

"They were the mules picking up the payments," said the general manager of one of the sites, but they led police to "three other operatives" and eventually disrupted a criminal enterprise that was extorting gambling sites globally. More often, however, infiltration at the periphery did not lead to indictments of members at the core of the enterprise because the nodal subnetworks were dispersed and not easy to track. By engaging independent contractors, cyberextortionists masked their identities and reduced the risk that network members would assist law enforcement detect and dismantle their illicit enterprises.[63]

Vertical power arrangements were not entirely absent. There existed small-scale intra-subnetwork hierarchies within relatively egalitarian nodal-network structures. For example, in the money-mover node, a primitive leader-follower structure allocated several "mules" to collect the "takes" at the behest of a few "bankers" who arranged for the flow of ransom payments. Similarly, the executor's node comprised several hackers, crackers, worm writers, and information merchants who worked in software and hardware production under the guidance of an intelligence controller who divided tasks, coordinated actions, determined deadlines, and launched attacks. While there was direction and guidance provided by organizers, there was little evidence of what Lemieux[64] calls "degree" or "closeness centrality" with multiple direct ties between actors in the networks or intense actor connections around one nodal source. To the contrary, virtual networks that brought down gambling sites were dynamic, decentered international "pods" of hit-and-run associates. At best, intermediary positions in the enterprise that linked most subnetworks together assumed the mantle of "network core", but only fleetingly.[65] The network supplied "contact points" to assemble criminal endeavors and develop retaliative actions against competitors or governments after which it disassembled.[66] Like confidence tricksters in traditional con games, members of Internet extortion networks seldom came into contact with one another, often did not know who they were working for except on a project basis, and quickly disappeared after "hits," only to resurface later when needed. There was a remarkable redundant characteristic to cyberextortion rings. Like rhizome plants that grow just below the surface of the ground and, when broken, start up again, bot-net armies were reassembled, new recruits were found and trained, new targets were identified for attack, and new Web networks reformed along their old communications lines, thus ensuring a measure of organizational competence and persistence.[67]

THE RULE OF LAW AND THE PROBLEM OF SECURITY

The success of malicious Ddos attacks and extortion depended not only on technical competence and organizational acumen, but as well on the ability of the online gambling industry and the state to control them. Generally speaking, there are three types of strategies used by industry and government to control crime in cyberspace: traditional law enforcement using regulatory compliance models or criminal intervention, third-party multilateral policing partnerships between private interest groups and government bodies, and self protection by prospective victims using market-based technical solutions.[68]

---

[63] Walker, *supra* note 28; Roberts, *supra* note 28; Ratliff, *supra* note 6.
[64] Lemieux, *supra* note 38, at 8–10.
[65] *Id.* at 9.
[66] Brenner, *supra* note 5, at 44.
[67] Lemieux, *supra* note 38; Williams, *supra* note 5; Brenner, *supra* note 5, at 44–45.
[68] D. Bayley & C. Shearing, The Future of Policing, *in* THE CRIMINAL JUSTICE SYSTEM: POLITICS AND POLICIES 150–167 (G. Cole & M. Gertz, eds., 7th ed., Belmont, Cal: Wadsworth Publishing) (1998); P. Grabosky, *Computer Crime: A Criminological Overview* (paper presented at the Tenth United Nations Congress on the Prevention of Crime and the Treatment of Offenders, Vienna, Apr. 15, 2000); P. GRABOSKY, R.G. SMITH & G. DEMPSEY, ELECTRONIC THEFT: *Unlawful Acquisition in Cyberspace* (New York: Cambridge University Press) (2001); Williams, *supra* note 5; A. Reiss, *Selecting Strategies of Social Control over Organizational Life, in* ENFORCING REGULATION 23–36 (K. Hawkins & J.M. Thomas, eds., Boston, Kluwyer-Nijhoff Publications) (1984); G.J. SMITH & H. WYNNE, GAMBLING IN CANADA. TRIUMPH, TRAGEDY OR TRADEOFF? (Calgary, Canada: West Foundation) (1999).

The ubiquity of sovereignty and the absence of legal guardianship

Transnational cyberextortion posed major challenges to these three law enforcement strategies. The first problem was the variation in the definition of cyberextortion. Criminal law typically deals with the protection of clearly defined tangible goods against human attacks, but cybercrimes often violated intangible values that were hard to define in general legal terms. As a result, cyberextortions were not always reported as separate offenses. What was defined as a cyberextortion in one sovereign jurisdiction was not always so defined in another. The laws were especially imprecise as to where offenses occurred (i.e. in the country where the criminal network was based or in the country where the crimes occurred), where evidence was to be collected, what laws applied, what courts prevailed, and what sanctions were appropriate.

Basic due diligence issues concerning authorization to conduct business, the disposition of transaction records, account confidentiality, record secrecy, and the collection and sharing of electronic information diverged dramatically from one sovereign jurisdiction to the other and revealed the absence of international legal norms for cyberspace and the governance of cyberextortion. Those operators with higher legal norms of propriety were undermined by the weak oversight policies of their neighbors leading to a cascading downward scheme of legal accountability.[69] A 2004 survey on computer security exposed the magnitude of the problem and demonstrated that information safe havens insulated illicit businesses from legal detection so that cyberextortion could operate with a minimum of interference.[70]

The ubiquity of law was compounded by the fissured structure of law enforcement within and between nation-states and this constituted a second problem for controlling cyberextortion. Even in the cases where the laws' applicability was determined, the logistics of search and seizure in real time, the volume of evidentiary materials, the encryption of information, and the ambiguity surrounding prior judicial approval for obtaining electronic stored computer data and accessing stored transaction data made the policing of cyberextortion complicated, costly, and laggard. The transfer of police evidence and decisions took weeks or months to accomplish while computer data for Ddos attacks was transferred by crime networks in minutes. Incriminating data was erased or altered in seconds, and data traffic revealing the origins of communications was stored secretly and for short periods of time by extortion rings thus undermining predigital police investigation techniques. When the police in one jurisdiction started to search a computer system in premise A, the perpetrators easily erased the relevant data in the storage devices in premise B, thus confounding the chain of communication needed to identify the sender data.[71]

Many police forces simply did not possess the capacity to investigate crimes that were committed from remote places in multiple sovereign jurisdictions where the criminals were not even present. U.S. policing agencies, including the Federal Bureau of Investigation, the Central Intelligence Agency, and state services, were preoccupied with terrorist activities and were not equipped to take on the additional task of monitoring Internet-based gambling crime.[72] The FBI typically took a month to process Ddos complaints and often forwarded them to local authorities that had neither the time nor resources to investigate them. The National High-Tech Crime Unit monitored Web site attacks and advised companies not to pay ransoms, but beyond that there was little direct action from them.[73] As the deputy director of the computer science laboratory of SRI international put it, the botnet-hunting community is "two or three years behind in terms of response mechanisms[.]"[74]

---

[69] COUNCIL OF EUROPE, *supra* note 5; WILSON & MOLANDER, *supra* note 5, at 45–46; Paul Toscano, *Taming the Cyber-Frontier: Security is Not Enough!*, CROSSTALK, Nov. 2000, <http://www.stsc.hill.af.mil/crosstalk/2000/11/toscano.html>; Working Group on Internet Governance, *Draft Issue Paper on Cybersecurity and Cybercrime* 2–3 (2005), <http://www.wgig.org/docs/WP-cybersec.pdf>.
[70] Williams, *supra* note 5; McAfee, *supra* note 12, at 9.
[71] COUNCIL OF EUROPE, *supra* note 5, at 11.
[72] G. Fields & J.R. Wilke, *F.B.I.'s new focus places big burden on local police*, WALL ST. J., June 30, 2003, at A1, A12.
[73] Ratliff, *supra* note 6; FBI, *Just Say No . . . To Cyber Extortion*, 2004, <http://www.fbi.gov/page2/jan04/cyber012304.htm>.
[74] Ryan Naraine, *Is the Botnet Battle Already Lost?*, EWEEK.COM Oct. 16, 2006, <http://www.eweek.com/article2/0,1759,2029720,00.asp>.

Furthermore, policing agencies lacked the trained staff to enforce gambling-related laws in cyberspace. All levels of law enforcement—international, national, and regional—had modest resources and limited numbers of specialized technical officers to meet the high requests for their services.[75] In Russia, high-tech unit officers were untrained and poorly paid, and some were "on the take" to organized crime groups.[76] Policing services around the world could not supply the demand for expert computer crime investigators, and when special units were formed, they were typically underfunded and overstretched. The National High-Tech Crime Unit, for example, had only 60 agents to monitor all cybercrimes from child pornography to identity theft. While it had a few successes in tracking down extortion networks, its policing approach was ad hoc, reactive, and slow.[77] Berlind summed up the dilemma well: "Given all that your local cops have to deal with and how thin their resources are stretched, don't expect a technological attack that very few can comprehend to get added to their list of priorities."[78]

Nor was law enforcement between nation-states especially well designed to operate in cyberspace. Cyberextortion committed from across the globe easily circumvented regulations based on local territorial-based laws and structures. Law enforcement agencies lacked adequate transborder computer crime management assistance and effective forensic tools.[79] A resident of Costa Rica who fell victim to a cyberextortion ransom originating in the United States, for example, received little assistance from law enforcement agencies in either jurisdiction. As Menn notes, "Costa Rican law enforcement was ill-equipped to deal with computer hackers thousands of miles away. Given the shaky legality of offshore betting, seeking help from U.S. authorities wasn't an attractive option."[80]

E-Money.Inc., an online payment company that was held ransom for $500,000, for example, called the FBI, but, because the attacks were coming from Russia, U.S. authorities could not remedy the situation. No extradition treaties existed, and law enforcement agencies neither detained nor arrested members of the ironically named "expert group protection

against hackers".[81] Indeed, the costs of extraterritorial law enforcement were prohibitive. The time, money, and personnel required by international investigations, and the uncertainty surrounding extradition proceedings and mutual legal assistance treaties were so high as to preclude attention to all but the most serious offending. Taken together, the overall enforcement structure was decentered and fragmented. Not surprisingly, victimized gambling companies remained reluctant to enlist the help of law enforcement agencies, resulting in victim compliance, low public visibility of cyberextortion, few successful prosecutions, and occasional paltry penalties.[82]

The limits of multilateral policing

The absence of legal guardianship and the limitations of calibrating transborder policing encouraged third party policing by private sector gambling companies, Internet security firms, and state agencies, but this too proved to be a third uncertain buttress for the legal control of cyberextortion. Two problems arose in attempting to establish multilateral policing.

[75] Grabosky, *supra* note 68, at 18–19; Williams, *supra* note 5; A.J. Surin, *To Catch a Cybercriminal*, COMPUTER CRIME RESEARCH CENTER, <http://www.crime-research.org/library/Cybercriminal.html> (last visited Oct. 12, 2007).
[76] Walker, *supra* note 17; Marcel-Eugène LeBeuf, *Organized Crime and Cybercrime: Criminal Investigations on the Cutting Edge* (Canadian Police College, Technical report, Ottawa, 2001), <http://www.cpc.gc.ca/rcd/ocrime_e.pdf>.
[77] Ratliff, *supra* note 6.
[78] D. Berlind, *In search of a cure for Ddos attacks*, ZDNET: TECHUPDATE Mar. 18, 2004, <http://www.techupdate.zdnet.com/techupdate/stories/main>.
[79] H. STAMBAUGH ET AL., ELECTRONIC CRIME NEEDS ASSESSMENT FOR STATE AND LOCAL LAW ENFORCEMENT (Washington, D.C.: National Institute of Justice) (2001); SMITH & H. WYNNE, *supra* note 68; K. Lenk, *The challenge of cyberspatial forms of human interaction to territorial governance and policing* in THE GOVERNANCE OF CYBERSPACE 126–36 (B. Loader, ed., London: Routledge) (1997); A.D. Smith, *Controversial and Emerging issues associated with cybergambling (e-casinos)*, 28 ONLINE INFO. REV. 435–43 (2004); Surin, *supra* note 75; T. Spring, *Who's Catching the Cyber-crooks?*, PC-WORLD, Aug. 26, 2005, *available at* <www.PCWorld.com/news/articles>.
[80] J. Menn, *Online companies facing huge losses in battling web extraction*, COMPUTER CRIME RESEARCH CENTER, Nov. 14, 2004, <www.crime-research.org/news>.
[81] Walker, *supra* note 17.
[82] LeBeuf, *supra* note 76.

First, while security firms were able to discover "zombie armies" and observe attacks in progress, the handoff to law enforcement was often unsuccessful.

The case of Don Best Sports, which was under attack for a $200,000 ransom in 2003, is illustrative. A computer security company tracked the attackers to a chat room in Kazakhstan, but when they notified the FBI and the Secret Service the latter "threw up their arms because it was in Kazakhstan" said the C.E.O. of the private security company.[83]

Second, even when international cooperation did result in arrests and prosecutions, it did not lead to enduring private/public law enforcement relations. For example, in the wake of the BetCris extortions in 2003, Digi Defense International teamed up with detectives from the National High-Tech Crime Unit and the FBI. Two computer engineers found the chat channel that controlled the zombies, infiltrated the network by pretending to be herders, earned the trust of a hacker, built up a profile of the extortion team, discovered their IP address and telephone number, and informed law enforcement of their identity and whereabouts.[84] A few months later, the Russian police, aided by the National High-Tech Crime Unit arrested an operative in the network. But the National High-Tech Crime Unit never credited the security firm for their role in the arrest, even though it did all the costly undercover work and set up the sting to entrap the network. One security engineer observed: "the N.H.T.C.U. and the F.B.I. were kind of using us".[85]

The conundrums of commercial cybersecurity

Extending the rule of law into cyberspace to create a secure digital environment for online gambling remains a work in progress and many gambling companies have opted for immediate commercial solutions that rely upon access control and authentication technologies and technologies of encryption and anonymity.[86] Self-protection was their first line of defense. This meant investing in opportunity reduction remedies such as identification services, antivirus software, computer incident response schemes, intrusion detection systems, enhanced firewall technologies, and patch and configuration sys-

tems to prevent malware infections of gambling sites and speed up the road to recovery after Ddos attacks had hit them[87] and investing in intelligent Web-based products such as parallel network intrusion prevention architectures and second generation self-correcting security software to monitor and divert "illegitimate packages" from targeted gambling sites.[88] Some private security firms, for example, configured "tech-boxes" that channeled all traffic to onsite or offsite data centers that then layered the data flow, segmented it for patterns, filtered out malicious messages by using a technique called "deep packet inspection", and created holding pens for zombie armies so that they could be disarmed.[89] Other companies designed traffic anomaly detectors and guards that identified deviant attack patterns and rerouted and eliminated them from Web sites while allowing legitimate gamblers to access gambling sites.[90] "Imagine 50,000 people showed up at your office and you got 50,000 calls at the same time—you probably wouldn't get much work done" explained the CEO at Prolexic. "So we would line up those 50,000 people and interrogate each one. If they were illegitimate, we'd shoot them in the head[.]"[91]

---

[83] Ratliff, *supra* note 6.

[84] Computer Crime Research Center, *supra* note 43.

[85] Ratliff, *supra* note 6.

[86] D. Denning, *The future of cryptography*, in THE GOVERNMENT OF CYBERSPACE 175–89 (B. Loader, ed., London: Routledge) (1997).; D. Denning, INFORMATION WARFARE AND SECURITY (Boston: Addison Wesley) (1999); P. Tang, *Multimedia information products and services a need for 'cybercops'?*, in THE GOVERNANCE OF CYBERSPACE 190–208 (B. Loader, ed., London: Routledge) (1997).

[87] J. McGeahy, *Keeping Things Secure*, in INTERNET GAMBLING REPORT IV 125–29 (A. Cabot, ed., Las Vegas: Trace Publications) (2001)., Computer Emergency Response Team, Creating a Computer Security Incident Response Team: a Process for Getting Started, 2002, <http://www.cert.org/csirts/Creating-A-CSIRT.html>; Cullingworth, *supra* note 7; Surin, *supra* note 75; Karshmer, *supra* note 7; S. NORTHCUTT, CYBERTHREAT AND RESPONSE – 2006 AND BEYOND (New York, SANS Institute) (2005); M. Ward, *Rings of Steel Combat Net Attacks*, BBC News, Sept. 14, 2005, <http://news.bbc.co.uk/1/hi/technology/4169223.stm>.

[88] Morgan, *supra* note 27, at 4; Grabosky, *supra* note 68, at 12–14.

[89] Walker, *supra* note 28; Ratliff, *supra* note 6.

[90] CISCO, *supra* note 13; Morgan, *supra* note 27, at 4; Pappalardo & Messmer, *supra* note 30; Murpy et al., *supra* note 13.

[91] Myser, *supra* note 12.

Internet service providers were especially proactive. They monitored Web site habits, checked so-called "master-slave traffic" on gambling sites, detected zombie machines, dissected the bots to discover the chat room addresses, and then actively pursued the herders. Using "center track", "packet marking", and "content filtering" techniques, they diverted attacks via an overlay network passing through a router. Then "hop by hop" or "controller-agent" tracking was used to identify the router and scan and crack the data using an algorithm to reveal the signature of the Ddos attack.[92] Some security firms and ISPs even posed as undercover bot-net herders for gambling sites in an effort to infiltrate crime networks and disrupt cyberextortion schemes on behalf of their clients.[93] Others formed "fingerprint alliance" teams that compared and shared attack profiles and teamed up to target crimes involving hacking, virus attacks, fraud, blackmail, and extortion.[94]

Despite the security makeover to manage risk on behalf of the online industry, problems still persisted for many gambling companies. First, the costs of rolling out and maintaining Ddos resistant architecture were prohibitive. Betwwts.com spent over $250,000 on security since their first attack in 2003, Protx spends $500,000 a year to protect itself from cyberextortion (50 times the original ransom demand), and Blue Square.com pays $2,000 an hour to consult with its cybersecurity experts.[95] While anti Ddos services cost around $12,000 to $15,000 a month, many gambling companies could not afford the high investments in hardware, software, and operating costs. They had to decide between the service provider and the extortionist. The risks of economic loss, damage to corporate reputations, customer switching, and the costs of Web site recovery encouraged many companies to continue "to drop ransoms into Swiss or Cayman Island bank accounts controlled by criminal organizations[.]"[96]

Second, a global patchwork of private self-protection schemes created little industry-wide certainty about safety and protection and little consensus about the best devices to stop attacks early and at a distance from their gambling Web sites. While some sectors of the industry managed to balance self-regulation with market-efficient solutions to control some of the darker corners of cyberspace, many remained vulnerable to extortion. In the networked world, no island is ever an island. Because cyberextortion was managed separately and secretly by Web site owners and their security experts, coordinated efforts by private security firms and Internet service providers to use commercial protection tools to defend the industry remained uneven, incomplete, and uncertain.[97]

Third, authentication and encryption technologies were vulnerable to criminal manipulations. This created a cottage industry in devices and schemes to circumvent these security technologies.[98] While firewalls stopped some malware, hackers got smarter and subverted the firewalls. While intrusion detection systems detected malware, the times between detect and correct were often too great, causing repeated interruptions in betting and casino services. While patches thwarted some malware, they also created internal information system breaks that were time consuming and expensive to fix because they were often outside the management capacity of the information technology systems. Paradoxically, the technical remedies sometimes created information entropy where the defensive systems for the gambling sites or their proxies were so complex that important data about Ddos attacks were either not retrieved or were trapped in segregated data silos that could not interact with other parts of the protection system. As cybersecurity evolved, the higher level plans of extortionists disguised attacks at their points of ingress into Web site's networks, tested the guards, switches and detectors for anomalies and vulnerabilities, and probed the new operating police-like systems for gaps, lapses, and stupid-

---

[92] Biever, *supra* note 21; Murpy et al., *supra* note 13.
[93] Computer Crime Research Center, *supra* note 43.
[94] Morgan, *supra* note 27, at 4; Surin, *supra* note 75.
[95] Karshmer, *supra* note 7; Ratliff, *supra* note 6.
[96] Pappalardo & Messmer, *supra* note 30.
[97] McGeahy, *supra* note 87, at 129–32; Working Group on Internet Governance, *supra* note 69 at 3.
[98] Tang, *supra* note 86; Lenk, *supra* note 79.

ity.[99] A never-ending cycle of technology-enhanced detection and counter detection measures emerged that made the initial investment in security procedures either worthless or in need of constant costly upgrades. If the earmark of criminal organization is its rational ability to "handle the technical problems of crime and negotiate social control",[100] then the next five years will likely bring more threats, more attacks, and more emergencies to the online gambling industry in the form of software piracy, information theft, identity fraud, and extortion.

CYBEREXTORTION AND THE FUTURE GOVERNANCE OF E-GAMBLING

This study raises several challenges for the future governance of the online gambling marketplace: calibrating the rule of law, creating extraterritorial law enforcement, and creating and managing market technical solutions.

Global harmonization

Since national governments remain the dominant authority for regulating criminal behavior, the first challenge is to revise standard territorial laws and regulations so that they are technologically up to date. While it is naive to believe that the weak state of global legal protections against cyberextortion or other forms of cybercrime can suddenly be transformed into a uniform world system of stable lawmaking, it may be possible to develop an approach similar to the Council of Europe or the United Nations Convention against Transnational Organized Crime, which harmonized legal definitions to cover virtual acts of trespass, breaking and entering, fraud, forgery, data interception and modification, network interference and sabotage, aiding and abetting, and unauthorized access to systems or data, so that crimes in one national jurisdiction have the same status and carry the same penalties in other national jurisdictions. These arrangements may then be extended as models to countries like Latvia, Malta, Gibraltar, Kazakhstan, Russia, and China—with the caveat that these extraterritorial applications of national laws are not "one size fits all" models and must be negotiated with, not imposed on, other sovereign jurisdictions.[101]

Regulatory supervision also merits reform. To start, the licensing issue must be resolved so that the national rules and criteria governing permissible operators of Internet gambling, banking, and cyberpayment schemes are similar from one jurisdiction to another and can act as effective measures against international based fraud, cyberextortion, and money laundering at online gambling sites. In addition, transaction thresholds regarding suspicious cyberspace fund transfers and record transactions should be globalized so that evidence obtained in one legal jurisdiction has the same admissibility in the courts of a neighboring jurisdiction. Finally, the techniques for on-site inspections of gambling operators and payment systems should be strengthened and rationalized so that commercial Web sites are subjected to independent, comparable, and collaborative audits and record inspections, applying an international code of practice.

Transborder enforcement

Extraterritorial issues related to the detection, investigation, and prosecution of offenders is the second obvious challenge for the governance of cyberextortion in the future. Policing cyberspace is a pluralistic endeavor, but the policing practices of many states have lagged behind the changing information and communication technologies of cyberspace and their criminal exploitation in the digital age. Eight challenges are apparent:

1. Can an international system of law enforcement be established that distinguishes between the search and seizure of stored data in a fixed computer and the interception of data flows that are sent from one computer

---

[99] Surin, *supra* note 75; Murpy et al., *supra* note 13; Northcutt, *supra* note 87; McConnell International, *supra* note 43.

[100] McIntosh, *supra* note 8, at 73.

[101] McConnell International, *supra* note 43; McAfee, *supra* note 12; Williams, *supra* note 5; Working Group on Internet Governance, *supra* note 69; K. Karofi & J. Mwanza, *Globalization and Crime*, 3 BANGLADESH J. SOC. 15–16. (2006).

to another or are communicated within a linked computer system for purposes of Web site attacks and extortion?[102]

2. Can international policing standards harmonize the seizure of intangible materials in such a manner that it need not require the seizure of the difficult-to-obtain physical medium (i.e. CDs, discs, hard drives) on which the data is typically located?[103]

3. Can new forms of judicial approval or probable cause be created for the search and seizure of highly mobile electronic stored data and records of service, the preservation of elusive intercept materials, and the decryption of secretly coded data so that they are transnational and admissible in multilateral judicial contexts?[104]

4. Where zombie armies are operating, can a single legal warrant permit searches into international connected data systems to collect evidence, or as legal officials hop and search from one system to another to detect the source of Ddos attacks and trace money flows, will they continue to require multiple warrants to act?[105]

5. Since data and records concerning hacking and extortion are held by telecommunication operators and Internet service providers, is there an international legal mechanism that can govern the future retention, disposal, and disclosure of this data to law enforcement authorities? For example, can law enforcement bodies in one country compel suspects or third parties in another to hand over data, passwords, encryption keys or algorithms?[106]

6. If private security organizations are engaged to assist in interceptions of Ddos attacks and site extortions, how will this process be managed to preserve the integrity and admissibility of the data as evidence for either national or multinational court proceedings?

7. As transborder search and seizures become more common to track cyberextortion, what national or multinational legal permissions, notifications, and conventions will apply, and what authorities need to be contacted to provide them? For example, if the data concerning the location of a Ddos attack site resides in Canada, will Canadian law permit foreign law officials to search and seize that

data through interconnected computer systems, and who will oversee the search and seizure process?

8. How will human rights, confidentiality of information, and privacy be safeguarded in the digital extension of the rule of law in pursuit of Internet based crime?[107]

Private security

Cyberspace is not the first policy domain to exist beyond the control of nation states. Air traffic control, nuclear testing, environmental pollution, and the transfer of bank funds, for example, have resulted in international legal cooperation and compromises.[108] Governments and businesses, therefore, have consistently had to balance legal imperatives with technology and market forces in controlling transnational problems. Managing market solutions is therefore the third challenge facing the future governance of crime at online gambling sites. Five issues are critical:

1. Can the relations between current private and public online companies and the emergent commercial cybersecurity industry be rationalized and extended to offer an economically affordable alternative to criminal ransoms on an industry-wide basis?

2. Can the information technology industry calibrate agreed-upon standards to benchmark the quality of system-protection tools, develop an accepted methodology to determine how much investment in security is sufficient, and provide a cost-effective plan to address prevention and to build interindustry partnerships?

3. Can electronic recordkeeping of e-gambling authorization measures such as digital signatures and biometric identification, and network-borne tracking systems be com-

---

[102] WILSON & MOLANDER, *supra* note 5, at 39–40.
[103] Working Group on Internet Governance, *supra* note 69.
[104] WILSON & MOLANDER, *supra* note 5, at 48–49.
[105] Grabosky, *supra* note 68; GRABOSKY, SMITH & DEMPSEY, *supra* note 68.
[106] Surin, *supra* note 75; Berlind, *supra* note 78.
[107] Working Group on Internet Governance, *supra* note 69; WILSON & MOLANDER, *supra* note 5, at 48–49.
[108] Grabosky, *supra* note 68, at 17.

bined into an infrastructure capable of surveying transactional data to discern criminal activities and reduce their associated costs and harms?

4. Can these technological solutions occur at what Kessler calls "the speed of thought"?[109] Web site attacks are now instantaneously automated to find any targets to exploit. In the world of information intrusion, extortionists know when to attack and launch their software with less need for perfection than Web site owners, security experts, and regulators require to deflect the attacks and manage their defenses.

5. Even if these technologies are available, can commercial firms and governments work together to strengthen market-driven, victim-based solutions and to create new or modified legal frameworks within which these technologies can operate and provide cybersecurity that has widespread international consensus and support?

The answers to these challenges are by no means easy or obvious as prohibitionist and regulationist positions about e-gambling harden. On the one hand, prohibition efforts typically drive legitimate businesses underground or out of the market and reduce the effectiveness of what little regulation they currently receive from governments, thereby increasing the chances of cybercrime, fraud, and deception. Regulatory efforts, on the other hand, promise discernible advantages such as tax benefits, consumer protection, job creation, and enhanced security. But the global nature of the Internet makes local or even nationally based solutions to the criminal problems of e-

gambling difficult to apply. Legalization does not de-facto guarantee security.

At the very least, the future governance of online gambling should be fixed with utmost good-faith duties that apply in an area like insurance law that also legislates similar features of risk and vulnerability and trust and representation. This entails placing a higher obligation on gambling operators than that which governs usual commercial transactions that are controlled by fair trading laws and consumer protection acts because the already high level of vulnerability associated with buying a risk in terrestrial legal gambling is further amplified in digital environments. Securing the safety of the e-gambling environment, then, should evince stringent thresholds that prioritize the common-law principle that "in high risk situations, the burden is on the person knowing the risk to inform the other of its extent[.]"[110] Strict liability on matters of trust and representation should prevail. As gambling moves into bedrooms, backyards, and basements, the industry and its overseers should not conceal what they privately know and should ensure that online gambling sites, products, procedures and operations are as free as possible from criminal exploitation. Only then may online gambling claim to be starting up the rocky road to legal respectability and social responsibility.

---

[109] Gary Kessler, *Security at the Speed of Thought*, INFO. SECURITY MAG., Nov. 2000, *version available at* <http://www.garykessler.net/library/thought.html>.
[110] G.E. Minchin, *Buying A Risk: An Application of Insurance Law to Legal Gaming*, 2 E COMMUNITY INT'L J. MENTAL HEALTH & ADDICTION 9–14 (2004).

Part II
Harmonisation of Computer Crime Laws – The Council of Europe Convention on Cyber Crime and the Additional Protocol to the Council of Europe Convention

[5]

THE COUNCIL OF EUROPE CONVENTION ON CYBERCRIME

MIKE KEYSER[*]

Table of Contents

I. INTRODUCTION

The Internet is often referred to as the new "Wild West."[1] This maxim holds true, because the Internet is so similar to the turn of the century Western Frontier.[2] Like the Wild West, the Internet has brought with it opportunity and millions of new jobs.[3] The Internet also brings with it very real dangers. Although the specific dangers may be different from those faced on the American Frontier, a web surfer's exposure to dangers which are new, difficult to police, and difficult to prevent, is very similar.[4] The only significant difference may be that the Internet is a virtual society

---

* J.D. candidate, Seattle University School of Law (May 2003); B.A., Washington State University (May 2000). The author would like to thank Bob Menanteaux, reference librarian at Seattle University School of Law, for all of his help and guidance.

1. Henry E. Crawford, Internet Calling: FCC Jurisdiction over Internet Telephony, 5 COMM. L. CONSPECTUS 43, 43 (1997) (discussing the Internet and analogizing it to the Wild West).

2. Id.

3. Mohit Gogna, The World Wide Web Versus the Wild Wild West, at http://home.utm.utoronto.ca/~mohit/ (last visited Dec. 4, 2002). For example, in 1996, 1.1 million jobs were created. Id.

4. Id.

288   J. TRANSNATIONAL LAW & POLICY   [Vol. 12:2

rather than a tactile one; a virtual society existing only in networks and information packets.[5] However, the harms committed against both individual citizens and businesses are very real.[6] These citizens are extremely vulnerable as criminal activity on the Internet continues to run rampant.[7]

This article is intended to expand upon the existing wealth of knowledge regarding cybercrimes. However, it takes the analysis one step further. This is the first article to consider the impact of a new, powerful, and timely piece of international legislation: The Council of Europe's Convention on Cybercrime.[8] Section II of this comment begins with a survey of the cyber-landscape. It illustrates citizenry and critical infrastructures extremely vulnerable to international, as well as domestic, cyber attacks. Section II ends with a case example—the case of Raymond Torricelli and his Internet exploits. Section III is an in-depth analysis of the newly signed, but not yet ratified, Cybercrime Convention. Section III examines the entire Convention, article by article, taking into account critical opinion, as well as drafter intent. Select provisions of importance are analyzed in greater depth by looking at their improvements upon existing law, in addition to their pitfalls. The fourth and final section concludes the comment by projecting toward the future, forecasting some aspects of the Convention's impact upon our lives as it enters into force, as well as the likely objections individuals, businesses, and interest groups will have to treaty provisions.

---

    5. Joginder S. Dhillon & Robert I. Smith, Defensive Information Operations and Domestic Law: Limitations on Governmental Investigative Techniques, 50 A.F.L. REV. 135, 138 (2001) (explaining the composition of the Internet and how information is transferred).

    6. Many of the crimes committed against individuals and businesses are legislated against in the European Convention on Cybercrime, and include identity theft, child pornography, and fraud, among others. Convention on Cybercrime, opened for signature Nov. 23, 2001, Europ. T.S. No. 185 [hereinafter Convention], available at http://conventions.coe.int/ Treaty/EN/ projets/FinalCybercrime.htm (last visited Dec. 4, 2002).

    7. Aaron Craig, Gambling on the Internet, 1998 COMPUTER L. REV. & TECH. J. 61 (1998) (discussing the seriousness of the effects of crime on the Internet), available at http://www.smu.edu/csr/Spring98-2-Craig.PDF.

    8. Convention, supra note 6.

II. Your Network Neighborhood

A. Crime on the "Net"

The 2001 Computer Crime and Security Survey, conducted by the Computer Security Institute and the FBI's San Francisco office, is prime evidence of the extent of lawlessness on the Internet:

> 1. 47 percent of the companies surveyed had their systems penetrated from the outside;[9]

> 2. 90 percent reported some form of electronic vandalism;[10]

> 3. 13 percent reported stolen transaction information (meaning personal data and credit card numbers).[11]

This figure is daunting since only a small percentage of companies responded, while hundreds of companies whose systems have been compromised, and whose information has been stolen, remain in the dark.[12] Numerous reasons exist which explain why businesses are reluctant to report system intrusions.[13] Most commonly, this reluctance is attributed to the fear that a public report would compromise a competitive position in their respective market.[14] In other words, they may lose business if the public perceives the company as vulnerable to attack or unable to keep personal identification secure.[15] The FBI estimates that the cost of electronic crime exceeds ten billion dollars per year.[16]

Cybercrimes are not limited to businesses. The Federal Trade Commission reported that identity theft and bogus Internet scams topped the list of consumer fraud complaints in 2001.[17] Identity theft, arguably the most prevalent crime on the Internet, comprised 42 percent of the total complaints.[18] With figures like these, it is no

---

9. John Galvin, Meet the World's Baddest Cyber Cops, ZIFF DAVIS SMART BUS. FOR THE NEW ECON. (Oct. 1, 2001), at 78 (on file with the Journal of Transnational Law & Policy).

10. Id.

11. Id.

12. Id.

13. Dhillon & Smith, supra note 5, at 140 (discussing the reluctance of companies to report intrusions on its systems).

14. Id.

15. Id.

16. Id. at 139.

17. Jay Lyman, ID Theft and Web Scams Top Consumer Complaints, NEWSFACTOR NETWORK (Jan. 24, 2002), at http://www.newsfactor.com/perl/story/15965.html.

18. Id.

290   J. TRANSNATIONAL LAW & POLICY   [Vol. 12:2

secret that cybercrimes pose an ongoing and significant threat to the security of the United States and its citizens.[19]

B. Greater Dependency on Technology

As our lives become more advanced, we depend on computers and technology to even greater degrees. For example, one should consider the increasing trend of Internet sales. The convenience and privacy of online consumer spending is leading towards a growing use of the Internet as a consumer's primary purchasing location. In the year 2000, online retail sales totaled $5 billion, while total sales were $42.4 billion.[20] "Total U.S. spending on online sales increased from $4.9 billion in November to $5.7 billion in December" of 2001.[21] Consumer online sales for the third quarter of 2002 reached $17.9 billion, a 35 percent increase over the third quarter of 2001.[22] Online sales through the third quarter of 2002 totaled $52.5 billion.[23] As online sales continue to increase, and personal and credit card information is transferred over the Internet, the American public also increases its chances that it will become the victim of a "cybercrime."

C. What is a Cybercrime & Who are Cybercriminals?

"The Department of Justice ("DOJ") defines computer crimes as 'any violations of criminal law that involve a knowledge of computer technology for their perpetration, investigation, or prosecution.'"[24] The types of people who commit cybercrimes vary as much as the multitude of crimes that can be committed.[25] "Computer criminals can be youthful hackers, disgruntled employees and company insiders, or international terrorists and spies."[26] These criminals become "cybercriminals" when their crimes involve the use of a computer. "[A] computer may be the 'object' of a crime," or in other words, "the criminal targets the computer itself."[27] "[A] computer may [also] be the 'subject' of a crime," or in other words, it "is the

---

19. Galvin, supra note 9.
20. CyberAtlas Staff, December Rakes in the E-Commerce Dough, at http://cyberatlas. internet.com/markets/retailing/article/0,,6061_961291,00.html (last visited Feb. 11, 2003).
21. Id.
22. Robyn Greenspan, Shoppers Gearing Up for Season, at http://cyberatlas.internet. com/markets/retailing/article/0,,6061_1494231,00.html#table1 (last visited Feb. 11, 2003).
23. Id.
24. Sheri A. Dillon et al., Note, Computer Crimes, 35 Am. Crim. L. Rev. 503, 505 (1998) (defining "computer crime") (quoting National Institute of Justice, U.S. Dep't of Justice, Computer Crime: Criminal Justice Resource Manual 2 (1989)).
25. Dillon et al., supra note 24, at 506.
26. Id.
27. Id. at 507.

physical site of the crime, or the source of, or reason for, unique forms of asset loss."[28] Examples of this type of crime are viruses, logic bombs, and sniffers.[29] Finally, "a computer may be [the] 'instrument' used to commit traditional crimes."[30] For example, a computer might be used to commit the most common type of cybercrime to date—identity theft.[31]

D. Identity Theft

Identity theft is now being called "the signature crime of the digital era."[32] "Identity theft is the illegal use of another's personal identification numbers."[33] Examples include a person using a stolen "credit card, or social security number to purchase goods,"[34] withdraw money, apply for loans, or rent apartments.[35] While these types of crimes have existed for a long time in the form of pick pocketing, the Internet facilitates their frequency and ease.[36] Without faces or signatures, the only thing preventing a person from posing as another is a password, which can be intercepted without much difficulty by an experienced criminal.[37]

E. Taking a Bite out of Crime, Domestically Speaking

In the United States, laws intended to combat cybercrimes are already in place.[38] Congress treats cybercrimes as distinct federal offenses through a multitude of acts, most notably the Computer

---

28. Id.
29. Id.
30. Id.
31. See Lyman, supra note 17.
32. Michael McCutcheon, Identity Theft, Computer Fraud and 18 U.S.C. § 1030(G): A Guide to Obtaining Jurisdiction in the United States for a Civil Suit Against a Foreign National Defendant, 13 LOY. CONSUMER L. REV. 48, 48 (2001) (discussing identity theft).
33. Id.
34. Id.
35. Id.
36. Id.
37. Id. at 49.
38. See, e.g., 18 U.S.C. § 875 (2000) (originally enacted as Act of June 25, 1948, ch. 645, 62 Stat. 741) (interstate communications: including threats, kidnapping, ransom, and extortion); 18 U.S.C. § 1029 (2000) (possession of access device); 18 U.S.C. § 1030 (2000) (fraud and related activity in connection with computers); 18 U.S.C. § 1343 (2000) (originally enacted as Act of July 16, 1952, ch. 879, § 18(a), 66 Stat. 722, and amended by Act of July 11, 1956, ch. 561, 70 Stat. 523) (fraud by wire, radio, or television); 18 U.S.C. § 1361 (2000) (based on Act of Mar. 4, 1909, ch. 321, § 35, 35 Stat. 1095; Act of Oct. 23, 1918, ch. 194, 40 Stat. 1015; Act of June 18, 1934, ch. 587, 48 Stat. 996; Act of Apr. 4, 1938, ch. 69, 52 Stat. 197) (injury to government property or contracts); 18 U.S.C. § 1362 (2000) (based on Act of Mar. 4, 1909, ch. 321, § 60, 35 Stat. 1099) (communication lines, stations, or systems); Economic Espionage Act of 1996, 18 U.S.C. § 1831, et seq. (2000).

292   J. TRANSNATIONAL LAW & POLICY   [Vol. 12:2

Fraud and Abuse Act of 1986[39] and the National Information Infrastructure Protection Act of 1996.[40] These laws are designed to incriminate domestic hackers. A good example is the case of twenty-year old Raymond Torricelli, known by the hacking code name, "rolex."[41]

Torricelli was the head of a notorious hacking group known as "#conflict."[42] Operating out of his New Rochelle, New York home, Torricelli "used his personal computer to run programs designed to search the Internet, and seek out computers which were vulnerable to intrusion."[43] Once a computer was "located, Torricelli's computer obtained unauthorized access . . . by uploading a program known as 'rootkit.'"[44] When run on a foreign computer, rootkit "allows a hacker to gain complete access to all of a computer's functions without having been granted these privileges by the authorized users of that computer."[45]

"One of the computers Torricelli accessed was used by NASA [the National Aeronautics and Space Administration] to perform satellite design and mission analysis concerning future space missions."[46] Another computer Torricelli accessed was used by NASA's Jet Propulsion Laboratory "as an e-mail and internal web server."[47]

After gaining unauthorized access to these computers, Torricelli "used many of the computers to host chat-room discussions."[48] "[I]n these discussions, he invited other chat participants to visit a website which enabled them to view pornographic images."[49] "Torricelli earned 18 cents for each visit a person made to that website," ultimately netting $300-400 dollars per week from this activity.[50]

Torricelli's criminal activities were far from over. He also intercepted "usernames and passwords [by] traversing the computer networks" of San Jose State University.[51] In addition, he stole

---

39. Pub. L. No. 99-474, § 2, 100 Stat. 1213 (1986) (amending 18 U.S.C. § 1030).

40. Pub. L. No. 104-294, tit. 2, § 201, 110 Stat. 3488, 3491-94 (1996) (amending 18 U.S.C. § 1030). For a discussion of laws currently in place, see Dillon et al., supra note 24, at 508.

41. Press Release, United States Dep't of Justice, Hacker Sentenced in New York City for Hacking into Two NASA Jet Propulsion Lab Computers Located in Pasadena, California (Sept. 5, 2001), available at http://www.usdoj.gov/criminal/cybercrime/ torricellisent.htm.

42. Id.

43. Id.

44. Id.

45. Id.

46. Id.

47. Id.

48. Id.

49. Id.

50. Id.

51. Id.

passwords and usernames from numerous other sources "which he used to gain free Internet access, or to gain unauthorized access to still more computers."[52] When Torricelli "obtained passwords which were encrypted, he would use a password cracking program known as 'John-the-Ripper' to decrypt the passwords."[53]

Torricelli was still not finished. He also obtained stolen credit card numbers and "used one such credit card number to purchase long distance telephone service."[54]

> [M]uch of the evidence obtained against Torricelli was obtained through a search of his personal computer. . . . [I]n addition to thousands of stolen passwords and numerous credit card numbers, investigators found transcripts of chat-room discussions in which Torricelli and members of '#conflict' [his hacker group] discussed, among other things, (1) breaking into other computers . . . (2) obtaining credit card numbers belonging to other persons and using those numbers to make unauthorized purchases . . . and (3) using their computers to electronically alter the results of the annual MTV [Music Television] Movie Awards.[55]

---

52. Id.
53. Id.
54. Id.
55. Id.

294   J. TRANSNATIONAL LAW & POLICY   [Vol. 12:2

III. Taking a Bite out of Crime

A. The Internationalization of Cybercrime

Due to the nature of cybercrimes and an undeveloped international body of law on the topic, cybercrimes often occur internationally. For example, perpetrators "across the United States and Europe were indicted by a federal grand jury [in May, 2000] for allegedly conspiring to infringe the copyright of more than 5,000 computer software programs. . . ."[56] These programs were "made available through a hidden Internet site located at a university in Quebec, Canada."[57]

Some of the perpetrators:

> allegedly were members . . . of an international organization of software pirates known as "Pirates with Attitudes," ["PWA"] an underground group that disseminates stolen copies of software, including programs that are not yet commercially available....
> [Others] were employees of Intel Corp., four of whom allegedly supplied computer hardware to the piracy organization in exchange for obtaining access . . . to the group's pirated software, which had a retail value in excess of $1 million.[58]

PWA is "one of the oldest and most sophisticated networks of software pirates anywhere in the world."[59] Officials are aware of this because "previous software piracy investigations that have focused on smaller sites have turned up numerous copyrighted software files bearing annotations reflecting that the files were supplied to the sites through PWA."[60]

International crime syndicates often communicate "in real time on private Internet Relay Chat ["IRC"] channels," or in code via open Internet chat rooms.[61] "PWA allegedly maintained numerous File Transfer Protocol ["FTP"] sites configured for the transfer of

---

56. Press Release, United States Dep't of Justice, U.S. Indicts 17 in Alleged International Software Piracy Conspiracy (May 4, 2000), available at http://www.cybercrime.gov /pirates.htm.

57. Id.

58. Id.

59. Id. (quoting Scott R. Lassar, United States Attorney for the Northern District of Illinois).

60. Id.

61. Id.

software files and stored libraries of pirated software on each of these sites."[62]

PWA's website "was not accessible to the general public, but instead was configured so that it was accessible only to" those people who knew its Internet Protocol ("IP") address.[63] In order for users to maintain their ability to access the website and download pirated software, they were required "to 'upload,' or provide files, including copyrighted software files obtained from other sources and, in return, were permitted to 'download'" pirated files provided by other users.[64] At one point, "more than 5,000 copyrighted computer software programs were available for downloading. . . ."[65]

Software pirates are often assigned different tasks, which shields the overall organization from a governmental "bust."[66] PWA followed this organizational scheme assigning some members to the role of "cracker," which are people who strip "away the copy protection that is embedded in [the] . . . software."[67] Others were assigned as "couriers" whose job it was to transfer software to PWA, or as "suppliers" who were funneling "programs from major software companies to the group."[68]

In this case, the United States had jurisdiction over those nationals involved in the piracy scheme.[69] But what about PWA members that live outside U.S. borders in countries that do not have an extradition treaty with the United States? It seems that United States laws might not apply to those international criminals or cannot reach their criminal actions. This problem poses a serious concern for many government officials because many computer systems can be easily accessed through a "global telecommunications network from anywhere in the world."[70] Furthermore, it becomes a roll of the dice as to whether the criminal's host country has laws stringent enough to bring the criminal to justice, or if the host country is even willing to cooperate in the first place.[71] Thus, in order to successfully combat cybercrime, it is clear that the world needs a better international legal system in which to catch and convict cybercriminals.

---

62. Id.
63. Id.
64. Id.
65. Id.
66. Id.
67. Id.
68. Id.
69. Id.
70. Dillon et al., *supra* note 24, at 539 (discussing computer systems and ease of access).
71. Id.

296 J. TRANSNATIONAL LAW & POLICY [Vol. 12:2

B. The Council of Europe Cybercrime Convention

The forty-one nation Council of Europe ("COE") drafted the Cybercrime Convention[72] after four years and twenty-seven drafts.[73] It was adopted by the Committee of Ministers during the Committee's 109th Session on November 8, 2001.[74] The Convention was opened for signature in Budapest, on November 23, 2001.[75] Thirty-five countries have signed the treaty, with Albania and Croatia having ratified it as well.[76] The Convention will come into force when five states, three of which must be COE members, have ratified it.[77] The treaty is intended to create a common cross-border "criminal policy aimed at the protection of society against cybercrime . . . by adopting appropriate legislation and fostering international co-operation."[78]

1. Importance

The COE's Convention on Cybercrime is important international legislation because it binds countries in the same way as a treaty. "An international convention, or treaty, is a legal agreement between governments that spells out a code of conduct."[79] Once a large number of states have ratified a treaty, then it becomes acceptable to treat it as general law.[80] Treaties are the only machinery that exist for adapting international law to new conditions and strengthening the force of a rule of law between states.[81] Thus, it seems very important for an international regime to be set up to combat these types of crimes in a growing and

---

72. Convention, supra note 6.

73. Peter Piazza, Cybercrime Treaty Opens Pandora's Box, SECURITY MGMT. (Sept. 2001), available at http://www.securitymanagement.com/library/001100.html.

74. Convention, supra note 6.

75. Id.

76. Council of Europe, Chart of Signatures and Ratifications, available at http://conventions.coe.int/Treaty/EN/CadreListeTraites.htm (last visited Dec. 6, 2002) (signatories include: United States; Albania; Armenia; Austria; Belgium; Bulgaria; Canada; Croatia; Cyprus; Estonia; Finland; France; Germany; Greece; Hungary; Iceland; Ireland; Italy; Japan; Malta; Moldova; Netherlands; Norway; Poland; Portugal; Romania; Slovenia; Spain; Sweden; Switzerland; South Africa; Ukraine; United Kingdom; and the former Yugoslav Republic of Macedonia).

77. Wendy McAuliffe, Council of Europe Approves Cybercrime Treaty, ZDNET UK NEWS (Sept. 21, 2001), at http://news.zdnet.co.uk/story/0,,t269-s2095796,00.html.

78. Convention, supra note 6, pmbl.

79. UNICEF, Laws and International Conventions, at http://www.unicef.org/turkey/laws_i_c/ (last visited Feb. 11, 2003).

80. JAMES LESLIE BRIERLY, THE LAW OF NATIONS: AN INTRODUCTION TO THE INTERNATIONAL LAW OF PEACE 57 (Humphrey Waldock ed., Oxford Univ. Press 6th ed. 1963) (1928).

81. Id.

integrated global society, which is becoming ever more vulnerable to cyber attacks.

2. Objectives

The Convention is intended to be the "first international treaty on crimes committed via the Internet and other computer networks."[82] Its provisions particularly deal with infringements of copyrights, computer-related fraud, child pornography, and violations of network security.[83] Its main objective, set out in the preamble, is to "pursue . . . a common criminal policy aimed at the protection of society against cybercrime . . . especially by adopting appropriate legislation and fostering international co-operation."[84]

3. Parties Involved

The Convention is open to worldwide membership.[85] Instrumental in its drafting were the forty-one COE "countries, which cover most of Central and Western Europe."[86] In addition, the United States, Canada, Japan, and South Africa also aided in its drafting.[87] As stated earlier, as of the date of this publication, thirty-five countries have signed the treaty.[88]

4. Scope

The Convention is broken up into four main segments, with each segment consisting of several articles. The first section outlines the substantive criminal laws and the common legislation all ratifying countries must adopt to prevent these offenses.[89] The second section delineates the prosecutorial and procedural requirements to which individual countries must adhere.[90] The third section sets out guidelines for international cooperation that most commonly involve joint investigations of the criminal offenses set out in section one.[91] Finally, the fourth section contains the articles pertaining to the signing of the Convention, territorial application of the Convention,

---

82. Convention, supra note 6, pmbl.

83. Id.

84. Id.

85. Lawrence Speer, Computer Crime: Council of Europe Cybercrime Treaty Attacked by ISPs, Business at Hearing, 6 COMPUTER TECH. L. REP. 100 (Mar. 16, 2001).

86. Robyn Blumner, Cyberfear Leading to International Invasion of Privacy, MILWAUKEE J. SENTINEL, June 6, 2000, at 17A.

87. Id.

88. Council of Europe, Chart of Signatures, supra note 76.

89. Convention, supra note 6.

90. Id.

91. Id.

298   J. TRANSNATIONAL LAW & POLICY   [Vol. 12:2

declarations, amendments, withdrawals, and the ever-important, federalism clause.[92]

5. Convention Section 1 – Definitions and Criminal Offenses

Article 1 initially defines four terms vital to the treaty.[93] These terms are vital because they are heavily relied upon throughout the treaty. The treaty first defines "Computer system" as a device consisting of hardware and software developed for automatic processing of digital data.[94] For purposes of this Convention, the second term, "computer data," holds a meaning different than that of normal computer lingo.[95] The data must be "in such a form that it can be directly processed by the computer system."[96] In other words, the data must be electronic or in some other directly processable form.[97]

The third term, "service provider" includes a broad category of entities that play particular roles "with regard to communication or processing of data on computer systems."[98] This definition not only includes public or private entities, but it also extends to include "those entities that store or otherwise process data on behalf of" public or private entities.[99]

The fourth defined term is "traffic data," which has created some controversy in this Convention. "Traffic data" is generated by computers in a "chain of communication in order to route" that communication from an origin to its destination.[100] Thus, it is auxiliary to the actual communication.[101] When a Convention party investigates a criminal offense within this treaty, "traffic data" is used to trace the source of the communication.[102] "Traffic data" lasts for only a short period of time and the Convention makes Internet Service Providers ("ISPs") responsible for preservation of this data.[103] The increased costs placed upon ISPs as a result of the Convention's stricter rules regarding preservation of "traffic data" is one issue of concern for many ISPs. Another concern is the

---

92. Id.

93. Id. art. 1.

94. Explanatory Report of the Comm. of Ministers [of the Convention on Cybercrime], 109th Sess. (adopted on Nov. 8, 2001), art. 1(a), ¶ 23 [hereinafter Explanatory Report] (on file with the Journal of Transnational Law & Policy).

95. Id. art. 1(b), ¶ 25.

96. Id.

97. Id.

98. Id. art. 1(c), ¶¶ 26, 27.

99. Id.

100. Id. art. 1(d), ¶¶ 28-31.

101. Id.

102. Id.

103. Id.

requirement of rapid disclosure of "traffic data" by ISPs.[104] While rapid disclosure may be necessary to discern the communication's route, in order to collect further evidence or identify the suspect, some civil libertarians express concern over its infringement upon individual rights—namely the right to privacy.

The drafters intended that "Convention parties would not be obliged to copy [the definitions] verbatim into their domestic laws...."[105] It is only required that the respective domestic laws contain concepts that are "consistent with the principles of the Convention and offer an equivalent framework for its implementation."[106]

After defining the vital terms, Article 1 lays out the Convention's substantive criminal laws. The purpose of these criminal laws is to establish a common minimum standard of offenses for all countries.[107] Uniformity in domestic laws prevents abuses from being shifted to a Convention party with a lower standard.[108] The list of offenses is based upon the work of public and private international organizations, such as the United Nations and the Organization for Economic Cooperation and Development.[109]

"All of the offenses contained in the Convention must be committed 'intentionally' for criminal liability to apply."[110] In certain cases, additional specific intentional elements form part of the offense.[111] The drafters have agreed that the exact meaning of "intentional" will be left to the Convention parties to interpret individually.[112] A mens rea requirement is important to filter the number of offenders and to distinguish between serious and minor misconduct.

The criminal offenses in Articles 2 thru 6 were intended by the drafters "to protect the confidentiality, integrity and availability of computer systems or data."[113] At the same time, however, the drafters did not criminalize "legitimate and common activities inherent in the design of networks, or legitimate . . . practices."[114]

---

104. Convention, supra note 6, arts. 17, 30.
105. Explanatory Report, supra note 94, art. 1, ¶ 22.
106. Id.
107. Id. ch. 2, § 1, ¶ 33.
108. Id.
109. Id. ch. 2, § 1, ¶ 34.
110. Id. ch. 2, §1, ¶ 39.
111. Id.
112. Id.
113. Id. tit. 1, ¶ 43.
114. Id.

a. Article 2 – Illegal Access[115]

Article 2 relates to "illegal access," or access to a computer system without right.[116] Examples of unauthorized intrusions are hacking, cracking, or computer trespassing; like those our friend Raymond Torricelli had demonstrated earlier. Intrusions such as these allow hackers to gain access to confidential data, such as passwords and identification numbers.[117] "Access" deals with the entering of any part of a computer system such as hardware components and stored data, but it "does not include the mere sending of an e-mail message" to a file system.[118] Convention parties are granted great latitude with respect to the legislative approach they take in criminalizing this action.[119] Parties can take a wide approach, or a more narrow one, by attaching such qualifying elements as infringing upon security measures, requiring specific intent to obtain computer data, or requiring a dishonest intent justifying criminal culpability.[120]

The analogous United States law to this Article is the Computer Fraud and Abuse Act of 1986 ("CFAA").[121] This Act makes it unlawful to either knowingly access a computer without authorization or to exceed authorization and obtain protected or restricted data.[122] The case of United States v. Ivanov,[123] is an example of the way in which courts would be able to utilize Article 2 in international prosecutions. Ivanov, a Russian computer hacker, was "charged with conspiracy, computer fraud and related activity, extortion, and possession of unauthorized access devices" after hacking into a Connecticut e-commerce corporation's computer files and stealing passwords and credit card information.[124] He then threatened the corporation with extortion while he was in Russia.[125] Ivanov moved to dismiss the indictment "on the ground that court lacked subject matter jurisdiction."[126] Essentially, Ivanov contended that because he was in Russia, the laws of the United States did not apply extraterritorially to him. The district court held that the taking of the corporation's data occurred in Connecticut, the

---

115. Id.
116. Convention, supra note 6, art. 2.
117. Explanatory Report, supra note 94, art. 2, ¶ 47.
118. Id. art. 2, ¶ 46.
119. Id. art. 2, ¶ 49.
120. Id. art. 2, ¶ 50.
121. 18 U.S.C. § 1030 (2000).
122. 18 U.S.C. § 1030(a)(1).
123. 175 F. Supp. 2d 367 (D. Conn. 2001).
124. Id. at 368.
125. Id.
126. Id.

violation of the CFAA occurred when his email was received in Connecticut, and thus the CFAA applied to Ivanov.[127] It would appear on its face that the CFAA is the United States equivalent to this Article. However, the Convention improves upon the CFAA by applying an across the board rule to all signatories thereby ensuring compliance. For instance, in this case, Russia cooperated with United States authorities in extraditing Ivanov to the United States for trial. But if Russia was not so cooperative, Ivanov would have broken a United States law, caused serious damage to a United States corporation and hundreds of citizens, and would be a free man living in another country. This is a situation in which the Convention's global law enforcement network would succeed.

b. Article 3 – Illegal Interception

Article 3, "illegal interception," outlaws the interception, without right, of nonpublic transmissions of computer data, whether it be by telephone, fax, email, or file transfer.[128] This provision is aimed at protecting the right to privacy of data communication.[129] One element of this offense is that the interception occur through "technical means," which is the surveillance of communications "through the use of electronic eavesdropping or tapping devices."[130] The offense also only applies to "nonpublic" transmissions of computer data.[131] This qualification relates only to "the nature of the transmission . . . and not the nature of the data" being transferred.[132] In other words, the data being transmitted may be publicly available, but the parties communicating may wish to remain confidential.[133] This communication can take place from computer to printer, between two computers, or from person to computer (such as typing into a keyboard).[134] For example, the use of common commercial practices, such as "cookies" used to track an individual's surfing habits, are not intended to be criminalized because they are considered be "with right."[135]

This provision does not exhaustively define what sorts of interception are lawful and which ones are unlawful. Therefore, according to the DOJ cybercrime website, nothing in this provision

127. Id. at 374.
128. Convention, supra note 6, art. 3.
129. Explanatory Report, supra note 94, art. 3, ¶ 51.
130. Id. art. 3, ¶ 53.
131. Convention, supra note 6, art. 3.
132. Explanatory Report, supra note 94, art. 3, ¶ 54.
133. Id.
134. Id. art. 3, ¶ 55.
135. Id. art. 3, ¶ 58.

"would change the U.S. wiretap statute (18 U.S.C. 2511(2)(a)(I)), which specifically allows monitoring by a service provider of traffic on its own network undertaken to protect its rights and property."[136]

c. Article 4 – Data Interference

Article 4, criminalizing the destruction of data, aims "to provide computer data and computer programs with protection similar to that enjoyed by" tangible objects against the intentional infliction of damage.[137] The input of malicious codes, viruses, and Trojan horses is thus covered under this criminal code.[138] Convention parties are granted the freedom to require that "serious harm" be committed when legislating this crime, in which the interpretation of what constitutes "serious harm" is left to the respective government.[139]

The United States' statutory equivalent is the Computer Fraud and Abuse Act of 1986.[140] This section prohibits a person from knowingly transmitting "a program, information, code, or command, and as a result of such conduct, intentionally" causing "damage without authorization, to a protected computer."[141] A "protected computer" is defined as a computer "which is used in interstate or foreign commerce or communication."[142] Damage must also occur to "one or more persons,"[143] but courts have held that "one or more persons" includes corporations.[144] In United States v. Middleton, a disgruntled former employee obtained illegal access to his former company's computer system, changed all the administrative passwords, altered the computer's registry, deleted the entire billing system (including programs that ran the billing software), and deleted two internal databases.[145] In response, company employees spent a considerable amount of time repairing the damage and buying new software.[146] The former employee, arrested under section 1030(a)(5)(A), moved to dismiss by alleging that the company was not an "individual" for purposes of the statute.[147] The

---

136. United States Dep't of Justice, Frequently Asked Questions and Answers About the Council of Europe Convention on Cybercrime, at http://www.usdoj.gov/criminal/cybercrime/COEFAQs.htm (last visited Feb. 13, 2003) [hereinafter Frequently Asked Questions].
137. Explanatory Report, supra note 94, art. 4, ¶ 60.
138. Id. art. 4, ¶ 61.
139. Id. art. 4, ¶ 64.
140. Pub. L. No. 99-474, § 2, 100 Stat. 1213 (1986) (amending 18 U.S.C. § 1030).
141. 18 U.S.C. §1030(a)(5)(A).
142. Id. §1030(g)(e)(2)(B).
143. 18 U.S.C. § 1030(e)(8)(A).
144. United States v. Middleton, 231 F.3d 1207, 1210-1211 (9th Cir. 2000).
145. Id. at 1209.
146. Id.
147. Id.

Court of Appeals disagreed, holding that Congress intended the word "individual" to include corporations.[148]

d. Article 5 – System Interference

Article 5, criminalizing "system interference," aims to prevent "the intentional hindering of the lawful use of computer systems."[149] "Hindering," as used in this Article, must be serious enough to rise to the level of criminal conduct.[150] "The drafters considered as 'serious' the sending of data to a particular system in such a form, size, or frequency that it has a significant detrimental effect on the ability of the owner or operator to use the system, or to communicate with other systems. . . ."[151] A common example of a hack criminalized under this section would be a "denial of service attack," a malicious code, such as a virus, that prevents or substantially slows the operation of a computer system leaving the common web surfer unable to access a web page.[152] A questionable example is "spamming," a practice whereby a person or program sends huge quantities of email to a voluminous amount of recipients for two possible purposes: (1) to block the communicating function of the system,[153] or (2) to over-expose enough consumers to advertising that sales of a product are generated.[154] It is arguable that spamming could fall under Article 5 when it reaches the point of computer sabotage in the slowing or shutting down of a computer network or service provider. However, a violation under Article 5 must be committed intentionally, and whether a "spammer" who merely mass advertises has the requisite mens rea will be an important issue that the Council and individual countries will need to resolve.[155]

Besides invoking Article 4 (Data Interference), the spreading of a computer virus would fall under this Article as well. One should consider, for example, the "Melissa" virus, which was launched in 1999 and ultimately caused eighty billion dollars in damage.[156] The virus was set to invade a person's address book and send up to fifty

---

148. Id. at 1211.

149. Explanatory Report, supra note 94, art. 5, ¶ 65.

150. Id. art. 5, ¶ 67.

151. Id.

152. Id.

153. Id.

154. Arosnet Policies, Newsgroup and Email Spamming: What is Spamming? at http://www.aros.net/policies/spam.shtml (last visited Feb. 12, 2003).

155. Explanatory Report, supra note 94, art. 5, ¶ 69.

156. Damien Whitworth & Dominic Kennedy, Author Could Escape Arm of the Law, TIMES (LONDON), May 5, 2000, at A1, available at 2000 WL 2888574.

e-mail messages to addresses stored on the computer.[157] With the rapid spread of the virus and subsequent massive strings of e-mails being sent and received by infected users, companies were forced to shut down their servers.[158]

e. Article 6 – Misuse of Devices

Article 6 establishes, as separate and independent offenses, the intentional commission of illegal acts regarding certain devices that are used in the commission of the named offenses of this Convention.[159] In many cases, black markets are established to facilitate the sale or trade of "hacker tools," or tools used by hackers in the commission of cybercrimes.[160] By prohibiting the production, sale, or distribution of these devices, this Article intends to combat these black market activities.[161] This Article not only covers tangible transfers but also the creation or compilation of hyperlinks facilitating hacker access to these devices.[162] A troubling issue arose with regard to "dual-use devices," or devices that have both a good and evil purpose.[163] In order for the dragnet not to sweep up devices that serve a useful purpose, the drafters intended this Article to relate to devices that "are objectively designed, or adapted, primarily for the purpose of committing an offen[s]e."[164] Finally, in order to avoid overcriminalization, the Article requires both a general intent and also a "specific . . . intent that the device is used for the purpose of committing any of the offen[s]es established in Articles 2 [thru] 5 of the Convention."[165]

f. Article 7 – Computer-Related Forgery

Article 7 outlaws computer-related forgery, or the intentional "input, alteration, deletion, or suppression of computer data resulting in inauthentic data with the intent that it be considered or acted upon for legal purposes as if it were authentic. . . ."[166] The purpose of this Article is to create a parallel offense to the forgery

---

157. Kelly Cesare, Prosecuting Computer Virus Authors: the Need for an Adequate and Immediate International Solution, 14 TRANSNAT'L LAW. 135, 143 (2001) (discussing the impact of the Melissa virus).

158. Id.

159. Explanatory Report, supra note 94, art. 6, ¶ 71.

160. Id.

161. Id. art. 6, ¶ 72.

162. Id.

163. Id. art. 6, ¶ 73.

164. Id.

165. Id. art. 6, ¶ 76.

166. Convention, supra note 6, art. 7.

of tangible documents."[167]   National concepts of forgery differ greatly.[168] Some countries base forgery on the "authenticity as to the author of the document," others base forgery on "truthfulness of the statement contained in the document."[169] In either case, the drafters intended that the minimum standard be the authenticity of the issuer of the data, regardless of the correctness of the actual data.[170] Convention parties are permitted to further define the genuineness of the data if they so choose.[171]

g. Article 8 – Computer-Related Fraud

Article 8 makes computer-related fraud illegal.[172] Computer-related fraud is the intentional causing of a loss of property by deletion or alteration of computer data, "interference with the functioning of a computer system, with fraudulent or dishonest intent of procuring without right, an economic benefit for oneself or for another person."[173] Assets such as electronic funds, deposit money, and credit card numbers have become the target of hackers, who feed incorrect data into the computer with the intention of an illegal transfer of property.[174] This Article is specifically intended to criminalize a direct economic or possessory loss of property if the "perpetrator acted with the intent of procuring an unlawful economic gain...."[175] In addition to the general intent requirement, this Article also "requires a specific fraudulent or other dishonest intent to gain an economic or other benefit. . . ."[176] This specific intent requirement is another effort by the drafters to filter serious misconduct from minor crimes.

This Article is an international tool of legislation that is greatly needed. Computer-related fraud in online auction houses, such as eBay, is a growing business for many criminals. The Internet Fraud Complaint Center ("IFCC"), a partnership between the Federal Bureau of Investigation ("FBI") and the National White Collar Crime Center ("NW3C"), reported that 1.3 million transactions per day take place on Internet auction sites.[177] Auction fraud through

---

167. Explanatory Report, supra note 94, art. 7, ¶ 81.

168. Id. art. 7, ¶ 82.

169. Id.

170. Id.

171. Id.

172. Convention, supra note 6, art. 8.

173. Id.

174. Explanatory Report, supra note 94, art. 8, ¶ 86.

175. Id. art. 8, ¶ 88.

176. Id. art. 8, ¶ 90.

177. INTERNET FRAUD COMPLAINT CENTER, FEDERAL BUREAU OF INVESTIGATION, INTERNET AUCTION FRAUD, May 2001, at http://www1.ifccfbi.gov/strategy/AuctionFraud Report.pdf (last

306   J. TRANSNATIONAL LAW & POLICY   [Vol. 12:2

the Internet ranks as the most prevalent type of fraud committed over the Internet, and it comprises sixty-four percent of all fraud reported.[178] This fraud results in a loss of almost four million dollars per calendar year.[179] The creation of a uniform criminal structure that outlaws the practice of fraud across the globe and facilitates the cooperation of countries in policing and preventing fraud in the sales of merchandise online, is a positive step toward securing the Internet as a safe place to do business. This Article will strengthen consumer confidence on the Internet and promote greater usage and integration into our lives.

h. Article 9 – Offenses Related to Child Pornography

Article 9 seeks to strengthen protective measures against sexual exploitation of children by modernizing current criminal law provisions.[180] Many countries, like the United States, already criminalize the traditional production and distribution of child pornography.[181] However, unlike the United States, some countries fail to expand this prohibition to electronic transmissions.[182] The treaty uses the term "minor" to refer to children under the age of eighteen.[183] This is in accordance with the definition of child under the United Nations Convention on the Rights of the Child.[184] However, the drafters recognized that some countries have a lower age for "minors" and allow Convention parties to set "a different age-limit, provided it is not less than 16 years [of age]."[185]

The United States already has a law on the books dealing with child pornography.[186] The Protection of Children from Sexual Predators Act makes it illegal to knowingly possess one or more child pornographic images that have been transmitted in interstate or foreign commerce, which includes possession of such images on a computer.[187] If the treaty were to be ratified, it is likely the defenses attempted by defendants to prosecution under United States law would also be attempted in prosecutions under the Convention. Defendants have argued, albeit unsuccessfully, that

---

visited Feb. 12, 2003).

178. Id.

179. Id.

180. Explanatory Report, supra note 94, art. 9, ¶ 91.

181. Id. art. 9, ¶ 93.

182. Id.

183. Id. art. 9, ¶ 104.

184. Id.

185. Id.

186. 18 U.S.C. § 2252 (2000), as amended by Protection of Children from Sexual Predators Act of 1998, Pub. L. No. 105-314, § 203(a)(1), 112 Stat. 2977, 2978 (1998).

187. See id. § 2252(a)(4)(B).

computer files are not "visual depictions" as defined in the United States Code.[188] This apparently would not change, since the treaty makes it a crime to possess child pornography on a computer system, thus making any child pornographic image on a computer a criminal offense.[189] Defendants have also argued that the images had been deleted, and thus, the images were not in their "possession" within the meaning of section 2252.[190] However, the government can point to other sources of evidence to prove possession, such as floppy disks, CD-Roms, and computer logs.[191]

Article 9 also makes virtual child pornography unlawful. Virtual child pornography is similar to real child pornography in that it appears to depict minors in sexually explicit situations, but it has one significant difference: it is produced through means that do not involve the use of children.[192] This can be accomplished through the use of adult actors that look like children, through computer-generated images, or through a process known as "morphing."[193] Morphing is the alteration of innocent pictures of children into sexually explicit depictions.[194]

The production, possession, and distribution of virtual child pornography was unlawful under 18 U.S.C. §§ 2252 and 2256. However, in Ashcroft v. Free Speech Coalition, the United States Supreme Court held that two key provisions of § 2256 were overbroad and unconstitutional.[195] This holding has tremendous impact on any future ratification of the Convention into United States law. Ashcroft held that the statute criminalized speech that is protected under the First Amendment.[196] The government, in arguing in favor of criminalizing virtual child pornography, made similar arguments to those of the drafters of the Convention.[197] First, the government argued that virtual child pornography can be used to lure or seduce children into performing illegal acts.[198] The Court found this argument unpersuasive because it was not the least restrictive means necessary to accomplish the government's objective.[199] The Court stated that many inherently innocent objects could be used to seduce children, including candy and video games,

---

188. United States v. Hocking, 129 F.3d 1069, 1070 (9th Cir. 1997).

189. Convention, supra note 6, art. 9.

190. United States v. Lacy, 119 F.3d 742, 747 (9th Cir. 1997).

191. Id.

192. Ashcroft v. Free Speech Coalition, 535 U.S. 234, 239 (2002).

193. Id. at 242.

194. Id.

195. Id. at 258 (holding 18 U.S.C. §§ 2256(8)(B), 2256(8)(D) unconstitutional as overbroad).

196. Id. at 256-58.

197. Explanatory Report, supra note 94, art. 9, ¶ 93.

198. Ashcroft, 535 U.S. at 251.

199. Id. at 252-54.

and therefore it is axiomatic that the government cannot ban speech intended for adults merely because it may fall into the hands of children.[200] Next, like the Convention's drafters, the government argued that virtual child pornography whets the appetites of pedophiles and encourages them to engage in illegal conduct.[201] The Court responded that this is also not a justification for the statute, because the government "cannot constitutionally premise legislation on the desirability of controlling a person's private thoughts."[202] This is a cornerstone upon which the First Amendment was built.[203] The government next argued that virtual images are indistinguishable from real ones, part of the same market, and often exchanged.[204] The Court found this unpersuasive as well, stating that virtual images cannot be "virtually indistinguishable," because otherwise the illegal images would be driven from the market by the indistinguishable substitutes. The Court reasoned that "few pornographers would risk prosecution by abusing real children if fictional, computerized images would suffice."[205]

Finally, the government argued that the "possibility of producing images by using computer imaging makes it . . . difficult . . . to prosecute those who produce pornography by using real children."[206] The government felt it would have difficulty in saying whether the pictures were made by using real children or by using computer imaging, and therefore the only solution is to prohibit both kinds of images.[207] The Court was unpersuaded by this argument as well, holding that the government cannot prohibit lawful speech as a means to ensnare unlawful speech.[208]

The application of the arguments made in Ashcroft are extremely relevant to the justifications for Article 9, as their policy justifications and prohibitions run parallel. As the situation currently stands, with sections 2256(8)(B) and 2256(8)(D) unconstitutional, the United States would be forced to take a limited reservation to Article 9 should it decide to ratify the Convention.

---

200. Id.
201. Id. at 253.
202. Id. (quoting Stanley v. Georgia, 394 U.S. 557, 566 (1969)).
203. Ashcroft, 535 U.S. at 253.
204. Id. at 254.
205. Id.
206. Id.
207. Id.
208. Id.

i. Article 10 – Offenses Related to the Infringements of Copyright and Related Rights

Additionally, Article 10 relates to those offenses that "are among the most commonly committed offen[s]es on the Internet. . . . The reproduction and dissemination on the Internet of protected works, without the approval of the copyright holder, are extremely frequent."[209] Copyright offenses "must be committed 'willfully' for criminal liability to apply."[210] "Willfully" was substituted for "intentionally," because this term is employed in the Agreement on Trade-Related Aspects of Intellectual Property Rights ("TRIPS"), which governs the obligations to criminalize copyright violations.[211]

j. Article 11 – Attempt and Aiding or Abetting

Article 11 establishes offenses related to attempting or aiding and abetting "the commission of the offenses defined in the Convention."[212] Liability under this Article arises when "the person who commits a crime established in the Convention is aided by another who also intends that the crime be committed."[213] For example, the transmission of a virus is an act that triggers the operation of a number of articles of the Convention. However, transmission can only take place through an ISP. "A service provider that does not have the requisite criminal intent cannot incur liability under this section."[214] Therefore, there is no duty under this section for an ISP to actively monitor content in order to avoid criminal liability under this section.[215]

k. Article 12 – Corporate Liability

This Article "deals with the liability of legal persons."[216] Four conditions must be met in order to establish liability.[217] First, a described offense must have been committed.[218] Second, it must have been committed to benefit a legal person.[219] Third, a person who is in a "leading position" must be the one who committed the

---

209. Explanatory Report, supra note 94, art. 10, ¶ 107.
210. Id. art. 10, ¶ 113.
211. Id.
212. Id. art. 11, ¶ 118.
213. Id. art. 11, ¶ 119.
214. Id.
215. Id.
216. Id. art. 12, ¶ 123.
217. Id. art. 12, ¶ 124.
218. Id.
219. Id.

offense, which could include a director.[220] Finally, "the person who has a leading position must have acted . . . within the scope of his or her authority to engage the liability of the legal person."[221] In the case of an offense committed by an agent or employee of the corporation, the offense must have been made possible by the leading person's "failure to take appropriate and reasonable measures to prevent employees or agents from committing criminal activities on behalf of the [corporation]. . . ."[222] Appropriate and reasonable measures are determined by examining the type of business, its size, the standards or established business practices, and other like factors.[223] However, liability of a corporation does not exclude individual liability.[224]

l. Article 13 – Sanctions and Measures

Article 13 completes Section 1 of the Convention by requiring Convention parties to provide criminal sanctions that are "effective, proportionate, and dissuasive" and "include the possibility of imposing prison sentences."[225] The drafters intended that this Article leave discretionary power to Convention parties "to create a system of criminal offences and sanctions" that are compatible with their existing national legal systems.[226]

6.   Convention Section 2 – Prosecutorial and Procedural Requirements

The articles in this section describe procedural measures that Convention parties must take "at the national level for the purpose of criminal investigation of the offences established in Section 1."[227] This section is intended to overcome some of the challenges associated with policing the ever-expanding information highway.[228] Some of those challenges are: (1) the difficulty in identifying the perpetrator, (2) the difficulty in determining "the extent and impact of the criminal act," (3) the difficulty in dealing with the volatility of electronic data, and (4) the difficulty in maintaining the speed and secrecy vital in the success of a cybercrime investigation.[229]

---

220. Id.
221. Id.
222. Id. art. 12, ¶ 125.
223. Id.
224. Id. art. 12, ¶ 127.
225. Id. art. 13, ¶ 128.
226. Id. art. 13, ¶ 130.
227. Id. art. 13, § 2, ¶ 131.
228. Id. art. 13, § 2, ¶ 132.
229. Id. art. 13, § 2, ¶ 133.

These challenges pose major problems for investigators since electronic data can be altered, moved, or deleted within seconds, which may very well be the only evidence in a criminal investigation.[230]

One way in which the Convention overcomes these problems is by adapting traditional procedures, like search and seizure, to an ever-changing technological landscape.[231] However, in order to make these traditional crime investigation methods effective, new measures have been created.[232] Examples of those measures include the expedited preservation of data, "[the] real-time collection of traffic data, and the interception of content data."[233]

a. Article 15 – Conditions and Safeguards

Article 15 establishes minimum safeguards upon the procedures instituted within Convention party legal systems, which may be provided constitutionally, legislatively, or judicially.[234] Parties are to ensure that their safeguards provide for the adequate protection of human rights and liberties.[235] However, the Convention only refers to parties who have human rights obligations under previously signed treaties.[236] The Convention seemingly leaves the point moot for parties that have not signed any international human rights treaties.[237] Opponents to the Convention argue that the treaty infringes upon basic human rights and liberties, most notably the right to privacy.

b. Article 16 – Expedited Preservation of Stored Computer Data

Article 16 relates to the expedited preservation of stored computer data, a new measure implemented in order to facilitate the investigation of cybercrimes.[238] This Article applies only to data that has already been collected and retained by ISPs.[239] One must not confuse "data preservation" with "data retention."[240] For purposes of this Article, data retention merely relates to the protection from deterioration of data already existing in stored

---

230. Id.
231. Id. art. 13, § 2, ¶ 134.
232. Id.
233. Id.
234. Id. art. 15, ¶ 145.
235. Id.
236. Convention, supra note 6, art. 15.
237. Id.
238. Id. art. 16.
239. Explanatory Report, supra note 94, tit. 2, ¶ 149.
240. Id. art. 15, tit. 2, ¶ 151.

form.[241] On the other hand, data retention, or the process of storing and compiling data, does not apply under this Article.[242] The concept of "data preservation" is a new legal power in many domestic laws, brought about by because of the ability for computer data to be destroyed or lost through careless handling and storage processes.[243] The statute operates in one of two ways: (1) the competent authorities in the Convention party country simply access, seize and secure the relevant data, or (2) where a reputable business is involved, competent authorities can issue an order to preserve the relevant data.[244] Convention parties are thus required to introduce a power that would enable law enforcement authorities to order the preservation of data for a particular period of time not exceeding 90 days.[245] Data such as this is frequently stored only for short periods of time, since these laws are designated to protect privacy and because the costs are high when preserving this type of data.[246]

c. Article 17 – Expedited Preservation and Partial Disclosure of Traffic Data

Article 17 establishes specific obligations with respect to the preservation of "traffic data" under Article 16. In addition, it provides for quick disclosure of some "traffic data," so authorities can identify the person or persons who have distributed such things as child pornography or computer viruses.[247] Recall that "traffic data" merely indicates where and how a virus or email was transmitted, but not who transmitted it or what it contained.[248] This section is most important when considering the following example. Often, more than one service provider is

> involved in the transmission of a communication. Each service provider may possess some 'traffic data' related to the transmission of the specified communication, which either has been generated and retained by that service provider in relation to the

---

241. Id.
242. Id. art. 15, tit. 2, ¶¶ 151, 152.
243. Id. art. 15, tit. 2, ¶ 155.
244. Id.
245. Id. tit. 2, ¶ 156.
246. Id. art. 17, ¶ 166.
247. Id. art. 17, ¶¶ 165, 166.
248. Id. art. 1(d), ¶¶ 28-31.

[actual] passage of the communication through its system or has been provided [by] other [ISPs].[249]

For commercial, security or technical purposes, sometimes "traffic data" is shared among the service providers involved.[250]

> In such a case, any one of the service providers may possess the crucial traffic data that is needed to determine the source or destination of the communication. Often, however, no single service provider possesses enough of the [important 'traffic data'] to be able to determine the actual source or destination of the communication. Each possesses one part of the puzzle, and each of these parts needs to be examined in order to identify the source or destination.[251]

The preferred method for accomplishing the expedited preservation and partial disclosure of "traffic data" is to enact legislation enabling authorities to obtain a single order, the scope of which would apply to all ISPs involved in a communication and "[t]his comprehensive order could be served sequentially on each service provider identified in the order."[252]

d. Article 18 – Production Order

Article 18 relates to production orders, which specifically allow "competent authorities to compel a person in its territory to provide specified stored computer data" or to compel an ISP to provide subscriber information.[253] This Article strictly relates to production of stored or existing data, not "traffic data" or "content data related to future communications."[254] Production orders precede search and seizure as a means of obtaining specific data.[255]

e. Article 19 – Search and Seizure of Stored Computer Data

Article 19, which relates to search and seizure, aims at modernizing and harmonizing differing domestic laws.[256] In many

---

249. Id. art. 17, ¶ 167.
250. Id.
251. Id.
252. Id. art. 17, ¶ 168.
253. Id. art. 18, ¶ 170.
254. Id.
255. Id. art. 18, ¶ 175.
256. Id. art. 19, ¶ 184.

314   J. TRANSNATIONAL LAW & POLICY   [Vol. 12:2

countries, stored computer data is not considered a tangible object, and thus, cannot be searched and seized in the same manner as a tangible object.[257] This Article aims to establish an equivalent search and seizure power ranging from tangible objects to stored computer data.[258] The preconditions required to search and seize traditional property, such as probable cause, will remain the same.[259]

However, additional procedural provisions are necessary "to ensure that computer data can be obtained in a manner . . . equally effective to a search and seizure [for] a tangible data carrier."[260] There are a number of reasons for this:

> [F]irst, the data is in intangible form. . . . Second, while the data may be read with the use of computer equipment, it cannot be seized and taken away in the same sense as [tangible goods]. . . . Third, due to [interconnected networks], data may not be stored in the particular computer that is searched, but such data may be readily accessible to that system.[261]

In the second case, either the physical medium on which the intangible data is stored must be seized or taken away, or a copy of the data must be made in either tangible form, such as a computer printout, or in intangible form, such as a diskette, before the tangible or intangible medium containing the copy can be seized and taken away.[262]

f. Article 20 – Real-Time Collection of Traffic Data

Article 20 takes into account the importance of collecting "traffic data" to determine the source or destination of the cybercrime being committed.[263] "Like real-time interception of content data, real-time collection of 'traffic data' is only effective if undertaken without the knowledge" of the suspect.[264] Therefore, ISPs knowledgeable about the interception must be required to maintain complete secrecy in order for this to be successful.[265] One way to achieve the necessary

---

257. Id.
258. Id.
259. Id. art. 19, ¶ 186.
260. Id. art. 19, ¶ 187.
261. Id.
262. Id.
263. Id. art. 20, ¶ 216.
264. Id. art. 20, ¶ 225.
265. Id.

secrecy is by relieving the service provider of any contractual or legal obligation to notify its customers about the data being collected.[266] This can be accomplished through a law requiring confidentiality, or by threatening an obstruction of justice charge against the ISP should it fail.

g. Article 21 –Interception of Content Data

Article 21, "interception of content data," has traditionally been carried out through governmental monitoring of telephone conversations.[267] However, recently, the rising popularity of communication through the Internet has made "tapping the net" a priority for law enforcement officials. The fact that computers are capable of transmitting not only words but also visual images and sounds makes it even easier for crimes to be committed.[268] "Content data refers to the communication content of the communication," or in other words, the gist of the message.[269]

h. Article 22 – Jurisdiction

Article 22 simply establishes that member countries must enact laws enabling them to have jurisdiction over all the previous crimes described above should they occur in any one of four places: (1) in the member country's territory, (2) on board a ship flying the flag of that country, (3) on board an aircraft registered under the laws of that country, or (4) outside the territory of the country but committed by one of its nationals.[270] A party would establish territorial jurisdiction if the person attacking the computer system and the victim were located within the country, or where the victim was inside the territory but the attacker was not.[271] The remaining jurisdictional sections are rather self-explanatory.

7. Convention Section 3 – International Cooperation

This section contains a series of provisions relating to the mutual legal assistance member countries must afford each other under the Convention.[272] This section causes grave concern for many United States businesses and interest groups.[273] This concern

---

266. Id. art. 20, ¶ 226.
267. Id. art. 21, ¶ 228.
268. Id.
269. Id. art. 21, ¶ 229.
270. Convention, supra note 6, art. 22.
271. Explanatory Report, supra note 94, art. 22, ¶ 233.
272. Id. ch. 3, ¶ 240.
273. See Mike Godwin, International Treaty on Cybercrime Poses Burden on High Tech

stems from the fact that although it may not be such a big deal to have the United States government wield greater power, the same new powers will also be given to member countries that may not "have a strong tradition of checks and balances on police power."[274] United States companies do not want foreign investigators searching through domestic computer systems based on a warrant issued under the Convention.[275]

The following example illustrates why United States companies should have cause for concern. Suppose a Seattle University law student, while researching a potential research topic, corresponds by e-mail with an Al-Qaeda member in Italy. A few days later the unknowing student finds federal agents examining the files on his home computer. The agents also visit the student's ISP, Seattle University, to retrieve records of the student's computer usage. The agents are basing their authority on a warrant that was issued by Italian authorities, which allows them to search for Al Qaeda locations and documents. Italian officials framed their warrant in terms of "suspected terrorist activity." Maybe the student should have anticipated this scenario, given the vigor with which the world is cracking down on Al-Qaeda members. Even if the law student is willing to run the risk, and bear the burden, of this kind of search, should Seattle University?

Larger ISPs, such as America Online, get dozens of search warrants and subpoenas every month. This treaty would change everything by not only requiring them to respond to those submitted by United States law enforcement officials, they would also have to respond to warrants and court orders from dozens of nations. All ISPs, phone companies, and other businesses would be forced into cooperating with investigations. This equates to higher storage, investigative and retrieval costs for this extra data. These higher costs would likely be passed down to the consumer in the form of higher monthly service rates.

The opposing argument is plausible, however; ISPs should expect this sort of intrusion as a cost of doing business in the Internet era. The problem again lies in the fact that these added costs will be passed down to the consumer. Additionally, if two companies have cabled together two computers, the second company could be forced to comply with investigations of other ISPs, which would cause even more problems.

Companies, IP WORLDWIDE, Apr. 4, 2001, at http://www.law.com/servlet/ContentServer?pagename=OpenMarket/Xcelerate/View&c=LawArticle&cid=1015973978355&live=true&cst=1&pc=0&pa=0.
274. Id.
275. Id.

a. Article 23 – General Principles Relating to International Cooperation

Article 23 begins this section by outlining "general principles" of mutual legal assistance. Cooperation is to be extended for all crimes described above, as well as for the collection of data and evidence in electronic form for the criminal offense.[276]

b. Article 24 – Extradition

Article 24 deals with extradition of criminals between member countries. "The obligation to extradite applies only to" those crimes committed in Articles 2 thru 11.[277] A threshold penalty also exists to minimize the massive extradition of criminals.[278] Under certain offenses, like illegal access (Article 2) and data interference (Article 4), member countries are permitted to impose short periods of incarceration.[279] Accordingly, extradition can only be sought where the maximum penalty is at least one year in jail.[280]

Important policy considerations are furthered by adding an extradition provision. By all the countries prosecuting the same crimes and sending criminals from one jurisdiction to another, criminals effectively cannot hide from the law when committing a crime within the Convention's jurisdiction. Because the deterrence of crime is an important policy goal of any criminal law statute, as well as this Convention, the extradition provision strengthens the entire Convention. In fact, extradition laws governing computer crimes are "hopelessly outdated and therefore, lagging behind the forces they are trying to regulate."[281] This lack of uniformity results in lax treatment of cybercriminals, allowing them to escape law enforcement officials by fleeing to countries unwilling to extradite a suspected criminal. This Convention provision is an important step in harmonizing extradition laws between member countries and bringing reluctant countries up to date.

---

276. Explanatory Report, supra note 94, art. 23, ¶ 243.

277. Id. art. 24, ¶ 245.

278. Id.

279. Id.

280. Id.

281. Cesare, supra note 157, at 153 (quoting John T. Soma et. al., Transnational Extradition for Computer Crimes: Are New Treaties and Laws Needed? 34 HARV. J. ON LEGIS. 317, 317-18 (1997)).

c. Article 25 – General Principles Relating to Mutual Assistance

Article 25 requires mutual assistance "to the widest extent possible."[282] Provisions from this Article include communications which are made through email and other means. For the most part, this treaty section is considered harmless, and therefore this section is uncontested by civil libertarians.

d. Article 26 – Spontaneous Information

Article 26 discusses "spontaneous information" and refers to those times when a member country obtains vital information to a case that it believes may assist another member country in a criminal investigation or proceeding.[283] In these situations, the member country that does not have the data may not even know it exists, and thus will never generate a request for such data. This section empowers the country with the "spontaneous information" to forward it to applicable foreign officials without a prior request.[284] While this might seem obvious and needless to a United States citizen, this provision is very useful in an multilateral treaty such as this, because under the laws of some member states, "a positive grant of legal authority is needed in order to" effectuate the provision of assistance absent a request.[285]

e. Article 27 – Procedures Pertaining to Mutual Assistance Requests In the Absence of Applicable International Agreements

Article 27 relates to mutual assistance in the absence of applicable international agreements. In other words, it establishes a mutual set of rules when parties are not already obliged under the European Convention on Mutual Assistance in Criminal Matters and its Protocol, or other similar treaties.[286] The terms of applicable agreements can be supplemental to the Convention as long as member countries continue to also apply the terms of this provision.[287] Parties must establish a central authority "responsible for sending and answering requests for [assistance]."[288] This is particularly helpful in expediting the rapid transmission of information in combating and prosecuting cybercrimes.[289]

---

282. Explanatory Report, supra note 94, art. 25, ¶ 253.
283. Id. art. 26, ¶¶ 260, 261.
284. Id. art. 26, ¶ 260.
285. Id.
286. Id. art. 27, ¶ 262.
287. Id. art. 27, ¶ 263.
288. Convention, supra note 6, art. 27.
289. Explanatory Report, supra note 94, art. 27, ¶ 265.

One important objective of this section "is to ensure that its domestic laws governing the admissibility of evidence are fulfilled," so that the evidence can be used before the court.[290] To ensure that this result is accomplished, member countries are required to "execute requests in accordance with procedures specified by the requesting party" so its domestic laws are not infringed.[291] This is required, unless the request violates the host country's domestic laws, then the county is not obliged to follow.[292] For example, a procedural requirement of one party may be that a witness statement be given under oath. "Even if the requested party does not" have this requirement, "it should honur [sic] the requesting party's request."[293]

f. Article 28 – Confidentiality and Limitation on Use

Article 28 specifically provides for confidentiality and limitations on use of information in order to preserve sensitive materials of a host country. This Article only applies when no mutual assistance treaty exists.[294] When such a treaty already exists, its provision apply in lieu of this provision, unless the countries agree otherwise.[295] Two types of confidentiality requests can be made by member countries. First, a party "may request that the information or material furnished be kept confidential where the request could not be complied with in the absence of such condition."[296] "Second, the requested party may make furnishing of the information or material dependent upon the condition that it not be used for investigations or proceedings other than those stated in the request."[297]

g. Article 29 – Expedited Preservation of Stored Computer Data

Article 29, mutual assistance related to the expedited preservation of stored computer data, is in most respects identical to Article 16, except that it relates to international cooperation. Drafters agreed that a mechanism needed to be in place to ensure the availability of this type of data when a lengthier and more involved process of a mutual assistance request is handled.[298]

---

290. Id. art. 27, ¶ 267.
291. Id.
292. Id.
293. Id.
294. Id. art. 28, ¶ 276.
295. Id.
296. Id. art. 28, ¶ 277.
297. Id. art. 28, ¶ 278.
298. Id. art. 29, ¶ 282.

h. Article 30 – Expedited Disclosure of Preserved Traffic Data

Likewise, Article 30, mutual assistance related to the expedited disclosure of preserved "traffic data," is the mutual assistance arm of Article 17.[299] Therefore, it needs little discussion.

i. Article 31 – Mutual Assistance Regarding Accessing of Stored Computer Data

Article 31 requires that each member country have the ability to search, access, or seize "data stored by means of a computer system located within its territory" for the benefit of another member country.[300] Paragraph one authorizes a member country to request this type of assistance, and paragraph two requires the host country to provide it.[301]

j. Article 32 – Trans-Border Access to Stored Computer Data With Consent or Where Publicly Available

Article 32 deals with "[t]rans border access to stored computer data with consent or where publicly available," which merely makes it permissible for a publicly available source of data to be available to a member country unilaterally and without a mutual assistance request, while at the same time, not preparing a comprehensive, legally binding system.[302]

k. Article 33 – Mutual Assistance Regarding the Real-Time Collection of Traffic Data

Article 33 makes it law that each party is obliged to collect real time "traffic data" for another member country.[303]

l. Article 34 – Mutual Assistance Regarding the Interception of Content Data

Article 34 is another hot button issue in this treaty because it discusses the cooperation and sharing of information obtained through means such as eavesdropping and wiretapping. In addition, it relates to the mutual assistance regarding the interception of content data.[304] The assistance provided in this

---

299. Id. art. 30, ¶ 290.
300. Id. art. 31, ¶ 292.
301. Id.
302. Id. art. 32, ¶ 293.
303. Id. art. 33, ¶ 295.
304. Id. art. 34, ¶ 297.

provision is limited by the mutual assistance regimes already in place and the domestic laws already enacted.[305]

m. Article 35 – 24/7 Network

Article 35 is a very interesting provision. The "24/7 network" is a way to effectively combat crimes committed through the use of computer systems when those crimes require a rapid response. This Article obligates each country to designate a point of contact that is available 24 hours per day, 7 days a week.[306] This Article was considered by the drafters to be one of the most important means of effectively responding to law enforcement challenges posed by cybercrimes.[307]

8. Convention Section 4 – Final Provisions

a. Article 36 – Signature and Entry Into Force

Article 36, entitled "Signature and entry into force," allows non-COE states to become signatories, in addition to COE states who had participated in drafting the Convention.[308] The Convention does not enter into force until five countries have ratified it, three of which must be COE states.[309]

b. Article 37 – Accession to the Convention

Article 37 deals with those states which have not participated in the drafting but, nevertheless, are interested in signing and ratifying the treaty.[310] A formal procedure is required "to invite a non-member State to accede" which requires a two-thirds majority to be present in addition to a "unanimous vote of the representatives of the contracting parties" in order for the state to accede.[311]

c. Article 38 – Territorial Application

Article 38, "territorial application," simply provides that a member country must express to which territories it intends the Convention to apply upon signature and ratification.[312]

---

305. Id.
306. Id. art. 35, ¶ 298.
307. Id.
308. Id. art. 36, ¶ 304.
309. Id. art. 36, ¶ 305.
310. Id. art. 37, ¶ 306.
311. Id.
312. Convention, supra note 6, art. 38(1).

322   J. TRANSNATIONAL LAW & POLICY   [Vol. 12:2

d. Article 39 – Effects of Convention

Article 39 relates to the Convention's relationship with other international agreements, particularly how pre-existing conventions of the COE should relate to each other or to other treaties concluded outside the COE.[313] In particular, member countries should adhere to "the rule of interpretation lex specialis derogat legi generali," or in other words, precedent should be given to the rules contained in this Convention.[314]

e. Article 40 -- Declarations

Article 40, "[d]eclarations," refers to certain articles contained within the Convention that permit parties to include specific "additional elements which modify the scope of the provisions."[315] Also, these elements were added to accommodate certain legal differences between member countries.[316] These "should be distinguished from 'reservations,' which permit a party to exclude or modify the legal effect of certain obligations set forth in the Convention."[317]

f. Article 41 – Federalism Clause

Article 41 is another important clause added to the Convention. The "federalism clause" allows for a special kind of declaration that is intended to accommodate the difficulties certain countries might face with regimes that distribute power between central and regional authorities.[318] The Convention was originally crafted with countries that had non-federalist governmental regimes in mind. In other words, the Convention was crafted with European countries in mind, which have one single police power. Countries such as the United States that have federal—as well as state—laws, would have been unable to sign the treaty without a federalism clause.[319] The reason is that some computer crimes committed wholly within a state would be considered state crimes, even though the federal government could ratify the treaty. Additionally, if the individual states did not consent to the Convention application, or consent to the new federal law, then the treaty would not extend to all

---

313. Explanatory Report, supra note 94, art. 39, ¶ 308.
314. Id. art. 39, ¶ 309.
315. Id. art. 40, ¶ 315.
316. Id.
317. Id.
318. Id. art. 41, ¶ 316.
319. Id. art. 41, ¶ 317.

territories within a state.[320] The COE added this clause so
countries, such as the United States, would ratify this agreement.
This clause is a source of controversy for many non-federalist
countries because they are skeptical of the extent to which non-
federalist countries can convince their constituent state
governments to adhere to the treaty provisions.

g. Articles 42 & 43 – Reservations and Status and Withdrawal
of Reservations

Articles 42 and 43 allow certain reservations to be made at the
time of signature or ratification for those allowable reservations
enumerated within the Convention.[321]

h. Article 44 -- Amendments

Article 44 allows for amendments to be made to the
Convention.[322] Any amendments adopted would come into force only
when all of the member countries "have informed the Secretary
General of their acceptance."[323]

i. Article 45 – Settlement of Disputes

Article 45 "provides that the European Committee on Crime
Problems ("CDPC") should be kept informed about the
interpretation and application of the provisions of the
Convention."[324] Three means of dispute resolution are provided
within this section, which are the CDPC, "an arbitral tribunal or the
International Court of Justice" ("ICJ").[325]

j. Article 46 – Consultation of the Parties

Article 46 creates a framework for the Parties to consult
regarding implementation of the Convention, the effect of significant
legal, policy or technological developments pertaining to the subject
of computer or computer related crime and the collection of evidence
in electronic form, and the possibility of supplementing or amending
the Convention.[326]

---

320. See id.
321. Id. art. 42, ¶¶ 320, 321.
322. Convention, supra note 6, art. 44.
323. Explanatory Report, supra note 94, art. 44, ¶ 325.
324. Id. art. 45, ¶ 326.
325. Id. art. 45, ¶ 327.
326. Id. art. 46, ¶ 328.

k. Article 47 -- Denunciation

Article 47 permits a member country to denounce the Convention.[327] A country's denunciation would "become effective on the first day of the month following the expiration of a period of three months after the date of receipt" and notification by the Secretary General.[328]

l. Article 48 – Notification

Article 48 requires notification to member countries of signatories and ratifications when they occur.[329]

m. Secret "Second Protocol"

Additionally, the COE may add a secret 'Second Protocol' to the treaty, which would cover the decoding of terrorist messages on the Internet.[330] It is certain that this new addition will come under heavy attack, particularly since privacy groups and civil libertarians have strongly voiced their opposition to the "existing cybercrime treaty for the last two years."[331]

IV. THE ROAD AHEAD

Before ratification by the United States, the Convention will face a myriad of oppositional forces. Those opposing the Convention make a number of compelling arguments: (1) the Convention curtails freedom of expression online, (2) the Convention overextends the investigative powers of police and governmental organizations, (3) the Convention demands too much of companies and individuals by requiring them to provide law enforcement with far greater information than is now the norm under most telecommunications laws, and (4) the Convention infringes upon citizen civil liberties.

The second argument made by those opposed to the Convention is that the government is granted an excessive amount of investigatory power, which is best illustrated in the example of call data vs. "traffic data." Presently, law enforcement agencies are allowed to seek call related data, which includes the phone numbers that are dialed and the duration of the calls. However, under the

---

327. Convention, supra note 6, art. 47(1).
328. Id. art. 47(2).
329. Id. art. 48.
330. Council of Europe—Treaty Change May Allow Greater Surveillance of Terrorists, PERISCOPE-DAILY DEF. NEWS CAPSULES, Feb. 21, 2002, available at 2002 WL 5970273.
331. Id.

Convention, law enforcement authorities would have the right to wide-ranging "traffic data," which includes the source, destination, and duration of calls, as well as the type of traffic or the sort of services consulted. Such a request could force an ISP to inform law enforcement agencies that a client visited a particular website for thirty minutes, downloaded ten images, and then sent emails to three specific addresses. Whether this is a violation of a person's right to privacy is an issue hotly contested.

The third argument touches upon the corporate opponents' Convention concerns. ISPs and other related businesses are reluctant to divulge their confidential client records, known as "subscriber data," at the whim of an investigating governmental agency. Companies are also concerned with the increased costs associated with retaining and preserving data should an order be served upon the company to do so. In all likelihood, however, these costs will be passed along to the consumer in the form of higher connection and subscriber fees. Thus, it is ultimately the consumer that will need to weigh the importance of policing cybercrime with the increased cost associated with Internet access when deciding whether to support the Convention.

The fourth argument, that civil liberties will be infringed, appears to be an unfounded concern. Article 15 requires member countries "to establish conditions and safeguards to be applied to the" governmental powers established in Articles 16 thru 21.[332] Those conditions and safeguards are required "to protect human rights and liberties."[333] Article 15 in fact "lists some specific safeguards, such as requiring judicial supervision, that should be applied where appropriate in light of the power or procedure concerned."[334]

V. Conclusion

Cybercrimes are not confined within national borders. A criminal armed with a computer and a connection has the capability to victimize people, businesses, and governments anywhere in the world. The criminal can commit violent crimes, participate in international terrorism, sell drugs, commit identity theft, send viruses, distribute child pornography, steal intellectual property and trade secrets, and illegally access private and commercial computer systems. These criminals can hide their tracks by weaving their communications through numerous ISPs.

---

332. Frequently Asked Questions, supra note 136.
333. Id.
334. Id.

For example, consider a computer hacker in Vancouver, British Columbia, who disrupts a corporation's communications network in Seattle, Washington. Before accessing the corporation's computer, he routes his communication through ISPs in Japan, Italy, and Australia. In such a case, Canadian law enforcement would need assistance from authorities in Tokyo, Rome and Sydney before discovering that the criminal is right in their own backyard.

International crimes such as these have impeded law enforcement efforts in ways never before contemplated. While the Internet is borderless for criminals, law enforcement agencies must respect the sovereignty of other nations. Thus, cooperation with foreign law enforcement agencies in fighting cybercrimes is paramount to any effort to catch these criminals. Unfortunately, differing legal systems and disparities in the law often present major obstacles. This article is intended to be the first inclusive survey and analysis of the Council of Europe's Convention on Cybercrime; the first international legislation designed to harmonize legal systems and those disparities in the law that make combating cybercrime so difficult. This article analyzed critical opinion as well as the drafters' intent regarding specific Convention provisions, while also explaining the purpose of the different articles. It also examined a select number of provisions in depth, determining their impact upon existing United States cybercrime laws. Finally, the author of this article has intended to remain neutral on the topic of whether the Convention is ultimately a positive or negative step forward for both the United States and the world, with the intent that the reader can form his or her own educated opinion upon weighing some of the issues raised in this comment.

[6]

THE CONVENTION ON CYBERCRIME: A HARMONIZED IMPLEMENTATION OF INTERNATIONAL PENAL LAW: WHAT PROSPECTS FOR PROCEDURAL DUE PROCESS?

MIRIAM F. MIQUELON-WEISMANN†

[C]riminal law harmonization is indispensable where a national control is no longer possible . . .: where there is an antagonism between globally operating perpetrators and national criminal law systems . . . In this global area of 'cyberspace,'at least common minimum rules are necessary . . . . On the other hand, there is no urgency to harmonize the *organizational rules* of criminal procedural law . . . highly related to [national differences] in cultural and historical developments . . . .[1]

I. INTRODUCTION

A. THE OPERATIVE DOCUMENTS

The CoE Convention provides a treaty-based framework that imposes three necessary obligations on the participating nations to:

1. enact legislation criminalizing certain conduct related to computer systems;
2. create investigative procedures and ensure their availability to domestic law enforcement authorities to investigate cybercrime offenses, including procedures to obtain electronic evidence in all of its forms; and,
3. create a regime of broad international cooperation, including assistance in extradition of fugitives sought for crimes identified under

---

† Associate Professor, Southern New England School of Law, formerly United States Attorney Southern District of Illinois and served as Assistant Special Counsel to the Office of Special Counsel, John C. Danforth, WACO Investigation.
1. Prof. Dr. Ulrich Sieber, *Memorandum On A European Penal Code*, in Juristenzeitung 369, §§ C(1)(a), C(2)(b) (1997), (available at http://www.jura.uni-muenchen.de/einrichtungen/ls/sieber/article/EMPC/EMPC_englisch) (copy on file with Author).

the CoE Convention.[2]

Notably, the CoE Convention contains significant restrictive language in the areas of transborder search and seizure and data interception, deferring authority to domestic laws and territorial considerations.[3] Also, it does not supercede pre-existing mutual legal assistance treaties ("MLATs") or other reciprocal agreements between parties.

The Official Explanatory Report, accompanying the CoE Convention, was formally adopted by the CoE's Committee of Ministers on November 8, 2001 (the "CoE Explanatory Report").[4] The CoE Explanatory Report provides an analysis of the CoE Convention. Under established CoE practice, such reports reflect the understanding of the parties in drafting treaty provisions and are accepted as fundamental bases for interpretation of CoE conventions,[5] but they do not provide an authoritative interpretation.[6]

B. What is Cybercrime?

Both international cybercrime and domestic cybercrime embrace the same offense conduct, namely, computer-related crimes and traditional offense conduct committed through the use of a computer. International cybercrime expert, Dr. Professor Ulrich Sieber, observes that:

> The ubiquity of information in modern communication systems makes it irrelevant as to where perpetrators and victims of crimes are situated in terms of geography. There is no need for the perpetrator or the victim of a crime to move or to meet in person. Unlawful actions such as computer manipulations in one country can have direct, immediate effects in the computer systems of another country . . . ."[7]

However, the ongoing debate among experts about a precise definition for "computer crime" or a "computer-related crime" remains unresolved. In fact, there is no internationally recognized legal definition of these terms.[8] Instead, functional definitions identifying general offense

---

2. *Letter Of Submittal To President Bush From Secretary Of State Colin Powell*, United States Department of State, reprinted in Convention on Cybercrime, 108th Congress, 1st Session, Treaty Doc.108-11 (2003) at vi.

3. *See Id.* (The United States does not require implementing legislation once the treaty is ratified. According to the Secretary of State's Letter to the President, existing federal law is adequate to meet the requirements of the treaty).

4. Council of Europe *Convention On Cybercrime*, http://conventions.coe.int/Treaty/en/Treaties/Html/185.htm (accessed May 25, 2005) [hereinafter Council of Europe, *Treaty*].

5. *Id.*

6. Council of Europe, *Glossary on the Treaties*, http://conventions.coe.int/Treaty/EN/Glossary.htm (accessed Jan. 17, 2005) [hereinafter Council of Europe, *Glossary*].

7. *See* Sieber, *supra* n. 1.

8. United Nations Crime and Justice Information Network, *International Review of Criminal Policy-United Nations Manual on the Prevention and Control of Computer Re-*

categories are the accepted norms.[9] Thus, the focus shifts away from reaching a global consensus over particular legal definitions, to identifying general categories of offense conduct to be enacted as penal legislation by each participating country.

The targeted unlawful conduct falls into several generally recognized categories. These categories, identified by the United Nations[10] as part of its study of cybercrime, include: fraud by computer manipulation,[11] computer forgery,[12] damage to or modifications of computer data or programs,[13] unauthorized access to computer systems and services,[14] and the unauthorized reproduction of legally protected computer pro-

---

lated Crime ¶ 7, http://www.uncjin.org/Documents/EighthCongress.html (accessed May 25, 2005) [hereinafter *U.N. Manual*].

   9. *Id.*

   10. *See id.* at ¶ 13 (Interestingly, the categories of computer crime identified in the *U.N. Manual* in 1995 appear to serve as the model for the same offense conduct targeted by the Council of Europe Convention on Cybercrime).

   11. *See id.* at ¶¶ 13-14 (Intangible assets represented in data format, such as money on deposit and confidential consumer information, are the most common targets. Improved remote access to databases allows the criminal the opportunity to commit various types of fraud without ever physically entering the victim's premises. The *U.N. Manual* underscores the fact that computer fraud by input manipulation is the most common computer crime, as it is easily perpetrated and difficult to detect. Often referred to as "data diddling" it can be committed by anyone having access to normal data processing functions at the input stage. The *U.N. Manual* also identifies "program manipulation" through the use of a "Trojan Horse" covertly placed in a computer program to allow unauthorized functions and "output manipulation" targeting the output of computer information as other examples of unlawful manipulation).

   12. *See id.* at ¶ 14 (Computer forgery can occur in at least two ways: 1) altering data in documents stored in a computerized form; and, 2) using the computer as a tool to commit forgery through the creation of false documents indistinguishable from the authentic original).

   13. *See id.* at ¶ 15 (This is a form of "computer sabotage" perpetrated by either direct or covert unauthorized access to a computer system by the introduction of new programs known as viruses, worms or logic bombs. A "virus" is a program segment that has the ability to attach itself to legitimate programs, to alter or destroy data or other programs, and to spread itself to other computer programs. A "worm" is similarly constructed to infiltrate and harm data processing systems, but it differs from a virus in that it does not replicate itself. A "logic bomb" is normally installed by an insider based on a specialized knowledge of the system and programs the destruction or modification of data at a specific time in the future. All three can be used as an ancillary part of a larger extortionate scheme that can involve financial gain or terrorism).

   14. *See id.* at ¶ 16 (The motives of the "cracker" or "hacker" may include sabotage or espionage. Access is often accomplished from a remote location along a telecommunication network. Access can be accomplished through several means including insufficiently secure operating system software, lax security, "cracker programs" used to bypass passwords or obtain access through the misuse of legitimate maintenance entry points in the system, or activating illicitly installed "trap doors on the system").

grams.[15] Recent additions to this list include child pornography[16] and the use of computers by members of organized crime and terrorist groups to commit computer-related crimes and/or a wide variety of crimes involving traditional offense conduct.[17]

C. HISTORICAL DEVELOPMENT OF INTERNATIONAL CYBERCRIME LAW

United States Senator Ribikoff introduced the first piece of cybercrime legislation in the U.S. Congress in 1977.[18] While the legislation did not pass, it is credited for stimulating serious policy-making activity in the international community.[19] In 1983, the Organisation for Economic Co-operation and Development ("OECD")[20] conducted a study of existing cybercrime legislation in international states and considered the possibility of unifying these divers systems into a unitary international response.[21] On September 18, 1986, the OECD published *Computer-Re-*

---

15. *See Id.* (The problem has reached transnational dimensions through the trafficking of unauthorized reproductions over modern telecommunication networks at a substantial economic loss to the owners).

16. U.S. Department of Justice, Computer Crime and Intellectual Property Section, *International Aspects of Computer Crime* § C(6), http://www.cybercrime.gov/intl.html (accessed May 25, 2005) (In 1996, the Stockholm World Congress Against the Commercial Exploitation of Children examined the recommendations and proposed initiatives in many countries and regions. In September, 1999, the Austria International Child Pornography Conference drafted the Convention on the Rights of the Child, building on the Stockholm World Congress initiatives, to combat child pornography and exploitation on the Internet).

17. *See* International Narcotics Control Board, *Report of the International Narcotics Control Board for 2002* ¶ 121, http://www.incb.org/e/ind_ar.htm (accessed May 21, 2005) (2002) (reporting that narcotics traffickers are using computers and the Internet to conduct surveillance of law enforcement, to communicate, and to arrange the sale of illegal drugs); *see also* Bruce Swartz, Dep. Asst. Atty. Gen. Crim. Div., State. before Sen. Comm. on For. Rel., *Multilateral Law Enforcement Treaties* (June 17, 2004) (available at http://www. cybercrime.gov/swartzTestimony061704.htm) (stating that "criminals around the world are using computers to commit or assist a great variety of traditional crimes, including kidnapping, child pornography, child sexual exploitation identity theft, fraud, extortion and copyright piracy. Computer networks also provide terrorist organizations and organized crime groups the means with which to plan, coordinate and commit their crimes").

18. S.R. 1766, 95th Cong., vol. 123, part 17, p. 21,023.

19. Stein Schjolberg, *The Legal Framework – Unauthorized Access to Computer Systems: Penal Legislation in 44 Countries*, http://www.mosstingrett.no/info/legal.html (last updated April 7, 2003) (Judge Schjolberg is the Chief Judge, Moss District Court, Norway).

20. *See generally* Organisation for Economic Development, *About OECD*, http://www. oecd.org (last visited Feb.29, 2005) (The OECD is an intergovernmental organization that promotes multilateral dialogue and international cooperation on political, social and economic issues. While it does not have legal authority, it has been a significant influence in policy making among member and non-member states and the United Nations. It is comprised of 29 countries, including the United States).

21. *See* Schjolberg. *supra* n. 19, at n.1 (A group of experts met in Paris on May 30, 1983 representing France, the United Kingdom, Belgium, Norway and Germany).

THE CONVENTION ON CYBERCRIME

lated Crime: An Analysis of Legal Policy.[22] The report surveyed existing laws in several countries and recommended a minimum list of offense conduct requiring the enactment of penal legislation by participating international states.[23] The recommendations included fraud and forgery, the alteration of computer programs and data, the copyright and interception of the communications or other functions of a computer or telecommunication system, theft of trade secrets, and the unauthorized access to, or use of, computer systems.[24] The OECD envisioned this list as a "common denominator" of acts to be addressed through legislative enactment by each member country.[25]

Following the completion of the OECD report, the Council of Europe ("CoE")[26] initiated its own study to develop categories of proposed offense conduct and guidelines for enacting penal legislation, taking into account the immediate and critical need for enforcement without affronting due process and abrogating individual civil liberties.[27] The CoE issued Recommendation No. R(89)9 on September 13, 1989.[28] That Recommendation expanded the list of offense conduct proposed by the OECD to include matters involving privacy protection, victim identification, prevention, international search and seizure of data banks, and international cooperation in the investigation and prosecution of international crime.[29]

On September 11, 1995, the CoE adopted Recommendation No. R(95)13.[30] Significantly, this Recommendation goes beyond the identification of substantive offense categories and explores procedural issues

---

22. *U.N. Manual, supra* n. 8, at ¶ 9.

23. OECD Report, ICCP No. 10, *Computer Related Analysis of Legal Policy* (1986).

24. *Id.*

25. Schjolberg, *supra* note 19, at ¶ 118.

26. *See* U.S. Department of Justice, *Frequently Asked Questions and Answers about the Council of Europe Convention on Cybercrime,* http://www.usdoj.gov/criminal/cybercrime/ new COEFAQs.html (The Council of Europe ("CoE") was established in 1949 to strengthen human rights, promote democracy and the rule of law in Europe. The organization currently consists of 46 member states, including all of the members of the European Union. The United States is not a member state; http://www.coe.int/DefaultEN.asp (last updated Mar. 24, 2005).

27. *U.N. Manual, supra* n. 8, at ¶¶ 144-45.

28. Council of Europe, *Computer Related Crime,* http://www.oas.org/juridico/english/ 89-9& Final%20Report.pdf (accessed May 22, 2005) (Recommendation No. R(89)9, adopted by the Committee of Ministers of the Council of Europe (1989) and Report by the European Committee on Crime Problems (1990)).

29. *U.N. Manual, supra* n. 8, at ¶¶ 119-22.

30. Council of Europe, Committee of Ministers, *Recommendation No. R(95)13 of the Committee of Ministers to Member States Concerning Problems of Criminal Procedural Law Connected With Information Technology,* www.coe.int/T/CM/home_en.asp, *select* Documents A-Z index/ Recommendations of the Committee of Ministers to member states/Results pg. 12/Rec(95)13/11 September 1995/PDF (Sept. 11, 1995) [hereinafter Council of Europe, *Recommendation (95)13*].

334   JOURNAL OF COMPUTER & INFORMATION LAW   [Vol. XXIII

concerning the need to obtain information through conventional criminal procedure methods, including search and seizure, technical surveillance, obligations to cooperate with investigating authorities, electronic evidence, and the use of encryption. The Recommendation emphasizes a need to protect civil rights by minimizing intrusions into the privacy rights of individuals during an investigation, but offers no specific proposals.

The next important development in international law came in 1997, when the CoE appointed the Committee of Experts on Crime in Cyberspace ("PC-CY") to identify new crimes, jurisdictional rights and criminal liabilities related to Internet communications.[31] Canada, Japan, South Africa, and the United States were invited to meet with the PC-CY and participate in the negotiations.[32] In 2001, the PC-CY issued its Final Activity Report styled as the Draft Convention on Cyber-crime and Explanatory Memorandum Related Thereto.[33] The Report became the master blueprint for the first international treaty. Finally, after several years of intense effort, the Ministers of Foreign Affairs adopted the CoE Convention on November 8, 2001[34] and thereafter, it was opened for signature to member and non-member states.[35]

D. PRACTICAL IMPEDIMENTS TO INTERNATIONAL INVESTIGATION
AND ENFORCEMENT

Historical impediments to the investigation and prosecution of cybercrime underscore the serious need for a global response to the problem. Cybercrime operates outside of any geographical constraints and light years ahead of national planning and implementation. Simply put,

31. Schjolberg, *supra* n. 19, § I.

32. The G-8 (United States, Japan, Germany, Britain, France, Italy, Canada and Russia) also convened in 1997 to discuss and recommend international cooperation in the enforcement of laws prohibiting computer crimes. United States Department of Justice, *Meeting of the Justice and Interior Ministers of the Eight, Communique*, http://www.cybercrime.gov/communique.htm (last updated Feb. 18, 1998).

33. European Committee on Crime Problems, *Final Activity Report*, http://www.privacy international.org/issues/cybercrime/coe/cybercrimefinal.html (accessed Dec. 13, 2004).

34. Council of Europe, *Treaty*, *supra* n. 4.

35. Other developments in the closely related fields of information security and information infrastructures overlap with CoE efforts. The Commission of European Communities (EC) issued the Communication from the Commission to the Council, the European Parliament, the European Economic and Social Committee and the Committee of the Regions: Network and Information Security: Proposal for a European Policy Approach, COM (2001) 298 final (2001) (*available at* http://europa.eu.int/eur-lex/en/com/cnc/2001/com2001_0298en01.pdf). The United States responded to the EC with formal comments on the proposal to protect information infrastructure on November 21, 2001. U.S. Dept. of Just., *Comments of the U.S. Government: Communication from the European Commission: "Network and Information Security: Proposal for a European Policy Approach"*, http://www.usdoj.gov/criminal/cybercrime/intl/netsec_USComm_Nov_final.pdf (Nov. 21, 2001).

the laws, criminal justice systems and levels of international cooperation have lagged behind escalating unlawful conduct despite the concerted efforts of the United Nations and the CoE.[36] The explanation for that lies, in part, in the magnitude and complexity of the problem when elevated from the national arena to the international venue,[37] particularly where many countries have yet to enact domestic legislation prohibiting the targeted offense conduct. Specific practical impediments to enforcement and prosecution[38] include:[39]

1. the absence of a global consensus on the types of conduct that constitute a cybercrime;

2. the absence of a global consensus on the legal definition of criminal conduct;

3. the lack of expertise on the part of police, prosecutors and courts in the field;

4. the inadequacy of legal powers for investigation and access to computer systems, including the inapplicability of seizure powers to computerized data;

5. the lack of uniformity between the different national procedural laws concerning the investigation of cybercrimes;

6. the transnational character of many cybercrimes; and

7. the lack of extradition and mutual legal assistance treaties,[40] synchronized law enforcement mechanisms that would permit international cooperation in cybercrime investigations, and existing treaties that take into account the dynamics and special requirements of these investigations.

The United States, in its response to the "Cybercrime Communication Issued by the European Commission," emphasized the problem: "With the globalization of communications networks, public safety is increasingly dependent on effective law enforcement cooperation with foreign governments. That cooperation may not be possible, however, if a country does not have substantive laws in place to prosecute or extradite

---

36. *U.N. Manual, supra* n. 8, at ¶ 5.

37. According to INSEAD/World Economic Forum: The Network Readiness Index (2003-2004), by 2002 the number of Internet users worldwide increased to 600 million from only 300 million in 1999. A 2004 survey of 494 U.S. corporations found 20 percent had been subject to "attempts of computer sabotage and extortion among others through denial of service attacks." CBS News.com, *Cybercrime A Worldwide Headache,* http://www.cbsnews.com/stories/2004/09/16/tech/main643897.shtml (last updated Sept.16, 2004).

38. For an interesting discussion of the investigative and enforcement hurdles faced in the prosecution of two high profile cybercrime cases, the "Rome Labs" and "Invita" cases, *see* Susan Brenner and Joseph Schwerha, *Transnational Evidence Gathering and Local Prosecution of International Cybercrime,* 20 J. Marshall J. Computer & Info. L. 347 (2002).

39. *See U.N. Manual, supra* n. 8, at ¶ 7 (identifying these impediments to investigation and enforcement as a result of its in-depth study and analysis in 1995).

40. *See infra,* section III (discussing the availability and practical uses of MLATs).

336   JOURNAL OF COMPUTER & INFORMATION LAW   [Vol. XXIII

a perpetrator."[41] Thus, in a very real sense, international cooperation is limited to the particular participants and/or treaty signatories who have affirmatively enacted domestic cybercrime legislation. Inadequate domestic legislation, combined with the failure of unanimous global cooperation, creates a gap in enforcement that provides "safe data havens"[42] for targeted conduct.[43] Meaningful international prosecutive efforts remain tenuous at best without a singular global consensus supported by the unanimous participation of all nations.[44]

II. THE COUNCIL OF EUROPE CONVENTION ON CYBERCRIME

A. SUMMARY OF TREATY PROVISIONS

The CoE Convention consists of forty-eight articles divided among four chapters: (I) "Use of terms;" (II) "Measures to be taken at the national level;" (III) "International cooperation;" and, (IV) "Final provisions."[45]

Chapter II, Section 1, Articles two through thirteen address substantive law issues and include criminalization provisions and other related provisions in the area of computer or computer-related crime. Specifically, they define nine offenses grouped into four different categories. The offenses include: illegal access, illegal interception, data interference, system interference, misuse of devices, computer-related forgery, computer-related fraud, offenses related to child pornography

---

41. U.S. Dept. of Just., *Comments of the United States Government on the European Commission Communication on Combating Computer Crime,* http://www.usdoj.gov, *search* Comments of the United States Government on the European Commission on Combating Computer Crime, *select* link No. 1 (accessed Dec. 17, 2004).

42. Dr. Prof. Ulrich Sieber, *Computer Crime and Criminal Information Law-New Trends in the International Risk and Information Society,* Hearings of the Permanent Subcommittee on Investigations, Committee on Government Affairs 19 http://www.uplink.com.au/lawlibrary/Documents/Docs/Doc122.html (accessed May 21, 2005).

43. Addressing the Southeastern European Cybersecurity Conference in Sophia, Bulgaria on Sept. 8, 2003, Lincoln Bloomfield said:

  Ensuring the safety and security of networked information systems – what we call cybersecurity – is very important to the United States . . . cybersecurity is very different from traditional national security issues. The government alone cannot ensure security – we must have partnerships within our societies and around the world.

Lincoln Bloomfield, *U.S. Says Cybersecurity is a Global Responsibility,* http://usinfo.org/wf-archive/2003/030909/epf213.htm (accessed May 25, 2005).

44. Yet, even with this recognition, the continuing slow response of the international community to act on the cybercrime problem seriously impedes meaningful international enforcement. At the CoE 2004 International Conference on Cybercrime, the forty-five nation participants agreed that governments are "dragging their heels" in implementing needed international reform through the final ratification of the treaty. CBS News, *supra* n. 37.

45. Council of Europe, *Treaty, supra* n. 4.

and offenses related to copyright.[46] Section 1 also addresses ancillary crimes and penalties.

Chapter II, Section 2, Articles fourteen through twenty-one address procedural law issues. Section 2 applies to a broader range of offenses than those defined in Section 1, including any offense committed *by means of* a computer system or evidence of which is in electronic form.[47] As a threshold matter, it provides for the common conditions and safeguards applicable to all procedural powers in the chapter.[48] Specifically, Article 15 requires the parties to provide for safeguards that are adequate for the protection of human rights and liberties. According to the CoE Explanatory Report, the substantive criteria and procedure authorizing an investigative power may vary according to the sensitivity of the data being sought in the investigation.[49]

The procedural powers include: expedited preservation of stored data, expedited preservation and partial disclosure of traffic data, and interception of content data.[50] Traditional application of search and seizure methodology is provided for within a party's territory along with other procedural options, including real-time interception of content data.[51] The second chapter ends in Article twenty-two with an explanation of the jurisdictional provisions.[52]

Chapter III addresses traditional and cybercrime-related mutual assistance obligations as well as extradition rules.[53] Traditional mutual assistance is covered in two situations:

1. where no legal treaty, reciprocal legislation or other such agreement exists between the parties; and

2. where such pre-existing legal relationship exists between the parties.

In the former situation, the provisions of the CoE Convention apply. In the latter situation, however, pre-existing legal relationships apply "to provide further assistance" under the CoE Convention.[54] It bears em-

---

46. Council of Europe, Convention On Cybercrime, ETS 185, Explanatory Report, at 28, ¶ 18 (Nov. 2001) (*available at* http://conventions.coe.int/Treaty/en/Treaties/Html/185. htm) [hereinafter "CoE Explanatory Report"].

47. *See id.* at 29, ¶ 19.

48. The issue of providing adequate procedural safeguards to protect the civil rights and privacy of putative defendants was a major discussion point during treaty negotiations. Based on those discussions, the United States asserted "six reservations and four declarations" that qualify its participation as a party. *See* Powell, *supra* n. 2, at vi.

49. CoE Explanatory Report, *supra* n. 46, at 31, ¶ 31.

50. *See id.* at 29, ¶ 19.

51. *See id.* at 48, ¶ 143.

52. *See id.* at 29, ¶ 19.

53. The provisions addressing computer or computer related crime assistance provide the same range of procedural powers as defined in Chapter II.

54. CoE Explanatory Report, *supra* n. 46, at 29, ¶ 20.

phasizing that the three general principles of international cooperation in Chapter III do *not* supercede the provisions on international agreements on mutual legal assistance and extradition, reciprocal agreements between parties, or relevant provisions of domestic law applying to international cooperation.[55]

Finally, Chapter III provides transborder access to stored computer data not requiring mutual assistance because there is either consent or the information is otherwise publicly available.[56] There is also provision for the establishment of a "24/7 network" for ensuring speedy assistance between the parties.[57]

B. APPLICATION AND ANALYSIS OF SIGNIFICANT TREATY PROVISIONS

1. *Four Basic Definitions*

The drafters of the CoE Convention agreed that parties need not incorporate verbatim the particular definitions contained in the CoE Convention, provided that each nation's domestic laws cover these concepts in a manner "consistent with the principles of the convention and offer an equivalent framework for its implementation."[58] The United Nations identified uniformity in law and consensus over definitional terms as two of the impediments that had to be overcome in order to achieve meaningful cooperation and successful enforcement.[59] The CoE Convention accomplishes this goal using four principal definitions.

A "computer system" is defined,[60] *inter alia,* as a device consisting of hardware and software developed for automatic processing of digital data.[61] It may include input, output, and storage facilities. It may stand alone or be connected in a network. A "network" is an interconnection of two or more computer systems.[62] The Internet is a global network consisting of many interconnected networks, all using the same protocols. It

---

55. *See id.* at 69, ¶¶ 233-34. This basic principle of international cooperation is explicitly reinforced in Articles 24 (extradition), 25 (general principles applying to mutual assistance), 26 (spontaneous information), 27 (procedures pertaining to mutual legal assistance in the absence of applicable international agreements), 28 (confidentiality and limitations on use), 31 (mutual assistance regarding accessing of stored computer data), 33 (mutual assistance regarding the real-time collection of traffic data) and 34 (mutual assistance regarding the interception of content data).

56. *Id.*

57. *Id.*

58. *See id.* at 29, ¶ 22.

59. *See* Point I (d), *supra.*

60. Council of Europe, *Treaty, supra* n. 4, at art. 1(a).

61. "[P]rocessing of data" means that data in the computer system is operated by executing a computer program. A "computer program" is a set of instructions that can be executed by the computer to achieve the intended result. CoE Explanatory Report, *supra* n. 46, at 29, ¶ 23.

62. Council of Europe, *Treaty, supra* n. 4, art. 1(a).

is essential that data is exchanged over the network.[63]

"Computer data" means any representation of facts, information or concepts in a form suitable for processing in a computer system, including a program suitable to cause a computer system to perform a function.[64] Computer data that is automatically processed may be the target of one of the criminal offenses defined in the CoE Convention as well as subject to the application of one of the investigative measures defined by the CoE Convention.[65]

The term "service provider" encompasses a very broad category of persons and/or entities that provide users of its services with the ability to communicate by means of a computer system. Both public and private entities that provide the ability to communicate with one another are covered in the definition of "service provider."[66] The term also includes persons or entities that process or store computer data on behalf of such communication services or users of communication services.[67] However, a mere provider of content, such as a person who contracts with a web hosting company to host his Web site, is not included in the definition if the content provider does not also offer communication or related data processing services.[68]

Finally, "traffic data" means *any* computer data relating to a communication by means of a computer system, generated by a computer system that formed a part of the chain of communication, indicating the communication's origin, destination, route, time, date, size, duration or type of underlying service.[69] Collecting traffic data in the investigation of a criminal offense committed in relation to a computer system is critical.[70] The traffic data is needed to trace the source of the communication as a starting point for the collection of further evidence, or as evidence of part of the offense.[71] Because of the short lifespan of traffic data, it is necessary to order its expeditious preservation and to provide rapid disclosure of the information to law enforcement to facilitate quick discovery of the communication's route before other evidence is deleted, or to

---

63. CoE Explanatory Report, *supra* n. 46 at 30, ¶ 24.

64. Council of Europe, *Treaty*, *supra* n. 4, art. 1(b).

65. CoE Explanatory Report, *supra* n. 46 at 30, ¶ 25.

66. *Id.* at 30, ¶ 26.

67. Council of Europe, *Treaty*, *supra* n. 4, art.1(c).

68. CoE Explanatory Report, *supra* n. 46, at 30, ¶ 27.

69. Council of Europe, *Treaty*, *supra* n. 4, art. 1(d).

70. CoE Explanatory Report, *supra* n. 46, at 30, ¶ 29. Specifically, the evidence that may be obtained from traffic data can include a telephone number, Internet Protocol address ("IP") or similar identification of a communication facility to which a service provider render service, the destination of the communication, and type of underlying service being provided (ie, file transfer, electronic mail, or instant messaging).

71. *Id.*

identify a suspect.[72] The collection of this data is legally regarded to be less intrusive because it doesn't reveal the content of communication that is viewed as more privacy sensitive.[73]

2. *Procedural Safeguards*

The CoE Convention addresses the complicated problem of guaranteeing civil rights protection to citizens living in different cultures and political systems.[74] Concluding that it was not possible to detail all of the conditions and safeguards necessary to circumscribe each power and procedure provided for in the CoE Convention, Article 15 was drafted to provide "the common standards or minimum safeguards to which Parties to the Convention must adhere."[75] These minimum safeguards reference certain applicable human rights instruments including: the 1950 European Convention for the Protection of Human Rights and Fundamental Freedoms ("ECHR") and its additional Protocols No.1, 4, 6, 7 and 12;[76] the 1966 United Nations International Covenant on Civil and Political Rights; and "other international human rights instruments, and which shall incorporate the principle or mandates that a power or procedure implemented under the Convention shall be proportional to the nature and circumstances of the offense."[77] Thus, domestic law must limit the overbreadth of protection orders authorized, provide reasonableness requirements for searches and seizures, and minimize intrusion regarding interception measures taken with respect to the wide variety of offenses.[78]

The CoE Explanatory Report loosely identifies procedural safeguards "as [those] appropriate in view of the nature of the power or procedure, judicial or independent supervision, grounds justifying the application of the power or procedure and the limitation on the scope or duration thereof."[79] The bottom line is that "[n]ational legislatures will have to determine, in applying binding international obligations and established domestic principles, which of the powers and procedures are sufficiently intrusive in nature to require implementation of particular

---

72. *Id.*

73. *Id.*

74. *See id.* at 49, ¶ 145. This sensitivity to the differences in legal responses to criminality based upon different legal cultures and traditions was emphasized in the recommendations of the Association Internationale de Droit Penal ("AIDP") in the Draft Resolution of the AIDP Colloquium held at Wurrzburg on October 5-8, 1992. *U.N. Manual, supra* n. 8, at ¶¶ 270-3.

75. CoE Explanatory Report, *supra* n. 46, at 49, ¶ 145.

76. *See id.* at 49, ¶ 145, ETS Nos. 005, (4), 009, 046, 114, 117,& 117.

77. *See id.* at 50, ¶ 146.

78. *Id.*

79. *Id.*

conditions and safeguards."[80] Thus, other than aspirational language, couched in terms of legally non-binding human rights instruments, the treaty offers no specific minimal procedural guarantees of due process incident to treaty implementation.

3. *Methods of Collecting Evidence*

The four methods for securing evidence are found in Article 18 ("Production Order"), Article 19 ("Search and Seizure of Stored Computer Data"), Article 20 ("Real time collection of traffic data"), and Article 21 ("Interception of Collection Data").[81] While attempting to overcome the territorial sensitivity of each nation to transborder evidence collection, the CoE Convention carefully limits the scope of these powers by deferring to domestic legislative requirements as mandated by the CoE Convention, qualified by a strong admonition encouraging mutual cooperation between the parties as provided for in Article 23.[82] In short, transborder access to evidence will be whatever the participating nation decides is appropriate in conformity with the parameters of the treaty. Thus, uniformity of evidence gathering remains an unresolved issue among participating nations. However, the CoE Convention does require the enactment of certain minimal procedures by a party.

Under Article 18, a party must be able to order a person within its territory, including a third party custodian of data, such as an ISP, to produce data, including subscriber information, that is in the person's possession or control.[83] Production orders are viewed as a less intrusive measure than search and seizure for requiring a third party to produce information. A production order is similar to subpoena powers in the United States.[84] However, the Article does not impose an obligation on the service provider to compile and maintain such subscriber informa-

---

80. *Id.* This section is the subject of the due process analysis at point V, *infra.*

81. Notably, Articles 16 and 17 of the CoE Convention refer only to data preservation and not data retention. The CoE Explanatory Report observes that data preservation for most countries is an entirely new legal power or procedure in domestic law. Likewise, it is an important new investigative tool in addressing computer crime, especially committed through the Internet. Because of the volatility of computer evidence, it is easily subject to manipulation or change. Thus, valuable evidence of a crime can be easily lost through careless handling or storage practices, intentional manipulation, or deletion designed to destroy evidence or routine deletion of data that is no longer required to be maintained. *See* CoE Explanatory Report, *supra* n. 46, at 51, ¶ 155.

82. Article 23 of the CoE Convention sets forth three general principles with respect to international co-operation. First, international co-operation is to be extended between the parties "to the widest extent possible." Second, co-operation is to be extended to all criminal offenses described in paragraph 14. Finally, co-operation is to be carried out through the provisions of the CoE Convention along with all pre-existing international mutual assistance and reciprocal agreements.

83. CoE Explanatory Report, *supra* n. 46, at 56-57, ¶ 177.

84. *See id.* at 55, ¶ 170.

tion in the ordinary course of their business. Instead, a service provider need only produce subscriber information that it does in fact keep, and is not obliged to guarantee the correctness of the information.[85] The application of the "proportionality principle," that is, the scope of the intrusion being limited to its purpose, is reemphasized in the CoE Explanatory Report.[86]

Significantly, the provision does not contain any minimal requirements concerning confidentiality of materials obtained through a production order. Except in the area of real-time interception of communications, there are no confidentiality provisions attendant to any of the evidence gathering tools provided for in the CoE Convention, nor are there any proposed minimal requirements.[87] Again, this is an area left to the domestic legislative discretion of the parties, leaving the issue of uniformity in the method of handling confidential information between nations unresolved. Standards of protection in one nation may differ materially from those in another nation and may impact dissemination of seized evidence. The legal contours of information dissemination remain unresolved by the treaty.

Article 19 is intended to enable investigating authorities, within their own territory, to search and seize a computer system, data stored in a computer system and data stored in storage mediums, such as diskettes.[88] However, two significant limitations curb the power to search and seize. First, and most important, Article 19 does not address "transborder search and seizure" whereby one country could search and seize data in the territory of other countries without first having to go through usual channels of mutual legal assistance.[89] Second, the measures contained in Article 19 are qualified by reference to the wording "in its territory," as a "reminder" that this provision – which qualifies all of the articles in this section – concerns only measures that are required to be taken at the national level.[90] Again, these measures operate between parties either through the tool of "international cooperation," or through channels of pre-existing mutual legal assistance arrangements.

Article 19 addresses the hugely problematic absence in many jurisdictions of laws permitting the seizure of intangible objects, such as stored computer data, which is generally secured by seizing the data medium on which it is stored. Such national domestic legislation is necessary, not only to protect the preservation of easily destroyed data, but also to provide available enforcement tools to assist other countries.

---

85. *See id.* at 57, ¶¶ 181 & 188.
86. *See id.* at 56, ¶ 174.
87. *See id.* at 56, ¶ 175.
88. *See id.* at 58, ¶¶ 187-89.
89. CoE Explanatory Report, *supra* n. 46, at 60, ¶ 195.
90. *See id.* at 59, ¶ 192.

Without these laws, a nation investigating a transborder crime is effectively prevented from seeking international cooperation in a country that fails to authorize lawful search and seizure within its territory.

Accordingly, paragraph 1 requires the parties to empower law enforcement authorities to access and search computer data, which is contained either within a computer system or part of it or on an independent data storage medium (such as a CD-ROM or diskette).[91] Paragraph 2 allows investigating authorities to extend their search or similar access to another computer system if they have grounds to believe that the data required is stored in the other system. However, this system must also be within the party's own territory.[92] Paragraph 3 authorizes the seizure[93] of computer data that has been accessed under the authority of paragraphs 1 and 2.[94] Paragraph 4 is a "coercive measure" that allows law enforcement authorities to compel systems administrators to assist during the search and seizure as may reasonably be required.[95]

While Article 19 applies to "stored computer data,"[96] Articles 20 and 21 provide for the real-time collection of traffic data and the real-time interception of content data associated with specified communications transmitted by a computer system.[97] Additionally, confidentiality considerations are addressed here.[98]

Specifically, Articles 20 and 21 require parties to establish measures to enable their competent authorities to collect data associated with specified communications in their territory at the time of the data's communication, meaning in "real time." However, Article 20 contains a provision allowing a party to make a "reservation" to the CoE Convention limiting the types of crimes to which Article 20 applies.[99]

Under Articles 20 and 21, subject to the party's actual technical capabilities,[100] a party is generally required to adopt measures enabling its

---

91. *See id.* at 59, ¶ 190.

92. *See id.* at 59, ¶ 193.

93. In the Convention, seizure means "to take away the physical medium upon which data or information is recorded, or to make and retain a copy of such data or information." Seize also means, in this context, the right to secure data. *See id.* at 59, ¶ 197.

94. *See id.* at 59, ¶ 196.

95. CoE Explanatory Report, *supra* n. 46, at 61, ¶ 200.

96. *Id.*

97. *See id.* at 61-62, ¶ 205.

98. *Id.*

99. Greater limitations may be employed with respect to the real-time collection of content data than traffic data. *See id.* at 62-63, ¶ 210. The United States has taken the position that a formal reservation is not needed because federal law already makes the mechanism generally available for criminal investigations and prosecutions. *See* Powell, *supra* n. 2, at xv.

100. CoE Explanatory Report, *supra* n. 46, at 65, ¶ 221. There is no obligation to impose a duty on service providers to obtain or deploy new equipment or engage in costly reconfiguration of their systems in order to assist law enforcement.

competent authorities to:

1. collect or record data themselves through application of technical means on the territory of that party; and

2. compel a service provider, to either collect or record data through the application of technical means or cooperate and assist competent authorities in the collection or recording of such data.[101]

The CoE Explanatory Report recognizes a critical distinction in the nature and extent of the possible intrusions into privacy between traffic data and content data.[102] With respect to the real-time interception of content data, laws often limit interception to investigations of serious offenses or serious offense categories, usually defined by certain maximum periods of incarceration.[103] Whereas, the interception of traffic data, viewed as less intrusive, is not so limited and in principle applies to every offense described by the CoE Convention.[104] In both cases, the conditions and procedural safeguards specified in Articles 14 and 15 apply to qualify the use of these interception provisions.[105]

4. *Crimes*

Section 1, Articles 2-13 of the CoE Convention establish a "common minimum standard of relevant offenses."[106] The Convention requires that all of the offenses must be committed "intentionally,"[107] although the exact meaning of the word will be left to national interpretation.[108] Laws should be drafted with as much clarity and specificity as possible in order to guarantee adequate forseeability regarding the type of conduct that will result in a criminal sanction.[109] As noted above, the United States maintains that its legislative structure adequately covers the offenses described in the CoE Convention and that no further implementing legislation will be required for ratification.[110]

---

101. *Id.*

102. *See id.* at 66, ¶ 227.

103. *See id.* at 63, ¶ 212.

104. *See id.* at 63, ¶ 214.

105. *See id.* at 63-64, ¶ 215.

106. CoE Explanatory Report, *supra* n. 46, at 31, ¶¶ 33-34. Notably the list is based on the guidelines developed earlier by the CoE in Recommendation No. R(89)9. *See U.N. Manual, supra* n. 8.

107. CoE Explanatory Report, *supra* n. 46, at 32, ¶ 39.

108. *Id.*

109. *See id.* at 33, ¶ 41.

110. The Computer Fraud and Abuse Act ("CFAA") was originally enacted in 1984 as the "Counterfeit Access Device and Computer Fraud and Abuse Act." Pub. L. No. 98-473, 2101(a), 98 Stat. 2190 (1984) (codified at 18 U.S.C. § 1030). In 1986 the statute was substantially revised and the title was changed to CFAA. The Act was revised and the scope of the law was expanded in 1988, Pub. L. No. 100-690, 102 Stat. 4404 (1988); 1989, Pub. L. No. 101-73, 103 Stat. 502 (1989); 1990, Pub. L. No. 101-647, 104 Stat. 4831, 4910, 4925 (1990); and 1994, Pub. L. No. 103-322, 108 Stat. 2097-99 (1994). In 1996, the CFAA was

The offenses described in Chapter II, Section I of the CoE Convention include:

Title 1, Articles 2-6, *Offenses against the confidentiality, integrity and availability of computer data and systems:* illegal access, illegal interception, data interference, system interference, misuse of devices;

Title 2, Articles 7-8, *Computer-related offenses:* computer-related forgery and computer-related fraud;

Title 3, Article 9, *Content-related offenses:* offenses related to child pornography;

Title 4, Article 10, *Offenses related to infringements and related rights:* offenses related to infringements of copyright and related rights; and

Title 5, Articles 11-13, *Ancillary Liability and sanctions:* attempt and aiding or abetting, corporate liability, and sanctions and measures.

The CoE Explanatory Report includes several caveats regarding the intent and application of these provisions. For example, criminal offenses defined under Articles 2-6 are intended to protect the confidentiality, integrity and availability of computer systems or data, and are not intended to criminalize legitimate and common activities inherent in the design of networks, or legitimate and common operating and commercial practices.[111] Each section is also subject to Article 8 of the ECHR, guaranteeing the right to privacy where applicable.[112] Again, these provi-

---

amended by the National Information Infrastructure Protection Act of 1996 ("NIIPA"), Pub. L. No. 104-294, tit. II, § 201, 110 Stat. 3488, 3491-96 (1996) (Economic Espionage Act of 1996, Title II). The CFAA proscribes 7 areas of offense conduct: (a)(1) knowing and willful theft of protected government information, (a)(2) intentional theft of protected information, (a)(3) intentional gaining of access to government information, (a)(4) fraud through a protected computer, (a)(5)(A) intentionally causing damage through a computer transmission, (a)(5)(B) recklessly causing damage through unauthorized access, (a)(5)(c)) causing damage through unauthorized access, (a)(6) fraudulent trafficking in passwords, and (a)(7) extortion. Portions of § 1030 were amended and expanded by provisions of the antiterrorism legislation entitled Uniting and Strengthening America by Providing Appropriate Tools Required to Intercept and Obstruct Terrorism Act of 2001, Pub. L. No. 107-56, § 814 (d)(1), 115 Stat. 272 (2001) (also referred to as the USA Patriot Act of 2001). Congress also enacted the Cybersecurity Enhancement Act of 2002, Pub. L. No. 107-296, § 225, 116 Stat. 2135, 2156 (2002). These provisions are discussed in more detail in section VII of this article, *infra*. Additionally, other traditional federal criminal laws may be used to prosecute computer related crimes, such as charges of copyright infringement, 17 U.S.C. § 506 (1997); conspiracy, 18 U.S.C. § 371 (1994); wire fraud, 18 U.S.C. § 1343 (2002); illegal transportation of stolen property, 18 U.S.C. § 2314 (1994); Electronic Communications Privacy Act, 18 U.S.C. §§ 2510-21, 2701-10 (2002); illegal interception devices and equipment, 18 U.S.C. § 2512 (2002); and unlawful access to stored communications, 18 U.S.C. §§ 2701 et. seq. (2002).

111. CoE Explanatory Report, *supra* n. 46, at 33, ¶ 43.

112. *See id.* at 34, ¶ 51 (The "catch" is that signatories who are non-member countries are not bound by the ECHR which is itself closed for signature to non-member countries).

346   JOURNAL OF COMPUTER & INFORMATION LAW   [Vol. XXIII

sions are the minimum offense categories that each party is obliged to implement through domestic legislation.

5. *Jurisdiction and Extradition*

Article 22 undertakes the monumental task of resolving the question of "who has jurisdiction" over the commission of computer-related offenses committed both within a territory and across sovereign borders. First, a series of criteria, grounded in international law principles,[113] is applied under which the parties are then obligated to establish jurisdiction over the criminal offenses enumerated in Articles 2-11.[114]

Article 22(1)(a) provides that each party "shall adopt" legislative measures to establish jurisdiction to prosecute the offenses listed in Articles 2-11 when committed "in its territory."[115] This provision is grounded upon the principle of territoriality[116] which is based on mutual respect of sovereign equality between States and is linked with the principle of nonintervention in the affairs and exclusive domain of other States.[117]

The "ubiquity doctrine" may also apply to determine the "place of commission of the offense."[118] Under this doctrine, a crime is deemed to occur "in its entirety" within a country's jurisdiction if one of the constituent elements of the offense, or the ultimate result, occurred within that country's borders. Jurisdiction applies to co-defendants and accomplices as well.[119]

Article 22(d) requires the parties to establish jurisdictional principles when the offense is committed by one of a party's nationals, if the offense is punishable under criminal law where it was committed, or if the offense is committed outside the territorial jurisdiction of any state. This provision is based on the principle of nationality, a different jurisdictional principle from the other subsections of the article.[120] It provides that nationals are required to abide by a party's domestic laws even when they are outside its territory. Under subsection (d), if a national commits an offense abroad, the party must have the ability to prosecute even if the conduct is also an offense under the law of the coun-

---

113. For an in depth discussion of international jurisdictional principles, *see* Julie O'Sullivan, *Federal White Collar Crime*, 735-50 (2d ed. 2003).

114. CoE Explanatory Report, *supra* n. 46, at 67, ¶ 232.

115. Council of Europe, *Treaty*, *supra* n. 4, at art. 22(1)(a).

116. CoE Explanatory Report, *supra* n. 46, at 67, ¶ 233. Note that subparagraph (b) and (c) are based upon a "variant of the principle of territoriality" where the crime is committed aboard a ship or aircraft registered under the laws of the State. *See id.* at 68, ¶ 235.

117. *U.N. Manual*, *supra* n. 8, at ¶ 249.

118. CoE Explanatory Report, *supra* n. 46, at 70-71, ¶ 250.

119. *Id.*

120. *See id.* at 67, ¶ 236.

try in which it was committed.[121]

However, the treaty does not resolve the central jurisdictional dilemma where more than one country has a "jurisdictional claim" to the case. The CoE Explanatory Report, interpreting Article 22(5) addresses this situation as follows:

> In the case of crimes committed by use of computer systems, there will be occasions when more than one Party has jurisdiction over some or all of the participants in the crime. . .the affected parties are to consult in order to determine the proper venue for prosecution. In some cases, it will be most effective for the States concerned to choose a single venue for prosecution; in others, it may be best for one State to prosecute some participants, while one or more other States pursue others. . . . Finally, the obligation to consult is not absolute, but is to take place "where appropriate."[122]

Additionally, in those instances where a party refuses a request to extradite on the basis of the offender's nationality[123] and the offender's presence in the territory of a party, (where the request is made under Article 24), paragraph 3 of Article 22 requires the party to enact jurisdictional provisions enabling prosecution domestically.[124] Ostensibly, this provision should avoid the possibility of offenders seeking safe havens from prosecution by fleeing to another country. The bottom line is that a party must either extradite or prosecute.[125]

Article 24, entitled "Extradition," does not provide any mechanism to implement or expedite extradition when a request is made by a party. Instead, subparagraph 5 merely provides that "[e]xtradition shall be subject to the conditions provided for by the law of the requested Party or by applicable extradition treaties, including the grounds on which the Party may refuse extradition."[126] However, the treaty does require each party to include as extraditable offenses those contained in Articles 2-11 of the CoE Convention.[127]

---

121. *Id.*

122. *See id.* at 68, ¶ 239.

123. *See* Powell, *supra* n. 2, at xvii. United States law permits extradition of nationals, accordingly no implementing legislation is required.

124. CoE Explanatory Report, *supra* n. 46, at 68, ¶ 237.

125. This article resembles the text of Articles 15(3) and 16 (10) of the UN Convention on Transnational Organized Crime, which is incorporated by reference into the Protocol to Prevent, Suppress, and Punish Trafficking in Persons, Especially Women and Children Supplementing the United Nations Convention Against Transnational Organized Crime (*available at* http://untreaty.un.org/English/notpubl/18-12E.doc and http://untreaty.un.org/English/TreatyEvent2005/List.asp) (accessed Feb.29, 2005). Those provisions require the views of the requesting nation to be taken into account and require the prosecuting nation to act diligently.

126. Council of Europe, *Treaty, supra* n. 4, at art. 24(5).

127. *See id.* at art. 24(2).

Finally, Article 35 requires each party to designate a point of contact available on a 24 hours, 7 days per week basis. This ensures co-operation in the investigation of crimes, collection of evidence or other such assistance.

III. MUTUAL LEGAL ASSISTANCE TREATIES ("MLATS") AND OTHER INTERNATIONAL COOPERATION AGREEMENTS

A. THE RELATIONSHIP TO THE CoE CONVENTION

As explained above, the CoE Convention addresses both the situation where a traditional pre-existing legal relationship either in the form of a treaty, reciprocal legislation, memorandum of understanding ["MOU"][128] or other such agreement exists between the parties, and the situation where there is no such pre-existing relationship. Where there is a pre-existing relationship, that legal relationship applies "to provide further assistance" under the CoE Convention.[129] Traditional pre-existing legal relationships are not superceded by the CoE Convention.

Additionally, the three general principles of international cooperation in Chapter III of the CoE Convention do not supercede the provisions of international agreements on mutual legal assistance and extradition, reciprocal agreements between parties, or relevant provisions of domestic law applying to international cooperation.[130]

The U.S. Department of State describes Mutual Legal Assistance Treaties or "MLATs" as a means of "impro[ving] the effectiveness of judicial assistance and to regularize and facilitate procedures" with foreign nations.[131] The treaties typically include agreed upon procedures for summoning witnesses, compelling the production of documents and

---

128. For example, the Securities and Exchange Commission has "case-by-case" informal MOUs to facilitate production with Switzerland, Japan, Canada, Brazil, Netherlands, France, Mexico, Norway, Argentina, Spain, Chile, Italy, Australia, the United Kingdom, Sweden, South Africa, Germany, Luxembourg and Hungary, as well as Joint Statements of Cooperation with the European Union (EU). *See* U.S. Dept. of St., *Mutual Legal Assistance in Criminal Matters Treaties (MLATs) and Other Agreements*, http://travel.state.gov/law/mlat.html (accessed May 21, 2005) [hereinafter *MLAT*].

129. CoE Explanatory Report. *supra* n. 46, at 29, ¶ 20.

130. *See id.* at 69, ¶¶ 233-34. This basic principle of international cooperation is explicitly reinforced in Articles 24 (extradition), 25 (general principles applying to mutual assistance), 26 (spontaneous information), 27 (procedures pertaining to mutual legal assistance in the absence of applicable international agreements), 28 (confidentiality and limitations on use), 31(mutual assistance regarding accessing of stored computer data), 33 (mutual assistance regarding the real-time collection of traffic data) and 34 (mutual assistance regarding the interception of content data).

131. *See MLAT, supra* n. 128.

other evidence, issuing search warrants and serving process.[132]

B. REMEDIAL IMBALANCES

Notably, these remedies are available only to prosecutors. The Office of International Affairs ("OIA"), Criminal Division, United States Department of Justice, is responsible for administering procedures under the MLATs and assisting domestic prosecutions by the respective United States Attorneys Offices. Thus, to the extent that the MLATs "supercede" the CoE Convention,[133] defense attorneys are effectively excluded from participating in that part of the process of international enforcement activity.

The operative provisions of MLATs often have the effect, whether intended or not, of limiting international enforcement efforts. Many such agreements require "dual criminality," that the crime for which information is being sought by a requesting country must also be offense conduct in the nation possessing the needed information. Where the nation has not criminalized targeted conduct, the investigation cannot proceed. For example in 1992, the United States requested information from Switzerland in connection with its investigation of a Swiss-based hacker who attacked the San Diego Supercomputer Center. Switzerland had not criminalized hacking and was, therefore, unable to assist in the investigation.[134]

In any event, the CoE Convention does not refer to the role or participation of defense counsel in the process at all. Defense attorneys must obtain evidence in criminal cases from foreign or "host" countries, pursuant to the laws of the host nation, through a procedure known as "Letters Rogatory."[135] To the extent that the United States maintains agreements with the various host nations, the State Department publishes "country specific information" to enable a litigant to avail himself of ex-

---

132. *Id.* The United States has bilateral Mutual Legal Assistance Treaties with Anguilla, Antigua/Barbuda, Argentina, Austria, Bahamas, Barbados, Belgium, Brazil, British Virgin Islands, Canada, Cayman Islands, Cyprus, Czech Republic, Dominica, Egypt, Estonia, Greece, Grenada, Hong Kong, Hungary, Israel, Italy, Jamaica, South Korea, Latvia, Lithuania, Luxembourg, Mexico, Montserrat, Morocco, Netherlands, Panama, Philippines, Poland, Romania, St. Kitts-Nevis, St. Lucia, St. Vincent, Spain, Switzerland, Thailand, Trinidad, Turkey, Turks and Caicos Islands, Ukraine, United Kingdom and Uruguay.

133. CoE Explanatory Report, *supra* n. 46, at 29, ¶ 20 & 67, ¶¶ 233-34. The three general principles of international co-operation in Chapter III of the CoE Convention do *not* supercede the provisions on international agreements on mutual legal assistance and extradition, reciprocal agreements between parties, or relevant provisions of domestic law applying to international co-operation.

134. ABA Privacy and Computer Crime Committee, *International Cybercrime Project*, http://www.abanet.org/scitech/computercrime/cybercrimeproject.html (accessed May 21, 2005).

135. *See MLAT, supra* n. 128.

traterritorial discovery.[136] There are strict requirements for the form of the request submission,[137] and the requesting party must pay all expenses associated with the process.[138] It is unclear if and to what extent the CoE Convention affects the rules with respect to treaties governing Letters Rogatory.

Letters Rogatory usually requires preauthorization by a judicial or administrative body and also requires transmission by a designated "central authority."[139] The process may be "cumbersome and time consuming"[140] and the treaties generally do not provide time lines for production of the requested information.[141] The Letters Rogatory was codified under 28 U.S.C. § 1781 (2000).[142] Under this section, the State Department is vested with the power in both civil and criminal cases to transmit the request for evidence to "a foreign or international tribunal, officer or agency to whom it is addressed."[143] The request may be used for providing notice, serving summons, locating individuals, witness examination, document inspection and other evidence production. The foreign tribunal can only honor requests that fall within its procedures and jurisdiction. Again, if criminal activity does not fall within the domestic legislation of the foreign country, then the Letters Rogatory request cannot be honored.

There are some limited international tools available to side step time-consuming and complicated procedures for obtaining information where the charge involves drug trafficking. For example, Article 7 of the United Nations Convention Against Illicit Traffic in Narcotic Drugs and

---

136. *See* United States Department of State, International Judicial Assistance, *Notarial Services and Authentication of Documents*, http://travel.state.gov/law/judicial_assistance. html (accessed May 21, 2005).

137. Organization of American States, *Additional Protocol to the Inter American Convention on Letters Rogatory*, art. 3 http://www.oas.org/juridico/english/treaties/b-46.html (accessed May 21,2005).

138. *Id.* at art. 5.

139. *E.g., id.* at art. 1 & 2.

140. *See MLAT, supra* n. 128.

141. *See* Organization of American States, *supra* n. 137.

142. *See* 28 U.S.C. § 1781 (2005). The section provides in pertinent part:

   (a) The Department of State has power, directly, or through suitable channels–

   . . .

      (2) to receive a letter rogatory issued, or request made, by a tribunal in the United States, to transmit it to the foreign or international tribunal, officer, or agency to whom it is addressed, and to receive and return it after execution. . .

   (b) This section does not preclude–

   . . .

      (2) the transmittal of a letter rogatory or request directly from a tribunal in the United States to the foreign or international tribunal, officer, or agency to whom it is addressed and its return in the same manner.

Id.

143. *Id.* at § 1781(a)(2).

Psychotropic Substances,[144] provides a procedure to obtain evidence from other participating nations without Letters Rogatory.[145]

Additionally, those international organizations, such as the Organization of American States ("OAS"), which do provide protocols for Letters Rogatory, have taken steps to encourage participating OAS nations to incorporate the CoE Convention into existing protocols. Specifically, the Ministers of Justice of the OAS in April 2004 called upon OAS members to accede to the CoE Convention and incorporate its principles into their national legislation.[146] In short, the defense is relegated in a very real sense to relying upon the limited discovery obligations of the prosecutor.[147] The limitations are obvious. The defendant's desire for specific information in the possession of the host country may materially differ from the information sought by the prosecution.

IV. PRINCIPLES OF HARMONIZATION: AN ONGOING DILEMMA

A. THE CONVENTION AS A HARMONIZATION MODEL

There are differing models for harmonization of penal enforcement in the European Community. The classical instrument of international cooperation is the convention.[148] The convention model has its genesis in the Treaty on European Union, TEU.[149] Specifically, the so-called

---

144. International Narcotics Control Board, United Nations Convention Against Illicit Traffic in Narcotic Drugs and Psychotropic Substances, 1988 http://www.incb.org/e/conv/1988/index.htm (accessed Nov. 16, 2004).

145. *See MLAT, supra* n. 128. This convention entered into force on November 11, 1990.

146. *See* Guy De Vel, Dir. Gen. of the Legal Affairs of the Council of Europe, Remarks, *The Challenge of Cybercrime* (Council of Europe, Conference on the Challenge of Cybercrime Sept. 15-17, 2004) (*available at* http://www.coe.int/T/E/Com/Files/Events/2004-09-cybercrime/disc_deVel.asp) (accessed May 21, 2005) (also recognizing the decision of APEC leaders in 2002 to recommend to their members to adopt laws against cybercrime in conformity with the CoE Convention).

147. Fed. R. Crim. P. 16(a)(1)(E)(i)-(iii).

148. *See See* Mareike Braeunlich, *European Criminal Law* 31 (unpublished Master Thesis, Lund University Spring, 2002) (on file with author) (available at www.jur.lu.se/. . ./english/essay/Masterth.nsf/0/94E4D9B5A0990798C1256BC900560788/$File/xsmall.pdf?, at 13. (Another model is the "directive." A directive leaves the choice of forms and method for achieving the desired results to the Member states. (Treaty of the European Community, ECT, Art. 249). Penal sanctions are never included in a directive. For example, a convention was used as the model to criminalize fraud against EC financial interests, whereas, in the case of money laundering, the EC utilized a directive. A third method, the "intergovernmental method" provides for a structure of cooperation and common decision making between nation states resting primarily on a network of multi-lateral agreements that allow nation states to retain sovereignty).

149. The TEU, also referred to as the Maastricht Treaty, entered into force in 1993. Cooperation on justice and home affairs was institutionalized under Title VI of the treaty, Article K. *See* Europa, *Title VI: Provisions of Cooperation in the Fields of Justice and Home Affairs, Article K*, http://europa.eu.int/en/record/mt/title6.html (accessed May 21, 2005).

352   JOURNAL OF COMPUTER & INFORMATION LAW   [Vol. XXIII

"third pillar area" of the TEU, Title V, Articles 29-45, provides for police
and judicial cooperation in criminal matters.[150] Simply, a convention is
a treaty signed by participating nations which is then adopted nationally
in accordance with the constitutional requirements of each Member
State.[151] Conventions take the form of traditional international law
agreements, enforceable as international treaties but not through any
central organizational mechanism.[152] Procedural criminal rule making
is addressed in the TEU, Title VI, Article K.2 as follows: judicial cooperation in criminal matters, rules combating fraud on an international scale
and police cooperation for purposes of combating serious forms of international crime "shall be dealt with in compliance with the European
Convention for the Protection of Human Rights and Fundamental Freedoms of 4 November 1950 [ECHR] . . . ." The impact of the ECHR on
penal matters in Europe is recognized as the most elementary guarantee
of procedural due process rights in the criminal law context.[153] The
ECHR is typically incorporated into crime control instruments that take
the form of treaties to which the member state may agree.[154] Section II,
Article 15 of the CoE Convention incorporates the ECHR as the principal
safeguard of procedural due process.[155]

---

150. The European Convention, Brussels, 31 May 2002 (03.06), CONV. 69/02, *Sub-
ject:Justice and Home Affairs-Progress Report and General Problems*, at 4.

151. *Id.* The sole difference between conventions and agreements, both under the rubric
of a treaty, is the form in which a State may express its consent to be bound. Agreements
may be signed with or without reservations as to ratification, acceptance or approvals.
Conventions require ratification. Council of Europe, *Glossary*, *supra* n. 6.

152. *See,* Braeunlich, *supra* n. 148, at 10.

153. *See id.* at 9.

154. The continuous development of fundamental rights in the European Union Treaties has been an evolving process, recently culminating with the Treaty Establishing A
Constitution For Europe. Beginning in 1986, the preamble to the Single European Act, 2/
28/1986, provides for the development of international law on the basis of "the fundamental
rights recognized in the constitutions and laws of the member states." Article 6.2 of the
Maastricht Treaty, TEU, 2/7/1992, requires the Union to "respect fundamental rights, as
guaranteed by the [ECHR]. . ." The Nice Treaty, 2/26/2001,(Official Journal C80 of 10
March 2001) may determine if there is a serious breach of Article 6 by a member state. The
Treaty on the European Union, the Amsterdam Treaty, 10/2/1997, confirms "their attachment to fundamental social rights. . .and respect for human rights and fundamental freedoms and the rule of law . . . ." The Official Journal of the European Union recently
released the Treaty Establishing A Constitution for Europe, intended to replace all existing
treaties and agreements relative to the formation of the EU, including The Treaty Establishing the European Community (Official Journal C325 of 24 December 2002) and the
Treaty on the European Union, (Official Journal C325 of 24 December 2002).Constitution,
Article IV-437. Further, Title VI, Article II, for the first time, formulates specific constitutional due process rights in the field of criminal prosecution that shall be binding on all
member states. Official Journal, C310 (Dec. 16, 2004) (*available at* http://europa.eu.int/
eur-lex/lex/JOHtml).

155. *See supra* Discussion, § II, B (2).

Conventions, as a harmonization model for international criminal enforcement, are criticized for several reasons. Several of these criticisms also underscore the flawed approach to procedural harmonization in the CoE Convention.

First, conventions may not come into force within a reasonable period of time for lack of ratification.[156] It is usual for countries to sign but never follow up with ratification. The United States is a case in point.[157] The United States signed the Criminal Law Convention on Corruption on October 10, 2000, but has never ratified it. The Convention on Cybercrime was signed on December 11, 2001, but is not ratified. While the United States ratified the Convention on Mutual Administrative Assistance in Tax Matters on February 13, 1991, an insufficient number of member states ratified until four years later when the convention finally entered into force on January 4, 1995.[158] The European Convention on Extradition, CETS No. 024, was open for signature and accession by non-member states on December 13, 1957. The United States has never signed that convention.[159]

Second, conventions do not include any follow-up measures to ensure that ratification is followed by compliance. Member States may express "reservations" that allow them to be exempted from certain operative provisions of the convention. In fact, the United States signed the CoE Convention subject to several reservations.[160]

Another problem is the failure of uniform interpretation based on linguistic and cultural differences. These differences translate into a serious concern about the prosecution of foreign nationals.[161] Specifically, there is no guarantee that an accused will understand the language or culture in the prosecution venue. Nor is there any guarantee that an

---

156. Ratification is an act by which the State expresses its definitive consent to be bound by the treaty. Then the state must respect the provisions of the treaty and implement it. Council of Europe, *Glossary, supra* n. 6.

157. The United States, a non-member country of the Council of Europe was given "observer Status" on December 7, 1995. Observer status was enacted on May 14, 1993 by the Committee of Ministers and extended to any nation wishing to cooperate with the CoE and "willing to accept the principles of democracy, the rule of law and respect for human rights and fundamental freedoms of all persons within its jurisdiction." Res(95)37 on observer status for the United States of America with the Council of Europe (*available at* http://www.coe.int?t?E?com/About_Coe/Member_states/eUSA.asp) (accessed Jan. 17, 2005).

158. Statistics *available at* http://conventions.coe.int/Treaty/Commun/ListeTraites. asp?PO=U, (accessed Jan. 17, 2005).

159. *Id.*

160. *See e.g.*, Powell, *supra* n. 2, at vii, x, xi, xii, xvi, xxi. "Federal Clause" reservations allow for variations between domestic law and Convention obligations permitting parties to "modify or derogate from specified Convention obligations."

161. International Law Association, London Conference, *The Final Report On The Exercise of Universal Jurisdiction in Respect of Gross Human Rights Offenses*, www.ila-hq.org/pdf/Human%20Rights%20Law/HumanRig.pdf (accessed May 25, 2005).

accused will be afforded the right to counsel or an interpreter, or even have the right to call or examine witnesses. The CoE Convention resolves none of the foregoing criticisms.

B. THE FALLBACK OF "CULTURAL DIVERSITY"

The recognition of cultural differences among nations appears to be the greatest stumbling block to achieving harmonization in the area of procedural due process. Each nation has its own notion about what constitutes criminality, the appropriateness of punishment, proportionality of punishments, and the rights accorded to the accused. Often, the rubric of cultural differences, ostensibly used to oppose harmonization, is merely a cover for opposition based upon "irrational historical reminiscences" and political opposition.[162] In an effort to reach a baseline consensus among nations, the CoE Convention employs "flexible harmonization,"[163] a model of uniform rule making confined to establishing parameters for acceptable substantive rules, leaving the formulation of procedural due process rules to the cultural peculiarities of each nation.[164] This paradigm of flexible harmonization facilitates diplomatic appeasement to national sovereignty enabling the CoE to accomplish law enforcement goals. However, the legitimacy of reaching law enforcement goals at the expense of fundamental fairness to the accused is contrary to the long term interests of international governance.

Added to the need for political appeasement is the perplexing phenomenon that often follows accommodation. Nations frequently enter into treaties and then fail to act in conformity with treaty obligations. The reasons that nations enter into treaties, only to later ignore them, remain sketchy.[165] Typically, successful implementation rests on the degree of one nation's willingness to voluntarily diminish its sovereignty over criminal enforcement for the common good of the international community. Not unexpectedly, compliance can be predicted where it is in the material interest of the participating nation to do so.

It bears repeating that the issue here is not whether international legal conventions work but rather, whether the CoE Convention, despite the aforementioned legal, cultural and political complications, provides a reliable guarantee of procedural due process of law. The watered down compromise of flexible harmonization offers little to motivate nations to voluntarily relinquish sovereignty in favor of international regulation.

---

162. *See* Sieber, *supra* n. 1, at 11, 16.
163. *Id.*
164. *Id.*
165. For an interesting discussion on this topic, *See,* Oona A. Hathaway, *The Promise and Limits of the International Law of Torture,* in *Foundations of International Law and Politics,* 228-238 (Oona A. Hathaway and Harold Hongju Koh eds., Foundation Press 2005).

Instead, the absence of procedural harmonization undermines predictable implementation and is contrary to a party's national interest to protect its own citizens abroad.

V. THE COE CONVENTION DOES NOT ADEQUATELY SAFEGUARD PROCEDURAL DUE PROCESS RIGHTS

A. WHAT IS PROCEDURAL DUE PROCESS?

The Fifth Amendment to the United States Constitution provides that "No person shall be . . . deprived of life, liberty or property, without due process of law . . . ." The Fourteenth Amendment contains the same language as expressly applied to the States.[166] The United States Supreme Court recognizes both procedural and substantive due process components.[167]

Substantive due process provides the contours of what laws may proscribe or prohibit. Procedural due process focuses on the concept of fundamental fairness and the rules that provide fair procedures to ensure that an accused is not unfairly or unjustly convicted. Explicit procedural guarantees of due process are found in the Constitution and the Bill of Rights.[168] However, as discussed below, domestic juridical limitation on the application of procedural due process to aliens necessarily diminishes the United States' commitment to the general admonitions in the treaty.

B. WHAT IS THE MODEL FOR PROCEDURAL DUE PROCESS IN THE COE CONVENTION?

Section II, Article 15, entitled "Conditions and Safeguards" of the CoE Convention, leaves the responsibility for enactment of procedural due process rules to each party as "provided for under its domestic law. . . which shall provide for the adequate protection of human rights and liberties, including rights arising pursuant to obligations it has undertaken under the 1950 Council of Europe Convention for the Protection of Human Rights and Fundamental Freedoms [ECHR], the 1966 United

---

166. The due process clause finds its roots in a similar clause of the Magna Carta in which the King of England agreed in 1215 A.D. that "[n]o free man shall be taken, or imprisoned, or be disseised of his Freehold, or liberties, or free Customs, or be outlawed, or exiled, or any otherwise destroyed; nor will we pass upon him, nor condemn him, but by lawful Judgment of his peers, or by the Law of the Land." (available at http://www.bl.uk/collections/treasures/magnatranslation.html).

167. *Schriro v. Summerlin*, 124 S. Ct. 2519, 2523 (2004).

168. *See e.g.*, U.S. Const., art. III: right to a jury trial; amend. V: right to a grand jury indictment, prohibitions against double jeopardy and self-incrimination, right to due process of law; amend. VI: rights to a speedy and public trial, jury of one's peers, to confront and cross-examine witnesses, right to counsel; and amend. XIV right to due process as applied to the states.

356   JOURNAL OF COMPUTER & INFORMATION LAW   [Vol. XXIII

Nations International Covenant on Civil and Political Rights, and other
applicable international human rights instruments, and which shall incorporate the principle of proportionality."[169]

Specifically, these rules do not require judicial supervision, but may
include "other independent supervision."[170] The parties are also admon-
ished to "consider the impact of the powers and procedures in this section
upon the rights, responsibilities and legitimate interests of third parties."[171] The tone is limited to aspirational guidance.

The Explanatory Report underscores the point that there are no unified or minimal standards for procedural due process: "As the Convention applies to Parties of many different legal systems and cultures, it is
not possible to specify in detail the applicable conditions and safeguards
for each power or procedure."[172] Significantly, the Explanatory Report
acknowledges that the ECHR is only applicable "in respect of the European States that are Parties to them."[173] The United States is not a
party to the ECHR and thus, is not bound by its minimal standards. Indeed, any CoE Convention signatory, not a member state of the Council
of Europe, is not a party to the ECHR because the ECHR is not open for
signature to non-member states of the Council of Europe.[174]

The safeguard of "proportionality" is also left to the discretion of the
parties. "States will apply related principles of their law such as limitations on overbreadth of production orders and reasonableness for
searches and seizures."[175] In very sketchy fashion, the Explanatory Report homogenizes aspirational recommendations for protections against
self-incrimination and possible invasions of privacy rights through intrusive means of search and seizure:

> National legislatures will have to determine, in applying binding inter-
> national obligations and established domestic principles, which of the
> powers and procedures are sufficiently intrusive in nature to require
> implementation of particular conditions and safeguards. As stated in
> Paragraph 215, Parties should clearly apply conditions and safeguards
> such as these with respect to interception [of data communications],
> given its intrusiveness. At the same time, for example, such safeguards
> need not apply equally to preservation [of seized data communication].
> Other safeguards that should be addressed under domestic law include
> the right against self incrimination, and legal privileges and specificity

---

169. Council of Europe, *Treaty*, *supra* n. 4, at art.15, ¶ 1.

170. *Id.* at ¶ 2.

171. *Id.*

172. CoE Explanatory Report, *supra* n. 46, at ¶ 145.

173. *Id.*

174. Council of Europe, http://www.conventions.coe.int/Treaty/Commun/ListeTraites.
asp (accessed Jan. 17, 2005) (listing treaties open to the member states of the Council of
Europe).

175. CoE Explanatory Report, *supra* n. 46, at ¶ 146.

of individuals or places which are the object of the application of the measure.[176]

Using a legally non-binding treaty as the primary source of procedural due process, in lieu of specific minimal guidelines to protect an accused, results in a structural weakness in the treaty. More than mere advice is required where penal sanctions stand to deprive an accused of liberty.

C. The Dynamic of Self-Enforcement

Whether a particular party has enacted sufficient due process protections, or even extends existing domestic due process protections to aliens prosecuted within its borders, must necessarily remain untested until cases are actually prosecuted. The dynamic of self-enforcement of the treaty objectives remains within the domain of each respective national legislature. What are the prospects for extending procedural due process to aliens prosecuted for cybercrime in the United States?

Central to the model of procedural due process in the CoE Convention is the mandate that each nation recognize "rights arising pursuant to obligations it has undertaken under the 1950 Council of Europe Convention for the Protection of Human Rights and Fundamental Freedoms [ECHR], the 1966 United Nations International Covenant on Civil and Political Rights, and other applicable international human rights instruments, and which shall incorporate the principle of proportionality."[177] The Supreme Court of the United States, in rejecting an alien's claim for damages under the Aliens Tort statute arising out of an alleged arbitrary arrest and unlawful seizure,[178] concluded that neither the ECHR nor the other international treaties imposed any legal obligation on the United States. Therefore, federal courts had no power to enforce individual rights violations under these treaties, even where the United States was a signatory.

> Petitioner says that his abduction by [DEA operatives] was an 'arbitrary arrest' within the meaning of the Universal Declaration of Human Rights (Declaration), G.A. Res. 217A(III), U.N. Doc. A/810 (1948). And

---

176. *See id.* at ¶ 147.

177. Council of Europe, *Treaty, supra* n. 4, art.15, ¶ 1.

178. The petitioner was acquitted on charges arising out of the torture and murder of a DEA agent by Mexican nationals. In a related lower court decision, the Ninth Circuit found that DEA agents had no authority under federal law to execute an extra-territorial arrest of the petitioner indicted in a federal court in Los Angeles. *Alvarez-Machain v. U.S.*, 331 F.3d 604, 609 (9th Cir. 2003). In fact, the agents unlawfully kidnapped petitioner to bring him to the United States to stand trial. *Id.* Petitioner moved to dismiss his indictment based upon "outrageous government conduct" and a violation of the extradition treaty with Mexico. *Id.* The district court agreed, the Ninth Circuit affirmed and the Supreme Court reversed holding that the forcible seizure did not divest the federal court of jurisdiction. *United States v. Alavrez*, 504 U.S. 655 (1992).

> he traces the rule against arbitrary arrest not only to the Declaration, but also to article nine of the International Covenant on Civil and Political Rights (Covenant), Dec. 19, 1996, 999 U.N.T.S. 171, to which the United States is a party, and to various other conventions to which it is not. But the Declaration does not of its own force impose obligations as a matter of international law . . . . And, although the Covenant does not bind the United States as a matter of international law, the United States ratified the Covenant on the express understanding that it was not self-executing and so did not itself create obligations enforceable in the federal courts.[179]

Thus, the ECHR, along with the other human rights treaties, incorporated into Section II, Art. 15, creates no enforceable procedural due process rights in United States federal courts.

Moreover, the decision to extend the protections of the Bill of Rights to aliens is not an automatic one or implicit in the concept of ordered liberty, and so the courts have held. Specifically, the Supreme Court declined to extend the protection of the Fourth Amendment to an alien extradited to the United States for trial on criminal charges. The Court reasoned that:

> [A]liens receive constitutional protections when they have come within the territory of the United States and developed substantial connections with this country. . .but this sort of presence-lawful but involuntary [extradition]- is not the sort to indicate any substantial connection with our country.[180]

Further rejecting the alien's equal protection argument, to wit: that aliens should be afforded the same constitutional rights afforded U.S. citizens in criminal cases, the Court concluded: "They are constitutional decisions of this Court expressly according different protections to aliens than to citizens, based on our conclusion that the particular provisions in question were not intended to extend to aliens in the same degree as to citizens." Justice Kennedy, in his concurring opinion, concluded that:

> The distinction between citizens and aliens follows from the undoubted proposition that the Constitution does not create, nor do general principles of law create, any judicial relation between our country and some undefined, limitless class of non-citizens who are beyond our territory.[181]

These decisions leave little doubt that the Bill of Rights does not operate extraterritorially in relation to searches and seizures authorized under the CoE Convention or in relation to constitutional infringements of the right to privacy in seizing data communications used to prosecute aliens for cybercrime. Instead, the extension of existing procedural due

---

179. *Sosa v. Alavrez-Machain, et.al.*, 124 S.Ct. 2739, 2767 (2004).

180. *United States v. Verdugo-Urquidez*, 494 U.S. 259, 271 (1990).

181. *Id.* at 275.

process guarantees to aliens turns on the two-prong voluntariness and substantial connection analysis. That ad hoc determination leaves little room for predictability in the application of the treaty in the United States.

Accordingly, the procedural due process rhetoric of the CoE Convention has no demonstrable influence on American jurisprudence. As noted previously, the Secretary of State indicated that no implementing legislation was required to ratify the treaty, necessarily excluding any additional legislation to effectuate the rights of aliens in the United States consistent with Section II, Art. 15 of the treaty. The United States should expect no more protection with respect to its citizens similarly situated in other participating nations. The cycle of mistrust is inevitably self-perpetuating under these circumstances.

D.   REJECTING THE MESSY COMPROMISE IN FAVOR OF A STRUCTURAL FIX

The CoE Convention abdicates all responsibility for providing procedural due process of law to an accused charged with crimes arising under offense categories. The sole justification provided is that it is "impossible" to draft even minimal obligatory guidelines for due process based on "cultural differences." Is this reason justified?

The logic simply does not follow that culturally diverse parties can agree on offense conduct but not upon internationally recognized standards that preserve basic human freedoms. The treaty's use of flexible harmonization strikes an ostensibly workable compromise among sovereign nations, particularly where the imposition of procedural due process standards may be superior to those offered by a party's own domestic legislation.

Indeed, this glaring legal ambiguity in the CoE Convention underscores a core weakness in international law, namely, the deference to territoriality principles of regulation and enforcement based on national sovereignty. The decentralized nature of international law, relegating enforcement to domestic legislation, results from the decentralized structure of international society and the inability to enforce violations of binding legal rules.[182] Left to the questionable dynamic of self-enforcement by participating nations, the CoE Convention surrenders any attempt to navigate the problem.

However, the counter-argument is persuasive. It may be unreasonable to expect the CoE Convention, a discreet body of international crimi-

---

182. For a more in-depth discussion of the problems with decentralization in international law, see H.J. Morgenthal, *Politics Among Nations*, in *Foundations of International Law and Politics*, 31-42, (Oona A. Hathaway and Harold Hongju Koh eds., Foundation Press 2005).

nal law, to resolve the bigger issue of decentralization that characterizes the entire body of international law.

Yet, the CoE Convention recognizes that criminal enforcement typically requires serious privacy intrusions[183] to facilitate individual prosecution. The equation presented by the CoE Convention, allowing for enforcement without ascertainable measures of procedural due process, results in an imbalance disfavoring individual liberties implicated by the very nature of a criminal prosecution. Thus, the need to eradicate cybercrime cannot outweigh the equally important need to achieve a consensus on minimal standards for securing fundamental procedural due process guarantees.

Additionally, mutual cooperation, a centerpiece of the treaty,[184] will be less forthcoming where one participant cannot rely on another to guarantee fair treatment of its own citizens subject to prosecution. This may be a reason that the CoE Convention does not supercede, but merely supplements pre-existing MLATs. The dynamic of national self-enforcement may be easier to predict "one on one" than on a broader international scale where countries frequently fail to honor treaty obligations, or fail to ratify them at all.

One solution may be the addition of a Protocol[185] to the treaty, modeled after the proposed Treaty Establishing a Constitution for Europe,[186] [hereinafter "Constitution"], which does include specific minimal procedural due process formulations, extended to citizens of all participating nations. The Constitution is expected to come into force in 2006, replacing all international agreements that provide for European unification.[187] Specifically, the Constitution provides for the right to an effective remedy and to a fair trial,[188] presumption of innocence and right of defense,[189] principles of legality and proportionality of criminal offenses

---

183. Global Internet Liberty Campaign, *Member Letter on Council of Europe Convention on Cybercrime*, http://www.gilc.org/privacy/coe-letter-1000.html (accessed May 21, 2005) (The Global Internet Liberty Campaign, comprised of national and international organizations such as the American Civil Liberties Union, the Human Rights Network, Privacy International, and others, presented detailed objections to the CoE about the CoE Convention with respect to Data Protection, and privacy concerns. "We believe that the draft treaty is contrary to well established norms for the protection of the individual, that it improperly extends the police authority of national governments, that it will undermine the development of network security techniques, and that it will reduce government accountability in future law enforcement conduct").

184. Council of Europe, *Treaty, supra* n. 4, art. 23.

185. *See* Council of Europe, *Glossary, supra* n. 6 (explaining that a protocol is a legal instrument that compliments, amend or modifies the main treaty).

186. Constitution, *supra* n. 154.

187. *See id.* at Part IV, Art. IV-437(1).

188. *See id.* at Title IV, Art. II-107.

189. *See id.* at Title IV, Art. II-108.

and penalties,[190] and the prohibition against double jeopardy.[191] Additionally, the Constitution expressly prohibits any abuse of rights set forth in its other provisions.[192] This structural fix is, therefore, consistent with the prevailing international movement toward true harmonization.

VI. CONCLUSION

The decentralized nature of international law, particularly in the sphere of criminal law enforcement, may explain the CoE Convention's accommodation of flexible harmonization to achieve law enforcement goals aimed at the timely eradication of cybercrime. Having a sense for "what will fly" in the international body politic, heavily dependent upon cultural understandings and differences, must always be a practical and necessary concern.

However, cybercrime prosecutions will most certainly raise issues relating to concurrent jurisdiction and/or the application of domestic law to foreign nationals. While the particular offense conduct may be properly circumscribed, the means of investigating and prosecuting the conduct will not be predictable. The rights of an accused suffer where true procedural harmonization is excised from the convention model. Nowhere is this legal defect more apparent than in the disconnect between the treaty's incorporation of human rights treaties as the due process model, and the American constitutional legal precedent rejecting the same treaties as a source of rights protections for aliens.

In its present form, the CoE Convention allows state intrusions into the sphere of individual privacy rights to gather evidence for use in subsequent criminal prosecutions without adequate guarantees of procedural due process. One solution may be the addition of a Protocol to the treaty, modeled after the proposed CoE Constitution providing minimal guidelines for procedural due process, extended to citizens of all participating nations. In this way, the CoE Convention on Cybercrime could become a blueprint for future international endeavors to harmonize penal law enforcement.

---

190. *See id.* at Title IV, Art. II-109.
191. *See id.* at Title IV, Art. II-110.
192. *See id.* at Title VII, Art. II-114.

[7]

In Search of a Balance Between Police Power and Privacy in the Cybercrime Treaty

By D.C. Kennedy[1]

---

[1] Ms. Kennedy graduated from Emory University School of Law in December 2001 and is a licensed attorney in Georgia. She has served as the Atlanta bureau chief for The Internet Law Journal and has worked as a research assistant for the Center for Social and Legal Research, a non-profit organization focused on privacy issues.

Introduction

Imagine that you wake up one morning, turn on your computer, and open an e-mail message with a catchy phrase in the subject line. Immediately after opening the e-mail's attachment, your personal computer is severely damaged. Obviously having a bad day, you head to your job as an attorney for a multinational corporation. By the time you arrive at work, there has been damage to company computers across the globe. The monetary costs of the damage, coupled with the downtime, are astronomical. The CEO of your company is furious. You hope to diffuse the situation by informing your boss that the person who released the virus has been apprehended. Unfortunately, soon after explaining the good news of the perpetrator's capture, you learn that the individual, who admits involvement with the e-mail virus, will not be prosecuted in his home state because that state had no laws on the books outlawing his behavior at the time of the incident. In fact, none of the states where damage occurred will be able to prosecute because of lack of jurisdiction. The damage is done and the perpetrator is free.

Although the situation may sound far fetched, this is the basic story of the events surrounding the dissemination of the I LOVE YOU virus. The perpetrator was allowed to go free because the Philippines did not have appropriate cybercrime laws instituted at the time the virus was released.[2] This high-profile case is a superb introduction to the difficult issues arising from the existence of cyberspace.[3]

---

[2] *See* CBS News Online, *Love Bug Suspect Off the Hook, at* http://www.cbsnews.com/stories/2000/08/21/tech/main226472.shtml (Aug. 21, 2000).
[3] *See generally* Jay Krasovec, *Cyberspace: The Final Frontier, for Regulation?,* 31 AKRON L. REV. 101, 103 n.1 (1997) (defining cyberspace generically "to encompass the use of electronic communications over computer networks mainly via the Internet.").

In this "Age of the Internet,"[4] access to information is unprecedented. This access can be positively used to contact friends and businesses around the world or can be negatively used to gain unauthorized access to information or to steal profitable data. With the threat of sinister uses for access comes the need for protection – protection from attacks such as the I LOVE YOU virus[5] and protection from prying eyes.[6] Even though protection from these threats is hampered because of the international scope of the threat, this same scope assists the cybercriminal. No longer must a criminal be located physically in the proximity of his crime. Instead, through the same technology that makes the Internet such a popular personal and business instrument, the criminal is able to cause damage regardless of national borders. The ability of the cybercriminal to cross national borders without effort, coupled with the relative ease of his causing harm, present problems for states that want to crack down on cybercrime. These states must determine effective ways to investigate activity that occurs outside of their national boundaries, including investigations in states that may not outlaw the activity. In addition, the states investigating these crimes must employ individuals with the appropriate technical training who can devote long hours to tracing the electronic trails of cybercriminals.

In an effort to address the difficulties of investigating cybercriminals, the Council of Europe put forward a cybercrime treaty to harmonize definitions of cybercrime in states that

---

[4] Susan Gindin, *Lost and Found in Cyberspace: Informational Privacy in the Age of the Internet*, 34 SAN DIEGO L. REV. 1153 (1997) (using term from title of Gindin's article).
[5] *See generally* James Evans, *Cyber-Crime Laws Emerge, but Slowly*, IDG.net, *available at* http://www.cnn.com/2000/TECH/computing/07/05/cyber.laws.idg/ (July 5, 2000) (describing how the "I Love You" virus brought attention to the need for domestic cybercrime laws).
[6] *See* Gavin Skok, *Establishing a Legitimate Expectation of Privacy in Clickstream Data*, 6 MICH. TELECOMM. & TECH. L. REV. 61, 61 (1999/2000) (explaining that the "prying eyes" concept refers to those who track individuals' activities on the Internet).

become parties to the treaty.[7] To assist law enforcement with investigation of these crimes, the

treaty provides for procedures to assist law enforcement in the search and seizure of computer

data and facilitates cooperative investigations by states affected in specific cybercrime incidents.[8]

The increase in police power that would result from the treaty concerns many privacy

advocates.[9] The basis for this concern is the limited protection available to support privacy of

information pertaining to individuals.[10]

    To examine the privacy issues at stake, this paper will first explore the increase in police

power granted by the treaty. The paper will follow this assessment by looking at the concerns

raised by the formulation of the treaty itself. It will then end by exploring the opportunity missed

by the treaty drafters to address fundamental privacy concerns. Part I will analyze the concept of

cybercrime in an effort to define the evil that the treaty is intended to address. As part of this

---

[7] *Crime in Cyberspace: First Draft of International Convention Released for Public Discu*ssion, *see infra* note 46 (criminalizing illegal access, interception, or interference with computer systems).

[8] Juliana Gruenwald, *Europeans Defining the Long Arm of The Cyberlaw, at* http://news.zdnet.co.uk/story/0,,s2081836,00.html (Sept. 25, 2000)(on file with the Richmond Journal of Law & Technology)(noting that the treaty requires states to "provide law enforcement authorities with the ability to conduct computer searches and seize computer data"); *see also id.* sec. 2, art. 15 (subjecting treaty powers to conditions and safeguards as provided for under national law).

[9] *See e.g.,* LIBERATING CYBERSPACE: CIVIL LIBERTIES, HUMAN RIGHTS AND THE INTERNET 2 (Liberty ed., 1999) ("Can the requirements of law enforcement be reconciled with individuals' right to privacy?"). Note that technological possibilities that would theoretically guarantee complete personal privacy would also likely prevent law enforcement from tracing crimes related to such information. *See* Toby Lester, *The Reinvention of Privacy,* THE ATLANTIC MONTHLY, Mar. 1, 2001, at 27 (detailing a piece of software that would allow the user to conduct business on the Internet in an anonymous way, to the extent that the provider would not have the names of the user to provide if subpoenaed).

[10] *See* ALAN F. WESTIN, PRIVACY AND FREEDOM 367 (Atheneum New York 1967) (detailing privacy concerns in the Information Age); *see also* Tony Lester, *The Reinvention of Privacy,* THE ATLANTIC MONTHLY, Mar. 1, 2001, at 27 (discussing the forward looking nature of the 1967 privacy book by Westin). The argument for protection of privacy assumes that individuals have an expectation of privacy concerning personal information, but that this expectation has, for the most part, not been protected by law. *See* LIBERATING CYBERSPACE: CIVIL LIBERTIES, HUMAN RIGHTS AND THE INTERNET 6 (Liberty ed., 1999).

discussion, Part I will examine the new 'tools' available to criminals in the Internet Age and, conversely, the new dilemmas that these 'tools' create for law enforcement. Part II will discuss the recently proposed cybercrime treaty. It will examine the provisions of the first publicly-released draft, the list of complaints that flooded into the Council of Europe after the release of the draft, and the revisions that resulted from the complaints. Part III will use two hypotheticals to study the impact of the treaty. In the hypotheticals, three Southeast Asian states – with privacy protection levels spanning from low to high – will interact with a European state in a cybercrime investigation. The paper will assert that the interaction that ensues, the very interaction contemplated by the treaty, will have the potential to lower privacy protections for the states involved. Part IV will explore the concept of privacy at the international level, paying particular attention to the definitions of privacy provided by the Universal Declaration of Human Rights and the International Covenant on Civil and Political Rights. It will compare the traditional international understandings of privacy – privacy of communication, freedom of expression, and criminal procedure protections – with the revolutionary change needed for the concept of privacy in the Internet Age. Part IV will end by arguing that this new conception of privacy should account for intrusions by governments, businesses, and rogue individuals. Part V will conclude by arguing that the increase in police power required by the treaty necessitates an offsetting increase in privacy protection for individuals. It will contend that the treaty should have included a privacy provision that required parties to enact, through domestic legislation, protection of informational privacy from unwanted violations by governments, businesses, or rogue individuals. In the absence of such a provision, there can only be a hope that governments will adopt such legislation on their own and that reinterpretations of international treaties will include protections for informational privacy.

I. The Problem of Cybercrime

A. Cybercrime and the Cybercriminal

In this Age of the Internet, 'cybercrime' has become a household word, but its definition is seldom explained. Books and articles written on the subject often assume that the reader understands the many facets of cybercrime. For many, however, computer hacking[11] and computer viruses[12] are the main images conveyed by the term. While these crimes comprise two important categories of cybercrime, many other crimes can be committed or facilitated utilizing computer networks. A non-exhaustive list of cybercrimes includes: fraud, forgery, counterfeiting, gambling, transmission of child pornography, transmission of threats, transmission of harassing communications, interception of communications, copyright infringement, and theft of trade secrets.[13]

The motivations of those who commit cybercrimes may be as varied as the nature of the cybercrime itself. Juveniles may be drawn by the prestige of outwitting adults.[14] Insiders may

---

[11] The term 'hacking' is somewhat confusing because people use the term to refer to different types of activities. A comprehensive definition of hacking includes numerous aspects of the term. A hacker is "[a] person who enjoys exploring the details of computers and how to stretch their capabilities." A hacker is "[a] malicious or inquisitive meddler who tries to discover information by poking around." A hacker is "[a] person who enjoys learning the details of programming systems and how to stretch their capabilities, as opposed to most users who prefer to learn on the minimum necessary." Sans Institute Resources, *NSA Glossary of Terms Used in Security and Intrusion Detection, at* http://www.sans.org/newlook/resources/glossary.htm (Apr. 1998).

[12] A virus is "[a] program or piece of code that is loaded onto [a] computer without [the user's] knowledge and runs against [the user's] wishes." Webopedia, *at* http://webopedia.internet.com/TERM/v/virus.html (last modified Feb. 5, 2002).

[13] David Goldstone & Betty-Ellen Shave, *International Dimensions of Crimes in Cyberspace*, 22 FORDHAM INT'L L.J. 1924, 1925 (1999); Gavin Skok, *Establishing a Legitimate Expectation of Privacy in Clickstream Data*, 6 MICH. TELECOMM. & TECH. L. REV. 61, 68 n.23 (1999/2000).

[14] In most instances, commentators distinguish juvenile cybercriminals, who are believed to be acting mischievously but not maliciously, from advanced criminals, who are expected to cause serious consequences by their actions. MODEL CODE OF CYBERCRIMES INVESTIGATIVE PROCEDURE Art. 1, § 2(c), *at* http://cybercrimes.net/MCCIP/art1.htm (2001).

be seeking retribution for a perceived wrong by a business or a former employer.[15] Hackers may

simply want bragging rights associated with compromising a particular computer system.[16]

Virus writers may be motivated by prestige, as well as by malicious feelings towards others.[17]

Criminal groups functioning on the Internet may seek monetary gain.[18] Foreign terrorists may

seek foreign intelligence.[19] Even with these various motivators, there is at least one common

characteristic of the people who commit cybercrimes. Yesterday's street criminal had "street

smarts"; today's cybercriminal has "computer smarts." In order to be successful at their craft,

cybercriminals need to possess a knowledge of computers that is far superior to the average

user's amateur skills. This knowledge allows the criminal to mask his criminal activity and to

divert the efforts of law enforcement officials.[20]

B. The New Tools of the Cybercriminal

Technology provides the cybercriminal with a new bag of 'tools' that make him more

effective at his craft. In this Internet Age, the 'tools' are not physical implements, but instead are

advantages for those who commit cybercrime. The first such 'tool' is the ability to hide evidence

pertaining to the cybercrime. The evidence is virtually hidden because of the instantaneous

transfer of data through computer systems.[21] The cybercriminal has the capacity to act at one

site in cyberspace and then, taking the evidence of the crime with him, to leave instantaneously.

The second 'tool' is the cybercriminal's ability to hide his identity. In effect, a skilled

---

[15] *See id.*
[16] *See id.*
[17] *See id.*
[18] *See id.*
[19] *See id.*
[20] *See id.*
[21] U. Sieber, *Computer Crime and Criminal Information Law – New Trends in the International Risk and Information Society,* Section E, Criminal Procedural Law, *at* http://www.uplink.com.au/lawlibrary/Documents/Docs/Doc122.html (last visited Sept. 17, 2002) (on file with the Richmond Journal of Law & Technology).

cybercriminal is able to attack computer systems leaving few, if any, clues as to his identity. His

identity is further concealed because he can easily commit the cybercrime without being

physically present in a jurisdiction.[22] The third 'tool' is the cybercriminal's ability to increase

his cybercriminal activity with minimal effort. The cybercriminal can ignore international

boundaries[23] by simultaneously targeting multiple victims in multiple states.[24] Ultimately, these

'tools' provide the cybercriminal with an international forum for cybercrime in a world where

laws criminalizing his behavior are limited to domestic borders.

C. Challenges for Law Enforcement

With each of the cybercriminal's new 'tools,' law enforcement officials face new

challenges.[25] The cybercriminal's first 'tool,' his instantaneous ability to hide data in computer

systems, creates a host of problems for law enforcement.[26] In domestic investigations, law

enforcement officials may discover that critical data is stored on a networked computer that is

located in another state. Law enforcement must then determine if their domestic court order is

sufficient to search the storage facility outside the state's territory or if mutual assistance must be

sought with law enforcement in the other state.[27] Even in the instance of information stored with

ISPs, the procedures that law enforcement need to follow are not uniform from state to state,

meaning that the task of obtaining the information may be quite time consuming.[28] If the

evidence is encrypted, there is a question as to whether a witness can be compelled to provide a

printout of encrypted data when questioned by law enforcement authorities or interrogated in

---

[22] David Goldstone & Betty-Ellen Shave, *International Dimensions of Crimes in Cyberspace*, 22
FORDHAM INT'L L.J. 1924, 1925 (1999).
[23] *See id.*
[24] *See id.*
[25] *See id.*
[26] Sieber, *supra* note 21.
[27] Goldstone & Shave, *supra* note 22, at 1937-38.
[28] *Id.* at 1937.

court. This situation becomes particularly daunting when an encryption key[29] is held by a second

person who is located outside the state's territory.[30] All of these inquiries take time and may

provide the cybercriminal the time frame needed to further conceal the incriminating data.

The second 'tool' to which law enforcement must respond is the cybercriminal's ability

to hide his identity. By skillfully using a computer system, the cybercriminal has the ability to

mask his identity or remain anonymous.[31] If the law enforcement cannot identify the

cybercriminal by the clues left in cyberspace, it may be extremely difficult to track the

criminal.[32] Because the cybercriminal can commit a crime without being present in a

jurisdiction, the cybercrime scene has no physical boundaries[33] and leaves law enforcement with

few, if any, physical leads as to the identity of the cybercriminal. Unlike the situation where a

criminal's location can be approximated by the distance that he could possibly have traveled

---

[29] One of the two forms of encryption is public-key encryption. Public-key encryption is "[a] cryptographic system that uses two keys – a public key known to everyone and a private or secret key known only to the recipient of the message. When John wants to send a secure message to Jane, he uses Jane's public key to encrypt the message. Jane then uses her private key to decrypt it. An important element to the public key system is that the public and private keys are related in such a way that only the public key can be used to encrypt messages and only the corresponding private key can be used to decrypt them. Moreover, it is virtually impossible to deduce the private key if you know the public key." Webopedia, *at* http://webopedia.internet.com/TERM/p/public_key_cryptography.html (last modified Oct. 29, 2001).

[30] Interview with Bill Thompson, Internet Privacy and Security Issues Expert for Special Services Group, in Atlanta, Ga. (Sept. 15, 2000); *see also* U. Sieber, *Computer Crime and Criminal Information Law – New Trends in the International Risk and Information Society,* Section E, Criminal Procedural Law, *at* http://www.uplink.com.au/lawlibrary/Documents/Docs/Doc122.html (last visited Sept. 17, 2002).

[31] The cybercriminal is able to remain anonymous not because the technology does not exist to track him, but because the resources needed to train and fund law enforcement in tracing techniques are generally not adequate. Interview with Bill Thompson, Internet Privacy and Security Issues Expert for Special Services Group, in Atlanta, Ga. (Sept. 15, 2000).

[32] David Goldstone & Betty-Ellen Shave, *International Dimensions of Crimes in Cyberspace,* 22 FORDHAM INT'L L.J. 1924, 1937 (1999); *see also* Nan Hunter, et al., *Contemporary Challenges to Privacy Rights,* 43 N.Y.L. Sch. L. Rev. 195, 198 (1999).

since the crime occurred, cybercriminals have no effective limitation on their distance from the

crime scene – even a second after the crime was committed.

The cybercriminal's third 'tool,' his ability to increase criminal activity by striking

multiple victims in multiple states, creates several problems. Law enforcement must first

determine whether domestic criminal laws are applicable to crimes committed by utilizing

international data networks.[34] If the domestic court system makes a determination that the laws

are not applicable, an investigation may be inappropriate, as no domestic laws have been

violated. Even if the domestic criminal law applies, jurisdictional issues must still be

addressed.[35] If a perpetrator has committed crimes in more than one state, the home state must

make a determination concerning extradition. In a crime involving multiple victim states, a

home state that is willing to extradite the accused must decide on one state to which to send the

accused. Conversely, a home state may be unable to extradite because the laws regarding

cybercrimes vary substantially in the two states.[36] In the case where extradition is not possible,

the home state may have the option of prosecuting the accused if jurisdiction can be established

by the presence of the accused in the home state. This solution may not satisfy the victim, as the

penalties for the cybercrime may be different in the home state and the victim state. In addition,

the victim may not believe that the same diligence will be used in the prosecution of the accused

in the home state as would be used in the victim state. The possibility also exists that the

---

[33] *See* MODEL CODE OF CYBERCRIMES INVESTIGATIVE PROCEDURE Art. VII, *at*
http://cybercrimes.net/MCCIP/art7.htm (2001)(obtaining evidence - search and seizure).
[34] U. Sieber, *Computer Crime and Criminal Information Law – New Trends in the International Risk and Information Society,* Section E, Criminal Procedural Law, *at*
http://www.uplink.com.au/lawlibrary/Documents/Docs/Doc122.html (last visited Sept. 17, 2002)
(on file with the Richmond Journal of Law & Technology).
[35] David Goldstone & Betty-Ellen Shave, *International Dimensions of Crimes in Cyberspace*, 22
FORDHAM INT'L L.J. 1924, 1938-39 (1999).
[36] *Id.*

accused committed no crime according to the laws of the home state; thus, he would face no penalty for his activity.[37]

While the term 'cybercrime' did not exist twenty years ago, today the number of attacks is increasing and the monetary damage from the crimes is staggering. Cybercriminals are able to benefit from the use of their new 'tools,' while law enforcement is plagued with a host of new cyberproblems. To even the playing field, law enforcement officials need increased police powers to combat the new 'tools' of cybercriminals.

II. Treaty on Cybercrime

A. Draft 19: The First Publicly-Released Version of the Cybercrime Treaty[38]

Although no treaty is likely to address the full scope of the problems created by cybercriminals' new 'tools,' the treaty drafted by the Council of Europe[39] endeavors to address several of the basic problems. The Council of Europe first examined the problems associated with the international nature of cybercrimes when it drafted a 1995 paper recommending that states adopt laws regarding cybercrime.[40] Realizing the need for a legally binding instrument,

---

[37] "In addition to the formal concerns related to substantive laws and procedural laws, international computer crime investigations are hampered by a variety of operational issues." *Id.* at 1939. These concerns include: "expertise and coordination," "communication," and "timeliness." *Id.*; *see also Cybercrime Part II – Law Enforcement Challenges*, 54 Mishpat Cyberlaw Informer, *at* http://mishpat.net/cyberlaw/archive/cyberlaw54.shtml (last visited Sept. 20, 2001).

[38] In April 2000, the treaty was released to the public via the Website of the Council of Europe. Drafters of the treaty had been working on the project since May 1997. Reuters, *Cybercrime Treaty Gets a Makeover, available at* http://news.zdnet.co.uk/story/0,,s2082557,00.html (Nov. 14, 2000).

[39] The Council of Europe is a "41-nation human rights watchdog." *Id.*

[40] Juliana Gruenwald, *Europeans Defining the Long Arm of The Cyberlaw, at* http://news.zdnet.co.uk/story/0,,s2081836,00.html (Sept. 25, 2000) (on file with the Richmond Journal of Law & Technology) (describing reaction to the release of Draft 19). As noted in Part I of the paper, problems associated with the international nature of the crimes include the cooperation needed between states to adequately investigate such crimes and the hurdles created when the activity is not illegal in one of the states involved.

the Council of Europe began deliberations on the cybercrime treaty in 1997.[41] The Council

invited observers from Canada, Israel, Japan, South Africa, and the United States[42] to take part in

the negotiations in the hopes that the resulting treaty would have international impact.[43] The

goal of these discussions was to create a cybercrime treaty which would "harmonize laws against

hacking, fraud, computer viruses, child pornography and other Internet crimes"[44] as well as

"make criminal investigations and proceedings concerning criminal offences related to computer

systems and data more effective and to enable the collection of electronic evidence of a criminal

offense."[45]

In April 2000, after nearly three years of negotiations, the Council posted to its website

the first publicly-released version of the proposed treaty.[46] The proposed treaty addressed four

principal areas: cybercrime, search and seizure, jurisdiction, and international cooperation.[47] In

the area of cybercrime, this draft of the treaty criminalized four categories of crime: access

crimes, data crimes, systems crimes, and crimes involving "illegal devices."[48] The first category,

---

[41] *Id.*

[42] James Evans, *Cyber-Crime Laws Emerge, but Slowly*, IDG.net, *available at* http://www.cnn.com/2000/TECH/computing/07/05/cyber.laws.idg/ (July 5, 2000).

[43] The council included these additional countries because of the high level of Internet activity in each country. Eighty percent of the world's Internet traffic emanates from the states participating in the negotiations. Reuters, *Cybercrime Treaty Gets a Makeover, available at* http://news.zdnet.co.uk/story/0,,s2082557,00.html (Nov. 14, 2000).

[44] *Id.*

[45] Preamble, *Final Draft Convention on Cyber-crime*, *at* http://conventions.coe.int/Treaty/en/Treaties/Html/185.htm (Nov. 23, 2001).

[46] The draft released was number 19. *Crime in Cyberspace: First Draft of International Conventional Released for Public Discussion, at* http://conventions.coe.int/Treaty/EN/ projets/cybercrime (on file with the Richmond Journal of Law & Technology). The current draft is available at http://conventions.coe.int/Treaty/en/Treaties/Html/185.htm (Nov. 23, 2001).

[47] In this paper, I have omitted discussion of Offenses Related to Child Pornography (Article 9), Intellectual Property (Article 10), Attempt and Aiding and Abetting (Article 11), and Corporate Liability (Article 12). *Id.*

[48] For a definition of "illegal devices," see infra note 57. Similar categories are also used in a report compiled by McConnell International concerning the state of cybercrime laws throughout the world. This report divided cybercrime into the categories of data crimes, network crimes,

access crimes, outlawed unauthorized access to data contained in a computer system and access to the computer system itself.[49] Under this provision of the treaty, it would be possible for a cybercriminal to be convicted of both gaining access to a computer system where desired data was stored and obtaining the desired data.[50] Data crimes, a second category of crime outlined in the treaty, made illegal the interception of data and interference with data.[51] The definitions of the two data crimes provided in the draft make it unclear whether data theft,[52] the outright taking or copying for the cybercriminal's use, was outlawed. The third category, systems crimes, outlawed actions that intentionally hindered the functionality of a computer system.[53] A clear example of such a violation is a denial of service attack.[54] Less clear is whether the

---

access crimes, and related crimes. The data crimes category included data interception, data modification, and data theft. Included in the network crimes category were network interference and network sabotage. The access crimes category included unauthorized access and virus dissemination. Included in the related crimes category were aiding and abetting cybercrimes, computer-related forgery, and computer-related fraud. MCCONNELL INT'L, CYBER CRIME… AND PUNISHMENT? ARCHAIC LAWS THREATEN GLOBAL INFORMATION, *at* http://www.mcconnellinternational.com/services/CyberCrime.htm (Dec. 2000).

[49] Article 2 defined illegal access as "intentional[]… access to the whole or any part of a computer system without right." Convention Draft, Convention Draft, *supra* note 46.

[50] Because the particulars of the offenses are enacted through domestic legislation, the act of breaching the system and the act of obtaining the data might or might not both be illegal in a particular state.

[51] Article 3 defined illegal interception as "intentional[]… interception without right, made by technical means, of non-public transmissions of computer data to, from or within a computer system, as well as electromagnetic emissions from a computer system carrying such data." Article 4 defined data interference as "intentional[]… damaging, deletion, deterioration, alteration, or suppression of computer data without right." Convention Draft, Convention Draft, *supra* note 46.

[52] MCCONNELL INT'L, CYBER CRIME… AND PUNISHMENT? ARCHAIC LAWS THREATEN GLOBAL INFORMATION, *at* http://www.mcconnellinternational.com/services/CyberCrime.htm (Dec. 2000).

[53] Article 5 defined system interference as "intentional[]…serious hindering without right of the functioning of a computer system by inputting, damaging, deleting, deteriorating, altering or suppressing computer data." Convention Draft, Convention Draft, *supra* note 46.

[54] A denial of service attack is "a type of attack on a network that is designed to bring the network to its knees by flooding it with useless traffic." Webopedia, *at* http://webopedia.internet.com/TERM/D/DoS_attack.html (last modified Feb. 6, 2002).

dissemination of a computer virus[55] or computer worm[56] would constitute a violation. The final

category of crime, "illegal devices," made it a crime to produce, sell, or obtain for use any device

created or changed to facilitate the commission of any of the crimes enumerated in the treaty.[57]

The illegal device provision raised the question as to how an individual who possessed a device

could establish innocence. The provision was written with the presumption that an individual

who possessed a device had the intent to use the device to engage in a cybercrime. Because the

same devices are used by cybercriminals and by those employed to check the security of

business systems, the presumed criminal intent was unfounded.[58]

The cybercrime articles included in the draft shared several common characteristics.

First, the illegality of each crime was to be executed through the adoption of domestic legislation

in each of the signator states.[59] Second, the definition of each cybercrime was to include the

requirements of "intentionally" and "without right."[60] With the foregoing provisions, the treaty

provided a framework to outlaw four categories of cybercrimes.

---

[55] A computer virus is "an insidious piece of computer code written to damage systems. Viruses can be hidden in executable program files posted online." Netdictionary, *at* http://www.netdictionary.com/html/v.html (last visited Sept. 20, 2001).

[56] A computer worm is "an insidious and usually illegal computer program that is designed to replicate itself over a network for the purpose of causing harm and/or destruction. While a virus is designed to invade a single computer's hard drive, a worm is designed to invade a network. The most infamous worm was created by Robert Tappan Morris in November 1988; it infiltrated over 6,000 network systems around the globe." Netdictionary, *at* http://www.netdictionary.com/html/w.html (last visited Sept. 20, 2001).

[57] Article 6 defined an illegal device as "a device…[used] for the purpose of committing any of the offenses established in accordance with Article 2-5." McConnell, *supra* note 48.

[58] Brian Krebs, *Tech Groups Still Wary of International Cyber-Crime Treaty, at* http://www.newsbytes.com/news/00/158848.html (last modified Dec. 1, 2000)(on file with the Richmond Journal of Law & Technology) (covering the continuing concerns of security professionals over the illegal devices provision of the cybercrime treaty even after revisions attempted to address the perceived problem).

[59] Convention Draft, Convention Draft, *supra* note 46.

[60] "Without right" is not fully defined in Articles 2-6. The draft provided the option for the state to add the requirement of dishonest intent to the criminal definition. Convention Draft, Convention Draft, *supra* note 46.

As the preamble of the proposed cybercrime treaty envisioned that one of the purposes of the instrument was as "an international agreement to regulate trans-border search and seizure,"[61] this draft of the treaty also addressed search and seizure issues. The proposed treaty empowered law enforcement officials with the authority to search and seize data stored on computer systems, when such actions were taken as part of an investigation of cybercrime.[62] As part of this search and seizure power, the treaty authorized the officials to retain copies of the data.[63] Another power granted to law enforcement was the authority to order persons in its territory to produce specific computer data.[64] In investigations where a lapse of time could lead to a loss of computer-stored evidence, the proposed treaty authorized law enforcement officials to expedite the preservation of stored data and of traffic data.[65] As to stored data, expediting referred to shortening the time required to obtain a search and seizure warrant or a production order. With traffic data, the draft authorized law enforcement officials to require that ISPs retain traffic related to a suspect. In addition, the service provider was required to reveal enough of the traffic so that law enforcement officials could track the path by which the communication was transmitted.

---

[61] Convention Draft, *supra* note 46 (draft number 19).

[62] Article 14 of draft number 19 "empower[ed] competent authorities to search or similarly access a computer system... and computer data stored therein." In the article, the "competent authorities" were empowered to "seize or similarly secure computer data accessed... in view of their possible use in criminal investigations and proceedings." Convention Draft, *supra* note 46.

[63] In addition to seizure, Article 14 of draft number 19 authorized "mak[ing] and retain[ing] a copy of those computer data" and "render[ing] inaccessible or remov[ing] those computer data." Convention Draft, *supra* note 46.

[64] Article 15 of draft number 19 authorized "competent authorities to order a person in its territory... to submit specified computer data under this person's control." Convention Draft, *supra* note 46.

[65] Article 16 of draft number 19 enabled "competent authorities to order...the expeditious preservation of data that is stored by means of a computer system, at least where there are grounds to believe that the data...is [] particularly vulnerable to loss or modification." Article 17 of the same draft "ensure[d] the expeditious preservation of [] traffic data [concerning a specific

As was the case with the categories of cybercrime, the search and seizure articles shared several characteristics. First, according to the proposed treaty, the provisions were to be implemented through domestic legislation in each of the signatory states. Second, in an effort to address privacy concerns, each of the articles specifically provided that "the powers and procedures referred to in the present article shall be subject to conditions and safeguards as provided for under national law."[66] Third, conspicuously absent from the search and seizure provisions was any mention of a requirement for judicial review for particular applications of the new law enforcement authority.[67] Without a judicial check on the power granted to law enforcement officials, individuals would have no guaranteed protection against abuses. As such, the foregoing provisions outlined the search and seizure powers granted under the treaty.

Jurisdiction was the third area addressed by the treaty.[68] According to the proposed treaty, jurisdiction was based either on territory or on the nationality of the accused. The draft skirted the issue of whether the term "territory" applied to the state where the harm occurred or to the state where the perpetrator was located at the time that the cybercrime was committed. Instead of settling this issue, the treaty provided that disputes over jurisdiction should be decided between the states involved. With the foregoing provisions, the drafters espoused a structure for jurisdictional concerns.

---

communication], regardless of whether one or more service providers were involved in the transmission of that communication." Convention Draft, *supra* note 46.

[66] Convention Draft, *supra* note 46.

[67] Margret Johnston, *US Companies Find Europe's Cyber Crime Treaty Too Vague: Americans Fear Individual Countries' Due-Process Laws Could be Violated,* IDG News Service, *at* http://www.e-businessworld.com/english/crd_treaty_321309.html (Dec. 8, 2000)(on file with the Richmond Journal of Law & Technology) (detailing concerns by US companies that cybercrime treaty has provisions that may cause harm to those with no intention of breaking the law).

[68] Article 19 of draft number 19 provided that a state had jurisdiction "when an offense [was] committed in whole or in part in its territory, or on a ship, an aircraft, or a satellite flying its flag or registered in that Party, or by one of its nationals." The article stated that it did "not exclude

The fourth and final area addressed by the proposed treaty was international cooperation.[69] Mutual cooperation for investigation of crimes was expected of states that became parties to the treaty. The mutual cooperation article was vague as to the procedures that would be necessary to carry out the assisted investigation. As to extradition, the draft ensured that either an existing instrument or this treaty could be used as the basis for extradition of a cybercriminal. The foregoing provisions thus provided a skeletal plan for international cooperation. As outlined in this section, the proposed treaty attempted to address the new 'tools' of cybercriminals by providing law enforcement with new powers to investigate the international nature of cybercrime. The inadequacies of the proposed treaty, which have been suggested in this section, did not pass unnoticed for long.

B. The Outcry

Until the public release of the proposed treaty in April 2000, member delegations had worked in virtual secrecy on the negotiations.[70] The Internet release of the treaty triggered

---

any criminal jurisdiction exercised in accordance with national law." Convention Draft, *supra* note 46.

[69] Article 20 in draft 19 provided for the "application of relevant international instruments on international co-operation in criminal matters." Article 21 concerned extradition. It stated that the criminal offences established in the treaty "shall be deemed as extraditable offences in any extradition treaty" existing between parties and for parties that do not have an extradition treaty the cybercrime treaty may be considered the basis for extradition. Article 22 provided for mutual assistance. In particular, the article provides for "mutual assistance to the widest extent possible for the purpose of investigations and proceedings concerning criminal offences relating to computer systems and data, or for the collection of electronic evidence of a criminal offence." Article 27 outlined access to computer data outside one's territory without the need for mutual assistance. In the case where computer data is publicly available, mutual assistance is not required regardless of the geographic location of the data. A state may also access computer data outside its territory, without the aid of mutual assistance, when it obtained the "voluntary consent of the person who has the lawful authority to permit the [state] access... to that data." Convention Draft, *supra* note 46.

[70] The Council has given no explanation for the lack of openness in the first three years of negotiations. Reuters, *Cybercrime Treaty Gets a Makeover, at* http://news.zdnct.co.uk/story/0,,s2082557,00.html (Nov. 14, 2000); Rick Perera, *UPDATE: Human Rights Groups Slam Cyber Crime Pact, at* http://www.idg.net/ic_273062_1794_9-

---

17

angered outcries from more than 400 e-mailers[71] and garnered the condemnation of a coalition of

29 international cyber-rights organizations, which represented the views of privacy experts, data

protection officials, and technical experts.[72] In a letter to the Council of Europe, the Global

Internet Liberty Campaign (GILC)[73] outlined its concerns with the proposed treaty.[74] Technical

experts complained that the treaty's broad provision concerning illegal devices[75] would

---

10000.html (Oct. 18, 2000). *See also* Juliana Gruenwald, *Europeans Defining the Long Arm of The Cyberlaw, at* http://news.zdnet.co.uk/story/0,,s2081836,00.html (Sept. 25, 2000) (on file with the Richmond Journal of Law & Technology). In the GILC letter, the coalition writes, "We also object in very strong terms to the manner under which this proposal was developed. Police agencies and powerful private interests acting outside of the democratic means of accountability have sought to use a closed process to establish rules that will have the effect of binding legislation. We believe this process violates requirements of transparency and is at odds with democratic decisionmaking." *Global Internet Liberty Campaign Member Letter on Council of Europe Convention on Cyber-Crime, at* http://www.gilc.org/privacy/coe-letter-1000.html (Oct. 18, 2000).

[71] Although it is unclear why the author of the article "Cybercrime Treaty Gets a Makeover" chose to state that the council was "inundated" with over 400 e-mails when there are millions of on-line users, a fair reading of the statement may take into consideration the relative obscurity of the proposal. Few Internet media sources covered the proposal, suggesting that the 400 people who e-mailed were interested enough to find the treaty by partaking of their own searches. Reuters, *Cybercrime Treaty Gets a Makeover, at* http://news.zdnet.co.uk/story/0,,s2082557,00.html (Nov. 14, 2000); *see also Global Internet Liberty Campaign Member Letter on Council of Europe Convention on Cyber-Crime, at* http://www.gilc.org/privacy/coe-letter-1000.html (Oct. 18, 2000).

[72] Robert Lemos, *Coalition Slams Cybercrime Treaty, at* http://www.zdnet.com/zdnn/stories/news/0,4586,2642290,00.html (Oct. 18, 2000).

[73] The Global Internet Liberty Campaign is a coalition of 29 international cyber-rights organizations that joined forced to speak out against the proposed treaty. Organizations included in the coalition are the U.S.'s American Civil Liberties Union, Bits of Freedom, U.K.'s Cyber-Rights and Cyber-Liberties, Electronic Frontiers Australia, Russia's Human Rights Network, France's IRIS, Spain's Kriptopolis, and South Africa's LINK Centre. *See* Robert Lemos, *Coalition Slams Cybercrime Treaty, at* http://www.zdnet.com/zdnn/stories/news/0,4586,2642290,00.html (Oct. 18, 2000); Rick Perera, *Update: Human Rights Groups Slam Cyber Crime Pact, at* http://www.idg.net/ic_273062_1794_9-10000.html (Oct. 18, 2000).

[74] *Global Internet Liberty Campaign Member Letter on Council of Europe Convention on Cyber-Crime, at* http://www.gilc.org/privacy/coe-letter-1000.html (Oct. 18, 2000). The letter also addresses copyright crimes, but that provision of the treaty is beyond the scope of this paper.

[75] Article 6 of the proposed treaty defined an illegal device as "a device...[used] for the purpose of committing any of the offenses established in accordance with Article 2-5." Convention Draft, *supra* note 46.

criminalize possession of devises used by security practitioners, educators, and researchers to increase the security of computer systems.[76] The concern centered on the fact that the devices used to ensure security within a system are the same ones utilized by hackers to gain unauthorized access to computer systems.[77] Those involved in securing systems worried that the provision of the treaty outlawed possession of such devices without regard to their intended use.[78] The coalition asserted that procedures for international investigations[79] had been omitted from the proposed treaty, and that such procedures should be agreed upon in order to ensure that a consistently high level of individual rights was maintained.[80] As to search and seizure,[81] the

---

[76] *Global Internet Liberty Campaign Member Letter on Council of Europe Convention on Cyber-Crime, at* http://www.gilc.org/privacy/coe-letter-1000.html (Oct. 18, 2000).

[77] Brian Krebs, *Tech Groups Still Wary of International Cyber-Crime Treaty, at* http://www.newsbytes.com/news/00/158848.html (last modified Dec. 1, 2000) (on file with the Richmond Journal of Law & Technology)(covering the continuing concerns of security professionals over the illegal devices provision of the cybercrime treaty even after revisions attempted to address the perceived problem).

[78] *Global Internet Liberty Campaign Member Letter on Council of Europe Convention on Cyber-Crime, at* http://www.gilc.org/privacy/coe-letter-1000.html (last modified Oct. 18, 2000).

[79] Article 20 provided for the "application of relevant international instruments on international co-operation in criminal matters." Article 21 concerned extradition. It stated that the criminal offences established in the treaty "shall be deemed as extraditable offences in any extradition treaty" existing between parties and for parties that do not have an extradition treaty the cybercrime treaty may be considered the basis for extradition. Article 22 provided for mutual assistance. In particular, the article provides for "mutual assistance to the widest extent possible for the purpose of investigations and proceedings concerning criminal offences relating to computer systems and data, or for the collection of electronic evidence of a criminal offence." Article 27 outlined access to computer data outside one's territory without the need for mutual assistance. In the case where computer data is publicly available, mutual assistance is not required regardless of the geographic location of the data. A state may also access computer data outside its territory, without the aid of mutual assistance, when it obtained the "voluntary consent of the person who has the lawful authority to permit the [state] access… to that data." *Convention Draft, supra* note 46.

[80] *Global Internet Liberty Campaign Member Letter on Council of Europe Convention on Cyber-Crime, at* http://www.gilc.org/privacy/coe-letter-1000.html (Oct. 18, 2000).

[81] Article 14 "empower[ed] competent authorities to search or similarly access a computer system… and computer data stored therein." In the article, the "competent authorities" were empowered to "seize or similarly secure computer data accessed… in view of their possible use in criminal investigations and proceedings." Article 15 authorized "competent authorities to order a person in its territory… to submit specified computer data under this person's control."

19

coalition stated that the treaty lacked any assurance of an independent judicial review in

particular instances were the search and seizure powers would be utilized.[82] The treaty's

provisions pertaining to the preservation of Internet traffic and the review of the content of

communications relating to an individual under investigation[83] raised a host of concerns. For the

ISPs, the requirement to preserve communications meant an increase in operating costs.

Additional costs incurred by the ISPs would include the personnel hours and the storage space

necessary to execute the requests of law enforcement.[84] For the cyber-rights organizations

involved in the coalition, the requirement that traffic and content information be made available

to law enforcement raised substantial privacy concerns. The coalition asserted that the treaty

would encourage "inappropriate monitoring of private communications,"[85] which would violate

accepted privacy norms.[86] One of the specific worries was that inappropriate monitoring would

lead to persecution of dissidents and minorities.[87] In summing up their position, the coalition

stated that the treaty improperly extended police power while failing to protect privacy of

---

Article 16 enabled "competent authorities to order...the expeditious preservation of data that is stored by means of a computer system, at least where there are grounds to believe that the data...is [] particularly vulnerable to loss or modification." Article 17 "ensure[d] the expeditious preservation of [] traffic data [concerning a specific communication], regardless of whether one or more service providers were involved in the transmission of that communication." Convention Draft, *supra* note 46.

[82] *Global Internet Liberty Campaign Member Letter on Council of Europe Convention on Cyber-Crime, at* http://www.gilc.org/privacy/coe-letter-1000.html (Oct. 18, 2000).

[83] Article 17 of the proposed treaty "ensure[d] the expeditious preservation of [] traffic data [concerning a specific communication], regardless of whether one or more service providers were involved in the transmission of that communication." Convention Draft, *supra* note 46.

[84] Steven Abood, *The Draft Convention on Cybercrime: What Every Internet Service Provider Should Know, at* http://www.tilj.com/content/webarticle02050101.htm (Feb. 5, 2001).

[85] *Global Internet Liberty Campaign Member Letter on Council of Europe Convention on Cyber-Crime, at* http://www.gilc.org/privacy/coe-letter-1000.html (Oct. 18, 2000).

[86] *Id.* (specifically citing a violation of the Data Protection Directive of the European Union).

[87] Nadine Strossen, *Contemporary Challenges to Privacy Rights*, 43 N.Y.L. SCH. L. REV. 195, 198 (1999) (pursuing the same line of reasoning).

communication, freedom of expression, or criminal procedure protections, all of which are

considered rights under the Universal Declaration of Human Rights.[88]

C. Draft 27: The Final Revision to the Treaty[89]

The criticism stunned the Council of Europe.[90] Peter Csonka, deputy head of the Council

of Europe's economic crime division,[91] said, "We were surprised by the violence of these

comments, ... We have learned we have to explain what we mean in plain language because

legal terms are sometimes not clear."[92] Through a series of drafts, the Council worked to address

the issues raised concerning illegal devices, procedural safeguards, and ISP retention of traffic[93]

and content data.[94] The drafters responded to the concern expressed by security personnel that

the treaty criminalized the mere use of certain devises by adding a provision, which provided that

those who possessed the devises without the intent of committing cybercrimes had not acted

---

[88]*Global Internet Liberty Campaign Member Letter on Council of Europe Convention on Cyber-Crime*, *at* http://www.gilc.org/privacy/coe-letter-1000.html (Oct. 18, 2000) (" We believe that the draft treaty is contrary to well established norms for the protection of the individual [and] it improperly extends the police authority of our national government . . . .").

[89] "A committee on crimes for the Council of Europe signed off . . . on the final draft of a broad treaty that aims to help countries fight cybercrime . . . . [The treaty] reached its 27th draft before being approved . . . . " Robert Lymos, *International Cybercrime Treaty Finalized*, *at* http://news.cnet.com/news/0-1003-200-6352408.html?tag=mn_hd (June 22, 2001).

[90] Reuters, *Cybercrime Treaty Gets a Makeover*, *at* http://news.zdnet.co.uk/story/0,,s2082557,00.html (Nov. 14, 2000).

[91] *Id.* (stating that the economic crime division of the Council of Europe is overseeing the creation of the treaty).

[92] *Id.*

[93] "Traffic data" is defined in Article 1.d. as "any computer data relating to a communication by means of a computer system, generated by a computer system that formed a part in the chain of communication, including the communication's origin, destination, route, time, date, size, duration, or type of underlying service." *Final Draft Convention on Cybercrime* art. 1, *at* http://conventions.coe.int/Treaty/en/Treaties/Html/185.htm/ (Nov. 23, 2001).

[94] "Content data" is not defined in the treaty, but is defined in the Explanatory Memorandum as "[t]he message or information being conveyed by the communication (other than the traffic data)." *Draft Convention on Cybercrime and Explanatory Memorandum Related Thereto* tit. 5, ¶ 209, *at* http://conventions.coe.int/treaty/EN/projets/FinalCyberRapex.htm (Nov. 8, 2001).

21

illegally.[95] In an effort to avoid the increased criminalization feared by GILC, the drafters

required that two types of intent be established for an individual to be convicted of the crime of

misuse of devises. The first type of intent was a general intent to engage in illegal activity.

Second, the specific intent to use the devise to commit one of four crimes outlined in the treaty –

illegal access, illegal interception, data interference, or system interference – had to be

established.[96]

With regards to criminal procedure issues, the drafters inserted an article requiring

minimum safeguards to adequately protect human rights and liberties.[97] The treaty required each

state to ensure, through domestic legislation, independent supervision of the treaty power in

question, justification of the use of the power, and a limitation on the scope and duration of the

power.[98] The decision as to which treaty powers are sufficiently intrusive to require the

safeguards set out in the article was left to the respective states.[99]

---

[95] Surprisingly, the main focus of the treaty, the harmonization of the definitions of cybercrimes, met with little opposition. One exception to this general acceptance of the definitions was the provision on illegal devices. "This article shall not be interpreted as imposing criminal liability where the production, sale, procurement for use… is not for the purpose of committing and offense… of this Convention, such as for the authorized testing or protection of a computer system." *Final Draft Convention on Cybercrime* art. 6, *at* http://conventions.coe.int/Treaty/en/Treaties/Html/185.htm (Nov. 23, 2001).

[96] *Draft Convention on Cybercrime and Explanatory Memorandum Related Thereto* tit. 1, ¶ 73-76, *at* http://conventions.coe.int/treaty/EN/projets/FinalCyberRapex.htm (Nov. 8, 2001).

[97] Article 15 is entitled "Conditions and safeguards." *Final Draft Convention on Cybercrime* art. 15, § 1, *at* http://conventions.coe.int/Treaty/en/Treaties/Html/185.htm (Nov. 23, 2001). These minimum safeguards are those to which the state is obliged under applicable international human rights treaties. Most of the states would be bound to those safeguards outlined in the International Covenant on Civil and Political Rights, *Draft Convention on Cybercrime and Explanatory Memorandum Related Thereto* tit.1, ¶ 145, *at* http://conventions.coe.int/treaty/EN/projets/FinalCyberRapex.htm (Nov. 8, 2001).

[98] In particular, the safeguards included "judicial or other independent supervision, grounds justifying application, and limitation on the scope and the duration of such power and procedure." *Final Draft Convention on Cybe-crime* art. 15, § 2, *at* http://conventions.coe.int/Treaty/en/Treaties/Html/185.htm (Nov. 23, 2001).

[99] *Draft Convention on Cybercrime and Explanatory Memorandum Related Thereto* tit. 1, ¶ 147, *at* http://conventions.coe.int/treaty/EN/projets/FinalCyberRapex.htm (Nov. 8, 2001).

To address the concerns pertaining to ISP retention of Internet traffic and content data, the drafters clarified the requirements by stipulating that the ISPs would only be asked to store specific data related to suspected crimes.[100] In these provisions, however, the drafters did not limit the time period for which the ISPs would be required to retain traffic and content data concerning alleged crimes. Although the drafters restricted the scope of the data to be maintained,[101] without a limitation concerning the time period for retention of data, ISPs could still incur significant business costs in adhering to the provisions of the treaty.[102] In addition, when law enforcement officials engaged service providers to collect data, the requirement that the providers keep confidential the fact that data was being collected[103] put the ISPs at odds with the privacy interests of their customers.[104]

---

[100] Two provisions of the treaty provide that ISPs can only be compelled to collect data associated with specific communications. The two articles are Article 20 -- Real-time Collection of Traffic Data and Article 21 -- Interception of Content Data. *Final Draft Convention on Cybercrime*, *at* http://conventions.coe.int/Treaty/en/Treaties/Html/185.htm (Nov. 23, 2001). The memorandum defines "traffic data" as relating to the time, duration, and size of the communication while "content data" refers to the actual text or visuals. *Draft Convention on Cybercrime and Explanatory Memorandum Related Thereto,* tit. 5, ¶ 227, *at* http://conventions.coe.int/treaty/EN/projets/FinalCyberRapex.htm (Nov. 8, 2001).

[101] "[T]he Convention does not require or authorize the general or indiscriminate surveillance and collection of large amounts of traffic data. It does not authorise the situation of 'fishing expeditions' where criminal activities are hopefully sought to be discovered . . . ." *Draft Convention on Cybercrime and Explanatory Memorandum Related Thereto,* tit. 5, ¶ 219, *at* http://conventions.coe.int/treaty/EN/projets/FinalCyberRapex.htm (Nov. 8, 2001).

[102] Business costs would include staff hours to track the data and storage space to keep records. Steven Abood, *The Draft Convention on Cybercrime: What Every Internet Service Provider Should Know,* The Internet Law Journal, *at* http://www.tilj.com/content/webarticle02050101.htm (Feb. 5, 2001).

[103] This provision was contained in both Article 20 and Article 21. *Final Draft Convention on Cybercrime*, *at* http://conventions.coe.int/Treaty/en/Treaties/Html/185.htm (Nov. 23, 2001).

[104] Recognizing this issue, the drafters required each state to adopt legislation to oblige the service provider to keep confidential the fact that the government was collecting data on the customer. *Id.* art. 20, § 2. According to the drafters, this would relieve the service provider of any contractual or legal obligation to notify the customer of the surveillance activity. *Draft Convention on Cybercrime and Explanatory Memorandum Related Thereto* tit. 5, ¶ 226, *at* http://conventions.coe.int/treaty/EN/projets/FinalCyberRapex.htm (Nov. 8, 2001).

While three of the revisions made by the drafters addressed specific concerns regarding

illegal devices, procedural safeguards, and ISPs' retention of data, additional modifications to the

treaty raised new issues. The treaty itself unnecessarily created four sets of problems concerning

sovereignty, jurisdiction, search and seizure of computer data, and international investigation. In

the arena of sovereignty, both the article concerning search and seizure and the article pertaining

to trans-border access to data without consent[105] permit law enforcement officials to cross state

boundaries without notifying or gaining permission from the intruded state.[106] Although some

experts argue, "[i]t may be legitimate and important for law enforcement to be allowed to

conduct a remote search of computers in a foreign country,"[107] it is unclear why the drafters have

allowed these intrusions of sovereignty when the treaty provides for mutual assistance between

states and provides for expedited mutual assistance when necessary.

---

[105] As in the original draft, trans-border access to stored computer data was allowed in certain
circumstances without the consent of the state where the information was located. Access was
permissible when the data was publicly available or when the investigating state obtained
consent from a person who has lawful authority to disclose the data. The article pertaining to
trans-border access, Article 32, provided, "A Party may, without obtaining the authorization of
another Party: a. access publicly available (open source) stored computer data, regardless of
where the data is located geographically; or b. access or receive, through a computer system in
its territory, stored computer data located in another Party, if the Party obtains the lawful and
voluntary consent of the person who has the lawful authority to disclose the data to the Party
through that computer system." *Final Draft Convention on Cybercrime, at*
http://conventions.coe.int/Treaty/en/Treaties/Html/185.htm (Nov. 23, 2001) (observing that no
precise definition is given for "publicly available" and that directly preceding the quoted words
are the words "open source" in parentheses).
[106] Under Article 19, this invasion was authorized if the person who owned the computer was
present in the state or if the ISP offered services in the state. *Id.* As to trans-border access without
consent of the intruded state, access was allowed if the data was publicly available or if
permission was gained from a person in the state who had legal authority to give such
permission. *Id.*
[107] David Goldstone & Betty-Ellen Shave, *International Dimensions of Crimes in Cybercrime*,
22 FORDHAM INT'L L.J. 1924, 1937-38 (1999).

In the area of jurisdiction, the drafters failed to address the problems raised by the existence of cyberspace.[108] No state has jurisdiction over cyberspace.[109] Thus, jurisdiction cannot simply be based on the place where the cybercrime took place. According to the treaty, jurisdiction was based primarily on territory and secondarily on nationality.[110] In an instance where more than one state claimed jurisdiction over an alleged offense, the treaty provided for the states involved to decide the "most appropriate jurisdiction for prosecution."[111] The "most appropriate jurisdiction" clause will likely be much invoked because of the ambiguity in the meaning of territory-based jurisdiction. The provision could be interpreted to provide jurisdiction to the state in which the perpetrator was located, as happened in the case of the I LOVE YOU virus where the Philippine government investigated the individual who released the virus from that state.[112] Unfortunately, this provision could just as easily be interpreted to give jurisdiction to the state in which the damage from the attack occurred. Alternatively, the provision could be construed to grant jurisdiction in either the host state or the victim state, with

---

[108] The provision concerning jurisdiction received only minor clarifications that did not address the main problem with the provision. One such minor clarification was that, under the first draft, jurisdiction based on territory could be established in relation to a satellite flying the flag of the state. Convention Draft, *supra* note 46. The mention of satellites was dropped from Draft 27 of the treaty. *Final Draft Convention on Cybercrime* art. 22, *at* http://conventions.coe.int/Treaty/en/Treaties/Html/185.htm (Nov. 23, 2001).

[109] Interview with Bill Thompson, Internet Privacy and Security Issues Expert for Special Services Group, in Atlanta, Ga. (Sept. 15, 2000).

[110] Under Article 22, jurisdiction over any offence in the treaty may be established if the offence was committed "in its territory, or on board a ship flying its flag, or on board an aircraft registered under the laws of that Party, or by one of its nationals, if the offence is punishable under criminal law where it was committed or if the offence is committed outside the territorial jurisdiction of any State." *Final Draft Convention on Cybercrime*, http://conventions.coe.int/Treaty/en/Treaties/Html/185.htm (Nov. 23, 2001).

[111] "When more than one Party claims jurisdiction over an alleged offence established in accordance with this Convention, the Parties involved shall, where appropriate, consult with a view to determining the most appropriate jurisdiction for prosecution." *Id.*

[112] James Evans, *Cyber-Crime Laws Emerge, but Slowly, at* http://www.cnn.com/2000/TECH/computing/07/05/cyber.laws.idg/ (July 5, 2000).

25

place of jurisdiction depending on the particular cybercrime at issue.[113] The drafters made no

attempt to solve this predicament.[114] It is unclear why the drafters simply did not choose one of

the above-mentioned meanings of the term 'territory.'

In search and seizure of computer data, the drafters clarified those who are subject to

orders that require production of specified computer data for use in law enforcement

investigations.[115] Under the newly crafted provision, any person physically located in the state

or any service provider offering services within the state would be required to submit data

---

[113] Examples involving two cybercrimes may help to clarify. In the instance of a computer virus, it may be easiest to try the perpetrator in the state where the individual was located at the time of the attack for two reasons. First, the law enforcement officials will likely be able to physically detain the individual. Second, because there are likely multiple victims in multiple states, the process of prosecuting will be simplified by occurring in only one state, namely the state where the individual is located. In a case of cybertheft, however, it may be that the drafters intended for the state where the theft occurred to have jurisdiction. Because there may only be one victim, the initial investigation of the cybertheft can easily begin by tracking the accused from the compromised computer in the victim state. This investigation can be accomplished without initially knowing where the perpetrator was located.

[114] Provisions concerning assistance between states changed little from the first publicly-released draft. Article 24 on extradition provided that the offenses in the treaty fulfilled the requirement of extraditable offenses for any existing extradition treaty between states and that the treaty would act as an extradition treaty for any states that lack such a treaty. Article 25, concerning general principles of mutual assistance, stipulated that the provisions on mutual assistance "shall be subject to the conditions provided for by the law of the requested Party or by applicable mutual assistance treaties." Mutual assistance regarding accessing of stored computer data, discussed in Article 31, provided, " A Party may request another Party to search or similarly access, seize, or similarly secure, and disclose stored data by means of a computer system located with the territory of the requested Party." Article 33, mutual assistance regarding the real-time collection of traffic data, stipulated that "[t]he Parties shall provide mutual assistance to each other with respect to the real-time collection of traffic data associated with specified communications in its territory transmitted by means of a computer system." Mutual assistance regarding the interception of content data, Article 34, provided, "The Parties shall provide mutual assistance to each other with respect to the real-time collection or recording of content data of specified communications transmitted by means of a computer system to the extent applicable by their applicable treaties and domestic laws." Articles 29 and 30 allowed for law enforcement officials to expedite requests for preservation of stored data and disclosure of preserved data. *See* Convention Draft, *supra* note 46.

[115] In the initial draft, Draft 19, production orders applied to "a person in its territory." No clarification of "person" or " in the territory" was provided. Convention Draft, *supra* note 46.

requested by means of a production order.[116] According to this language, production could be required from a computer outside the state so long as it belonged to an individual who was physically present in the state or to a service provider that provided services within the state. A complimentary provision provided for search and seizure of stored computer data.[117] The draft empowered competent authorities to search and seize computer data within the state. Reading the two provisions together would allow for data produced from outside the state, pursuant to a production order, to be seized once in the state.

Generally speaking, the problems created by the treaty are unnecessary. The treaty is intended to encourage uniform definitions of cybercrime and through such uniformity to enhance the ability of law enforcement to investigate these cybercrimes. A carefully written treaty with well-defined provisions could have avoided much unnecessary confusion. The question remains as to whether overall privacy concerns have been adequately addressed by the revisions to the treaty. In international investigations, the drafters omitted any clear procedures that could have ensured high levels of protection for individual rights.[118] In an effort to address broad privacy concerns, the "powers and procedures" provision of the articles on expedited preservation of stored computer data, expedited preservation and partial disclosure of traffic data, production orders, search and seizure of stored computer data, real-time collection of traffic data, and

---

[116] Article 18, Production Orders, empowers [a state's] competent authorities to order a person in [the state's] territory as well as a service provider offering its services in a territory to submit computer data under its possession or control to law enforcement officials. *Final Draft Convention on Cyber-crime, at* http://conventions.coe.int/Treaty/en/Treaties/Html/185.htm (Nov. 23, 2001).

[117] Article 19 empowers competent authorities to search a computer system and to seize a computer system or a computer-data storage medium in a search. *Id.*

[118] *Global Internet Liberty Campaign Member Letter on Council of Europe Convention on Cyber-Crime, at* http://www.gilc.org/privacy/coe-letter-1000.html (Oct. 18, 2000).

interception of content data are all "subject to Article 14 and 15."[119] These two articles provide

that the powers and procedures are subject to the safeguards provided under domestic law and

under applicable international human rights treaties.[120] Thus, critical to an understanding of the

privacy protections afforded by the treaty is knowledge of the safeguards provided by domestic

law and by pertinent international human rights treaties.

III. Examples of Privacy Protections Provided Under Domestic Laws

A. Treaty Expected to Become International Standard

While the focus of the treaty is to increase police power to allow law enforcement

officials to effectively battle the new 'tools' of cybercriminals, there is a concern that the

increase in police power will not be properly rebalanced with the privacy rights of individuals.[121]

In an attempt to rebalance the scales between police power and privacy, the treaty protects

privacy through safeguards provided under domestic laws and under applicable human rights

treaties. Because the first set of safeguards provided under the treaty are those found in domestic

laws,[122] the first part of the answer to the question of whether the treaty adequately addresses

Internet-Age privacy concerns must be found by examining domestic protections of privacy.

---

[119] Articles 16, 17, 18, 19, 20, and 21, respectively. *Final Draft Convention on Cyber-crime, at* http://conventions.coe.int/Treaty/en/Treaties/Html/185.htm (Nov. 23, 2001).
[120] Article 14 calls for each state to establish the "powers and procedures" necessary for "the purpose of specific criminal investigations or proceedings." Article 15 states that the powers and procedures shall be subject to the conditions and safeguards provided for under the domestic law of each Party concerned, with due regard for the adequate protection of human rights. It further states that "such conditions and safeguards shall, as appropriate in view of the nature of the power or procedure concerned, inter alia, include judicial or other independent supervision, grounds justifying application, and limitation on the scope and the duration of such power or procedure." *Final Draft Convention on Cyber-crime, at* http://conventions.coe.int/Treaty/en/Treaties/Html/185.htm (Nov. 23, 2001).
[121] *See* Fletcher N. Baldwin, Jr., *Cybercrime: The Dawning of the Age of the Internet, in* 1 CYBERCRIME & SECURITY 18 (Alan E. Brill et al. eds., 1998).
[122] *Final Draft Convention on Cybercrime* art. 15, *at* http://conventions.coe.int/Treaty/en/Treaties/Html/185.htm (Nov. 23, 2001).

The key to understanding the privacy protections afforded by current domestic laws is two-fold, meaning that a recognition of the policies enacted in the states is needed as well as a grasp of the impact of each state's policies when two or more states interact. The policies adopted by states will first be examined to determine the goals that the state desires to further with its Internet crime control policy in addition to exploring the ability of the government to prosecute the crime and the capacity of the victim to recover for his losses. The outcomes of interactions between states with differing levels of privacy protection will then be explored.

B. Three Examples of Southeast Asian States with Differing Levels of Privacy Protection

As it is not possible to examine every state, several states in Southeast Asia have been chosen to illustrate the overall approach to privacy protection afforded by the treaty.[123] Three Southeast Asian states were selected to illustrate the first prong of the approach, privacy protection afforded by domestic laws. Southeast Asian states were selected because their history of colonialism, which they subsequently replaced with emerging capitalist economies, represents the experience of many of the states that exist outside of Europe.[124] Singapore, Thailand, and the Special Administrative Region of Hong Kong have been specifically chosen because each provides an example of a differing level of privacy protection. For each of these three, Internet crime control policies will be examined. The second prong of the approach, which examines the

---

[123] Even though the treaty will originally be open only to the 41 members of the Council of Europe and limited non-members, such as Canada, Israel, Japan, South Africa and the United States, there is a belief that the treaty will at some point become global in scope. As such, the hypotheticals examine interactions that include states not initially signatories to the treaty. *See* Press Release, Council of Europe, Crime in Cyberspace: First Draft of International Conventional Released for Public Discussion, *at* http://conventions.coe.int/treaty/en/projets/cyber.htm (Apr. 27, 2000).

[124] Several countries in this region are known as Asian Tigers due to fast growing economies that create vast concentrations of wealth. In addition, this area of the world has a significant population.

outcomes of the interactions between states with differing levels of privacy protection, will be

illustrated with two hypothetical interactions between a European state and the three Southeast

Asian states.

1. Singapore: An Example of a Low Level of Privacy Protection

The kind of society that a state supports determines the goals concerning privacy

protection that underlie the Internet crime control policy of that state.[125] Totalitarian states

oppose privacy rights while liberal democratic systems support individual privacy rights and

freedoms.[126] These two abstract kinds of societies lie on opposite poles of the political

spectrum.[127] Singapore is known for its near totalitarian regime. In support of the doctrine that

the kind of society determines the level of privacy protection, Singapore has a reputation for

aggressively using surveillance for social control.[128] In its approach to Internet crime control, the

goal of the government is to shield its citizens from any undesirable influences.[129] In an effort to

---

[125] *See* C. Keith Boone, *Privacy and Community*, 9 SOC. THEORY & PRAC. 1 (1983), *reprinted in* RICHARD C. TURKINGTON & ANITA L. ALLEN, PRIVACY LAW: CASES AND MATERIALS 16 (West 1999). "[W]hether or not privacy and community are antagonistic depends on the *kind* of society in question." *Id.*

[126] "Consider two kinds of societies lying at opposite poles of the political spectrum, as in the cases of a statist totalitarian society and a liberal democracy. Essential to the development of the totalitarian society is the full expansion of the public into the private sphere, such that no society may properly be termed totalitarian until it has 'simply liquidated the whole sphere of privacy.'

. . .

By contrast, consider a liberal democratic system committed to long-standing political concepts of equal liberty, individual rights and freedoms, and an open, nonrepressive [sic] democratic process. . . . Linked as it is to the moral and material well-being of individuals, liberal social philosophy emphasizes the importance of nourishing individuality and liberty in its citizenry.

. . .

. . . It is apparent, then, that within the normative framework of a liberal democracy, it is the suppression of privacy, not its invigoration, that is antagonistic to community." *Id.* at 16-18.

[127] *Id.* at 16.

[128] *See* PRIVACY INT'L, PRIVACY AND HUMAN RIGHTS 2000: COUNTRY REPORT ON SINGAPORE, *at* http://www.privacyinternational.org/survey/phr2000 (2000).

[129] Baldwin, *supra* note 122, at 17. Singapore's general approach to Internet policy is censorship. *See* Steven M. Hanley, *International Internet Regulation: A Multinational*

ensure government supervision of Internet usage, all ISPs are government-owned or government-controlled companies.[130] The Telecommunications Authority of Singapore has extensive authority to monitor any activity considered to be a threat to national security.[131] The Authority routinely monitors phone conversations and Internet use.[132]

Singapore has no constitutionally protected right to privacy against government acts.[133] Although government officials are normally required to obtain court-issued search warrants, exceptions exist to this general warrant rule. Law enforcement may search without a warrant if they believe the intrusion is necessary to preserve evidence and warrantless searches are permitted in drug-related and organized-crime-related incidents.[134] Specific to Internet-related crime, the police do not need a warrant to search computers under the Electronic Transactions Act (ETA).[135]

Singapore has passed criminal laws that enable the prosecution of perpetrators of Internet crime. The Computer Misuse Act (CMA)[136] prohibits unauthorized access to computer data,

---

Approach, 16 J. MARSHALL J. COMPUTER & INFO. L. 997, 1012 (1998); Lewis S. Malakoff, *Are You My Mommy, or My Big Brother? Comparing Internet Censorship in Singapore and the United States*, 8 PAC. RIM L. & POL'Y J. 423; Joseph C. Rodriguez, *A Comparative Study of the Internet Content Regulations in the United States and Singapore: The Invincibility of Cyberporn*, 1 ASIAN-PAC. L. & POL'Y J. 9 (2000); Peng Hwa Ang & Berlinda Nadarajan, *Censorship and Internet: A Singapore Perspective, at* http://www.isoc.org/HMP/PAPER/132/txt/paper.txt (last modified May 4, 1995).

[130] PRIVACY INT'L, PRIVACY AND HUMAN RIGHTS 2000: COUNTRY REPORT ON SINGAPORE, *at* http://www.privacyinternational.org/survey/phr2000 (2000).

[131] *Id.*

[132] *Id.*

[133] *Id.*

[134] U.S. DEPT. OF STATE, COUNTRY REPORTS ON HUMAN RIGHTS: PRACTICES FOR 1996: SINGAPORE, http://www.privacy.org/pi/reports/hr96_privacy_report.html (Jan. 1997).

[135] Electronics Transactions Act ch. 88, pt. XII, § 53 (Sing.), *at* http://www.lawnet.com.sg/free/vldb.htm (July 10, 1998); *see also* PRIVACY INT'L, *supra* note 131.

[136] Computer Misuse Act ch. 50A, pt. III, § 16 (Sing.), *at* http://www.lawnet.com.sg/free/vldb.htm (1998); *see also* PRIVACY INT'L, *supra* note 131.

unauthorized modification of computer data, unauthorized obstruction of the use of computers,

and unauthorized disclosure of access codes.[137] The ETA imposes a duty of confidentiality on

individuals who possess data obtained under the act and imposes sanctions for disclosing such

data without authorization. [138]

As to whether Singapore has jurisdiction over such crimes, the policy of Singapore is to

extend the territorial principle[139] in cases where there is some nexus between the territory and the

crime.[140] In particular, the CMA grants to courts jurisdiction over anyone who commits a crime

under the act. Regardless of citizenship, the accused is treated as if he was in Singapore at the

time of the incident or as if the computer, the program, or the data was in Singapore at the time

of the incident.[141]

As to recovery of losses by the victim, no general data protection or privacy laws exist in

Singapore.[142] However, in association with criminal prosecution against businesses and rogue

individuals, the CMA requires the perpetrator to pay compensation, which the victim can recover

through civil debt procedures.[143] Even in cases where a criminal prosecution was not achieved,

---

[137] Under the CMA, police may access any computer at any time, including data that is
encrypted. Anyone refusing to assist the police in a cybercrime investigation may be prosecuted.
The police are authorized to arrest, without warrant, any person who is reasonably expected to
have committed an offense under the CMA. Computer Misuse Act ch. 50A, pt. III, § 15(1)(a)
(Sing.), *at* http://www.lawnet.com.sg/free/vldb.htm (1998).
[138] Electronics Transactions Act ch. 88, pt. XII, § 48 (Sing.), *at*
http://www.lawnet.com.sg/free/vldb.htm (July 10, 1998).
[139] "[E]quality of states and non-interference in domestic affairs of a state are the foundations of
the international order. Hence, territoriality was the accepted basis of exercising jurisdiction as it
accorded with these organising principles of international law." M. Sornarajah, *Globalisation
and Crime: The Challenges to Jurisdictional Principles*, 1999 SINGAPORE J. OF LEGAL STUD.
409, 411-12 (1999), *available at* http://www.law.nus.edu.sg/sjls/articles.htm.
[140] *Id.* at 412.
[141] Computer Misuse Act ch. 50A, pt. III, § 11 (Sing.), *at*
http://www.lawnet.com.sg/free/vldb.htm (1998); *see also* PRIVACY INT'L, *supra* note 131.
[142] Ravi Chandran, *Privacy in Employment*, 2000 SINGAPORE J. LEGAL STUD. 263, 265 (2000).
[143] Computer Misuse Act ch. 50A, pt. 3, § 13 (Sing.), *at* http://www.lawnet.com.sg/free/vldb.htm
(1998).

the victim can sue the business or rogue individual based on tort law, in an action for breach of confidence.[144] To be successful, the victim must establish that the data is not trivial, that he had a legitimate expectation of privacy in the data, and that the use of the data was unauthorized.[145] In Singapore, the government can prosecute cybercrime and the victim has a means to recover damages that result from the cybercrime. As the goal of the Internet crime control policy is social control, Singapore is an example of a low level of privacy protection.

2. Thailand: An Example of an Intermediate Level of Privacy Protection

On the totalitarian/liberal democracy spectrum, Thailand falls into the middle of the range. The government's concerns over national security and public morals drive its privacy policies.[146] On the privacy-of-communications front, Thailand's Constitution provides for the protection of privacy.[147] Specifically, the constitution stipulates a protection of communication. Although the state guarantees privacy by law, in reality privacy is not protected. Activities such as illegal wiretapping are commonplace in Thailand.[148] As for protection against unreasonable government intrusion, in most instances, law enforcement officers are required to obtain a

---

[144] Ravi Chandran, *Privacy in Employment*, 2000 SINGAPORE J. LEGAL STUD. 263, 265 (2000) (examining employee/employer context, but generally applicable to situations that arise in Singapore).

[145] *Id.* at 265-281(including a discussion of how the tort applies to e-mail).

[146] THAIL. CONST. § 37 (1997), *available at* http://www.krisdika.go.th/law/text/lawpub/e11102540/text.htm (last visited Sept. 17, 2002) (stating that persons "shall enjoy the liberty of communication by lawful means" and providing an exception for action taken "by virtue of the law specifically enacted for security of the State or maintaining public order or good morals"); *see also* PRIVACY INT'L, PRIVACY AND HUMAN RIGHTS 2000: COUNTRY REPORT ON KINGDOM OF THAILAND, *at* http://www.privacyinternational.org/survey/phr2000 (2000).

[147] THAIL. CONST. § 34, 37 (1997), *available at* http://www.krisdika.go.th/law/text/lawpub/e11102540/text.htm (last visited Sept. 20, 2001) (section 34 states that "the right of privacy shall be protected" and section 37 protects freedom of communications); *see also* PRIVACY INT'L, PRIVACY AND HUMAN RIGHTS 2000: COUNTRY REPORT ON KINGDOM OF THAILAND, *at* http://www.privacyinternational.org/survey/phr2000 (2000).

warrant prior to a search. A major exception to this protection however allows police to issue

warrants; such warrants are not subject to judicial review.[149]

Thailand is one of the world's many countries that has no specific legislation on

cybercrime. This means that it would be difficult, if not impossible, to prosecute a perpetrator of

cybercrime who was located in Thailand.[150] Thailand has no specific laws that protect personal

information. This means that currently the victim could not recover for losses. Realizing the

need to "prevent misuse of information and give rights to data owners," Thailand officials are

finalizing a data protection law.[151] In Thailand, the government has no means to prosecute

cybercrime and the victim has no avenue to recover damages that result from the cybercrime.

Because the goal of the Internet crime control policy is driven by concerns over morals but does

not rise to the level of social control, Thailand is an example of an intermediate level of privacy

protection.

3. Hong Kong: An Example of a High Level of Privacy Protection

On the political spectrum that ranges from totalitarian to liberal democracy, the Special

Administrative Region of Hong Kong falls near the liberal democratic end. Until 1997, Hong

Kong was part of the British Commonwealth, mirroring many British traditions including

---

[148] PRIVACY INT'L, PRIVACY AND HUMAN RIGHTS 2000: COUNTRY REPORT ON KINGDOM OF THAILAND, *at* http://www.privacyinternational.org/survey/phr2000 (2000).

[149] U.S. DEPT. OF STATE, COUNTRY REPORTS ON HUMAN RIGHTS: PRACTICES FOR 1996: THAILAND, *at* http://www.usis.usemb.se/human/1996/eastasia/thailand.html (Jan. 1997)(stating that the issuance of warrants by the police requires prior approval from the Ministry of Interior or the provincial governor).

[150] *See* Fletcher N. Baldwin, Jr., *Cybercrime: The Dawning of the Age of the Internet, in* 1 CYBERCRIME & SECURITY 17 (Alan E. Brill et al. eds., 1998)(arguing that although it is possible that Thailand has no political agenda concerning Internet crime control, it is more likely that Thailand has yet to perceive such crime as a significant threat because of the low numbers of its citizens that have access to the Internet).

democratically elected government officials and trial by jury.[152] According to the Basic Law of

Hong Kong, the agreement hammered out between Great Britain and China before the 1997

handover to China, Hong Kong's form of government will remain unchanged until 2047.[153]

Hong Kong remains a party to the International Covenant on Civil and Political Rights; this

treaty creates an international obligation for the government to protect privacy.[154] Although

there is some concern that the Chinese government will modify the policy,[155] Hong Kong's

---

[151] Karnjana Karnjanatawe, *Data Protection Laws Under Discussion*, BANGKOK POST, July 4, 2001, *available at*
http://scoop.bangkokpost.co.th/bkkpost/2001/july2001/db040701/040701_database02.html.

[152] U.S. DEPARTMENT OF STATE, COUNTRY REPORTS ON HUMAN RIGHTS PRACTICES FOR 1996: HONG KONG, *at* http://www.usis.usemb.se/human/1996/eastasia/hong_kong.html (Jan. 30, 1997)(detailing Hong Kong's past).

[153] The Basic Law of the Hong Kong Special Administrative Region ch. 1, art. 5 (1990), *at* http://www.tdctrade.com/blaw/index.htm. (the Basic Law is referred to as the "mini constitution" of Hong Kong).

[154] The Basic Law of the Hong Kong Special Administrative Region ch. 3, art. 39 (1990), *at* http://www.tdctrade.com/blaw/blaw_ch1.htm (assuring that the International Covenant on Civil and Political Rights shall remain in force even though Hong Kong is now a Special Administrative Region of China); *see also* United Nations International Covenant on Civil and Political Rights (entered into force Mar. 23, 1976), *at* http://www.un.org/Depts/Treaty/final/ts2/newfiles/part_boo/iv_boo/iv_4.html (last visited Sept. 11, 2002) (China is not a signator of the treaty).

[155] *See* Steven M. Hanley, *International Internet Regulation: A Multinational Approach*, 16 J. MARSHALL J. COMPUTER & INFO. L. 997, 1012 (1998).

Even though China is not considered part of Southeast Asia, the domestic policies of China are included here because of its new governance of Hong Kong, the fourth largest financial center in the world. (Additionally, China is an undeniable force in the geographic region because of its enormous population coupled with its new-found interest in becoming a world economic power.)

Hong Kong democratic activists are concerned that China will be able to circumvent the law. China's Computer Information and Internet Security Regulations raises concerns as it provides, "These regulations [referring to the act as a whole] should be consulted with regards to the implementation of the security, protection, and management of computer information networks connecting to networks in the Hong Kong Special Administrative Region . . . ." Computer Information Network and Internet Security, Protection and Management Regulations ch. V, art. 24 (1997), *at* http://www.qis.net/chinalaw/prclaw54.htm (last modified Apr. 7, 1998).

In Chinese law, there is a provision for the secrecy of communication. In practical terms, however, this has little or no impact since the Chinese government has, for centuries, kept meticulous records on its people. PRIVACY INTERNATIONAL AND THE ELECTRONIC PRIVACY INFORMATION CENTER, PRIVACY AND HUMAN RIGHTS 2000: COUNTRY REPORT ON CHINA, *at*

general Internet policy is based on self-regulation and a concern for economic well-being.[156] As

to privacy of communications, the Basic Law of Hong Kong provides for privacy of

communications.[157] The law stipulates that this privacy can only be compromised through

---

http://www.privacyinternational.org/survey/index.html (last visited Sept. 20, 2001). China's
newly enacted criminal procedure law provides that "when a search is conducted, a search
warrant must be shown to the person searched." Criminal Procedural Law art. 111
(P.R.C.)(1996), *available at* http://product.chinawe.com/cgi-bin/lawdetail.pl?LawID=288.
Seizure of the targeted items is proper when the object "may be used to prove a criminal
suspect's guilt or innocence." Criminal Procedural Law art. 114 (P.R.C.)(1996), *available at*
http://product.chinawe.com/cgi-bin/lawdetail.pl?LawID=288.
     In an effort to modernize the country, China views the adoption of the Internet as "a
necessary communication tool for successful economic competition." Scott Feir, *Regulations
Restricting Internet Access: Attempted Repair of Rupture in China's Great Wall Restraining the
Free Exchange of Ideas,* 6 PAC. RIM. L. & POL'Y J. 361, 361 (1997). While believing that this
technology is necessary for economic development, the government is concerned that access to
information is a threat to its ability to control the population. *Id.* In response to the perceived
threat, the Chinese government required that a nation-wide firewall be developed – a technology
that has limited information entering the country. ISPs must abide by the requirements of the
Great Firewall of China. Scott Feir, *Regulations Restricting Internet Access: Attempted Repair of
Rupture in China's Great Wall Restraining the Free Exchange of Ideas,* 6 PAC. RIM. L. & POL'Y
J. 361, 361 (1997).   China has also set up a special Internet police force to ensure compliance
with its Internet policies. PRIVACY INTERNATIONAL AND THE ELECTRONIC PRIVACY INFORMATION
CENTER, PRIVACY AND HUMAN RIGHTS 2000: COUNTRY REPORT ON CHINA, *at*
http://www.privacyinternational.org/survey/index.html (last visited Sept. 20, 2001). China's
Computer Information Network and Internet Security, Protection and Management Regulations
(CINISPMR) require that Internet users register with the State security forces. Computer
Information Network and Internet Security, Protection and Management Regulations art. 10, 13
(1997), *at* http://www.qis.net/chinalaw/prclaw54.htm (last modified Apr. 7, 1998).
     CINISPMR protects the freedom and privacy of network users from intrusion by
individuals, but provides no protection from the activity of the State. The article also requires
that those who engage in Internet businesses must assist the State in "discovering" and "properly
handling" law violations involving computer activities. Computer Information Network and
Internet Security, Protection and Management Regulations art. 7 (1997), *at*
http://www.qis.net/chinalaw/prclaw54.htm (last modified Apr. 7, 1998).
China's approach to governance restricts the rights of individuals while strengthening control by
the government. The general approach to Internet policy is one of censorship, to limit access to
information. *See* Steven Stanley, *International Internet Regulation: A Multinational Approach,*
16 J. MARSHALL J. COMPUTER & INFO. L. 997, 1012 (1998).
[156] Office of the Privacy Commissioner for Personal Data, Hong Kong, The Personal Data
(Privacy) Ordinance, Slide 4, *at* http://www.pco.org.hk/misc/hk_apdpf/sld004.htm (Aug.3,
1995).
[157] U.S. DEPARTMENT OF STATE, BACKGROUND NOTE: HONG KONG, *at*
http://www.state.gov/r/pa/ei/bgn/2747.htm (Nov. 2001).

means of legal procedures that allow for protection of public security or investigation of criminal activity.[158] With regard to government intrusion, police are required to obtain court-issued warrants before obtaining evidence.[159]

In the realm of Internet crime control policy, Hong Kong has enacted the Personal Data Privacy Act (PDPA) that regulates the collection, use, and security of personal data.[160] The PDPA covers "any data relating directly or indirectly to a living individual" if from the data it is possible to ascertain the individual's identity and if the data "is in a form in which access of processing is practicable."[161] The PDPA applies to any person who directs the collection, processing, or use of personal data.[162] The PDPA applies to both public and private sectors,

---

[158] Article 30 of the Basic Law provides "the freedom and privacy of communications of Hong Kong residents." According to the article, these rights may not be infringed "except...[by] relevant authorities [who] may inspect communications in accordance with legal procedures to meet the needs of public security or of investigation into criminal offenses." The Basic Law of the Hong Kong Special Administrative Region ch. 3, art. 30 (1990), *at* http://www.tdctrade.com/blaw/blaw_ch3.htm; *see also* PRIVACY INTERNATIONAL AND THE ELECTRONIC PRIVACY INFORMATION CENTER, PRIVACY AND HUMAN RIGHTS 2000: COUNTRY REPORT ON SPECIAL ADMINISTRATIVE REGION OF HONG KONG, *at* http://www.privacyinternational.org/survey/phr2000/countriesag.html#Heading9 (last visited Sept. 20, 2001) (stating that although Hong Kong generally protects privacy, an exception exists for crime involving organized crime because of Hong Kong's history and thus stricter measures are used in this area).

[159] Although the Independent Commission Against Corruption, a body created to address historical corruption problems, once had the independent authority to issue search warrants, it must now utilize the court system to obtain such warrants. U.S. DEPARTMENT OF STATE, COUNTRY REPORTS ON HUMAN RIGHTS PRACTICES FOR 1996: HONG KONG, *at* http://www.usis.usemb.se/human/1996/eastasia/hong_kong.html (Jan. 30, 1997).

[160] Office of the Privacy Commissioner for Personal Data, Hong Kong, Personal Data Privacy Ordinance, *at* http://www.pco.org.hk/english/ordinance/ordglance.html (Aug. 3, 1995); *see also* PRIVACY INTERNATIONAL AND THE ELECTRONIC PRIVACY INFORMATION CENTER, PRIVACY AND HUMAN RIGHTS 2000: COUNTRY REPORT ON SPECIAL ADMINISTRATIVE REGION OF HONG KONG, *at* http://www.privacyinternational.org/survey/phr2000/countriesag.html#Heading9 (last visited Sept. 20, 2001).

[161] Office of the Privacy Commissioner for Personal Data, Hong Kong, Personal Data Privacy Ordinance, *at* http://www.pco.org.hk/english/ordinance/ordglance.html (Aug.3, 1995).

[162] *Id.*

although many of the exceptions to the act apply primarily to the public sector.[163] Under the

PDPA, the government can prosecute cybercrime[164] and the victim has the ability to recover

damages that result from the cybercrime.[165] As the goal of Internet crime control is to root out

crime without impinging on privacy protections, Hong Kong is an example of a high level of

privacy protection. In Southeast Asia, Hong Kong provides significant protections for individual

privacy while Singapore and, to a more limited degree, Thailand support state control to the

detriment of individual privacy protections. As the Internet enables access across borders, there

is a concern about how states with differing levels of privacy protections will interact under the

cybercrime treaty.

C. Interactions between Southeast Asian States and a European State

The critical question to determine in deciding if the cybercrime treaty adequately protects

privacy through domestic laws is whether the outcomes from interactions between states enhance

or at least maintain the protections currently afforded in the states involved. In the following two

hypotheticals, three Southeast Asian states will be examined in interaction with a European

---

[163] PRIVACY INTERNATIONAL AND THE ELECTRONIC PRIVACY INFORMATION CENTER, PRIVACY AND HUMAN RIGHTS 2000: COUNTRY REPORT ON SPECIAL ADMINISTRATIVE REGION OF HONG KONG, *at* http://www.privacyinternational.org/survey/phr2000/countriesag.html#Heading9 (last visited Sept. 20, 2001).

[164] "There are a variety of offences, for example non-compliance with an enforcement notice served by the Privacy Commissioner carries a penalty of a fine at Level 5 (at present $25,001 to $50,000) and imprisonment for 2 years." Office of the Privacy Commissioner for Personal Data, Hong Kong, Personal Data Privacy Ordinance (Aug. 3,1995), *at* http://www.pco.org.hk/english/ordinance/ordglance1.html#offences/ (last visited Sept. 11, 2002); *see generally* Office of the Privacy Commissioner for Personal Data, Hong Kong, Personal Data Privacy Ordinance, *at* http://www.pco.org.hk/english/ordinance/section_68.html (Aug. 3, 1995) (detailing the entire list of offenses).

[165] "An individual who suffers damage, including injured feeling, by reason of a contravention of the Ordinance in relation to his or her personal data may seek compensation from the data user concerned." Office of the Privacy Commissioner for Personal Data, Hong Kong, Personal Data Privacy Ordinance, *at* http://www.pco.org.hk/english/ordinance/ordglance1.html#offences/ (Aug. 3, 1995); *see generally* Office of the Privacy Commissioner for Personal Data, Hong Kong,

state.[166] In each hypothetical, the relevant questions to be answered are whether the evidence

can be gathered, whether the accused can be prosecuted in the state, and whether the victim can

recover damages. If the outcomes of these interactions enhance or at least maintain the

protections currently afforded to privacy in the states involved, then the treaty has successfully

increased police power while maintaining guarantees of privacy.

1. Hypothetical One: European perpetrator and Southeast Asian victims

In this first hypothetical, a European perpetrator has instigated a denial-of-service

attack[167] affecting computer systems in Singapore, Thailand, and Hong Kong. All three

Southeast Asian states investigate with the aim of prosecuting the perpetrator. Each state must

determine if access to evidence is possible and subsequently if prosecution is possible. In

addition, a determination needs to be made as to whether the victim can recover for his losses.

Because the attack did not commence in Singapore, Thailand, or Hong Kong, under the

cybercrime treaty the states can explore avenues to access information that both require[168] and do

not require mutual assistance[169] from the European state. As to those provisions that do not

require mutual assistance, the production order provision of the treaty[170] provides that law

---

Personal Data Privacy Ordinance, *at* http://www.pco.org.hk/english/ordinance/section_68.html
(Aug. 3, 1995).

[166] Because of the European Union's comprehensive data protection directive, all European
states have a high level of privacy protection, search and seizure by court-issued warrant, and
regulation of the cybercrimes listed in the treaty. Although there are distinctions between the
European states, for the hypothetical "European state" will be used to refer to an entity that
promotes the general policies of any of these states. *See* Susan E. Gindin, *Lost and Found in
Cyberspace: Informational Privacy in the Age of the Internet*, 34 SAN DIEGO L. REV. 1153, 1182
(1997).

[167] A denial-of-service attack is "a type of attack on a network that is designed to bring the
network to its knees by flooding it with useless traffic." Webopedia, *at*
http://webopedia.internet.com/TERM/D/DoS_attack.html (last modified Feb. 5, 2002).

[168] *Final Draft Convention on Cybercrime* art. 27, 31, 33, 34, *at*
http://conventions.coe.int/Treaty/en/Treaties/Html/185.htm/ (Nov. 23, 2001).

[169] *Id.* art. 32.

[170] *Id.* art. 18.

enforcement may gain access to data that is outside their territory if the person who owns the computer is in their territory or if the ISP concerned provides service in their territory. In this hypothetical, it is unlikely that the European perpetrator will travel to any of the effected Southeast Asian states. The provision concerning ISPs,[171] however, may be helpful in certain states. Singapore substantially restricts those who can operate ISPs in the state's territory,[172] so it is unlikely that the European perpetrator utilized an ISP from which the Singapore authorities can obtain assistance. The laws concerning ISPs in Thailand and Hong Kong are not so restrictive, so it is possible that the perpetrator will have utilized an ISP operating both in the victim state and in the European state. Noting the likely sophistication of the cybercriminal, odds favor the fact that he will have used more than one ISP to instigate the attack. If this is the case, then the authorities in Thailand and Hong Kong may be able to trace part of the path of the perpetrator, but will likely be frustrated once the perpetrator's path switches to a second ISP. Under the trans-border access provision of the treaty,[173] any of the three victim states can access information if it is publicly available on the Internet or if the perpetrator gives consent for the authorities to access the information. It is unlikely that either of these conditions will be met.

Because it is unlikely that the above mentioned treaty articles will provide access to critical evidence, Singapore, Thailand, and Hong Kong may utilize the mutual assistance articles of the treaty.[174] Singapore, Thailand, and Hong Kong will be required to satisfy the conditions provided for by the law of the European state, the state from whom the information is requested.[175] The laws of the European state require a warrant for search and seizure. Hong

---

[171] *Id.* arts. 20, 21.

[172] *See* PRIVACY INT'L, *supra* note 131.

[173] *Final Draft Convention on Cybercrime* art. 20, 21, *at* http://conventions.coe.int/Treaty/en/Treaties/Html/185.htm/ (Nov. 23, 2001).

[174] *Id.* arts. 25, 31, 33, 34.

[175] *Id.* art. 25, § 4.

Kong easily meets this standard, as their domestic laws require court-issued warrants.[176] It is unclear whether Thailand's normal procedure in search and seizure cases would meet the requirement of the European state. Thailand's laws require a warrant before the search and seizure is undertaken, but in many cases the police issue the warrant.[177] Thai officials may be required to secure a warrant from a judge – a process not provided for under their domestic law. The Singapore situation is also complicated. Under Singapore's Electronics Transaction Act (ETA),[178] no warrant is required in Internet cases. Regardless of this domestic law, Singapore officials may be required to secure a warrant from a judge in order to benefit from mutual assistance.

As to collecting evidence, it is likely that Thailand and Hong Kong could retrieve data from an ISP, but less likely that the ISP used by the European perpetrator would have been one who operated in Singapore – thus decreasing the likelihood that Singapore authorities would obtain useful information from a Singapore-affiliated ISP. As for mutual assistance, Hong Kong could easily obtain mutual assistance from the European state, while Thailand and Singapore could face potentially irreconcilable complications.

If the investigations were successful, each of the victim states would desire to prosecute the European perpetrator. To do so, the individual state must have a domestic law that outlaws the specific activity in question. Thus, Thailand could not prosecute until after such time as it adopted cybercrime legislation. Because Thailand has no laws under which to prosecute, it

---

[176] U.S. DEPARTMENT OF STATE, COUNTRY REPORTS ON HUMAN RIGHTS PRACTICES FOR 1996, *at* http://www.privacy.org/pi/reports/hr96_privacy_report.html (Jan. 30, 1997)(Hong Kong).
[177] *Id.* (Thailand).
[178] *See* Electronics Transactions Act ch. 88, pt. XII, § 53 (July 10, 1998)(Sing.), *at* http://www.lawnet.com.sg/free/vldb.htm; PRIVACY INTERNATIONAL AND THE ELECTRONIC PRIVACY INFORMATION CENTER, PRIVACY AND HUMAN RIGHTS 2000: COUNTRY REPORT ON REPUBLIC OF SINGAPORE, *at*

would have to request that the European state prosecute and argue that jurisdiction was proper

for the European state because the perpetrator was physically located there.[179] In contrast, Hong

Kong could prosecute under its Personal Data Privacy Act[180] and Singapore could prosecute the

perpetrator under its Computer Misuse Act.[181] To proceed with prosecution, Hong Kong and

Singapore would need to establish jurisdiction over the European perpetrator. Under the

cybercrime treaty, jurisdiction is conferred by territory,[182] among other provisions. Hong Kong

would have to argue that this provision refers to the territory where the damage occurred.[183]

Singapore would site its Computer Misuse Act,[184] which clarifies any jurisdictional confusion by

stating that jurisdiction extends to anyone who commits a crime under the act. As to

prosecution, Thailand could not prosecute while Hong Kong and Singapore could prosecute, if

they could establish jurisdiction.

Regarding recovery of damages by the victim, the victim could not currently recover in

Thailand because the state has no laws concerning recover for damages incurred as a result of

---

http://www.privacyinternational.org/survey/phr2000/countriesru.html (last visited Sept. 20, 2001).

[179] Both Hong Kong and Singapore would object to the assertion that the European state had jurisdiction to prosecute. Both would argue for extradition of the perpetrator to their respective state.

[180] Office of the Privacy Commissioner for Personal Data, Hong Kong, Personal Data Privacy Ordinance ch. 486, pt. IX (Aug. 3,1995), *at* http://www.pco.org.hk/english/ordinance/section_68.html (last visited Sept. 20, 2001).

[181] Computer Misuse Act ch. 50A (Sing.)(1998), *at* http://www.lawnet.com.sg/free/vldb.htm; PRIVACY INTERNATIONAL AND THE ELECTRONIC PRIVACY INFORMATION CENTER, PRIVACY AND HUMAN RIGHTS 2000: COUNTRY REPORT ON REPUBLIC OF SINGAPORE, *at* http://www.privacyinternational.org/survey/phr2000/countriesru.html (last visited Sept. 20, 2001).

[182] *Final Draft Convention on Cybercrime* art. 18, *at* http://conventions.coe.int/Treaty/en/Treaties/Html/185.htm (Nov.23, 2001).

[183] As stated earlier in the article, one argument regarding jurisdiction proposes that territorial jurisdiction refers to the place where the perpetrator is located. *See* Section II.C; *see generally Final Draft Convention on Cybercrime, at* http://conventions.coe.int/Treaty/en/Treaties/Html/185.htm (Nov. 23, 2001).

[184] *See* Computer Misuse Act, *supra* note 181.

Internet crimes. In Hong Kong, the victim has the ability to recover damages under the Personal Data Privacy Act.[185] In Singapore, the victim could recover under the Computer Misuse Act.[186] Thus, the victim in Thailand could not recover for damages while a victim in Hong Kong or Singapore likely could recover. As is demonstrated by this hypothetical, the outcomes under the treaty would vary greatly based on the domestic laws in the states.

2. Hypothetical Two: Southeast Asian perpetrators and European victim

In the second hypothetical, a European person has been the victim of cybertheft at the hands of three Southeast Asian perpetrators – one from Singapore, one from Thailand, and one from Hong Kong. The European state wants to investigate with the aim of prosecuting the perpetrator. First, the European state must determine if access to evidence is possible. Next, the state must decide if prosecution is viable. In addition, a determination needs to be made as to whether the victim can recover damages.

While the European state faces the same basic problems as those faced by the victim states in first hypothetical, the mutual assistance request sheds light on a particularly illuminating result that arises under the treaty. When requesting mutual assistance, the European state will be required to satisfy the conditions provided for by the law of the state from which it is requesting assistance.[187] The European state will successful meet the requirements of Hong Kong's domestic laws because both the European state and Hong Kong require court-issued warrants.[188] In requesting information from Thailand and Singapore, the European state will encounter a

---

[185] Office of the Privacy Commissioner for Personal Data, Hong Kong, Personal Data Privacy Ordinance ch. 486, pt. IX *at* http://www.pco.org.hk/english/ordinance/section_68.html (Aug. 3, 1995).

[186] *See* Computer Misuse Act, *supra* note 181.

[187] *Final Draft Convention on Cybercrime* art. 25, § 4, *at* http://conventions.coe.int/Treaty/en/Treaties/Html/185.htm (Nov. 23, 2001).

[188] U.S. DEPARTMENT OF STATE, COUNTRY REPORTS ON HUMAN RIGHTS PRACTICES FOR 1996, *at* http://www.privacy.org/pi/reports/hr96_privacy_report.html (Jan. 30, 1997).

troublesome situation for privacy advocates. Thailand does not require a court-issued warrant[189] and Singapore requires no search warrant.[190] Thus, the European state would not be required to procure a search warrant to obtain information from Thailand or Singapore.

This second hypothetical highlights the problems associated with the treaty utilizing safeguards provided under domestic laws. As privacy advocates have lamented, the treaty lacks necessary search and seizure procedural safeguards.[191] By requiring no specified procedures in trans-border search and seizure, the treaty allows the European state to benefit from investigations undertaken without protections that would be required if the search were undertaken in the European state. The lack of required search and seizure procedures may allow a 'race to the bottom' in regards to protection of privacy. Because the outcome of an interaction between states with differing levels of domestic privacy protection likely decreases the currently provided protection in at least some of the states involved, the treaty has not successfully maintained, much less increased, guarantees of privacy while increasing police power.

IV. Why the Outcry over Privacy and Why it is Likely to Continue

A. Current International Concept of Privacy

Because the treaty affords the protections found in domestic laws as well as the protections found in international treaties, the second set of safeguards examined are provided by relevant human rights treaties. To appreciate the protections provided by international treaties, one must grasp the meaning of the term privacy and understand the specific aspects of privacy granted protection under international law. Alan Westin, one of the world's foremost authorities

---

[189] *Id.*

[190] *See* Computer Misuse Act, *supra* note 181.

[191] "Requirements for search and seizure of stored computer data lack necessary procedural safeguards to safeguard the rights of the individual and to ensure due process of law. In particular, there is no effort to ensure that an independent judicial review." *Global Internet*

on privacy, explains privacy as "the voluntary and temporary withdrawal of a person from the general society through physical or psychological means . . ."[192] In the legal realm, this equates to "the claim of individuals, groups, or institutions to determine for themselves when, how, and to what extent information about them is communicated to others."[193] Due to the multi-faceted nature of the legal term, privacy has been divided into four general categories: privacy of association, privacy in making intimate decisions, privacy from unwanted intrusions, and privacy of personal information.[194] Associational privacy is freedom from interference of relationships with individuals or groups.[195] Decisional privacy involves freedom from interference in intimate personal decisions.[196] Privacy from unwanted intrusions relates to physical and electronic invasion.[197] Privacy of personal information concerns "the rights of individuals to control information about themselves."[198]

Liberty Campaign Member Letter on Council of Europe Convention on Cyber-Crime, at http://www.gilc.org/privacy/coe-letter-1000.html (Oct. 18, 2000).

[192] ALAN F. WESTIN, PRIVACY AND FREEDOM 367 (Atheneum New York 1967).

[193] *Id.*

[194] *See* Fletcher N. Baldwin, Jr., *Impact of the Cyberspace on the Right to Privacy, in* 3 CYBERCRIME & SECURITY IIIA1.5 (Alan E. Brill et al. eds., 1998)(combining ideas of Constitutional and common law privacy).

[195] *Id.* at IIIA.1-6.

[196] *Id.*

[197] *Id.* at IIIA.1-5 to IIIA.1-6. Lessig suggests an alternative categorization of privacy components with three intertwined meanings. One of these meanings seeks to minimize intrusion. The test for a violation of this type of privacy is the burden of the state's intervention; if the intrusion is minimally burdensome, then the protection against the intrusion should be minimal. A second category of privacy hinges on the concept of dignity. Under this doctrine, even if the individual did not notice a search, it is nonetheless an invasion of privacy because it is an offense to dignity. The third category views privacy as a way to constrain the power of government to regulate. *See* LAWRENCE LESSIG, CODE AND OTHER LAWS OF CYBERSPACE 146 (Basic Books, A Member of the Persus Books Group 1999).

[198] Baldwin, *supra* note 195, at IIIA.1-6. As to the concept of privacy generally, another explanation is that privacy incorporates "ideas of bodily and social autonomy, of self-determination, and of the ability to create zones of intimacy and exclusion that define and shape our relationships with each other." Yet another definition of privacy is "'the right of individuals' to decide for themselves how much they wish to share with others in terms of thoughts, feelings, and facts of personal life." SUSAN DRUCKER & GARY GUMPERT, REAL LAW @ VIRTUAL SPACE:

The current international understanding of privacy encompasses the protections secured

in the Universal Declaration of Human Rights (UDHR) and in the International Covenant on

Civil and Political Rights (ICCPR).[199] Under the UDHR, privacy of communication, freedom of

expression, and criminal procedure protections are secured.[200] Privacy of communication is

protected from arbitrary government interference.[201] As to freedom of expression, the UDHR

protects an individual's right to hold a belief and to exchange information and ideas through any

media.[202] In the area of criminal procedure protections, the UDHR protects individuals from

arbitrary arrest and detention.[203] The ICCPR clarifies the general guidelines of privacy put forth

in the UDHR.[204] In the ICCPR, communications are protected primarily from divulgence to

anyone but the intended recipient and against interruption or interference.[205] The safeguards

---

REGULATION IN CYBERSPACE 326 (1999). In all of the conceptions of privacy mentioned in this paper, control over personal information is a component of the understanding of privacy. A. Michael Froomkin, *The Death of Privacy?*, 52 STAN. L. REV. 1461, 1463 (2000).

[199] Regional treaties are not here included because such treaties do not bind states that are not signatories. *Draft Convention on Cybercrime and Explanatory Memorandum Related Thereto* ¶ 110, *at* http://conventions.coe.int/treaty/EN/projets/FinalCyberRapex.htm (Nov. 8, 2001).

[200] *Universal Declaration of Human Rights*, U.N. GAOR, 3d Sess., pt. 1 at 71 arts. 12,19, U.N. Doc. A/RES/217 A (III).

[201] Article 12 of the UDHR states "no one shall be subjected to arbitrary interference with his privacy, family, home or correspondence.... Everyone has the right to the protection of the law against such interference or attacks." *Id.* at art. 12.

[202] Article 19 states, "Everyone has the right to freedom of opinion and expression; this right includes freedom to hold opinions without interference and to seek, receive and impart information and ideas through any media and regardless of frontiers." *Id.* at art. 19.

[203] *Id.* at art. 9.

[204] Fernando Volio, *Legal Personality, Privacy, and the Family*, in THE INTERNATIONAL BILL OF RIGHTS: THE COVENANT ON CIVIL AND POLITICAL RIGHTS 190 (Louis Henkin ed., 1981). Article 17 states that "no one shall be subjected to arbitrary or unlawful interference with his privacy, family, home or correspondence . . .[and that] [e]veryone has the right to the protection of the law against such interferences or attacks." International Covenant on Civil and Political Rights, *opened for signature* Dec. 19, 1966, 6 I.L.M. 360, 373.

[205] Volio, *supra* note 205, at 197; *see* HENRY STEINER AND PHILIP ALSTON, INTERNATIONAL HUMAN RIGHTS IN CONTEXT: LAW, POLITICS, AND MORALS 529 (1996).

only apply to "arbitrary or unlawful" interference.[206] According to the ICCPR, freedom of expression is protected "regardless of frontiers."[207] However, special responsibilities are attached to the rights associated with freedom of expression, meaning that the rights may be restricted under certain circumstances.[208] Approved justifications for governments to implement laws to restrict freedom of expression include protection of national security or public order and respect for the rights of others.[209] In the criminal procedure arena, pertinent protections in the ICCPR pertain to lawful arrests, judicial control for criminal procedures concerning arrests, and judicial review of the legality of arrests.[210] This means judicial review ensures privacy protection against unreasonable intrusions by government actors engaged in investigation or arrest activities. The General Assembly of the United Nations made the provisions of the ICCPR applicable to violations by governments, businesses, and rogue individuals.[211]

When examined in light of the categories of privacy introduced at the beginning of the section, the international understanding of privacy touches all the categories but does not provide full coverage to the ideas encompassed in the categories. Both privacy of communication and freedom of expression provide some protection in the area of associational privacy by allowing an individual to maintain secret communications with groups or individuals disfavored by governments. Decisional privacy is peripherally guarded by freedom of expression because this protection allows an individual to receive or impart information concerning a sensitive decision.

---

[206] Volio, *supra* note 205, at 191. Those involved in drafting the ICCPR discussed "unlawful" as being "itself contrary to human rights" and "arbitrary" as meaning that "even when [the act] is not in violation of positive law [the act] is arbitrary or capricious." *Id.*; *see* STEINER, *supra* note 206, at 524.
[207] International Covenant on Civil and Political Rights, *supra* note 205, at 374, art.19, § 2.
[208] *Id.* at 374, art.19, § 3.
[209] *Id.*
[210] STEINER, *supra* note 205, at 156.

Privacy of communication provides some protection in the area of privacy of personal information by guarding communications from interruption or interference as well as keeping the communications from anyone except the intended recipient. Criminal procedure protections provide defense from unwanted intrusions and protect personal information by limiting a government's ability to intrude upon personal information. (See Chart 1.)

B. Privacy Concept in the Internet Age

In revisions to the treaty, the drafters added a provision that would guard human rights in accordance with currently existing protections provided in international treaties.[212] Those involved with GILC envisioned a "forward-looking" interpretation[213] of these international instruments, arguing the privacy of communication, freedom of expression, and criminal procedure protections extend to cyberspace.[214] The problem with this "forward-looking" assessment by members of GILC is that the philosophers and diplomats whose ideas shaped the current international standard did not and could not consider the vast privacy concerns associated with the Internet.

---

[211] The ICCPR Committee stated "effective measures have to be taken by States to ensure that information concerning a person's private life does not reach the hands of persons who are not authorized by law to receive, process and use it . . ." *Id.* at 529.

[212] Article 15 provides that the powers and procedures granted in the treaty ". . . shall be subject to . . . due regard for the adequate protection of human rights, in particular as provided in applicable international human rights instruments." *Final Draft Convention on Cybercrime* art. 15, *at* http://conventions.coe.int/Treaty/en/Treaties/Html/185.htm (Nov. 23, 2001).

[213] *Global Internet Liberty Campaign Member Letter on Council of Europe Convention on Cyber-Crime, at* http://www.gilc.org/privacy/coe-letter-1000.html (Oct. 18, 2000).

[214] *See Id.* Part II.B. The argument proposed by GILC is that the cybercrime treaty violates the guarantees of privacy of communication and freedom of expression as well as criminal procedure protections in existing international instruments. For this argument to be valid, it must first be established that these protections extend into cyberspace. This has yet to be established on the international scene. The term cyberspace "encompasses the use of electronic communications over computer networks mainly via the Internet." Jay Krasovec, *Cyberspace: The Final Frontier for Regulation?*, 31 AKRON L. REV. 101, 101, n.1 (1997).

These privacy concerns center on the collection and possible misuse of data.[215] The

potential opportunities to exploit data are growing exponentially because technological

developments are lowering the cost of data collection and surveillance while increasing the

quality and quantity of the data.[216] In this Age of the Internet, consumers are concerned that

governments are selling personal information – ranging from driver's license data, to health

records, to tax documents – to make a profit[217] and that e-companies are using consumer

preferences for business advantages. In essence, the all-seeing eye from George Orwell's *1984*

"need not necessarily belong to the government, as many in the private sector find it valuable to

conduct various forms of surveillance or to 'mine' data collected by others."[218] Today's privacy

concerns encompass violations from governments, businesses, and rogue individuals.[219]

The drafters of this treaty had the opportunity to address this monumental development in

the privacy arena by requiring signatory states to adopt new domestic laws guaranteeing privacy

rights against governments, businesses, and rogue individuals. Although the rights would vary

---

[215] *See* Paul M. Schwartz, *Internet Privacy and the State*, 32 CONN. L. REV. 815, 819 (2000); *see also* Susan E. Gindin, *Lost and Found in Cyberspace: Information Privacy in the Age of the Internet*, 34 SAN DIEGO L. REV. 1153, 1156-58 (1997).

[216] A. Michael Froomkin, *The Death of Privacy?*, 52 STAN. L. REV. 1461, 1463 (2000). Access is available because personal data is stored on networked computers, is collected by Web sites, and is available due to the underlying technical structure of the Internet which allows simultaneous collection and transmission of information. Schwartz, *supra* note 215, at 820; Gindin, *supra* note 215, at 1156. In addition, generation of comprehensive records of online behavior is possible. Schwartz, *supra* note 216, at 818; *see* Gavin Skok, *Establishing a Legitimate Expectation of Privacy in Clickstream Data*, 6 MICH. TELECOMM. TECH. L. REV. 61, 61 ¶ 1 (2000), *at* http://www.mttlr.org/volsix/skok.html.

[217] Andrew Ecclestone, *Freedom of Information: An Electronic Window Onto the Government*, *in* LIBERATING CYBERSPACE: CIVIL LIBERTIES, HUMAN RIGHTS AND THE INTERNET 62 (Liberty ed., 1999).

[218] Froomkin, *supra* note 217, at 1463.

[219] Lawrence Lessig, *Cyberspace and Privacy: A New Legal Paradigm? Foreward*, 52 STAN. L. REV. 987, 998-99 (2000). The concern of experts is that "traditional legal doctrines appear ill equipped to deal with contemporary [privacy] problems that originate in cyberspace." Amy E. Wells, *Criminal Procedure: The Fourth Amendment Collides with the Problem of Child Pornography and the Internet*, 53 OKLA. L. REV. 99, 99 (2000).

from state to state, this could have been a major step in protecting informational privacy,[220]

which is as critically important in the Internet Age as the ability to prosecute cybercrimes.

V. Solutions for balancing the scales between police power and privacy

The cybercrime treaty addresses the need to expand police power in an age when one

individual in the Philippines unleashed a computer virus[221] that succeeded in creating $8 billion

worth of damage to computer systems around the world.[222] The treaty, however, creates an

imbalance in the scales that weigh police power and privacy by introducing new procedural

powers for police to search and seize computer data, to investigate cybercrimes outside their

state, and to receive mutual assistance in cross-border investigations, without increasing

protection for personal privacy.[223] Although the drafters of the treaty were "mindful of the need

to ensure a proper balance between the interests of law enforcement and respect for fundamental

human rights,"[224] the treaty largely sidesteps this balancing act by failing to address protection of

privacy in the Age of the Internet.

---

[220] *See infra* pt. V.A. (definition of this term).

[221] A computer virus is "an insidious piece of computer code written to damage systems. Viruses can be hidden in executable program files posted online." Netdictionary, *at* http://www.netdictionary.com/html/v.html (last visited Sept. 20, 2001).

[222] James Evans, *Cyber-Crime Laws Emerge, But Slowly, at* http://www.cnn.com/2000/TECH/computing/07/05/cyber.laws.idg/ (July 5, 2000).

[223] To increase police power in cybercrime investigations without increasing privacy protections "may result in serious disturbances of the complicated balance between the necessary powers of intervention of the [investigating and] prosecuting authorities on the one hand and civil liberties on the other hand." U. Sieber, *Computer Crime and Criminal Information Law, New Trends in the International Risk and Information Society,* Section E, Criminal Law Procedure, *at* http://www.jura.uni-muenchen.de/einrichtungen/ls/sieber/mitis/ComCriCriInf.htm (last visited Sept. 22, 2001) (on file with the Richmond Journal of Law & Technology).

[224] Preamble, *Final Draft Convention on Cybercrime* (Nov. 23, 2001), *at* http://conventions.coe.int/Treaty/en/Treaties/Html/185.htm. The drafters of the treaty realized the need to include privacy protections in the treaty. Henrik Kaspersen, chairman of the Committee on Experts on Crime in Cyber-Space for the Council of Europe, said, "We do not want to leave privacy apart from the convention." *COE Cyber Crime Treaty Debated, at* http://techlawjournal.com/crime/20001208.asp (Dec. 11, 2000). Even with this realization, the drafters did not adequately address privacy concerns.

A. The theoretical answer

To understand the missed opportunity to increase privacy protection, it is necessary to examine an Internet-Age concept of privacy – informational privacy. While the general concept of privacy encompasses associational privacy,[225] decisional privacy,[226] privacy from unwanted intrusions,[227] and privacy of personal information,[228] informational privacy focuses only on the last two of these classifications. Today's most talked about privacy violations are those where e-mails are obtained by governments and where clickstreams[229] are tracked by businesses. These are violations related to how information was obtained; in these examples, information was obtained by means of unwanted electronic intrusions. In most instances, the person whose privacy was violated generated the data that was later captured. In the government invasion, the person had written the e-mails. When the business intruded, the person had created a clickstream as he viewed numerous Web pages. These unwanted electronic invasions are one type of violation of a person's privacy. Violations related to privacy of personal information are a second type common in the Internet Age; these violations pertain to a person's ability to control how information about him is used. In this category, the information may or may not have been generated by the person. An example of personal information not generated by the individual is a Social Security number. The number is assigned by the government, yet is considered to be personal information that helps to verify the identification of the individual. In this category of

---

[225] Associational privacy is freedom from interference of relationships with individuals or groups. Fletcher N. Baldwin, Jr., *Impact of the Cyberage on the Right to Privacy, in* 3 CYBERCRIME & SECURITY IIIA.1-5 to IIIA.1-6 (Alan E. Brill et al. eds., 1998).

[226] Decisional privacy involves freedom from interference in intimate personal decisions. *Id.*

[227] Privacy from unwanted intrusions relates to physical and electronic invasion. *See id.*

[228] Privacy of personal information concerns "the rights of individuals to control information about themselves." *Id.* at IIIA.1-6.

[229] A clickstream is "[t]he series of electronic footprints created when a Web user moves about in cyberspace . . . ." Gavin Skok, *Establishing a Legitimate Expectation of Privacy in Clickstream Data,* 6 MICH. TELECOMM. TECH. L. REV. 61, 61 (2000).

privacy, the information may or may not be physically controlled by the individual. An example

of information not held by the person is the record of an individual's bank account, which is

stored on the bank's computer system. These foregoing examples sketch an outline of aspects of

informational privacy that could have been protected by the treaty.

Because informational privacy may be violated by governments as well as by businesses

and rogue individuals, the concept may be divided into four categories – privacy from unwanted

intrusions by governments, privacy of personal information against governments, privacy from

unwanted intrusions by businesses and rogue individuals, and privacy of personal information

against businesses and rogue individuals. (See Chart 2.) For each of these categories, a

prominent U.S. legal scholar has written a forward-looking account that provides insight into the

concept of informational privacy in the Internet Age.[230]

Justice Louis Brandeis addressed the issue of privacy from unwanted government

intrusion in a U.S. Supreme Court case concerning whether such privacy protection extended to

invasions that were not physical in nature.[231] Arguing in his famous 1928 *Olmstead* dissent[232]

that the protection did indeed extend to non-physical invasions, Brandeis asserted, "It is not...

the rummaging of his drawers that constitutes the offense, but it is the invasion of his

indefeasible right of personal security, personal liberty and private property...."[233] Brandeis

contended that the individual should be protected from any form of unreasonable government

---

[230] *See infra* notes 232-60.

[231] Olmstead v. United States, 277 U.S. 438, 471-78 (1928). The case centered around a conviction based on evidence gathered from a wiretap. Brandeis' argument was based primarily on the Fourth Amendment of the United States Constitution. In particular, his assertion was based on the provision that states, "[t]he right of the people to be secure in their persons, houses, papers, and effects, against unreasonable searches and seizures, shall not be violated..." *Id.* (quoting U.S. CONST. amend. IV.).

[232] *Id.*

[233] *Id.* at 474-75. This proposition asserted by Brandeis in 1928 was not adopted by the United States Supreme Court until *Mapp v. Ohio.* Mapp v. Ohio, 367 U.S. 643, 659 (1961).

intrusion because the privacy protection stemmed from a person's most basic right, the right to

be left alone.[234] He argued that government violated this fundamental right of privacy with every

unjustified intrusion, regardless of the means that might be developed to effectuate the

invasion.[235] In the dissent, Brandeis' foreshadowed government invasion of e-mail messages by

suggesting that, in the future, the government would be able to reproduce personal information in

court without removing the papers from the person's house.[236] Brandeis' forward-looking legal

thinking laid the groundwork for the assertion that individuals have a right against unreasonable

electronic intrusion by government.[237]

A second category of informational privacy focuses on yet another right against

unreasonable government imposition. Justice William Brennan discussed this second category,

privacy of personal information against government, in his dissent in the 1976 U.S. Supreme

Court case of *United States v. Miller*.[238] The case centered on whether the defendant had a right

of privacy in personal information that was not under his physical control; in this case the data

had been technologically captured[239] in bank records.[240] Even though the individual had

physically released the information from his control, Brennan argued that the defendant had a

---

[234] "The makers of our Constitution undertook to secure conditions favorable to the pursuit of happiness. . . . They sought to protect Americans in their beliefs, their thoughts, their emotions and their sensations. They conferred, as against Government, the right to be let alone – the most comprehensive of rights and the right most valued by civilized men." *Olmstead*, 277 U.S. at 478.
[235] "To protect that right [the right to be let alone], every unjustifiable intrusion by the Government upon the privacy of the individual, whatever the means employed, must be deemed a violation of the Fourth Amendment." *Id.*
[236] " Ways may some day be developed by which the Government, without removing papers from secret drawers, can reproduce them in court." *Id.* at 474. "Discovery and invention have made it possible for the Government, by means far more effective than stretching upon the rack, to obtain disclosure in court of what is whispered in the closet." *Id.* at 473.
[237] *See* ALAN F. WESTIN, PRIVACY AND FREEDOM 370-77 (Atheneum New York 1967).
[238] United States v. Miller, 425 U.S. 435, 447-56 (1976).
[239] The bank maintained most of the records on microfilm. The bank made copies of deposit slips and checks. *Id.* at 438.
[240] *Id.* at 441-42.

reasonable expectation that the data would remain confidential between the bank and him,[241]

unless the government provided sufficient documentation to garner a warrant or subpoena.[242]

Brennan warned that the door had been opened for abuse of government power because the

Court had affirmed the government's obtaining the information at issue without first

demonstrating to a judicial official the need for such information.[243] His concern was that

unfettered government access to personal information could be used to create a "virtual . . .

biography," which could reveal "many aspects of . . . [a person's] affairs, opinions, habits, and

associations."[244] Brennan advocated for a right against unreasonable invasion of personal

information by government.

While forward-looking discussions of the two categories of informational privacy that

address government violations arose in U.S. Supreme Court cases, discussions of these

categories of informational privacy in relation to violations by businesses and rogue individuals

appeared in two preeminent journal articles. In an influential piece on privacy, William

Prosser[245] explained the tort of unwanted intrusion by businesses and rogue individuals.[246]

Prosser agreed with Brandeis' assertion that the invasion need not be physical in nature[247] and

outlined a two-part test for violation of the tort. First, he asserted that there must be prying,

meaning that the intrusion must be of a nature that would be offensive to a reasonable person.[248]

---

[241] *Id.* at 448-49.

[242] *Id.* at 441.

[243] "To permit a police officer access to these records merely upon his request, without any judicial control as to the relevancy or other traditional requirements of legal process, and to allow the evidence to be used in any subsequent criminal prosecution against a defendant, opens the door to a vast and unlimited range of very real abuses of police power." *Id.* at 451.

[244] *Id.*

[245] Prosser was the former Dean of the University of California School of Law at Berkeley.

[246] Prosser classified four torts: intrusion, public disclosure of private facts, false light in the public eye, and appropriation. William Prosser, *Privacy*, 48 CAL. L.REV. 383, 389-407 (1960).

[247] *Id.* at 390.

[248] *Id.* at 391.

The second requirement explained by Prosser was that the information at issue must be entitled to be private, meaning that there be no legal requirement that it be public and that it not be public information.[249] Prosser's work advocated for the torts of privacy, particularly the tort of unwanted intrusion by businesses and rogue individuals.

Louis Brandeis and Samuel Warren wrote the seminal article on the issue of privacy in 1890.[250] Brandeis and Warren spoke of the right to keep information about oneself out of the public eye.[251] Although much of the focus was on publicity afforded to the creations of an author,[252] Brandeis and Warren stepped beyond this narrow focus. The two declared that protection should be afforded to information that concerns the "private life, habits, acts, and relations of an individual."[253] Their advocacy was for the protection of privacy of personal information against businesses and rogue individuals. In their scheme, recovery from businesses and rogue individuals would be provided through tort law.[254] The outcome of the tort action would be driven by the facts of the specific case[255] and would be balanced against the demands of public welfare and private justice.[256] As in the case of unwanted invasion by government,

---

[249] *Id.*

[250] Louis Brandeis & Samuel Warren, *The Right to Privacy,* 4 HARV. L. REV. 195 (1890). For a discussion of the article, see Fletcher N. Baldwin, Jr., *Impact of the Cyberage on the Right to Privacy, in* CYBERCRIME & SECURITY IIIA.1-3 (Alan E. Brill et al. eds., 1998) and William Prosser, *Privacy,* 48 CAL. L. REV. 383, 383-84 (1960).

[251] "In every such case the individual is entitled to decide whether that which is his shall be given to the public." Louis Brandeis & Samuel Warren, *The Right to Privacy,* 4 HARV. L. REV. 193, 199 (1890). The authors refer to a right not to publish, which is equated with a right to keep certain information from the public. *Id.* at 212.

[252] "No other has the right to publish his [the author's] productions in any form, without his consent. This right is wholly independent of the material on which, or the means by which, the thought, sentiment, or emotion is expressed." *Id.* at 199. "The principle which protects personal writings and any other productions of the intellect or of the emotions, is the right to privacy...." *Id.* at 213.

[253] *Id.* at 213, 216.

[254] *Id.* at 219.

[255] *Id.* at 215-16.

[256] *Id.* at 214.

Brandeis envisioned privacy of personal information as part of "the more general right of the individual to be let alone."[257]

While Brandeis linked the differing aspects of privacy under the umbrella term of the right "to be let alone,"[258] this section has laid out the aspects of another umbrella term, informational privacy. In the preceding paragraphs, protection of informational privacy from violation by government has been explored as a right[259] while tort law[260] has been examined as a means to address violations by businesses and rogue individuals. Unfortunately, the drafters of the treaty simply failed to address any protection of informational privacy.

B. The Practical Balancing Act

The particular increase in government police power provided for under the treaty will result in the loss of particular types of privacy for all individuals. Under the treaty, an individual's expectation of privately storing data in computer systems will be lessened because such data will be available for search and seizure in criminal investigations.[261] Anonymity of communications will also likely be compromised. To rebalance the scales between police power and privacy, a guaranteed protection of individual privacy needs to offset the increase in police power. As additional police power was called for because of the nature of the Internet, an increase in privacy protection is warranted in Internet-related activity to rebalance the police

---

[257] *Id.* at 205.

[258] Olmstead v. United States, 277 U.S. 438, 478 (1928); Louis Brandeis & Samuel Warren, *The Right to Privacy,* 4 HARV. L. REV. 195, 205 (1890).

[259] "Right" defined as "a legally enforceable claim that another will do or will not do a given act; a recognized and protected interest the violation of which is a wrong." BLACK'S LAW DICTIONARY 1322 (7th ed. 1999).

[260] "Tort" defined as "a civil wrong for which a remedy may be obtained, usually in the form of damages . . . . " BLACK'S LAW DICTIONARY 1496 (7th ed. 1999).

[261] This will be true regardless of whether the data is physically located within the state where the investigation is taking place. *See Final Draft Convention on Cybercrime* art. 26, 31, 33, 34, *at* http://conventions.coe.int/Treaty/en/Treaties/Html/185.htm (Nov. 23, 2001).

power/privacy scales. Particularly, the offsetting measure should involve increased informational privacy protection for individuals against unwanted invasion, whether by governments, businesses, or rogue individuals.

While the ideal solution to the issue of informational privacy would be for all states to adopt domestic legislation that protected individuals from unreasonable invasions by governments, businesses, and rogue individuals, it is impractical to believe that every state would currently adopt such a policy.[262] The best alternative available would have been for the drafters to have advocated for increased privacy protections in those states that were willing to adopt an informational privacy system while assuring that at least some minimal protections were guaranteed in all states that become parties to the cybercrime treaty.

In those states that are interested in protecting informational privacy, a system that provides a remedy for invasion would best protect the individual. While some argue that the content of cyberspace should be regulated,[263] it makes little sense to argue for such a scheme when discussing personal data. Personal data may be used in as many ways that may benefit the individual as that may harm the individual. Thus, to require that personal data be removed from cyberspace would create an unmanageable system. Instead, the individual should be guaranteed the right to pursue legal action against governments, businesses, and rogue individuals when

---

[262] The drafters found it impossible to include one international standard for privacy protection in the treaty. Margret Johnston, *US Companies Find Europe's Cyber Crime Treaty Too Vague: Americans Fear Individual Countries' Due-process Laws Could Be Violated,* IDG News Service, *at* http://www.e-businessworld.com/english/crd_treaty_321309.html (Dec. 8, 2000)(on file with the Richmond Journal of Law & Technology).

[263] In essence the argument is that it should be a crime for certain information to be on the Internet. A competing theory is that sanctions should only apply to the individual who places the information onto the Internet or who retrieves the information from the Internet.

personal information is used in unacceptable ways.[264] The particulars of this system would be developed through domestic law.

For those states that are not willing to guarantee this level of informational privacy, the treaty should have, nonetheless, required some level of protection. Henrik Kaspersen, chairman of the Committee on Experts on Crime in Cyber-Space for the Council of Europe, explained that the drafters did not want to leave privacy out of the treaty but found it impossible to include one international standard for privacy protection.[265] As such, the goal should not been one world standard but an incremental increase from the level of informational privacy protection currently provided by each state. This increase in informational privacy would have been an important step in rebalancing the police power and privacy scales of justice.

Conclusion

Today, cyberspace allows for many of the same activities as Main Street. Individuals can engage in cybershopping, cyberdating, and cyberlearning. As with Main Street, however, there is also a sinister element at work that is engaged in cybertheft, cyberfraud, and cyberdamage. To deal with these new cybercrimes, law enforcement officials require increased powers to investigate crimes involving computers systems. The cybercrime treaty will provide law enforcement with these needed powers. Such an increase in police power raises concerns about privacy protections. A treaty provision that ensured an incremental increase in informational privacy would have been an important step in allaying privacy concerns. As the treaty stands,

---

[264] *See* Gavin Skok, *Establishing a Legitimate Expectation of Privacy in Clickstream Data*, 6 MICH. TELECOMM. TECH. L. REV. 61, 82-83 (1999/2000); Susan Gindin, *Lost and Found in Cyberspace: Informational Privacy in the Age of the Internet*, 34 SAN DIEGO L. REV. 1153, 1182 (1997).
[265] Margret Johnston, *US Companies Find Europe's Cyber Crime Treaty Too Vague: Americans Fear Individual Countries' Due-process Laws Could Be Violated,* IDG News Service, *at* http://www.e-businessworld.com/english/crd_treaty_321309.html (Dec. 8, 2000)(on file with the Richmond Journal of Law & Technology).

individuals must rely on domestic laws and international treaties for protection. Without new domestic laws and revitalized interpretations of old international human rights treaties, the provided protections may prove to be paltry.

[8]

GO TO JAIL—DO NOT PASS GO, DO NOT PAY CIVIL DAMAGES: THE UNITED STATES' HESITATION TOWARDS THE INTERNATIONAL CONVENTION ON CYBERCRIME'S COPYRIGHT PROVISIONS

ADRIENNE N. KITCHEN*

There are millions of people with personal computers to make copies. That is exactly one of the reasons I think you want to be very careful. You do not want to be accidentally taking a large percentage of the American people, either small business or citizens, into the gray area of criminal law.[1]

INTRODUCTION

In the summer of 2001, a young Russian man named Dmitri Skylarov traveled to Las Vegas to take part in the Defcon 9 computer hacker conference.[2] As a cryptographer for Elcomsoft, a Russian corporation involved primarily in developing computer forensic utility software,[3] Skylarov gave a presentation before hundreds of computer programmers entitled, "ebook Security: Theory and Practice."[4] The presentation consisted of a demonstration of Elcomsoft's "Advanced ebook Processor" software that allowed a user to view, edit, and copy books and other documents written in Adobe Systems' portable document format (PDF), formerly considered to be "unalterable."[5]

Skylarov did not return home to Russia for another six months.[6] On the evening following his demonstration, he was arrested by the F.B.I. at his hotel.[7] An unwilling guinea pig, Skylarov became one of the first persons to be prosecuted under the 1998 Digital Millennium Copyright Act ("DMCA")[8] for trafficking in software to circumvent

---

* J.D. Candidate, June 2003, The John Marshall Law School. B.A. in English & Rhetoric, Univ. of Ill. at Urbana-Champaign, 2000. The author wishes to thank Prof. Doris Estelle Long for her insights and Karl Maersch for his editorial assistance.

[1] United States v. LaMacchia, 871 F. Supp. 535, 544 (D. Mass. 1994) (quoting the Vice-President and General Counsel of the Computer and Communications Industry Association in Hearing on S. 893, Aug. 12, 1992).

[2] Jennifer B. Lee, *U.S. Arrests Russian Cryptographer as Copyright Violator*, N.Y. TIMES, July 18, 2001, at C8, *available at* LEXIS News Library, N.Y. Times File.

[3] *Id.* Interestingly enough, Elcomsoft's clients include many United States government agencies, including the F.B.I. and the C.I.A. *Id.*

[4] *Russian Computer Programmer Arrested for US Copyright Infringement*, AGENCE FRANCE PRESSE, July 18, 2001, *available at* LEXIS Library, News Group File, Most Recent Two Years [hereinafter *Russian Programmer*].

[5] *Id.*

[6] *Id.*

[7] *Id.*

[8] Digital Millennium Copyright Act, Pub. L. No. 105-304, 112 Stat. 2827 (1998). The DMCA was enacted by the Clinton administration on October 28, 1998 and implemented the obligations of the World Intellectual Property Organization into United States law. *Id.* The DMCA prohibits the use of anti-circumvention devices, which allow a person to bypass technological protection measures so that he may access or copy a work. Pamela Samuelson, *Intellectual Property and the Digital Economy: Why the Anti-Circumvention Regulations Need to be Revised*, 14 BERKELEY TECH. L.J.

copyrighted materials on electronic books.[9] Suddenly, this twenty-seven-year-old father of two was faced with a potential five-year jail sentence and a $500,000 fine for demonstrating software that was "perfectly legal" in his own country.[10] By the time of his indictment by a California grand jury, the charges against him had grown to include conspiracy to traffic in circumvention technology, which would bump his potential jail sentence up to twenty-five years with a monetary fine up to $2.25 million.[11] Advocates of the prosecution initially hoped that Skylarov's incarceration would "send a message to Russian and European hackers that software tampering and pirating would be aggressively pursued across borders."[12]

Internet liberty advocates quickly jumped to Skylarov's defense, contending that the dispute between Adobe and Elcomsoft was clearly of a commercial, not criminal, nature.[13] Asserting that free speech was at risk, they voiced protests that software programmers and computer security researchers joined nationwide.[14] Within a week, Adobe retracted their support of Skylarov's prosecution, conceding that it "was not conducive to the best interests of any of the parties involved or the industry."[15] Despite this, the U.S. Department of Justice pressed on, determined to make an example of the Russian who would dare show how to decrypt an e-book code.

519, 519 (Spring 1999). The DMCA also prohibits circumvention in general. *Id.* The DMCA was intended to protect the rights of copyright holders, but it also protects Internet service providers ("ISPs") from liability for end-user infringement. *Id.* The DMCA contains five main sections: Title I, dealing with WIPO treaty implementation; Title II, establishing ISP liability limitations; Title III, establishing exemption from liability for copyright infringement done in the course of restoring or repairing software programs on computers; Title IV, covering miscellaneous provisions; and Title V, dealing with protection of certain original designs. Jo Dale Carothers, Note, *Protection of Intellectual Property on the World Wide Web: Is the Digital Millennium Copyright Act Sufficient?*, 41 ARIZ. L. REV. 937, 939 (Fall 1999). Congress included a clause that a fair use defense to infringement may still be applied despite the restrictions on anti-circumvention measures, but failed to establish what exactly a fair use is on the Internet. *Id.* at 944-45. Interestingly enough, the DMCA anti-circumvention laws did not go into effect until two years after its enactment, which is suggestive of the problems Congress faced in adapting the law to increasingly complex technology issues. *Id.* at 952-53.

    [9] *Russian Programmer, supra* note 4.

    [10] Lee, *supra* note 2, at C8; *see also* Sabrina Tavernise, *Russians Deem Arrest Insult to Their Industry,* N.Y. TIMES, Aug. 30, 2001, at C3, *available at* LEXIS News Library, N.Y. Times File (quoting a Russian programmer who denounced the U.S. actions as "rubbish" and "crazy," and who analogized that, "[i]t's the same as buying a loaf of bread, and when you find the middle isn't baked, you come back to show the baker and get put in jail").

    [11] Adam Creed, *Skylarov Indicted, Could Face 25 Years in Jail,* NEWSBYTES, Aug. 28, 2001, *available at* LEXIS News Library, Newsgroup File, Most Recent Two Years.

    [12] *See Russian Programmer, supra* note 4; *see also* Tavernise, *supra* note 10, at C3 (remarking that even prior to Skylarov's prosecution, Russia struggled with its reputation as a country that bred software piracy). With the collapse of the Communist state, Russia's economy collapsed as well, breeding and marketing software piracy that still exists on nearly every street corner there today. *Id.*

    [13] *Fate of Russian Arrested for Hacking Undecided,* AGENCE FRANCE PRESSE, July 23, 2001, *available at* LEXIS News Library, News Group File, Most Recent Two Years.

    [14] *Id.*

    [15] *U.S. Company Backs Down on Prosecuting Russian Hacker,* AGENCE FRANCE PRESSE, July 24, 2001, *available at* LEXIS News Library, Newsgroup File, Most Recent Two Years.

Insisting he had done nothing wrong, Skylarov pled not guilty to the charges against him.[16]

In November 2001, while Skylarov remained in California, the Council of Europe ("CoE") called upon their member and observer-status countries to adopt the Council's Convention on Cybercrime. The Convention was the first treaty to seek harmonization of cybercrime laws, like those contained within the DMCA. With the initiative of the Convention, countries around the world began to discuss the line separating copyright infringement from criminal activity, whether new and harsher laws are needed, and how to make such laws effective worldwide. These issues beg the questions: What should be done with people like Skylarov? Did Congress intend to punish his conduct criminally? In a growing global economic community, who will be responsible for pursuing the copyright offender and determining whether the punishment fits the crime?

This Comment discusses the goals, scope, and effectiveness of the world's first international cybercrime treaty and its criminal copyright provisions. Part I.A discusses the evolution of cybercrime and its impact on the global economy. Part I.B examines the history and structure of the CoE and its relationship with the United States. Part I.C then explains the purpose and goals of CoE's Draft International Convention on Cybercrime.

Part II.A describes the criminal standards and penalties imposed by the terms of the Convention. Part II.B contrasts the Convention with current United States copyright and cybercrime statutes, particularly the No Electronic Theft Act and Title 18 of the United States Code, to determine what copyright infringement the United States criminalizes and why. Part II.C dissects the major purported objections and challenges to the Convention from an American legal and Constitutional standard.

Part III proposes that the United States Congress refuse to take the final step of ratification of the Convention treaty as it exists now. Part III also suggests that while the issue of cybercrime prevention and penalty is ripe, the United States needs to quickly address the issue of criminal copyright infringement in a broader form. Finally, Part IV advocates that the need for an effective international force against cybercrime is real and concludes that fundamental American values and rights need not be sacrificed at the expense of a hasty preemptive strike at cybercrime.

I. THE COUNCIL OF EUROPE, CYBERCRIME, AND THE DRAFT INTERNATIONAL CONVENTION

A. *The Evolution of Cybercrime and its Global Consequences*

Cybercrime is a relatively new term for crimes that involve computer networks.[17] In this age of digitalization, companies all over the world rely heavily on computer

---

[16] Colin McMahon, *Russian Hacker Cuts Freedom Deal,* CHI. TRIB., Dec. 21, 2001, at 35, *available at* LEXIS News Library, Chicago Tribune File. While awaiting trial, Skylarov made a deal with the United States in which he admitted to the facts of his situation but not illegal activity, and effectively secured his freedom and a trip back to Moscow. *Id.*

[17] *See* BLACK'S LAW DICTIONARY 319 (7th ed. 1999). The term cybercrime is a general term that encompasses such illegal acts as "cybersquatting," "cyberstalking," and "cybertheft." *Id.* Cybersquatting is the act of reserving a domain name on the Internet, especially a name that would

networks for transferring and storing information, as well as communicating with other businesses and consumers.[18] Computer users, known as "hackers," use their knowledge of computer systems to break into complex databases and networks to commit various crimes.[19]

The Internet finds itself conducive to fraud, copyright infringement, child pornography, and other crimes because its content can be easily dispersed all over the world in a relatively anonymous manner.[20] Cybercrime also has the potential to cause serious public safety problems, most notably when critical infrastructure operation systems are targeted.[21]

As such networks reach across international lines, the crimes committed have great jurisdictional range.[22] Cybercrimes, including criminal copyright infringement, have been increasing in both frequency and severity in recent years as hackers and other criminals keep up with the latest technological encryption and protection advances.[23]

For example, a survey conducted by the Computer Emergency Response Team ("CERT") Coordination Center at Carnegie-Mellon University indicated a 183% jump in the number of hacking incidents over a one-year span.[24] Also, the Spring 2000 Computer Security Institute ("CSI")/FBI Computer Crime and Security Survey projected monetary losses exceeding $265 million in 2000, up from $100 million in 1997; those may in fact be underestimated figures, because only forty-two percent of respondents were able to quantify their losses.[25] A more recent study by an independent research institute, Computer Economics, indicated that the spreading of the "I Love You" virus from the Philippines, as well as copycat viruses, resulted in $6.7 billion in damages to businesses worldwide.[26] Virus attacks also resulted in

---

be associated with a company's trademark, and then seeking to profit by selling or licensing the name to the company that has an interest in being identified with it. *Id.* Cyberstalking is the act of threatening, harassing, or annoying someone through multiple e-mail messages, through the Internet. *Id.* Cybertheft is the act of using an online computer service, such as one on the Internet, to steal someone else's use and enjoyment of property. *Id.*

[18] *See* U.S. Dept. of Justice Frequently Asked Questions About the Council of Europe Convention on Cybercrime, *available at* http://www.usdoj.gov/criminal/cybercrime/COEFAQs.htm [hereinafter Dept. of Justice—Convention FAQs] (last visited Nov. 4, 2001).

[19] *See* Agent Steal, *available at* http://www.agentsteal.com (last visited Nov. 4, 2001). Articles, written by Agent Steal, otherwise known as Justin Petersen, include titles such as "Everything a Hacker Needs to Know About Being Busted by the Feds," and "Tapping Data Phone Lines." *Id.*

[20] *See generally* Susan W. Brenner, *Is There Such a Thing as Virtual Crime?,* 4 CAL. CRIM. LAW REV. 1 (2001) (noting that most "cybercrimes" are just regular crimes that are capable of being carried out via the use of a computer, including theft and embezzlement, fraud, forgery, pornography, obscenity, stalking, vandalism, burglary, common trespass, as well as inchoate offenses).

[21] *See* Dept. of Justice—Convention FAQs, *supra* note 18 (offering an example of a case in which a juvenile disabled a telephone company computer that supported communications services to an airport, forcing the FAA to close its control tower for several hours).

[22] *See id.* (offering an example of the international scope of cybercrime). In 1998, Vladimir Levin was convicted of hacking into a major international bank from Russia and transferring $12 million from accounts located around the world. *Id.*

[23] *See id.*

[24] *Id.*

[25] *Id.*

[26] *Id.* Also known as the "Love Bug," the "I Love You" virus took VBScript form and called itself VBS_LOVELETTER. *Id.* The virus used Microsoft Outlook to send e-mail to all on its

more than $12.1 billion in damages to businesses during 1999 alone, with such figures projected to rise in the following years.[27]

B. The History and Structure of the Council of Europe

The Council of Europe ("CoE"), organized in 1948,[28] is an intergovernmental organization[29] comprised of forty-three European member countries.[30] Any European country is welcome to become a member of CoE provided it accepts the principle of the rule of law and guarantees human rights and fundamental freedoms to everyone under its jurisdiction.[31] CoE states four goals of its assembly: (1) to protect human rights, pluralist democracy, and the rule of law; (2) to promote awareness and encourage the development of Europe's cultural identity and diversity; (3) to seek solutions to problems facing European society;[32] and (4) to help consolidate

---

address list with a subject line reading, "ILOVEYOU". *Id.* The body of the message read, "kindly check the attached LOVELETTER coming from me," and included the lethal attachment file entitled, "LOVE-LETTER-FOR-YOU.TXT.VBS." *Id.* When the attachment was opened, the virus would overwrite the computer's files with specific extensions for its codes, which effectively wiped out the host codes and replaced them with the infected codes, ready to be forwarded on to other unsuspecting e-mailers. *Id.* The virus also replicated itself through the mIRC chat program, where one infected user would inadvertently spread the virus to everyone in that user's chat channel. *Id.;* see Virus Encyclopedia, *available at* http://www.antivirus.com/vinfo/virusencyclo/ (last visited Jan. 10, 2002).

[27] *See* Dept. of Justice—Convention FAQs, *supra* note 18.

[28] *See* A Short History of the Council of Europe, *available at* http://www.coe.int/portalt.asp (last visited Nov. 4, 2001) (explaining how CoE sprung out of a movement dedicated to European unity and rebuilding the continent after the liberation of the European States following World War II). Winston Churchill proposed "a remedy which, as if by miracle, would transform the whole scene and in a few years make Europe as free and happy as Switzerland is today. We must build a kind of United States of Europe." *Id.*

[29] *See* Council of Europe: an Overview, *available at* http://www.coe.int/portalt.asp [hereinafter Overview of Council of Europe] (last visited Nov. 4, 2001) (clarifying that CoE is not to be confused with the European Union, which is a distinct organization comprised of 15 member countries). All fifteen European Union states are also members of the Council of Europe. *Id.* The official languages of CoE are English and French; however, the Parliamentary Assembly also uses German, Italian, and Russian as working languages, and other languages may be interpreted during debates. *Id.*

[30] *See* Council of Europe: the Parliamentary Assembly, *available at* http://www.coe.int/portalt.asp (last visited Nov. 4, 2001) (listing member countries of the Council of Europe and their number of representatives: Albania (4), Armenia (4), Andorra (2), Austria (6), Azerbaijan (6), Belgium (7), Bulgaria (6), Croatia (5), Cyprus (3), Czech Republic (7), Denmark (5), Estonia (3), Finland (5), France (18), Georgia (5), Germany (18), Greece (7), Hungary (7), Iceland (3), Ireland (4), Italy (18), Latvia (3), Liechtenstein (2), Lithuania (4), Luxembourg (3), Malta (3), Moldova (5), Netherlands (7), Norway (5), Poland (12), Portugal (7), Romania (10), Russia (18), San Marino (2), Slovakia (5), Slovenia (3), Spain (12), Sweden (6), Switzerland (6), "the former Yugoslav Republic of Macedonia" (3), Turkey (12), Ukraine (12), United Kingdom (18)).

[31] *See* Overview of Council of Europe, *supra* note 29 (noting that the Council also grants consultative status to over 350 non-governmental organizations ("NGO") so that they may work together to represent the ordinary public). NGO's are consulted via discussions and colloquies with members of the Parliamentary Assembly to ensure a free-flowing dialogue between the two sectors. *Id.*

[32] *See id.* (noting that such problems include discrimination against minorities, xenophobia, intolerance, environmental protection, human cloning, AIDS, drugs, organized crime, and others).

democratic stability in Europe by backing political, legislative and constitutional reform.[33]

The framework upon which CoE stands is comprised of the Parliamentary Assembly, which serves to hear deliberations on issues,[34] and a Committee of Ministers, which makes decisions on the issues at hand.[35] The Assembly meets four times a year for a week at a time in plenary session in the Chamber of the Palais de l'Europe in Strasbourg.[36] An essential role of the Assembly is to create treaties with the effect of harmonizing European legal systems.[37] The United States, as a non-member State, holds observer status in the Committee of Ministers' decision-making activities, and may choose to adopt or reject the conventions enacted by CoE at its discretion.[38]

---

[33] *See id.* (stating that CoE's work reaches into such areas as human rights, media, legal co-operation, social and economic questions, health, education, culture, heritage, sport, youth, local democracy and trans-frontier co-operation, the environment and regional planning). CoE receives financing for its projects and activities from the governments of its member states, who each contribute an amount proportionate to their population and wealth. *Id.* CoE's 2002 budget is roughly 169 million Euros. *Id.*

[34] *See* Council of Europe: the Parliamentary Assembly, *available at* http://www.coe.int/portalt.asp (last visited Nov. 4, 2001) (articulating that the Assembly is comprised of 602 members (301 representatives and 301 substitutes) drawn from each of the 43 represented nations). Every country contributes between 2 and 18 representatives depending on population size. *Id.* Five political groups are officially represented: the Socialist Group, the Group of the European People's Party, the European Democratic Group, the Liberal, Democratic and Reformers' Group, and the Group of the Unified European Left. *Id.*

[35] *See* Council of Europe: the Committee of Ministers, *available at* http://www.coe.int/t/e/committee_of_ministers/public (last visited Nov. 4, 2001) (describing that the Foreign Ministers of the member states meet at least twice a year to review political issues and matters of European co-operation and to give the necessary political impetus to CoE's activities). The Committee of Ministers functions not only as the decision-making body of CoE, but also as the facilitator of its enacted international agreements. *Id.*

[36] *See* Council of Europe: the Parliamentary Assembly, *supra* note 34 (describing that each session involves political debates on issues of importance to European nations and serves to create international treaties, known as conventions in Europe, to be ratified by the Committee of Ministers and to be effective upon all member countries). In an effort to create dialogue between representatives and experts on vital social and political issues, the Assembly also holds regular conferences, symposiums, and public parliamentary hearings. *Id.*

[37] *See* Council of Europe: Legal Co-operation, *available at* http://www.coe.int/portalt.asp/ (last visited Nov. 4, 2001) (identifying measures the Council is taking to shape European legislation).

[38] *See* Council of Europe's Member States, *available at* http://www.coe.int/portalt.asp (last visited Nov. 4, 2001) (describing the rules of membership). The United States gained observer status to the Committee of Ministers on October 1, 1996, meaning that it may participate in discussions and may adopt CoE enactments, but is not technically bound to comply with all CoE decisions, member states must. *Id.* Other countries with observer status to the Committee are: Canada, Holy See, Japan, and Mexico. *Id.* Canada, Israel, and Mexico hold observer status to the Parliamentary Assembly. *Id.* Additionally, two countries, Bosnia-Herzegovina and the Federal Republic of Yugoslavia, are deemed Special Guests to the Parliamentary Assembly. *Id.*

[1:364 2002]   John Marshall Review of Intellectual Property Law   370

C. History, Purpose, and Goals of the Council of Europe's International Convention on Cybercrime

Recognizing the increasing growth of computer and Internet technology on a global scale, the CoE began discussions about combating cybercrimes in the late 1980's.[39] In 1989, CoE created its first official recommendation that new substantive laws be developed that would criminalize certain conduct committed through computer networks.[40] Twelve years later, in April 2001, the Committee of Ministers and the Parliamentary Assembly approved the final draft of the International Convention on Cybercrime. Because the Convention draft differs in several respects to United States statutes, the treaty has been signed by the United States, but Congress has not yet ratified it.[41]

"The Convention covers three main topics: harmonisation of the national laws which define offences, definition of investigation and prosecution procedures to cope with global networks, and establishment of a rapid and effective system of international co-operation."[42] Offenses criminalized by the Convention include offenses against the confidentiality and integrity of computer systems, computer-related offenses such as forgery and fraud, content-related offenses, and copyright infringement offenses.[43] Although United States law encompasses the majority of these offenses, the Convention creates an international minimum standard for criminal behavior, a procedural format for enforcement, and most notably, a requirement of international cooperation and assistance in investigation and prosecution of such cybercrimes.[44]

---

[39] *See* First International Treaty to Combat Crime in Cyberspace, *available at* http://conventions.coe.int/Treaty/EN/cadreprojets.htm (last visited Mar. 1, 2002) (noting that traditional international cooperation efforts would not be sufficient to keep up with the explosive growth of technology and its capacity for use in criminal pursuits).

[40] *See* Council of Europe Press Service, *available at* http://www.press.coe.int (last visited Nov. 4, 2001) (identifying a second study and recommendation on corresponding procedural law which was completed in 1995). In February 1997, the Council of Europe's Committee of Ministers devised a new committee, the Committee of Experts on Crime in Cyberspace, to prepare a binding legal document that would incorporate issues such as substantive criminal offenses, the use of coercive powers, and jurisdiction in cybercrime cases. *Id.* Between April 1997 and December 2000, the Committee held ten meetings, and the drafting group held fifteen meetings to debate and draft the Convention. *Id.* In April 2000, the draft text was declassified and published on Internet, so that specialists and network users could comment. *Id.* In March 2001, the Parliament invited international experts to a special hearing to debate the major premises as well as the fine points of the Convention. *Id.* Following this, the Committee of Ministers asked the Assembly for an opinion on the draft, which it adopted, with several amendments, at its April 2001 session. *Id.*

[41] *Council of Europe Signs Draft Cybercrime Treaty*, THE INDUSTRY STANDARD.COM, June 22, 2001, *available at* LEXIS, News Library, The Industry Standard file. The United States signed the treaty on June 22, 2001. *Id.*

[42] *See generally* Main Lines of the Convention, *available at* http://www.press.coe.int (last visited Nov. 4, 2001).

[43] *Id.*

[44] *See* Dept. of Justice—Convention FAQs, *supra* note 18; *see also* Main Lines of the Convention, *supra* note 42 (stating that the international enforcement of the criminal provisions would require law enforcement authorities in different countries to collect and exchange information as well as computer-based evidence, though purportedly not to facilitate "transfrontier" searches; the system was intended to be fast-paced and operating at all times to ensure immediacy of investigation).

II. COMPARISON AND CONTRAST OF THE COPYRIGHT REGULATIONS AND PENALTIES OF
CURRENT U.S. STATUTES AND THE CRIMINAL COPYRIGHT PROVISIONS OF THE
CONVENTION

A. United States Statutes Involving Criminal Copyright Violations

Copyright protection serves to promote the progress of science and the useful
arts by granting exclusive rights to the copyright holder.[45] Copyright law in the
United States is currently governed mainly by four statutes: the Copyright Act of
1976;[46] the No Electronic Theft Act;[47] the Audio Home Recording Act of 1992;[48] and
the Digital Millennium Copyright Act.[49] Generally, United States copyright law does
not exist to criminalize copyright offenses; the majority of remedies are civil.[50]
Nonetheless, the No Electronic Theft Act ("NET Act") consists of amendments to the
Copyright Act of 1976 that were created "to provide greater copyright protection by
amending criminal copyright provisions, and for other purposes."[51] The NET Act[52]
applies criminal infringement remedies in § 506(a) to one who willfully infringes a
copyright[53] either:

   (1) for purposes of commercial advantage or private financial gain,[54] or

   (2) by the reproduction or distribution, including by electronic means,
   during any 180-day period, of 1 or more copies or phonorecords, or more
   copyrighted works, which have a total retail value of more than $1,000.[55]

---

   [45] U.S. CONST. art. I, § 8, cl.8 ("The Congress shall have Power To . . . promote the Progress of
Science and useful Arts, by securing for limited Times to Authors and Inventors the exclusive Right
to their respective Writings and Discoveries.").
   [46] Copyright Act of 1976, 17 U.S.C. §§ 101-810 (1994 & Supp. 2000).
   [47] No Electronic Theft Act, Pub. L. No. 105-147, 111 Stat. 2678 (1997).
   [48] Audio Home Recording Act, 17 U.S.C. §§ 1001-1010 (1992).
   [49] *See generally* DMCA, *supra* note 8.
   [50] *See* 17 U.S.C. §§ 501-505 (2000) (listing such civil remedies as injunctions, impounding and
disposition of infringing articles, damages (actual and statutory) and profits, and costs and
attorney's fees). The provisions make extensive use of the word "may" in explaining the powers that
the judiciary has to adjudicate such infringement actions. *Id.*
   [51] NET Act, 111 Stat. 2678 (1997); *see also* UCLA Online Institute for Cyberspace Law and
Policy: The 'No Electronic Theft' Act, *available at* http://www.gseis.ucla.edu/iclp/hr2265.html (last
visited Nov. 4, 2001) (remarking that the Act was meant to close a loophole in the previous criminal
copyright laws, where intentional copiers and distributors of copyrighted material over the internet
did not face criminal penalties so long as they did not profit from their actions).
   [52] *See generally* 17 U.S.C. §§ 1201-02, 1204 (2000) (discussing criminal infringement
remedies). The NET Act is discussed specifically because it provides the most comprehensive
criminal copyright provisions, while the Digital Millennium Copyright Act's criminal provisions, for
example, apply only to limited copyright violations such as circumvention of copyright protection
systems and tampering with copyright management information.
   [53] *See* Copyright Act of 1976, 17 U.S.C. § 101 (1994 & Supp. 2000) (failing to define the term
"willful"). *But see* 17 U.S.C. § 506(a)(2) (2000) ("For purposes of this subsection, evidence of
reproduction or distribution of a copyrighted work, by itself, shall not be sufficient to establish
willful infringement.").
   [54] *See* 17 U.S.C. § 101 (2000) ("The term 'financial gain' includes receipt, or expectation of
receipt, of anything of value, including the receipt of other copyrighted works.").
   [55] NET Act, 111 Stat. 2678 (1997).

[1:364 2002]   John Marshall Review of Intellectual Property Law   372

The penalties applied for criminal infringement are governed by 18 U.S.C. § 2319.[56] When a violation of the NET Act occurs, the offender is subject to a jail sentence and monetary fine, the respective length and amounts of which are contingent upon the degree of infringement.[57] The degree is measured by several factors: the number of infringing actions; the value of the copyrighted works; and the number of previous offenses by the infringer; the greater these factors, the more severe the punishment.[58]

Thus, turning a copyright violation that occurs by electronic means into a cybercrime was a somewhat difficult process under United States law, though the NET Act made prosecution a more viable option than it previously had been.[59]

---

[56] 17 U.S.C. § 506(a)(2) (2000).

[57] 18 U.S.C. § 2319 (2000). Section 2319 provides that one who violates 506(a) shall be punished in the following manner and in addition to any other applicable provisions of Title 17:

(b) Any person who commits an offense under section 506 (a)(1) of Title 17—

(1) shall be imprisoned not more than 5 years, or fined in the amount set forth in this title, or both, if the offense consists of the reproduction or distribution, including by electronic means, during any 180-day period, of at least 10 copies or phonorecords, of 1 or more copyrighted works, which have a total retail value of more than $2,500;

(2) shall be imprisoned not more than 10 years, or fined in the amount set forth in this title, or both, if the offense is a second or subsequent offense under paragraph (1); and

(3) shall be imprisoned not more than 1 year, or fined in the amount set forth in this title, or both, in any other case.

(c) Any person who commits an offense under section 506(a)(2) of Title 17, United States Code-

(1) shall be imprisoned not more than 3 years, or fined in the amount set forth in this title, or both, if the offense consists of the reproduction or distribution of 10 or more copies or phonorecords of 1 or more copyrighted works, which have a total retail value of $2,500 or more;

shall be imprisoned not more than 6 years, or fined in the amount set forth in this title, or both, if the offense is a second or subsequent offense under paragraph (1); and

shall be imprisoned not more than 1 year, or fined in the amount set forth in this title, or both, if the offense consists of the reproduction or distribution of 1 or more copies or phonorecords or 1 or more copyrighted works, which have a total retail value of more than $1,000.

Id.

[58] *Id.*

[59] *See generally* Business Software Alliance: First Guilty Verdict Under NET Act Draws Praise, *available at* http://www.bsa.org/usa/press/newsreleases/1999-08-20.181.phtml (last visited Nov. 4, 2001). While the NET Act was passed in 1997, the first conviction under the Act did not take place until May 11, 2001. *Id.* Christian Morley of Salem, Massachusetts was found guilty of conspiracy to infringe software copyrights as a member of the hacker organization "Pirates with Attitudes." *Id.* The group regularly distributed unauthorized copies of software, including unreleased versions. *Id.*

Copyright violations are still criminalized where illegal reproductions and distributions, including "sharing," knowingly occur on a relatively grand scale, but may also be criminalized for even smaller degrees of infringement.[60] The NET Act amendments reflect a desire to protect copyright owners while maintaining intent, value, and time restrictions, so as not to promote zealous and fruitless prosecutions of small-time offenders.[61]

Recognizing the need for copyright protection worldwide, the United States has also committed itself to international agreements such as the Berne Convention for the Protection of Literary and Artistic Property ("Berne Convention")[62] and the Universal Copyright Convention,[63] which provide that United States copyright law will be protected even where infringements occur in other countries.[64]

The United States is also a signatory to the Agreement on Trade-Related Aspects of Intellectual Property Rights, Including Trade in Counterfeit Goods ("TRIPS"), which is administered by the World Trade Organization ("WTO").[65] TRIPS provides for enforcement procedures that are "fair and equitable" and those that will permit "effective action against any act of infringement of intellectual property rights."[66]   Article 61 of TRIPS promotes criminal penalties including imprisonment and monetary fines "sufficient to provide a deterrent, consistently with

---

[60] *See* File-Sharing Primer, *available at* http://hotwired.lycos.com/webmonkey (last visited Nov. 4, 2001). File and software "sharing" is a popular trend amongst college students and adults alike. *Id.* Popular file-sharing applications include Napster, Macster (for Macintosh operating systems), Gnutella, and Scour Exchange. *Id.* These "peer-to-peer" applications allow file-sharers to swap music, videos, and other files amongst themselves. *Id.* Recently, Napster became the subject of a very public debate on the legal validity of file sharing. *Id.; see also* A & M Records, Inc. v. Napster Inc., 239 F.3d 1004 (9th Cir. 2001) (finding that by its transmission and database of peer-to-peer music files, Napster probably engaged in contributory and vicarious copyright infringement).

[61] *See* 17 U.S.C. § 507(a)-(b) (2000) (establishing a five-year statute of limitations, commencing after the cause of action first arose, for maintaining a criminal proceeding, and a three-year statute of limitations, beginning after the claim accrued, for bringing a civil suit).

[62] Berne Convention for the Protection of Literary and Artistic Works, Sept. 9, 1886, last revised in Paris, July 24, 1971, 828 U.N.T.S. 221. The United States did not become a member of the Berne Convention until March 1, 1989. *Id.*

[63] Universal Copyright Convention, Aug. 11, 1910, last revised in Paris, July 24, 1971, 6 U.S.T. 2731.

[64] International Copyright, *available at* http://www.loc.gov/copyright/fls/fl100.pdf (last visited Dec. 7, 2001). True "international copyright" does not exist to protect expression throughout the world. *Id.* Prior to these treaties, if an author's work was copyright-protected in the United States and then was used without authorization in another country, the author would only have redress according to the copyright laws—if any existed—in the other country. *Id.*

[65] General Agreement on Tariffs and Trade-Multilateral Trade Negotiations: Agreement on Trade-Related Aspects of Intellectual Property Rights, Including Trade in Counterfeit Goods, Apr. 15, 1994, 33 I.L.M. 81 [hereinafter TRIPS]. TRIPS sought to "establish a mutually supportive relationship between the WTO and the World Intellectual Property Organization (WIPO) as well as other relevant international organizations." *Id.* Both the TRIPS Agreement and the WIPO Copyright Treaty incorporate the Berne Convention as a foundation for their principles. *Id.*

[66] *Id.* art. 41(1). The most notable advance in protection contained in TRIPS is its establishment of procedural enforcement norms that signatory countries must incorporate into their domestic laws; the advance is substantial in comparison to the Berne Convention, which did not contain procedural enforcement norms. Doris Estelle Long, Enforcement and the TRIPS Agreement (excerpted) in *A Coursebook in International Intellectual Property Law* (Doris Estelle Long & Anthony D'Amato eds., 2000).

the level of penalties applied for crimes of a corresponding gravity."[67] What TRIPS does *not* do is require a harmonization of enforcement standards and procedures between nations, which the Convention purports to necessitate.[68]

B. *Criminal Standards and Penalties Imposed by the Convention*

The Convention on Cybercrime consists of four chapters encompassing forty-eight articles.[69] Copyright offenses comprise their own title within chapter two: measures to be taken at the national level.[70] Though brief, Article 10, "Offenses Related to Infringement of Copyright and Related Rights," takes a serious stance on the establishment and enforcement of criminal copyright provisions.[71] Specifically, Article 10[72] *requires* that signatory countries criminalize any instance of copyright infringement or related infringement "where such act[s] are committed wil[l]fully, on

---

[67] *See* TRIPS, *supra* note 65, art. 61.

[68] *See* The TRIPS Agreement and Trade Facilitation: Background Note by the Secretariat, *available at* http://docsonline.wto.org (last visited Nov. 20, 2001). "Wide disparities between levels of intellectual property protection cause problems in international trade as goods and services which may be produced and sold in one jurisdiction may be infringing in another. The approximation of legal standards and enforcement procedures tends to alleviate these problems, but the TRIPS Agreement will not eliminate them." *Id.*

[69] *See* Convention on Cybercrime, *available at* http://conventions.coe.int/treaty/en/projets.htm [hereinafter Convention](last visited Nov. 4, 2001).

[70] *Id.*

[71] *Id.*

[72] *Id.* Article 10 provides:

> 1. Each Party shall adopt such legislative and other measures as may be necessary to establish as criminal offences under its domestic law the infringement of copyright, as defined under the law of that Party, pursuant to the obligations it has undertaken under the Paris Act of 24 July 1971 revising the Berne Convention for the Protection of Literary and Artistic Works, the Agreement on Trade-Related Aspects of Intellectual Property Rights and the WIPO Copyright Treaty, with the exception of any moral rights conferred by such conventions, where such acts are committed wilfully, [sic] on a commercial scale and by means of a computer system.

> 2. Each Party shall adopt such legislative and other measures as may be necessary to establish as criminal offences under its domestic law the infringement of related rights, as defined under the law of that Party, pursuant to the obligations it has undertaken under the International Convention for the Protection of Performers, Producers of Phonograms and Broadcasting Organisations (Rome Convention), the Agreement on Trade-Related Aspects of Intellectual Property rights and the WIPO Performances and Phonograms Treaty, with the exception of any moral rights conferred by such conventions, where such acts are committed wilfully, on a commercial scale and by means of a computer system.

> 3. A Party may reserve the right not to impose criminal liability under paragraphs 1 and 2 of this article in limited circumstances, provided that other effective remedies are available and that such reservation does not derogate from the Party's international obligations set forth in the international instruments referred to in paragraphs 1 and 2 of this article.

a commercial scale and by means of a computer system."[73] The copyright provisions state that each country must establish laws that would create criminal copyright offenses, pursuant to the countries' obligations under the Berne Convention, TRIPS Agreement, and WIPO Copyright Treaty, in cases of willful infringement on a commercial scale by the use of a computer system.[74] Further, the Convention's copyright provisions provide for criminal laws enforcing the infringement of related rights with the same requirements of willful infringement on a commercial scale by the use of a computer system.[75] Lastly, the Convention copyright provisions allow for a country to reserve its right *not* to impose criminal liability on a copyright infringer, but only where other "effective" measures are in place that would not clash with the Convention's rules within Article 10.[76]   Thus, the Convention establishes international rules intended to harmonize copyright laws between nations, with the plain intent to take a stricter stance on criminal copyright liability.

In contrast to the United States' NET Act, copyright infringement actions that merely meet the three aforementioned requirements are automatically delineated as criminal, with no minimum damage amount, time frame, or number of copies made.[77] Any infringement that is done with knowledge that it is illegal, on a commercial scale,[78] by the use of a computer system makes the infringer criminally liable and subject to criminal punishment under the law of that country.[79] However, unlike in the TRIPS Agreement, there is no provision for "effective enforcement" of the types of punishment enumerated in the Convention.[80] Hence, the Convention creates blanket substantive laws but does not address their application and enforcement.

C. The United States' (and Other) Objections to the Convention's Criminal Provisions for Copyright

The Convention drafters recognized that their proposed treaty would be met with intense scrutiny.[81]   Problems acknowledged by the drafters include: the

---

[73] *Id.; see also* Berne Convention for the Protection of Literary and Artistic Works, July 24, 1971; TRIPS Agreement; and WIPO Copyright Treaty, December 20, 1996.

[74] *See* Convention, *supra* note 69.

[75] *Id.*

[76] *Id.; see also Explanatory Report, infra* note 117, *available at* http://www.conventions.coe.int /Treaty/en/Reports/Html/185.html (last visited Mar. 1, 2002) (explaining that the clause was not intended to extend the protection that authors, film producers, performers, phonogram producers, broadcasting companies, and other right holders have to those that are not eligible under their own domestic copyright laws or under international copyright agreements).

[77] *Id.; see also* 17 U.S.C. § 506 (2000); 18 U.S.C. § 2319 (2000).

[78] *See* E-Commerce News: Convention on Cybercrime, *available at* http://www.wilmer.com/ docs/news_items/ACFD9E.pdf (last visited Nov. 4, 2001) (noting that "commercial scale" is never defined in the Convention, leaving the phraseology open to questions of whether personal-use file-sharing is to be automatically criminalized as well as infringement for profit).

[79] *See* Convention, *supra* note 69, art. 10.1 (last visited Nov. 4, 2001) ("Each Party shall adopt such legislative and other measures as may be necessary to establish as criminal offences under its domestic law the infringement of copyright.").

[80] *See* TRIPS, *supra* note 65.

[81] *See* Council of Europe, *Big Brother or Free-for-All—How Can the Law Strike a Balance?*, *available at* http://www.coe.int/T/E/Communication_and_Research/Press/Themes_Files/cybercrime/ e_bigbrother.asp#topofpage (last visited Nov. 4, 2001) (observing an ensuing "clash" in the

[1:364 2002]   John Marshall Review of Intellectual Property Law   376

potential denial of civil liberties;[82] overreaching government power;[83] lack of privacy rights;[84] reduction of the free-flow of information by tighter restraints;[85] and imposition of third-party content liability for Internet Service Providers ("ISPs").[86]

Some of the most intense criticisms of the Convention come from organizations such as the Global Internet Liberty Campaign ("GILC"),[87] which argue that the Convention threatens free speech and privacy rights by improperly and dangerously extending the reach of the policing authority of national governments.[88] Additionally, GILC asserts that the broad extension of copyright crimes in Article 10 is objectionable, because it is not yet established that criminal penalties are the appropriate remedies for instances of copyright infringement in the majority of States.[89]   Furthermore, Article 10 allows for mutual assistance in prosecuting copyright crimes without dual-criminality. However, when one country deems an instance of copyright infringement to be a crime and another country does not, how can they work together to prosecute that offense?[90]

Convention between individual rights to free speech and privacy, state rights to combat cybercrime, society's need for secure information networks, and a general corporate need to protect its business interests in an electronically-driven market).

[82] *See* ACLU/EPIC, *Comments on CoE Cybercrime Convention,* at http://www.pili.org/lists/piln/archives/msg00777.html (last visited Nov. 4, 2001) (noting that Article 19.4 of the Convention appears to require countries to adopt laws that force users to provide their encryption keys and the plain text of the encrypted files, which raises the issue of the right against self-incrimination).

[83] *See* Associated Press, *Cybercrime Treaty Raises Concern,* at http://www.jsonline.com/bym/tech/ap/oct00/ap-europe-cybercri102800.asp (last visited Nov. 4, 2001) (remarking that the Convention gives law enforcement officials a basis to investigate any crime where evidence may be stored on a computer, and that it also gives the government an overreaching power to collect private information).

[84] *Id.*

[85] *See* Convention, *supra* note 69.

[86] *Id.*

[87] *See* Global Internet Liberty Campaign, *Statement of Principles at* http://www.gilc.org/about/principles (last visited Nov. 4, 2001). Primarily a privacy watchdog group, the GILC advocates, among other things, ending prior censorship of Internet communication, sustaining free speech on the Internet and in other digital communications with limited government restrictions, and the unrestricted encryption and protection of digital information. *Id.*

[88] *See* GILC Member Letter, *at* http://www.gilc.org/privacy/coe-letter-1000.html (last visited Nov. 4, 2001) (posting a letter objecting to the Convention that was signed by the following groups: American Civil Liberties Union (US), Association for Computing Machinery (International), Associazione per la Libertà nella Comunicazione Elettronica Interattiva (IT), Bits of Freedom (NL), Canadian Journalists for Free Expression (CA), Center for Democracy and Technology (US), Computer Professionals for Social Responsibilities (US), Crypto-Rights Foundation (US), Cyber-Rights & Cyber-Liberties (UK), Derechos Human Rights (US), Digital Freedom Network (US), Digital Rights (DK), Electronic Frontier Foundation (US), Electronic Frontiers Australia (AU), Electronic Privacy Information Center (US), Equipo Nizkor (ES), Feminists Against Censorship (UK), FITUG e.V.(DE), Foundation for Information Policy Research (UK), Human Rights Network (RU), Internet Freedom (UK), Internet Society – Bulgaria (BG), Internet Society, IRIS – Imaginons un réseau Internet solidaire (FR), Kriptopolis (ES), Liberty (UK), The Link Centre, Wits University, Johannesburg (ZA), NetAction (US), Networkers Against Surveillance Taskforce (JP), Opennet, PGP en Français (FR), Privacy International (UK), quintessenz (AT), Verein für Internet Benutzer (AT), and XS4ALL (NL)).

[89] *Id.* "New criminal penalties should not be established by international convention in an area where national law is so unsettled." *Id.*

[90] *Id.*

Besides the problems that lie within the Convention document, there are many objections to the procedural manner in which the Draft Convention was drawn.[91] Only law enforcement groups were involved in the drafting of the language, without any non-governmental organization or industry input.[92] Without consumer or industry input, the document lists the rules but lacks the economic realities of enforcement. Additionally, the Final Draft was only made available on the Internet for general public comment in April, 2000, roughly four years after drafting began.[93]

The Convention, most notably, does not provide for "effective" enforcement of the laws and penalties it creates. When compared to the TRIPS agreement, promulgated five years before it, the Convention seems to take a step back by not specifying the level of penalties and other remedies available. What remains is a virtually ineffective set of laws designed to apply to everyone but actually enforceable upon few. The Convention takes a harsher tone than TRIPS, and threatens more, but fails to ultimately and effectively punish copyright infringers. At the same time, the Convention overreaches, giving great power to law enforcement to reach into databases, retrieve private information, and prohibit content. Thus, there is less protection of copyright offered than United States citizens already receive via TRIPS, despite the illusion of harsher standards.

III. CONGRESS SHOULD REFUSE TO RATIFY THE CONVENTION TREATY IN ITS CURRENT FORM

On November 23, 2001, the Convention on Cybercrime was opened for signature in Budapest, Hungary.[94] The United States signed only after provisions banning racist and xenophobic content were dropped.[95] Concerns with the Convention, well

---

[91] *See* ACLU/EPIC Comments on CoE Cybercrime Convention, *supra* note 82 (commenting that while the Convention's proposed laws require transparency and harmonization, the manner in which they were promulgated was rather opaque, with extremely limited opportunity for public comment or criticism).

[92] *Id.*

[93] *See* The Council on Europe, *The Draft International Convention*, *available at* http://www.coe.int/T/E/Communication_and_Research/Press/Themes_Files/Cybercrime/e_projconve ntion.asp#TopOfPage (last visited March 22, 2002) (providing a timeline for drafts that stretches four years).

[94] *Id.* The following thirty countries have signed the Convention: Albania, Armenia, Austria, Belgium, Bulgaria, Croatia, Cyprus, Estonia, Finland, France, Germany, Greece, Hungary, Iceland, Ireland, Italy, Malta, Moldova, the Netherlands, Norway, Poland, Portugal, Romania, Spain, Sweden, Switzerland, the "Former Yugoslav Republic of Macedonia", Ukraine, the United Kingdom, Canada, Japan, South Africa, and the United States. *Id.*

[95] Paul Meller, *Hate Crime Footnote Added to Council of Europe Cybercrime Treaty*, InfoWorld Daily News, November 9, 2001. Such provisions would clash with the First Amendment freedom of speech guarantees in the U.S. Constitution. *Id.* However, a "footnote" or "protocol" has been added to the Convention, allowing countries who agree to it to sign on and those who don't to refuse, while still abiding by the main text of the Convention. *Id.* Those who refuse to sign onto the protocol, however, are still expected to enforce the racist-content bans when such content originates in their country and is aimed at a country that makes them illegal. *Id. See also* Council of Europe, *Elaboration of an Additional Protocol to the Convention on Cybercrime, Dealing with the Criminalization of Acts of Racist or Xenophobic Nature Committed through Computer Networks at* http://www.legal.coe.int/economiccrime/cybercrime/AP_Protocol(2002)5E.pdf (last visited Mar. 1, 2002). CoE suggests that many countries are in strong favor of criminalizing racist and xenophobic

[1:364 2002]   John Marshall Review of Intellectual Property Law   378

voiced in the months prior to the signing, remain high as the Convention merely needs ratification before becoming substantive United States law.[96]

Why is the Convention so threatening to the United States' interests? Primarily, the Convention establishes criminal penalties for copyright infringement—actions not traditionally considered to be deserving of criminal punishment. Dmitri Skylarov was arrested under the Digital Millennium Copyright Act, but Adobe quickly dropped its support of the prosecution. Why? Adobe received bad publicity for punishing the "poor foreigner" who was only doing something in America that was perfectly legal in his own country.[97] The United States is not ready to criminalize people like Skylarov. What he did was legal in his own country, and while copyright infringement is a serious offense and can cost copyright holders millions of dollars, few United States citizens accept it as criminal on the same level as fraud or embezzlement. College students everywhere downloaded songs off of Napster.[98] Should the United States make an example out of these kids? While staunch defenders of copyright protection shout "yes," the economics of enforcement may weigh against such prosecutions.

The CoE seems to want to "get things done" without answering the most important question: How will it all work? The copyright laws offered by the Convention seek to bind all signatory countries to vague enforcement protocols. Copyright laws are already in effect in the United States—through our own statutes, TRIPS, WIPO, and other international agreements.[99]

---

content. *Id.* The protocol, then, is intended to be an extension of the Convention's scope of substantive, procedural, and enforcement rules in order to additionally prohibit "such behaviour." *Id.* "Racist or xenophobic material" is defined by CoE as "any written material, any image or any other representation of thoughts or theories, which advocates, promotes, incites (or is likely to incite) acts of violence, hatred, or discrimination against any individual or group of individuals, based on race, colour, (religion, descent, nationality), or national or ethnic origin." *Id.* Expression of the intent to be bound by the protocol is evidenced by either signature without reservation as to acceptance or by signature subject to acceptance and followed by acceptance. *Id.* However, any country has the option to reject their acceptance of the protocol by notifying the CoE Secretary General. *Id.; see also* Edouard Launet, *Council of Europe Secretary General: The aim is to harmonise criminal law* LIBERATION March 9, 2002 *at* http://www.coe.int/T/E/ Communication_and_Research/Press/Themes_Files/Cybercrime/e_InterviewSGLiberation.asp#TopO fPage (last visited Mar. 12, 2002) (interviewing the Secretary General of the CoE). The CoE Secretary General noted that an additional protocol that would criminalize the dissemination of terrorist messages may be drawn, and that CoE was in the process of assembling a committee of terrorism experts to gain their opinion on such a protocol. *Id.*

[96] *See* European Forum on Harmful and Illegal Cyber Content, *available at* http://press.coe.int/cp/2001/884a(2001).htm (last visited Mar. 1, 2002). In a move contradictory to United States free speech policies and indicative of CoE's enforcement priorities, CoE announced on November 28, 2001 that they had organized a European forum on harmful and illegal cyber content. *Id.* CoE intended to bring in experts in content-regulation fields to establish procedures for determining what would be allowed legally on the Internet. *Id.* The focus of the forum dealt with combining the efforts of the public and private sectors to regulate "offensive" content such as child pornography, racist statements, and xenophobic sites. *Id.*

[97] *See* McMahon, *supra* note 16. Skylarov presented detailed anti-encryption instructions to hundreds of people, and his company dealt with the United States government on a regular basis. *Id.* Hence, it is difficult to seriously view him as innocent and completely oblivious to U.S. law. *Id.* In fact, several Russian programmers admitted that Skylarov bragged about breaking the law, and that he and Elcomsoft "were trying to push the limit." *Id.*

[98] *See* A & M Records v. Napster, 239 F.3d 1004 (9th Cir. 2001).

[99] *See* TRIPS, *supra* note 65.

The United States should first take a hard look at its goals to determine the best way to accomplish them. Initially, Congress should determine whether the laws in place are sufficient and consist of an effective way to protect intellectual property holders. The real purpose of copyright laws is to encourage creativity and thus stimulate the economy with new products, not to overly punish those who violate the law by criminalizing violations at any cost. The drafters of the Convention, being mainly law-enforcement officials, lost sight of this goal despite their good intentions. It is difficult to see how imposing a prison sentence on a college student sharing music files with another student in Great Britain could be justified or viewed as reasonable. If Skylarov's arrest taught the United States anything, it may be that Americans do not necessarily want copyright infringement to be a criminal offense on the same level as embezzlement or assault.

The United States should look to other platforms for addressing copyright law harmonization outside of its existing laws and the new Convention. One such platform may be an economic trade agreement. The United States-Jordan Free Trade Agreement[100] is one of the first bilateral trade agreements to address intellectual property rights protection.[101] The initial question may be: Is a trade agreement a proper forum for the establishment of copyright laws? The answer is a resounding yes. The difference between the Jordan Free Trade Agreement and the Cybercrime Convention, insofar as copyright provisions are concerned, is the context in which they are presented.[102] The Convention, created mainly by the United States Department of Justice and other law enforcement officials, presents its two paragraphs of copyright infringement policies in the context of a harmonization treaty that covers the infinitely broad topic of "cybercrime." But copyright infringement, standing alone, is difficult to equate with stealing or arson as a "criminal" act for a majority of people unless it is placed in a more appropriate context where those people will be able to understand what makes criminal copyright infringement laws publicly justifiable. The Jordan Free Trade Agreement, in contrast to this, presents the issue in context of economic relations, as copyright protection ultimately affects consumers and valuable intellectual property rights. This premise should be presented in a context, such as that of an economic agreement that provides clear justification of the criminal consequences. Presenting criminal punishments for copyright infringement to the public in the context of preventing economic harm would likely lead to their acceptance more easily than doing so without a context or in a broad, all-encompassing one.

IV. CONCLUSION

Had the drafters of the Convention considered not only what the law and punishment would be, but also how to make the entire process effective at deterring copyright infringement, their rules would appear as more than scare tactics. Without

---

[100] U.S.-Jordan Free Trade Agreement, Oct. 24, 2000, *at* http://www.ustr.gov/regions/eu-med/middleeast/ textagr.pdf (last visited Nov. 4, 2001).

[101] *See id.* The Free Trade Agreement was scheduled to enter into force on December 17, 2001. *Id.* The most well-known trade agreement incorporating intellectual property rights protection is the aforementioned WTO Agreement. *See* TRIPS, *supra* note 65.

[102] *See* U.S.-Jordan Free Trade Agreement, *supra* note 100.

economic and practical considerations, the Convention stands as an ineffective tool with no force. One example of a potentially proper venue would be a trade agreement. With incorporation of substantive copyright provisions in its text, a trade agreement is a practical forum through which laws may be created and effectively enforced in the marketplace, the niche where copyright fits. Jordan adopted and ratified the WIPO Copyright Treaties, which protects copyrighted works in a digital network environment. In the "Enforcement of Intellectual Property Rights" section, the Jordan Free Trade Agreement sets out distinct and explicit protocols for enforcement, including fines sufficiently high to deter "with a policy of removing the monetary incentive to the infringer," seizure of suspected copyright goods, payment of compensatory damages to the right-holder and repayment of profits made by infringer to the right-holder.[103]

Another way to tackle the issue in a broader form may be to devote an entire international treaty to the subject of digital copyright infringement, so that the issue is not, as it is in the Convention, a smaller part of a larger ideal. This would put the proper perspective on the substantive and procedural laws and would lead to more focused enforcement efforts. First, the treaty would identify the interests and rights of individual and corporate copyright holders, specifically those of Internet users and website authors. Then, the treaty would establish substantive and procedural norms to which all signing countries could conform. Finally, such a treaty would reflect an international policy consensus on enforcement procedures, with carefully delineated guidelines as to what conduct is deserving of criminal punishment. Also included should be rules concerning how such punishments would be executed when one country's established laws differ from another, or in situations where one country has copyright laws and another does not.

Proponents of the Convention assert that it, and specifically the copyright provisions, are a brazen step forward in computer-user and network security, because harmonization is essential in a global and digital environment.[104] Without this harmonization treaty, they argue, American substantive and procedural law may clash with the laws of other countries, punishing those who would go free in their homeland and freeing those who would be punished.[105]

---

[103] *Id.*

[104] *See* Cyber-crime: The Law Moves In, *available at* http://www.coe.int/T/E/ Communication_and_Research/Press/Themes_Files/Cybercrime/e_intro.asp#TopOfPage (last visited Jan. 10, 2002). CoE sought to "bring legal and ethical standards into an area where—for good or ill, and in liberty's name—only the laws of the market have applied so far." *Id.* Additionally, the U.S. Department of Justice comments that a multilateral treaty such as the Convention, that erases jurisdictional obstacles that hamper international investigations and prosecutions of cybercrimes, is particularly desirable because of the United States' reliance on the Internet as a communication, business, and educational tool. *See* Dept. of Justice—FAQ's, *supra* note 18.

[105] One limited example of how clashing laws affect judgments in internet-crime cases may be found in the recent discussion of *Yahoo!, Inc. v. La Ligue Contre Le Racisme et L'Antisemitisme*, 169 F. Supp. 2d 1181 (N.D. Cal 2001). In *Yahoo!*, a French Court found the Yahoo! Internet Company criminally liable for allowing nearly 1,000 Nazi and Third Reich objects to be sold on the Yahoo.com auction site, which is also linked to on the Yahoo.fr (France) site. *Id.* at 1184. Yahoo!, which is based in the United States, sought a declaratory judgment to make the French court's ruling unenforceable under U.S. law, arguing that banning such anti-Semitic materials would infringe impermissibly upon its First Amendment free speech rights. *Id.* at 1186. Concerned with the potential of "chilling protected speech that occurs simultaneously within our borders," Judge Jeremy Fogel opined:

Some Americans opposed to the Convention retort that the laws that the United States has enacted are sufficient, and that "new" laws (i.e., the Convention) are unnecessary.[106] This point of view is naïve, however, since it discounts the possibility that as the digital environment expands, American-owned businesses will increasingly be put at risk by infringers. This argument also does not take into account the variety of substantive and procedural laws that exist throughout the world, and it does not touch the question of whose system of laws should preside in the cyberworld. While such conflicts have already appeared in the Internet speech and encryption software arenas, one may anticipate that the same conflict will arise in all areas subject to cybercrime—including digital copyright infringement.

This Comment does not suggest that the Convention's goals of harmonization are wrong, or that its aims are off the mark. There must be harmonization and cooperation between nations in preventing and investigating digital copyright infringements that span borders in seconds. But, the United States cannot afford to sacrifice the cornerstones of its democracy in order to make music-loving college kids criminals.

In drafting a treaty that fails by both overreaching and shrinking from its goals, CoE attacks a very real problem by proposing an ineffective and uncertain solution. CoE should have treated the criminal copyright provisions of Article 10 with a determined aim at a deterrent effect.[107] The United States Congress should reject the Convention because of its faulty Article 10, as well as the entire document. Instead, legislation should be drafted that will specifically address harmonization of copyright infringement laws in a significantly broader form, such as within a trade agreement or by encompassing its own treaty. We cannot criminalize all copyright

---

> Absent a body of law that establishes international standards with respect to speech on the internet and an appropriate treaty or legislation addressing enforcement of such standards to speech originating within the United States, the principle of comity is outweighed by the Court's obligation to uphold the First Amendment.

Id. at 1193.

[106] At a Congressional hearing, Harris Miller, President of the Information Technology Association of America, testified:

> We don't believe the U.S. laws by and large need to be changed. There are a lot of other countries around the world where there are huge holes in the ability of those countries to prosecute cyber-criminals. So most of the work to be done is not necessarily in the U.S. code or in state laws. Most of the work that is to be done is around the world.

Security Risks in Electronic Commerce: Hearing Before the Senate Commerce, Science, Technology and Space Subcommittee, 108th Cong. (2001) [hereinafter Senate Hearing].

> Bruce Schneier, Chief Technical Officer of Counterpane Internet Society, testified:
> We need old laws applied cleanly to the new environment, because the crimes are the same, the people are the same, the environment is the same. The techniques are different, but you don't want the same crime to be suddenly much worse or much better if a computer is used. Fraud is fraud, theft is theft. And just because the tool is different, doesn't mean the ramifications should change.

Id.

[107] *See* Janet Reno, *Statement by the Attorney General, Symposium of the Americas: Protecting Intellectual Property in the Digital Age* (Sept. 12, 2000), *available at* http://www.cybercrime.gov/ipsymposium.htm (last visited Jan. 10, 2001) (advocating the Justice Department's strong commitment to prosecuting cases and making sure that "serious IP criminals go to jail for significant prison terms" and that "[t]here is no safe place to hide.").

infringement, but we need to provide routine, international deterrence.[108] There is no doubt that there exists a need to prevent copyright infringement, but it must be done the right way.

---

[108] *See* Senate Hearing, *supra* note 106 (quoting Vinton Cerf, Senior Vice-President for Internet Architecture and Technology, WorldCom).

> For this to work on a global scale, there will have to be some degree of collaboration and work to make the laws of the national boundaries somehow be at least compatible, so that law enforcement can work across international boundaries. This is not new. It's just perhaps made more visible, more highlighted by the global nature of the Internet.

Id.

[9]

COMBATING CHILD PORNOGRAPHY ON THE INTERNET: THE COUNCIL OF EUROPE'S CONVENTION ON CYBERCRIME

Dina I. Oddis

"Do ye hear the children weeping . . .
in the playtime of the others,
in the country of the free?"[1]

I. INTRODUCTION

Images flicker across the computer screen: a four-year-old girl in pigtails, pain and fear etched into her young face.[2] A man removing the diaper from a three-month-old girl, inserting his finger into her vagina and then raping her.[3] A young boy posing naked before the camera with his wrists and ankles bound in chains.[4] A man sodomizing a seven-year-old boy, while in the background the screams of a young girl being abused are clearly audible.

These images are not cartoons.[5] They are not cute.[6] They are not "soft-core pictures of precociously seductive fifteen-year-olds."[7] They *are* stomach churning.[8] They turn children into sexual objects, forever destroying their childhood.[9] They fan the appetites of pedophiles globally who clamor

---

1. ELIZABETH BARRETT BROWNING, *The Cry of the Children, in* POETIC WORKS OF ELIZABETH BARRETT BROWNING 156 (1974).
2. *See* Lenny Savino, *Child Porn Dragnet: 30,000 Web Customers are Investigators' Next Target with Assist from Local Police, Judges*, PITTSBURGH POST GAZETTE, Aug. 15, 2001, at A-8, *available at* LEXIS, News Group File, Most Recent Two Years.
3. *The Child Protection Society, at* http://geocities.com/CapitolHill/5021 (last visited Oct. 22, 2001).
4. J.F.O. McAllister, *Depravity Online*, TIME (International Edition), Feb. 26, 2001, at 27, *available at* LEXIS, Individual Publications File.
5. *See The Darker Side of Cuteness*, THE ECONOMIST, May 8, 1999 (U.S. Ed.), *available at* LEXIS, News Library, Individual Publication File. In Japan, where approximately four-fifths of the world's child pornographic literature is produced, pornographic comic books depicting school girls dressed in their uniforms and in obscene sexual poses are extraordinarily popular with adults, selling in the millions [hereinafter THE ECONOMIST].
6. *Id.* "Kawaii desu ne" ("Oh, how cute") has guided the format and "illustrations" in adult Japanese pornographic comic books and has even become the prototypical female model for the Japanese woman, who is often expected to speak in a "little girl" voice and comport herself in a childlike manner.
7. PHILIP JENKINS, BEYOND TOLERANCE: CHILD PORNOGRAPHY ON THE INTERNET 9 (2001) [hereinafter JENKINS].
8. Ben Taylor, *Paedophile Ring Smashed*, PERTH SUNDAY TIMES, Jan. 14, 2001, *available at* LEXIS, News Group File, Most Recent Two Years.
9. *See Sexual Abuse of Children, Child Pornography and Paedophilia on the Internet:*

incessantly for new images.[10] Even worse, they can be "dangerously addictive," leading a person to discover his own pedophiliac tendencies and potentially act out those tendencies with live children.[11]

This is the world of child pornography, a world whose expansion has paralleled that of the Internet. As the number of Internet users has skyrocketed (to an estimated 304 million by March 2000, compared with fewer than 90,000 in 1993), so has the popularity of child pornography sites.[12] Non-profit watch groups around the world are reporting mammoth increases in the number of "hits" to such sites.[13] In the United States, U.S. News & World Report estimates that at least 40,000 "sex-oriented" sites exist, with possibly thousands more.[14] In the year 2000, the FBI investigated 2,856 cases of online child pornography and child sex exploitation.[15] In 1996, it investigated only 113.[16] Since the launch of its CyberTipline in March 1998, the National Center for Missing and Exploited Children has analyzed approximately 37,000 reports about child sex exploitation.[17]

International organizations have struggled to stem this horrifying plague. In a 1999 conference in Paris on Internet pedophilia and child pornography, UNESCO (the United Nations' organization dedicated to the promotion of education, science, and culture and which has become an acknowledged leader in championing the protection of children and children's rights) called for the formulation of a joint plan providing for "practical and justifiable solutions" within well-defined social, economic, and political parameters.[18] On May 25, 2000, the United Nations itself promulgated the Optional Protocol to the Convention on the Rights of the Child on the Sale of Children, Child Prostitution, and Child Pornography.[19] The European Union has adopted several Council Decisions regarding the regulation and prevention of electronic child pornography and should, by

---

An International Challenge, Expert Meeting, UNESCO, Paris, Jan. 18-19, 1999, *available at* http://www.unesco.org/webworld/child_screen/conf_index.html [hereinafter UNESCO].

10. *Id.*

11. JENKINS, *supra* note 7, at 23.

12. STATE OF THE INTERNET 2000, U.S. Internet Council and ITTA Inc., *available at* http://www.usci.org/papers/stateoftheinternet2000/intro.html.

13. *See* Internet Watch Foundation, *available at* http://www.iwf.org.uk.

14. Brendan I. Koerner, *A Lust for Profits,* U.S. NEWS & WORLD REPORT, Mar. 27, 2000, at 36.

15. Rod Nordland & Jeffrey Bartholet, *The Web's Dark Secret,* NEWSWEEK, Mar. 19, 2001, at 44.

16. *Online Child Pornography,* Federal Bureau of Investigation, *at* http://www.fbi.gov.hq/cid/cac/ubbicebt.htm.

17. Nordland & Bartholet, *supra* note 15.

18. UNESCO, *supra* note 9.

19. The Protocol, which is currently open for ratification, has been signed by seventy-three States, including three Contracting Parties, will not enter into force until three months after the tenth instrument of ratification or accession has been deposited with the Secretary-General of the United Nations. *See* http://untreaty.un.org/English/TreatyEvent 2001.

year-end 2001 or early 2002, issue a proposal for a Framework Decision through its Commission which will include specific provisions for approximating laws and sanctions on computer-related crime and child pornography throughout its Member states.[20] Additionally, in June 2001, the Council of Europe publicized its Draft Convention on Cybercrime, which was formally adopted by the Committee of Ministers on September 19, 2001.[21] That document is the first international, legally binding instrument "designed to protect network and user security."[22] More important, an entire section of the Convention (Title 3, Article 9) is devoted to the criminalization and definition of child pornography distributed through a computer system.[23]

The Council of Europe's Convention on Cybercrime has been the subject of much protest from the United States, Japan, Australia, and South Africa, as well as twenty-two associations in nine European countries (Austria, France, Germany, Italy, the Netherlands, Spain, Ukraine, and the United Kingdom).[24] These protests center around concerns that the Convention does not go far enough in protecting privacy and freedom of speech,[25] despite the Council's firm commitment to protecting those and other fundamental human rights, as espoused in its European Convention for the Protection of Human Rights and Fundamental Freedoms.[26] Specifically, the protesting associations of the Global Internet Liberty

---

20. *See* Communication from the Comm'n to the Council, the European Parliament, the Econ. and Soc. Comm. & the Comm. of the Regions, COM(00)890 final, *available at* http://europea.eu.int/ISPO/eif/InternetPoliciesSite/Crime/CrimeCommEn.html (last visited Jan. 18, 2003). On October 7, 2002, the Presidency of the European Union communicated a Note to the Council of the European Union regarding the "Draft Council Framework Decision on combating the sexual exploitation of children and child pornography," Doc. 12418/02 DROIPEN 68 MIGR 92, after having resolved initial concerns of the European Parliament regarding appropriate definitions for child pornography in cyberspace. The current Draft, if recommended by the Parliament and then adopted by the Council, would criminalize across the European Union: (a) the production of child pornography; (b) the distribution, dissemination or transmission of child pornography; (c) the supplying or making available child pornography; and (d) the acquisition of possession of child pornography, whether undertaken by means of a computer system or not. The threshold age is set at 18 years. The Draft provides for terms of imprisonment from one to three years.

21. *See The Convention on Cybercrime*, Council of Europe Press Service, http://press.coe.int/pres.asp? (Nov. 23, 2001).

22. *Id.*

23. *Id.*

24. *Id.*

25. *See* Letter, Comments of the American Civil Liberties Union, the Electronic Privacy Information Center and Privacy International on Draft 27 of the Proposed COE Convention on Cybercrime, Global Internet Liberty Campaign (GILC), *available at* http://www.gilc.org/privacy/coe-letter-0601.html (June 7, 2001).

26. The Council approved the European Convention in 1950. That Convention, which entered into force in 1953, protected fundamental human rights to "life, liberty, and security of the person," as well as privacy and freedom of expression. *See* NEWMAN & WEISSBRODT, INTERNATIONAL HUMAN RIGHTS 468 (1996).

480   TEMPLE INT'L & COMP. L.J.   [Vol. 16.2

Campaign (GILC) point to the enforcement remedies proposed: continued surveillance and interception of electronic communications, as well as the mandated disclosure of individual and corporate encryption keys.[27]

Never before has a balancing of interests been so clearly delineated: the rights of privacy and freedom of expression on one hand, and the global protection of children and their rights on the other. This Comment looks at the Council's efforts to regulate child pornography on the Internet through the Convention. Part II focuses on the technological evolution of the Internet, Usenet, and newsgroups, which seem so peculiarly and devastatingly favored as the "medium of choice" of child pornographers. Part III looks at how the Internet has fostered the growth of virtually untraceable child pornography "clubs." After a brief introduction to the history of the Council of Europe, Part IV traces the formulation of the European Court of Human Rights' jurisprudence regarding the protection of privacy and freedom of expression as applied to sexually explicit materials and behavior. It also looks at the Court's development of the "margin of appreciation" approach toward States' rights to freely develop legislation appropriate to achieving the Council's goals. Part V examines the Council's Draft Convention on Cybercrime, specifically Title 3, Article 9 on child pornography, in light of those doctrines.

This paper concludes that the Council of Europe's Draft Convention on Cybercrime establishes much-needed universal standards for regulating electronic child pornography. The containment remedies proposed, while seemingly draconian and worthy of police states rather than freedom-loving democracies, are appropriately tuned to deal with the elusive nature of today's virtual "loli-lover" community, with "picture" sites that disappear after only a few hours into cyberspace without a trace. More important, because the Convention on Cybercrime has been fashioned within the context and the legal arena of the Council of Europe's Convention for the Protection of Human Rights and Fundamental Freedoms, the Convention on Cybercrime successfully balances the rights of privacy and freedom of expression of the individual, on the one hand, with the preservation of the structural integrity of a democratic society and of the public health and morals of its citizens.

II. THE INTERNET, USENET, AND NEWSGROUPS

A. The Internet: Its Origins and Development

The development of the Internet started as a response to the USSR's early success with Sputnik in 1957.[28] In the face of "rising American Cold

---

27. *Id.*

28. Richard T. Griffiths, *History of the Internet, Internet for Historians (and Just About Everyone Else),* (Leiden University) [hereinafter Griffiths], *at*

War paranoia about military inferiority,"[29] the U.S. Defense Department created the Advanced Research Projects Agency (ARPA) to conduct long-term research and development in various fields. ARPA employed several hundred top scientists in a think-tank environment that focused on space, ballistic missiles, and nuclear test monitoring, maintaining all the while its overriding interest in computer technology.[30] ARPA also had a keen interest in computer communications that would provide direct links between its home base and its numerous sub-contractors, including various university research facilities such as Stanford Research Institute, University of California at Santa Barbara, University of California in Los Angeles, and the University of Utah.[31]

In 1962, two major events occurred. In August, John C.R. Licklider of the Massachusetts Institute of Technology published a series of memoranda on what he termed the "Galactic Network," a worldwide system of interconnected computers that would enable users to access data and programs from any site.[32] In October, ARPA organized a computer research program – the Information Processing Techniques Office (IPTO) – and appointed Licklider to head that effort.[33] From October 1962 through July 1963 when he left IPTO, Licklider's main mission was not to design military tools, but rather to implement his own personal vision of human-computer interaction.[34]

That type of interaction required three fundamental technologies: a data assembly technology that would facilitate message transmission, a physical network that would connect computers, and a communication link, or common language, that would be recognized by all connected computers and enable the exchange of data and information. The first technology developed was "packet switching," a method of breaking down one message into standard-sized "packets" that could travel independently from one another along a communication channel.[35] Each packet was unique, with locating information about its origin and destination, as well as coordinates denoting its place in the original message so that the receiving computer could reassemble the message appropriately once all the pieces were received.[36]

http://www.let.leidenuniv.nl/history/ivh/frame-theorie.html (last updated Oct. 5, 2001.)

29. Jesper Vissing Laursen, *The Internet: Past, Present and Future – Internet & WWW History* [hereinafter Laursen], *at* http://www.vissing.dk/inthist.html (last visited Jan. 18, 2003)..

30. Griffiths, *supra* note 28.

31. *Id.*

32. Barry M. Leiner et al., *A Brief History of the Internet*, Internet Society [hereinafter *Leiner et al.*], *at* http://www.isoc.org/internet/history/brief.shtml (last visited Jan. 18, 2003)..

33. Griffiths, *supra* note 28.

34. Laursen, *supra* note 29.

35. *See* Leiner et al., *supra* note 32.

36. Dave Marsh, *History of the Internet* [hereinafter Marsh], *at* http://www.internetvalley.com/archives/mirrors/davemarsh-timeline-1.htm (last visited Jan. 18, 2003).

This technology facilitated long-distance transmission, made it more difficult to eavesdrop on messages, and enabled packets to follow more than one route to the assigned destination.[37] These advantages were important from a military point of view because the network, as a whole, would continue to function even if a portion were destroyed in a nuclear attack.[38] (Keep in mind that ARPA's first priority, as a unit within the Defense Department, was developing advanced computer technology that would assure the superiority of the United States during the Cold War era.)

The second technology was a network that would link all the computers together and form the conduit over which messages, data, and information would be sent.[39] In 1969, special network computers, or Interface Message Processors, were developed and sited at each of the research facilities that IPTO had enlisted to help develop this technology.[40] This step formed an important link to the academic world, which would soon be the prime force in the development of Usenet and newsgroups.[41]

The third technology, common computer communication protocols developed by a special task force, was put in place toward the end of 1969.[42] Those protocols handled communication between the computers on the network and also between the computers and the network itself, tracking log-ins and file transfers.[43] The development of a program to send messages across a distributed network soon followed, culminating in the invention of e-mail in 1971.[44]

Parallel with the ever-expanding ARPANET (the Internet's precursor), other groups developed purpose-built networks for their own researchers and scholars.[45] The U.S. Department of Energy established MFENet for its research department in magnetic fusion energy; NASA developed SPAN; and computer scientists developed CSNET under the aegis of the U.S. National Science Foundation (NSF).[46] While the NSF was later to play a particularly important role in developing offshoot networks in the academic community throughout the United States,[47] at this point its original network was like that of other groups – restricted for its own use and incompatible on a protocol basis with other networks, i.e., computers on CSNET could communicate only with other computers on that network.[48] There was no

---

37. *See id.*

38. *See The Internet, at* http://whatis.techtarget.com/sDefinition/0,,sid26_gci212370,00 .html (last visited Jan. 18, 2003).

39. Laursen, *supra* note 29.

40. *Id.*

41. Griffiths, *supra* note 28.

42. Laursen, *supra* note 29.

43. *Id.*

44. Marsh, *supra* note 36.

45. Leiner et al., *supra* note 32.

46. *Id.*

47. Laursen, *supra* note 29.

48. Leiner et al., *supra* note 32.

linked communication possible between a SPAN-linked computer and one on MFENet or between networks themselves.

One major event that changed this was the Defense Department's formal adoption of Transmission Control Protocol/Internet Protocol (TCP/IP) in 1980 as the controlling protocol on the fast-developing Internet (still officially dubbed ARPANET).[49] TCP/IP, had an important advantage over its predecessor Network Control Protocol (NCP). While NCP was limited to governing communication along a single network, with no possibility of overseeing and regulating communication with networks linked to the original one (in this case, ARPANET), TCP/IP could efficiently satisfy the requirements of an "open-architecture network environment," where individual networks with different technological designs could be developed for specific purposes and user groups, but could still communicate with each other for the exchange of data, information, and news.[50]

B. The Usenet: Development

The facilitating feature of TCP/IP became critical to the evolution of Usenet, the civilian counterpart to ARPANET created in 1979.[51] Developed by graduate students Tom Truscott of Duke University and Jim Ellis of the University of North Carolina,[52] Usenet originally used the Unix-to-Unix Protocol (UUCP) developed at AT&T's Bell Laboratories in 1969 as its underlying communication program.[53] This fostered a ready-made network for Usenet throughout university circles, as UNIX was the main operating system employed by universities and AT&T distributed UUCP free to all UNIX computer users.[54] Through this medium, Truscott and Ellis organized a hierarchy of discussion groups to accommodate a growing number of interests among university graduate students across the nation,[55] with administrators informally moderating traffic at major locations and developing standard operating procedures for adding newsgroups and distributing messages.[56] However, by the summer of 1986, the main file used to track the newsgroups had become too cumbersome to operate efficiently.[57] This led to a restructuring of Usenet (called "The Great

---

49. Laursen, *supra* note 29.

50. Leiner et al., *supra* note 32.

51. Laursen, *supra* note 29.

52. *Id.*

53. Marsh, *supra* note 36. Today, Usenet uses the Network News Transfer Protocol. *See SearchNetworking.com Definitions: Networking, at* http://searchnetworking.techtarget. com/sDefinition/0,,sid7_gci214588,00.html (last visited Jan. 18, 2003).

54. Griffiths, *supra* note 28.

55. Laursen, *supra* note 29.

56. *See The Usenet: Modern Hierarchies, at* http://www.livinginternet.com/ u/ui_modern.htm (last visited Jan. 18, 2003).

57. *Id.*

484   TEMPLE INT'L & COMP. L.J.   [Vol. 16.2

Renaming") into the eight major newsgroup hierarchies in use today,[58] while the original administrators became known as the "Backbone Cabal."[59]

The new Usenet and its hierarchies required a formalized application process to add a new group. This process included formulating a charter to explain the group's purpose and discussion topic, opening a thirty-day discussion period and taking a general vote.[60] If the voting favored a new group's creation by a two-thirds majority, a general message was posted on "news.announce.newgroups" with pertinent information.[61] Not everyone felt this process was amenable to true free speech, and the "alt." hierarchy was developed as an "alternative" communication channel.[62]

Unlike the Usenet hierarchy newsgroup, alt. groups could be created by anyone without publicizing the group's purpose or topic and without rules to limit its creation.[63] Only the site's administrator would decide whether or not to carry the new group. In fact, that decision process proved a mere formality. "[F]or simplicity, many sites automatically honor[ed] all requests to create a new group and (by default) ignore[d] all requests to remove groups."[64] Another feature of alt. newsgroups became readily apparent: these groups could not be dismantled, removed, extinguished, or even renamed.[65] Alt. newsgroups were immortal, fading away only if "people stop[ped] reading [them]."[66] These characteristics made alt. newsgroups attractive to pedophiles seeking "like-minded" people with whom to communicate and exchange images of pre-teen, early teen, toddler, or even infant children engaged in explicit sexual conduct.[67]

C. Newsgroups and Bulletin Boards: A New Home for Child Pornography

Even before the development of alt. newsgroups, pedophiles and child pornography enthusiasts had computerized their activities. By the mid-1980s in the United States, virtually all access to this type of material had been

---

58. *See Usenet, at* http://livinginternet.com/u/ui.htm. These eight subdivisions include comp (computer subjects), humanities (humanities subjects, added in 1996), misc (miscellaneous groups), news (news topics) rec (recreational subjects), sci (science topics), soc (sociological subjects) and talk (controversial topics).

59. *Id.*

60. *See The Usenet: Creating Usenet & Newgroups, at* http://livinginternet.com/ (last visited Jan. 18, 2003).

61. *Id.*

62. *See The Usenet: The Alt Hierarchy, at* http://www.livinginternet.com/u/ui_alt.htm (last visited Jan. 18, 2003).

63. *Id.*

64. David Barr, *So You Want to Create an Alt Newsgroup,* Internet FAQ Archives, *at* http://www.faqs.org/faqs/alt-creation-guide/ (last visited Jan. 18, 2003).

65. *Id.; See also The Usenet: The Alt Hierarchy;* Laursen, *supra* note 29.

66. *Id.*

67. JENKINS, *supra* note 7 *passim.*

eliminated.[68] But computers offered a new communication medium by then. Modem connections made the first dial-up bulletin board services, such as Compuserve, technologically possible, although still relatively costly.[69] "Real-time" chat became a reality, and the early 1980s witnessed the establishment of the first bulletin boards devoted to child pornography.[70] At the same time, Usenet and UUCP were instrumental in fostering networking on an international scale, with Usenet connections established to Europe and Australia.[71] With the TCP/IP protocol already adopted as the underlying communication program of ARPANET, the development of the Network News Transfer Protocol (NNTP) in 1987 enabled Usenet to be carried on the TCP/IP networks.[72] By that time, the "Great Renaming" had occurred and alt. newsgroups were born.[73]

Within that new hierarchy, pedophiles using pseudonyms such as "Godfather Corleone," "Curious George," "Darkstar," and "Lolig@gger" created chat rooms where they could exchange updated information, the newest series of pictures available,[74] the latest law enforcement agency attempts to track "like-minded people," and where to find actual pictures.[75] The alt. newsgroups devoted to such discussions were, and still are, difficult to find because of their intentionally complicated names and because they are so numerous, with an estimated 40,000 sites devoted to this type of material.[76]

It is even more difficult to track those sites from which actual pictures can be downloaded into personal libraries. Because such files are large and contain literally thousands of images, they are usually found under one main alt. hierarchy known as "alt. binaries," with extensions added to this generic name to indicate that pictures are available for downloading.[77] Child pornography sites such as "alt.binaries.pictures.erotica.pre-teen" and "alt.binaries.pictures.erotica.ll-series" contained hundreds of thousands of images when still in use.[78] Once law enforcement agents discovered those sites, the original files were transferred to a new Uniform Resource Locator (URL) within hours.[79] Devotees relayed locator information regarding the

---

68. *Id.* at 41.

69. *Id.* at 41-42.

70. *Id.* at 47.

71. Laursen, *supra* note 29.

72. *Id.*

73. *See id.* at 9-10.

74. "Series" commonly refers to a group of pictures "starring" the same child or group of children engaged in explicit sexual conduct. Often these series are named for the principal "star," such as the "hel-lo" (Helen/Lolita) series, the Karen series, etc. *See* JENKINS, *supra* note 7 *passim*.

75. *Id.*

76. Nordland & Bartholet, *supra* note 15.

77. Barr, *supra* note 64.

78. JENKINS, *supra* note 7, at xi.

79. *Id.* at 68.

486   TEMPLE INT'L & COMP. L.J.   [Vol. 16.2

new sites on "pedo boards,"[80] being careful to camouflage the new URLs so that their own transmissions, even if monitored by some law enforcement agency (LEA, a popular "pedo board" acronym), could not be traced back to their own computers.[81]

III. THE INTERNATIONALIZATION OF CHILD PORNOGRAPHY

A. *International Child Pornography Clubs*

The global scale of child pornography clubs has become all too apparent over the past several years. On September 2, 1998, in a series of coordinated raids in the United States and thirteen other countries, law enforcement officials broke up an international child pornography club known as "Wonderland."[82] More than one million images of child pornography were seized in raids in Australia, Austria, Belgium, Britain, Finland, France, Germany, Italy, Norway, Portugal, and Sweden.[83] In the United Kingdom alone, over 750,000 images depicting children engaged in various sexual activities with adults as well as with other children were seized.[84] In the United States, over 500,000 images of similar nature were confiscated as evidence.[85] Officials believed that over 180 individuals spanning forty-seven countries were members of this "club."[86] New members were sponsored by long-standing participants and paid "dues" by uploading 10,000 "new" images to a club file before being given the password ("Wonderland" spelled with a zero instead of the letter "o") to pass the first level of security,[87] with another five to six levels to pass before finally gaining entrance to the club.[88] In addition, the club employed sophisticated encryption software developed by the KGB during the Cold War era.[89]

---

80. *Id.* at 68-69.

81. *Id.* at 69-70.

82. Michael Grunwald, *Global Internet Child Porn Ring Uncovered*, WASH. POST, Sept. 3, 1998, at A12, *available at* LEXIS News Group File, Beyond Two Years.

83. Tim Bryant, *St. Charles Man Admits His Role in Child Porn Ring*, ST. LOUIS POST-DISPATCH, Nov. 17, 1998, at B3, *available at* LEXIS News Group File, Beyond Two Years.

84. Nick Davies & Jeevan Vasagar, *Global Child Porn Ring Broken*, THE GUARDIAN (LONDON), Jan. 11, 2001 [hereinafter *Davies & Vasagar*], at 8, *available at* LEXIS News Group, Individual Publications Library file.

85. Elaine Shannon, *Main Street Monsters*, TIME, Sept. 14, 1998, at 59, *available at* LEXIS News Group, Individual Publications Library file.

86. *Id.*

87. Davies & Vasagar, *supra* note 84.

88. *See* Steve Gold, *Seven Jailed in World's Largest Internet Pedophile Ring*, NEWSBYTES, Feb. 14, 2001, *available at* LEXIS, News Group File, Most Recent Two Years. *See also* Maria Hawthorne, *Wonderland Paedophile Cases Wind Up*, AAP NEWSFEED, Feb. 14, 2001, *available at* LEXIS, News Group File, Most Recent Two Years.

89. *FY2000 Treasury Appropriations: Hearing with the Customs Service Before the Subcomm. On Treasury, Gen. Govt. & Civil Service of the Senate Committee on*

A second Internet club was discovered during the "Wonderland" investigation. British authorities believed that the two U.S. founders of "Wonderland" formed "Our Place."[90] U.S. Customs officials learned from Shawn C. Moseman, a thirty-year-old former Coast Guardsman and "Wonderland" member arrested in September 1999, that "Our Place" counted between forty and fifty members.[91] Moseman, apparently determined to belong to "Our Place," was instrumental in voting in new members and establishing the club's rules.[92]

Authorities believe that a newer third club exists, with pornography material produced and circulated by Eric Franklin Rosser, a fifty-two-year-old keyboard musician who collaborated on a 1980 John Cougar Mellencamp album.[93] The club, named "Teenboys," is devoted to images of boys around twelve years of age and allegedly was formed by a South London caretaker.[94] Its supposed membership of 1,800 pedophiles far outstrips the "Wonderland" club, thought at the time to be the largest child pornography club in existence.[95]

Clubs of this nature are to be differentiated from child pornography "rings," which have a distinctly commercial cast. The "Blue Orchid," allegedly operated by Russians Sergey Garbko and Vsevolol Solntsev-Elbe out of Moscow, produced and distributed videos showing boys aged eight years and older being physically and sexually abused,[96] in addition to offering a child pornography series entitled "Russian Flowers."[97] Another commercial ring, managed by Russian and Indonesian webmasters, was run by a Fort Worth, Texas couple who functioned as "gatekeepers" for the site.[98] "Landslide Industries, Inc." counted 250,000 subscribers worldwide

---

Appropriations of the S. Appropriations Comm., 106th Cong. (1999) (statement of Commissioner Raymond W. Kelly, Commissioner, Customs Service), *available at* LEXIS, Federal Document Clearing House Congressional Testimony Apr. 15, 1999.

90. Sean O'Neill, *Net Child Porn Gang Facing Jail,* THE DAILY TELEGRAPH (AUSTRALIA), Feb. 13, 2001, at B7, *available at* LEXIS, News Group File, Most Recent Two Years.

91. *Chesapeake Man Pleads Guilty to Child Pornography Charges,* THE VIRGINIAN PILOT, Feb. 9, 2001, at B7, *available at* LEXIS, News Group File, Most Recent Two Years.

92. *Id. See also Child-Porn Defendant Gets 12-Year Term,* THE VIRGINIAN PILOT, May 19, 2001, at B7, *available at* LEXIS, News Group File, Most Recent Two Years.

93. Jason Burke, *Most Wanted Paedophile May Be in U.K.,* THE OBSERVER (U.K.), Jun. 17, 2001, at 11, *available at* LEXIS, News Group File, Most Recent Two Years.

94. *Id.*

95. Peter Rose, *1,800 Beasts in Child Porn Ring,* THE NEWS OF THE WORLD, June 10, 2001, *available at* LEXIS, News Group File, Most Recent Two Years.

96. Press Release, U.S. Customs Service, Russian Police Take Down Global Child Pornography Web Site (Mar. 26, 2001), *available at* http://www.customs/gov/hot-new/pressre1/2001. In a cooperative effort between the Moscow City Police, the Moscow U.S. Customs Attaché, and U.S. Customs officials in the United States, the first U.S. customers of "Blue Orchid" wares were indicted on March 23, 2001. More indictments are expected to follow. *Id.*

97. *Id.*

98. Naftali Bendavid, *Huge Child Porn Web Site Broken Up,* CHICAGO TRIBUNE,

488   TEMPLE INT'L & COMP. L.J.   [Vol. 16.2

(30,000 of them in the United States) who paid $29.95 a month for access to sites named "Child Rape," "Cyber Lolita," and "Children Forced to Porn."[99] Although damaging enough, these sites have a strictly commercial goal. Clubs such as "Wonderland" and "Our Place" are formed to perpetuate the virtual community of pedophiles and to satisfy their needs for new and more images of children engaged in sexual activity.[100] In so doing, they rob children of their childhood and of themselves.[101]

B. Creating a "Virtual Community"

International pornography clubs represent only a very small percentage of the activity that exists in the pedophiles' virtual world. Quantification is difficult because pedophiles believe that their behavior is completely normal and do not seek treatment voluntarily.[102] Cyberspace increases this sense of normalcy and legitimization because newsgroups and chat rooms have made it easier for "like-minded people" to find each other and develop a sense of community.[103] Alt. newsgroups are truly global in their reach: One message posted in one newsgroup on one Internet Service Provider (ISP) will be carried throughout the entire Internet by ISPs on their own servers located in dozens of countries.[104] Deleting the message from one ISP server does not remove it from any other server, or from the Internet.[105]

Images enjoy the same immortality. Once uploaded to an "alt.binaries" file, they endure for years, as demonstrated by the "hel-lo" images that first surfaced in the late 1980s and are considered by the most jaded pedophiles to be the best series of all.[106] Named after the child "star" portrayed, those images feature Helena (a seven- or eight-year-old British girl) in a series of sexual acts with Gavin (a boy of approximately the same age) and with a man, presumably Helena's father.[107] Older, more experienced pedophiles recommend this series to novices just starting to build their own libraries.[108]

Aug. 9, 2001, at 9, *available at* LEXIS, News Group File.

99. *Id. See also* Christopher Marquis, *U.S. Says It Broke Ring That Peddled Child Pornography,* N.Y. TIMES, Aug. 9, 2001, at A1, *available at* LEXIS, Individual Publications File; Eric Lichtblau. *Sting Nets 100 Arrests in Internet Child Porn,* L.A. TIMES, Aug. 9, 2001, at A1, *available at* LEXIS, News Group File.

100. JENKINS, *supra* note 7 *passim. See also* UNESCO, *supra* note 9.

101. *See* UNESCO, *supra* note 9.

102. *Id.*

103. JENKINS, *supra* note 7, at 185.

104. Yaman Akdeniz, *Child Pornography on the Internet,* 148 NEW L. J. 451 (1998), *available at* LEXIS, U.K. Law Journals File.

105. *Id.*

106. JENKINS, *supra* note 7, at 2. "Hel-lo" is the abbreviation for "Helen/Lolita," with "Lolita" signifying an underage girl, generally prepubescent (below the age of puberty, around thirteen years old). *See id.* at xii.

107. *Id.*

108. *Id.*

And, whether beginner or advanced, the pedophile considers that library his most cherished possession, meriting the most meticulous care, preservation, and security.[109]

IV. THE COUNCIL OF EUROPE

To address the pedophiles' pervasive use of electronic technology in expanding their virtual world, the Council of Europe has devoted an entire section of its recently promulgated Convention on Cybercrime to the criminalization of computer-generated child pornography. The Council's history as the first and foremost champion of human rights and fundamental freedoms in the European theatre uniquely qualify it as the leader in formulating the principles necessary for the detection, containment, and penalization of electronic pornographic images.

A. Brief Introduction

The Council of Europe was born amid the devastation and ruin which all but buried Europe after World War II. Winston Churchill's vision of a "United States of Europe," expressed in his speech in Zurich on September 19, 1946, indicated the road of the future.[110] From the various movements springing up all over the Continent, one organization – the International Committee of the Movements for European Unity – soon achieved a leadership position.[111] That organization assembled the Congress of Europe, which met in The Hague on May 7, 1948, and which was attended by over a thousand delegates from twenty countries.[112] Almost a year later to the day, on May 5, 1949, at St. James's Palace in London, that impetus bore fruit in the form of a treaty establishing the Council of Europe.[113] Ten European countries signed the treaty, known as the Statute of the Council of Europe: Belgium, France, Luxembourg, the Netherlands, the United Kingdom, Ireland, Italy, Denmark, Norway, and Sweden.[114] Those governments felt that the international protection of human rights should not be the province solely of the United Nations and its members,[115] but should form the backbone of a European international body dedicated to upholding

---

109. *See* UNESCO, *supra* note 9.

110. *A Short History of the Council of Europe*, Council of Europe [hereinafter *Short History*], http://www.coe.int/T/E/Communication_and_Research/Contacts_with_the_public/About_Council_of_Europe/A_Short_Story/ (last visited Oct. 7, 2002).

111. *Id.*

112. *Id.*

113. *Id.*

114. *Id.*

115. FRANK NEWMAN & DAVID WEISSBRODT, INTERNATIONAL HUMAN RIGHTS: LAW, POLICY, AND PROCESS 468 (2d ed. 1996).

490   TEMPLE INT'L & COMP. L.J.   [Vol. 16.2

fundamental principles of democracy and human rights.[116] The Council of Europe was made the guardian of those principles and rights, the recognition of which was to function simultaneously as the "entrance ticket" for a country's admission to the Council and also a permanent, enduring obligation on the part of its members.[117]

Headquartered in Strasbourg, France, the Council set to work immediately to formulate this new philosophy and gave tangible evidence of Europe's commitment to an integrated economic and social arena. The European Convention for the Protection of Human Rights and Fundamental Freedoms (the Convention) was signed in Rome on November 1950 and came into force September 3, 1953.[118] More important, the Convention was the first international instrument to enumerate human rights in treaty form,[119] creating a "collective guarantee of human rights"[120] which all Member States to the Council would uphold by binding themselves to respect the fundamental principles of democracy.[121] Within its territory, each signatory State would formulate the necessary rules to establish and protect the guaranteed rights and freedoms enumerated in the Council's Convention.[122]

B. The European Convention on Human Rights

The Convention was a response to events both current and past in Europe. On the one hand, the spread of communism into the central and eastern European states after World War II sparked a need to thwart communism.[123] On the other, the Convention was also a reaction to the egregious human rights violation that had occurred in Europe during World War II.[124]

The Convention is one of several international treaties that protects those rights first detailed in the *Universal Declaration of Human Rights 1948* of the United Nations.[125] While the Universal Declaration defines two broad

---

116. Peter Leuprecht, *Introduction to the Symposium: Innovations in the European System of Human Rights Protection: Is Enlargement Compatible with Reinforcement?*, 8 TRANSNAT'L L. & CONTEMP. PROBS. 313 (1998).

117. *Id.*

118. *Short History, supra* note 110.

119. J.G. MERRILLS, THE DEVELOPMENT OF INTERNATIONAL LAW BY THE EUROPEAN COURT OF HUMAN RIGHTS 1 (1988) [hereinafter MERRILLS].

120. A.H. ROBERTSON, THE COUNCIL OF EUROPE: ITS STRUCTURE, FUNCTIONS AND ACHIEVEMENTS 161 (1961).

121. *Id.*

122. *Id.*

123. HARRIS ET AL., LAW OF THE EUROPEAN CONVENTION ON HUMAN RIGHTS 1 (1995) [hereinafter HARRIS ET AL.].

124. *Id.* at 2.

125. Universal Declaration of Human Rights, G.A. Res. 217A (III), GAOR, at 71, U.N. Doc. A/810 (1948).

categories of rights – civil and political rights in the first category, and economic, social, and cultural rights in the second – the Convention shields mainly civil and political rights.[127] At the time that it was drawn up and adopted (1949-50), there was an overwhelming need for a short, non-controversial text that governments could readily accept without lengthy deliberations and while public opinion still favored such an agreement.[128] Thus, the social and political values that dominated Western Europe, fortified in the aftermath of World War II's totalitarian revolution, dictated a document limited to those political and civil rights necessary for an "effective political democracy."[129]

However, those rights were not to be secured without regard for the needs of a democratic society.[130] As the Convention's Preamble itself stated, the Members of the Council of Europe:

[R]eaffirm[ed] their profound belief in those Fundamental Freedoms which are the foundation of justice and peace in the world and are best maintained on the one hand by an effective political democracy and on the other by a common understanding and observance of the Human Rights upon which they depend ...[131]

Thus, the Convention sought a balance between the demands of the general, democratic community interest and the requirements implied in the protection of individual fundamental rights.[132] This balance becomes strikingly clear in Articles 8-11 of the Convention, which protect the "personal freedoms" of the right to respect for private and family life (Article 8), the right to freedom of religion (Article 9), the right to freedom of expression (Article 10), and the right to freedom of assembly (Article 11).[133] However, those articles also contain "limitation clauses" that detail instances where the rights enumerated may be curtailed by the State.[134]

---

126. *See* Universal Declaration of Human Rights, G.A. Res. 217A (III), GAOR, at 71, U.N. Doc. A/810 (1948).

127. HARRIS ET AL., *supra* note 123, at 3.

128. *Id.* at 4. There was consensus among the drafting parties that economic, social, and cultural rights were too thorny to be resolved quickly and were thus best left for a later date. Those rights are now protected by the European Social Charter 1961. *Id.; See also id.* n. 19 at 4.

129. European Convention for the Protection of Human Rights and Fundamental Freedoms, Preamble, Apr. 11, 1950 , 213 U.N.T.S. 222 (entered into force Sept. 21 1953, as amended by Protocols No. 11 entered into force Nov. 1, 1998) [hereinafter European Convention for Human Rights].

130. HARRIS ET AL., *supra* note 123, at 11.

131. *Id. See also* European Convention for Human Rights, Preamble, *supra* note 129.

132. HARRIS ET AL., *supra* note 123, at 11.

133. *See* European Convention for Human Rights, *supra* note 131, art. 8-11.

134. *Id.*

492   TEMPLE INT'L & COMP. L.J.   [Vol. 16.2

While the wording varies for each article, in general a restriction is permitted only where "necessary in a democratic society in the interests of national security, public safety or the economic well-being of the country, for the prevention of disorder or crime, [or] for the protection of health or morals."[135] Where to draw the line on such State restrictions was ultimately left to the judicial organs that the Convention created: the European Commission on Human Rights (the Commission), and the European Court on Human Rights (the Court). In drawing that line, the Court and its Commission (now no longer in existence)[136] developed early on the doctrine of the "margin of appreciation," which strikes a balance between the Court's supervisory function over the Member States and the right of each State to govern its citizenry through the full exercise of its sovereignty.

C. The Jurisprudence of the Court

1. The Margin of Appreciation

Before delving into the intricacies of this doctrine, the reader must understand the Court's role in the system of protection of human rights as envisioned by the Council and implemented by the Convention. It is not a "court of last resort" to which applicants can appeal the final decision of their national courts.[137] The initial and primary responsibility for human rights protection must originate with the Member States themselves.[138] The Court comes into play when one Member State requests a review of the "observance of national law by the national authorities" of another Member State.[139] A Member State can request such a review if it feels that the national law of the Member State as implemented does not adequately insure the rights guaranteed by the Convention, that the national courts themselves of that Member State have improperly interpreted the Convention in securing those rights, or some combination of both. It is an appropriate application of the margin of appreciation that enables the Court

---

135. *Id.* at art. 8-11, ¶ 2.

136. Protocol No. 11, which entered into effect November 1, 1998, streamlined the adjudicatory process, eliminated the Commission whose pre-screening function was melded into those of the Court, and provided for a full-time Court, which heretofore had functioned on only a part-time basis. The new Court is now divided into three bodies, which screen applications for appropriate jurisdiction and adjudicate those matters: Committees (with three judges); Chambers (with seven judges), and a Grand Chamber (with seventeen judges). The plenary Court no longer hears disputes, limiting itself to administrative matters (appointing the President Judge of each Chamber, constituting Chambers, adopting Court rules of procedure, etc.). HARRIS ET AL., *supra* note 123, at 708-09.

137. *Id.* at 15.

138. *Id.* at 14.

139. *Id.* at 15.

to either severely check or give broad discretion to State conduct in the matter.[140]

The doctrine of a margin of appreciation acknowledges that the national authorities, whether judicial or legislative, are generally in a better position than the international judge to determine what methods, laws, restrictions, and penalties are best suited to protect the human rights enumerated in the Convention.[141] By adopting this doctrine as its *modus operandi,* the Court never intended to appear weak, ineffective or, worse still, non-committed to the preservation of those fundamental rights of the Convention, as critics have often claimed (and most recently with respect to the Convention on Cybercrime).[142] On the contrary, the Court claimed a "subsidiary role" for the Convention, where the principles espoused in that document supported the national legal systems of the contracting parties.[143] Thus, the Court recognized the "superiority of the organs of a state in fact-finding and in the assessment of what the local circumstances demand by way of limitation of rights."[144]

This doctrine was clearly detailed in *Handyside v. U.K.,*[145] a 1976 case concerning whether a conviction for possessing an obscene article could be justified under Article 10(2) as a limitation on the right to freedom of expression necessary for the protection of morals.[146] In *Handyside,* a publication intended for school children (*The Little Red Schoolbook*) contained diverse controversial material, including a large chapter on sex.[147] The British publisher was successfully prosecuted under the Obscene Publications Acts of 1959 and 1964, and over a thousand copies of the books were seized.[148] The publisher claimed a violation of his Article 10(1) rights of freedom of expression.[149] Although the Court recognized that his freedom of expression had been "curtailed," the Court held that the interference was

---

140. *Id.*

141. HARRIS ET AL., *supra* note 123, at 291-92.

142. *Id.*

143. *Id.* at 292.

144. *Id.*

145. Handyside v. U.K., 24 Eur. Ct. H.R. (ser. A) (1976). This case may also be found in LEADING CASES OF THE EUROPEAN COURT OF HUMAN RIGHTS 28 (R.A. Lawson & H.G. Schermers eds.) [hereinafter LEADING CASES].

146. Art. 10(1) of the Convention states in part: "Everyone has the right to freedom of expression. This right shall include freedom to hold opinions and to receive and impart information and ideas without interference by public authority and regardless of frontiers." Art. 10(2), its limitations clause, states in part: "The exercise of these freedoms, since it carries with it duties and responsibilities, may be subject to such formalities, conditions, restrictions or penalties as are prescribed by law and are necessary in a democratic society, in the interests of national security, territorial integrity or public safety, for the prevention of disorder or crime, [or] for the protection of health or morals." *See* European Convention for Human Rights, *supra* note 129, art. 10.

147. MERRILLS, *supra* note 119, at 100.

148. *Id.* at 145.

149. Handyside, 24 Eur. Ct. H.R, 14 note 145, at ¶ 42.

494   TEMPLE INT'L & COMP. L.J.   [Vol. 16.2

justified under Article 10(2) as "prescribed by law and . . . necessary in a democratic society . . . for the protection of morals."[150] In upholding this action of the British government, the Court reiterated that the "machinery of protection" established by the Convention was *subsidiary* to the national systems, not superior.[151] Such subsidiarity was even more important in the absence of a "European consensus" as to what constituted "morality,"[152] which varied "from time to time and from place to place" and regarding which there was no uniform application of domestic law of the various Contracting States.[153] The Court also emphasized that:

> By reason of their direct and continuous contact with the vital forces of their countries, State authorities are, in principle, in a better position than the international judge to give an opinion on the exact content of these requirements as well as on the "necessity" of a "restriction" or "penalty" intended to meet them.[154]

While the margin of appreciation fostered the co-existence of diverse systems aimed at human rights protection, each with its own definition of what those rights are, there was also the danger that the objective and universal standards set forth by the Convention could be overrun by national determinations of what constituted "in the public interest."[155] By shifting the burden of proving the necessity to interfere with a guaranteed right onto the State, the Convention and the Court "preserve[d] the superior character of the protected rights."[156] In requiring that the State demonstrate a "pressing social need" for such interference, the Court raised the standard of proof beyond mere "good faith" to one of relevancy and sufficiency regarding the measures of interference actually taken by the State.[157]

2. Morality and the Right to Freedom of Expression

With "tolerance and broad-mindedness" two of the "hallmarks" of the Court's conception of a democratic society, it became manifest that the entire Convention inclined against justifying interferences from the State to

---

150. MERRILLS, *supra* note 119, at 145.

151. *Id.* at 145-46.

152. HOWARD CHARLES YOUROW, THE MARGIN OF APPRECIATION DOCTRINE IN THE DYNAMICS OF EUROPEAN HUMAN RIGHTS JURISPRUDENCE 46 (1996).

153. MERRILLS, *supra* note 119, at 146.

154. Handyside, *supra* note 145, at ¶ 48.

155. HARRIS ET AL., *supra* note 123, at 292.

156. *Id.*

157. *Id.* ¶ 50.

protect the intolerance and narrow-mindedness of others.[158] As the Court itself declared in *Handyside*:

> Freedom of expression constitutes one of the essential foundations of a [democratic] society, one of the basic conditions for its progress and for the development of every man. Subject to paragraph 2 of Article 10, it is applicable not only to "information" or "ideas" that are favourably received or regarded as inoffensive but also to those that offend, shock or disturb the state or any sector of the population. Such are the demands of that pluralism, tolerance and broadmindedness without which there is no "democratic society."[159]

Unlike the United States Supreme Court's interpretation of the First Amendment of its Constitution that more greatly emphasized what freedom of speech or expression is (i.e., what is included enjoys protection and what is not included does not), the Convention considers all expression, regardless of content, as falling within Article 10(1).[160] For example, obscenity has been excluded from First Amendment protection, whereas under Article 10(1), it is "expression," but such expression may be restricted or limited within the meaning of Article 10(2).[161]

In a fashion somewhat similar to *Handyside*, *Müller et al. v. Switzerland*[162] juxtaposed public morality with freedom of artistic expression. In *Müller*, a Swiss artist was invited by nine other artists to exhibit three of his paintings at an exhibition celebrating the 500th anniversary of the Canton of Fribourg's entry into the Swiss Confederation.[163] The exhibition, widely advertised in the press and on posters throughout the city, was open to the general public, while a catalogue prepared for the exhibition's preview contained photographic reproductions of the paintings.[164] Acting on a complaint from one exhibit viewer whose minor daughter had "reacted violently" to the paintings on display, the chief public prosecutor for the Canton reported to the investigating judge that at least some of the paintings appeared to violate Article 204 of the Swiss Criminal Code, which proscribed obscene publications and mandated their confiscation and destruction.[165]

---

158. HARRIS ET AL., *supra* note 123, at 295.

159. Handyside, 24 Eur. Ct. H.R. Art ¶ 49.

160. HARRIS ET AL., *supra* note 123, at 375 n. 2.

161. *Id.* at 375.

162. Müller v. Switzerland, 13 Eur. Ct. H.R. 212 (1988), *available at* http://www.echr.coe.int/Hudoc.htm.

163. *Id.* ¶ 10.

164. *Id.* ¶ 11.

165. *Id.* ¶ 12.

496 TEMPLE INT'L & COMP. L.J. [Vol. 16.2

The subject matter of the paintings – sodomy, fellatio, bestiality, the erect penis – was characterized as "obviously morally offensive to the vast majority of the population" by the district court.[166] Although the works were not physically destroyed, they were segregated in the Art and History Museum of the Canton of Fribourg where they would be made available "only to a few serious specialists capable of taking an exclusively artistic or cultural interest in them as opposed to a prurient interest."[167]

After exhausting all available national remedies, the applicants complained of the confiscation of their paintings to the still-existing Commission, claiming a violation of their rights to freedom of expression as guaranteed by Article 10(1) of the Convention.[168] The Court's considerations focused on the three cardinal points of Article 10's limitations clause,[169] which detailed under what circumstances restrictions imposed on an individual's right to freedom of expression by the State were permissible: whether the penalties and restrictions levied on the artists (criminal conviction and confiscation of the paintings) were "prescribed by law," whether those measures were meant to achieve one of the aims enumerated under Article 10(2), and if those measures were in fact "necessary in a democratic society" to achieve the stated end.[170]

On the first point, the Court found that in order for a norm to be "prescribed by law," it had to be precise enough to possess a certain degree of "foreseeability" regarding the potential consequences of any given action.[171] The Court conceded that "[t]he need to avoid excessive rigidity and to keep pace with changing circumstances" meant that obscenity laws would be inevitably couched in vague terms[172] to maintain a certain consonance between law and continually changing prevailing social mores.[173] On the second point, the Court accepted, as the Swiss government argued, that Article 204 was indeed enacted to protect public morals, and there was no reason to believe that the Swiss courts intended anything incompatible with the Convention.[174]

Expounding on the third point of whether such restrictions were "necessary in a democratic society," the Court reiterated that "necessary" implied a "pressing social need," and elaborated on its own role in that determination: "The Contracting States have a certain margin of

---

166. *Id.* ¶ 14.

167. Müller, 13 Eur. Ct. H.R., ¶ 14.

168. *Id.* ¶ 23.

169. *See* European Convention for Human Rights, *supra* note 129, for the text of art. 10(2).

170. Müller, 13 Eur. Ct. H.R. at ¶ 28.

171. *Id.* ¶ 29 (explaining that the "foreseeability requirement" inherent in the phrase "prescribed by law" grew out of the Court's own case law and had become part of the body of interpretative rules regarding the Convention.)

172. *Id.*

173. HARRIS ET AL., *supra* note 123, at 288.

174. Müller, 13 Eur. Ct. H.R. at ¶ 30.

appreciation in assessing whether such a need exists, but this goes hand in hand with a European supervision, embracing both the legislation and the decisions applying it."[175] The Court elegantly applied this balancing test, on the one hand recognizing that artists contribute to that freedom of exchange of ideas and opinions so fundamental to a democratic society and that the State had an obligation not to interfere unduly with that freedom.[176] On the other hand, the Court also recognized that the paintings in question (which crudely depicted sexual relations, particularly between men and animals) were "liable grossly to offend the sense of sexual propriety of persons of ordinary sensitivity," despite the fact that sexual ideas and mores had changed significantly in recent years.[177]

Both *Handyside* and *Müller* illustrate that the Court has generally granted a wide margin to the State where the State claims to act for the protection of morals, allowing it to define morals and what it must do to protect them.[178] In both cases, the nature of the targeted audience (the school children in *Handyside*) or recipient (the minor daughter in *Müller*) of sexually explicit material bolstered the right of the State to intervene.[179] Thus, the intended audience or market is a significant factor for the Court in determining whether an interference with the right to freedom of expression is justified.[180]

3. Morality and the Right to Privacy

The Court has also been asked to decide on what grounds State interference is justified with respect to private sexual activities or practices. Paragraph 1 of Article 8 of the Convention guarantees "the right to respect for [a person's] private and family life, his home and his correspondence."[181] The right described here is not to *privacy*, which more narrowly connotes secrecy or seclusion, but to *respect for private life*, which embraces the concept of relationships between individuals.[182] This was clearly articulated in *Niemietz v. Federal Republic of Germany,*[183] where the Court elucidated that

---

175. *Id.* ¶ 32. The bright line rule that "necessary" implies a "pressing social need" is a view consistently held by the Court in its own jurisprudence. *Id.*

176. *Id.* ¶ 33.

177. *Id.* ¶¶ 18, 36.

178. HARRIS ET AL., *supra* note 123, at 392.

179. *Id.* at 393.

180. *Id.* at 407.

181. *See* European Convention of Human Rights, *supra* note 129, at art 8(1).

182. HARRIS ET AL., *supra* note 123, at 303.

183. Niemietz v. Federal Republic of Germany, 251 Eur. Ct. H.R. (ser. A) (1992). Also in LEADING CASES 493. In *Niemietz*, German law enforcement authorities searched the law office premises of Mr. Niemietz in hopes of finding indications of the identity of someone who had written an insulting letter under a false name, a criminal offense in Germany. Mr. Niemitz claimed that this violated his right to respect for his home and correspondence as guaranteed by Article 8 of the Convention. The Court agreed,

"[r]espect for private life must also comprise to a certain degree the right to establish and develop relationships with other human beings."[184] A further refinement was developed in *X and Y v. Netherlands*,[185] where the Court specifically delineated "private life" as "a concept which covers the physical and moral integrity of the person, including his or her sexual life."[186]

A person's sexual activities involve the "most intimate aspect of private life," as the Court expressed in *Dudgeon v. U.K.*[187] Given this, "there must exist particularly serious reasons before interferences on the part of the public authorities can be legitimate for the purposes of paragraph 2 of Article 8."[188] In this case, the applicant Mr. Dudgeon claimed that the continued existence of a Northern Ireland law prohibiting consensual adult homosexuality constituted "a justified interference with his private life, protected under Article 8 of the Convention."[189] The government argued that the disputed legislation fell well within the state's right to protect the morals of its citizens, as provided by the limitations clause of Article 8.[190] The question before the Court was not only whether the criminalization of homosexuality was "necessary in a democratic society" but also "whether the interference complained of was proportionate to the social need claimed for it."[191] The Court added a significant factor to its deliberations on this issue,

---

concluding that "the notion of "private life" should [not] be taken to exclude activities of a professional or business nature." While the interference had a legitimate aim (that of preventing crime and of protecting others), it was not proportionate to the aims claimed because "the search impinged on professional secrecy to an extent that appears disproportionate in the circumstances." *Id.* ¶¶ 29, 37.

184. *Id.* ¶ 29.

185. X & Y v. Netherlands, 91 Eur. Ct. H.R. (ser. A) (1985). Also in LEADING CASES 156. In *X and Y v. Netherlands*, a sixteen-year-old mentally handicapped girl was sexually abused while residing in a special home for mentally-handicapped children. Because she was mentally and legally incompetent to file a complaint, her father did so in her stead. Proceedings were never initiated against the perpetrator because of a gap in Dutch law which required that the girl, being of the age of legal consent (sixteen years old), file the complaint herself. Even though law enforcement authorities themselves recognized and agreed that the girl was incapable of doing so, the Court of Appeal dismissed the father's appeal that action be taken. The father applied to the Commission for redress, which referred the case to the Court. In its turn, the Court found that Dutch law did not provide the applicant with "practical and effective protection," and that she had in effect been a victim of an Article 8 violation. *Id.* ¶ 31.

186. *Id.* ¶ 22.

187. Dudgeon v. U.K., 45 Eur. Ct. H.R. (ser. A) (1981) ¶ 52. Also in LEADING CASES 124.

188. *Id.*

189. *Id.*

190. Dudgeon, 45 Eur. Ct. H.R. at ¶ 42. Article 8(2) states: "There shall be no interference by a public authority with the exercise of this right except such as is in accordance with the law and is necessary in a democratic society in the interests of national security, public safety or the economic well-being of the country, for the prevention of disorder or crime, for the protection of health or morals, or for the protection of the rights and freedoms of others." *See* European Convention of Human Rights, *supra* note 129.

191. MERRILLS, *supra* note 119, at 148.

stating that "not only the nature of the aim of the restriction but also the nature of the activities involved [would] affect the scope of the margin of appreciation."[192]

The Court arrived at a two-pronged decision. First, it found the law in violation of Article 8(1) because, although the authorities had not actively enforced the law against those over twenty-one in recent years, the mere fact that it was still retained as a legal statute caused "detrimental effects . . . on the life of a person of homosexual orientation like the applicant."[193] The Court added that mere public shock, offense, or repugnance was not enough to warrant penal sanctions for homosexual behavior as long as "consenting adults alone" were involved in that behavior.[194] However, the Court justified the State's interference with this "most intimate aspect of private life" in dismissing Mr. Dudgeon's complaint that the law prevented him from having sexual relations with males under twenty-one. Some degree of control over homosexual conduct was necessary to prevent the exploitation and corruption of underage youth, and "it [fell] in the first instance to the national authorities to decide on the appropriate safeguards of this kind required for the defence of morals in their society and, in particular, to fix the age under which young people should have the protection of the criminal law."[195]

The privacy of one's sexual activities and the State's rightful need to prevent harm to others clashed head-on in the 1995 case of *Laskey, Jaggard, and Brown v. U.K.*.[196] During a routine investigation, the police came into possession of a number of video films which depicted sado-masochistic encounters between the applicants and over forty other homosexual men.[197] The applicants were charged with a series of offenses relating to those sado-masochistic activities which had taken place over a ten-year period.[198] The acts included maltreatment of the genitalia and ritualistic beatings with either bare hands or implements, such as stinging nettles, spiked belts, or a cat-o'-nine tails.[199] These activities were consensual and conducted in private, specially equipped "chambers" at various locations for the sole purpose of sexual gratification.[200] New "members" were actively recruited and videotapes of the activities were distributed among the "members."[201] The applicants pleaded guilty to the assault charges, were convicted and

---

192. *Id.*
193. Dudgeon, 45 Eur. Ct. H.R. at ¶ 60.
194. *Id.*
195. *Id.* ¶ 62.
196. Laskey, Jaggard, and Brown v. U.K., 24 Eur. H.R. Rep. 39 (1997).
197. *Id.* ¶ 8.
198. *Id.*
199. *Id.*
200. *Id.* ¶ ¶ 8, 9.
201. Laskey et al., *supra* note 196, ¶ 36.

sentenced to terms of imprisonment, with Mr. Laskey being separately charged and convicted for possession of an indecent photograph of a child.[202]

The applicants then appealed to the British Court of Appeal, Criminal Division, and to the House of Lords, where those appeals were denied.[203] However, in his comment on the case, Lord Mustill raised the question of whether such acts would be permitted under Article 8 of the Convention, since "the decisions of the European authorities clearly favoured the right of the appellants to conduct their private life undisturbed by the criminal law."[204] This may have prompted Laskey, Jaggard, and Brown to apply to the European Commission, complaining that their convictions were "an unforeseeable application of a provision of the criminal law which, in any event, amounted to an unlawful and unjustifiable interference with their right to respect for their private life."[205]

Before the Court, the applicants argued that the consensual nature of their activities rendered them "sexual expression, rather than violence" and that their behavior "formed part of private morality which [was] not the State's business to regulate."[206] In its stead, the Government argued that some of the acts could be compared to "genital torture" which a Contracting State was not obligated to tolerate just because "they were committed in the context of a consenting sexual relationship."[207] The Government also contended that such forms of behavior should be deterred not only on public health grounds but also on grounds that they "undermine the respect which human beings should confer upon each other."[208]

The Court agreed. The presence of "a significant degree of injury or wounding" distinguished the instant case from previous cases dealing with "consensual homosexual behaviour in private between adults."[209] The extreme nature of the practices, the very number of assault charges, and the long duration of the activities led the Court to find that the national authorities' actions in prosecuting and convicting the applicants were appropriate to safeguard public health within the meaning of Article 8(2).[210]

The 1997 case of *A.D.T. v. U.K.*[211] reaffirmed the Court's stance on state interference with private sexual activities. The applicant, a practicing homosexual, was charged with gross indecency between men after videotapes portraying the applicant and up to four other adult men engaged in homosexual acts in his home were seized and viewed by police

---

202. *Id.* ¶ 11.
203. *Id.* ¶ ¶ 14-23.
204. *Id.* ¶ 22.
205. *Id.* ¶ 32.
206. Laskey et al., *supra* note 196, ¶ ¶ 39, 45.
207. *Id.* ¶ 40.
208. *Id.*
209. *Id.* ¶ 45.
210. *Id.* ¶ 50.
211. A.D.T. v. U.K. (July 31, 2000) *at* http://www.echr.coe.int/eng/Judgments.htm.

authorities.[212] He was not charged with distribution of sexual material but with participating in homosexual acts with more than two people, which automatically conferred a "public nature" to the activities.[213] The offence was not the videotaping but the fact that homosexual activity occurred with more than two people present.[214] The tapes themselves were made in the privacy of applicant's home and were never intended for distribution or publication.[215] There was no element of physical harm or sado-masochism involved, and no organized activity or risk of injury to any of the participants.[216] The applicant emphasized that "had it not been for the prosecution, the video tape would not have been distributed in any real sense whatever."[217]

The Court found that the applicant's right to respect for his private life had, in fact, been violated.[218] Although it agreed that sexual activities could justify state interference for the protection of health or morals, in *A.D.T.* there was little risk of public exposure to those activities.[219] The group of friends involved was restricted, the activities were carried out in the privacy of applicant's home, the video tapes were not for public distribution, and the applicant was prosecuted for the activities themselves, not for endangering public morals or health.[220] Thus, the Court concluded that the absence of public health considerations and the purely private nature of the behavior were "not sufficient to justify the legislation and the prosecution."[221]

V. THE CONVENTION ON CYBERCRIME

Having recognized that the fundamental changes in society wrought by the "revolution in information technologies" had also given birth to new types of crimes committed in an as yet unregulated territory (cyberspace),[222] the Council of Europe established a working group in 1996 to hammer out the terms of the first legally binding instrument that would lay out universal definitions and standards for defining and criminalizing "cybercrime," and that at the same time would provide a procedural framework for its

---

212. *Id.* ¶ 8-9.

213. The Sexual Offences Act of 1967 provided that "homosexual acts in private between consenting adult men were no loner an offence." Section 1(2) of the Act stated that an act was not private if, inter alia, more than two persons took part or were present. *Id.* ¶ 16.

214. *Id.* ¶ 28.

215. *Id.* ¶ 9.

216. *Id.* ¶ ¶ 10, 22.

217. A.D.T., *supra* note 211, ¶ 22.

218. *Id.* ¶¶ 38-39.

219. *Id.* ¶ 37.

220. *Id.*

221. *Id.*

222. *Draft Convention on Cybercrime and Explanatory Memorandum Related Thereto*, http://conventions.coe.int, ¶ 1 [hereinafter *Explanatory Memorandum*].

detection, investigation, and prosecution.[223] The Council invited four non-Council Member States to participate in the drafting, negotiating, and final signing of this groundbreaking document: Canada, Japan, South Africa, and the United States. Their inclusion extends the Convention's coverage to most of the world's traffic data.[224]

Open to the current forty-four Member States of the Council of Europe, the Convention on Cybercrime is the first instrument that deals with cybercrime within the sphere of international law and which is based on measures of international cooperation.[225]

A. *Criminalizing Cybercrime in General*

The Convention on Cybercrime keeps the criminal law "abreast of th[ose] technological developments which offer highly sophisticated opportunities for misusing facilities of the cyberspace and causing damage to legitimate interests."[226] Because cyberspace is not restricted by geographical limitations or national boundaries,[227] criminal activity occurring in such boundless territory must be addressed by international law through appropriate international legal instruments.[228]

Accordingly, the Convention has three principal aims. It attempts to meld together, across the panorama of participating Members, domestic substantive law regarding cybercrime offenses and related provisions.[229] Second, it establishes a criminal procedural framework that empowers each participating Member to investigate and prosecute offenses committed by means of, or with the assistance of, a computer system. It also provides for the gathering and preservation of evidence in electronic form that is related to the commission of such offenses.[230] Third, it sets up a regime designed to

---

223. *Id.* ¶ 9.

224. *Background of the Convention on Cybercrime,* found at the Council of Europe's website, http://www.coe.int (last visited Jan. 18, 2003).

225. Convention on Cybercrime, *opened for signature* Nov. 23, 2001, Europ. T.S. 185 [hereinafter Cybercrime Convention]. The Convention will enter into force after five signatories have ratified it, of which at least three must be Member States of the Council of Europe. As of this writing, twenty-nine of the current forty-four Member States of the Council of Europe have signed the Convention: Albania, Armenia, Austria, Belgium, Bulgaria, Croatia, Cyprus, Estonia, Finland, France, Germany, Greece, Hungary, Iceland, Ireland. Italy, Malta, Moldova, Netherlands, Norway, Poland, Portugal, Romania, Spain (by referendum), Sweden, Switzerland, FYR Macedonia, Ukraine, and the United Kingdom. Albania recently moved to formal ratification of the Convention on June 20, 2002. Additionally, the four non-Member States invited to participate in the negotiations and drafting of the Convention have signed it: Canada, Japan, South Africa, and the United States. Explanatory Memorandum, *supra* note 223, ¶ 9.

226. Explanatory Memorandum, *supra* note 222, ¶ 9.

227. *Id.* ¶ 5.

228. *Id.* ¶ 6.

229. *Id.* ¶ 15.

230. *Id.*

foster effective international cooperation.[231] In achieving those aims, the Convention respects the major doctrines developed throughout the European Court's juridical literature, i.e., the margin of appreciation, the right to freedom of expression, and the right to privacy, as those doctrines relate to the investigation and prosecution of cybercrime in general, and electronic child pornography, in particular.

The Convention first defines at what point conduct qualifies as "criminal." Conduct rises to the level of a criminal offense when it is (1) committed deliberately, i.e., with intent,[232] and (2) committed "without right."[233] The meaning of the phrase "without right" is left to be derived from the surrounding context of each Party's own domestic law.[234] "Without right" may refer to actions taken without lawful authority, regardless of what type of "authority" (legislative, executive, administrative, judicial, or other) proscribes that action.[235] It may refer to conduct not covered by affirmative defenses, justifications, or excuses.[236] Moreover, it grants each Party the liberty to exempt certain types of conduct from that proscription. For example, with particular regard to computer-generated child pornography, a Party may decide not to criminalize the procuration or possession of child pornography through or in a computer system.[237] It may also decline to criminalize pornographic material that shows "a person appearing to be a minor engaged in sexually explicit conduct" or "realistic images representing a minor engaged in sexually explicit conduct."[238] This flexibility accorded to the meaning of "without right" permits full expression of, and adherence to, the doctrine of margin of appreciation, a cornerstone of the European Court's jurisprudence.

Through three major sections, the Convention develops universal standards for the criminalization, prosecution, and sanctioning of cybercrime. Chapter I defines four categories of offenses that fall within the Convention's coverage. The first category (offenses against the confidentiality, integrity, and availability of computer data and systems) includes illegal access, illegal interception, data interference, system interference, and misuse of devices.[239] The second category (computer-related offenses) comprises computer-related forgery and computer-related fraud.[240] The third category details content-related offenses and is largely dedicated to the production, dissemination, and possession of child

---

231. Explanatory Memorandum, *supra* note 222, ¶ 15.

232. *Id.* ¶ 39.

233. *Id.* ¶ 38.

234. *Id.*

235. *Id.*

236. Explanatory Memorandum, *supra* note 222, ¶ 38.

237. Cybercrime Convention, *supra* note 225, arts. 9(1)(d), (e).

238. *Id.* arts. 9(2)(b), (c).

239. Explanatory Memorandum, *supra* note 222, ¶ 17.

240. *Id.*

504   TEMPLE INT'L & COMP. L.J.   [Vol. 16.2

pornography.[241] The fourth category deals with offenses related to copyright and related rights.[242]

Chapter II develops a two-part procedural framework within which computer crimes are to be prosecuted. The first part sets forth the common conditions necessary for criminal investigations or proceedings related to cyber-crime: the enactment of specific legislative and other measures to establish the powers and procedures, the direct applicability of such powers and procedures to the offenses defined in Chapter I,[243] and those safeguards which shall "provide for the adequate protection of human rights and liberties."[244] By definition, safeguards for the protection of human rights and liberties will fulfill two general conditions. Internally, within the Party's political boundaries, they will conform to those safeguards provided for by each Party's domestic law, whether through constitutional, judicial, or legislative instruments.[245] Externally, on an international level, such safeguards will conform to standards set forth in those human rights instruments (see, e.g., the European Convention for the Protection of Human Rights and Fundamental Freedoms, the International Covenant on Civil and Political Rights, etc.) to which the Party has adhered. The second part of Chapter II sets out specific procedural powers regarding the expedited preservation of stored data; expedited preservation and partial disclosure of traffic data; production orders; searches and seizures of computer data; real-time collection of traffic data; and the interception of content data.[246]

Chapter III details three main principles buttressing international cooperation in the cyber-crime arena. First, cooperation between Parties is to be "to the widest extent possible,"[247] requiring Parties to cooperate with each other and to minimize obstacles obstructing the sharing of information and evidence at the international level.[248] Second, that cooperation must extend not only to all criminal offenses involving computer systems and data, but also to the gathering of electronic evidence proving such offenses.[249] Third, where an existing legal agreement exists (e.g., a mutual legal assistance treaty or reciprocal legislation), the existing arrangements shall be applicable also to assistance under the Convention.[250] Where no such legal basis exists, the Convention's provisions shall apply *in toto*.[251] A fourth and final chapter contains those provisions that are standard in Council of

---

241. *Id.*
242. *Id.*
243. Cybercrime Convention, *supra* note 225, art. 14.
244. *Id.* art. 15.
245. Explanatory Memorandum, *supra* note 222, ¶ 145.
246. *Id.* ¶ 18.
247. Cybercrime Convention, *supra* note 225, art. 23.
248. Explanatory Memorandum, *supra* note 222, ¶ 242.
249. *Id.* ¶ 243.
250. *Id.*
251. *Id.*

Europe treaties (signature and entry into force, accession to the Convention, declarations and reservations, settlement of disputes, etc.).[252]

B. *Criminalizing Electronic Child Pornography in Particular*

An appropriate evaluation of the Council of Europe's Convention on Cybercrime pertinent to its regulation and criminalization of computerized child pornography should examine three conceptual areas: (1) the establishment of universal standards to be adopted on a state level; (2) the formulation of procedural law uniquely tuned to the complexities of criminalizing and prosecuting computerized child pornography; and (3) appropriate safeguards designed to protect individual rights from arbitrary state or national law enforcement interference.

1. Establishing Universal Standards

As the first legally binding international instrument to establish universal standards regarding the criminalization of computerized child pornography, the Cybercrime Convention takes an important step toward containing this offense on a global scale. Paragraph 1 of Article 9 proscribes producing, offering or making available, distributing or transmitting, procuring or possessing child pornography in a computer system or on a computer-data storage medium.[253] Paragraph 2 continues the Convention's groundbreaking development in defining child pornography as pornographic material that depicts a minor (Article 9(2)(a)), a person appearing to be a minor (Article 9(2)(b)), or realistic images representing a minor, engaged in sexually explicit conduct (Article 9(2)(c)).[254] Paragraph 3 defines a "minor" as one under the age of eighteen, but permits States to lower that threshold age to sixteen.[255]

Paragraph 2 stands out in extending the criminalization of child pornography to electronic images, an area not always covered by existing State child pornography laws.[256] The Convention bridges that gap by applying homogeneous terms acceptable to a majority of parties. It also provides for limited reservations in Paragraph 4 for those parties who would find themselves in conflict with their state constitutions or with domestic legal principles.[257]

---

252. Cybercrime Convention, *supra* note 225, arts. 36-48.

253. *Id.* art. 9(1).

254. *Id.* art. 9(2).

255. *Id.* art. 1, ¶ 3.

256. Explanatory Memorandum, *supra* note 222, ¶ 79: "States must examine their existing laws to determine whether they apply to situations in which computer systems or networks are involved. If existing offences already cover such conduct, there is no requirement to amend existing offences or enact new ones."

257. *See infra* note 259 and accompanying text.

However, the Convention adheres to the European Court's doctrine of margin of appreciation and does not mandate supplanting State law with its specific Articles. It sets a guideline for criminalizing certain conduct within the jurisdiction of those States who adopt the Convention's provisions. Whether that criminalization comes from already existing laws or new ones enacted in order to implement the Convention's requirements is of no import.[258] While a country might need to adopt Article 9 to its fullest extent to satisfy the Convention's threshold requirements, its own legislature might balk, absent some external motivation. This is Japan's quandary, where law enforcement and liberal government officials are embarrassed by the quantity of electronic child pornography available. Interpol estimates that eighty percent of all child pornography available on worldwide websites is "Made in Japan," yet the "Old Guard" in control of the government either will not or cannot comprehend the necessity for effective regulation.[259] Legislation passed within the past several years is overly broad, vague, and weakly worded, making prosecution difficult.[260] Having signed the Convention, Japan must now enact appropriate legislation to fulfill its international obligations under it, legislation that almost certainly will be strongly opposed by its elder politicians.

This margin of appreciation accorded to national legal systems is visible also in Paragraph 4 of Article 9, which permits each Party to make certain reservations, i.e., to not apply certain Convention definitions. Such reservations extend to procuring, possessing, or storing child pornography with the aid of a computer system or data storage medium.[261] Italy may very well make this reservation. The Italian Court of Cassation recently ruled that possession of "hard core" child pornographic images on a computer was not a crime if those images were for personal use only and did not involve a financial motive.[262] A second set of reservations concerns the Convention's definition of pornographic material as depicting "a person appearing to be a minor engaged in sexually explicit conduct" or "realistic images representing a minor engaged in sexually explicit conduct."[263] This is at least one of the reservations that the United States is likely to make, given its Supreme Court's recent decision rendering unconstitutional certain portions of the 1996 Child Pornography Prevention Act.[264]

---

258. *Id.*

259. Tim Larimer, *Japan's Shame*, TIME, Apr. 19, 1999, at 34, *available at* LEXIS, Individual Publications File.

260. *Id.*

261. *See* Cybercrime Convention, *supra* note 225, art. 9(1).

262. JENKINS, *supra* note 7, at 194, (citing "La Cassazione, a Sezioni unite, ha respinto un ricorso: Se le foto hard sono per uso proprio, il reato non c'è" ["The Plenary Session of the Court of Cassation has denied an appeal: If hard core photos are for one's own use, there is no crime."], *La Repubblica,* May 31, 2000).

263. Cybercrime Convention, *supra* note 225, art. 9(2)(b), (c).

264. On Oct. 30, 2001, the U.S. Supreme Court heard oral arguments challenging the constitutionality of that portion of the 1996 Child Pornography Protection Act which criminalized all visual depictions that "appear to be" or "convey the impression" of minors

No one should think that these reservations rise to "negotiating" human rights, as argued by the GILC, an international non-governmental organization "determined to preserve civil liberties and human rights on the Internet."[265] The Council's *Explanatory Memorandum* clarifies important points regarding these reservations. First, the Council deemed it prudent to permit some reservation possibilities, given the new criminal law and procedures being established by the Convention.[266] Second, the reservations were intended to permit the largest number of States to sign the Convention while fostering consistency with their own national legal systems.[267] Third, the reservations were limited in number and scope to ensure the largest and most uniform application of the Convention possible.[268] Fourth, as provided by Article 43 and in consonance with the Council's margin of appreciation, no set time period was mandated for the withdrawal of reservations to help avoid any conflict that Parties might have with their "constitutional or fundamental legal principles."[269] Lastly, permitting the Secretary General the possibility of "periodic" inquiries regarding a State's future withdrawal of its reservations enables the Parties to proceed with such withdrawals as quickly and as far as possible, as dictated by their own domestic exigencies.[270]

2. Formulating Procedural Law

The Convention formulates important procedural law critical to the successful investigation and eventual prosecution of computerized child pornography. Measures such as the preservation of computer data (Article 16), the preservation and partial disclosure of traffic data (Article 17), the production on demand of stored computer data (Article 18), the search and seizure of stored computer data (Article 19), the real-time collection of traffic data (Article 20), and the interception of content data (Article 21) may seem worthy of police states rather than democratic societies. However, when viewed in the light of criminalizing and containing child pornography on the Internet, such measures seem not only appropriate but imperative in obtaining and preserving evidence. It must be remembered that the above-mentioned articles are subject to, and limited by, the provisions of Article 14

---

engaged in explicit sexual conduct.' On Apr. 16, 2002, the Court held that the phrases "appear to be" and "convey the impression" were overbroad and vague, and thus unconstitutional. *See* Ashcroft v. The Free speech Coalition, 122 S. Ct. 1389, 2002 WL 552476 (U.S.); *see also* The Free Speech Coalition v. Reno, 220 F.3d 1113 (9th Cir. 2000). *See also* FAQs About the Council of Europe Convention on Cybercrime, Dec. 1, 2000, http://www.usdoj.gov.criminal/cybercrime/COEFAQs.htm.

265. *GILC Newsletter*, Vol. 5, Issue 4, June 26, 2001, *available at* http://www.gilc.org/alert (on file with Temple University Beasley School of Law Library).

266. Explanatory Memorandum, *supra* note 222, ¶ 321.

267. *Id.*

268. *Id.*

269. *Id.*

270. *Id.*

(which circumscribes those measures to apply for the purposes of specific criminal investigations or proceedings)[271] and the provisions of Article 15 (which provide conditions and safeguards for the "adequate protection of human rights and liberties").[272]

Article 16's preservation of computer data is aimed at specific computer information already in existence, already stored by a computer system and which has been targeted in relation to specific criminal investigations or proceedings.[273] Data preservation denotes the protection of already stored data that might be subject to alteration, modification, or destruction.[274] In the case of child pornographic images which are hoarded in massive personal computer libraries, measures to preserve that evidence of wrongdoing (just possessing such images is criminalized) are necessary.

Obtaining information on where specific computer traffic has originated is crucial in identifying distributors of child pornography.[275] Article 17's provisions would facilitate tracking the transmissions of child pornography webmasters who use anonymous proxy servers to disguise the point of origin of their wares. Those provisions require that each Party enact appropriate legislation to insure that traffic data is preserved on a timely basis, regardless of how many service providers were involved in the transmission of the communication under investigation and to insure the disclosure of enough of that traffic data to properly identify the service providers involved in transmitting the alleged illegal communication and the path of that communication.[276] Such provisions would be useful in tracking those elusive "floating" libraries that occupy one URL for only a few hours before being shut down and transferred to another. Article 17 would also help piece together data regarding the transmission of information, pictures, or movies that may have passed through more than one service provider in an effort to avoid source identification.[277]

Article 18's "production order" resembles more a subpoena *duces tecum* than a search and seizure mechanism. This provision facilitates ordering a suspected pedophile to submit specified computer data stored in his computer (e.g., pornographic images of minors).[278] For service providers, it affords an appropriate legal basis for cooperation with law enforcement authorities that relieves them from liability, a consequence much feared by defenders of the "free Internet."[279] Additionally, the production of specified computer data also implies furnishing decryption keys necessary to access

---

271. Cybercrime Convention, *supra* note 225, art. 14.
272. *Id.* art. 15.
273. Explanatory Memorandum, *supra* note 222, ¶ 321.
274. *Id.*
275. *Id.* ¶ 166.
276. Cybercrime Convention, *supra* note 225, art. 17.
277. Explanatory Memorandum, *supra* note 222, ¶ 167.
278. *Id.* ¶ 173.
279. *Id.* ¶ 171.

encrypted images. As demonstrated in the "Wonderland" club, such keys are used knowledgeably by pedophiles to protect their pornographic libraries. Without the legal means provided by Article 18 for obtaining these keys, evidence important in prosecuting these malefactors will remain beyond the reach of the law.

Article 19, providing for the search and seizure of stored computer data, is intended to harmonize domestic law across countries.[280] In a number of jurisdictions, pornographic images of children may not be considered a tangible object legally capable of being seized,[281] and any attempt to secure those images for criminal proceedings would be legally invalid. Article 19 closes that gap, identifying such images as tangible objects capable of being seized and thus bringing them under legal power.[282]

Article 20 (the real-time collecting of traffic data) and Article 21 (the interception of content data) provide important steps in tracking the computerized transmission of pornographic images of minors. Real-time collection of data is an important investigative measure because it enables law enforcement authorities to determine the source or destination and time, date, and duration of pornographic transmissions,[283] obviating the need for the elaborate retrospective cross-checking currently required to verify that a particular site on a given day and at a given hour was used to display hard-core child porn images.[284] Also, because pedophiles change such sites continually to avoid detection and identification, historic traffic data is either no longer available or has become irrelevant.[285]

Article 21, a companion provision to Article 20, provides the necessary legal weaponry to intercept transmissions of entire pornographic libraries, thus alerting authorities to new "picture sites" as they open. "[G]iven that computer technology is capable of transmitting vast quantities of data, including visual images and sound, it has greater potential for committing crimes involving distribution of illegal content (e.g., child pornography)."[286] The value of this in containing child pornography on the Internet is inestimable, when one considers that by the time an ISP provider is aware that a floating pornographic site has opened on its network, the site has already uploaded into cyberspace countless new images of children suffering sexual abuse.

---

280. *Id.* ¶ 184.
281. *Id.*
282. *Id.*
283. Explanatory Memorandum, *supra* note 222, ¶ 216.
284. JENKINS, *supra* note 7, at 69.
285. *Id.*
286. *Id.* ¶ 228.

3. Mandating Conditions and Safeguards

Some have found that the Convention has not "attended adequately" to the protection of individual human rights.[287] Those States that are not signatories of the European Convention on Human Rights "have not necessarily entered into national law the principles of protection of these rights."[288] The Convention has "missed an important opportunity to ensure that minimum standards consistent with the European Convention on Human Rights and other international human rights accords were actually implemented."[289] There is little foundation for these criticisms.

First, the fundamental freedoms present in the Council of Europe's Convention on Human Rights and exemplified in the judicial history of the European Court of Human Rights form the building blocks on which the Council builds its Convention on Cybercrime. States are legally bound to guarantee their citizens certain rights (privacy, expression, religion, association, etc.) unless there is a social pressing need for State interference. Such interference must be in accordance with domestic law, be necessary in a democratic society, and conform to the principle of proportionality (the measure or provision must be proportionate to its aim). The four States signing the Cybercrime Convention that are not bound by the Convention for Human Rights (Canada, Japan, South Africa, and the United States) are, however, bound by their accession to the United Nations Charter and their adherence to the Universal Declaration of Human Rights and the International Covenant on Civil and Political Rights. Those international accords promote the recognition, respect, and protection of international human rights, including but not limited to freedom from arbitrary interference with one's privacy and freedom of expression.[290] Additionally, these rights (as expressed in the Universal Declaration of Human Rights) are now part of customary international law and enjoy universal application and enforcement.[291]

---

287. *GILC Member Letter* of Dec. 12, 2000, *supra* note 244.

288. *Id.*

289. Comments of the American Civil Liberties Union, *supra* note 25.

290. *See* Charter of the United Nations, June 26, 1945, 59 Stat. 1031, T.S. No. 993, *entered into force* Oct. 24, 1945. ("We the peoples of the United Nations determine to reaffirm faith in fundamental human rights, in the dignity and worth of the human person, in the equal rights of men and women and of nations large and small."); *see also* Universal Declaration of Human Rights, *supra* note 126 (protecting the right to life, liberty and the security of the person and the right to freedom from arbitrary interference with his privacy, family, home, or correspondence); *and* International Covenant on Civil and Political Rights, G.A. res. 2200A (XXI), 21 U.N. GAOR Supp. (No. 16) at 52, U.N. Doc. A/6316 (1966), 999 U.N.T.S. 171, *entered into force* Mar. 23, 1976, Art. 17 (protecting freedom from arbitrary or unlawful interference with one's privacy, family, home or correspondence) and Art. 19 (freedom to hold opinions without interference).

291. *See* Filartiga v. Pena-Irala, 630 F.2d 876, 883 (2d Cir. 1980) (holding that for a Declaration to be recognized as expressing customary law, it must "create an expectation of adherence" and that expectation must be "gradually justified by State practice"). The

Second, Paragraph 1 of Article 15 of the Cybercrime Convention explicitly provides for the protection of human rights and liberties, "including rights arising pursuant to obligations [each Party] has undertaken under the 1950 Council of Europe Convention for the Protection of Human Rights and Fundamental Freedoms, the 1966 United Nations International Covenant on Civil and Political Civil Rights, and other applicable international human rights instruments."[292] The *Explanatory Memorandum* clarifies that the "application of the powers and procedures" specifically described in the Convention "shall include conditions or safeguards . . . that balance the requirements of law enforcement with the protection of human rights and liberties."[293] Each Party's adherence to one or more of the above-mentioned international human rights instruments thus establishes a floor of protection for those rights.

Third, Convention procedures and powers shall "incorporate the principle of proportionality,"[294] which derives directly from the European Convention on Human Rights and is applicable to those European countries adhering to the Council of Europe. Stated simply, "[T]he power or procedure shall be proportional to the nature and circumstances of the offence."[295] Other non-European States will apply their own related principles of law and impose constitutional limitations and requirements of reasonableness on those procedures.[296]

Finally, ensuring that minimum standards for the protection of human rights have been implemented rests on the Parties themselves through the application of whatever dispute resolution mechanism has been made available. In the case of the Cybercrime Convention, any dispute arising between Parties regarding the interpretation or application of the Convention's provisions shall be submitted to one of three entities for peaceful settlement: (1) the European Committee on Crime Problems; (2) an arbitral tribunal whose decision shall be binding on the Parties to the dispute; or (3) to the International Court of Justice itself.[297]

U.N. Universal Declaration of Human Rights enjoys that status.

   292. Cybercrime Convention, *supra* note 225, art. 15, ¶ 1.

   293. Explanatory Memorandum, *supra* note 222, ¶ 146.

   294. Cybercrime Convention, *supra* note 225, art. 15, ¶ 1.

   295. Explanatory Memorandum, *supra* note 222, ¶ 146.

   296. *Id.*

   297. Cybercrime Convention, *supra* note 225, art. 45.

VI. CONCLUSION

Rapidly advancing information technologies continually transform our society. From wireless modems on laptops that can tap into the Web to hand-held electronic data organizers, electronic technology has pervaded almost every aspect of our daily life. The telecommunications sector, in particular, has been revolutionized by incredibly small yet extraordinarily powerful microprocessors that enable the transmission of vast amounts of text, voice, music, and pictures, both still and moving. We experience virtually limitless possibilities in exchanging and disseminating information. The World Wide Web has illuminated every corner of the globe.

There is a darker side to this, however. Child pornography, once almost completely stamped out in the United States, has taken on new life in cyberspace communities devoted to the sexual abuse of children at the hands of pedophiles, men who not only fantasize about sex with children, but who constantly clamor for new pictures to whet their near insatiable appetites. Although child pornography has been outlawed in its more normal media (still pictures and movies), the criminalization of "computer-generated images of fictitious children engaged in imaginary but explicit sexual conduct" has sparked a fierce debate between would-be regulators and civil libertarians. And because the "scene of the crime" defies definition and jurisdiction, how to contain the modern-day equivalent of the Black Plague and still protect privacy and freedom of expression interests remains a serious matter of contention.

The Council of Europe's Convention on Cybercrime is the first international and legally binding instrument to criminalize electronic child pornography. It establishes universal standards and definitions for that conduct, mandates national enforcement of those standards, and balances the expected range of protections and safeguards of international human rights with measures appropriately fine-tuned to deal with the elusive nature of child pornography on the Internet. Critics of the Convention on Cybercrime contend that its provisions will severely constrict the absolute freedom necessary for the Internet to survive, inhibit its growth by making service providers themselves liable for crimes committed through their networks of which they might have no knowledge, and effectively destroy the privacy of computerized communications.

However, the Convention on Cybercrime is firmly embedded in those fundamental freedoms and human rights which have been championed so strongly by the European Convention for Human Rights and stalwartly upheld by over forty years of distinguished jurisprudence from the European Court of Human Rights. Moreover, the Convention on Cybercrime draws strength from the United Nations Charter, the Universal Declaration of Human Rights, the International Covenant on Civil and Political Rights, and other international human rights instruments. If the Convention has a weakness, it is that the crime of electronic child pornography is categorized as one of several "content-related computer offenses" and, as such, does not enjoy the exclusive attention that the severity and egregious ramifications of its perpetrations warrants.

The provisions and measures adopted by the Convention that are specifically aimed at criminalizing and sanctioning electronic child pornography are groundbreaking. They provide the first solid legal framework for proscribing and punishing a real crime committed in a virtual jurisdiction at each step in the chain, from production to possession. Not only is computer-generated child pornography itself a crime, in the hands of a pedophile it becomes "a tool for the future criminal abuse and exploitation of other children."[298] Until it is outlawed universally, and regardless of how or where it occurs, children will be robbed of their childhoods, and they will cry "in the playtime of the others, in the country of the free."[299]

VII. POSTSCRIPT

The United States Supreme Court's recent decision striking down certain portions of the 1996 Child Pornography Prevention Act (CPPA) compels the addition of this postscript. On April 16, 2002, in *Ashcroft v. The Free Speech Coalition*,[300] the High Court declared as unconstitutional certain phrases which go to the heart of the definition of computer-generated child pornography. Relying on two decisions that established model definitions for obscenity (*Miller v. California*[301]) and child pornography (*New York v. Ferber*[302]), the Court held that the CPPA's attempt to expand those

---

298. Akdeniz, *supra* note 104.

299. *See* BROWNING, *supra* note 1.

300. Ashcroft v. The Free Speech Coalition, 122 S. Ct. 1389 (2002), 2002 WL 552476 (U.S.).

301. Miller v. California, 413 U.S. 15, 93 S. Ct. 2607 (1973). In *Miller*, the defendant was convicted of mailing unsolicited sexually explicit brochures to a restaurant in Newport Beach, California, thereby violating a California statute. The brochures depicted explicit sexual activity between men and women in groups of two or more, with the genitalia of the participants prominently displayed. In vacating the California Appellate Court's affirmation of that conviction, the Supreme Court established a three-pronged test for obscenity. Works would be considered "obscene" if, according to the judgment of an average person applying community standards, such works (1) appealed to the "prurient interest;" (2) depicted or described in an offensive way sexual conduct as defined by the applicable state statute; and (3) when taken as a whole, lacked "serious literary, artistic, political or scientific value." *Id.* at 17, 18, 24.

302. New York v. Ferber, 458 U.S. 747, 102 S. Ct. 3348 (1982). In *Ferber*, a bookstore promoter was convicted of selling films depicting young boys masturbating, in violation of a New York statute proscribing promoting the sexual performance by a child under the age of sixteen. The statute defined "sexual performance" as any performance that included sexual conduct by a child, and "sexual conduct" as "actual or simulated sexual intercourse, deviate sexual intercourse, sexual bestiality, masturbation, sado-masochistic abuse, or lewd exhibition of the genitals." In formulating what constituted child pornography, the *Ferber* Court focused on the *actual* participation of a child in the production of sexually explicit material, which resulted in the sexual exploitation of that

definitions to include a "virtual" aspect exceeded the bounds previously set and did not pass constitutional muster.[303] Specifically, "computer-generated images, as well as images produced by more traditional means, do not involve, let alone harm, any children in the production process."[304]

The definition that "virtual child pornography" cannot harm, exploit, or abuse children in any way because no real child is involved in the production of such material (a definition directly derived from *Ferber*[305]) is diametrically opposed to the concept expressed by the Council of Europe in its Cybercrime Convention, which contains language nearly identical to that ruled unconstitutional by the United States Supreme Court.[306] (The Convention's language pertinent to virtual child pornography states, in part, that child pornography shall include material that depicts "a person appearing to be a minor engaged in sexually explicit conduct" and "realistic images representing a minor engaged in sexually explicit conduct."[307] Compare the relevant statutory language of the CPPA that defines child pornography as any visual depiction or computer-generated image or picture of a person that "is, or appears to be, a minor engaging in sexually explicit conduct."[308]) This legal divergence between the Council of Europe and the Supreme Court is understandable when one considers the difference in approach adopted by the two institutions. The Council of Europe's broadly encompassing definition of virtual child pornography is footed on the concept that the nature of the targeted audience of sexually explicit material is critical in determining whether or not the material is to be proscribed by

---

child on two levels. First, material produced with the participation of children formed a permanent record of that participation, aggravating the psychological, emotional, and mental harm to the child's health. Second, the ongoing production of child pornographic materials continuously fueled demand for more material and resulted in further exploitation and abuse. In the Court's eyes, the only remedy was to completely dismantle the distribution network necessary to market the product by imposing severe criminal sanctions on those involved in promoting such material in any fashion. Lamentably, the Court suggested that either employing a younger-looking person or "simulation outside of the prohibition of the statute" (i.e., virtual imaging) would be constitutionally acceptable alternatives. *Id.* at 747, 759-60, 763.

303. The definition of virtual child pornography and the proscription of pandering of virtual child pornography are codified at 18 U.S.C. § 2256(8)(B) and 18 U.S.C. § 2256(8)(D), respectively. In part, those provisions state:

"(8) child pornography" means any visual depiction, including any photograph, film, video, picture, or computer or computer-generated image or picture, whether made or produced by electronic, mechanical, or other means, of sexually explicit conduct, where . . . (B) such visual depiction is, or appears to be, or a minor engaging in sexually explicit conduct; (D) such visual depiction is advertised, promoted, presented, described, or distributed in such a manner that conveys the impression that the material is or contains a visual depiction of a minor engaging in sexually explicit conduct . . . ."

304. *Ashcroft*, 122 S. Ct. at 1397.

305. *See Ferber*, 458 U.S. at 747, 759-60, 763.

306. *See* Explanatory Memorandum, *supra* note 222.

307. Cybercrime Convention, *supra* note 225, art. 9, ¶ 2(b), (c).

308. *See* 18 U.S.C. § 2256 (8)(B), (D).

law.[309] The United States Supreme Court's narrower definition dictates that, unless a real child is used in the production of potentially pornographic material, there is no exploitation or abuse, and thus the material remains protected by the First Amendment (as long as it does not run afoul of the *Miller* definition of obscenity[310]).

This ideological skirmish carries significant implications for the United States and any other country signatory of the Cybercrime Convention. The definition of child pornography detailed in Paragraph 2 of Article 9 of the Convention expressly includes material that visually depicts, *inter alia*, "a person appearing to be a minor engaged in sexually explicit conduct" or "realistic images representing a minor engaged in sexually explicit conduct."[311] The Council itself correctly recognized the equally harmful effect that such "imaginary" images might have:

> "[W]hile not necessarily creating harm to the 'child' depicted in the material, as there might not be a real child, [computer-generated images or morphed images of natural persons] might be used to encourage or seduce children into participating in such acts, and hence form part of a subculture favouring child abuse."[312]

That such harm may be merely "probable" is sufficient, for the Council, to warrant such a definition. And, when we consider the electronic and technological expertise that pervades virtual pedophile communities, such a definition – and the criminalization accompanying it – seems appropriate and all too necessary to ward off future permutations of child pornography that escape legal prosecution under present standards.

The majority opinion in *Ashcroft*, on the other hand, negates the possibility that the mere viewing of computer-generated images can lead to criminal conduct, claiming that "the causal link [between such images and actual instances of child abuse] is contingent and indirect."[313] There are indications to the contrary. In Japan, pornographic comic books depicting schoolgirls dressed in their uniforms and in obscene sexual poses are extraordinarily popular with adults, selling in the millions.[314] One of the most popular "sexual activities" of Japanese businessmen is "enjo kosai," (compensated dating), or schoolgirl prostitution.[315] Whether the comic books give birth to the behavior or vice versa is of no import; each reinforces the other.

---

309. *See* HARRIS ET AL., *supra* note 123.

310. *Ashcroft*, 122 S. Ct. at 1396.

311. Cybercrime Convention, *supra* note 225, art. 9, ¶ 2(b), (c).

312. Explanatory Memorandum, *supra* note 222, ¶ 102.

313. *Ashcroft*, 122 S. Ct. at 1402.

314. *See* THE ECONOMIST, *supra* note 5.

315. *Id.*

In hearings before the Senate Judiciary Committee on the CPPA, Dr. Victor Cline, a clinical psychologist and psychotherapist specializing in, among other things, the treatment of sexual compulsions and addictions, stated emphatically:

> "[P]edophiles, in my experience, use child pornography and/or create it to stimulate and whet their sexual appetites which they masturbate to then later use as a model for their own sexual acting out with children ... The man always escalates to more deviant material, and the acting out continues and escalates despite very painful consequences ... Some also use it to seduce children into engaging in sexual acts with themselves."[316]

Bruce A. Taylor, President and Chief Counsel of the National Law Center for Children and Families, argued convincingly during the same hearings that images created with modern graphics programs are undetectable from the "real thing," and are "every bit as dangerous to society as actual child pornography."[317] Organizations on the frontlines in the investigation and prosecution of sexual abuse of children continually see evidence of the direct and proximate role that computer-generated child pornography plays in that abuse. The Office of Juvenile Justice and Delinquency Prevention of the United States Department of Justice, in cooperation with the Federal Bureau of Investigation, has published a portable guide outlining "the highly predictable behavioral patterns of preferential sex offenders in relation to their use of computers."[318] The National Center for Missing and Exploited Children, in its manual for law enforcement officers investigating the sexual exploitation of children by acquaintance molesters, details how the use of computers and of computer-generated images are important tools of seduction in the pedophile's arsenal.[319] Moreover, as a psychosexual disorder with a "pathological use of

---

316. *Child Pornography Prevention Act of 1995: Hearing on S. 1237 Before the S. Jud. Comm.*, 104th Cong. (1996) (statement of Dr. Victor Cline, Emeritus Professor in Psychology, University of Utah, clinical psychologist & psychotherapist) [hereinafter *Senate Hearings*] *available at*, LEXIS, Federal Document Clearing House Congressional Testimony, June 4, 1996, Tuesday.

317. *Id.* (statement of Bruce A. Taylor, President & Chief Counsel of the Nat. L. Center for Children and Families).

318. *See* U.S. Dept of Justice Office of Juvenile Justice and Delinquency Prevention, *Use of Computers in the Sexual Exploitation of Children,* authored by Daniel S. Armagh, Director, National Center for Prosecution of Child Abuse; Nick L. Battaglia, Sergeant, San Jose Police Department, San Jose, California; and Kenneth V. Lanning, M.S., former Supervisory Special Agent, FBI, National Center for the Analysis of Violent Crime, FBI Academy, Quantico, Virginia.

319. *See generally* National Center for Missing and Exploited Children, *Child Molesters: A Behavioral Analysis* 70 (2001) ("Child pornography and erotica are used ... to lower children's inhibitions ... If other children are involved, the child might be led to

sexual fantasies, behaviors, or objects as a stimulus for sexual excitement" focused on prepubescent children (generally thirteen years or younger in age),[320] pedophilia manifests itself characteristically in need-driven behavior that is uncontrollable by the pedophile, and is "persistent, compulsive, and fantasy-driven."[321] The pedophiles' "criminal sexual behavior is rooted in their sexual fantasies and need to turn fantasy into reality."[322] This pathology suggests that reclassifying pedophilia as a compulsive illness, where the gap between "fantasy" (thought) and "reality" (criminal behavior) is practically non-existent, would be prudent for law enforcement purposes. Thus, the nexus between "thoughts or impulses and any resulting child abuse"[323] would form a direct link between virtual images and criminal conduct. The acknowledgment of that link would compel the subsequent legal recognition of virtual images as an instrumentality of child abuse, thus warranting appropriate criminalization.[324]

At least one Supreme Court Justice believes that such a link exists and offers an alternate "narrowing" interpretation of the CPPA language struck down that would pass constitutional muster. In her dissenting opinion, Justice O'Connor agrees that child pornographic images may be used by pedophiles to seduce young children.[325] Further, she suggests that the CPPA's phrase "appears to be ... of" is better, and more narrowly, interpreted as meaning "virtually indistinguishable from."[326] Specifically, she writes:

> Not only does the text of the statute comfortably bear this narrowing interpretation, the interpretation comports with the language that Congress repeatedly used in its findings of fact ... Finally, to the extent that the phrase "appears to be ... of" is ambiguous, the narrowing interpretation avoids constitutional problems such as overbreadth and lack of narrow tailoring.[327]

---

believe that the activity is acceptable."), *available at* http://www.missingchildren.org (last visited Jan. 18, 2003) [hereinafter *Child Molesters*].

320. AMERICAN PSYCHIATRIC ASSOCIATION: *Diagnostic and Statistical Manual of Mental Disorders* 568, 571, Fourth Edition, Text Revision, Washington, D.C., American Psychiatric Association, 2000 [hereinafter *DSM-IV-TR*].

321. *Child Molesters, supra* note 318, at 24.

322. *Id.*

323. *Ashcroft*, 122 S. Ct. at 1403.

324. *See generally* Child Molesters, *supra* note 318 (discussing the behavioral characteristics of pedophiles who use child pornography as part of their need-driven sexual ritual in acting out their fantasies); *see also* DSM-IV-TR, *supra* note 318, at 78 (defining the clinical traits and characteristics of pedophilia for diagnostic purposes).

325. *Ashcroft*, 122 S.Ct. at 1409 (O'Connor, J., dissenting).

326. *Id.*

327. *Id.*

Once the Cybercrime Convention becomes effective and projects into international law its definition of computer-generated child pornography, it is logical to infer that any State signing the Convention that does not fully apply that definition through its legislative process will more than likely become a nation host to a myriad of pedophile and commercial pornographic sites. The United States is not exempt from this disturbing prospect. Given the *Ashcroft* decision, it is almost unavoidable that the United States will make a reservation to Art. 9, para. 2(b) and 2(d) of the Convention on Cybercrime[328] and will not apply the definition of virtual child pornography espoused in the Convention. Any new United States legislation enacted to replace the offending parts of the CPPA will, of necessity, contain more narrowly tailored language than that originally contained, thus leaving a legislative gap between domestic usage (virtual images are only thought that does not give rise to criminal conduct) and international custom (fictitious pornographic images are just as harmful to children as real images and therefore equally proscribed). This legal lacuna will make the United States an appealing playground for pedophiliac virtual "frolicking." Horrifically, pedophiles and commercial pornographers will be able to exchange and distribute "computer-generated images of fictitious children engaged in explicit but imaginary sexual conduct"[329] *legally*. Those images will fuel the continued global degradation, exploitation, and abuse of children *legally*. Every child will be exposed to extreme moral and physical depravity *legally*. Neither the United States, nor any other country dedicated to the protection of its children, should be a party to such subversion.

---

328. *See* Explanatory Memorandum, *supra* notes 222; Ashcroft, 122 S.Ct. at 1396.

329. The phrase is based on the Ninth Circuit's opinion in The Free Speech Coalition v. Reno, 198 F.3d 1083, 1086 (9th Cir. 1999) ("[T]he First Amendment prohibits Congress from enacting a statute that makes criminal the generation of images of fictitious children engaged in imaginary but explicit sexual conduct."). Additional phrasing was culled from the author's research. *See, e.g.,* Alison R. Gladowsky, Note, *Has the Computer Revolution Placed Our Children in Danger? A Closer Look at the Child Pornography Prevention Act of 1996*, 8 Cardozo Women's L.J. 21, 32 ("The court held that the First Amendment prohibits Congress from enacting a statute that criminalizes the generation of images of fictitious children engaged in imaginary but explicit sexual conduct."); Rikki Solowey, Comment, *A Question of Equivalence: Expanding the Definition of Child Pornography to Encompass "Virtual" Computer-generated Images*, 4 Tul. J. Tech. & Intell. Prop. 161, 179-80 ("Congress also found that when child pornography is used as a means of seducing or breaking down a child's inhibitions, the images are equally as effective regardless of whether they are real or computer-generated photographs."); *see also supra* note 303 and accompanying text regarding the original codified definitions of virtual child pornography rendered unconstitutional by Ashcroft v. The Free Speech Coalition.

[10]

Internet Hate Speech: The European Framework and the Emerging American Haven

Christopher D. Van Blarcum[*]

Table of Contents

    *   Candidate for J.D., Washington and Lee University School of Law, May 2005; B.A.,
The George Washington University, June 2001. I would like to thank all the people who have
made this Note possible. I would especially like to thank Professor Joan Shaughnessy, Carter
Williams, and Kevin White for their instrumental feedback. I would also like to thank Professor
Ronald J. Krotozynski, Professor Frederick Kirgis, and Bruce Boyden for their advice. Finally,
I would like to thank my parents, David and Linda Van Blarcum, without whose guidance and
support this Note would not be possible.

In this advance, the frontier is the outer edge of the wave—the meeting point between savagery and civilization.

Frederick Jackson Turner, The Closing of the American Frontier.[1]

I. Introduction

The civilization of the Internet has been the great quandary facing Internet regulators over the past decade. The Internet, like Turner's frontier,[2] was not a *tabula rasa*—at its formation, traditional laws were still available.[3] But the Internet raised new problems that made the enforcement of old laws problematic, and the Internet soon developed its reputation as an entity free

---

1. FREDERICK JACKSON TURNER, THE FRONTIER IN AMERICAN HISTORY 3 (Henry Holt and Co. 1921) (1920). *But see* Paul Weingarten, *Historians Clash Over Less-Romantic View of Old West*, CHI. TRIB., Jan. 28, 1990, at C6, 1990 WL 2939410 (stating that many new historians assert that Turner's version of the frontier is "racist, sexist, overly romantic and simply wrong").

2. *See* TURNER, *supra* note 1, at 38 ("There is not *tabula rasa*. The stubborn American environment is there with its imperious summons to accept its conditions; the inherited ways of doing things are also there . . .").

3. *See* Jack L. Goldsmith, *Against Cyberanarchy*, 65 U. CHI. L. REV. 1199, 1250 (1998) ("Cyberspace transactions are no different from 'real space' transnational transactions.").

from government regulation.[4] The greatest obstacles to enforcement of traditional laws are the Internet's anonymity and its multijurisdictionality.[5] Anonymity makes it hard for local prosecutors and victims to discover the identity of the party responsible for illegal conduct.[6] Even if the party can be identified, however, multijurisdictionality means that the prosecutor or victim may not have jurisdiction or face great obstacles in bringing suit against the offending party.[7]

The problem with enforcement of the inherited laws was not so much a product of a defect in the language of the laws as it was a product of the inherent structure of the Internet.[8] As a result, it should come as no surprise that despite unilateral efforts by the United States and almost every other nation to attempt to civilize the Internet, "the closing of the Internet frontier" remains far from a reality. Although governments have extended traditional laws to the Internet and have attempted to pass new laws regulating the Internet, these laws have had limited effectiveness reigning in unwanted conduct.[9]

The global accessibility of information on the Internet allows an individual or a business that disagrees with the rules in one jurisdiction to move to a more lenient country and resume its business with its website remaining accessible for viewing in the country it fled.[10] The global nature of the Internet results in those countries with less civilized Internet standards becoming havens for actors who wish to continue their "savage" manners untouched by the laws of the objecting country.

---

4. *See* JOSEPH KIZZA, CIVILIZING THE INTERNET xi (1998) (stating that the Internet is a place "where laws are self-made and observed (or broken) at will").

5. *See* Lawrence Lessig, *The Law of the Horse: What Cyberlaw May Teach*, 113 HARV. L. REV. 501, 505 (1999) (stating that many believe that "[t]he anonymity and multi-jurisdictionality of cyberspace makes [sic] control by government in cyberspace impossible").

6. *See* Jay Krasovec, *Cyberspace: The Final Frontier, For Regulation?*, 31 AKRON L. REV. 101, 109–10 (1997) (stating that the use of pseudonyms and remailer services allows individuals to engage in communication on the Internet anonymously).

7. *See* Goldsmith, *supra* note 3, at 1216 ("The Island of Tobago can *enact* a law that purports to bind the rights of the whole world. But the effective scope of this law depends on Tobago's ability to *enforce* it.").

8. *See* Lessig, *supra* note 5, at 506 (asserting that those who believe government control of the Internet is impossible are wrong because they erroneously assume that the architecture of the Internet is fixed and cannot be changed).

9. *See, e.g.*, Metro-Goldwyn-Mayer Studios, Inc. v. Grokster, 259 F. Supp. 2d 1029, 1045–46 (C.D. Cal. 2003) (dismissing a copyright infringement suit filed against distributors of peer-to-peer file-sharing software because the software had noninfringing uses and the distributors had no control over the files shared by users of the software).

10. *See* Agence-France Press, *Neo-Nazi Web Sites Reported to Flee Germany*, N.Y. TIMES, Aug. 21, 2000, at A5 (reporting that ninety rightist groups had transferred their sites to the United States in the wake of German authorities cracking down on Internet hate speech).

The "haven" problem can generally be avoided in two ways. The first is for the victimized country to attempt to block odious content from reaching its Internet browsers. Spain has recently implemented this approach by passing legislation authorizing judges to block sites that do not comply with Spanish national law.[11] This approach, however, is onerous on the victimized country, as it forces the country to search out the content and block it, without placing a deterrent on the producer of the content to refrain from putting the content on the Internet in the first place.

The other option to solve the "haven" problem is in the form of regional and multilateral efforts to regulate the Internet. The greatest benefit of a multilateral compact is its ability to negate the multijurisdiction problem. If the offending party is located in a country also a party to the multilateral compact, it becomes much easier for the victimized country to push the host country to take action against the offender or to extradite the offender to the victimized country. The removal of the multijurisdiction obstacle, it is hoped, will make the laws much easier to enforce and is seen as more efficient than unilateral blocking of sites because it attempts to deter the objectionable content from being placed on the Internet from the outset.[12]

The first major multilateral compact aimed at Internet crimes was the Council of Europe's Convention on Cybercrime.[13] The purpose of the Convention on Cybercrime is to pursue "a common criminal policy aimed at the protection of society against cybercrime . . . by adopting appropriate legislation and fostering international co-operation" that defends copyright holders by making the laws more uniform and providing for international cooperation in enforcement.[14] The Convention on Cybercrime focuses primarily on infringements of copyright, computer-related fraud, child pornography, and violations of network security.[15] As of January 11, 2004, thirty-three countries

---

11. *See* Julia Scheeres, *Europeans Outlaw Net Hate Speech*, WIRED.COM, *at* http://www.wired.com/news/business/0,1367,56294,00.html (Nov. 9, 2002) ("Spain recently passed legislation authorizing judges to shut down Spanish sites and block access to U.S. Web pages that don't comply with national laws.") (on file with the Washington and Lee Law Review).

12. *See* Catherine P. Heaven, Note, *A Proposal for Removing Road Blocks From the Information Superhighway By Using an Integrated International Approach to Internet Jurisdiction*, 10 MINN. J. GLOBAL TRADE 373, 400–01 (2001) (suggesting the creation of a regulatory body to propose Internet regulations for the globe).

13. Convention on Cybercrime, European Treaty Series, No. 185, *at* http://conventions.coe.int/Treaty/en/Treaties/Html/185.htm (Nov. 23, 2001) (on file with the Washington and Lee Law Review).

14. *Id.*

15. Summary of Convention on Cybercrime, Council of Europe, *at* http://conventions.coe.int/Treaty/en/Summaries/Html/185.htm (last visited Jan. 27, 2005) (on file with the

have signed the Convention, including some nonmembers of the Council of Europe (the United States, Japan, South Africa, and Canada).[16]

As an addendum to the Convention on Cybercrime, the Council of Europe recently has proposed an additional protocol to the Convention (Additional Protocol) that concerns Internet hate speech. That protocol is the focus of this Note. This Note first discusses the problem of hate speech generally[17] and then examines the Council of Europe and the relationship of the United States to that body.[18] This Note then details the provisions of the Additional Protocol and examines how they will affect current law in Europe.[19] It then analyzes the ability of an implemented Protocol to reach conduct originating in the United States and considers whether the Protocol will cause the United States to become a haven for Internet hate speech.[20] Lastly, this Note examines solutions that the United States and Europe could adopt to reduce the probability of the United States becoming a haven for Internet hate speech.[21]

II. Hate Speech Regulations Preceding the Protocol

European regulation of hate speech can be traced to the after-effects of World War II. After the Holocaust, European countries moved to take steps to prevent similar atrocities from ever happening again, and hate speech was targeted for elimination. As a consequence of the interest in proscribing hate speech, many countries passed laws proscribing the speech and took part in international agreements aimed at eliminating the speech. The primary international agreement on hate speech is Article 4 of the International

---

Washington and Lee Law Review). The Summary states:

> The Convention is the first international treaty on crimes committed via the Internet and other computer networks, dealing particularly with infringements of copyright, computer-related fraud, child pornography and violations of network security. It also contains a series of powers and procedures such as the search of computer networks and interception.

Id.

16. *See* Chart of Signatures and Ratifications of a Treaty, Convention on Cybercrime, European Treaty Series, No. 185, *at* http://conventions.coe.int/Treaty/Commun/ChercheSig. asp?NT=185&CM=14&DF=27/01/05&CL=ENG (last visited Jan. 27, 2005) (showing a table of countries that have signed or ratified the Convention) (on file with the Washington and Lee Law Review).

17. *Infra* Part II.

18. *Infra* Part III.

19. *Infra* Part IV.

20. *Infra* Part V.

21. *Infra* Part VI.

Convention on the Elimination of All Forms of Racial Discrimination (ICERD).[22] Article 4 provides that parties shall (1) criminalize the dissemination of ideas based on racial superiority or hatred, (2) declare illegal and prohibit organizations that promote and incite racial discrimination and shall recognize participation in such organizations or activities as an offense punishable by law, and (3) prohibit public authorities and public institutions from promoting or inciting racial discrimination.[23] As of January 1, 2000, 155 states have signed ICERD, including all but four members of the Council of Europe.[24] The list of countries that have ratified ICERD includes the United States, but the United States made a reservation indicating its refusal to undertake any measures that violate the First Amendment.[25]

As a result of ICERD, all European nations have adopted legislation aimed at repressing hateful speech.[26] France's extensive legislation on combating racism includes criminalizing the following: (1) inciting hatred or discrimination on basis of race; (2) wearing emblems reminiscent of crimes against humanity; and (3) defending or disputing crimes against humanity.[27] The criminal law in Germany makes it a crime to incite hatred and violence against segments of the population and to disseminate publications that are morally harmful to young persons (including those that stimulate or incite racial hatred).[28] The laws

---

22. International Convention on the Elimination of All Forms of Racial Discrimination, Mar. 7, 1966, 660 U.N.T.S. 195.

23. *Id.* at 220.

24. *See* SWISS INSTITUTE OF COMPARATIVE LAW, EUROPEAN COMMISSION AGAINST RACISM AND INTOLERANCE, LEGAL INSTRUMENTS TO COMBAT RACISM ON THE INTERNET 66 (2000) [hereinafter LEGAL INSTRUMENTS] (stating that 155 states were party to ICERD as of January 1, 2000, including all member states of the Council of Europe, except Andorra, Liechenstein, Moldova, and San Marino), *available at* http://www.coe.int/T/E/human_rights/Ecri/1-ECRI/3-General_themes/3-Legal_Research/2-Combat_racism_on_Internet/CRI(2000)27.pdf (on file with the Washington and Lee Law Review).

25. *See id.* at 67 ("The United States of America indicated its refusal to accept any obligation under Art. 4 which would require restriction of the protection afforded by its constitution and laws to the freedoms of speech, expression and association.").

26. *See id.* at 13 (stating that its previous report showed that "all European countries have at their disposal a more or less effective legislative arsenal to repress hateful expressions" and that a minimum standard imposed by the United Nations Convention on the Elimination of Racial Hatred is applicable to hateful expressions disseminated via the Internet).

27. *See* SWISS INSTITUTE OF COMPARATIVE LAW, EUROPEAN COMMISSION AGAINST RACISM AND INTOLERANCE, LEGAL MEASURES TO COMBAT RACISM ON THE INTERNET (2001) [hereinafter LEGAL MEASURES] (documenting the criminal laws in France designed to combat racism), *available at* http://www.coe.int/T/E/human_rights/Ecri/1-ECRI/3-General_themes/3-Legal_Re search/1-National_legal_measur es/default.asp#TopOfPage (on file with the Washington and Lee Law Review).

28. *See id.* (documenting the criminal laws in Germany designed to combat racism). For a general discussion of Germany's laws combating hate speech, see generally Ronald J.

governing hate speech have generally been found to extend to the Internet to the extent the legislation is written in a technically neutral manner.[29]

Given this background, the laws necessary to combat racism exist in Europe. The anonymity and multijurisdictionality of the Internet, however, have proved problematic for enforcement of these laws. Although all European countries regulate hate speech, they each have different laws and different levels of enforcement, frustrating countries with stronger hate speech regulations.[30] As a result, in order to combat hate speech most effectively, European nations desired a uniform law. The Council of Europe was given the task of drafting such a law.

III. The Council of Europe

A. Functions of the Council of Europe

Established in 1949, the Council of Europe promotes intergovernmental cooperation in securing democracy in Europe and in preventing the recurrence of gross violations of human rights.[31] Although the Council of Europe had only ten founding members, it now has forty-five members, all of which are located in the European region.[32] The Council of Europe has a larger membership than

---

Krotoszynski, *A Comparative Perspective on the First Amendment: Free Speech, Militant Democracy, and the Primacy of Dignity as a Preferred Constitutional Value in Germany,* 78 TUL. L. REV. 1549 (2004).

29. *See* LEGAL INSTRUMENTS, *supra* note 24, at 13 ("As a general rule, the laws governing the right of communication are drafted in a technically neutral manner, which takes into account any dissemination of information irrespective of the medium; consequently, they are fully applicable to messages distributed on the Internet.").

30. *See id.* ("[T]he problem therefore lies not so much in the absence of adequate material rules as in obstacles to their application in the form of characteristics peculiar to the network of networks, namely its polycentric structure, its ubiquity and the cover of anonymity."); *see also infra* notes 47–52 and accompanying text (detailing the problems found by the Council of Europe in its reports on hate speech).

31. *See* CONNIE PECK, SUSTAINABLE PEACE: THE ROLE OF THE UN AND REGIONAL ORGANIZATIONS IN PREVENTING CONFLICT 101 (1998) (stating that the Council of Europe "was set up in response to Europe's traumatic experience with the Nazi regime, and its main aim was to secure democracy in Europe and to prevent the recurrence of gross violations of human rights").

32. *See id.* at 101–02 (stating that the Council of Europe had ten founding members); *see also* About the Council of Europe, Council of Europe, *at* http://www.coe.int/T/e/Com/about_coe/ (last visited Jan. 27, 2005) (stating that the Council of Europe currently has forty-six members, including twenty-one from Central and Eastern Europe) (on file with the Washington and Lee Law Review). The Council of Europe also has one candidate for membership, Belarus, and five observer countries—Canada, the Holy See, Japan, Mexico, and the United States. *See*

the European Union, which has only twenty-five members.[33] For membership, the Council requires a country to achieve and maintain certain standards of democracy and human rights; these standards include a democratically-elected parliament, a legal system in line with democratic principles, and a system for the protection of national minorities.[34] Besides size of membership, the Council of Europe also differs from the European Union in another way: Actions by the Council of Europe have no legal effect without signature and ratification by the member countries of the Council.[35] As a result, the Council of Europe is primarily a treaty-making entity.[36] Since its formation, the Council of Europe has concluded 195 treaties.[37]

B. The Relationship of the United States to the Council of Europe

Although the United States is not a member of the Council of Europe, participation in the Council of Europe's treaty-making process is not exclusive to its members.[38] The Council of Europe has granted the United States observer status, which allows the United States to appoint a permanent observer to the Council of Europe; however, observer status does not give the United States a seat on the Committee of Ministers or in the Council's Parliamentary Assembly.[39] The Council of Europe invites nonmember states to sign and ratify

The Council of Europe's Member States, The Council of Europe, *at* http://www.coe.int/T/E/Com/About_Coe/Member_states/default.asp (last visited Jan. 27, 2005) (listing the members of Council of Europe) (on file with the Washington and Lee Law Review).

33.   The EU at a Glance, Europa, *at* http://europa.eu.int/abc/keyfigures/index_en.htm (last visited Jan. 27, 2005) (on file with the Washington and Lee Law Review).

34.   *See* PECK, *supra* note 31, at 102–03 (stating the requirements to become a member of the Council of Europe).

35.   *See* JÖRG POLAKIEWICZ, TREATY-MAKING IN THE COUNCIL OF EUROPE 10 (1999) ("It should be stressed that the treaties are not legal instruments of the Organisation as such, but owe their existence to the consent of those member states that sign and ratify them.").

36.   *See id.* at 7 (stating that "treaties are the most visible contribution of the Council of Europe").

37.   *See* Complete List of the Council of Europe's Treaties, The Council of Europe, *at* http://conventions.coe.int/Treaty/Common/ListeTraites.asp?CM=8&CL=ENG (last visited Jan. 27, 2005) (stating that 196 treaties have been concluded since the formation the Council of Europe) (on file with the Washington and Lee Law Review).

38.   *See* POLAKIEWICZ, *supra* note 35, at 33 (stating that "[p]articipation in most Council of Europe treaties is not exclusively limited to the member states of the Council of Europe").

39.   *See* The United States of America and the Council of Europe, The Council of Europe, *at* http://www.coe.int/T/E/Com/About_Coe/Member_states/e_usa.asp (last visited Jan. 27, 2005) (stating that countries with observer status can "appoint a permanent observer to the Council of Europe and send observers to the committees of experts open for participation to all member states; [however,] [o]bserver status gives no right to be represented on the Committee

its treaties when the Council wishes to broaden the scope of the treaty to include non-European countries.[40] The United States has signed five treaties in the course of its contact with the Council of Europe and has ratified two of them.[41] Among the most prominent treaties the United States has signed is the Council of Europe's Convention on Cybercrime, which provides a multilateral framework for combating various Internet crimes, including copyright infringement, fraud, and child pornography.[42] The United States, however, has yet to ratify the Convention.[43]

C. The Council of Europe's Involvement in Hate Speech

Over the past few years, the Council of Europe has become increasingly involved in the problems posed by racism, xenophobia, and anti-Semitism in Europe. In 1993, the Council of Europe issued a Declaration and Plan of Action on Combating Racism, Xenophobia, Anti-Semitism, and Intolerance.[44] The Plan of Action provided for a "European Youth Campaign against Racism, Xenophobia, Anti-Semitism and Intolerance."[45] Additionally, the Council

---

of Ministers or the Parliamentary Assembly unless a specific decision has been taken by one of these organs on its own behalf") (on file with the Washington and Lee Law Review).

40.   *See* POLAKIEWICZ, *supra* note 35, at 33 (stating that open treaties are open to accession by nonmember states—even non-European states—provided that they have been formally invited to accede by the Committee of Ministers of the Council of Europe).

41.   *See* United States: All legal acts accomplished as of Jan. 12, 2004, The Council of Europe, *at* http://conventions.coe.int/Treaty/Commun/ListeTraites.asp?CM=14&MA=999& PO=USA&SI=1&CL=ENG (last visited Jan. 27, 2005) (stating that as of Jan. 27, 2005, the United States has signed five Council of Europe treaties and has ratified two of them) (on file with the Washington and Lee Law Review).

42.   *See supra* notes 10–13 and accompanying text (detailing the provisions of the Convention on Cybercrime).

43.   *See* Chart of Signatures and Ratifications of a Treaty, *supra* note 16 (showing that the United States has not ratified the Convention). *But see* President George W. Bush, *Message to the Senate of the United States, at* http://www.whitehouse.gov/news/releases/2003/11/2003 1117-11.html (Nov. 23, 2003) (showing that President Bush only recently transmitted the Convention to the United States Senate for its consideration) (on file with the Washington and Lee Law Review).

44.   Council of Europe, Declaration and Plan of Action on Combating Racism, Xenophobia, Antisemitism, and Intolerance, *at* http://www.coe.int/T/E/human_rights/Ecri/5-Archives/2-Other_texts/2-Vienna_Summit/Plan_of_Action/Plan_of_Action_Vienna_Summit. asp (Oct. 9, 1993) [hereinafter Declaration and Plan of Action] (on file with the Washington and Lee Law Review); *see also* Peck, *supra* note 31, at 108 ("Alarmed by the upsurge of racism, xenophobia, and antisemitism, the 1993 meeting of the council's Heads of State and Government adopted a Declaration and Plan of Action.").

45.   *See* Declaration and Plan of Action, *supra* note 44 (launching "a broad European Youth Campaign to mobilise the public in favour of a tolerant society based on the equal dignity

asked governments to re-examine their legislation, and the European Commission Against Racism and Intolerance (ECRI) was established to review member states' legislation and policies and propose further action at the local, national, and regional levels.[46]

In reporting on the conditions faced by minorities and immigrants, the Commission examined the rights accorded these groups, and the protections available to them, in each member country.[47] The Commission also examined portrayals in the media, including the Internet, and found several concerns. For example, the Commission expressed concern regarding the steep rise in the number of racist websites in Germany.[48] In Austria, the Commission expressed concern in regard to the amount of circulation of anti-Semitic material through the Internet.[49] The Commission cited the Internet as one of the main focal points of anti-Semitic propaganda in the Netherlands and stated that there has been a reported rise of discrimination on the Internet in that country towards Jews, Turks, and Moroccans.[50] The Commission was also troubled by the lack of enforcement of Internet-content regulations in some countries[51] and by

of all its members and against manifestations of racism, xenophobia, antisemitism and intolerance"); *see also* Peck, *supra* note 31, at 108 (stating that its Plan of Action included a European Youth Campaign against Racism, Xenophobia, Anti-Semitism and Intolerance, which "includes training courses, high-profile events, seminars, and the production of educational materials").

46. *See* Declaration and Plan of Action, *supra* note 44 (inviting members to re-examine their legislation and setting up a committee of governmental experts to review members' policies, propose further action, formulate general policy recommendations, and examine international legal instruments).

47. *See, e.g.*, COMMISSION AGAINST RACISM AND INTOLERANCE, THIRD REPORT ON GERMANY *passim* (2004) (examining Germany's Constitution, citizenship laws, criminal laws, and civil and administrative laws), *available at* http://www.coe.int/T/E/human_rights/Ecri/1-ECRI/2-Country-by-country_approach/Germany/third_report_Germany.pdf (on file with the Washington and Lee Law Review).

48. *See id.* at 15 ("ECRI is concerned about the steep rise in numbers of racist internet sites originating in Germany . . . .").

49. *See* EUROPEAN COMMISSION AGAINST RACISM AND INTOLERANCE, SECOND REPORT ON AUSTRIA 14 (2001) ("[A]ntisemitism is still present in Austria and manifests itself in a variety of ways. These include circulation of antisemitic material (notably via the Internet) . . . ."), *available at* http://www.coe.int/T/E/human_rights/Ecri/1-ECRI/2-Country-by-country_app roach/Austria/PDF_CBC2Austria.pdf (on file with the Washington and Lee Law Review).

50. *See* EUROPEAN COMMISSION AGAINST RACISM AND INTOLERANCE, SECOND REPORT ON THE NETHERLANDS 14, 16 (2001) (stating that, according to MDI, racist offenses have been on the rise, with most of the offenses of an anti-Semitic nature, but also discrimination against Turks and Moroccans), *available at* http://www.coe.int/T/E/human_rights/Ecri/1-ECRI/2-Country-by-country_approach/Netherlands/CBC2%20Netherlands.pdf (on file with the Washington and Lee Law Review).

51. *See, e.g.*, EUROPEAN COMMISSION AGAINST RACISM AND INTOLERANCE, SECOND REPORT ON GREECE 14, *at* http://www.coe.int/T/E/human_rights/Ecri/5-Archives/1-EC

European countries with less stringent regulations acting as a safe haven for content.[52]

In response to its findings, the ECRI adopted a general policy recommendation on December 15, 2000.[53] The ECRI recommended that the Council of Europe include the issue of suppression of hate speech in the pending Convention on Cybercrime in order to strengthen international cooperation and allow law enforcement to take more efficient action against the dissemination of hate speech.[54] While an Internet hate speech protocol was initially added to the Convention on Cybercrime, it was removed when it became apparent that the United States (whose signature was desired for the other provisions) would not sign the Convention if the Internet hate speech provisions were attached.[55] Instead, the Council of Europe made the Internet hate speech measure a separate protocol. On November 7, 2002, the Committee of Ministers of the Council of Europe adopted the "Additional Protocol to the Convention on cybercrime, concerning the criminilisation of acts of a racist and xenophobic nature committed through computer systems."[56] The Additional Protocol was opened for signature on January 28, 2003, and, as of January 10, 2004, has been signed by twenty-three members of the Council of Europe, including Austria, France, Germany, the Netherlands, Poland, and

---

RI's_work/5-CBC_Second_Reports/Greece/CBC2%20Greece.pdf (2000) ("Although there are legal provisions condemning incitement to racial hatred in general as well as legal and other provisions aimed at combating racism and intolerance in the electronic media, these are virtually unused.") (on file with the Washington and Lee Law Review).

52. *See* LEGAL INSTRUMENTS, *supra* note 24, at 27 ("This problem of 'safe havens' is not limited to racist contents, but also concerns revisionist sites whose existence has to do with the fact that there is no criminal legislation in that regard in certain European countries.").

53. EUROPEAN COMMISSION AGAINST RACISM AND INTOLERANCE, GENERAL POLICY RECOMMENDATION NO. 6: COMBATING THE DISSEMINATION OF RACIST, XENOPHOBIC, AND ANTISEMITIC MATERIEL VIA THE INTERNET 1, *at* http://www.coe.int/T/E/human_rights/ Ecri/1-ECRI/3-General_themes/1-Policy_Recommendations/Recommendation_N%B06/Rec% 206%20en.pdf (2001) (on file with the Washington and Lee Law Review).

54. *See id.* at 5 (listing the recommendations of the European Commission against Racism and Intolerance).

55. *See* Michelle Madigan, *Internet Hate-Speech Ban Called 'Chilling'*, PCWorld.com, *at* http://www.pcworld.com/resource/printable/article/0,aid,107499,00.asp (Dec. 2, 2002) ("The Council of Europe's original Convention on Cybercrime in 2001 also contained a hate-speech measure, but it was dropped at the last minute to gain support from the United States . . . .") (on file with the Washington and Lee Law Review).

56. Additional Protocol to the Convention on cybercrime, concerning the criminalization of acts of a racist and xenophobic nature committed through computer systems, Jan. 28, 2003, Europ. T.S. No. 189 [hereinafter Additional Protocol].

792   *62 WASH. & LEE L. REV. 781 (2005)*

Sweden; however, as of that date, only two countries had ratified the treaty.[57] The Additional Protocol will take force once five countries ratify it.[58]

IV. *The Additional Protocol on Internet Hate Speech*

A. *The Provisions of the Additional Protocol*

The provisions of the Additional Protocol can be divided into five types of conduct that parties to the Protocol are required to criminalize. First, it requires each party to criminalize "distributing, or otherwise making available, racist and xenophobic material to the public through a computer system."[59] But a party may choose not to make the conduct criminal if the conduct is not associated with hatred or violence and other effective civil or administrative remedies are available.[60] A party may also reserve the right not to apply this provision to speech that is purely discriminatory, and not associated with hatred or violence, if the country cannot criminalize purely discriminatory speech because of established principles in its legal system.[61] The requirement that the communication be "to the public" excludes emails and private communications from the provision.[62] The scope of the Protocol was limited to public communications because of concerns that private communications are protected

---

57. Council of Europe, Chart of Signatures and ratifications of a treaty, Europ. T.S. No. 189, *at* http://conventions.coe.int/Treaty/Commun/ChercheSig.asp?NT=189&CM=8&DF=27/ 01/05&CL=ENG (last visited Jan. 27, 2005) (on file with the Washington and Lee Law Review).

58. *See* Additional Protocol, *supra* note 56, at 11 (stating that the Protocol will "enter into force on the first day of the month following the expiration of a period of three months after the date on which five States have expressed their consent to be bound by the Protocol, in accordance with the provisions of Article 9").

59. *Id.* at 8.

60. *See id.* at 8–9 (stating that a party may reserve the right not to attach criminal liability where material advocates, promotes, or incites discrimination that is not associated with hatred or violence, provided that other effective remedies are available); *see also* Explanatory Report, Additional Protocol to the Convention on cybercrime, concerning the criminalization of acts of a racist and xenophobic nature committed through computer systems, Jan. 28, 2003 [hereinafter Explanatory Report], ¶ 32, Europ. T.S. No. 189 (stating that such other remedies may be civil or administrative).

61. *See* Additional Protocol, *supra* note 56, at 9 ("[A] Party may reserve the right not to apply paragraph 1 to those cases of discrimination for which, due to established principles in its national legal system concerning freedom of expression, it cannot provide for effective remedies as referred to in the said paragraph 2.").

62. *See* Explanatory Report, *supra* note 60, ¶ 29 ("The term . . . makes it clear that private communications or expressions communicated or transmitted through a computer system fall outside the scope of this provision.").

by the European Convention on Human Rights.[63] But "to the public" does include exchanging such material in a chat room or posting similar messages in newsgroups, which can include content that would require a password to access (if the password would be given to anyone meeting certain criteria).[64]

Second, the Additional Protocol requires each country to criminalize the act of directing a threat to a person through the Internet purely because of race, national origin, or religion.[65] This provision does not include the reservation right present in some of the other articles of this Protocol, so parties are not allowed to opt-out of this provision.[66] Third, the Protocol requires each country to criminalize the act of publicly insulting a person through a computer system because of the person's race, national origin, or religion.[67] A party, however, may choose to require the condition that the victim be exposed to hatred, contempt, or ridicule, or a party may reserve the right to refrain from applying this article altogether.[68]

Fourth, each party must pass legislation making it a crime to distribute or make available through the Internet "material which denies, grossly minimises,

---

63. *See id.* (stating that private communications "are protected by Article 8 of the ECHR.").

64. *Id.* ¶ 31.

65. *See* Additional Protocol, *supra* note 56, at 9 (criminalizing racist and xenophobic motivated threats). Article 4 states:

Each Party shall adopt such legislative and other measures as may be necessary to establish as criminal offences under its domestic law, when committed intentionally and without right, the following conduct: threatening, through a computer system, with the commission of a serious criminal offence as defined under its domestic law, (i) persons for the reason that they belong to a group, distinguished by race, colour, descent or national or ethnic origin, as well as religion, if used as a pretext for any of these factors, or (ii) a group of persons which is distinguished by any of these characteristics.

Id.

66. *See id.* (providing for no right of reservation in Article 4); *id.* at 11 (stating that parties may only avail themselves of the reservations provided for in Articles 3, 5, and 6 of this Protocol and in Article 22 of the Convention, and that no other reservations may be made).

67. *See id.* at 9 (criminalizing racist and xenophobic motivated insults). Article 5 states:

Each Party shall adopt such legislative and other measures as may be necessary to establish as criminal offences under its domestic law, when committed intentionally and without right, the following conduct: insulting publicly, through a computer system, (i) persons for the reason that they belong to a group distinguished by race, colour, national or ethnic origin, as well as religion, if used as a pretext for any of these factors; or (ii) a group of persons which is distinguished by any of these characteristics.

Id.

68. *See id.* (providing for options for parties to limit the scope of Article 5).

approves or justifies acts constituting genocide or crimes against humanity."[69] This provision includes not only the Holocaust, but also genocides and crimes established by other international courts, such as the tribunals established to study genocides in the former Yugoslavia and in Rwanda.[70] The Protocol provides, however, that a country may reserve the right not to have this section apply to it.[71] A country may also choose to require that the conduct be committed with the intent to "incite hatred, discrimination or violence against any individual or group of individuals, based on race, colour, descent or national or ethnic origin, as well as religion."[72] Finally, the Protocol requires parties to criminalize "aiding or abetting" the commission of any of the offenses established by the Protocol.[73]

In addition to criminalizing conduct, the Protocol also makes prosecution of offenders easier because it provides for extradition between parties by extending the scope of the extradition provisions of the Convention on

---

69.   *See id.* at 9–10 (criminalizing denial, gross minimization, approval or justification of genocide or crimes against humanity). Article 6 states:

> Each Party shall adopt such legislative measures as may be necessary to establish the following conduct as criminal offences under its domestic law, when committed intentionally and without right: distributing or otherwise making available, through a computer system to the public, material which denies, grossly minimises, approves or justifies acts constituting genocide or crimes against humanity, as defined by international law and recognised as such by final and binding decisions of the International Military Tribunal, established by the London Agreement of 8 April 1945, or any other international court established by relevant international instruments and whose jurisdiction is recognised by the Party.

Id.

70.   *See* Explanatory Report, *supra* note 60, ¶ 40 (stating that the scope of the provision is not only limited to crimes committed by the Nazi regime and established as such by the Nuremberg Tribunal but also extends "to genocides and crimes against humanity established by other international courts," such as the International Criminal Tribunals for the former Yugoslavia, for Rwanda, and the Permanent International Criminal Court); *see also* Jonathan Band, *Banning Hate Speech Poses Hidden Risks*, THE JERUSALEM REP., Dec. 30, 2002, at 55 (expressing concern that the language of the Protocol could be held to include genocides recognized by the Arab League and subjecting to liability those historians and reporters who deny Israel's guilt for the plight of Arab refugees or for minimizing the scope of Jenin).

71.   *See* Additional Protocol, *supra* note 56, at 5 (stating that a party may "reserve the right not to apply, in whole or in part, paragraph 1 of this article").

72.   *Id.*

73.   *See id.* (criminalizing aiding and abetting). Article 7 states:

> Each party shall adopt such legislative and other measures as may be necessary to establish as criminal offences under its domestic law, when committed intentionally and without right, aiding or abetting the commission of any of the offences established in accordance with this Protocol, with intent that such offence be committed.

Id.

Cybercrime to include the Internet hate speech crimes established by the Additional Protocol.[74]

B. Liability Under the Protocol: Internet Users and Internet Service Providers

The Protocol primarily provides for liability of individuals who actually post the racist content on the Internet, and limits the liability of Internet Service Providers (ISPs) who serve as mere conduits of the speech. All of the offenses listed in the Protocol have a requirement that the conduct be "intentional."[75] The Protocol does not define what can be considered "intentional" conduct and leaves its meaning up to each party.[76] The Explanatory Report, however, states that the "intent" requirement will limit the liability of ISPs that merely serve as a conduit for a website or bulletin board containing the racist or xenophobic material.[77] As a result, the effect of the requirement should be to limit the liability of ISPs. Individuals who post the material will generally meet the intent requirement as long as they intentionally posted the material on the Internet, and liability therefore will fall on Internet users.

Although the Protocol limits the liability of ISPs, if a country adopts an expansive definition of "intent," an ISP could be held liable. For instance, nothing in the Protocol prevents a country from finding a "permissive intent" when an ISP receives notification of the racist or xenophobic speech by a country or third party and fails to take steps to remove the odious content.[78]

---

74. See id. ("The Parties shall extend the scope of application of the measures defined in Articles 14 to 21 and Articles 23 to 35 of the Convention, to Articles 2 to 7 of this Protocol."); see also Convention on Cybercrime, Europ. T.S. No. 185 (Nov. 23, 2001) (providing, in Article 24, for parties to include criminal offenses described as extraditable offenses), available at http://conventions.coe. int/Treaty/en/Treaties/Html/185.htm (on file with the Washington and Lee Law Review); see also Explanatory Report, supra note 60, ¶ 3 (stating that one of the purposes of the Additional Protocol is to facilitate extradition).

75. See Explanatory Report, supra note 60, ¶ 25 ("All the offences contained in the Protocol must be committed 'intentionally' for criminal liability to apply.").

76. See id. ("The drafters of the Protocol, as those of the Convention, agreed that the exact meaning of 'intentionally' should be left to national interpretation.").

77. Id. The Explanatory Report states:

It is not sufficient, for example, for a service provider to be held criminally liable under this provision, that such a service provider served as a conduit for, or hosted a website or newsroom containing such material, without the required intent under domestic law in the particular case. Moreover, a service provider is not required to monitor conduct to avoid criminal liability.

Id.

78. See id. (stating that an ISP cannot be held liable as a conduit "without the required

This situation is similar to Germany's Information and Communications Service Act of 1997, which holds ISPs liable if they know of the content, have the ability to block it, and fail to take remedial action.[79]

Although the Protocol does not require countries to define "intent" in any particular manner, members of the European Union[80] that sign the Protocol must implement the Protocol in accordance with the European Union's Directive on Electronic Commerce—this Directive limits the liability of ISPs. Article 12 of the Directive says that ISPs are not liable for information transmitted on the condition that the provider "(a) does not initiate the transmission; (b) does not select the receiver of the transmission; and (c) does not select or modify the information contained in the transmission."[81] The Directive additionally provides that ISPs have no duty to monitor conduct; Article 15 states that countries may not impose "a general obligation on providers . . . to monitor the information which they transmit or store, nor a general obligation actively to seek facts or circumstances indicating illegal activity."[82]

In addition to limiting the liability of ISPs acting as mere conduits and providing that ISPs have no duty to monitor content, the Directive limits the liability of ISPs when they are hosting information. Nonetheless, ISPs still have obligations. Article 14 of the Directive states that providers are not liable for information that they store, on the condition that the provider does not have actual knowledge of illegal activity or acts expeditiously to

---

intent under domestic law in the particular case").

79.   *See* JOSEPH KIZZA, CIVILIZING THE INTERNET: GLOBAL CONCERNS AND EFFORTS TOWARD REGULATION 121 (1998) ("Service providers are not responsible for outside content that they keep ready for usage without having an influence on it unless the content is known to them and they have the technical capabilities to prevent its dissemination.").

80.   *See supra* notes 32–33 and accompanying text (stating that the Council of Europe has a larger membership than the European Union; the Council of Europe has forty-five members, and the European Union has only twenty-five).

81.   Directive 2000/31/EC of the European Parliament and of the Council of 8 June 2000 on certain legal aspects of information society services, in particular electronic commerce, in the Internal Market 12, *at* http://europa.eu.int/ISPO/ecommerce/legal/documents/2000_31ec/ 2000_31ec_en.pdf (2000) [hereinafter EU Directive on Electronic Commerce] (on file with the Washington and Lee Law Review). But this Article does not "affect the possibility for a court or administrative authority, in accordance with Member States' legal systems, of requiring the service provider to terminate or prevent an infringement." *Id.* at 13.

82.   *Id.* at 13. Member states may, however, "establish obligations for ISP's [sic] to inform the competent public authorities of alleged illegal activities undertaken or information provided by recipients of their service or obligations to communicate to the competent authorities, at their request, information enabling the identification of recipients of their service with whom they have storage agreements." *Id.*

remove or disable access to the information upon obtaining such knowledge.[83]

As a result, when Germany implemented the Directive, it kept its provisions requiring ISPs to remove illegal content of which they are aware and which they have the capability of removing. Section 10 of Germany's Act on Utilization of Teleservices[84] states that an ISP will not be liable for storing third-party information if the ISP "acts expeditiously to remove or to disable access to the information."[85]

The limited liability of ISPs for criminal conduct will also govern how countries implement the Protocol for the crime of "aiding and abetting" the commission of any of the offenses.[86] The Protocol requires the same *mens rea* for aiding and abetting as for the other offenses.[87] The explanatory report states that "although the transmission of racist and xenophobic material through the Internet requires the assistance of service providers as a conduit, a service provider that does not have the criminal intent cannot incur liability under this action."[88] This is consistent with the way "aiding and abetting" has been defined in other European countries, for purposes of establishing liability of ISPs. For instance, in Switzerland, a director of a telephone company was convicted for aiding and abetting by failing to take

---

83.   *See id.* (stating when ISPs can be held liable for hosting illegal content). Article 14 states:

> Where an information society service is provided that consists of the storage of information provided by a recipient of the service, Member States shall ensure that the service provider is not liable for the information stored at the request of a recipient of the service, on condition that: (a) the provider does not have actual knowledge of illegal activity or information and, as regards claims for damages, is not aware of facts or circumstances from which the illegal activity or information is apparent; or (b) the provider, upon obtaining such knowledge or awareness, acts expeditiously to remove or to disable access to the information.

Id.

84.   In Germany, this Act is entitled Elektronischer Geschäftsverkehr-Gesetz (EGG). The text of the Act is available in German at http://www.rws-verlag.de/volltext/01egg01.pdf.

85.   Shigenori Matsui, *The ISP's Liability for Defamation on the Internet* 7, *at* http://www.iias.or.jp/research/res_houmodel/20021129/820Matsui.pdf (last visited Jan. 27, 2005) (on file with the Washington and Lee Law Review).

86.   *See supra* note 73 and accompanying text (concerning the criminalization of aiding and abetting).

87.   *See* Explanatory Report, *supra* note 60, ¶ 45 ("Liability arises for aiding or abetting where the person who commits a crime established in the Protocol is aided by another person who also intends that the crime be committed.").

88.   *Id.* The Explanatory Report further states that there is no duty on a service provider to monitor content actively to avoid criminal liability under this provision. *Id.*

corrective action to thwart sex chatlines operated by his company after the company was notified of the criminal conduct by the Attorney General.[89]

C. *Civil Liability Under the Protocol*

The Additional Protocol primarily contemplates criminal liability for engaging in conduct prohibited by the Protocol.[90] The lone contemplation of civil liability in the text of the Protocol is a provision allowing parties the option not to create a criminal offense for distributing racist and xenophobic material to the public through a computer system if the conduct is not associated with hatred or violence and other effective remedies are available (including civil remedies).[91] Despite the Protocol's very limited reference to civil liability, offenders can still face civil liability as a result of the Protocol.

France, a signator of the Protocol, allows persons who have been victimized by the commission of a criminal offense to commence an *action civile* (civil action) against the party who has committed the criminal offense.[92] As the result of an *action civile*, the victim can receive damages, restitution, and recovery of legal costs.[93] Although an *action civile* is generally reserved only for those victims who have "personally suffered the harm directly caused by the offence," France allows associations to commence the action where provided for by law.[94] Most relevantly, French law provides that antiracism groups may commence an *action civile* with respect to certain offenses.[95] The ability of an antiracist group

---

89. *See* LEGAL INSTRUMENTS, *supra* note 24, at 47 (stating that a PTT director was convicted of aiding and abetting the publication of obscene material because of the sex chatlines operated by individuals via the telephone networks (making them accessible to minors) and that the Attorney General's department had on several occasions drawn the PTT's attention to the possibility that children might listen to or participate in pornographic conversations and the criminal conduct, but PTT took no action).

90. *See supra* notes 59–73 and accompanying text (discussing the Protocol's criminalization of certain hate speech).

91. *See supra* note 60 and accompanying text (noting a condition of the Protocol under which parties can choose not to make certain conduct criminal).

92. *See* CHRISTIAN DADAMO & SUSAN FARRAN, THE FRENCH LEGAL SYSTEM 201–03 (2d ed. 1996) (stating generally the procedures for commencing an *action civile* in France).

93. *See id.* at 201 (stating remedies available to victims who commence an *action civile*).

94. *See id.* at 202 (stating who has the right to commence an *action civile*).

95. *See* THE FRENCH CODE OF CRIMINAL PROCEDURE, REV. 41 art. 2–1 (Kock and Frase, trans. 1988) (providing under which Penal Code statutes and under what conditions an association that proposes to fight racism may exercise the rights granted a civil party); *see also* DADAMO & FARRAN, *supra* note 92, at 202 (stating that consumer associations, antiracism, antisexual violence, and protection of children associations have the right to sue in respect of certain offenses); Richard Vogler, *Criminal Procedure in France, in* COMPARATIVE CRIMINAL

to commence an *action civile* was most prominently displayed in *Yahoo!, Inc. v. La Ligue Contre Le Racisme et L'Antisemitisme.*[96] In this case, two French student unions, La Ligue Contre Le Recisme et L'Antisemitisme (LICRA) and L'Union Des Etudiants Jurifs de France (UEJF) brought an *action civile* against Yahoo! because Yahoo!'s website advertised Nazi memorabilia for sale, in violation of a French criminal statute.[97]

Given France's generous laws allowing associations formed to combat racism to bring civil actions against producers of hate speech, in implementing the Protocol, France will probably continue to allow these associations to bring an action against individuals or corporations. As a result, although the Protocol primarily contemplates criminal sanctions for violations, violators may also find themselves subject to civil liability.

D. Impact of the Additional Protocol in Europe

All European countries have in place laws aimed at repressing hate speech, and these laws often extend to hate speech posted on the Internet.[98] However, the

---

PROCEDURE 14, 26 (John Hatchard et al. eds., 1996) ("A group or organisation (e.g. a bank of society) may become a civil party provided that its overall interests, and not merely those of individual members, have been clearly prejudiced.").

96.   Yahoo!, Inc. v. La Ligue Contre Le Racisme et L'Antisemitisme, 379 F.3d 1120 (9th Cir. 2004). La Ligue Contre Le Racisme et L'Antisemitisme (LICRA) and L'Union Des Etudiants Juifs De France (UEJF) are French nonprofit organizations dedicated to eliminating anti-Semitism. Yahoo!, Inc. v. La Ligue Contre Le Racisme et L'Antisemitisme, 169 F. Supp. 2d 1181, 1183 (N.D. Cal. 2001), *rev'd*, 379 F.3d 1120 (9th Cir. 2004). On April 5, 2000, LICRA sent a "cease and desist" letter to Yahoo!'s Santa Clara headquarters informing Yahoo! that the sale of Nazi- and Third Reich-related goods through its auction services violates French law and threatening Yahoo! with legal action unless it took corrective action. *Id.* at 1184. LICRA and UEJF subsequently utilized the United States Marshal's Office to serve Yahoo! with process in California and filed a civil complaint against Yahoo! in French court. *Id.* The French court found that approximately 1000 Nazi- and Third Reich-related objects were being offered for sale on Yahoo!'s auction site. *Id.* The French court concluded that the Yahoo! auction site violated the French Criminal Code, which prohibits exhibition of Nazi propaganda and artifacts for sale, and issued an order requiring Yahoo! to prohibit French citizen access to those auctions. *Id.* at 1184–85. Yahoo! subsequently commenced action in the United States District Court seeking a declaratory judgment that the French order was not enforceable. *Id.* at 1186. The United States District Court granted the declaratory judgment on the grounds that the posting of the material on Yahoo!'s website was protected speech. *Id.* at 1193–94. The Ninth Circuit reversed on the ground of lack of personal jurisdiction over LICRA and UEJF. *Yahoo!, Inc.*, 379 F.3d at 1123.

97.   *See id.* at 1184 (stating that LICRA and UEJF filed a civil complaint against Yahoo! in the Tribunal de Grande Instance de Paris for Yahoo!'s violation of Section R645-1 of the French Criminal Code).

98.   *See* LEGAL INSTRUMENTS, *supra* note 24, at 13 (stating that its previous report showed

Council of Europe's Additional Protocol would make significant changes to the legislation already in place. The most visible change is greater restrictions on posting revisionist literature challenging the existence of genocides.[99] The Additional Protocol includes broad language making it a crime to deny or minimize genocides.[100] However, only France and Switzerland currently have in place legislation comparative in its breadth to that of the Council of Europe's.[101] Germany, Belgium, and Austria have in place similar legislation, but it is limited to denials of genocide committed by the Nazis.[102] However, the Additional Protocol does allow countries the option not to apply that Article, so it is unclear how many countries will choose to reserve that right.[103]

The other major effect of the Protocol will be to further intergovernmental cooperation in prosecution of offenders by removing obstructions to prosecutions when the source is located in another European country.[104] The Explanatory Report states that one of the primary reasons for the adoption of the Protocol is to facilitate international cooperation, especially extradition and mutual legal assistance.[105] A complaint present in the reports of the European Commission on Racism and Intolerance was the disparity in the enforcement and the language of the laws.[106] The Protocol should provide the increased cooperation and the uniformity needed to close that gap.

---

that all European countries have at their disposal an effective legislative arsenal to repress hateful expressions, and that a minimum standard imposed by the United Nations Convention on the Elimination of Racial Hatred is applicable to hateful expressions disseminated via the Internet); *id.* at 30 (stating that in many European countries, Internet sites are treated like the press).

99. *See id.* at 27 (stating that revisionist sites have a safe haven in those countries that do not criminalize posting revisionist literature on the Internet).

100. *See* Additional Protocol, *supra* note 56, at 9–10 (requiring parties to criminalize distributing, through a computer to the public, material that denies, grossly minimizes, approves, or justifies acts constituting genocides or crimes against humanity).

101. *See* LEGAL INSTRUMENTS, *supra* note 24, at 14 (stating that in France it is an offense to "dispute crimes against humanity," and that Switzerland punishes the offense).

102. *See id.* (stating that in Germany, Belgium, and Austria, it is a crime to deny genocide committed by the Nazis).

103. *See supra* notes 69–71 and accompanying text (discussing a provision in the protocol that states that a country may choose to opt-out of the provision requiring countries to criminalize speech minimizing or denying the existence of a genocide).

104. *See* Explanatory Report, *supra* note 60, ¶ 3 (stating that the Additional Protocol facilitates international cooperation, especially extradition and mutual legal assistance).

105. *Id.*

106. *See* EUROPEAN COMMISSION AGAINST RACISM AND INTOLERANCE, SECOND REPORT ON GREECE, *supra* note 51, at 14 ("Although there are legal provisions condemning incitement to racial hatred in general as well as legal and other provisions aimed at combating racism and intolerance in the electronic media, these are virtually unused."); *see also* LEGAL INSTRUMENTS,

Although the Protocol will create greater uniformity of laws, the reservations present in the Protocol will still result in some disparity. The Protocol does not state whose law would control in a conflict, but in a dispute involving an ISP and a conflict of law between two countries that are members of the European Union,[107] the European Union Directive on Electronic Commerce would govern. Article 3 of the European Union Directive on Electronic Commerce provides that ISPs are governed by the laws of the member state in which they are established.[108] However, the Directive provides for an exception to that choice of law when the recipient country's choice of law is necessary for the prevention, investigation, detection and prosecution of criminal offenses, including "the fight against any incitement to hatred on grounds of race, sex, religion or nationality, and violations of human dignity concerning individual persons."[109] This exception is likely to encompass criminal Internet hate speech legislation, so the general rule that ISPs are only subject to the law of the country in which they are established does not appear to apply to Internet hate speech. But even if Internet hate speech falls into this exception, the European Union Directive still governs the procedure that a country must follow before taking action against an ISP established in another member country. The Directive provides that the enforcing country must first ask the country of establishment to take action, and if the country of establishment does not take such measures, or the measures taken are inadequate, the enforcing country must notify the Commission and the country of establishment of its intention to take such action against the ISP.[110]

---

supra note 24, at 27 ("This problem of 'safe havens' . . . also concerns revisionist sites whose existence has to do with the fact that there is no criminal legislation in that regard in certain European countries.").

107.   *See supra* notes 32–33 and accompanying text (stating that the Council of Europe has forty-five members and the European Union has only twenty-five members).

108.   *See* EU Directive on Electronic Commerce, *supra* note 81, at 9 ("Member States may not, for reasons falling with the coordinated field, restrict the freedom to provide information society services from another Member State."); *id.* at 4 ("[I]n order to effectively guarantee freedom to provide services and legal certainty for suppliers and recipients of services, such information society services should in principle be subject to the law of the Member State in which the service provider is established.").

109.   *Id.* at 9.

110.   *See id.* at 10 (listing the steps a Member State must take before commencing action against an ISP established in another member State). Article 3(b) states:

> [B]efore taking the measures in question and without prejudice to court proceedings, including preliminary proceedings and acts carried out in the framework of a criminal investigation, the Member state has:
>
> -- asked the Member State referred to in paragraph 1 to take measures and the latter did not take such measures, or they were inadequate,
>
> -- notified the Commission and the Member State referred to in paragraph 1 of its intention to take such measures.

The Protocol will only have effect if it is actually ratified by the members of the Council of Europe. So far, only two countries have ratified the Additional Protocol.[111] However, this should not be taken as a sign of dilatoriness of European countries to implement the Additional Protocol, nor does this mean these treaties will not be implemented. The Council of Europe has a good track record for implementation of its agreements:[112] Of the 195 treaties approved by the Council of Europe, only 35 of them have not yet entered into force, and many of those treaties have only been opened for signature within the past five years.[113] It is common for ratification of treaties and their entering into force to take a few years, so the lack of rapid accession to the Protocol is not unusual.[114] Additionally, because many European countries have prior laws regulating hate speech on the Internet, animosity to the Additional Protocol in Europe is unlikely. The problem of hate speech in Europe was also recently highlighted by the publication of photographs of Prince Harry wearing a Nazi swastika at a costume party.[115] Because of the European interest in curbing hate speech, ratification is likely.[116]

E. Attempts by European Countries To Enforce Their Internet Laws Against Foreign Content

The effect of the Protocol and the hate speech legislation adopted by Europe is likely to extend beyond the parties to the agreement. European nations have a history of attempting to enforce their Internet content laws

---

Id.

111. *See* Chart of Signatures and Ratifications of a Treaty, Europ. T.S. No. 189, *at* http://conventions.coe.int/Treaty/EN/searchsig.asp?NT=189&CM=8&DF=24/11/03 (last visited Jan. 27, 2005) (showing that only two countries have ratified the Additional Protocol) (on file with the Washington and Lee Law Review).

112. *See* POLAKIEWICZ, *supra* note 35, at 14 ("It can be said, however, that the record of ratifications of Council of Europe treaties is more favourable than that of many other international or European organisations.").

113. *See* Complete List of the Council of Europe's Treaties, *supra* note 37 (listing all of the treaties opened for signature and stating when they entered into force).

114. *See id.* (showing the date the treaty was opened for signature and the date the treaty entered into force).

115. *See* Alan Cowell, *A Prince Who Forgot History Angers Many,* N.Y. TIMES, Jan. 14, 2005, at A12 (concerning photographs published by the British tabloid *The Sun* of Prince Harry wearing a Nazi swastika armband).

116. *See* LEGAL INSTRUMENTS, *supra* note 24, at 13 (stating that "all European countries at their disposal have a more or less effective legislative arsenal to repress hateful expressions," and that these criminal provisions are applicable to hateful expressions disseminated via the Internet).

against content uploaded from sources outside Europe, and they view their jurisdiction based on where the content was read. Such litigation has produced three high-profile cases: *Toben*, *Somm*, and *Yahoo!*.

1. Toben

Frederick Toben is an Australian immigrant from Germany.[117] From Australia, he runs the Adelaide Institute and its companion website, but the site appears to be hosted on an American server.[118] One of the arguments of the Institute is that the Nazis never used gas chambers to murder Jews and others during the Holocaust.[119] Although the website is not maintained in Germany and is written in English, this site is accessible by German Internet users and contains content in violation of a German law prohibiting the dissemination of material challenging the existence of the Holocaust.[120] Frederick Toben was arrested in 1999 when he was on a visit to Germany and was charged for violating the German statute because of the content of his site and because of pamphlets he had distributed while in Germany.[121] A lower court sentenced Toben for the distribution of the pamphlets, but held that the German statute

---

117. *See* Robyn Weisman, *Germany Bans Foreign Web Site for Nazi Content*, NEWSFACTOR NETWORK, *at* http://www.newsfactor.com/story.xhtml?story_id=6063 (last visited Jan. 27, 2005) ("Though German-born, Toben has lived in Australia for most of his life and is a citizen of that country.") (on file with the Washington and Lee Law Review).

118. *See* Adelaide Institute, *at* http://www.adelaideinstitute.org (last visited Dec. 1, 2004) (hosting the website of the Adelaide Institute) (on file with the Washington and Lee Law Review); *see also* Terry Lane, *Censoring the Adelaide Institute's Web Site is Futile*, ONLINEOPINION, *at* http://www.onlineopinion.com.au/view. asp?article=1126 (Nov. 30, 2000) ("Now we have the Internet, and Dr. Toben's Adelaide Institute website appears to be located on an American server.") (on file with the Washington and Lee Law Review). The location of the Adelaide Institute's website on an American server stems from Australian law. Australia, like Germany, prohibits hate speech, and it has ordered Frederick Toben to shut down his website. *See generally* Toben v. Jones (2003) 129 F.C.R. 515 (affirming determination of the Australian Human Rights and Equal Opportunity Commission that Toben's website is likely to offend, insult, humiliate, or intimidate Jews, and that website was not reasonable and in good faith academic belief).

119. *See* Jones v. Toben, (2002) 71 A.L.D. 629 ("'We are not "holocaust deniers." We proudly proclaim that to date there is no evidence that millions of people were killed in homicidal gas chambers.'" (quoting *About the Adelaide Institute*)).

120. *See* Arrest Warrant for Dr. Frederick Toben, Institute for Historical Review, *at* http://www.ihr.org/other/990409warrant.html (last visited Jan. 27, 2005) (stating that German authorities had downloaded the content from the Adelaide Institute's website and charging that the content is in violation of the German Criminal Code) (on file with the Washington and Lee Law Review).

121. *See id.* (stating the facts on which Frederick Toben was arrested).

could not reach Toben's website because the site was based in Australia.[122] However, this determination was reversed on appeal, and Germany's High Court, the Bundesgerichthof, ruled that "German authorities may take legal action against foreigners who upload content that is illegal in Germany—even though the Websites may be located elsewhere."[123] The outcome of this case demonstrates that Germany views its jurisdiction broadly and will determine jurisdiction based on where the content was viewed rather than on where it was published or targeted.

2. Somm

The *Somm* case raised a similar question concerning liability for content entering German borders from outside the country; however, Somm involved the liability of an ISP for content stored on a server in a foreign country, rather than the liability of the individual who posted the content. Felix Somm was an executive of CompuServe Deutschland.[124] Somm was prosecuted by German authorities for providing access to illegal pornographic material to CompuServe subscribers, on the grounds that he should have filtered out the contents.[125] Although Somm was found guilty, his conviction was reversed on appeal.[126] The conviction was reversed because Somm was only the manager of a subsidiary of CompuServe and did not have the power to block the content,[127] a necessary element required by Germany's Information and Communications Services Act of 1997 in order to hold an ISP liable for content.[128] This case adds to the rule of the Toben case: Although Germany will determine jurisdiction based on where the content is posted, Germany will not assign liability to officers of foreign subsidiaries who have no control over the content.

---

122.   *See* Weisman, *supra* note 117 (stating that a lower court ruled that only websites based in Germany were liable).

123.   *Id.*

124.   Edmund Andrews, *German Court Overturns Pornography Ruling Against Compuserve*, N.Y. TIMES, Nov. 18, 1999, at C4.

125.   *See id.* (stating that a Munich court sentenced Somm to two years probation and a fine of 100,000 marks ($180,000) because CompuServe could have done more to block access to illegal pornographic websites).

126.   *Id.*

127.   *See id.* (stating that the Bavarian court found Somm "a slave of the parent company" and that he could not have done much more than he did to block the content).

128.   *See* KIZZA, *supra* note 79, at 121 ("Service providers are not responsible for outside content that they keep ready for usage without having an influence on it unless the content is known to them and they have the technical capabilities to prevent its dissemination.").

3. Yahoo!

ISP liability for content originating from the United States was also at issue in *Yahoo!, Inc. v. La Ligue Contre Le Racisme et L'Antisemitisme* (LICRA).[129] Two French student organizations, LICRA and UEJF, instituted an action in French court against Yahoo! for violating a French law prohibiting the offering for sale of Nazi merchandise.[130] Yahoo! offered the merchandise for sale on its auction website.[131] The court issued an order requiring Yahoo! to "eliminate French citizens' access to any material on the Yahoo.com auction site that offers for sale any Nazi objects, relics, insignia, emblems, and flags."[132] On a motion to reconsider the Order, the court affirmed its earlier judgment and stated that although it is difficult to identify the national identity of the Internet user, a combination of geographical identification of the IP address and declaration of nationality would result in a filtering success rate of 90%.[133] The court ordered that Yahoo! had three months to comply with the Order or it would be subject to a penalty of 100,000 francs per day.[134]

In response to this Order, Yahoo! sought and received in U.S. District Court for the Northern District of California a declaratory judgment stating that French authorities cannot impose and collect fines on Yahoo!.[135] Before deciding the merits of the case, the district court first concluded that it had jurisdiction to hear the dispute based on the actions of LICRA in targeting Yahoo!'s California headquarters with a cease and desist letter, effecting

---

129. Yahoo!, Inc. v. La Ligue Contre Le Racisme et L'Antisemitisme, 379 F.3d 1120 (9th Cir. 2004).

130. *See* Yahoo!, Inc. v. La Ligue Contre Le Racisme et L'Antisemitisme, 169 F. Supp. 2d 1181, 1184 (N.D. Cal. 2001) (stating that two French student unions filed a civil complaint against Yahoo! alleging that Yahoo! violated French law), *rev'd*, 379 F.3d 1120 (9th Cir. 2004).

131. *See id.* (finding that items for sale included Adolf Hitler's *Mein Kampf, The Protocol of the Elders of Zion*, and purported evidence that the gas chambers of the Holocaust did not exist).

132. *Id.*

133. *See* La Ligue Contre Le Racisme et L'Antisemitisme v. Yahoo!, Inc., T.G.I. Paris 14 (Nov. 20, 2000) ("The combination of two procedures, namely geographical identification of the IP address and declaration of nationality, would be likely to achieve a filtering success rate approaching 90%."), *available at* http://www.cdt.org/speech/international/001120yahoofrance. pdf (on file with the Washington and Lee Law Review).

134. *See id.* at 20 ("We order YAHOO Inc. to comply within 3 months from notification of the present order with the injunctions contained in our order of 22nd May 2000 subject to a penalty of 100,000 Francs per day of delay effective from the first day following expiry of the 3 month period.").

135. *See* Yahoo!, Inc. v. La Ligue Contre Le Racisme et L'Antisemitisme, 169 F. Supp. 2d 1181, 1194 (N.D. Cal. 2001) (granting Yahoo!'s motion for a declaratory judgment prohibiting the enforcement of the French order against Yahoo!), *rev'd*, 379 F.3d 1120 (9th Cir. 2004).

service through the use of United States Marshals, and garnering a French judgment that requires Yahoo! to perform specific physical acts in California.[136] In granting summary judgment for Yahoo!, the district court stated that the enforcement of foreign judgments is based on the "comity of nations."[137] The district court issued the declaratory judgment because the content is protected by the First Amendment, and the court "may not enforce a foreign order that violates the protections of the United States Constitution by chilling protected speech that occurs simultaneously within our borders."[138] On appeal, the Ninth Circuit reversed and found that there was no basis for jurisdiction because LICRA and UEJF had insufficient contacts with the forum state.[139]

In an amici curiae brief filed to the United States Court of Appeals for the Ninth Circuit by the United States Chamber of Commerce and several industry associations, an alterative reason for issuing the declaratory judgment was offered: the lack of jurisdiction of the French court.[140] The lack of jurisdiction argument was based on the notion that Yahoo! was an American company that "provides Internet services in English, targeted at American citizens, from host computers located in the United States."[141] The brief pointed to decisions holding that the maintenance of a passive website is not sufficient to meet the requirements of the "minimum contacts" test for jurisdiction.[142] The brief also stated that requiring Internet users to search out laws of all foreign nations and block illegal content from visibility in that nation is technologically impossible

---

136. *See* Yahoo!, Inc. v. La Ligue Contre Le Racisme et L'Antisemitisme, 145 F. Supp. 2d 1168, 1174 (N.D. Cal. 2001) (stating that LICRA sent a cease and desist letter to Yahoo!'s California headquarters, requested that a French court require Yahoo! to perform specific physical acts in Santa Clara, and effected service through United States Marshals, leading to purposeful availment by LICRA of California laws).

137. *See Yahoo!*, 169 F. Supp. 2d at 1192 ("The extent to which the United States, or any state, honors the judicial decrees of foreign nations is a matter of choice, governed by 'the comity of nations.'" (quoting Hilton v. Guyot, 159 U.S. 113, 163 (1895))).

138. *Id.*

139. Yahoo!, Inc. v. La Ligue Contre Le Racisme et L'Antisemitisme, 379 F.3d 1120, 1123 (9th Cir. 2004).

140. Brief Amici Curiae of Chamber of Commerce of the United States et al., Yahoo!, Inc. v. La Ligue Contre le Racisme et L'Antisemitisme, at 18 (9th Cir. 2002) (Case No. 01-17424) [hereinafter Brief] (stating that the French court's judgment "is unenforceable for a second, independent reason—the French court's expansive jurisdiction is inconsistent with due process requirements"), *available at* http://www.cdt.org/jurisdiction/020507yahoo.pdf (on file with the Washington and Lee Law Review).

141. *Id.* at 19–20.

142. *See id.* at 20 ("As this court has held, the maintenance of a passive website does not, as a matter of law, demonstrate that the corporation has '*purposefully* (albeit electronically) directed his activity in a *substantial* way to the forum state.'" (quoting Cybersell, Inc. v. Cybersell, Inc., 130 F.3d 414, 418 (9th Cir. 1997)) (emphasis added by Brief)).

and, even if possible, would be expensive to implement.[143]   Given these problems, the filers were troubled by the chilling effect that could result from enforcement: "Faced with the fear of such prosecution, companies and individuals would inevitably feel pressured to remove material that might be unlawful in any jurisdiction, thus giving the most restrictive jurisdictions in the world a de facto veto over the content available."[144]   The district court and the Ninth Circuit did not reach this question because the case was decided on other grounds. As a result, it is unclear to what extent lack of jurisdiction can act as an alternative bar to enforcement.

After the decision by the district court, a second action was filed against Yahoo! and its former Chief Executive Tim Koogle, charging that the sale of Nazi memorabilia on Yahoo!'s website justified war crimes.[145] This action was commenced by French Holocaust survivors.[146] However, Yahoo! was found not guilty in this second suit.[147] The dismissal was not based on a finding of lack of jurisdiction, but a failure to meet the merits. The French court said that the auction pages on Yahoo!'s site did not meet the description of glorifying or favorably presenting Nazi war crimes.[148]

F. The United States and the Protocol

Although the Council of Europe has made the Additional Protocol available for the signature of the United States[149] and the United States has

---

143. See id. at 13–14 (stating that it is not technologically possible to identify with certainty the geographic location of an Internet user, and even if it were, it is not economically feasible for the vast majority of web publishers to deploy).

144. Id. at 11.

145. French Court Clears Yahoo in Nazi Case, SILICONVALLEY.COM, at http://www.siliconvalley.com/mld/siliconvalley/news/editorial/5156629.htm (Feb. 11, 2003) (stating that plaintiffs accused Yahoo! of justifying war crimes and crimes against humanity) (on file with the Washington and Lee Law Review).

146. See id. (stating that this action was launched by French Holocaust survivors, who were joined by a group called the Movement Against Racism and For Friendship Between People).

147. See id. (stating that the French court threw out the accusations leveled against Yahoo!).

148. See id. ("But the Paris court said Tuesday that 'justifying war crimes' means 'glorifying, praising, or at least presenting the crimes in question favorably.' Yahoo and its auction pages did not fit that description, the court said.").

149. See Additional Protocol, supra note 56, at 10 (providing in Article 9 that the protocol is open for signature to all states that have signed the Convention).

808   *62 WASH. & LEE L. REV. 781 (2005)*

signed the underlying treaty,[150] the Bush Administration has indicated that the United States will not become a party to the Additional Protocol.[151] A Department of Justice spokesman said of the Additional Protocol: "The important thing to realize is that the U.S. can't be a party to any convention that abridges a constitutional protection."[152] The decision of the United States to refrain from signing the Additional Protocol is not surprising as the United States had indicated that it would not have signed the underlying treaty if the Internet hate speech language was included.[153] The Additional Protocol also faced strong opposition from interest groups on both sides of the American political spectrum, including the American Civil Liberties Union and the Heritage Foundation.[154]

V. Enforcement of European Internet Hate Speech Laws Against United States Internet Users and Providers

A. Hate Speech and the First Amendment

Although the United States has decided against signing the Protocol, the Yahoo! case and the other cases mentioned above illustrate that this does not necessarily mean that Europe will refrain from attempting to hold the United States liable for hate speech posted from the United States.[155] Europe has a

---

150.   *See* Council of Europe, Chart of Signatures and ratifications of a treaty, Europ. T.S. No. 185, *at* http://conventions.coe.int/Treaty/EN/searchsig.asp?NT=185&CM=8&DF=23/ 11/03 (last visited Jan. 27, 2005) (showing that the United States signed the Convention on Cybercrime on Nov. 23, 2001) (on file with the Washington and Lee Law Review). The Convention on Cybercrime concerns copyright infringement, computer-related fraud, and child pornography on the Internet. Convention on Cybercrime, Europ. T.S. No. 185 (Nov. 23, 2001), *available at* http://conventions.coe.int/Treaty/en/Treaties/Html/185.htm (on file with the Washington and Lee Law Review).

151.   *See* Declan McCullagh, *U.S. Won't Support Net "Hate Speech" Ban*, CNET NEWS.COM, *at* http://news.com.com/U.S.+won't+support+Net+%22hate+speech%22+ban/2100-1023_3-965983.html (Nov. 15, 2002) (stating that the Bush Administration will not support the Additional Protocol) (on file with the Washington and Lee Law Review).

152.   *Id.*

153.   *See* Madigan, *supra* note 55 ("The Council of Europe's original Convention on Cybercrime in 2001 also contained a hate-speech measure, but it was dropped at the last minute to gain support from the United States . . . .").

154.   *See id.* (quoting a Heritage Foundation fellow concerned about the vagueness of the protocol); McCullagh, *supra* note 151 (quoting an American Civil Liberties Union director applauding the decision of the United States not to sign the Additional Protocol).

155.   *See supra* Part IV.E (discussing the prosecutions of Frederick Toben, Felix Somm, and Yahoo! for content posted to the Internet outside the enforcing country).

broad reading of its jurisdiction based on where the content was viewed. The Yahoo! case demonstrates that the First Amendment can play an important role in determining the enforceability of judgments against American users and providers for hate speech content posted in America.[156] Therefore, an overview of the protections accorded to hate speech by the First Amendment is necessary. In many cases, the First Amendment will decide the ability of a foreign nation to enforce a judgment in an American court. Generally, the First Amendment protects hate speech from government regulation. Speech is subject to proscription in some instances, but the contexts are limited.[157] In *Chaplinsky v. New Hampshire*,[158] the Supreme Court said that restrictions upon the content of speech are allowed where the speech is "of such slight social value as a step to truth that any benefit that may be derived from [it] is clearly outweighed by the social interest in order and morality."[159] For hate speech, there are two primary tests for determining if the speech is proscribable: (1) if the speech presents a true threat,[160] or (2) if the speech equates to "fighting words."[161]

---

156.   *See* Yahoo!, Inc. v. La Ligue Contre Le Racisme et L'Antisemitisme, 169 F. Supp. 2d 1181, 1192 (N.D. Cal. 2001) (stating that the court "may not enforce a foreign order that violates the protections of the United States Constitution by chilling protected speech that occurs simultaneously within our borders"), *rev'd*, 379 F.3d 1120 (9th Cir. 2004).

157.   *See* Mari J. Matsuda, *Public Response to Racist Speech*, WORDS THAT WOUND: CRITICAL RACE THEORY, ASSAULTIVE SPEECH, AND THE FIRST AMENDMENT 17, 34–35 (Mari J. Matsuda et al. eds., 1993) (stating that unprotected speech includes some false statements, private facts about a private individual, defamatory speech, obscene speech, "fighting words," and "true threats").

158.   Chaplinsky v. New Hampshire, 315 U.S. 568 (1942). Chaplinsky was alleged to have told the City Marshal that the Marshal was a "God damned racketeer" and "a damned Fascist and the whole government of Rochester are Fascists or agents of Fascists." *Id.* at 569–70. Chaplinsky was charged and convicted for violating a New Hampshire statute prohibiting any person from addressing "any offensive, derisive or annoying word to any other person who is lawfully in any street or other public place, nor call him by any offensive or derisive name." *Id.* at 569. The Supreme Court upheld the statute and Chaplinsky's conviction. *Id.* at 574. The Court stated that the First Amendment does not protect "fighting" words that "by their very utterance inflict injury or tend to incite an immediate breach of the peace." *Id.* at 572. The Court upheld the statute because it was "narrowly drawn and limited to define and punish specific conduct lying within the domain of state power, the use in a public place of words likely to cause a breach of the peace." *Id.* at 573.

159.   *Id.* at 572.

160.   *See* Brandenburg v. Ohio, 395 U.S. 444, 447 (1969) (holding that the First Amendment protects speech that advocates violence, so long as the speech is not directed to inciting or promoting lawless action and is not likely to incite or produce such action); *see also* Planned Parenthood of Columbia/Willamette, Inc. v. Am. Coalition of Life Activists, 290 F.3d 1058, 1086 (9th Cir. 2002) (holding that the posting of names and addresses of abortion providers on a website of anti-abortion organization constituted a "true threat" and was not entitled to First Amendment protection).

161.   *See Chaplinsky*, 315 U.S. at 574 (upholding conviction under a New Hampshire

The "true threat" test was established in *Brandenburg v. Ohio*.[162] The *Brandenburg* test states that the "constitutional guarantees of free speech and free press do not permit a State to forbid or proscribe advocacy of the use of force or of law violation except where such advocacy is directed to inciting or producing imminent lawless action and is likely to incite or produce such action."[163] The Supreme Court held that a Ku Klux Klan meeting involving the burning of a cross, derogatory comments about Negroes and Jews, and the presence of weaponry was not sufficient to rise to the level of inciting "imminent lawless action" because it was "mere advocacy," and reversed the conviction on First Amendment grounds.[164]

The *Brandenburg* test faces questionable application to the Internet, as the Internet's impersonal contact cannot be seen as readily meeting the "true threat" requirement of being likely to incite "imminent lawless action."[165] The first real application of the "true threat" test to the Internet was in *Planned Parenthood of Columbia/Willamette, Inc. v. American Coalition of Life Activists*.[166] The

---

statute that made it a crime to use in a public place words likely to cause a breach of peace). *But see* R.A.V. v. City of St. Paul, 505 U.S. 377, 391 (1992) (holding unconstitutional a Minnesota ordinance that prohibited the display of a symbol that one knows or has reason to know "arouses anger, alarm or resentment in others on the basis of race, color, creed, religion, or gender").

162. *See* Brandenburg v. Ohio, 395 U.S. 444, 445–49 (1969) (reversing the conviction of a KKK rally organizer because the statute he was convicted under purported to proscribe mere advocacy of speech, which is protected by the First Amendment). In *Brandenburg*, the defendant was convicted for violating the Ohio Criminal Syndicalism Statute for "advocat[ing] ... the duty, necessity, or propriety of crime, sabotage, violence, or unlawful methods of terrorism as a means of accomplishing industrial or political reform" and for "voluntarily assembl[ing] with any society, group, or assemblage of persons formed to teach or advocate the doctrines of criminal syndicalism." *Id.* at 444–45. The defendant was identified by videotapes as a speaker at a KKK rally, at which KKK members were gathered around a wooden cross, that they burned, made derogatory statements about Negroes and Jews, and carried weapons. *Id.* at 445–47. The Supreme Court held the Ohio Criminal Syndicalism Statute unconstitutional. *Id.* at 449. The statute purported "to punish mere advocacy and to forbid, on pain of criminal punishment, assembly with others merely to advocate the described type of action," and did not distinguish between mere advocacy and incitement to imminent lawless action. *Id.* at 448–49. Advocacy of the use of force can only be proscribed "where such advocacy is directed to inciting or producing imminent lawless action and is likely to incite or produce such action." *Id.* at 447. Because the Ohio statute failed to make this distinction, it was ruled unconstitutional. *Id.* at 449.

163. *Id.* at 447.

164. *Id.* at 449.

165. *See* Yulia A. Timofeeva, *Hate Speech Online: Restricted or Protected? Comparison of Regulations in the United States and Germany*, 12 J. TRANSNAT'L L. & POL'Y 253, 273 (2003) ("Indeed, it does not seem highly probable that impersonal, or even personal messages on the computer screen would directly cause someone to get involved in violence or disorder.").

166. Planned Parenthood of Columbia/Willamette, Inc. v. Am. Coalition of Life Activists, 290 F.3d 1058 (9th Cir. 2002). The ACLA published "Deadly Dozen" posters containing

American Coalition of Life Activists (ACLA) published posters and also provided the names and locations of abortion providers to a website (the "Nuremberg Files").[167] After being featured on posters, three abortion providers were murdered.[168] On the website, the names of abortion providers who had been murdered were lined through in black, and names of those who had been wounded were lined through in gray.[169] Given the context of the posters and the Files, the Ninth Circuit held that the Nuremberg Files constituted a "true threat" because the defendants knew that the doctors would feel threatened by them.[170] As a result, the content was not protected by the First Amendment.[171]

In addition to "true threats," "fighting words" are also proscribable and are not protected speech. In *Chaplinsky*, the Supreme Court defined "fighting

---

information on physicians who perform abortions. *Id.* at 1064–65. The ACLA also published on its website the "Nuremberg Files," containing the names of 200 physicians and 200 judges, politicians, law enforcement officers, spouses, and abortion rights supporters. *Id.* at 1065. The "Nuremberg Files" crossed out in black the names of abortion providers who had been murdered, and lined through in gray those who had been wounded. *Id.* at 1080. Dr. David Gunn, Dr. George Patterson, and Dr. John Bayard Britton had been shot after posters containing their name and workplace had been circulated. *Id.* at 1063–64. Physicians brought suit against the ACLA under the Freedom of Access to Clinics Entrances Act (FACE), 18 U.S.C. § 248, which provides aggrieved persons a right of action against whoever by "threat of force . . . intentionally . . . intimidates . . . any person because that person is or has been . . . providing reproductive health services." *Id.* at 1062. ACLA argued that the poster and the Nuremberg Files were protected political speech, and were not "true threats." *Id.* at 1072. The Ninth Circuit applied a "reasonable speaker" true threat test to determine the definition of "threat of force" under FACE: [W]hether a reasonable person would foresee that the statement would be interpreted by those to whom the maker communicates the statement as a serious expression of intent to harm or assault." *Id.* at 1074. The court concluded that the posters were not just political statements, even if the first couple of posters were purely political messages; "the poster format itself had acquired currency as a death threat for abortion providers." *Id.* at 1079. As a result, the court held that the use of the posters and the listing in the Nuremberg Files constituted a "true threat." *Id.* at 1088. However, the Nuremberg Files still constitute "protected speech" and personal information may only not be used "with the specific intent to threaten" the physicians. *Id.*

167.   *See id.* at 1064–65 (stating that the ACLA published a "Deadly Dozen" poster listing the names and offices of a dozen abortion providers, and provided information on abortion providers to a website hosting the names of abortion providers).

168.   *See id.* at 1063–64 (stating that Dr. David Gunn, Dr. George Patterson, and Dr. John Bayard Britton had all been shot and killed after appearing on posters).

169.   *See id.* at 1080 ("[N]ames of abortion providers who have been murdered because of their activities are lined through in black, while names of those who have been wounded are highlighted in grey.").

170.   *See id.* at 1088 (stating that the posters and the "Nuremberg Files" constitute true threats, and the ACLA realized that the posters had a threatening meaning that physicians would take seriously).

171.   *See id.* at 1086 ("Like 'fighting words,' true threats are proscribable.").

words" as words that by their very utterance "inflict injury or tend to incite an immediate breach of the peace."[172] The Supreme Court has recently fleshed out this doctrine in *R.A.V. v. City of Saint Paul*,[173] which held unconstitutional a Saint Paul ordinance that criminalized "plac[ing] on public or private property a symbol . . . including, but not limited to, a burning cross or Nazi swastika, which one knows or has reason to know arouses anger, alarm or resentment in others on the basis of race, color, creed, religion or gender."[174] The Court said that even if the statute only reached speech proscribable under the "fighting words" doctrine, it was still unconstitutional because it prohibited speech based purely on the basis of the subjects the speech addressed.[175] The statute only criminalized "fighting words" on the basis of "race, color, creed, religion, or gender," and permitted the use of "fighting words" on every other subject.[176] As a result, the statute created "the possibility that the city is seeking to handicap the expression of particular ideas."[177]

---

172. Chaplinsky v. New Hampshire, 315 U.S. 568, 572 (1942).

173. R.A.V. v. City of St. Paul, 505 U.S. 377 (1992). Petitioner, R.A.V., allegedly assembled a cross and burned the cross inside the fenced yard of a neighbor who lived across the street from R.A.V. *Id.* at 379. Petitioner was charged for violating a Saint Paul ordinance that provides that it is disorderly conduct to "place[ ] on public or private property a symbol . . . including, but not limited to, a burning cross or Nazi swastika, which one knows or has reason to know arouses anger, alarm or resentment in others on the basis of race, color, creed, religion or gender." *Id* at 380. Petitioner moved "to dismiss this count on the ground that the Saint Paul ordinance was substantially overbroad and impermissibly content based and therefore facially invalid under the First Amendment." *Id.* The trial court granted this motion, but the Minnesota Supreme Court reversed. *Id.* The Minnesota Supreme Court said that the statute was not overbroad because it was limited to content that is proscribable under the *Chaplinsky* "fighting words" doctrine. *Id.* Further, the Minnesota Supreme Court said that the statute was not impermissibly content-based because it was narrowly tailored. *Id.* at 381. The United States Supreme Court reversed the determination of the Minnesota Supreme Court. *Id.* For its review, the Court assumed that the only content the statute could reach was content proscribable as "fighting words" under the *Chaplinsky* formulation. *Id.* However, the Court held that the statute was impermissibly content-based because it prohibited speech purely on the basis of the subjects the speech addresses. *Id.* Although the statute prohibited "fighting words" on the basis of "race, color, creed, religion, or gender," it did not reach political affiliation, union membership, or homosexuality. *Id.* at 391. The Court said that the "First Amendment does not permit Saint Paul to impose special prohibitions on those speakers who express views on disfavored subjects." *Id.*

174. *Id.* at 380.

175. *See id.* at 381 ("Assuming, *arguendo*, that all of the expression reached by the ordinance is proscribable under the 'fighting words' doctrine, we nonetheless conclude that the ordinance is facially unconstitutional in that it prohibits otherwise permitted speech solely on the basis of the subjects the speech addresses.").

176. *See id.* at 391 ("Those who wish to use 'fighting words' in connection with other ideas—to express hostility, for example, on the basis of political affiliation, union membership, or homosexuality—are not covered.").

177. *Id.* at 394.

The Court did say that Saint Paul could prohibit cross burning consistent with the First Amendment; the city just failed to do so in that case.[178] Another attempt to prohibit cross burning was found unconstitutional in *Virginia v. Black*.[179] Although *R.A.V.* is a "fighting words" case, *Virginia v. Black* is a "true threat" case.[180] Unlike the ordinance in *R.A.V.*, Virginia's cross burning statute did not single out any particular individual or group;[181] instead, it generally provided that it "shall be unlawful for any person or group of persons, to burn, or cause to be burned, a cross on the property of another, a highway or other public place."[182] Given the history of cross burnings as a form of intimidation, the Court said that it was consistent for Virginia to outlaw cross burnings done with the intent to intimidate, as it met the "true threat" threshold.[183] However, the Court held the statute unconstitutional because it provided that any burning of a cross constituted "prima facie evidence of an intent to intimidate."[184] The Court stated that the history of cross burnings indicates that a burning cross is "not always intended to intimidate,"[185] and the

---

178.   *See id.* at 396 ("St. Paul has sufficient means at its disposal to prevent such behavior without adding the First Amendment to the fire.").

179.   Virginia v. Black, 538 U.S. 343 (2003). Defendants were convicted separately for violating Virginia's cross-burning statute, which provides that it is unlawful for any person "with the intent of intimidating any person or group of persons, to burn, or cause to be burned, a cross on the property of another, a highway or other public place." *Id.* at 348. The statute further provides that any "such burning of a cross shall be prima facie evidence of an intent to intimidate a person or group of persons." *Id.* The Supreme Court held that it is consistent with the First Amendment for a state to ban cross burning carried out with the intent to intimidate. *Id.* at 363. However, by making the burning of a cross prima facie evidence of intent to intimidate, the statute crossed the line between what may be proscribable threatening speech, and what is merely core political speech. *Id.* at 365–66. Even though a cross burning at a political rally may arouse anger in a vast majority of citizens, that is not sufficient to ban all cross burnings. *Id.* at 366. Because the statute fails to distinguish between cross burnings directed at an individual from cross burning directed at a group of like-minded believers, the statute was ruled unconstitutional. *Id.* at 365–66.

180.   *See id.* at 360 (stating that intimidation is a type of "true threat" and that respondents do not contest that some cross burnings fit within this meaning of intimidating speech).

181.   *See id.* at 362 ("Unlike the statute at issue in *R.A.V.*, the Virginia statute does not single out for opprobrium only that speech directed toward 'one of the specified disfavored topics.'").

182.   *Id.* at 348.

183.   *See id.* at 363 ("Instead of prohibiting all intimidating messages, Virginia may choose to regulate this subset of intimidating messages in light of cross burning's long and pernicious history as a signal of impending violence.").

184.   *See id.* at 367 ("For these reasons, the prima facie evidence provision, as interpreted through the jury instruction and as applied in Barry Black's case, is unconstitutional on its face.").

185.   *Id.* at 365.

statute failed to distinguish between "a cross burning at a public rally or a cross burning on a neighbor's lawn."[186] The prima facie evidence provision, the Court stated, "ignores all of the contextual factors that are necessary to decide whether a particular cross burning is intended to intimidate."[187] In order to be a "true threat," there must be intent to intimidate, and the prima facie evidence provision constituted an impermissible shortcut.[188]

One could argue that *Black* backtracks from the Court's opinion in *R.A.V.* that the First Amendment cannot be proscribed based on the content of the speech. The prohibition on cross burnings seems aimed particularly at cross burnings done with a racial animus. However, the Court does distinguish the two statutes, likely preserving the *R.A.V.* rule. Justice O'Connor distinguished the Virginia statute from the St. Paul ordinance by saying that in the Virginia statute, "[i]t does not matter whether an individual burns a cross with intent to intimidate because of the victim's race, gender, or religion, or because of the victim's 'political affiliation, union membership, or homosexuality.'"[189] As a result, the statute did not result in a targeted prohibition because it targeted all cross burnings and not just those directed to intimidate a particular group, and the Court cited a few cases where cross burnings were intended to intimidate but were not done with a racial animus.[190] This distinction seems to indicate that the Court is not backtracking on its statement in *R.A.V.* that the First Amendment does not allow the government to proscribe speech on the basis of the subject of the speech.

B. The Protocol and the First Amendment

The preceding cases demonstrate that for the United States to proscribe hate speech, the United States must meet the high burden required by the tests for "true threat" or for "fighting words." Even though the United States has stated it will not enact the Protocol, the constitutionality of the provisions will affect the ability of a party to enforce its hate speech legislation in American

---

186.   *Id.* at 366.

187.   *Id.* at 367.

188.   *See id.* ("The First Amendment does not permit such a shortcut.").

189.   *Id.* at 362 (quoting R.A.V. v. City of St. Paul, 505 U.S. 377, 391 (1992)).

190.   *See id.* at 362–63 (noting instances of cross burnings directed at union members, the case of a defendant who burned a cross in the yard of a lawyer who had previously represented him and who was currently prosecuting him, and the case of defendants who burned a cross in a neighbor's yard possibly because they were angry that their neighbor had complained about the presence of a firearm shooting range in defendants' yard).

courts.[191] As a result, an analysis of the constitutionality of each of the provisions of the Protocol is necessary. Given the high burden set by the Court, if the United States were to enact the Protocol, most of the provisions of the Protocol would likely be held unconstitutional.

Article 3 of the Protocol requires each party to criminalize "distributing, or otherwise making available, racist and xenophobic material to the public through a computer system."[192] This Article does not distinguish between purely political speech and speech intended to intimidate, so it would not meet the constitutional requirements of a "true threat." This statute is analogous to the statute ruled unconstitutional in *Black*: Like Virginia placed a blanket prohibition on cross burning,[193] the Council of Europe is placing a blanket prohibition on distribution of racist and xenophobic materials. The Virginia statute failed to distinguish between cross burnings at a political rally for the benefit of like-minded individuals and a cross burning on a neighbor's lawn.[194] The Council of Europe has failed to distinguish between racist and xenophobic materials directed to other racists and xenophobes and material intended to intimidate. As a result, this Article will not meet the "true threat" test.

Article 3 also will not meet the requirements of the "fighting words" test. *Chaplinsky* limits the "fighting words" doctrine to those words that "by their very utterance inflict injury or tend to incite an immediate breach of the peace."[195] It is doubtful the mere distribution of racist material over the Internet will result in an "immediate breach of the peace."[196] However, even if it is accepted that the distribution of racist and xenophobic material on the Internet would cause an "immediate breach of the peace," the Article would run into the *R.A.V.* problem of singling out certain speech for criminalization. The Protocol only criminalizes racist and xenophobic speech, which is similar to how the

---

191.   *See* Yahoo!, Inc. v. La Ligue Contre Le Racisme et L'Antisemitisme, 169 F. Supp. 2d 1181, 1184 (N.D. Cal. 2001) (issuing a declaratory judgment that a French order requiring Yahoo! to disable French access to auctions of Nazi memorabilia is unenforceable in the United States because of the protections afforded speech by the First Amendment), *rev'd*, 379 F.3d 1120 (9th Cir. 2004).

192.   Additional Protocol, *supra* note 56, at 8.

193.   *See* Virginia v. Black, 538 U.S. 343, 348 (2003) ("It shall be unlawful for any person or persons, with the intent of intimidating any person or group of persons, to burn, or cause to be burned, a cross on the property of another, a highway or other public place.").

194.   *See id.* at 366 ("It does not distinguish between a cross burning at a public rally or a cross burning on a neighbor's lawn. It does not treat the cross burning directed at an individual differently from the cross burning directed at a group of like-minded believers.").

195.   Chaplinsky v. New Hampshire, 315 U.S. 568, 572 (1942).

196.   *See* Timofeeva, *supra* note 165, at 272 ("Indeed, it does not seem highly probable that impersonal, or even personal messages on the computer screen would directly cause someone to get involved in violence or disorder.").

Saint Paul ordinance only criminalizes the posting of symbols likely to arouse anger on the basis of "race, color, creed, religion or gender."[197] The Saint Paul ordinance was held unconstitutional on this basis because the First Amendment "does not permit St. Paul to impose special prohibitions on those speakers who express views on disfavored subjects."[198] Given this precedent, even if the Protocol were found to criminalize only conduct rising to the level of "fighting words," it will be held unconstitutional because it only criminalizes speech concerning certain disfavored subjects.

A similar analysis would lead to the unconstitutionality of Article 6, which criminalizes the denial or minimization of a genocide.[199] The denial of genocide is not likely to result in intimidation, and, even if it does, the statute does not distinguish between denials of genocide intended to intimidate and denials not intended to intimidate. As a result, it is not likely to meet the *Black* "true threat" test. The Article does allow a country to reserve the right to require that the denial be accompanied by "intent to incite hatred, discrimination or violence against any individual or group."[200] However, even with a requirement of intent, this Article is still likely to be found unconstitutional under a "true threat" analysis. The reservation still requires criminalization of intent to incite hatred and discrimination, which are not true threats—only intent to incite violence is a true threat.[201] Even if it can be assumed that denials of genocide are likely to lead to an "immediate breach of peace" under the "fighting words" analysis and the other problems did not exist, this Article still would be unconstitutional because it is singling out a particular viewpoint for criminalization. The Article states that only denials of genocide are to be criminalized under the Protocol, so it is criminalizing a "disfavored subject" based on the speaker's viewpoint, which is unconstitutional under *R.A.V.*[202]

Article 5, criminalizing the act of publicly insulting a person for the reason that they belong to a group distinguished by race, is also likely to be

---

197. R.A.V. v. City of St. Paul, 505 U.S. 377, 379 (1992).

198. *Id.* at 391.

199. *See supra* notes 69–71 and accompanying text (stating that Article 6 requires each party to criminalize the denial or minimization of a genocide, unless the party reserves the right not to apply this Article).

200. Additional Protocol, *supra* note 56, at 10.

201. *See* Planned Parenthood of Columbia/Willamette v. Am. Coalition of Life Activists, 290 F.3d 1058, 1088 (9th Cir. 2002) (stating that the Nuremberg Files are only unprotected to the extent physicians are threatened with being next on a hit list).

202. *See* R.A.V. v. City of St. Paul, 505 U.S. 377, 391 (1992) ("The First Amendment does not permit St. Paul to impose special prohibitions on those who speakers who express views on disfavored subjects.").

unconstitutional.[203] Insulting someone in public is likely to result in an "immediate breach of the peace," which would make it a candidate for proscription under *Chaplinsky*.[204] However, the Internet involves less reason for thinking that a public insult would lead to an immediate breach of the peace, so it is doubtful this would rise to the level of "fighting words" in the context of the Internet.[205] Even if it did rise to the level of "fighting words," this Article would be unconstitutional because it impermissibly concerns the subject of the speech. In *R.A.V.*, the Supreme Court assumed that the ordinance only reached conduct proscribable as "fighting words," but held the ordinance unconstitutional because it only criminalized conduct likely to arouse anger on the basis of "race, color, creed, religion or gender."[206] Similarly, the Protocol only criminalizes publicly insulting someone on the basis of the person's "race, colour, descent or national or ethnic origin."[207] Because the Article singles out for punishment those speakers who "express views on disfavored subjects," it will likely be found unconstitutional.[208]

The Article that comes the closest to being constitutional is Article 4, which requires parties to criminalize "threatening . . . with the commission of a serious criminal offense . . . (i) persons for the reason that they belong to a group, distinguished by race, colour, descent or national or ethnic origin . . . or (ii) a group of persons which is distinguished by any of these characteristics."[209] This Article seems to make the necessary distinction between speech likely to result in "imminent lawless action" and speech not likely to result in such action because it is limited only to cases where a person threatened another person with the "commission of a serious criminal offense." As a result, the conduct described in this Article appears to be proscribable as a true threat. However, even though it is proscribable conduct, the statute is likely to fail the First

---

203.   *See* Additional Protocol, *supra* note 56, at 4 (requiring parties to adopt measures criminalizing "insulting publicly . . . persons for the reason that they belong to a group distinguished by race, colour, descent or national or ethnic origin").

204.   *See* Chaplinsky v. New Hampshire, 315 U.S. 568, 569, 573 (1942) (holding that it is constitutional for New Hampshire to criminalize addressing any offensive word to any other person in a public place because it is likely to result in an "immediate breach of the peace").

205.   *See* Timofeeva, *supra* note 165, at 272 ("Indeed, it does not seem highly probable that impersonal, or even personal messages on the computer screen would directly cause someone to get involved in violence or disorder.").

206.   *See* R.A.V. v. City of St. Paul, 505 U.S. 377, 380, 396 (1992) (holding the St. Paul ordinance unconstitutional).

207.   Additional Protocol, *supra* note 56, at 5.

208.   *See* R.A.V., 505 U.S. at 391 ("The First Amendment does not permit St. Paul to impose special prohibitions on those speakers who express views on disfavored subjects.").

209.   Additional Protocol, *supra* note 56, at 9.

Amendment analysis because it violates the *R.A.V.* rule that it is impermissible to proscribe speech based on the subject of the speech. The Protocol only targets true threats where the threat was instigated because of the person's "race, colour, descent or national or ethnic origin," making it a regulation of the basis of speech, and not a regulation based on the conduct or effect of the speech. One could argue that, in *Black*, the Supreme Court became more receptive to regulation based on the subject of the speech, but the statutes appear to be distinguishable enough to the point where *R.A.V.* remains good law.[210]

C. Enforcement of Criminal Liability

The First Amendment analysis demonstrates that each of the provisions of the Protocol would likely be found unconstitutional under American law if the United States adopted these provisions, with the possible exception of Article 4's true threat provisions. However, the United States has indicated that it will not sign the Protocol, so a legislative enactment is not presently at issue.[211] Instead, the First Amendment jurisprudence provides insight into the enforceability of European judgments in American courts. Because of the protections the First Amendment accords speech, it is doubtful the European nations that enact the Protocol will be able to reach most hate speech posted from the United States.

American Internet users who post hate speech on the Internet generally do not need to worry about criminal liability unless they engage in foreign travel. As the *Toben* case illustrates, European courts view their jurisdiction broadly, and hold users who post speech on the Internet liable under their nations' law, even if the content is uploaded to the Internet from outside their nations.[212] However, Toben made the mistake of visiting Germany and was arrested while on German soil.[213] For a criminal trial, the defendant generally must be present.[214] If Toben never visited Germany, in order for Germany to press

---

210. *See supra* notes 189–90 and accompanying text (analyzing the differences between the statutes at issue in *R.A.V.* and in *Black*).

211. *See* McCullagh, *supra* note 151 (stating that the Bush Administration will not support the additional protocol).

212. *See supra* Part IV.E.1 (concerning the criminal prosecution by Germany of Frederick Toben).

213. *See* Matthew Abraham, *History's Rewriter Faces German Jail*, THE AUSTRALIAN, July 8, 1999, at 4 (stating that Toben was arrested while making a visit to the local prosecutor's office to discuss his Holocaust research).

214. *See* DADAMO & FARRAN, *supra* note 92, at 193 ("Moreover, unlike in a civil trial, the

criminal charges against Toben, the prosecutors would have needed to extradite Toben from Australia to Germany.

Extradition in the United States is governed by treaties; the United States cannot seize a fugitive criminal and surrender him to a foreign power in the absence of a treaty.[215] Extradition treaties are either multilateral or bilateral. An example of a multilateral extradition treaty would be the underlying Convention on Cybercrime's extradition provisions.[216] However, a party to the Convention on Cybercrime is not obligated to extradite defendants sought for prosecution for violating provisions of the Additional Protocol,[217] and there are no other multilateral treaties on point.[218] Therefore, a country seeking a fugitive defendant from the United States would need to rely on its bilateral treaty with the United States.

The United States does not have any bilateral extradition treaties with European nations that would obligate it to hand over defendants to be charged in connection with the posting of hate speech on the Internet. The United States' bilateral extradition treaty with Germany contains a list of thirty-three extraditable offenses, and, additionally, provides for extradition for any offense not listed, provided it is punishable under the federal laws of the United States and Germany.[219] The posting of hate speech on the Internet neither falls within any of the listed extraditable offenses, nor is it a crime punishable under the federal laws of the United States, so it would not be an extraditable offense.

---

defendant must be personally present at his trial before a criminal court . . . and cannot be simply represented as in civil proceedings.").

215. *See* Valentine v. United States *ex rel.* Neidecker, 299 U.S. 5, 9 (1936) ("[I]n the absence of a conventional or legislative provision, there is no authority vested in any department of the government to seize a fugitive criminal and surrender him to a foreign power."); M. CHERIF BASSOUINI, INTERNATIONAL EXTRADITION: UNITED STATES LAW AND PRACTICE 36 (4th ed. 2002) ("[T]he United States requires a treaty, as does the United Kingdom and most common law countries.").

216. *See* Convention on Cybercrime, Nov. 23, 2001, art. 24, Europ. T.S. No. 185 (providing in Article 24 for extradition for crimes established by the Convention), *available at* http://conventions.coe.int/Treaty/en/Treaties/Html/185.htm (on file with the Washington and Lee Law Review).

217. *See id.* (stating that the extradition provisions of the Convention on Cybercrime only concern criminal offenses established in accordance with Articles 2–11 of the Convention); *see also* Additional Protocol, *supra* note 56 (stating in Article 8 that the scope of application of measures defined in Article 24 is extended to signatories of the Additional Protocol).

218. *See* BASSOUINI, *supra* note 215, at 913–23 (listing multilateral conventions containing provisions on extradition).

219. *See* Extradition, Jun. 20, 1978, U.S.-F.R.G., art. 2, 32 U.S.T. 1485, 1489 (providing extradition for offenses described in the Appendix to the treaty, and for offenses, whether listed in the Appendix or not, provided they are punishable under the laws of the United States and the laws of the Federal Republic of Germany).

The extradition treaty of the United States with France has similar language to the treaty with Germany, with a list of extraditable offenses, on the condition that acts are punished as crimes or offenses by the laws of both States.[220] As a result, just like with Germany, the United States cannot extradite an individual to France for posting hate speech on the Internet.

The other extradition treaties of the United States with European nations contain similar language.[221] Because there are no treaties providing for extradition by the United States of individuals sought for criminal prosecution for posting hate speech on the Internet, the prosecuting country will be unable to extradite the offender from the United States. This bars criminal prosecution unless, like Toben, the defendant engages in foreign travel.

Although the individual poster of the content would need to engage in foreign travel, an ISP may have an office or subdivision in the country that is charging the defendant for the conduct. However, the *Somm* case demonstrates that liability is not likely to be imposed on corporate subdivisions for conduct of the parent company. Because the German subdivision in that case had no control over servers located in America, the charges were dismissed against Felix Somm.[222] If courts follow this precedent, no liability is likely to be imposed on American ISPs or their foreign subdivisions for content posted on American servers.

D. *Enforcement of Civil Liability*

Although the defendant must be present for a criminal trial, no presence is required for a civil trial. If the defendant is not present, a court is likely to issue a default judgment against an Internet user who posts hate speech on the Internet once the judge determines that the claim is admissible and well founded.[223] However, this judgment will be helpful to the enforcing country only if the defendant has assets in the country issuing the default judgment.[224]

---

220. *See* Extradition, Feb. 12, 1970, U.S.-Fr., art. 2, 22 U.S.T. 407, 409 (providing that extradition shall be granted for certain acts if they are punished as crimes or offenses by the laws of both countries).

221. *See* Goldsmith, *supra* note 3, at 1220 ("A pervasive feature of modern extradition treaties is the principle of double criminality. This principle requires that the charged offense be criminal in both the requesting and the requested jurisdictions.").

222. *See supra* Part IV.E.2 (stating that Felix Somm's conviction was reversed on appeal because he had no control over content posted on American servers).

223. *See* DADAMO & FARRAN, *supra* note 92, at 178 ("A judgment may be entered in the absence of the defendant once the judge has ensured that the claim is admissible and well founded.").

224. *See* Goldsmith, *supra* note 3, at 1217 (stating that the defendant's physical presence or

Otherwise, the issuing country would need to attempt to enforce the judgment in the United States, if all the assets of the defendant are located there.

If a country seeks to enforce a civil judgment in an American court against an individual who posts hate speech on the Internet, a court is likely to refuse to enforce the judgment. Enforcement of foreign judgments is based on comity.[225] However, the outcome would likely be the same as that reached in the *Yahoo!* case. The First Amendment protections accorded free speech will likely be enough to prevent enforcement of foreign civil judgments in American courts.[226] However, it is questionable whether the First Amendment protects all of the provisions of the Protocol—particularly Article 4's true threat provisions. Even if a court were to find that the true threat on the basis of race is proscribable based on *Black*, the court may still fall back on the second reason offered by the amici curiae in the *Yahoo!* case: The foreign court has no jurisdiction over a web site posted in the United States and targeted at American Internet users.[227] In the United States, the mere passive presence of a website as viewable in another jurisdiction will not be enough for a court to allow jurisdiction.[228] For jurisdiction, American courts generally require that the website target the forum or that the website is highly interactive.[229] Because presence is not sufficient, unless one of these other requirements is met, even if the content is proscribable, the judgment is still unlikely to be enforced because

assets within the territory remains the primary basis for a nation or state to enforce its laws, and that the large majority of persons who transact in cyberspace have no presence or assets in the jurisdictions that wish to regulate their information flows in cyberspace).

225. *See* Yahoo!, Inc. v. La Ligue Contre Le Racisme et L'Antisemitisme, 169 F. Supp. 2d 1181, 1192 (N.D. Cal. 2001) ("The extent to which the United States, or any state, honors the judicial decrees of foreign nations is a matter of choice, governed by 'the comity of nations.'" (quoting Hilton v. Guyot, 159 U.S. 113, 163 (1895))), *rev'd*, 379 F.3d 1120 (9th Cir. 2004).

226. *See id.* at 1193 ("Absent a body of law that establishes international standards with respect to speech on the Internet and an appropriate treaty or legislation addressing enforcement of such standards to speech originating within the United States, the principle of comity is outweighed by the Court's obligation to uphold the First Amendment.").

227. *See supra* notes 140–43 and accompanying text (concerning the alternative argument promoted by the amici curiae for granting Yahoo! the declaratory judgment: The lack of jurisdiction of the French court).

228. *See* Zippo Mfg. Co. v. Zippo Dot Com, Inc., 952 F. Supp. 1119, 1124 (W.D. Pa. 1997) ("A passive Website that does little more than make information available to those who are interested in it is not grounds for the exercise [of] personal jurisdiction.").

229. *See id.* at 1126–27 (holding that the Pennsylvania court has jurisdiction over a case filed against a California website, after finding that the website is highly interactive, has subscribers in Pennsylvania, has contracts with Internet-access providers to furnish its services to customers in Pennsylvania, and the harm occurred in Pennsylvania). *But see* Hy Cite Corp. v. Badbusinessbureau.com, L.L.C., 297 F. Supp. 2d 1154, 1158–67 (W.D. Wis. 2004) (rejecting the sliding scale of website interactivity approach adopted in *Zippo*, and instead applying traditional jurisdiction tests).

822   *62 WASH. & LEE L. REV. 781 (2005)*

of the lack of jurisdiction of the foreign court. As a result, given the protections accorded free speech by the First Amendment and America's requirements for establishing personal jurisdiction, it is doubtful that a foreign judgment would be enforceable in an American court against an individual who posts hate speech on the Internet from America.

If the person posting the hate speech is not a unique individual, but instead a corporation or an ISP, the same analysis would apply. Although the foreign court would likely find jurisdiction to hear the case and issue a judgment, unless the corporation has foreign assets available, the judgment would need to be enforced in an American court, and the outcome would be the same as in the *Yahoo!* case.[230] The American court would find the judgment contrary to the First Amendment or would find that the foreign court has no jurisdiction over the matter.[231]

E. Effect of Inability of European Laws To Reach American Conduct

As European countries are unable to extradite American offenders and are not able to enforce civil judgments in American courts, the posting of hate speech from American servers will go largely unpunished. The effect of the protections accorded racist speech by American laws will be that America will become a haven for hate speech. An American haven can take two possible forms: (1) no foreign web sites will come to America, but American web sites will provide a leak to European web users; or (2) European webmasters, fearing liability for posting hate speech in Europe, will be attracted to America. If the former occurs, America will not face a policy problem, as it will not result in an escalation of hate speech taking place on its territory. However, if the latter occurs, more hate-speakers will come to America, which could create a potential policy problem for America.

America does act as a leak of hate speech to the world: Before the Protocol, it was already the case that most hate sites on the Internet were based in America.[232] This number largely represents sites, such as

---

230. *See* Goldsmith, *supra* note 3, at 1217 ("A defendant's physical presence or assets within the territory remains the primary basis for a nation or state to enforce its laws.").

231. *See* Yahoo!, Inc. v. La Ligue Contre Le Racisme et L'Antisemitisme, 169 F. Supp. 2d 1181, 1193 (N.D. Cal. 2001) ("Absent a body of law that establishes international standards with respect to speech on the Internet and an appropriate treaty or legislation addressing enforcement of such standards to speech originating within the United States, the principle of comity is outweighed by the Court's obligation to uphold the First Amendment."), *rev'd*, 379 F.3d 1120 (9th Cir. 2004).

232. *See* Scheeres, *supra* note 11 (stating that, according to a Council of Europe report,

Stormfront.org,[233] that target an American audience. However, the number also includes sites that have moved to America in response to hate speech legislation in other countries: Reports indicate that Germany's actions against hate speech led many hate groups to transfer their sites from Germany to the United States.[234] As a result, it appears that an American haven does have the effect of causing some hate-speakers to move their sites to America to take advantage of America's protection of free speech.

If the trend of transferring sites from European countries to the United States continues, with a greater crackdown on racist sites in Europe, more of these websites will likely flee to the United States. Given the protections accorded hate speech by the First Amendment, the United States will have no constitutional way to combat them. This may or may not pose a policy problem for the United States. If the speakers are merely utilizing American servers, and otherwise maintaining their presence in foreign territory, then the site will have minimal effect on American culture. The greatest effect would be greater animosity toward the United States from countries that have criminalized the content and are seeking to remove such content from the Internet. However, if these individuals continue to maintain presence outside the United States, then foreign countries would be able to assert jurisdiction over these individuals based on presence even if the website is not located in the enforcing country.[235]

But if the transference of websites to the United States alone proves insufficient to protect speakers of hate from liability under the growing global framework against hate speech, then the speakers may take the next logical step—transference of their presence to the United States. Although the United States has a rich tradition for the protection of free speech and the welcoming of different ideological viewpoints, the transference of presence could pose a policy problem for the United States. An influx of hate speakers into the United States would likely result in an increase of hate groups in the United States, which would have the effect of increasing racial tension. As a

---

2500 out of 4000 racist websites were created in the United States).

    233.   Stormfront, *at* http://www.stormfront.org (last visited Jan. 27, 2005) (on file with the Washington and Lee Law Review).

    234.   *See* Agence-France Press, *Neo-Nazi Web Sites Reported to Flee Germany*, N.Y. TIMES, Aug. 21, 2000, at A5 ("In a report on neo-Nazi activities, [N.D.R.] radio said that around 90 rightist groups had transferred their sites to the United States . . . .").

    235.   *See* Goldsmith, *supra* note 3, at 1216–17 (stating that a nation can enforce its laws against a person with physical presence or assets within the territory).

result, steps consistent with the Constitution may be necessary to help prevent the United States from becoming a haven for Internet hate speech.

VI. Ways To Mitigate the United States as a Haven for Internet Hate Speech

Although the Protocol will be largely ineffective against hate speech originating in America and the First Amendment prevents America from joining in the Protocol, there are several policy alternatives available to policymakers that could mitigate the ability of the United States to act as a haven for Internet hate speech. These policies include steps Europe can take to clog the American leak, and steps America can implement to prevent an escalation of racist speech.[236]

A. European ISPs Blocking Foreign Hate Speech Sites

European nations can adopt the approach that Spain has taken with American websites. Spain has passed a law authorizing judges to order the blocking of websites that do not comply with national law.[237] The increasing use of blocking software may lead some racist speakers to determine that setting up a racist website in the United States is not worth the effort if the site will not be available around the globe. However, as stated above, this approach can be problematic. Namely, it is onerous on the victimized country because it forces the victimized country to search out the illegal content.[238] As a result, this approach may not be effective in deterring the content from being placed on the Internet in the first place.

---

236. In addition to the policy proposals suggested below, there are also means users can take to block hate speech from their computers. The Anti-Defamation League has developed a free filter available for download, which blocks websites of those organizations which, in the judgment of the Anti-Defamation League, advocate hatred, bigotry, or violence towards Jews or other groups on the basis of their religion, race, ethnicity, sexual orientation, or other characteristics. For more information on the Anti-Defamation League's HateFilter, see http://www.adl.org/hatefilter/default.asp.

237. *See* Scheeres, *supra* note 11 ("Spain recently passed legislation authorizing judges to shut down Spanish sites and block access to U.S. Web pages that don't comply with national laws.").

238. *See supra* note 11 and accompanying text (stating that the Spanish law does not place a deterrent on the producer of the content to not put the content on the Internet on the first place).

B. Increased Cooperation by American ISPs Against Hate Speech

European countries can also increase dialogue with American ISPs and try to create voluntary agreements for the suppression of hate speech. Even though the United States government cannot proscribe most hate speech, the First Amendment does not require a private party to publish and make available the speech.[239] As a result, ISPs are able to restrict the speech published on their websites. In recognizing the limitations the Protocol would have in reaching conduct originating in the United States, the European Commission on Racism and Intolerance endorsed this approach.[240] ISPs have indicated a willingness to cooperate on this front: In the wake of the French actions against Yahoo!, Yahoo! announced that it would ban auctions of Nazi artifacts on its site.[241] However, the cooperation of ISPs would only be successful to the extent the websites in question do not maintain their own server. Even if they are not on their own server, this may only just lead to displacement of hate speech, with speakers leaving censored servers and placing their content on uncensored servers.

C. Extradition Treaty

Another policy solution would be for the United States to enter into a treaty providing for the extradition of speakers of hate speech.[242] However, this approach is unlikely to pass constitutional muster under the current framework proposed by the Council of Europe. Extradition must be done by treaty.[243] A

---

239. *See* Hudgens v. NLRB, 424 U.S. 507, 520–21 (1976) (holding that striking union members have no First Amendment right to enter a mall for the purpose of advertising their strike against one of the stores therein because a mall is not a state actor).

240. *See* LEGAL INSTRUMENTS, *supra* note 24, at 90 ("The prudent course, therefore, would be to enter into a dialogue with all service providers, in particular the Americans, in order to convince them that they themselves must take the appropriate measures to combat racist sites (by blocking sites, filtering, refusing anonymity to authors of sites, etc.).").

241. *See* Lori Enos, *Yahoo! to Ban Nazi-Related Auctions*, E-COMMERCE TIMES, http://www.ecommercetimes.com/perl/story/6432.html (Jan. 3, 2001) ("Responding to pressure from anti-hate groups and concerned users, Yahoo! announced . . . it will ban auctions of Nazi artifacts and other items 'that are associated with groups which promote or glorify hatred and violence.'") (on file with the Washington and Lee Law Review).

242. *See* Alexander Tsesis, *Prohibiting Incitement on the Internet*, 7 VA. J.L. & TECH. 5, ¶ 89 (2002) (proposing an extradition treaty as a way to prevent the United States from becoming a safe harbor for hate speech), *available at* http://www.vjolt.net/vol7/issue2/v7i2_a05-Tsesis.pdf.

243. *See* BASSOUINI, *supra* note 215, at 36 ("[T]he United States requires a treaty, as does the United Kingdom and most common law countries.").

court would be unlikely to allow the extradition of a defendant to a foreign country if the extradition would be inconsistent with the Bill of Rights. Although Congress can sometimes accomplish by treaty what it cannot legislate under the Commerce Clause,[244] a treaty must still be consistent with the Bill of Rights.[245] An extradition treaty would likely be ruled unconstitutional if the crime for which the fugitive was being sought would result in an action unconstitutional in the United States.[246] It appears as though none of the provisions of the Protocol would be constitutional, with the possible exception of the Article concerning true threats.[247]

However, an extradition treaty can still provide a solution. Even though the "true threat" Article of the Protocol would likely be found unconstitutional because it impermissibly regulates on the basis of the subject of the speech, "true threats" are proscribable in the United States. The United States could enter an extradition treaty providing for extradition of "true threats," as long as the criminal statute in question is not subject-based. As a result, it is possible for Europe to rewrite the language of the "true threat" Article in a way that would be consistent with the First Amendment, allowing the United States to take part in an extradition treaty if it chooses to do so.

D. A Constitutional Moment?

A final policy alternative would be for the United States to adopt the tort action suggested by Richard Delgado and the administrative and criminal remedies suggested by Mari Matsuda. Delgado argued for the creation of a tort action available to victims of hate speech in his seminal Article, *Words that*

244.	*See* Missouri v. Holland, 252 U.S. 416, 434–35 (1920) (holding constitutional the Migratory Bird Treaty Act, which gives effect to a treaty between the United States and Great Britain, even though Congress has no power to legislate migratory birds under the Commerce Clause).

245.	*See* Reid v. Covert, 354 U.S. 1, 17–19 (1957) (holding unconstitutional an executive agreement authorizing military jurisdiction for crimes committed abroad by civilian dependents of servicemen, as a violation of rights guaranteed by the Bill of Rights).

246.	*Cf.* BASSOUINI, *supra* note 215, at 929 (stating that in July 1996, the Italian Constitutional Court declared its extradition treaty with the United States unconstitutional because the United States recognizes the death penalty, which is unconstitutional under Italian law).

247.	*See supra* Part IV.B (analyzing the constitutionality of each of the crimes provided for by the Protocol); *see also* Tsesis, *supra* note 242, ¶ 89 (stating that the United States would likely qualify its participation in an extradition treaty to those cases where incitements pose an imminent threat of harm).

Wound.[248] Delgado's cause of action is not based so much on the idea of "true threat" or "fighting words" that characterizes most legislation aimed at repressing racist speech, but instead on the idea of harassment and emotional distress.[249] To bring a cause of action under Delgado's tort theory, the plaintiff would be required to prove that: "Language was addressed to him or her by the defendant that was intended to demean through reference to race; that the plaintiff understood as intended to demean through reference to race; and that a reasonable person would recognize as a racial insult."[250]

Expanding on Delgado's tort action, Mari Matsuda argues for criminal and administrative sanctions for hate speech.[251] Matsuda's approach provides for three prerequisites to prosecution for hate speech: (1) "The message is of racial inferiority;" (2) "The message is directed against a historically oppressed group;" and (3) "The message is persecutory, hateful, and degrading."[252] According to Matsuda, her approach would restrict redress to only the most serious hate speech, and would appease civil libertarians' concerns of censorship, by leaving many forms of racist speech to private remedies.[253]

However, the adoption of the approaches suggested by Delgado and Matsuda has had mixed results, and despite the efforts of Delgado and Matsuda to propose their causes of action in line with the First Amendment,[254] the First Amendment has proved problematic. Outside of true threats and fighting words, racial insults have generally only been found actionable when they constitute battery, harassment, or emotional distress.[255] Delgado's and

---

248. *See* Richard Delgado, *Words that Wound: A Tort Action for Racial Insults, Epithets, and Name-Calling*, 17 HARV. C.R.-C.L. L. REV. 133, 149 (1982) ("Because racial attitudes of white Americans 'typically follow rather than precede actual institutional [or legal] alteration,' a tort for racial slurs is a promising vehicle for the eradication of racism.").

249. *See id.* ("The psychological, sociological, and political repercussions of the racial insult demonstrate the need for judicial relief.").

250. *Id.* at 179.

251. *See* Matsuda, *supra* note 157, at 17 ("Taking inspiration from Delgado's position, I make the further suggestion that formal criminal and administrative sanction—public as opposed to private prosecution—is also an appropriate response to racist speech.").

252. *Id.* at 36.

253. *See id.* at 50 ("[This chapter] suggests criminalization of a narrow, explicitly defined class of racist hate speech to provide public redress for the most serious harm, leaving many forms of racist speech to private remedies.").

254. *See* Delgado, *supra* note 248, at 172–79 (concluding that the government interest in regulating racial insults outweighs the speaker's free speech interests, as racial insults do not meet any of the four free speech interests articulated by Professor Emerson); Matsuda, *supra* note 157, at 35 ("In the following section I suggest that an explicit and narrow definition of racist hate messages will allow restriction consistent with first amendment values.").

255. *See* Fisher v. Carrousel Motor Hotel, Inc., 424 S.W.2d 627, 628–30 (Tex. 1967) (holding that the snatching of a plate from a Negro because he could not be served in the

Matsuda's causes of action run into problems with the First Amendment because they are based on the subject of the speech, as they both refer to targeting insults at a person on the basis of that person's race, running afoul of *R.A.V.*[256]

But if hate speech becomes a debilitating social problem in the United States, a "Constitutional moment" could occur. The exigencies of the Great Depression led to a Constitutional moment, according to Ackerman, that resulted in the United States Supreme Court abandoning a restrictive view of the Commerce Clause, expanding it to its modern interpretation as a broad bestowal of power to Congress.[257] Given the historical protections accorded free speech,[258] and the Court's generally strict adherence to precedent,[259] it is questionable if even a major influx of hate speech websites in America can provoke such a reassessment of the First Amendment. However, it remains possible. For instance, the Supreme Court has viewed with increasing favor the principles of the European Convention of Human Rights,[260] and the Convention's opposition to hate speech may be viewed favorably by the

---

cafeteria was a battery because the tort is designed to protect dignity as well as physical security); *see also* Contreras v. Crown Zellerbach Corp., 565 P.2d 1173, 1177 (Wash. 1977) (holding that a Mexican-American stated a claim for the tort of outrage—or intentional infliction of emotional distress—when continuously subjected to racial jokes and slurs by fellow employees).

256.   *See supra* notes 173–76 and accompanying text (stating that in *R.A.V.*, the Supreme Court held unconstitutional a St. Paul ordinance because, even if the statute only regulated "fighting words," the statute impermissibly prohibited speech based purely on the basis of the subject of the speech).

257.   *See* Bruce Ackerman, *Constitutional Politics/Constitutional Law*, 99 Yale L.J. 453, 488 (1989) (asserting that there have been three constitutional regimes in American history, and that these regimes were inaugurated by three constitutional moments: Founding, Reconstruction, and the New Deal).

258.   *See, e.g.*, Brandenburg v. Ohio, 395 U.S. 444, 447 (1969) (holding that the First Amendment protects speech that advocates violence, so long as the speech is not directed to inciting or promoting lawless action and is not likely to incite or produce such action). *But see* Abrams v. United States, 250 U.S. 616, 624 (1919) (upholding convictions of defendants who published material containing language disloyal about the form of the government). The Court's opinion in *Abrams* is famous for the dissent of Justice Oliver Wendell Holmes, who laid out the test the Court would later apply in *Brandenburg*: "[W]e should be eternally vigilant against attempts to check the expression of opinions that we loathe and believe to be fraught with death, unless they so imminently threaten immediate interference with the lawful and pressing purposes of the law that an immediate check is required to save the country." *Id.* at 630 (Holmes, J. dissenting).

259.   *See* Ackerman, *supra* note 257, at 488 (naming only three Constitutional moments in American history).

260.   *See* Lawrence v. Texas, 539 U.S. 558, 573 (2003) (citing a decision of the European Court of Human Rights finding sodomy laws in violation of the European Convention on Human Rights).

Court.[261] The protections the United States accords speech increasingly counter the values and regulations of the rest of the world, and the Court could view American exceptionalism as a persuasive reason to change the interpretation of the First Amendment.

This approach does not necessarily mean that the United States entirely needs to throw out the *Brandenburg* "true threat" framework: The effect could be as minimal as tossing out the rule in *R.A.V.* that speech cannot be proscribed on the basis of the subject of the speech. If that requirement is eliminated, then the United States could have more discretion to proscribe "true threats" that harm or target a particularly vulnerable group. The rule has been challenged by some for making limited logical sense because the Court acknowledges that "true threats" are not protected, but nevertheless finds content-based statutes unconstitutional because the statutes treat some "true threats" different from others.[262] If content is allowed to be proscribed on the basis of the subject of the speech, then it would be possible for the remedies offered by Delgado and Matsuda to be adopted. Even if the United States does not join the Protocol, the adoption of their proposals would give the United States the ability to proscribe some hate speech and enable the United States to enact a deterrent to hate speech, making the United States a less attractive haven for hate speech.

VII. Conclusion

Although the Council of Europe's Internet Hate Speech Protocol is not likely to result in any additional criminal or civil liability for American Internet users and providers, it will still have an effect on American society. With the increased cooperation of European countries to combat hate speech on the Internet in Europe, America is likely to become a haven for hate speech. This would be caused by both the visibility of pre-established American sites in Europe and America's status as an attractive home for European sites escaping the restrictions on speech present in Europe. However, there are steps that can

---

261. *See* The European Convention on Human Rights, art. 10 (Nov. 4, 1950) (stating that everyone has the right to freedom of expression, but that is limited by those restrictions necessary in a democratic society, including the protection of health or morals and for the protection of the reputation or the rights of others), *available at* http://www.hri.org/docs/ECHR50.html (on file with the Washington and Lee Law Review); *id.* art. 14 (stating that the enjoyment of rights and freedoms set forth in the Convention shall be secured without discrimination on any ground such as race, colour, national origin, or association with a national minority).

262. *See* STEVEN H. SHIFFRIN, DISSENT, INJUSTICE, AND THE MEANINGS OF AMERICA 63 (1999) (stating that Scalia's content-neutral alternative in *R.A.V.* would drive from the marketplace the very same ideas and viewpoints, along with others).

be taken to mitigate the problem. Most effectively, European nations should engage in a discourse with ISPs and seek their voluntary assistance in trying to cut down on the speech. If that approach does not work, and the problem becomes extremely severe, it may lead to a Constitutional moment, where the Supreme Court reverses its First Amendment jurisprudence. This would allow speech proscriptions on the basis of the subject of the speech, giving the United States greater constitutional authority to proscribe hate speech.

Part III
Investigation, Jurisdiction and Sentencing Issues

[11]

THE CRITICAL CHALLENGES FROM INTERNATIONAL HIGH-TECH AND COMPUTER-RELATED CRIME AT THE MILLENNIUM

MICHAEL A. SUSSMANN[*]

I consider high-tech crime to be one of the most serious issues demanding my attention, and I am doing everything in my power to ensure that the United States actively responds to these challenges.

U.S. Attorney General Janet Reno, January 21, 1997[1]

I. INTRODUCTION

There is a revolution going on in criminal activity. It creates major problems for law enforcement in almost every part of the world—problems that have rarely been as systemic and pervasive.

The revolution lies in the ways that networked computers and other technologies permit crimes to be committed remotely, via the Internet and wireless communications. A criminal no longer needs to be at the actual scene of the crime (or within 1,000 miles, for that matter) to prey on his victim. The possibility of an international element has been added to almost any crime, which means that cumber-

---

[*] Senior Attorney, Computer Crime and Intellectual Property Section, U.S. Department of Justice. From 1993-96, the author was Special Assistant to the Assistant Attorney General for the Criminal Division of the U.S. Department of Justice. The views expressed in this article are those of the author and do not necessarily represent the views of the United States. The author wishes to thank the following individuals for providing materials and editing manuscript drafts: Drew Arena, Scott Charney, Claudia Flynn, James Freund, Sam Hollander, Adam Isles, and Sara Maurizi.

1. U.S. Attorney General Janet Reno, Keynote Address to the Meeting of the G-8 Senior Experts' Group on Transnational Organized Crime, Chantilly, VA (Jan. 21, 1997) (transcript available at <http://www.usdoj.gov/criminal/cybercrime/agfranc.htm>) [hereinafter Reno, Chantilly Keynote Address]. The G-8 is an international multilateral group consisting of Canada, France, Germany, Italy, Japan, Russia, the United Kingdom, and the United States. During the 1990s, there were different names for this group, such as "G-7 plus Russia," "P-8," "The Eight," and "G-8," but all of the different monikers refer to the same group of countries. Use throughout this Article of different G-8 names is for accurate referral to source materials and is not intended to confer any other meaning. The genesis, mandate, and current work of the G-8 are discussed at length, *infra*, at Section IV(C).

452   DUKE JOURNAL OF COMPARATIVE & INTERNATIONAL LAW   [Vol 9:451

some mechanisms for international cooperation can slow or derail many more investigations than ever before.[2] Because everything from banks to phone systems to air traffic control to our military relies so heavily on networked computers, few individuals and institutions are impervious to this new and threatening criminal activity.[3]

Take the case of a criminal sitting in Russia who routes a communication through Sweden and Italy before hacking into a bank in New York. The Federal Bureau of Investigation (FBI) may not be able to solve the crime without the immediate help of Russian, Swedish, and Italian authorities. And the immediacy is critical because a criminal's trail often ends as soon as he disconnects from the Internet. To make matters worse, technical solutions, laws and legal processes, and cooperation among governments and with industry are far behind where they need to be for law enforcement to stay a step ahead of the bad guys. Finally, not enough people realize this threat exists on the scale it does. Commenting recently about the public's awareness of the threat to our nation's computers from invisible attacks, Richard Clarke, the current White House "terrorism czar" said:

> [CEOs of big corporations] think I'm talking about a 14-year-old hacking into their Web sites. I'm talking about people shutting down a city's electricity, shutting down 911 systems, shutting down telephone networks and transportation systems. You black out a city, people die. Black out lots of cities, lots of people die. It's as bad as being attacked by bombs .... Imagine a few years from now: A President goes forth and orders troops to move. The lights

---

2. *See, e.g.,* Scott Charney & Kent Alexander, *Computer Crime,* 45 EMORY L.J. 931, 948 (1996) (stressing the need for an organized international response to the worldwide problem of computer crime).

3. *See Hearings on Infrastructure Protection Before the Subcomm. on Technology, Terrorism and Government Information of the Senate Judiciary Comm.,* 105th Cong. (1998), *available in* 1998 WL 12761104 (statement of Michael A. Vatis, Deputy Assistant Director, Federal Bureau of Investigation and Chief, National Infrastructure Protection Center) [hereinafter Vatis Testimony]. "This Nation depends on the stable, consistent operation of our critical infrastructures for our way of life, our well-being and our security. These include: telecommunications, energy, banking and finance, water systems, and emergency services, both government and private .... And the infrastructures are more interdependent than in the past, with the result that debilitation or destruction of one could have cascading, destructive effects on others." *Id. See generally* PRESIDENT'S COMMISSION ON CRITICAL INFRASTRUCTURE PROTECTION, CRITICAL FOUNDATIONS: PROTECTING AMERICA'S INFRASTRUCTURES 3-20 (1997). The President's Commission on Critical Infrastructure Protection was created by President Clinton under Executive Order 13010 to study the problem of infrastructure protection in depth and develop proposed solutions. *See id.* at vii.

go out, the phones don't ring, the trains don't move. That's what we mean by an electronic Pearl Harbor.[4]

At the dawn of the new millennium, at least some modern-day Paul Reveres are raising the alarm. A growing number of law enforcement officials in the United States and abroad are increasing awareness and calling for enhancement of high-tech crime-fighting abilities.[5] Likewise, the international community is beginning to take important action to address this threat to public safety.[6] But in many ways we are just scratching the surface; the long road ahead is going to require leadership, innovation, and persistence.

This Article will, first, examine the specific challenges posed by criminals who use computers and networked communications to ply their craft; second, discuss what needs to be done to effectively combat high-tech crime; and third, examine what steps are currently being taken in this area by some of the major multilateral organizations, such as the Council of Europe, the European Union, and the G-8. I will offer my assessment of the work being performed by international groups, and will draw specific attention to areas where efforts are inefficient or non-existent.

II. THE CHALLENGES

Imagine this scene out of tomorrow's headlines: A hacker, going on-line through the Internet, breaks into computers that the Federal Aviation Administration (FAA) uses for air traffic control. He dis-

---

4. Tim Weiner, *The Man Who Protects America From Terrorism*, N.Y. TIMES, Feb. 1, 1999, at A3. Mr. Clarke has a sign in his office that reads "Think Globally/Act Globally." *See id.*

5. *See, e.g.*, Paul Boateng, Minister of State for the Home Office (U.K.), Tomorrow's Challenges for Law Enforcement, Keynote Address to the Second International Conference for Criminal Intelligence Analysts (Mar. 1, 1999) (transcript on file with the *Duke Journal of Comparative and International Law*) (announcing the formation of a Ministerial Committee on computer misuse).

> [C]ommercial organisations may find it ever more problematic securely to maintain their business transactions, and . . . criminals and criminal enterprises may find an increasing number of opportunities to manipulate systems to their advantage . . . By virtue of the interconnectivity of computer systems in both the private and the public sectors, there is also the growing danger that a criminal attack on one part of a system could lead to the failure of the rest. Moreover, the perpetrator can now just as easily be a 15 year old 'surfer' in Wigan—tomorrow's cyberwarrior—as a professional gang of 50 year old fraudsters in Wisconsin. We must prevent such people from making these attacks.

Id. at 7. (The Minister of State for the Home Office in the United Kingdom is equivalent in rank to the Deputy Attorney General of the United States.)

6. *See infra* Section IV (discussing work in this area being done by international multilateral organizations).

454   DUKE JOURNAL OF COMPARATIVE & INTERNATIONAL LAW   [Vol 9:451

rupts a regional air traffic network, and the disruption causes the crash of a DC-10 in the Rocky Mountains, killing all aboard. The FAA and the FBI know there has been a hacker intrusion, originating through the Internet, but nothing else. Since anyone can access the Internet from anywhere in the world, the FBI has no idea where the hacker may be located. Moreover, they do not know the motive of the attack or the identity of the attackers. Is it a terrorist group, targeting the United States and likely to strike again at any time, or is it a fourteen-year-old hacker whose prank has spun tragically out of control?

Let us follow this scenario a bit further. Within thirty minutes of the plane crash, the FBI tracks the source of the attack to an Internet Service Provider (ISP) in Germany. Assuming the worst, another attack could occur at any time, and hundreds of planes in flight over the United States are at risk. The next investigative step is to determine whether the ISP in Germany is a mere conduit, or whether the attack actually originated with a subscriber to that service. In either case, the FBI needs the assistance of the German ISP to help identify the source of the attack, but it is now 3:00 a.m. in Germany.

- Does the FBI dare wait until morning in Europe to seek formal legal assistance from Germany or permission from the German government to continue its investigation within their borders?

- Does the Department of Justice authorize the FBI's computer experts to conduct a search, without German consent, on the German ISP from their terminals in Washington?

- Does the FBI agent need a U.S. court order to access private information overseas? What would be the reach of such an order?

- If the FBI agent plows forward and accesses information from computers in Germany, will the German government be sympathetic to the U.S. plight, will the violation of German sovereignty be condemned, or both?

- What are the diplomatic and foreign policy implications of the United States remotely (and without advance notice) conducting a search that may intrude into German sovereignty?

The legal and policy implications of possible "transborder searches," such as the one contemplated in this scenario, are quickly becoming a concern for law enforcement agencies around the globe as they grapple with new challenges posed by networked communications and new technologies.[7] Traditional investigative procedures—and particularly the often cumbersome procedures that govern investigations at the international level—may not be adequate to meet the need in computer crime cases for immediate law enforcement action reaching beyond national borders.[8] The globalization of criminal activity has created vexing problems that, in some cases, defy simple solutions.[9]

Before we explore some of the challenges that new high-tech and computer-related crimes pose, it is important to describe the three ways that criminals use computers.[10] First, a criminal may target or attack a computer or a system controlled by a computer (e.g., hackers disrupting local phone service). Second, a criminal may use a computer to commit a "traditional" crime such as fraud or theft (e.g., promoting bogus investments on a Web page). Third, a criminal may use a computer in a way that is incidental to the offense, but where the computer nonetheless contains evidence of a crime (e.g., drug dealers using personal computers to store records of drug sales and "clients").[11]

The first two kinds of criminal activity can be carried out remotely, and often from great distances. Likewise, evidence of a crime can be stored at a remote location, either for the purpose of concealing the crime from law enforcement and others, or simply because of the design of the network. "Hackers are not hampered by the existence of international boundaries, since information and property can be transmitted covertly via telephone and data networks. A hacker needs no passport and passes no checkpoints. He simply types a command to gain entry."[12] This element of remoteness takes the investigation and prosecution of these crimes out of the exclusive purview of any single nation, thereby creating challenges and obstacles to crime-solving.[13]

---

7. The topic of transborder search and seizure, under which these issues fall, is discussed *infra* Section III(D)(2).

8. *See* Charney & Alexander, *supra* note 2, at 948.

9. *See, e.g., infra* Section III(D) (discussing difficulties in locating and identifying criminals who commit crimes remotely, via networked communications).

10. *See* Charney & Alexander, *supra* note 2, at 934.

11. *See id.*

12. Reno, Chantilly Keynote Address, *supra* note 1. *See generally* Carolyn P. Meinel, *How Hackers Break in . . . And How They Are Caught*, SCI. AM., Oct. 1998, at 98-107 (offering a fictionalized composite of many actual intrusions, or "hacks," and the attendant countermeasures that took place in cyberspace, all from remote locations).

13. Examples of criminals hop-scotching the globe by merely using a home computer and a phone line abound. Between June and October 1994, a hacker sitting in St. Petersburg, Rus-

456   DUKE JOURNAL OF COMPARATIVE & INTERNATIONAL LAW   [Vol 9:451

Not long ago, most crimes were local. The criminal or criminals, the actual crime, and the victim were all within the same state, if not the same city. Such television crime-stoppers as Tony Baretta, Sergeant Joe Friday, and Steve McGarrett of Five-O seldom had to go far to find their man (or woman).[14] Physical evidence of the crime could be found at or near the crime scene, and these cops rarely needed help from outside their precincts. It was the extraordinary set of facts—bank robbers fleeing across state lines, for example—that brought *The F.B.I.*'s Inspector Lewis Erskine (played by Efrem Zimbalist, Jr.) into the case. From 1965 to 1974, Inspector Erskine, roaming the United States, investigated counterfeiters, extortionists, organized crime figures, and bombings by political radicals. But, with the exception of the occasional Communist spy, the entirety of each case rested within the borders of the United States.[15]

Today, however, characters who seem to come more from Tom Clancy's world are taking advantage of powerful personal computers linked to the Internet and World Wide Web, the explosion of electronic commerce and e-mail, and wireless and satellite communications to bring a global dimension to an increasing amount of criminal activity.[16] Targeting computers with malicious programming codes[17] from thousands of miles away is no longer the fanciful idea of science

---

sia, pilfered $5 million from Citibank accounts worldwide and placed the money into his accomplice's accounts in the United States, Israel, Finland, Germany, the Netherlands, and Switzerland. *See* Saul Hansell, *Citibank Fraud Case Raises Computer Security Questions*, N.Y. TIMES, Aug. 19, 1995, at 31; THE WHITE HOUSE INTERNATIONAL CRIME CONTROL STRATEGY (May 1998). The culprit, Vladimir Levin, was extradited to the United States in 1997, pled guilty to conspiracy to commit bank fraud, and was sentenced to thirty-six months' imprisonment. Approximately $4.5 million of the stolen money was recovered. *Id.*

14. Baretta, Friday, and McGarrett are fictional characters, respectively, from the television police dramas *Baretta* (1975-78), *Dragnet* (1952-70), and *Hawaii Five-O* (1968-80). *See* TIM BROOKS & EARLE MARSH, THE COMPLETE DIRECTORY TO PRIME TIME NETWORK AND CABLE TV SHOWS 77, 289, 442-43 (1995).

15. Inspector Erskine was the lead character in the police drama *The F.B.I.* (1965-74). *See id.* at 326. The program won the commendation of real-life FBI Director J. Edgar Hoover, who gave the show full government cooperation and even allowed filming of some background scenes at FBI Headquarters in Washington, D.C. *See id.*

16. If it is true that art imitates life, then the action-thrillers written by Tom Clancy bear out these trends. Tom Clancy, the author of such Cold War bestsellers as THE HUNT FOR RED OCTOBER (1984), RED STORM RISING (1986), and THE CARDINAL IN THE KREMLIN (1988) is now churning out such titles as RUTHLESS.COM (1998) (co-authored with Martin Greenberg), and NET FORCE (1999) (co-authored with Steve Pieczenik).

17. "Malicious programming code" is code that is designed to cause unauthorized damage to computer systems.

fiction writers.[18] Today, such crimes are becoming the daily workload for some investigators and prosecutors.[19] A computer server running a Web page designed to defraud senior citizens might be located in the Seychelle Islands, and victims of the scam could be scattered throughout twenty-five different countries. Or an extortionist may commit blackmail by sending e-mails that run through the communications networks of five countries before reaching the intended recipient.

As we approach the 21st Century, the irrelevance of borders is making some old crime-solving paradigms and practices obsolete. The power of networks and Pentium-driven PCs makes every computer a potential tool for criminals and gives them the ability to reach across borders with great stealth—and then hang up the phone to disappear without a trace.[20] The globalization of criminal activity and the anonymity with which criminals can cross electronic "borders" is a real problem, with a potential to affect every country, every law enforcement officer, every citizen. So what are we to do?

III. WHAT NEEDS TO BE DONE

On December 9-10, 1997, U.S. Attorney General Janet Reno held the first-ever meeting of her counterparts from the G-8 countries (Canada, France, Germany, Italy, Japan, Russia, and the United Kingdom), with the focus on high-tech and computer-related crime.[21] That the first meeting ever held among the senior law-enforcement officials of the eight countries was centered on computer crime un-

---

18. *See, e.g.,* WILLIAM GIBSON, NEUROMANCER (1984) (describing futuristic hackers who remotely penetrate corporate security systems using intelligent viruses). Four years after *Neuromancer* was published, in 1988, a Cornell University student named Robert Morris developed a program known as a "worm," which he designed to attack computers through the Internet. A worm is a self-contained computer program (unlike a "virus," which must attach itself to other programs) that duplicates itself and then attempts to penetrate computer systems and cause damage. After Morris's worm penetrated the target computer, it would consume the computer's available memory, resulting in the shutdown of the computer. Before his worm could be neutralized, it had crippled approximately 6,200 computers and caused over $98 million in damage. *See* United States v. Morris, 928 F.2d 504 (2d Cir. 1991).

19. For example, the Computer Crime and Intellectual Property Section at the U.S. Department of Justice in Washington has a staff that includes eighteen attorneys. Likewise, the FBI has Infrastructure Protection/Computer Intrusion Squads in seven U.S. cities, with five more funded and scheduled to be operational by January 1, 2000.

20. *See* Marc D. Goodman, *Why the Police Don't Care About Computer Crime,* 10 HARV. J.L. & TECH. 465, 467 (1997).

21. *See* Janet Reno, On the Meeting of Justice and Interior Ministers of The Eight (Dec. 10, 1997) (visited Apr. 19, 1999) <http://www.usdoj.gov/criminal/cyber crime/commp8pr.htm>. The G-8 and its work on high-tech crime is discussed *infra* at Section IV(C).

458   DUKE JOURNAL OF COMPARATIVE & INTERNATIONAL LAW   [Vol 9:451

derscores the growing concerns that world leaders share about security in cyberspace.[22] In a statement to her colleagues, Attorney General Reno highlighted four areas where progress by the international
community is critical if law enforcement is to keep pace with both
technology and the criminals who exploit it:

- First, enactment of sufficient laws to appropriately criminalize computer and telecommunications abuses;
- Second, commitment of personnel and resources to combating high-tech and computer-related crime;
- Third, improvement in global abilities to locate and identify
  those who abuse information technologies; and
- Fourth, development of an improved regime for collecting
  and sharing evidence of these crimes, so that those responsible can be brought to justice.[23]

The joint Communiqué issued at the conclusion of the meeting
by all eight countries[24] as well as the ten Principles and ten-point Action Plan agreed to by the Ministers and Attorney General[25] reflected
concern for these issues. Each of these four areas is critical to pro-

---

22. *See* Clifford Krauss, *8 Countries Join in an Effort To Catch Computer Criminals*, N.Y.
TIMES, Dec. 11, 1997, at A12 (quoting Jack Straw, the British Home Secretary, as saying,
"We're using 19th-Century tools to face a 21st-century problem. One person can stay in the
same place and commit crimes in several countries without leaving his armchair.").

23. Telephone Interview with Scott Charney, Chief, Computer Crime and Intellectual
Property Section, U.S. Department of Justice and Chair, G-8 Subgroup on High-tech Crime
(Dec. 1, 1998).

24. *See* Meeting of the Justice and Interior Ministers of The Eight, Communique' (Dec.
10, 1997) (visited Apr. 19, 1999) <http://www.usdoj.gov/criminal/cybercrime/communique.
htm>.

   National laws apply to the Internet and other global networks. But while the enactment and enforcement of criminal laws have been, and remain, a national responsibility, the nature of modern communications networks makes it impossible for any country acting alone to address this emerging high-tech crime problem. A common
   approach addressing the unique, borderless nature of global networks is needed and
   must have several distinct components.

   Each country must have in place domestic laws that ensure that the improper use of
   computer networks is appropriately criminalized and that evidence of high-tech
   crimes can be preserved and collected in a timely fashion. Countries must also ensure
   that a sufficient number of technically-literate, appropriately-equipped personnel are
   available to address high-tech crimes.

   Such domestic efforts must be complemented by a new level of international cooperation, especially since global networks facilitate the commission of transborder offenses. Therefore, consistent with principles of sovereignty and the protection of human rights, democratic freedoms and privacy, nations must be able to collect and
   exchange information internationally, especially within the short time frame so often
   required when investigating international high-tech crimes.

Id.

25. *See id.* The full text of the Principles and Action Plan are provided *infra* note 135.

tecting public safety and ensuring that users of new technologies are not victimized in new ways. Each area also poses unique challenges to ingenuity, national leadership, and international cooperation. I will take up each of them separately in the following subsections.

A. Needed: Sufficient Laws to Punish Computer Crimes

When Country *A* criminalizes certain conduct and Country *B* does not, a bridge for cooperation in solving a crime committed in Country *A* may not be possible. The United States has entered into bilateral treaties of extradition with over 100 countries.[26] These treaties are either "list treaties," containing a list of offenses for which extradition is available, or they require dual criminality (i.e., require that the conduct under investigation is a crime in both the requesting and requested countries and is punishable by at least one year in prison).[27] With regard to treaties for international legal assistance such as those involving the issuance of subpoenas, interviewing of witnesses, or production of documents, some treaties permit assistance as long as the conduct under investigation is a crime in the requesting state. The United States strongly favors this approach.[28] Other treaties permit assistance only if dual criminality exits and if the offense is extraditable.[29] Therefore, if one country does not criminalize computer misuse (or provide for sufficient punishment), extradition and the collection of certain evidence may be prohibited. Consider the following two examples.

---

26. *See* 18 U.S.C. § 3181 (1998) (listing treaties of extradition).

27. Telephone Interview with Drew C. Arena, Counselor for Criminal Justice Matters, U.S. Mission to the European Union (Mar. 9, 1999). (From 1987 to 1992, Mr. Arena was the Director of the Office of International Affairs at the U.S. Department of Justice in Washington, D.C.).

28. *See id.* However, in the more sensitive area of search and seizure, some U.S. treaties either require dual criminality (e.g., Treaty on Mutual Legal Assistance, June 12, 1981, Neth.-U.S., T.I.A.S. No. 10734 art. 6, para. 1) or allow a party to refuse a request "if it relates to conduct in respect of which powers of search and seizure would not be exercisable in the territory of the Requested Party in similar circumstances." Treaty Between the United States of America and the United Kingdom of Great Britain and Northern Ireland on Mutual Assistance in Criminal Matters, Dec. 2, 1996, U.S.-Great Britain, S. TREATY DOC. NO. 104-2 (1996) [hereinafter US/UK MLAT], art. 14, para. 2.

29. *See* Council of Europe Convention on Mutual Assistance in Criminal Matters of 1959, Article 5(1)(a) and (b) (allowing parties to those conventions to limit "coercive measures," e.g., search warrants, to situations of either dual criminality or extractability of the underlying offense); Telephone Interview with Drew C. Arena, Counselor for Criminal Justice Matters, U.S. Mission to the European Union (Mar. 18, 1999).

460   DUKE JOURNAL OF COMPARATIVE & INTERNATIONAL LAW   [Vol 9:451

In 1992, hackers from Switzerland attacked the San Diego Supercomputer Center.[30] The United States sought help from the Swiss,
but the investigation was stymied due to lack of dual criminality, (i.e.,
the two nations did not have similar laws banning the conduct), which
became an impediment to official cooperation. Eventually, local police in Zurich did render informal assistance, and they prepared a list
of questions for U.S. authorities to answer, transmitted through official channels, so the case could be properly pursued. After the
United States answered those questions, but before follow-up questions could be answered through official channels, the hacking
stopped, the trail went cold, and the case had to be closed.[31]

Several years later a similar problem arose, when the United
States found itself unable to reach a criminal in order to bring him to
justice. From August 1995 until February 1996, the Naval Criminal
Investigative Service and the FBI investigated a hacker who was
stealing password files and altering log files in military, university,
and other private computer systems.[32] Many of these systems contained sensitive research on satellites, radiation, and energy-related
engineering.[33] U.S. authorities tracked the hacker to Argentina and
notified a local Argentine telecommunications carrier.[34] The carrier
contacted local law enforcement, which began its own investigation.
Subsequently, an Argentine judge authorized the search of the
hacker's apartment and the seizure of his computer equipment based
on potential violations of Argentine law.[35] Unfortunately, the treaty
between Argentina and the United States did not authorize the extradition of individuals for "computer crimes" (although it does for
more traditional crimes). The U.S. Attorney's Office in Boston
charged the perpetrator with several criminal violations, but it was
unclear whether or not the case would ever be resolved due to the

30. Telephone Interview with Scott Charney, Chief, Computer Crime and Intellectual
Property Section, U.S. Department of Justice and Chair, G-8 Subgroup on High-tech Crime
(Mar. 2, 1999).

31. *See id.*

32. *See* Pierre Thomas & Elizabeth Corcoran, *Argentine, 22, Charged With Hacking Computer Networks,* WASH. POST, Mar. 30, 1996, at A4; Telephone Interview with Stephen P.
Heymann, Deputy Chief, Criminal Division, U.S. Attorney's Office (D. Mass.) (Apr. 12, 1999)
(Mr. Heymann is the Computer and Telecommunications Coordinator (CTC) for the District
of Massachussets and was the lead prosecutor for this case).

33. *See First Internet Wiretap Leads to a Suspect,* N.Y. TIMES, Mar. 31, 1996, at A20.

34. *See* Thomas & Corcoran, *supra* note 32.

35. *See id.*

absence of uniformity between U.S. and Argentine laws.[36] Fortunately, the hacker agreed to a plea bargain wherein he waived extradition and agreed to plead guilty in the United States.[37]

These cases demonstrate how inadequate laws can allow criminals to go unpunished in one country, while they thwart the efforts of other countries to vindicate the rights of the state and protect its citizens. While the United States has amended its criminal code to specifically penalize a wide variety of computer crimes,[38] other countries have been slower to do so.[39] At a meeting of senior law enforcement officials from the G-8 countries in January 1997, Attorney General Reno stated:

---

36. *See id.*; *First Internet Wiretap Leads to a Suspect, supra* note 33; Telephone Interview with Stephen P. Heymann, *supra* note 32.

37. *See First Internet Wiretap Leads to a Suspect, supra* note 33; Telephone Interview with Stephen P. Heymann, *supra* note 32.

38. *See* The Computer Fraud and Abuse Act of 1984, Pub. L. 101-73, *codified as* U.S.C. § 1030 (1984), *amended by* the National Information Infrastructure Protection Act of 1996, Pub. L. No. 104-294 (1996). The law contains eleven separate provisions designed to protect the confidentiality, integrity, and availability of data and systems. For example, section 1030(a)(2) makes it a crime to access a computer without or in excess of authority and obtain (1) financial information from a financial institution or credit reporting company; (2) any information in the possession of the government; or (3) any private information where the defendant's conduct involves interstate or foreign commerce. Section 1030(a)(5) makes it a crime for anyone to knowingly cause the transmission of a computer program, information, code, or command, that results in unauthorized damage to a protected computer. (A "protected computer" is one used exclusively by the United States or a financial institution; one used partly by the United States or a financial institution, in which the defendant's conduct affects the government's or financial institution's operation of the computer; or any computer that is used in interstate or foreign commerce or communications. 18 U.S.C. § 1030(e)(2)). *See also* The National Information Infrastructure Protection Act of 1996, A Legislative Analysis, by the Computer Crime and Intellectual Property Section of the U.S. Dept. of Justice (visited Apr. 1, 1999) <http:www.usdoj.gov/criminal/cybercrime/1030_anal.html>; Charney & Alexander, *supra* note 2, at 949-54 (providing a summary and explanation of the individual provisions of the Computer Fraud and Abuse Act). The United States also is moving to update statutes concerning "traditional" crimes, where new technologies present new opportunities for criminals. *See, e.g.*, Child Pornography Prevention Act (CPPA), Pub. L. 104-208, 110 Stat. 3009-28. 18 U.S.C. § 2252A (1996) (criminalizing, among other things, the use of computers to create and/or transmit child pornography); United States v. Hilton, 167 F.3d 61 (1st Cir. 1999). "Congress enacted the CPPA to modernize federal law by enhancing its ability to combat child pornography in the cyberspace era . . . . Lawmakers wished to improve law enforcement tools to keep pace with technological improvements that have made it possible for child pornographers to use computers to 'morph' or alter innocent images of actual children to create a composite image showing them in sexually explicit poses." Hilton, 167 F.3d at 65.

39. For example, while unauthorized access to a computer, without further action, is a criminal offense in such countries as France, Canada and the United States, it currently is not a criminal offense in Russia or Japan. *See* Charney, *supra* note 23 (as chair of the G-8 Subgroup on High-tech Crime, Mr. Charney is compiling the results of a survey completed by G-8 law enforcement officials on those countries' legal systems with respect to computer crime).

462   DUKE JOURNAL OF COMPARATIVE & INTERNATIONAL LAW   [Vol 9:451

[U]ntil recently, computer crime has not received the emphasis that
other international crimes have engendered. Even now, not all affected nations recognize the threat it poses to public safety or the
need for international cooperation to effectively respond to the
problem. Consequently, many countries have weak laws, or no
laws, against computer hacking—a major obstacle to solving and to
prosecuting computer crimes.[40]

The solution to this problem is simple to state: "[countries] need
to reach a consensus as to which computer and technology-related activities should be criminalized, and then commit to taking appropriate domestic actions."[41] But it is not as easy to implement. An international "consensus" concerning the activities that universally should
be criminalized may take time to develop. Meanwhile, individual
countries that lack this kind of legislation will each have to pass new
laws, an often cumbersome and time-consuming process. In the
United States, for example, action by both the Congress and the
President is required for new legislation.

B.   Needed: Personnel and Resources to Combat High-tech Crime

In 1986, an astronomer-turned-systems-manager at the University of California at Berkeley found a seventy-five cent accounting error in the computer's billing program, which led to the discovery that
an unauthorized user had penetrated Berkeley's computer system.[42]
When the astronomer, Clifford Stoll, began to investigate further, he
discovered a hacker identified as "Hunter" was using Berkeley's
computer system as a conduit to break into U.S. government systems
and steal sensitive military information.[43] The hacker's objective
seemed to be to spy on the United States' "Star Wars" missile defense program.

Stoll encountered serious problems as he began to pursue the
hacker. To begin with, Stoll was unable to find computer literate law
enforcement personnel with an appreciation of the technical nature
of the criminal activity. He also found that the legal processes required to locate and identify the hacker while he or she was online
and thereby traceable were inadequate.[44] Various local and federal

---

40. Reno, Chantilly Keynote Address, *supra* note 1.

41. *Id.*

42. *See generally* CLIFFORD STOLL, THE CUCKOO'S EGG: TRACKING A SPY THROUGH
THE MAZE OF COMPUTER ESPIONAGE (1989) (describing the author's ten-month odyssey in
search of the hacker).

43. *See id.*

44. *See id.* at 43.

agencies that Stoll contacted, including the FBI and Central Intelligence Agency (CIA), initially expressed little interest in pursuing what at first looked like a computer prank.[45] When local police finally issued a California order to trace a phone call, the trail led to Virginia where the order had no force. When the call was finally traced to Germany, the German telecommunications carrier could not quickly ascertain the source of the attacks because the trace had to be accomplished through mechanical switches. As Stoll and those assisting him moved backwards through the labyrinth of telecommunications to its source, they found a dearth of law enforcement personnel with technical expertise who could help.[46]

Stoll's "investigation" brought to light a number of interdependent "personnel" and "resource" requirements that, unless fulfilled, will impede the success of law enforcement in this burgeoning area. It is critical that the requirements summarized below are met at the international level to eliminate weak links in the chain of an investigation.

1. Experts Dedicated to High-tech Crime. The complex technical and legal issues raised by computer-related crime require that each country have individuals who are dedicated to high-tech crime. These individuals are needed to support domestic law enforcement authorities faced with high-tech issues, and they will be the first point of contact for their international counterparts.[47]

---

45. Until government investigators learned of the potential threat to national security, they had no interest in pursuing a case which appeared to have damages valued at less than $1.00. *See id.* (describing how the FBI in Montgomery, Alabama would investigate a computer crime only after a million dollars was at stake); *see also* Goodman, *supra* note 20 (discussing law enforcement disinterest in pursuing computer crimes).

46. *See generally* STOLL, *supra* note 42. Since Hunter's trail evaporated each time he ended a communication, Stoll had to resort to generating phony official-looking data to keep the hacker interested and online long enough for the trace to be completed. Eventually, the source of the attacks was identified, and the hacker was prosecuted in Germany. Ironically, one of the reasons the investigation was successful is because Stoll worked directly with telephone company personnel, who in turn worked with other telecommunications providers, instead of working with the government. *See id.* at 53, 225.

47. *See* Reno, Chantilly Keynote Address, *supra* note 1 ("[We must ensure] that law enforcement personnel are capable of addressing high-tech crime by understanding two emerging and converging technologies simultaneously: computers and telecommunications. The complexity of these technologies, and their constant and rapid change, suggest that countries need to designate investigators and prosecutors to . . . work these cases on a full-time basis, immersing themselves in computer-related investigations and prosecutions."); Reno, *supra* note 21 ("Countries must also ensure that a sufficient number of technically-literate, appropriately-equipped personnel are available to address high-tech crimes.").

464   DUKE JOURNAL OF COMPARATIVE & INTERNATIONAL LAW   [Vol 9:451

2. *Experts Available on a Twenty-Four Hour Basis.* A unique feature of high-tech and computer-related crime is that it requires immediate action to locate and identify perpetrators. Due to a general lack of historical communications data, the trail of a criminal may be impossible to trace once a communication link is terminated. This lack of data is due, in part, to the fact that businesses no longer bill their customers by individual telephone call or Internet connection but, instead, by bulk billing (e.g., a single rate for one month of usage).[48] When bulk billing is employed, there is no longer a business need to record the transmission information (i.e., connection times or source and destination) for individual connections; therefore, traffic data may not be available at a later date. Thus, investigators and prosecutors with expertise in this field must be available twenty-four hours a day, at home and by pager, so that appropriate steps can be taken in a fast-breaking high-tech case.

3. *Continuous Training.* Because of the phenomenal rate at which computer technologies evolve, and because high-tech criminal techniques and capabilities change more rapidly than those in more traditional areas of criminal activity, experts must receive continuous training in the investigation and prosecution of high-tech cases. In addition to domestic training, countries should participate in coordinated training with other countries, so transnational cases can be pursued quickly and seamlessly.[49]

4. *Up-to-date Equipment.* To keep pace with computer criminals, law enforcement experts in this field must be properly equipped with the latest hardware and software. There was a time when police needed little more than a gun, handcuffs, flashlight, and a notepad. Today, providing them with proper equipment may prove to be one of the more difficult challenges, because the cost of purchasing sophisticated equipment and software to keep pace with

---

48. *See, e.g.,* James Peltz & Michael Hiltzik, *Takeover Possible at Earthlink,* L.A. TIMES, Jan. 26, 1999, at C7.

49. In the United States, high-tech prosecutors at the federal level attend a one-week training course every year, with training provided by both government and private sector personnel. Likewise, all federal investigative agencies provide high-tech training to their agents. The government's National Cybercrime Training Partnership is developing high-tech training for federal, state, and local law enforcement personnel. *See generally* Martin Kettle & Owen Bowcott, *Computer Crime: The Age of the Digital Sleuth,* THE GUARDIAN, Dec. 12, 1997, at 19.

rapid advances in technology places considerable burdens on the budget process.[50]

To get approval to hire and/or allocate dedicated personnel, to commit time and money to training, and to find millions of dollars for frequent purchases and upgrades of equipment and software, senior policy-makers—often acting under tight budget constraints—must become directly involved and provide strong leadership. In fact, to ensure that high-tech issues receive appropriate attention, the support of officials at the level of Attorney General, or Justice or Interior Minister may be required.[51]

C.   Needed: Improved Abilities to Locate and Identify Criminals

When a hacker disrupts the telephone network of a Baby Bell, when the White House receives an e-mail threatening the President, or when the files of a Fortune 500 company are stolen via the Internet, a primary investigative requirement is to locate the source of the attack. To do so requires tracing the "electronic trail" from the victim back to the attacker. As we enter the new millennium, law enforcement personnel chasing a hacker's trail face a landscape dramatically different from the recent pre-Internet era.

In today's communications environment, as a result of corporate divestiture, a single carrier usually does not carry a communication from end-to-end. The days when the police worked alone with "Ma Bell" to solve a crime are over. A hacker's transmission may pass from his or her computer to a local phone company, to an ISP, to a long-distance telephone carrier, to a university computer, across an ocean via satellite, on its way to a foreign corporate victim.[52] Consider that:

---

50. *Cf.* Goodman, *supra* note 20; Jon Bigness, *Dick Tracy Comes to Life,* CHI. TRIB., Dec. 15, 1997, at 1C.

51. Unfortunately, many of the senior policy-makers and budget gurus in government are unfamiliar with new computer and telecommunications technologies, and with the threats posed by computer criminals. If these individuals are not familiar with the technologies at issue and the new threats they pose, they may be hesitant to support law enforcement by seeking appropriate legislative and budgetary changes. *See, e.g.,* Weiner, *supra* note 4 ("In his office, ... [White House terrorism czar Richard Clarke] spoke passionately about the threat of cyberwar, invisible attacks on the nation's computers, a terror so insidious, so arcane he has trouble convincing corporate chieftains and political commissars that it is real.").

52. *See, e.g., Computer Hacker Sought; European Man Cracked Thousands of Passwords Worldwide,* DALLAS MORNING NEWS, July 29, 1998, at 5A (reporting a hacker detected in the network of the University of California at Berkeley math department after gaining Internet access by way of modem through a Swedish Internet Service Provider and passing his communications through such countries as the United Kingdom, Denmark and South Korea).

- a nefarious communication may pass through a large *number of carriers* (e.g., Sprint PCS to Bell Atlantic to CompuServe to AT&T to MCI to the Microsoft Network to Deutsche Telekom);
- the communication may pass through many different *types of carriers*, each with different technologies (e.g., local telephone companies, long-distance carriers, ISPs, wireless and satellite networks);[53] and
- the communication may pass through carriers in a number of *different countries*, each in different time zones and subject to different legal systems.

And, unfortunately, each of these differentiations may occur within one individual hacker attack.

Because tracing the trail from victim back to attacker may be possible only when the hacker is actually on line (since transmission information is often not recorded and retained), law enforcement officials must work at lightning-fast speed. However, the traditional international legal assistance regime often cannot accommodate requests for assistance that occur during a cyber-attack because responses cannot be handled in real-time.[54] Inefficient and overly bureaucratic instruments for mutual legal assistance need to give way to more practical approaches.

A further set of complications arises with each individual carrier approached by law enforcement. First, in order to be able to assist law enforcement officials, the technical infrastructure (i.e., the communications network and the computers and software that run it) needs to have been designed and configured to generate and preserve

---

53. Locating and identifying a criminal who is using an array of carriers becomes much more challenging when wireless communications are used. Previously, when a telephone was used in a crime, a telephone line physically connected the perpetrator to a specific location. If the call could be traced, police knew exactly where the call originated. At the same time, law enforcement could find out the name of the person who was being billed for the phone line, although that person may not, of course, have been actually using the phone at the time of the offense.

But today, mobile phones allow an individual to commit crimes while roaming around the globe. In certain cases, sophisticated technologies can permit law enforcement to identify the general area where a wireless call is coming from, but such information may not be specific enough to allow an arrest to be made. Even then, however, identifying the owner of a particular mobile phone can be difficult, because mobile phones can be altered to transmit phony identifying information. Moreover, as mobile phones become less expensive, criminals can use them as "disposable phones," so that evidence linking the perpetrator to the communication is destroyed immediately after the commission of the crime.

54. *See generally* STOLL, *supra* note 42.

critical traffic data, such as the information relating to the source and destination of a cyber-attack.[55] In certain instances, technologies to generate and preserve this data simply do not exist. Second, assuming the particular piece of the technical infrastructure is capable of generating and preserving needed data, carriers must in fact actually collect and retain such records.[56] Examples of current industry practices that leave carriers without critical data include offering free anonymous e-mail accounts where subscriber information is not requested or verified; implementing dynamic addressing systems at ISPs (i.e., Internet addresses for computers are re-assigned with each new connection); and deciding against generating or maintaining records for local telephone calls. Third, law enforcement must be allowed timely access to this information by the carrier. Accordingly, listed below are the steps that need to be taken so that law enforcement can navigate through the contours of this dynamic environment to find computer criminals.

1. Technical Standards Must Promote Public Safety. Countries need to reach a consensus as to the technical requirements and industry standards in hardware, software, Internet protocols, and related technologies that are most critical to law enforcement needs. Thereafter, countries must develop a process for encouraging technical specifications that promote public safety.

2. Critical Traffic Data Must be Preserved. Countries should ensure that telecommunications carriers and ISPs routinely store

---

55. The use by many ISPs of "modem banks" or "hunt groups," to address increasing demand for Internet access is an example of a network design that can obfuscate critical traffic data. Where a modem bank is used, an ISP may have hundreds (or thousands) of phone lines, but the ISP gives its customers just one access number (e.g., 555-1234). The ISP's network is configured to automatically route each incoming call to the "next" available line, but without linking a customer with a specific incoming line, it may be impossible to tell through which phone line a cyber-attack is transmitted.

56. In some countries, telecommunications carriers and ISPs are required by law to routinely retain data that later may be critical to a criminal investigation; in other countries, such retention is prohibited. And in the third case, a country's laws may be silent on this topic, leaving companies to weigh public safety concerns, privacy interests, and market forces in developing their practices. Of particular concern to U.S. law enforcement are the EU's 1995 and 1997 directives concerning the processing of personal data, which will require deletion of traffic data. *See* Directive 95/46/EC of the European Parliament and of the Council of 24 October 1995 on the Protection of Individuals with Regard to the Processing of Personal Data and on the Free Movement of Such Data, 1995 O.J. 31 (L 281); Directive 97/66/EC of the European Parliament and of the Council of December 15, 1997 Concerning the Processing of Personal Data and the Protection of Privacy in the Telecommunications Sector, 1997 O.J. 1 (L 24) (Jan. 30, 1998). *See* discussion *infra* Part IV.B. and accompanying footnotes.

468   DUKE JOURNAL OF COMPARATIVE & INTERNATIONAL LAW   [Vol 9:451

access logs and other key traffic data for certain minimum periods of time (e.g., ninety days). Countries also need to adopt legal processes that allow law enforcement to request that a carrier or ISP retain specific traffic data for longer periods of time, should that data be needed for a criminal investigation.[57]

    3.   Information Must Be Shared Quickly. When a communication travels through several carriers, law enforcement must obtain court orders in each successive jurisdiction through which a signal passes in order to trace the communication to its source.[58] If there are points of origin in different jurisdictions, investigators must go to separate courthouses to obtain necessary court orders. "This consumes valuable time and scarce resources and impedes identification of the perpetrator."[59]   Legal processes must be improved to account for new technologies and find ways to remove unwieldy, piecemeal mechanics from domestic and international investigations.[60]

    When information is sought from carriers in different countries, applications to obtain critical information currently need to be made separately in each country; the resulting delay can debilitate investigators in hot pursuit. Unfortunately, innovative solutions for expediting international cooperation have not yet been developed. We should consider whether traditional means of legal assistance (i.e., requests under mutual legal assistance treaties and use of letters rogatory) need to be supplemented with procedures that will facilitate the immediate sharing of traffic data, or whether other avenues should be explored.[61]

---

    57. *See infra* note 67. *See, e.g.,* 18 U.S.C. 2703(f) (requiring a telecommunications carrier or ISP to retain data for up to 180 days at the request of law enforcement). As law-making bodies take up the issue of data protection and other restrictions on the collection and storage of communications data, law enforcement agencies must work to ensure that new data protection policies do not create safe havens for computer criminals, but instead balance privacy concerns with public safety needs.

    58. *See generally* STOLL, *supra* note 42; 18 U.S.C.S. § 3121 (Supp. 1989) ("trap and trace" statute).

    59. Statement of Attorney General Janet Reno before the United States Senate Committee on Appropriations, Subcommittee on Commerce, Justice, State, and the Judiciary, *available in* 1999 WL 8084451 (Feb. 4, 1999).

    60. In Senate testimony, Attorney General Reno discussed a High-Technology Crime Bill being considered by the Department of Justice that would address "several technical and procedural infirmities that inhibit effective investigation and prosecution of cybercrime." One amendment to existing statutes would "allow federal judges to direct cooperation among successive communications providers that carry a particular communication." *Id.*

    61. *See* Reno, Chantilly Keynote Address, *supra* note 1.

4. Government/Industry Cooperation is Imperative. There is broad international consensus that cooperation with industry is integral, and indeed critical, to investigating high-tech crime and thereby protecting public safety.[62] Governments should recognize that the needs of law enforcement may place burdens on industry and thus take reasonable steps to minimize such burdens.[63] At the same time, industry ought to consider the safety of the public when responding to the needs of the market. Cooperation can be enhanced in two ways. First, by establishing investigative points-of-contact with critical communications carriers. Second, by standardizing procedures by which investigators seek assistance from industry. Above all, governments must foster an operational relationship with industry based on trust.[64]

D. Needed: Effective Means for Obtaining Evidence Internationally

Even if all countries have adequate computer crime laws, possess dedicated, well-trained and well-equipped experts who are available twenty-four hours a day, and have the ability to locate and identify criminals who use networked communications, there remains a significant hurdle to overcome. How does law enforcement collect electronic evidence that may be scattered across several different countries, can be deleted or altered with one click of a mouse, may be encrypted, and will ultimately need to be authenticated in another country's court? Again, these are areas where the challenges have been recognized but solutions either may not be apparent or may be difficult to implement.

1. *Protected Seizures or "Quick Freeze/Quick Thaw."* One characteristic of electronic evidence is that it can be altered, transferred or destroyed almost instantaneously, and from remote

---

62. *See* Reno, *supra* note 21. At their meeting in December 1997, Attorney General Reno and the G-8 Justice and Interior Ministers affirmed their commitment to broad cooperation with industry:

> The development of effective solutions will also require unprecedented cooperation between government and industry. It is the industrial sector that is designing, deploying and maintaining these global networks and is primarily responsible for the development of technical standards. Thus, it is incumbent on the industrial sector to play its part in developing and distributing secure systems that, when accompanied by adherence to good computer and personnel security practices, serve to prevent computer abuse. Such systems should also be designed to help detect computer abuse, preserve electronic evidence, and assist in ascertaining the location and identity of criminals. *Id.*

63. *See id.*

64. *See* Kettle & Bowcott, *supra* note 49.

locations, often with little more than a single keystroke.[65] These changes to evidence may result from a criminal trying to cover his tracks, or a system administrator routinely clearing old e-mails or other data from a company's servers. Whatever the case, critical evidence can be lost—long before an international request for assistance is ever transmitted. Traditional methods of obtaining evidence from foreign governments can include lengthy delays, as foreign legal processes, translations, and diplomacy slowly proceed.[66] Old modalities may not always be practical when considering new technologies.

Therefore, when electronic evidence is sought, there may be a need for mechanisms such as a "preservation of evidence request" or "protected seizure," which would work as follows. Where there is a particularized concern about the loss of electronic evidence, a country would make an informal international request that the data immediately be preserved. This could be accomplished in a number of ways, from having a telecommunications carrier or ISP copy and store a customer's data, to actually seizing a criminal's computer and securing, but not searching, it for a short period of time.[67] Once data is protected from loss, expedited processes would provide the foreign country with formal documentation to authorize the issuance of a domestic search warrant or similar process.[68]

2.   *Transborder Search and Seizure.*[69] Since paper documents must be within close proximity to be of use, they are usually located

---

65.   *See, e.g.*, STOLL, *supra* note 42; Kettle & Bowcott, *supra* note 49.

66.   In addition, immediately after a system intrusion, law enforcement authorities may be certain that a crime has occurred and may have identified a potential source, but they may be days away from providing the particularized information usually required by a foreign government before assistance can be granted. It is in that window, between the detection of the crime and formal request, that there is a great risk of deletion, alteration or destruction of evidence. *See generally* STOLL, *supra* note 42.

67.   The U.S. Code provides for a form of "preservation of evidence request." A telecommunications carrier or ISP is required, "at the request of a governmental entity, [to] take all necessary steps to preserve records and other evidence in its possession pending the issuance of a court order or other process." 18 U.S.C. § 2703(f)(1) (1994). The government can have these records retained for up to 180 days. 18 U.S.C. § 2703(f)(2). This is an important example of how legal processes can be modernized to account for advances in communications and related technologies; implementation of this process on an international level would greatly enhance existing modalities of international legal assistance. *See infra* note 135, Principle V, Action Item 4-6, 8.

68.   *See* Reno, Chantilly Keynote Address, *supra* note 1.

69.   The following discussion on transborder search and seizure is based on the substantial work of Scott Charney, Chief, Computer Crime and Intellectual Property Section, U.S. Department of Justice. Telephone Interviews with Scott Charney, Chief, Computer Crime and

in the same country as the person being investigated. By contrast, electronic documents are often stored remotely on computers, sometimes thousands of miles away from their author. This may be done because of the structure of a particular business (where data is maintained at company headquarters) or the architecture of the network.[70] At other times, data may be purposely stored in another country to keep it beyond the reach of law enforcement.

A transborder search occurs when a law enforcement agent in his or her own country accesses a computer in another country to obtain electronic evidence, perhaps in furtherance of the execution of a domestic warrant. For example, in the hypothetical discussed in Section II (where a hacker had broken into FAA computers), U.S. investigators would likely have conducted a transborder search due to exigent circumstances (i.e., the possibility of imminent death or serious injury to air travelers). Also, a law enforcement agent can unknowingly conduct a transborder search, when he is not aware that his search has led him across a border. If an investigator searches the computer of a domestic corporation, it may be difficult to know where data accessed through that domestic terminal is actually stored. One site may have a link to another site, and the investigator may not know his communication was routed from a server in Dallas to one in Toronto. Because searches made under exigent circumstances (including those where it is believed evidence will be destroyed if not seized) and inadvertent searches across borders are likely to occur, it may be wise for countries to consider developing rules and/or guidelines to govern a transborder search (e.g., regarding notice to the searched country).

Governments have three potential solutions at this juncture. First, governments could decide to forego the development of principles, allowing each country to decide for itself whether transborder searches constitute an acceptable law enforcement practice.[71] Sec-

---

Intellectual Property Section, U.S. Department of Justice and Chair, G-8 Subgroup on High-tech Crime (Dec. 1998 to Feb. 1999).

70. For example, while America Online provides service in the United States, Europe and Asia, all of its data is stored on its computers in Reston, Virginia. When two people in Japan use AOL accounts to e-mail one another, all of their data is stored in the United States. Thus, if Japanese law enforcement tries to investigate a local crime involving two people who live within the same square mile in Tokyo, the Japanese must seek the assistance of U.S. law enforcement to get at any e-mail on AOL's server. Perhaps inappropriately, the documents are accessible to the account-holders in Japan, but beyond the reach of Japanese law enforcement.

71. If this approach is taken, the most difficult scenario may arise where the searching country takes the view that a transborder search is, under some theory, permissible, and the

472   DUKE JOURNAL OF COMPARATIVE & INTERNATIONAL LAW   [Vol 9:451

ond, governments could limit transborder searches to cases where production of the data could otherwise be compelled through legal processes.[72] This approach expedites the gathering of certain critical evidence while allowing data outside the traditional reach of a country to remain so. The third solution involves creating principles permitting law enforcement agents to conduct transborder searches under clearly defined circumstances that are more broad than those above. Support for this approach may rest on a consensus that the need for effective law enforcement outweighs concerns over protecting data stored in a particular country.

Unfortunately, the area of transborder searches is one where agreement on a particular approach may represent only a tiny step toward resolving other seemingly intractable issues such as how jurisdiction over stored data should be perceived and defined. One senior British law enforcement official has offered the following:

> Jurisdiction over a database should not now depend only on where it happens to be physically stored. Where the owners of the system have set it up to be accessible from another jurisdiction, it should be regarded as present in that jurisdiction for law enforcement purposes.

> I recognise this raises difficult constitutional issues for all of us. I hope it will be clear that this [is] not international Governments acting together in an Orwellian idea of 'Big Brother.' Transborder search principles would need to be accompanied by agreed minimum standards and safeguards. But time is limited.[73]

Because the potential for transborder searches exists in almost every country, progress cannot be put off simply because of the difficult legal and policy issues that litter the path to a comprehensive solution. Although, as discussed in Section IV, debates on this topic

---

searched country responds that the execution of that search is not only prohibited in its country but constitutes unauthorized access to its computers and therefore is a criminal offense.

72. For example, when a foreign corporation is doing business in one of the fifty United States, it is subject to that state's (as well as U.S.) laws, and under certain circumstances the corporation can be compelled to produce documents stored in another country. *See* United States v. Bank of Nova Scotia, 691 F.2d 1384 (11th Cir. 1982) (enforcing grand jury subpoena duces tecum in tax and narcotics investigation of U.S. citizen, where subpoena called for production of records in branch office in the Bahamas and compliance would require bank to violate Bahamian bank secrecy rule).

73. Paul Boateng, *supra* note 5. This philosophy is not unlike that used by the court in United States v. Bank of Nova Scotia, 691 F.2d 1384. *See also* discussion *supra* note 72.

are currently taking place in multilateral fora, any outcome is far from certain.[74]

    3. *Encryption.* Encryption is a method of scrambling data to protect its confidentiality. Mathematical algorithms are used in conjunction with "keys" (frequently, the key is a password) to hide content, and the intended recipient of an encrypted e-mail message or the user of an encrypted file can only read the message or file if he or she has access to the key. Encryption is important to protect the confidentiality of e-mail traffic, stored data, and commercial transactions.[75]

    When encryption is used by criminals for communications or data storage, investigations can be severely hampered because encryption can prevent timely access to the content of seized or intercepted data. Debates concerning the regulation of encryption, as well as a possible management infrastructure for decryption keys, are underway within governments, between governments, and between governments and industry.[76] There has been a wealth of material already written on regulation, key management, and related topics,[77] and discussion on those points is beyond the scope of this article.

    What is worth noting, however, is that whatever the overall regime and the legislative and regulatory framework, mutual legal assistance arrangements between countries must include some manner of decryption support services and governments must have the legal ability to provide such support.[78] Consider the case where French law

---

    74. Unfortunately, a thorough discussion of transborder search and seizure issues is beyond the scope of this Article; many of these issues are still being framed and debated within and among governments.

    75. *See generally* BRUCE SCHNEIER, APPLIED CRYPTOGRAPHY: PROTOCOLS, ALGORITHMS, AND SOURCE CODE IN C (2d ed. 1996).

    76. For information concerning U.S. policy on encryption, see, for example, Department of Justice Frequently Asked Questions on Encryption Policy; Letter from Attorney General Reno and others to Members of Congress regarding law enforcement's concerns related to encryption; Senate Hearings on Privacy in a Digital Age: Encryption and Mandatory Access; and Testimony of Deputy Assistant Attorney General Robert S. Litt Before the Subcommittee on Telecommunications, Trade and Consumer Protection of the House Commerce Committee, Sept. 4, 1997 (visited Apr. 10, 1999) <http://www.usdoj.gov/criminal/cybercrime/crypto.html>.

    77. *See, e.g.,* STEPHEN KENT, ET AL., SPECIAL PANEL OF THE ASSOCIATION FOR COMPUTING MACHINERY U.S. POLICY COMMITTEE, CODES, KEYS AND CONFLICTS: ISSUES IN U.S. CRYPTO POLICY (1994); KENNETH DAM & HERBERT LIN, CRYPTOGRAPHY'S ROLE IN SECURING THE INFORMATION DAM, NATIONAL RESEARCH COUNCIL, COMMITTEE TO STUDY NATIONAL CRYPTOGRAPHY POLICY (1996).

    78. The United States has dozens of bilateral mutual legal assistance treaties in effect. The more modern treaties have flexibility to accommodate "newer" forms of assistance, such as decryption support. As an example, the U.S./U.K. MLAT art. 1, para. 2(h) provides for

474   DUKE JOURNAL OF COMPARATIVE & INTERNATIONAL LAW   [Vol 9:451

enforcement requests data from the United States that is needed for
a criminal investigation. Assume this request is contemplated under
French/U.S. legal assistance practices. If U.S. authorities retrieve the
data and it is encrypted, and the decryption key is stored in the
United States, the data will be of little use to the French if we supply
it to them as is. Further, the United States will be in the best position
to have the data decrypted, either by learning the password from the
target of the investigation, or by otherwise obtaining the key.[79] While
commitments to provide decryption support do not exist as such today, the need for them will become more dire as the use of powerful
encryption becomes more widespread.

    4. *Computer Forensics.* Imagine that you are handling a case
involving two business partners, Sam and Harry. Assume a particular
e-mail message is important to your proof. Your witness, Sam,
testifies that Harry made false statements when applying for a bank
loan. On cross-examination, Harry's lawyer tries to suggest that
Sam's testimony is a recent fabrication.

    To rebut the charge of recent fabrication, you introduce into
evidence an e-mail that Sam sent to another colleague, Bob, at the
time of Harry's false statements, that is consistent with Sam's testimony at trial.[80] Harry's lawyer calls Bob as a witness and introduces
Bob's copy of the e-mail into evidence—but this one is missing the

---

"such other assistance as may be agreed between Central Authorities." However, other treaties lacking such provisions could be construed to prohibit assistance that is not explicitly stated
in their texts. In those cases, an amending document may be required in order to make decryption support available. *See* U.S./U.K. MLAT, *supra* note 28.

    79. For an interesting examination of the legal issues raised by law enforcement's attempts
to gain access to plaintext (i.e., unencrypted or decrypted text) and keys, see Phillip Reitinger,
Compelled Production of Plaintext and Keys, The Law of Cyberspace, U. CHI. LEGAL. F. 171
(1996). The author determines the principal legal obstacle to law enforcement access to be the
Fifth Amendment privilege against self-incrimination, and he concludes that a grand jury subpoena can direct the production of the plaintext of encrypted documents, although a limited
form of immunity may be required; and a grand jury subpoena may direct the production of
documents that reveal keys. Whether law enforcement can compel production of keys that are
only known, rather than recorded, is an open question. *See id.* at 173.

    80. The document would fall outside the definition of hearsay and therefore be admissible
after a sufficient foundation is laid. *See* FED. R. EVID. 801(d)(1)(B) ("A statement is not hearsay if . . . [t]he declarant testifies at the trial or hearing and is subject to cross-examination concerning the statement, and the statement is . . . consistent with the declarant's testimony and is
offered to rebut an express or implied charge against the declarant of recent fabrication or improper influence or motive.").

paragraph which refers to Harry having lied.[81] So there are two copies of the "same" e-mail; one, however, contains text that is not contained in the other. What do you do?

Similar problems concerning authenticity of evidence can arise with digital images. By now we have all probably seen (but possibly not known we did) magazine covers with a celebrity's head seamlessly attached to a younger and more fit body.[82] Today, if a photo is being used as evidence, you have to ask: is it real, or was it created (or altered) by merely rearranging binary digits? Further, when information incidental to a document's content, such as the date it was created or last "saved," is important to your proof, how are you going to assure the judge (and jury) that this information was not inadvertently altered when your witness retrieved it from his computer? Put another way, how is the integrity of an electronic medium maintained when it is brought into the courtroom?

The emerging field which addresses these issues is known as "computer forensics."[83] It encompasses the development and use of scientific protocols and procedures for searching computers, analyzing data, and maintaining the authenticity of data that has been retrieved.[84] From a practical standpoint, there are two tasks that experts in this field perform, although the line between the two often can blur. First, they retrieve electronic evidence. Any lawyer can list and print the document files on a hard drive (e.g., the Word or WordPerfect documents on the "C" drive), but it may take an expert to gather evidence that has been deleted (sometimes with powerful programs or devices), hidden, encrypted, or protected with passwords, software time bombs, or other devices that could destroy the

---

81. This document, again, is not hearsay, because it is not being offered for the truth of the statement contained therein, but instead to show that Sam's copy of the e-mail has been doctored. *See* FED. R. EVID. 801(c).

82. *See, e.g.*, Mark Kennedy, *When Seeing Isn't Believing: Digital Altering of Celebrity Photos is Becoming the Norm*, THE STAR LEDGER, Sept. 1, 1997 (discussing such digital alterations as a TV Guide cover in 1989 featuring Oprah Winfrey's face superimposed on Ann Margaret's body; Time magazine having darkened O.J. Simpson's mug shot for its cover; and Premiere magazine having removed Harrison Ford's facial scar for its cover; and stating, "Now it's possible for anyone with a few hours on a mid-priced desktop computer . . . to alter the content of photos.")

83. *See generally* Joan E. Feldman & Roger I. Kohn, *The Essentials of Computer Discovery*, LW GLASS CLE 297 (1998); Gregory S. Johnson, *A Practitioner's Overview of Digital Discovery*, 1997-98 GONZ. L. REV. 347.

84. *See* FEDERAL BUREAU OF INVESTIGATION, U.S. DEPT. OF JUSTICE, FBI LABORATORY ANNUAL REPORT '98 6, 15 (1999); Michael G. Noblett, *Computer Analysis and Response Team (CART): The Microcomputer as Evidence*, 19 CRIME LABORATORY DIG. 10, 10 (Jan. 1992).

476   DUKE JOURNAL OF COMPARATIVE & INTERNATIONAL LAW   [Vol 9:451

evidence. The other aspect of this field is maintaining the authenticity of electronic data such that it can be probative in grand jury or courtroom proceedings.

In the United States, generally accepted protocols and procedures have been established so that (1) investigators searching computers have great success retrieving stored data, and (2) proof of authenticity and associated challenges are in keeping with those associated with physical evidence.[85] Outside of the United States, some countries have the same (or possibly greater) capabilities, but a significant number of others find themselves lacking in such proficiency.[86] The remedy to this disparity in abilities lies in international training and sharing of information and forensic tools. Organized efforts are currently underway to effect these changes.[87] With regard to authenticity, internationally recognized standards in computer forensics need to be adopted and implemented so that evidence gathered in one country can be introduced in proceedings in another country as a matter of course.

IV. WHAT IS BEING DONE BY MULTI-LATERAL ORGANIZATIONS?

To date, three multilateral organizations (i.e., groups with multiple-nation membership) are doing the bulk of the international policy work on high-tech and computer-related crime: the Council of Europe (COE), the European Union (EU) and its related institutions, and the G-8. To a lesser degree, some work in this area has been done by the Organization for Economic Cooperation and Development (OECD), and the United Nations.[88]

Of the three main groups, the G-8 has been particularly effective in making progress on several fronts. While the EU and COE have large European memberships, the G-8 has broader representation, with members from Europe, Russia, North America, and Japan.[89]

---

85. *See id.*; PROCEEDINGS OF THE 12TH INTERPOL FORENSIC SCIENCE SYMPOSIUM 14-51 (Richard Frank & Harold Peel eds. 1998).

86. *See* PROCEEDINGS OF THE 12TH INTERPOL FORENSIC SCIENCE SYMPOSIUM, *supra* note 85, at 8-43 (containing survey responses concerning specific aspects of computer forensics for fifteen countries, such as Australia, China, and Spain).

87. *See* discussion, *infra* Section IV.

88. *See* discussion of these multilateral groups *infra* Section IV.A-E. Work is being done in some instances on a bilateral (two-country) basis. But the broad international policy in this area is being done in the multilateral fora, and an examination of bilateral efforts underway is beyond the scope of this article.

89. *See infra* Section IV.C.

Because networked communications traverse every continent, and because leading communications and computer technology is developed in areas besides Europe (such as Asia and North America), regional efforts to solve universal crime problems will inevitably be either slower or less effective than similar efforts by policy-making bodies with a broad geographic base.

The heads of state of the G-8 countries meet annually. At their 1998 Summit, they adopted a comprehensive plan to fight high-tech and computer-related crime.[90] While the COE started addressing computer crime at the technical level in 1988, its heads of state have only met twice since 1949 when the COE was created, and have never addressed computer crime.[91] While EU heads of state called for a study of the subject and development of relevant policies, the heads of state from its member countries have not settled on a specific plan of action to combat computer crime.[92] Finally, unlike the COE and EU, the G-8 is neither governed by international convention nor constrained by a convention-created bureaucracy. It can therefore move faster and address new and emerging areas as the will of its leaders dictates.

A. The Council of Europe

The Council of Europe (COE) is an international organization based in Strasbourg, France.[93] It was established by ten Western European countries in the wake of the Second World War, with the signing of its founding treaty, known as the Statute of the Council of Europe, in 1949.[94] Today, it has a pan-European membership of forty countries, which include the Baltic states, Russia and Turkey.[95] It defines its main role as strengthening democracy, human rights, and the rule of law throughout its member states.[96] In the area of criminal law, twenty conventions and over eighty recommendations have been adopted, as well as a number of reports on crime issues.[97]

---

90. *See infra* Section IV.C.2 & note 135.

91. *See* Arena, *supra* note 29.

92. *See infra* Section IV.B.

93. *See About the Council of Europe* (last modified Jan. 27, 1999) <http://www.coe.fr/eng/present/about.htm>.

94. *See A Brief History of the Council of Europe* (last modified Jan. 28, 1998) <http://www.coe.fr/eng/present/history.htm>.

95. *See About the Council of Europe*, supra note 93.

96. *See id.*

97. *See* Peter Csonka, *Council of Europe Activities Related to Information Technology, Data Protection and Computer Crime*, 5 INFO. & COMM. TECH. LAW 177, 178 (1996).

In 1989, the Committee of Ministers[98] adopted a recommendation and report on computer-related crime, Recommendation No. R. (89) 9.[99] The recommendation called on member states to consider computer crimes when either reviewing or proposing domestic legislation, and the report contained guidelines in this area for legislators.[100] In 1995, the Committee adopted Recommendation No. R. (95) 13, which provided procedures for implementing Recommendation (89) 9, and contained principles "concerning problems of criminal procedure law connected with information technology" on such topics as search and seizure, technical surveillance, electronic evidence, encryption, and international cooperation.[101]

In February 1997, a Committee of Experts on Crime in Cyberspace (PC-CY) was formed to examine computer crime and related problems in criminal procedure law.[102] Its work is aimed at drafting a binding legal instrument (i.e., a "Cybercrime Convention") which defines cybercrime offenses, and addresses such topics as jurisdiction, international cooperation, search and seizure, data protection, and liability of ISPs.[103] The PC-CY first met in April 1997, and has had several additional meetings.[104] The PC-CY expects to have a draft Convention completed by December 31, 2000, at which time the draft will be forwarded to the Steering Committee on European Crime Problems (CDPC) (a committee of senior career bureaucrats). If the CDPC approves the draft, it will be forwarded to the Committee of Ministers for their approval. After approval by the Committee of

---

98. The Committee of Ministers is the decision-making organ of the Council of Europe, which comprises the foreign ministers from the member countries. (A European Foreign Minister is equivalent in rank to the U.S. Secretary of State.) *See Introduction to the Committee of Ministers of the Council of Europe* (last modified Mar. 22, 1999) <http://www.coe.fr/cm/intro/intro.0.html>.

99. *See* Csonka, *supra* note 97, at 179-80.

100. *See id.*

101. *Id.* at 186; *Recommendation No. R (95) 13 of the Committee of Ministers to Member States Concerning Problems of Criminal Procedure Law Connected with Information Technology* (last modified Dec. 3, 1998) <http://www.usdoj.gov/criminal/cybercrime/crycoe.htm> (adopted Sept. 11, 1995).

102. While membership of the PC-CY is limited to experts from fourteen European countries, representatives from the Canada, Japan, and the United States may attend meetings, but may not vote on any matter. *See Council of Europe's Fight Against Corruption and Organised Crime* (last modified June 10, 1997) <http://www.coe.fr/corrupt/epccy.htm> (Specific Terms of Reference, Committee of Experts on Crime in Cyberspace, 583rd Meeting, Feb. 4, 1997).

103. *See id.*; Telephone Interview with Drew C. Arena, *supra* note 29.

104. *See* THE WHITE HOUSE, INTERNATIONAL CRIME CONTROL STRATEGY 69 (May 1998).

Ministers, the Convention will be open for signature by COE members and non-member states which participated in its drafting.[105]

B. The European Union

The European Union (EU) has its roots in three organizations formed in the 1950s by Belgium, West Germany, France, Italy, Luxembourg, and the Netherlands: the European Coal and Steel Community (ECSC); the European Atomic Energy Community (Euratom); and the European Economic Community (EEC).[106] These three communities are still at the heart of the EU, and the treaties which founded them have since been revised and extended.[107] The Treaty on European Union, generally called the Maastricht Treaty, gives a single legal framework to the three European Communities.[108]

The EU now has fifteen member states, and its own flag, anthem and currency (the Euro).[109] The EU's objective is to "promote economic and social progress which is balanced and sustainable, assert the European identity on the international scene, and introduce a European citizenship for the nationals of the Member States."[110]

In the area of high-tech crime, the EU has issued several texts. In 1995, it promulgated a directive which established certain rights and protections for citizens concerning electronically processed data.[111] For example, the directive establishes the right of a citizen to know what electronic data a corporation maintains on that person, and provides protection against personal data being transferred to a

---

105. *See Council of Europe's Fight Against Corruption and Organised Crime, supra* note 102. If the United States were to become a signatory to the Convention (which is impossible to predict at this point), the U.S. Senate would have to ratify the Convention, as with any international treaty.

106. *See* DIRECTORATE-GENERAL FOR INFORMATION, COMMUNICATION, CULTURE AND AUDIOVISUAL MEDIA, EUROPEAN COMMUNITIES, HOW DOES THE EUROPEAN UNION WORK? 6-7 (2d ed. 1998). The founding treaties have been revised three times: in 1987 (the Single Act); in 1992 (the Treaty on European Union); and in 1997 (the draft Treaty of Amsterdam). *See The abc of the European Union - citizenship* (last modified Feb. 23, 1999) <http://europa.eu.int/abc-en.htm>.

107. *See The abc of the European Union - citizenship, supra* note 106.

108. *See id.*

109. *See id.* The member states are: Austria, Belgium, Denmark, Finland, France, Germany, Greece, Ireland, Italy, Luxembourg, the Netherlands, Portugal, Spain, Sweden, and the United Kingdom. *See What is the European Union? 15 Member States and Maps* (last modified Feb. 3, 1998) <http://europa.eu.int/en/eu/states.htm>.

110. *The abc of the European Union - citizenship, supra* note 106.

111. *See* Directive 95/46/EC *supra* note 56.

480   DUKE JOURNAL OF COMPARATIVE & INTERNATIONAL LAW   [Vol 9:451

non-EU country if that country has inadequate privacy protections.[112] Member states are required to establish mechanisms to enforce these rights.[113] In 1997, the EU issued a directive designed to ensure privacy relating to telecommunications data.[114] That directive requires telecommunications carriers to delete traffic data at the end of each transmission (with exceptions for billing purposes and for law enforcement and national security needs).[115] In light of these Directives, it is imperative that government policy decisions concerning electronic commerce and privacy be made in concert with decisions concerning public safety.

In 1997, the European Council[116] endorsed an action plan to combat organized crime, and assembled a Multidisciplinary Group on Organized Crime (MDG) to implement the action plan.[117] Recommendation Five of the action plan calls for a study on high-tech crime, and development of a policy addressing public safety which provides law enforcement and judicial authorities with the means to prevent and combat the misuse of new technologies.[118] Since its inception, the MDG has adopted the study of Dr. Ulrich Sieber on legal aspects of computer related crime,[119] and it is exploring what role Europol might play in combating computer crime.[120]

---

112. *See id.*

113. *See id.*

114. *See id.*

115. *See id.* The EU has issued a number of other documents relating to crime in cyberspace. *See, e.g.,* Decision No. 276/1999/EC of the European Parliament and of the Council of January 25, 1999, Official Journal of the European Communities, L33/1 (Feb. 6, 1999) (adopting an action plan on promoting safer use of the Internet by combating illegal and harmful content on global networks).

116. The European Council is comprised of the heads of state of the fifteen member countries of the EU. *See The Council of the European Union* (last modified Mar. 31, 1998) <http://europa.eu.int/inst/en/cl.htm#council>. The Council meets twice a year to provide input to the European Parliament about policy and development of the European Union. *See id.*

117. *See 2146.Council - Justice and Home Affairs Press Release, Brussels, 03-12-1998, Nr. 13673/98, Presse 427* (visited Mar. 27, 1999) <http://ue.eu.int/newsroom/main.cfm?LANG=1> (Press Release from the 2146th Council Meeting, Council of the European Union, General Secretariat, Justice and Home Affairs Report on the Follow-Up of the 1997 Action Plan on the Fight Against Organized Crime).

118. *See id.;* Telephone Interview with Drew C. Arena, *supra* note 29.

119. *See generally* Prof. Dr. Ulrich Sieber, *Legal Aspects of Computer-Related Crime in the Information Society—COMCRIME Study, in* SPECIAL LAW AND COUNTRY REPORTS (1998).

120. Europol is a European police office created by convention in 1998. Located at The Hague, Europol is an information clearing house and analysis center with law enforcement liaison officers from the member states. Europol is not a European police force; its mandate is to increase cooperation and communication between and among law enforcement agencies in the member states. *See* Telephone Interview with Drew C. Arena, *supra* note 29.

C. The G-8

1. *Background.* The present G-8 (or "Group of Eight") leading industrialized democracies originated in 1975 at an Economic Summit convened by President Valery Giscard d'Estaing of France and attended by leaders from Germany, Japan, the United Kingdom and the United States.[121] President Giscard and Chancellor Schmidt of Germany wanted to establish an informal forum for world leaders to discuss world economic issues.[122] Italy and Canada joined this original "Group of Five" in 1976-77 and the configuration became known as the Group of Seven, or "G-7."[123] G-7 meetings followed a limited agenda of economic issues, and were intended to provide an informal consultation forum.[124] In the 1980s, these annual meetings became more formalized, with an agreed statement, or communique, issued by the leaders at the conclusion of each summit.[125] Leaders such as President Reagan, French President Mitterand, German Chancellor Kohl, and British Prime Minister Thatcher brought increasingly broader agendas to the table.[126] At the end of the cold war, as democratic and economic reform got underway in Russia, Russian leaders were gradually integrated into the G-7.[127] In 1998, the group's name was formally changed to the "G-8," and the first full G-8 Summit was held in Birmingham in June of that year.[128]

In its current configuration, the G-8's membership includes the majority of the world's most powerful democracies—countries that are global leaders economically, technologically, legally, and politically. This small but powerful membership gives the G-8 certain ad-

---

121. *See What is G8?* (visited Mar. 27, 1999) <http://birmingham.g8summit.gov.uk/brief 0398/what.is.g8.shtml> (the British Foreign and Commonwealth Office web page for the 1998 Birmingham Summit).

122. *See id.*

123. *See id.*

124. *See id.*

125. *See id.* For example, the 1983 Williamsburg Summit, hosted by President Reagan, produced a G-7 agreement to support the deployment of U.S. Cruise and Pershing missiles to Europe to confront new Soviet SS20 missiles. Agreement on common opposition to global terrorism followed at the Tokyo Summit in 1986. *See id.*

126. *See What is G8?, supra* note 121.

127. *See id.* Former President Gorbachev attended a meeting in the margins of the London Summit in 1991. Likewise, in 1992 and 1993, President Yeltsin was invited to Summits to discuss financial assistance to the Russian economy, and in 1994 President Yeltsin first took part in foreign policy discussions. The Denver Summit in 1997 was called the "Summit of the Eight," in recognition of broader Russian involvement. *See id.*

128. *See id.*; Richard W. Stevenson, *Rich Leaders Turn Eye to Crime and Debt,* N.Y. TIMES, May 17, 1998, at A11.

vantages over more bureaucratic or cumbersome multilateral organizations.[129]

2. *Focus on High-tech Crime.* After the 1995 Summit in Halifax, Nova Scotia, a group of experts was brought together to look for better ways to fight international crime. In 1996 this group (which became known as the "Lyon Group") produced forty recommendations to combat international crime[130] that were endorsed by the G-8 heads of state at the Lyon Summit in June 1996. Recommendation Sixteen, in part, called for countries to "review their laws in order to ensure that abuses of modern technology that are deserving of criminal sanctions are criminalized and that problems with respect to jurisdiction, enforcement powers, investigation, training, crime prevention and international cooperation in respect of such abuses are effectively addressed."[131]

To implement Recommendation Sixteen and otherwise enhance the abilities of law enforcement in combating high-tech and computer-related crime, a subgroup of the Lyon Group was formed in January 1997 ("G-8 Subgroup on High-tech Crime"), and it held its first five meetings during that year.[132] In December 1997, Attorney General Reno hosted the first-ever meeting of her counterparts from the G-8 countries, and the meeting centered on computer crime.[133] At the conclusion of the meeting, the Ministers[134] adopted ten Principles and a ten-point Action Plan to combat high-tech crime, and issued a Communiqué.[135] At the 1998 G-8 Summit in Birmingham,

---

129. "Our small number allows us to act quickly, and our unique membership offers an opportunity to lead the world community that is rarely found in our history. And we are often on the cutting edge for example in responding to international terrorism, to international money laundering, to precursor chemicals." Reno, Chantilly Keynote Address, *supra* note 1.

130. *See G8 and International Crime* (visited Mar. 27, 1999) <http://birmingham.g8summit.gov.uk/crime/>.

131. P8 Senior Experts Group on Transnational Organized Crime, P8 Senior Experts Group Recommendations 3 (Apr. 12, 1996) (on file with the *Duke Journal of Comparative & International Law*) (the P8 Senior Experts Group is also known as the Lyon Group).

132. *See Computer Crime and Intellectual Property Section (CCIPS)* (last modified Nov. 24, 1998) <http://www.usdoj.gov/criminal/cybercrime/intl.html>.

133. *See id.*

134. "Ministers" is a convention that refers to the law enforcement heads from the G-8 countries, the majority of which are either Ministers of Justice or Ministers of the Interior.

135. The full text of the Principles and Action Plan adopted by the Ministers follows:
PRINCIPLES AND ACTION PLAN TO COMBAT HIGH-TECH CRIME
Statement of Principles
We hereby endorse the following PRINCIPLES, which should be supported by all countries:

I. There must be no safe havens for those who abuse information technologies.

II. Investigation and prosecution of international high-tech crimes must be coordinated among all concerned States, regardless of where harm has occurred.

III. Law enforcement personnel must be trained and equipped to address high-tech crimes.

IV. Legal systems must protect the confidentiality, integrity, and availability of data and systems from unauthorized impairment and ensure that serious abuse is penalized.

V. Legal systems should permit the preservation of and quick access to electronic data, which are often critical to the successful investigation of crime.

VI. Mutual assistance regimes must ensure the timely gathering and exchange of evidence in cases involving international high-tech crime.

VII. Transborder electronic access by law enforcement to publicly available (open source) information does not require authorization from the State where the data resides.

VIII. Forensic standards for retrieving and authenticating electronic data for use in criminal investigations and prosecutions must be developed and employed.

IX. To the extent practicable, information and telecommunications systems should be designed to help prevent and detect network abuse, and should also facilitate the tracing of criminals and the collection of evidence.

X. Work in this area should be coordinated with the work of other relevant international fora to ensure against duplication of efforts.

Communique Annex: Principles to Combat High-Tech Crime (last modified Mar. 30, 1998) <http://www.usdoj.gov/criminal/cybercrime/principles.htm>.

Action Plan

In support of these PRINCIPLES, we are directing our officials to:

1. Use our established network of knowledgeable personnel to ensure a timely, effective response to transnational high-tech cases and designate a point-of-contact who is available on a twenty-four hour basis.

2. Take appropriate steps to ensure that a sufficient number of trained and equipped law enforcement personnel are allocated to the task of combating high-tech crime and assisting law enforcement agencies of other States.

3. Review our legal systems to ensure that they appropriately criminalize abuses of telecommunications and computer systems and promote the investigation of high-tech crimes.

4. Consider issues raised by high-tech crimes, where relevant, when negotiating mutual assistance agreements or arrangements.

5. Continue to examine and develop workable solutions regarding: the preservation of evidence prior to the execution of a request for mutual assistance; transborder searches; and computer searches of data where the location of that data is unknown.

6. Develop expedited procedures for obtaining traffic data from all communications carriers in the chain of a communication and to study ways to expedite the passing of this data internationally.

7. Work jointly with industry to ensure that new technologies facilitate our effort to combat high-tech crime by preserving and collecting critical evidence.

8. Ensure that we can, in urgent and appropriate cases, accept and respond to mutual assistance requests relating to high-tech crime by expedited but reliable means of communications, including voice, fax, or e-mail, with written confirmation to follow where required.

9. Encourage internationally-recognized standards-making bodies in the fields of telecommunications and information technologies to continue providing the public and private sectors with standards for reliable and secure telecommunications and data processing technologies.

10. Develop and employ compatible forensic standards for retrieving and authenticating electronic data for use in criminal investigations and prosecutions.

484   DUKE JOURNAL OF COMPARATIVE & INTERNATIONAL LAW   [Vol 9:451

England, the Heads of State endorsed and agreed to implement their Ministers' Principles and Action Plan.[136] Essentially an international template for fighting high-tech crime, the Principles and Action Plan have been adopted by President Clinton, British Prime Minister Tony Blair, French President Jacques Chirac, Russian President Boris Yeltsin, and the other G-8 leaders. This is quite significant. It is the first time a group of powerful world leaders have jointly adopted a detailed plan for fighting computer crime.[137] Additionally, instead of referring the plan back to member countries for individual action, a subgroup of G-8 experts meets regularly to work cooperatively toward implementation of the Action Plan.

   3. *High-tech Crime Subgroup.* As of May 1999, the G-8 Subgroup on High-tech Crime had met fourteen times.[138] Its focus has been on enhancing the abilities of law enforcement to investigate and prosecute high-tech and computer-related crime. The Subgroup's progress and accomplishments include the following:

   a. High-tech Points of Contact. In March 1998, a network of high-tech points of contact for law enforcement in each of the G-8 countries was established.[139] These contacts are available twenty-four hours a day to respond to urgent requests for assistance in international high-tech crime investigations or cases involving electronic evidence.[140] Recruitment and education efforts are currently underway to expand this network to include many more Internet-connected countries. The hope is that in the near future, international investigations in this area will not be delayed because of the inability to locate the proper computer crime expert or because of differences in time zones.[141]

   b. International Training Conference. In November 1998, the Subgroup hosted an international computer crime training conference for G-8 law enforcement officials.[142] The conference,

---

Communique Annex: Action Plan to Combat High-Tech Crime (last modified Mar. 30, 1998) <http://www.usdoj.gov/criminal/cybercrime/action.htm>.

   136. *See The Birmingham Summit: Final Communique,* ¶ 21 (visited Mar. 30, 1999) <http://birmingham. g8summit.gov.uk/docs/final.shtml>. The *Final Communique* was established May 17, 1998. *See id.; see also* Stevenson, *supra* note 128; Susan Page, *Trade and Crime Were Also on Agenda,* USA TODAY, May 18, 1998, at 15A.

   137. The forty recommendations and the principles on high-tech crime agreed to in 1997 have recently been endorsed by the EU. In addition, the UN is considering changes to its model treaty on mutual legal assistance reflecting the work being carried out by the G-8. *See G8 and International Crime, supra* note 130.

which focused on technical and operational issues, allowed cybercrime experts to share knowledge regarding the latest trends and techniques of high-tech criminals, the technical problems encountered in high-tech investigations, and law enforcement solutions. This was the first such conference, and the participants expressed unanimous support for similar future conferences.[143]

c.   Review of Legal Systems. The Subgroup is in the process of comparing each country's legal system as it relates to high-tech crime.[144] The project covers substantive and procedural laws, data protection and privacy, search and seizure law, extradition, electronic surveillance (wiretapping), and abilities to secure traffic data (connection information) and subscriber information.[145] This is an important step for the G-8 to take to ensure that the member countries' legal systems appropriately criminalize computer crimes and promote their investigation.

d.   Locating and Identifying Computer Criminals ("Preservation of Traffic Data"). Substantial energy has been devoted to this critical topic, which includes access to historical traffic data and future ("real-time") traffic data. As a first step in this area, principles for transborder access to stored computer data have been adopted.[146]

e.   Principles for Transborder Searches and Seizures. The Subgroup reached a consensus on principles for transborder access to stored computer data.[147] Among other things, the principles include "fast freeze" recommendations on preserving data in anticipation of a formal request for mutual legal assistance, as well as on expedited processing of formal legal assistance requests. The principles also obligate states to ensure that their national laws and procedures permit them to secure rapid preservation of stored data in a

---

138. Telephone Interview with Scott Charney, Chief, Computer Crime and Intellectual Property Section, U.S. Department of Justice and Chair, G-8 Subgroup on High-tech Crime (May 7, 1999).

139. *See id.*

140. *See id.*

141. *See id.*

142. Telephone Interview with Scott Charney, *supra* note 138.

143. *See id.*

144. *See id.*

145. *See id.*

146. *See* discussion *infra* Part IV.C.3.e.

147. Telephone Interview with Scott Charney, *supra* note 138.

486   DUKE JOURNAL OF COMPARATIVE & INTERNATIONAL LAW   [Vol 9:451

computer system, even where necessary only to assist a foreign state; endorse some forms of consensual access; and affirm that no authorization from a searched state is required for transborder access to publicly available data.[148]   These principles are only recommendations on interim measures, and it is too early in the process to know if complicated issues concerning transborder searches and seizures can be resolved sufficiently to allow for their implementation.[149]

f.   Computer Forensics.   In recognition of the fact that the International Organization of Computer Evidence (IOCE) has broad representation that includes most of the G-8 countries, the Subgroup, through its Chair, referred to the IOCE the task of developing recommendations for international standards on the retrieval and authentication of electronic evidence.[150] The first step for the IOCE will be defining common terms, identifying methods and techniques to be used, and establishing a common format for forensics requests.[151]

g.   Cooperation with Industry. The Subgroup has followed the instruction of the G-8 Heads of State at their Summit in May 1998 for close cooperation with industry.[152] Representatives from hardware manufacturers, telecommunications carriers, and ISPs have made presentations at meetings, and have discussed concrete steps law enforcement and industry can take together to accelerate cooperation between the two.[153]

On going Subgroup work concerning industry includes the following: adopting a process that allows the companies that are developing technical standards, including next-generation Internet technologies, to take into account public safety needs; consulting within governments to ensure that new data protection policies do not provide havens for criminals; standardizing law enforcement requests for assistance to industry, in order to allow industry to respond more quickly and with less expense; and developing twenty-four-hour points-of-contact with critical ISPs. In addition, plans are underway

---

148. *See id.*

149. *See id.*

150. *See id.*

151. *See id.*

152. *See The Birmingham Summit: Final Communique, supra* note 136.

153. These representatives have included America Online (American ISP), NiftyServe (Japanese ISP), and Deutsche Telekom (German telecommunications carrier and ISP).

for a G-8 industry conference on high-tech crime which would bring together high-tech crime-fighters and private sector representatives from the G-8 countries.[154]

D. Organization for Economic Cooperation and Development (OECD)

The OECD is an organization of twenty-nine countries that provides member-governments with a forum to develop economic and social policy.[155] It was formed by convention in 1961 by twenty countries in North America and Western Europe, and since then its membership has been joined by Japan, Australia, New Zealand, Finland, Mexico, the Czech Republic, Hungary, Poland and Korea.[156] Membership is limited to countries which are committed to a market economy and pluralistic democracy.[157] Most work is done in one of the OECD's 200 committees, working groups, and expert groups, and over 40,000 government officials participate in OECD meetings each year. The OECD has a permanent secretariat in Paris, and the United States (like other nations) has an ambassador posted to the OECD.[158]

The OECD has developed and issued a number of documents related to computers and cyberspace. "Guidelines on the Protection of Privacy and Transborder Flows of Personal Data" were adopted in 1980.[159] The Guidelines were intended "to harmonise national privacy legislation and . . . to prevent at the same time interruptions in international flows of data."[160] "Guidelines for the Security of Information Systems" were adopted in 1992.[161] These guidelines were intended to raise awareness of risks to information systems and to provide reassurance as to the reliability of information systems. Governments and the private sector were urged to cooperate to cre-

---

154. Telephone Interview with Scott Charney, *supra* note 138.

155. *See About OECD: What is OECD?* (last modified Mar. 26, 1999) <http://www.oecd. org/about/general/ index.htm>.

156. *See About OECD: Membership* (last modified Mar. 26, 1999) <http://www.oecd.org/ about/general/member-countries.htm>.

157. *See About OECD: What is OECD?, supra* note 155.

158. *See id.*

159. *See Guidelines on the Protection of Privacy and Transborder Flows of Personal Data* (last modified Mar. 26, 1999) <http://www.oecd.org//dsti/sti/it/secur/prod/PRIV-EN.HTM>.

160. *Id.*

161. *See Guidelines for the Security of Information Systems* (last modified Mar. 26, 1999) <http://www.oecd.org//dsti/sti/it/secur/prod/e_secur.htm>.

ate an international framework for security of information systems.[162] In 1997, the OECD issued Cryptography Policy Guidelines and the Report on Background and Issues of Cryptography Policy.[163]

E. The United Nations

The United Nations is planning to increase awareness of computer crime issues by sponsoring a workshop on "Crimes Related to the Computer Network" at the Tenth United Congress on Crime Prevention and the Treatment of Offenders, scheduled to be held in Vienna in April 2000.[164] At the request of the Centre for International Crime Prevention in Vienna, the United Nations Asia Far Eastern Institute (UNAFEI) has assumed responsibility for coordinating the workshop.

In October 1998, UNAFEI hosted an experts meeting in Fuchu, Tokyo to begin preparations for this workshop. The group of experts, including representatives from Australia, Canada, India, the Netherlands, Japan, Korea, South Africa and the United States, are planning a workshop program that will demonstrate the legal and technical difficulties of tracking criminal activities over computer networks as well as the problems associated with searching and seizing evidence stored on computer networks. In addition, negotiations are currently underway on a UN Convention on transnational organized crime. It is likely that certain aspects of cybercrime will be addressed by the Convention.[165]

V. CONCLUSION

Criminality deriving from new technologies such as computers, the Internet, and wireless communications provides daunting challenges for law enforcement around the globe. Crimes can be committed remotely, without the criminal ever setting foot in the country where the misdeed occurs or the victim is located. Critical evidence may vanish the moment the culprit ends his transmission. And any hacker can route his communication through a foreign country, thereby adding an international element to his crime which may create insurmountable obstacles for law enforcement. Since the United

---

162. *See id.*

163. *See Cryptography Policy: The Guidelines and the Issues* (last modified Mar. 26, 1999) <http://www.oecd.org//dsti/sti/it/secur/prod/e-crypto.htm>.

164. *See* United Nations General Assembly Resolution 1997/52 of December 1997.

165. Telephone Interview with Greg Schaffer, Trial Attorney, Computer Crime and Intellectual Property Section, U.S. Dept. of Justice (March 8, 1999).

States depends on the stable, consistent operation of such critical infrastructures as banking, telecommunications, and emergency services—all of which have become increasingly automated—the stakes facing the public are quite high indeed.

Although law enforcement officials are loath to admit that any criminal has the upper hand, candid professionals acknowledge that they face an uphill battle in this arena. As technologies evolve, laws need updating so that international legal assistance can be provided, and criminals can be extradited and brought to justice. Countries must dedicate more experts to high-tech crime-fighting, and then provide them with the sophisticated and expensive equipment required for their tasks. The ability to locate and identify criminals must be improved dramatically, although it sometimes seems beyond the limits of existing technologies. And various issues posed by the need to gather electronic evidence of a crime from several countries—often in real-time—must be resolved. As a result, the ultimate outcome of this struggle to maintain public safety in our increasingly automated way of life is far from certain.

Many important steps have been taken in this regard by individual governments, and ambitious efforts are also underway in the international community. But so much more needs to be done. At every level, there must be a heightened appreciation of the threat posed by international high-tech and computer-related crime. Senior government officials have to provide leadership, be receptive to new ways of thinking, and come to understand that many of the old paradigms for crime-fighting no longer suffice.

Finally, these challenges cannot be met unless a true partnership between governments and the private sector comes into being. Policy-makers and law enforcement officials must recognize that law enforcement needs may place burdens on industry, which they should take reasonable steps to minimize. At the same time, industry ought to consider the safety of the public when responding to the needs of the market.

As we begin a new millennium, governments must work together to stay ahead of this next generation of criminal activity. They cannot allow cyberspace to become the new Wild West—a frontier bereft of the rule of law, where criminals prey on citizens with impunity. We must not permit the many benefits of the information age—such as electronic commerce and enhanced communications—to be seriously diminished by their vulnerability to illegal activity.

[12]

INTERNATIONAL CYBER-JURISDICTION: A COMPARATIVE ANALYSIS

Ray August[*]

Headline grabbing cases point out an issue of increasing concern: Who has jurisdiction over cyberspace? [1] In one recent case, a French

---

[*] Professor of Business Law, Washington State University; J.D., University of Texas at Austin; LL.M., University of Cambridge; Ph.D., University of Idaho. Author of INTERNATIONAL BUSINESS LAW (3d ed. Prentice Hall 2000) and PUBLIC INTERNATIONAL LAW (Prentice Hall 1995), and co-author of CYBERLAW (West 2000). Webmaster, ALSB J. INT'L BUS. L., *at* http://www.wsu.edu/~legal/ijrnl.

[1] In addition to headlines in the popular press, the issue of jurisdiction in cyberspace has also become a popular topic in law reviews and journals. Recent articles include: *American Bar Association Section Report: Achieving Legal and Business Order in Cyberspace: A Report on Global Jurisdiction Issues Created by the Internet*, 55 BUS. LAW. 1801 (2000) [hereinafter *ABA Section Report*]; Tyler Anderson, *An Analysis of Personal Jurisdiction and Conflict of Laws in the Context of Electronically Formed Contracts*, 37 IDAHO L. REV. 477 (2001); Ronald A. Brand, *Intellectual Property, Electronic Commerce and the Preliminary Draft Hague Jurisdiction and Judgments Convention*, 62 U. PITT. L. REV. 581 (2001); Joseph S. Burns & Richard A. Bales, *Personal Jurisdiction and the Web*, 53 ME. L. REV. 29 (2001); Melissa K. Cantrell, *The Taming of E-Health: Asserting U.S. Jurisdiction over Foreign and Domestic Websites*, 103 W. VA. L. REV. 573 (2001); William Crane, *Legislative Updates: The World-Wide Jurisdiction: An Analysis of Over-Inclusive Internet Jurisdictional Law and an Attempt by Congress to Fix It*, 11 J. ART & ENT. L. 267 (2001); Brian E. Daughdrill, *Poking Along in the Fast Lane on the Information Super Highway: Territorial-Based Jurisprudence in a Technological World*, 52 MERCER L. REV. 1217 (2001); Rochelle Cooper Dreyfuss, *An Alert to the Intellectual Property Bar: The Hague Judgments Convention*, 2001 U. ILL. L. REV. 421; Susan Nauss Exon, *A New Shoe Is Needed to Walk Through Cyberspace Jurisdiction*, 11 ALB. L.J. SCI. &

court assumed jurisdiction over Yahoo, an American online content provider, and ordered it to remove web pages showing Nazi memorabilia, material that is illegal to view in France but legal almost everywhere else.[2] In another case, a British court held a British subject liable for posting photographs on an American web server considered obscene in Britain but not in the United States.[3] Still another, an American court held the president of a gambling company organized and headquartered in Antigua liable for soliciting and accepting bets from Americans over the Internet.[4]

The challenge in determining if and when courts have jurisdiction over activities conducted on the Internet would not be great if the Internet were confined to a single geographical area, or if it were neatly divisible along territorial boundaries into distinct local networks. By its nature, however, the Internet is international: it disrespects local and national jurisdiction. The challenge, therefore, is to create rules that work smoothly across local, national, and international boundaries.

In devising new jurisdictional rules for cyberspace, judges, legislators, and treaty draftsmen are using analogy—the tried-and-true tool of legal reasoning—to modify existing rules to fit this new paradigm. Reasoning by analogy can have its problems, however,

TECH. 1 (2000); Adrian Goss, *Jay Cohen's Brave New World: The Liability of Offshore Operators of Licensed Internet Casinos for Breach of United States' Anti-Gambling Laws*, 7 RICH. J.L. & TECH. 32 (Spring 2001), *at* http://www.richmond.edu/jolt/v7i4/article2.html; Christopher Allen Kroblin, *Expanding the Jurisdictional Reach for Intentional Torts: Implications for Cyber Contacts*, 31 GOLDEN GATE U. L. REV. 51 (2001); Erica D. O'Loughlin, *The Times They Are A-Changin': Personal Jurisdiction in Cyberspace*, 66 MO. L. REV. 623 (2001); Francesco G. Mazzotta, *A Guide to E-Commerce: Some Legal Issues Posed by E-Commerce for American Businesses Engaged in Domestic and International Transactions*, 24 SUFFOLK TRANSNAT'L L. REV. 249 (2001); Sanjay S. Mody, *National Cyberspace Regulation: Unbundling the Concept of Jurisdiction*, 37 STAN. J. INT'L L. 365 (2001); Joseph Schmitt & Peter Nikolai, *Application of Personal Jurisdiction Principles to Electronic Commerce: A User's Guide*, 27 WM. MITCHELL L. REV. 1571 (2001); and Stephan Wilske & Teresa Schiller, *International Jurisdiction in Cyberspace: Which States May Regulate the Internet?* 50 FED. COMM. L.J. 117 (1997).

  [2] Ligue Contre la Racisme et l'Antisémitisme v. Yahoo, Inc. *See Yahoo Ordered to Bar French from Nazi Web Sites*, (Nov. 20, 2000), *at* http://news.zdnet.co.uk/story/0,,t269-s2082683,00.html.

  [3] Crown v. Waddon. *See* Chris Nuttal, *Police Hail Net Porn Ruling*, BBC News (July 1, 1999), *at* http://news.bbc.co.uk/hi/english/sci/tech/newsid_382000/382152.stm.

  [4] United States v. Galaxy Sports. Press Release, U.S. Department of Justice, (Feb. 28, 2000), *at* http://www.usdoj.gov/criminal/cybercrime/cohen.htm.

especially when differences in context are not taken into account.[5] Nevertheless, analogy is the reasoning tool of choice for creating new law, and existing analogous rules have to be considered in any description of cyber-jurisdiction as it currently stands.[6]

Jurisdiction, of course, defines three kinds of power: the power to prescribe, the power to adjudicate, and the power to enforce.[7] The first of these relates principally to the power of a government to establish and prescribe criminal and regulatory sanctions;[8] the second, to the power of the courts to hear disputes, especially civil disputes; and the third, to the power of a government to compel compliance or to punish noncompliance with its laws, regulations, orders, and judgments.[9]

Although prescriptive jurisdiction is exercised by legislatures and executive agencies (through the making of laws, rules, and regulations), it is most commonly challenged and tested in the courts. Similarly, legislatures and executive agencies can exercise adjudicative jurisdiction and enforcement jurisdiction (through hearings, arrests, and the like), but once again the scope of this power is usually challenged and tested in the courts. That being so, the discussion here will examine how the courts have defined and treated jurisdiction and, in particular, international jurisdiction in the realm of cyberspace.

The discussion begins with an examination of the traditional bases of international criminal and regulatory jurisdiction, with examples of how this jurisdiction is exercised in cyberspace. The discussion continues with an examination of international civil jurisdiction, followed by an examination of the jurisdiction to enforce, again with examples of how each of these sorts of jurisdiction applies in

---

[5] See the criticism of the use of analogy in Niva Elkin-Koren, *Copyright Law and Social Dialogue on the Information Superhighway. The Case against Copyright Liability of Bulletin Board Operators*, 13 CARDOZO ARTS & ENT. L.J. 345, 349 (1995).

[6] The *ABA Section Report*, *supra* note 1, examines traditional American case law and analogizes it to Internet-related jurisdictional issues. This useful study is limited by its decidedly American perspective.

[7] RESTATEMENT (THIRD) OF FOREIGN RELATIONS LAW OF THE U.S. § 401 (1987).

[8] *Id.* § 402; Harvard Law School, *Research in International Law: II. Jurisdiction with Respect to Crime*, 29 AM. J. INT'L L. 435 (Supp. 1935) [hereinafter Harvard, *Jurisdiction with Respect to Crime*.].

[9] RESTATEMENT (THIRD) OF FOREIGN RELATIONS LAW OF THE U.S. § 431 (1987).

534 / Vol. 39 / *American Business Law Journal*

cyberspace. It concludes with consideration of the jurisdictional problems, or issues, that have arisen with the advent of the Internet.

I. INTERNATIONAL CRIMINAL AND REGULATORY JURISDICTION

In order for a national court to adjudicate criminal and regulatory sanctions internationally, there must be some connection, or nexus, between the regulating nation (the forum) and the crime or criminal. This, as we shall see, is true whether the regulated conduct takes place in the physical world or in cyberspace.

Four nexuses have been invoked by courts to justify their exercise of jurisdiction.[10]

1. The *territoriality nexus* holds that the place where an offense is committed—in whole or in part—determines jurisdiction.[11]
2. The *nationality nexus* looks to the nationality or national character of the person committing the offense to establish jurisdiction.[12]
3. The *protective nexus* provides for jurisdiction when a national or international interest of the forum is injured by the offender.[13]
4. The *universality nexus* holds that a court has jurisdiction over certain offenses that are recognized by the community of nations as being of universal concern, including piracy, the slave trade, attacks on or the hijacking of aircraft, genocide, war crimes, and crimes against humanity.[14]

---

[10] *Id.* §§ 402, 404; Draft Convention on Jurisdiction with Respect to Crime, arts. 3-10, *reproduced in* Harvard Law School, *Jurisdiction with Respect to Crime, supra* note 8, at 439–42. For an analysis of these jurisdiction nexuses based primarily on longstanding American case law, see *ABA Section Report, supra* note 1.

[11] An offense does not have to be consummated within the forum's territory for the forum to have jurisdiction. If an offense is commenced within the forum, even if it is completed or consummated abroad, the forum will have jurisdiction. Harvard Law School, *Jurisdiction with Respect to Crime, supra* note 8, at 484–87. Logically, jurisdiction based on the place where an offense was commenced is the converse of jurisdiction based on the effects nexus, which focuses on the place where the offense is consummated. *See id.* at 487–94.

[12] RESTATEMENT (THIRD) OF FOREIGN RELATIONS LAW OF THE U.S. § 404 (1987).

[13] *Id.* § 404.

[14] The *Restatement* states that the universal nexus may "perhaps" include "certain acts of terrorism." *Id.* Section 404, comment b, asserts that "[u]niversal jurisdiction is increasingly accepted for certain acts of terrorism, such as assaults on the life or physical integrity of diplomatic personnel, kidnapping, and indiscriminate violent assaults on people at large," *id.* § 404 cmt. b, but it cites no cases or commentaries in support of its contention. It seems more likely, in light of the terrorist attacks on September 11, 2001, and the ensuing military action in Afghanistan, that the courts and commentators will treat terrorist acts as crimes against humanity. Crimes against humanity were originally defined in Article 6(c) of the

It is not enough that these nexuses exist; the connection between the forum and the person or activity also must be "reasonable."[15] In determining reasonableness, courts consider one or more of the following factors, depending on the circumstances of the particular case:

- the extent to which the criminal or regulated activity takes place, or has a substantial, direct, and foreseeable effect, within the territory of the forum;[16]
- the extent to which the defendant or the injured party has a "genuine link" (*i.e.*, an ongoing and real relationship) with the forum;[17]
- the character of the activity (that is, its importance to the forum, whether other countries regulate it, and the extent to which countries generally regard it as appropriate for regulation);[18]
- the extent to which justified expectations will be protected or harmed by the regulation;[19]
- the extent to which another country has an interest in regulating the activity and the likelihood of a conflict with those regulations;[20]
- the importance of the regulation to the international community;[21] and

---

Charter of the International Military Tribunal established after World War II (the Nuremberg Tribunal) as "murder, extermination, enslavement, deportation, and other inhumane acts committed against any civilian population." Charter of the International Military Tribunal, Nuremberg Trial Collection, The Avalon Project, Yale Law School, *at* http://www.yale.edu/lawweb/avalon/imt/proc/imtconst.htm. Because this broad definition includes the usual definition of terrorism (which is typically described as "the sustained clandestine use of violence, including murder, kidnapping, and bombings, for a political purpose) it seems unnecessary to separately define terrorism as one of the crimes covered by the universality nexus. *See* RAY AUGUST, PUBLIC INTERNATIONAL LAW 345–46 (1995).

[15] RESTATEMENT (THIRD) OF FOREIGN RELATIONS LAW OF THE U.S. § 403 (1987).

[16] *Id.* § 403(2)(b). The Draft Convention on Jurisdiction with Respect to Crime, *supra* note 10, art. 3, describes this same idea in terms of an "attempt" to commit a crime from outside the forum's territory. This attempt must be focused on conduct having its effect within the forum's territory.

[17] RESTATEMENT (THIRD) OF FOREIGN RELATIONS LAW OF THE U.S. § 403 cmt. e. The classic discussion of the genuine link requirement appears in the Nottebohm Case (Liech. v. Guat.), 1955 I.C.J. 4 (Second Phase – Judgment of April 6) in the context of a country's right to sponsor a national's suit before an international court.

[18] RESTATEMENT (THIRD) OF FOREIGN RELATION LAW OF THE U.S. § 403(2)(c).

[19] *Id.* § 403(2)(d).

[20] *Id.* § 403(2)(g), (h).

[21] *Id.* § 403(2)(e).

536 / Vol. 39 / *American Business Law Journal*

> the extent to which the regulation is consistent with the traditions of the international community.[22]

There is one final preliminary matter to note before we look at examples of cases in which the different nexuses have been used. That is: the nexuses are not mutually exclusive. Courts routinely rely on more than one in assuming jurisdiction.[23]

A. The Territoriality Nexus

The most basic and common jurisdictional nexus is the territoriality nexus.[24] Originally, it was based on the idea that a "territorial sovereign has the strongest interest, the greatest facilities, and the most powerful instruments for repressing crimes committed ... in his territory."[25] In other words, crime traditionally was a local matter that was best punished locally.

But crime is no longer exclusively a local concern. As the Harvard Law School faculty observed in 1935, in a statement that seems even more relevant today, "with the increasing facility of communication and transportation, the opportunities for committing crimes whose constituent elements take place in more than one State have grown apace."[26]

Today, accordingly, the territoriality nexus allows courts to assume jurisdiction over crimes and regulatory offenses committed or consummated "in part" within the forum's territory.[27] That is, jurisdiction can exist whenever "any essential element of the crime is accomplished" within the forum's territory.[28]

---

[22] *Id.* § 403(2)(f).

[23] For example, in the landmark international jurisdictional case of Attorney General of the Government of Israel v. Eichman, 36 I.L.R. 5 (Jm. D.C. 1968) (Isr.), the court relied on the protective and the universality nexuses in exercising jurisdiction to try an official of the Austrian Nazi party for war crimes committed in the course of duty on behalf of a foreign country outside the boundaries of the forum (Israel), before the forum came into existence, and against persons who were not citizens of the forum.

[24] RESTATEMENT (THIRD) OF FOREIGN RELATIONS LAW OF THE U.S. § 403 cmt. c.

[25] GEORGE C. LEWIS, FOREIGN JURISDICTION AND THE EXTRADITION OF CRIMINALS 30 (1857).

[26] Harvard Law School, *Jurisdiction with Respect to Crime, supra* note 8, at 484.

[27] Draft Convention on Jurisdiction with Respect to Crime, *supra* note 10, art. 3.

[28] Harvard Law School, *Jurisdiction with Respect to Crime, supra* note 8, at 494.

This development has created two subcategories of the territoriality nexus: the commencement nexus and the effects nexus. The first gives courts jurisdiction over crimes undertaken within the forum's territory but completed or consummated abroad.[29] The second allows courts to assert jurisdiction over crimes planned and plotted abroad, the effects of which take place locally.[30]

The effects nexus has become especially popular with U.S. courts as a mechanism for extending jurisdiction extraterritorially over foreign actors.[31] It is important to recognize, however, that it is really only one aspect of the territoriality nexus. That is, the territoriality nexus can be invoked whenever any "element" of a crime occurs within a forum's territory—from the planning and commencement of a crime to its final effect—and it is not limited to crimes that take place entirely within one territory.[32] Accordingly, in analyzing cases that involve conduct in cyberspace, it is especially important to consider every contact a defendant has with the forum territory and not just those that have effects there.

The importance of looking at all the elements that make up a criminal or regulatory offense is illustrated by the case of *Crown v. Waddon*.[33] That case involved an attempt by the defendant to escape the application of Britain's Obscene Publications Act at 1959, which imposes criminal sanctions on offenders who publish obscene materials in the United Kingdom. To avoid liability, Waddon posted pornographic materials on a server located in the United States. A British court, however, found that publication had occurred in the United Kingdom. It did so, the court said, because the defendant transmitted the pornographic materials from his computer in the United Kingdom to the U.S. server, and those materials were downloaded from the U.S. server for viewing on a computer in the United Kingdom.

---

[29] *Id.* at 484.

[30] *Id.* at 487–88.

[31] *See* United States v. Aluminum Co. of Am., 148 F.2d 416 (2d Cir. 1945) (establishing an effects nexus for violations of U.S. antitrust laws); Timberland Lumber Co. v. Bank of Am., 549 F.2d 597 (9th Cir. 1976) (setting out a balancing test for determining when jurisdiction can be reasonably asserted in antitrust cases).

[32] Harvard Law School, *Jurisdiction with Respect to Crime*, *supra* note 8, at 494.

[33] BBC News (July 1, 1999), *at* http://news.bbc.co.uk/hi/english/sci/tech/newsid_382000/382152.stm.

Similarly, a New York court assumed jurisdiction in *People v. World Interactive Gaming Corp.*,[34] which involved a New York-based[35] company's attempt to offer gambling service contrary to New York law by setting up an Antigua-based subsidiary and creating an online service hosted on a server in Antigua. Using much the same rationale as the British court in *Crown v. Waddon*, the New York Court held that the gambler's "act of entering the bet and transmitting the information from New York via the Internet" meant that there had been "gambling activity within New York state" in violation of state law.[36] Moreover, aside from the use of a subsidiary (which the New York-based parent company wholly dominated) and a Web server in Antigua, the defendant "operated its entire business from its corporate headquarters in Bohemia, New York."[37]

Territoriality was also a jurisdictional nexus for a German court in a suit against the head of CompuServe's German subsidiary for distributing child pornography. Neither CompuServe, an American Internet service provider, nor its officers were tried because CompuServe was not doing business in Germany. Instead, the court found that it had jurisdiction over Felix Somm, a Swiss national, because he was domiciled in Germany, because he was the head of CompuServe's wholly owned German subsidiary, and because the pornography was posted on the subsidiary's web servers located in Germany. Finding that it had jurisdiction, the court convicted Somm.[38]

The German Federal Supreme Court reached a similar conclusion in a suit against Frederick Töben, an Australian, who was prosecuted for violating a post-World War II German law outlawing the Nazi

---

[34] 714 N.Y.S.2d 844 (N.Y. App. Div. 1999).

[35] The company was headquartered in New York and incorporated in Delaware. *Id.* at 846.

[36] *Id.* at 850.

[37] *Id.* at 849.

[38] People v. Somm, Case 8340 Ds 465 Js 173158/95 (Amtsgericht, Munich, Bavaria 1999). An English translation of the court's judgment is available at http://www.cyber-rights.org/isps/somm-dec.htm.

On appeal, Somm's conviction was overturned because of a German law that exempts Internet service providers from liability if they have no reasonable mechanism for excluding illegal Web pages from being posted on their servers. The trial court's exercise of jurisdiction, however, was not questioned. *See Defense Counsel's Remarks*, at http://www.apnic.net/mailing-lists/apple/archive/1999/11/msg00010.html (last visited Dec. 30, 2001).

Party and forbidding any glorification of it.[39] Prior to 1999, Töben sent leaflets through the mails to Germany denying that the Nazis had ever perpetrated the Holocaust. He also posted the same information on an Australian Internet Web site.[40] On visiting Germany in April 1999, Töben was arrested and charged with inciting racial hatred and "defaming a segment of the national population." A trial court found Töben guilty of sending leaflets by mail to Germany. It dismissed the charges of posting materials on the Internet, however, holding that German law could not be applied to content on a foreign Web site. Both Töben and the prosecution appealed. On appeal, the German Federal Supreme Court (the *Bundesgerichtshof*) not only upheld Töben's conviction for mailing leaflets to Germany, it reversed the trial court's finding that Germany's anti-Nazi law does not apply to the Internet. The fact that material glorifying the Nazi Party—material that Germany considers highly offensive to its national interest—could be accessed from within Germany, was sufficient, the Federal Supreme Court held, to give German courts jurisdiction.[41] In other words, there was a sufficient nexus with German territory for the court to hear the case.

B. The Nationality Nexus

The right of a country to exercise jurisdiction based on the nationality of a defendant is universally recognized. A country is assumed to have nearly unlimited control of its nationals, so its "treatment of its nationals is not ordinarily a matter of concern to other States or to international law."[42]

In the context of cyberspace, however, the courts have yet to directly rely on nationality as a nexus for asserting jurisdiction. Nationality, nevertheless, may have been an important factor in several cases. In the *Somm* case, for example, CompuServe's German

---

[39] Töben's arrest warrants, translated into English, are available on the Institute for Historical Review's Web site at http://www.ihr.org/other/990409warrant.html and http://www.ihr.org/other/990503warrant.html (last visited Dec. 30, 2001).

[40] The Web site at http://www.adelaideinstitute.org/ (last visited Dec. 30, 2001) is maintained by Töben's Adelaide Institute in Adelaide, Australia.

[41] Töben, who returned to Australia after serving seven months of a ten-month sentence, is not inclined to return to Germany to serve any additional time. Steve Kettmann, *German Hate Law: No Denying It*, WIRED NEWS, (Dec. 15, 2000), *at* http://www.wired.com/news/politics/0,1283,40669,00.html.

[42] Harvard Law School, *Jurisdiction with Respect to Crime*, *supra* note 8, at 519.

subsidiary was incorporated in Germany and subject to German law.[43] In *World Interactive Gaming*, the defendant was headquartered in New York, incorporated in Delaware, and therefore a U.S. national company. As a consequence, the company's argument, that its wholly dominated Antiguan subsidiary was a foreign entity exempt from local jurisdiction, was rejected.[44]

Nationality was likely used as a jurisdictional nexus in the trial of Jay Cohen in *United States v. Galaxy Sports*.[45] Cohen, the president of World Sports Exchange (WSE), an online gambling organization headquartered in Antigua, was convicted of soliciting and accepting bets from Americans via WSE's Internet Web site. The federal District Court for the Southern District of New York refused to hear arguments that the court lacked jurisdiction.[46] Nevertheless, because Cohen was an American residing in the United States, the court seems to have concluded that he was subject to the court's jurisdiction based on his nationality.[47]

C. The Protective Nexus

Continental European courts, as well as courts in other civil law countries, regularly rely on the protective nexus[48] in assuming jurisdiction over foreign defendants. By comparison, U.S. courts and courts in common law countries generally look for a territoriality nexus, and especially the effects nexus, which is one of its subordinate forms.[49] This is due to differing definitions of the protective nexus. In common law countries, the protective nexus is limited to "acts

---

[43] People v. Somm, *supra* note 38.

[44] People v. World Interactive Gaming Corp., 714 N.Y.S.2d 884, 849 (N.Y. App. Div. 1999).

[45] *See* Press Release, U.S. Department of Justice (Feb. 28, 2000), *at* http://www.usdoj.gov/criminal/cybercrime/cohen.htm.

[46] Mike Brunker, *Net Betting Operator Isn't Wavering*, MSNBC, *at* http://www.msnbc.com/news/369978.asp (Aug. 10, 2000).

[47] *See* Perkins Coie Internet Case Summary *at* http://www.perkinscoie.com/casedigest/icd_results.cfm?keyword1=gambling&topic=Gambling (last visited Dec. 30, 2001). The Second Circuit Court of Appeals affirmed, but it did so without discussing the issue of jurisdiction. United States v. Galaxy Sports, 260 F.3d 68 (2d Cir. 2001).

[48] The protective nexus includes the passive personality nexus: the right of a nation to exercise jurisdiction when one of its nationals is injured. The passive personality nexus was affirmed as a jurisdictional basis recognized in international law in the classic international law case of The Lotus (Fr. v. Tur.) 1927 P.C.I.J. (ser. A) No. 10 (1927).

[49] *See supra* note 31 and accompanying text.

done abroad which affect the security of the state . . . ."[50] In civil law countries, however, the nexus is defined more expansively to include nearly all actions that injure the forum and "which concern it more than they concern other states . . . ."[51]

As is the case for the nationality nexus, the courts have yet to directly identify the protective nexus as a source they need to rely on to exercise jurisdiction. Even so, the protective nexus could properly have been asserted in several cyberspace cases.

In the *Töben* case (the case involving the Australian charged with inciting racial hatred for posting materials on a web site that denied the existence of the Holocaust) the German Federal Supreme Court could have assumed jurisdiction on the basis of a protective nexus. It could have done so because of Germany's avowed interest in protecting a substantial "segment of the national population" from being defamed.[52]

Furthermore, in the *Galaxy Sports* case,[53] which involved the New York-based company that operated an online gambling service through an Antigua-based subsidiary, the trial court, in addition to asserting jurisdiction based on territoriality, may also have relied on a protective nexus. The statute the defendant was charged with violating was the federal Wire Wager Act. That act, which imposes criminal liability on anyone who "knowingly uses a wire communication facility for the transmission in interstate or foreign commerce of bets or wagers,"[54] is based on a substantial national interest in "suppress[ing] . . . organized gambling activities."[55] That

---

[50] IAN BROWNLIE, PRINCIPLES OF PUBLIC INTERNATIONAL LAW 304 (4th ed. 1990). The same language ("against the security of the state") also appears in RESTATEMENT (THIRD) OF FOREIGN RELATIONS LAW OF THE U.S. § 402(3) (1987). The Draft Convention on Jurisdiction with Respect to Crime, *supra* note 10, art. 7, defines the protective nexus as extending to "any crime committed outside [the forum's] territory by an alien against the security, territorial integrity or political independence of the [forum] . . . ."

[51] GEORG DAHM, ZUR PROBLEMATIK DES VÖLKERSTRAFRECHTS 28 (1956).

[52] *See supra* notes 39–41 and accompanying text.

[53] *See supra* notes 45–47 and accompanying text.

[54] 18 U.S.C. § 1084(a) (1994).

[55] Letter from United States Attorney General Robert F. Kennedy to Speaker of the House of Representatives, Apr. 6, 1961, 2 U.S. CODE & CONGR. NEWS, 87th Congr., 1st Sess., pp. 2631, 2633.

being so, the court's assumption of jurisdiction, based on a protective nexus, would be logical.[56]

D. *The Universality Nexus*

Ordinarily, international law only applies to relations between nations. It is, first and foremost, "inter"-national law, law between nations. As such, it normally does not establish regulations or criminal sanctions that apply directly to individuals. The exception to this rule is for the small category of crimes that are covered by the universality nexus; that is, those crimes that are considered to be so egregious as to be of universal concern.

Because these crimes are established by international law (*delicta juris gentium*), and not national law, any court with competence to apply international law has jurisdiction to hear them.[57] There is no requirement that the crime be related to the forum or its territory. The only requirement is that the forum must properly have the defendant in its custody.[58]

The crimes covered by the universality nexus include, at least: piracy, the slave trade, attacks on or the hijacking of aircraft, war crimes, genocide, and crimes against humanity.[59] This list, however, has been expanding since the end of the World War II.[60] For example, the 1996 Draft Code of Crimes Against the Peace and Security of Mankind prepared by the International Law Commission includes an extensive list of acts that make up crimes against humanity, including murder, extermination, enslavement, torture, persecution (on political, racial, religious, or ethnic grounds), rape, enforced prostitution, and sexual abuse "when committed in a

---

[56] As noted earlier, the Second Circuit affirmed the trial court's judgment, but it did so without discussing the issue of jurisdictional basis. *See supra* note 47.

[57] BROWNLIE, *supra* note 50, at 304; RESTATEMENT (THIRD) OF FOREIGN RELATIONS LAW OF THE U.S. § 404 (1987).

[58] If the forum abducted the defendant from another nation, the general rule is that it may try the defendant so long as the nation from which the defendant was abducted does not protest. *See, e.g.*, Attorney General of the Government of Israel, 36 I.L.R. 5, ¶ 12 (I.M. D.C. 1961) (Is.); United States v. Alvarez-Machain, 504 U.S. 655 (1992). A few courts, however, allow the defendant to object to the abduction. *See* State v. Ebrahim, 1991 (2) SALR 553, 32 I.L.M. 277 (App. Div. 1991).

[59] RESTATEMENT (THIRD) OF FOREIGN RELATIONS LAW OF THE U.S. § 404.

[60] *Id.* § 404 cmt. a; Kenneth C. Randall, *Universal Jurisdiction Under International Law*, 66 TEX. L. REV. 785, 789 (1988).

systematic manner or on a large scale and instigated or directed by a Government or by any organization or group,"[61] and a lengthy list of war crimes, including murder, torture, and terrorism.[62]

To date there have been no cases in which the universality nexus has been applied to criminal conduct in cyberspace. There has been a great deal of interest, however, in the topic, especially since the terrorist attacks on September 11, 2001, and the U.S. government's assertion of a global war on international terrorism.[63] The Federal Bureau of Investigation, for example, is developing a tracking program named Magic Lantern in part to ferret out online terrorists;[64] the day after the terrorist attacks, the FBI served search warrants on a number of Internet service providers to get information about an e-mail address that it alleged was connected to the attacks.[65] More recently, the Justice Department proposed an Anti-Terrorism Act of 2001 that would expand the powers of the federal government to prosecute online terrorism-related activities.[66]

E. *The Effect of Multiple Criminal and Regulatory Nexuses*

The decisions in the *Waddon*, *CompuServe*, *World Interactive Gaming*, *Galaxy Sports*, and *Töben* cases highlight a dilemma for governments trying to control crime on the Internet. The existence of multiple and overlapping criminal regulatory nexuses give courts in many countries overlapping and conflicting jurisdictions. This puts online

---

[61] International Law Commission, Draft Code of Crimes Against the Peace and Security of Mankind, 1996, art. 18, *at* http://www.un.org/law/ilc/texts/dcodefra.htm.

The Draft Code was prepared by the International Law Commission at the direction of U.N. General Assembly. *See Current Development: Draft Code of Crimes Against the Peace and Security of Mankind*, 75 AM. J. INT'L L. 674 (1981).

[62] International Law Commission, Draft Code of Crimes Against the Peace and Security of Mankind, 1996, art. 20.

[63] Press Release, White House, Global War on Terrorism: The First 100 Days (Dec. 20, 2001), *at* http://www.whitehouse.gov/news/releases/2001/12/100dayreport.html.

[64] Statement of Donald M. Kerr to U.S. House of Representatives on Internet and Data Interception Capabilities Developed by FBI (July 24, 2000), *at* http://www.fbi.gov/congress/congress00/kerr072400.htm. The program, originally called "Carnivore," has been renamed "Magic Lantern." Elinor Mills Abreu, Reuters, *FBI Confirms 'Magic Lantern' Project Exists*, (Dec. 12, 2001), *at* http://dailynews.yahoo.com/htx/nm/20011212/tc/tech_magiclantern_dc_1.html.

[65] Associated Press *FBI Looking to Internet for Terrorism Clues*, (Sept. 12, 2001), *at* http://www.siliconvalley.com/docs/news/tech/018876.htm.

[66] H.R. 2896, 107th Cong. (1st Sess. 2001).

entrepreneurs at risk for committing a crime somewhere. This risk could adversely impact the growth of the global economy[67] and Internet commerce that governments everywhere are trying to promote.[68]

The conflict is especially apparent in the multiple and overlapping regulations that apply to online gambling. At least three Australian states have adopted laws legalizing, regulating, and taxing Internet gambling.[69] In Europe, several countries allow gambling operators to offer their services online, but only to residents of their own countries.[70] In the United Kingdom, the Gaming Board has stated that measures to outlaw online gambling would be futile and it has recommended that the government adopt legislation legalizing Internet gambling sites.[71] In the United States, the Wire Wager Act makes Internet gambling illegal except when the state where the gambler resides and the state where the gambling facility is located have both made it legal.[72]

It seems clear that conflict and confusion are the order of the day. Indeed, following the conviction of Jay Cohen in the *Galaxy Sports* case, a Costa Rican-based Internet gambling site, Betmaker.com, owned by U.S. nationals, sold out to Sportingbet.com, an online bookmaker located in the United Kingdom, for about fifteen million pounds. The sale was said to have progressed quickly because of concerns by Betmaker's U.S. owners that they could face prosecution in the United States.[73] Following the sale, Mark Blandford, the

---

[67] For efforts of the international community to promote global commerce, see the World Trade Organization web site in general and the "WTO in Brief" page in particular, at http://www.wto.org/english/thewto_e/whatis_e/inbrief_e/inbr00_e.htm (last visited Dec. 30, 2001).

[68] On the effort to promote Internet commerce, see U.S. Information Infrastructure Task Force, *A Framework for Global Electronic Commerce*, at http://iitf.doc.gov/eleccomm/execsu.htm (last visited Dec. 30, 2001) and Tony Blair, *The Knowledge Economy and Government Internet Policy*, (Sept. 13, 1999), *at* http://www.techlawjournal.com/internet/19990913sp.htm.

[69] Parliament of Australia, Senate Information Technologies Committee, *Netbets: A Review of Online Gambling in Australia*, 26, n.48 (Mar. 2000), *at* http://www.aph.gov.au/senate/committee/it_ctte/gambling/index.htm.

[70] *Id.*

[71] *Id.*

[72] 18 U.S.C. § 1084(b) (1994), *available at* http://caselaw.lp.findlaw.com/casecode/uscodes/18/parts/i/chapters/50/sections/section_1084.html.

[73] *U.S. Gets Online Gambling Boost*, FIN. TIMES, Aug. 10, 2000, at 4, http://news.ft.com/ft/gx.cgi/ftc? pagename=View&c=Article&cid=FT34TA2PQBC.

managing director of the U.K. bookmaker, said that he believed that his ownership of Betmaker.com, which targets the U.S. market, would not leave him open to prosecution. "I am wholly confident and that is not a view I have come to lightly," he said. "It's based on legal advice that the U.S. only has jurisdiction over its own citizens on what is actually taking place in the U.S."[74] Blandford should not be surprised, however, if a U.S. court chooses to assume jurisdiction on the basis of a territorial nexus (which only requires that some element of the crime take place within the forum's territory), the nexus that the *Galaxy Sports* trial court seems to have relied upon. Nor should he be surprised if a U.S. court chooses to find a protective nexus (based on the country's declared interest, set out in the Wire Wager Act, of suppressing illegal gambling), which the courts in both *Galaxy Sports* and *Töben* could have relied upon.

The solution, of course, would be for the international community to adopt a treaty harmonizing criminal jurisdiction in cyberspace. Indeed, on November 23, 2001, the Council of Europe[75] promulgated[76] for ratification its Convention on Cybercrime.[77] The treaty, however, is not especially satisfactory in resolving jurisdictional conflicts. It grants courts in signatory states jurisdiction over offenses committed "in its territory"[78] or by "one of its nationals, if the offence is punishable under criminal law where it was committed or if the offence is committed outside the territorial jurisdiction of any State,"[79] but it does not exclude those courts from using alternative jurisdictional nexuses. Indeed, it provides that "[t]his Convention does not exclude any criminal jurisdiction exercised in accordance

---

[74] *Id.*

[75] The Council of Europe, which is not to be confused with the European Union, is an intergovernmental organization founded in 1949 to promote the protection of human rights and the harmonization of its member states' laws. Currently it has forty-one members including all fifteen European Union member states. Its home page is http://www.coe.int/ (last visited Dec. 30, 2001).

[76] The drafting effort began in the late 1980s with the cooperation of the United States. *See* Reuters, *U.S. Embraces European Cybercrime Proposal*, (Dec. 4, 2000), *at* http://www.cnn.com/2000/TECH/computing/12/04/ crime.tech.reut/index.html.

[77] Convention on Cybercrime, Nov. 23, 2001, Europ. T.S. No. 185, http://conventions.coe.int/Treaty/EN/WhatYouWant.asp?NT=185.

[78] *Id.* art. 24(1)(a).

[79] *Id.* art. 24(1)(d).

546 / Vol. 39 / *American Business Law Journal*

with domestic law."[80]   As a consequence, rather than clearing up confusion about conflicting jurisdictional claims, it perpetuates and promotes them.

II. INTERNATIONAL CIVIL JURISDICTION

In order for a national court to exercise jurisdiction over international civil (noncriminal) disputes, there must be a nexus between the persons or property involved and the forum. That is, a court must have either *in personam* jurisdiction or *in rem* jurisdiction.[81]

A. *Jurisdiction over Persons*

In personam jurisdiction is the power of a court to hear disputes involving natural[82] and juridical[83] persons.   The universally recognized basis for a court to assume *in personam* jurisdiction is consent. This may be actual or implied.

1. Actual Consent

A person may give actual consent to a court's jurisdiction by incorporating or otherwise registering to do business in a forum, or by appearing before a court. Actual consent may also be given in a forum selection or choice-of-law clause. [84]   For example, Netscape Communications includes the following forum selection and choice of law provisions on its Web site:

---

[80] *Id.* art. 24(4).

[81] Another jurisdiction basis, which is a combination of both *in personam* and *in rem* jurisdiction, is *quasi-in rem* jurisdiction. This type of jurisdiction is based on a person's interest in property within the forum's territory, but unlike *in rem* jurisdiction it is used as a means to collect a money judgment against the person. In the last quarter-century, most countries have imposed the same kinds of fairness requirements for assuming *quasi-in rem* jurisdiction that apply to *in personam* cases. *See, e.g.*, Shaffer v. Heitner, 433 U.S. 186 (1977); Swiss Federal Debt Collection and Bankruptcy Statute, art. 271(1)(4) (effective Jan. 1, 1997).

[82] Natural persons are human beings.

[83] Juridical persons are legal entities created by national or international law and granted the privilege of carrying on many of the functions of natural persons, such as engaging in business, suing, and being sued. They include business firms, nonprofit organizations, international organizations, and governmental agencies.

[84] In civil law countries, codes of civil procedure recognize that parties may expressly consent to the jurisdiction of a court or agency. *See, e.g.*, CÓDIGO FEDERAL DE PROCEDI-MIENTOS CIVILES, art. 23, (Mex.) http://www.juridicas.unam.mx/ijure/fed/6/24.htm?s= (last visited Dec. 30, 2001).

This web site (excluding linked sites) is controlled by Netscape from its offices within the state of California, United States of America. It can be accessed from all 50 states, as well as from other countries around the world. As each of these places has laws that may differ from those of California, by accessing this web site both you and Netscape agree that the statutes and laws of the state of California, without regard to the conflicts of laws principles thereof, will apply to all matters relating to use of this web site.

You and Netscape also agree and hereby submit to the exclusive personal jurisdiction and venue of the Superior Court of Santa Clara County and the United States District Court for the Northern District of California with respect to such matters. Netscape makes no representation that materials on this web site are appropriate or available for use in other locations, and accessing them from territories where their contents are illegal is prohibited. Those who choose to access this site from other locations do so on their own initiative and are responsible for compliance with local laws.[85]

2. Implied Consent in Common Law Countries

The criteria for determining if a party has impliedly consented to a court's jurisdiction differs between common law and civil law countries. The two approaches are similar enough, however, that delegations from both groups are currently working, under the auspices of The Hague Conference on Private International Law, on a draft international convention that would harmonize the law in the area.

In common law countries, a person's consent to a court's assumption of jurisdiction can be implied from the person (1) having the nationality of the forum, (2) being domiciled in the forum, (3) having general contacts with the forum, or (4) having specific contacts with the forum. The first two of these implied forms of consent are based on the physical presence of a person and they have been recognized by the common law since ancient times.[86] The last two,

---

[85] *See* Netscape, Applicable Laws, *at* http://home.netscape.com/legal_notices/laws.html (last visited Dec. 30, 2001).

[86] *See* Burnham v. Superior Court of Cal., 495 U.S. 604 , 608–09 (1990) (discussing English common law rules); Robertson v. R.R. Labor Bd., 268 U.S. 619, 622–23 (1925) (same).

which are "based upon a kind of 'virtual' presence,"[87] are a more recent creation.

The establishment of implied consent based on a person's "virtual" contacts with a forum was brought about by legal and technological developments that occurred at the beginning of the twentieth century. At that time, corporations—"virtual" entities that lack a physical presence—became commonplace,[88] as did stocks, bonds, and other "virtual" properties. Likewise, automobiles and airplanes made populations mobile and more likely to be absent from their domiciles.[89]

In response to these developments, the U.S. Supreme Court, in its landmark *International Shoe Co. v. Washington* opinion,[90] recognized that implied consensual jurisdiction could be based on contacts other than nationality and domicile. As long as a person has sufficient contacts with a forum, the Court said, the exercise of jurisdiction by a court in that forum would not offend "traditional notions of fair play and substantial justice."[91]

From the Supreme Court's opinion in *International Shoe*, two modern forms of implied consensual jurisdiction have evolved.[92] One is based on "general contacts" with the forum. That is, the contacts with the forum must be systematic and continuous.[93] In such a case, a court may exercise general jurisdiction over a person, even when the proceeding is unrelated to the person's specific contacts with the forum.[94] For example, if a company maintains a branch office in a forum, a court there will have jurisdiction over the company even if the dispute has nothing to do with the branch office.

A second modern form of implied consensual jurisdiction is based on "specific contacts" with the forum. In this circumstance, a court

---

[87] Dan L. Burk, *Jurisdiction in a World Without Borders*, 1 VA. J.L. & TECH. 3, ¶ 26 (Spring 1997), *at* http://vjolt.student.virginia.edu/graphics/vol1/home_art3.html.

[88] *See* Int'l Shoe Co. v. Washington, 326 U.S. 310, 316-20 (1945).

[89] *See* Burk, *supra* note 87, ¶ 25.

[90] 326 U.S. 310.

[91] *Id.* at 316.

[92] Although the *International Shoe* case involved an international dispute, most of the case decisions in the United States involving a court's assumption of jurisdiction based on implied consent have involved disputes in which the parties were from different U.S. states. The same rules, nonetheless, apply to international disputes.

[93] 326 U.S. at 318.

[94] *See* Helicopteros Nacionales de Columbia, S.A. v. Hall, 466 U.S. 408, 414 n.9 (1984).

will have jurisdiction only if the facts giving rise to the proceeding arise out of the person's specific contacts with the forum. The contacts may be isolated or occasional, but they must be directed at the forum.[95] They also must be more than "minimum contacts" such that the person could anticipate having to participate in the particular type of proceeding within the forum.[96] Finally, the assumption of jurisdiction must be reasonable; it must not "offend traditional notions of fair play and substantial justice."[97] As the Supreme Court stated in *Hanson v. Denckla*:[98]

> The unilateral activity of those who claim some relationship with a nonresident defendant cannot satisfy the requirement of contact with the forum State. The application of that rule will vary with the quality and nature of the defendant's activity, but it is essential in each case that there be some act by which the defendant *purposefully avails* itself of the privilege of conducting activities within the forum State, thus invoking the benefits and protections of its laws.[99]

For example, a court would have jurisdiction over a foreign driver involved in an automobile accident within the forum, even if the driver had no other contacts with the forum. It would be enough that the driver availed him- or herself of the privilege of driving an automobile in the forum. By comparison, a court would not have jurisdiction over the manufacturer of a defective car if someone other than the manufacturer or its agents brought the car into the forum state—the factual situation in *Hanson v. Denckla*—because the manufacturer would not have availed itself of doing business in the state.

In the last few years, U.S. courts have extended the reach of their implied consensual jurisdiction based on specific contacts to persons whose contacts with the forum are confined to transactions made over the Internet. The leading Internet case is *Zippo Manufacturing Co. v. Zippo Dot Com, Inc.*[100] In *Zippo*, which involved a dispute over the ownership of an Internet domain name, the District Court for the

---

[95] 326 U.S. 317–18.
[96] *Id.*
[97] *Id.* at 316.
[98] 357 U.S. 235 (1958).
[99] *Id.* at 253 (emphasis added).
[100] 952 F. Supp. 1119 (W.D. Pa. 1997).

550 / Vol. 39 / *American Business Law Journal*

Western District of Pennsylvania applied the criteria set out in *International Shoe* to determine if the defendant had "specific contacts" with Pennsylvania. It reformulated the criteria as follows:

> A three-pronged test has emerged for determining whether the exercise of specific personal jurisdiction over a non-resident defendant is appropriate: (1) the defendant must have sufficient "minimum contacts" with the forum state, (2) the claim asserted against the defendant must arise out of those contacts, and (3) the exercise of jurisdiction must be reasonable.[101]

In applying this test, the *Zippo* court observed that the proper exercise of personal jurisdiction "is directly proportionate to the nature and quality of commercial activity that an entity conducts over the Internet."[102] After examining the decisions in other Internet cases, it concluded that commercial activity on the Internet can be arranged along a sliding scale.

> At one end of the spectrum are situations where a defendant clearly does business over the Internet. If the defendant enters into contracts with residents of a foreign jurisdiction that involve the knowing and repeated transmission of computer files over the Internet, personal jurisdiction is proper . . . . At the opposite end are situations where a defendant has simply posted information on an Internet Web site which is accessible to users in foreign jurisdictions. A passive Web site that does little more than make information available to those who are interested in it is not grounds for the exercise [of] personal jurisdiction . . . . The middle ground is occupied by interactive Web sites where a user can exchange information with the host computer. In these cases, the exercise of jurisdiction is determined by examining the level of interactivity and commercial nature of the exchange of information that occurs on the Web site . . . .[103]

In other words, there are three sorts of online activity that will determine whether a person has impliedly consented to the jurisdiction of a foreign forum:

1.   A person intentionally transmits files over the Internet to a resident within the forum—consent to the forum's jurisdiction will be implied.

---

[101] *Id.* at 1122–23.

[102] *Id.* at 1124.

[103] *Id.*

2. A person creates an interactive Web site that exchanges information with a resident within the forum—consent to the forum's jurisdiction will arise if the exchange is commercial and more than minimal.

3. A person creates a passive Web site that only provides information about a person—no consent to the jurisdiction will be implied.

Examples of each of these situations can be found in *Zippo* and in cases adopting and applying its three-part test.

In the *CompuServe, Inc. v. Patterson*[104] case, for instance, the Sixth Circuit Court of Appeals found that it had jurisdiction because the defendant intentionally sent information directed to the forum. In this case, Patterson, a Texas resident, entered into a contract to distribute trademarked shareware through CompuServe's Internet server located in Ohio and then electronically uploaded thirty-two master software files to the server. When CompuServe later began to market a product that Patterson believed to be similar to his own, he threatened to sue for trademark infringement. CompuServe brought an action in Ohio seeking a declaratory judgment that it had not infringed Patterson's trademarks. Patterson asked that the case be dismissed, contending that he had no contact with Ohio. On appeal, the Sixth Circuit denied Patterson's request for dismissal, reasoning that Patterson had sufficient contact with Ohio because he had intentionally directed his business activities toward that state. He had knowingly entered into a contract with an Ohio resident, the Sixth Circuit said, and then deliberately and repeatedly transmitted files to Ohio.[105]

In the *Zippo* case itself, the court held that it was "a 'doing business over the Internet' case in the line of *CompuServe.*" The court said:

> We are being asked to determine whether [the defendant] Dot Com's conducting of electronic commerce with Pennsylvania residents constitutes the purposeful availment of doing business in Pennsylvania. We conclude that it does. Dot Com has contracted with approximately 3,000 individuals and seven Internet access providers in Pennsylvania. The intended object of these transactions has been the downloading of the electronic messages that form the basis of this suit in Pennsylvania.[106]

---

[104] 89 F.3d 1257 (6th Cir. 1996).

[105] *Id.* at 1265.

[106] 952 F. Supp. at 1126–27.

552 / Vol. 39 / *American Business Law Journal*

Several courts have examined the extent of commercial activity on interactive Web sites in determining if personal jurisdiction existed. In *Euromarket Designs Inc. v. Crate & Barrel Ltd.*,[107] a federal district court in Illinois held that it had personal jurisdiction over an Irish retailer using the Crate & Barrel name. It declined to assert general consent jurisdiction, but found specific consent from the high level of interactivity on the defendant's Web site, which included an online catalog that allowed consumers to place orders online. Because this activity solicited all users, including Illinois residents, to buy goods, the court concluded that defendant was doing sufficient business over the Internet to establish jurisdiction in Illinois.[108]

By comparison, in *Dagesse v. Plant Hotel NV*,[109] the federal District Court for New Hampshire declined to find jurisdiction. In that case, Dagesse brought a personal injury suit against Plant Hotel, an Aruban company, after being injured in a fall at a resort owned by Plant Hotel in Aruba. Dagesse claimed the Plant Hotel's interactive Web site, which allowed for online reservations and listed a 1-800 telephone number, established sufficient contacts with New Hampshire for the court to assume jurisdiction. The court disagreed. It held that the contacts were not the factual and legal cause of Dagesse's injuries and that the defendant did not deliberately use its site for commercial transactions with New Hampshire residents.[110]

In *Soma Medical International v. Standard Chartered Bank*,[111] the Tenth Circuit Court of Appeals, affirming the *Zippo* test, found that the defendant's maintenance of a purely passive Web site did not give rise to personal jurisdiction in Utah.[112] The same result, based on similar

---

[107] 96 F. Supp. 2d 824 (N.D. Ill. 2000). Euromarket Designs, Inc., an Illinois company, owned the "Crate and Barrel" trademark in the United States and the European Union and it operated several stores in the United States using that name. For a non-internet version of the same dispute in a U.K. court see Euromarket Designs Inc v. Peters (Crate & Barrel) [2000] E.T.M.R. 1025 (Ch. 1999), (U.K.) http://www.hrothgar.co.uk/YAWS/reps/eurom.htm.

[108] 96 F. Supp. 2d at 834–35.

[109] 113 F. Supp. 2d 211 (D.N.H. 2000).

[110] *Id.* at 218.

[111] 196 F.3d 1292 (10th Cir. 1999).

[112] *Id.* at 1299.

facts, has been reached in *Nutrition Physiology Corp. v. Enviros Ltd.,*[113] *Bedrejo v. Triple E Canada, Ltd.,*[114] *Cybersell, Inc. v. Cybersell, Inc.,*[115] *Copperfield v. Cogedipresse,*[116] and in *Weber v. Jolly Hotels.*[117]

The criteria used in *Zippo* were recently adopted in Canada in *Braintech, Inc. v. Kostiuk.*[118] In that case, the British Columbia Court of Appeal found that a Texas court did not have jurisdiction to award a judgment against a Canadian company based solely on the fact that the company had a passive Web site accessible in Texas.[119]

Currently, the courts of other common law countries have not addressed the exercise of personal jurisdiction in civil proceedings based on transactions conducted on the Internet. However, the jurisdictional rules followed in all common law countries are essentially the same, so it is likely that they will—like the Canadians—adopt the rules set out in the U.S. cases.

3. Implied Consent in Civil Law Countries

In civil law countries, the rules for determining implied consent are set out in codes of civil procedure. Unlike the common law world, where statutory provisions must meet the due process requirement of

---

[113] 87 F. Supp. 2d 648 (N.D. Tex. 2000). The U.K. defendant, which was sued for patent infringement, maintained a web site that described the company and its products and directed those interested in obtaining more information to contact the company's local distributors. The court held that the web site did not establish minimum contacts with the State of Texas and dismissed the case.

[114] 984 P.2d 739 (Mont. 1999). The Canadian defendant, sued for product liability, maintained a passive web site that provided information about the motor homes it sold. The court held that the site did not establish minimum contacts with the State of Montana and dismissed the suit.

[115] 130 F.3d 414 (9th Cir. 1997). The Florida defendant, which was sued for trademark infringement, maintain a web site that directed interested parties to contact it by e-mail. The court held that this passive web site did not create minimum contacts with the State of Arizona and dismissed the case.

[116] 26 Med. L. Rptr. 1185 (C.D. Cal. 1997). A California court declined to assume jurisdiction over the French publishers of the *Paris Match* magazine in a defamation action, holding that the magazine's web site was merely passive advertising.

[117] 977 F. Supp. 327 (D.N.J. 1997). A New Jersey court refused to assumed jurisdiction over an Italian hotel operator in a personal injury case, holding that its web site amounted to mere passive advertising.

[118] [1999] BCCA 0169 (Can.), http://www.canlii.org/bc/cas/bcca/1999/1999bcca169 .html.

[119] [1999] BCCA 0169 ¶¶ 61–62.

minimum contacts, there is no similar judicial rule limiting the scope of the statutory codes.

The European Union's Regulation on Jurisdiction and the Recognition and Enforcement of Judgments in Civil and Commercial Matters, which came into effect in January 2001, harmonizes the E.U.'s jurisdictional rules.[120] It provides a good example, as a consequence, of jurisdictional provisions applicable in some of the most developed civil law countries.

The Regulation provides that "persons domiciled" in an E.U. Member State are only to be "sued in the courts of that Member State"[121] unless the Regulation provides otherwise.[122] The circumstances in which the Regulation provides for suits to be brought elsewhere are these:

1. (a) in matters relating to a contract, in the courts for the place of performance of the obligation in question;
2. in matters relating to maintenance, in the courts for the place where the maintenance creditor is domiciled or habitually resident . . . ;
3. in matters relating to tort, delict[[123]] or quasi-delict,[[124]] in the courts for the place where the harmful event occurred or may occur;
4. in as regards a civil claim for damages or restitution which is based on an act giving rise to criminal proceedings, in the court seized of those proceedings, to the extent that that court has jurisdiction under its own law to entertain civil proceedings;

---

[120] Council Regulation (EC) No. 44/2001 (Dec. 22, 2000), *at* http://europa.eu.int/smartapi/cgi/sga_doc? smartapi!celexapi!prod!CELEXnumdoc&lg=EN&numdoc=32001R0044&model=guichett [hereinafter Council Reg. No. 44/2001]. The Regulation replaces the 1968 Brussels Convention on Jurisdiction and the Enforcement of Judgments in Civil and Commercial Matters [hereinafter Brussels Convention], which was last amended in 1990. The consolidated text is published in European Union, OFFICIAL JOURNAL C 027, 26/01/1998 p. 0001-0027 *at* http://europa.eu.int/eur-lex/en/lif/dat/1968/en_468A0927_01. html (last visited Dec. 30, 2001).

The Regulation does not apply in Denmark. Council Reg. No. 44/2001, pmbl. ¶21. However, Denmark continues to be subject to the Brussels Treaty vis-à-vis the other E.U. member states. *Id.* at pmbl. ¶22.

[121] Council Regulation 44/2001, *supra* note 120, art. 2.

[122] *Id.* art. 3.

[123] A delict, in civil law countries, is a wrong that may be prosecuted by the state or by a private person.

[124] A quasi-delict is a delict committed without malice; that is, negligent wrongdoing.

5.   as regards a dispute arising out of the operations of a branch, agency
       or other establishment, in the courts for the place in which the
       branch, agency or other establishment is situated . . . .[125]

In addition, special rules apply to consumer contracts. (1) A
consumer contract can be concluded by "any means" including
contracts made over the Internet.[126] (2) The consumer may sue the
other party to a consumer contract (the merchant) "either in the
courts of the Member State in which [the merchant] is domiciled or
in the courts for the place where the consumer is domiciled."[127] (3)
The merchant, however, may sue the consumer "only in the courts
of the Member State in which the consumer is domiciled."[128] (4) A
merchant is subject to the consumer contract rules if it is domiciled or
has a branch, agency, or establishment in any Member State.[129]
Finally, (5) a forum selection clause is only valid if it is entered into
"after the dispute has arisen" or it specifies additional places where
the consumer may sue.[130]

The E.U. approach to consumer contracts, as one can see, is
dramatically different from the U.S. approach. Unlike the U.S.
jurisdictional rules, which require a court to find that there is a nexus
between the transaction and the forum, the E.U. Regulation entirely
abandons the requirement of a transactional nexus. Instead, it looks
solely to the domicile of the parties to determine jurisdiction. So,

---

[125] Council Regulation 44/2001, *supra* note 120, art. 5.

[126] *Id.* art. 15(1)(c). As originally proposed, the Regulation stated that it applied specifically
to "consumer contracts concluded via an interactive website accessible in the State of the
consumer's domicile." Commission Proposal for a Council Regulation (EC) on Jurisdiction
and the Recognition and Enforcement of Judgments in Civil and Commercial Matters (E.U.
Commission Doc. 599PC0348) § 6. However, "[t]he fact that a consumer simply had
knowledge of a service or possibility of buying goods via a passive website accessible in his
country of domicile [would] not [have] trigger[ed] the protective jurisdiction." *Id.* The final
language of the Regulation does not mention interactive websites, but the words "any
means" clearly cover such transactions.

[127] Council Regulation 44/2001, *supra* note 120, art. 16(1).

[128] *Id.* art. 16(2). The same rule is found in the Brussels Convention except that (1) the sale
must take place in the consumer's country of domicile; (2) the seller must solicit the sale
through advertising directed to the consumer or agree to accept payments in installments;
and (3) the seller must be domiciled in or have a branch, agency, or other establishment in
another member country. Brussels Convention, *supra* note 120, art. 13.

[129] Council Regulation 44/2001, *supra* note 120, art. 15(2).

[130] *Id.* at art. 17. The Brussels Convention, *supra* note 120, art. 15, makes all forum
selection clauses pertaining to consumer contracts void.

regardless of where the contract was made, the merchant can sue a consumer only in the Member State where the consumer is domiciled. Furthermore, the consumer can sue the merchant in the consumer's place of domicile or in any Member State where the merchant is domiciled, or has a branch, agency, or establishment. In effect, nearly every suit is going to be brought in the Member State where the consumer is domiciled; this is especially so as forum selection clauses in consumer contracts are made entirely ineffective.

For non-consumer sales, the E.U. Regulation takes just the opposite approach, completely ignoring the parties' place of domicile and looking to the primary transactional nexus: the place where the contract is to be performed.[131] In tort cases, the same transactional approach is taken: the place where the injury occurs is the place where jurisdiction exists.[132]

This tort rule was important in two recent Internet-related cases. In *Mecklermedia Corp. v. DC Congress GmbH*,[133] an English Chancery court held that it had jurisdiction to hear a dispute brought by an American company and its English subsidiary against a German company alleging that the defendant had committed the tort of "passing off" in misusing a trademarked name ("Internet World") on an Internet Web site accessible from England.

A French court assumed jurisdiction in the case of *Ligue Contre la Racisme et l'Antisémitisme v. Yahoo*[134] when Yahoo was sued for posting Nazi memorabilia on Web pages accessible from France. Yahoo argued that it was an American company and that the materials it had posted were not in violation of American law. The judge

---

[131] Council Regulation 44/2001, *supra* note 120, art. 5(1). The same rule appears in the Brussels Convention, *supra* note 120, art. 5(1). For an example of a similar provision in a non-European code of civil procedure, see the Law of Civil Procedure of the People's Republic of China, art. 243, *at* http://www.qis.net/chinalaw/prclaw34.htm#chap25 (last visited Dec. 30, 2001).

[132] Council Regulation 44/2001, *supra* note 120, art. 5(3); *see also* Brussels Convention, *supra* note 120, art. 5(3).

[133] 1998 Ch. 40, [1998] 1 All E.R. 148, [1997] 3 W.L.R. 479, 1997 F.S.R. 627 (Eng. Ch. 1997). A summary description is at http://www.rhysroberts.co.uk/articles/copy.html.

[134] Summary orders of May 22, 2000 and Aug. 11, 2000 (Paris T.P.I.). English translations are at http://www.gyoza.com/lapres/html/yahen.html and http://www.gyoza.com/lapres/html/yahen8.html. The permanent order was issued on Nov. 20, 2000. *See* Crispian Balmer Review, Reuters, *Yahoo Ordered to Bar French from Nazi Web Sites*, (Nov. 20, 2000), *at* http://dailynews.yahoo.com/h/nm/20001120/ wr/france_yahoo_dc_2.html.

responded that the materials were in violation of a provision of the French Penal Code (under which a private person is authorized to prosecute in France as a delict or tort), and concluded that because "the harm is suffered in France, our jurisdiction is therefore competent over this matter pursuant to Article 46 of the New Code of Civil Procedure."[135]

4. Implied Consent under the Draft Hague Convention

The Hague Conference on Private International Law,[136] which is an intergovernmental organization with fifty-seven member states (including all the E.U. Member States and the United States)[137] organized to promote "the progressive unification of the rules of private international law,"[138] is in the process of drafting a Convention on Jurisdiction and Foreign Judgments in Civil and Commercial Matters.[139] This convention is closely related to the E.U.'s Regulation on Jurisdiction and Foreign Judgments in Civil and Commercial Matters, as one can tell—in part—from its title.[140]

---

[135] Summary order of May 22, Council Regulation 44/2001, *supra* note 120, art. 2.2000.

[136] The Conference's home page is *at* http://www.hcch.net/index.html (last visited Dec. 30, 2001).

[137] The membership as of December 6, 2001 was: Argentina, Australia, Austria, Belarus, Belgium, Bosnia and Herzegovina, Brazil, Bulgaria, Canada, Chile, China, Croatia, Cyprus, Czech Republic, Denmark, Egypt, Estonia, Finland, The former Yugoslav Republic of Macedonia, France, Georgia, Germany, Greece, Hungary, Ireland, Israel, Italy, Japan, Jordan, Republic of Korea, Latvia, Lithuania, Luxembourg, Malta, Mexico, Monaco, Morocco, Netherlands, Norway, Peru, Poland, Portugal, Romania, Russian Federation, Slovakia, Slovenia, Spain, Sri Lanka, Suriname, Sweden, Switzerland, Turkey, United Kingdom of Great Britain and Northern Ireland, United States of America, Uruguay, Venezuela, and Yugoslavia. Hague Conference on Private International Law: Member States, *at* http://www.hcch.net/e/members/members.html (last visited Dec. 30, 2001).

[138] Statute of The Hague Conference on Private International Law, 1955, art. 1, *at* http://www.hcch.net/e/conventions/text01e.html.

[139] The Conference's work program for drafting the Convention is available at http://www.hcch.net/e/workprog/jdgm.html (last visited Dec. 30, 2001). An October 1999 Draft, which is the latest complete draft, is at http://www.hcch.net/e/conventions/draft36e .html. A June 2001 Working Revision with proposed changes to the October 1999 Draft is at ftp://hcch.net/doc/jdgm2001draft_e.doc (last visited Dec. 30, 2001).

[140] The draft Hague Convention and the E.U. Regulation on Jurisdiction were both based on the Brussels Convention on Jurisdiction and Enforcement of Judgments in Civil and Commercial Matters, Sept. 27, 1968, 1968 O.J. (L 299) 32, at http://www.curia.eu.int/ common/recdoc/convention/en/c-textes/_brux-textes.htm. The E.U. Regulation replaces

Like the E.U. Regulation on Jurisdiction, the draft Hague Convention would allow a person to bring an action in contract—other than a consumer contract—in the country where the contract was to be performed[141] and an action in tort or delict in the country where the act or omission happened or where the injury occurred.[142] In the case of a consumer contract, a consumer could sue the in the country where he or she is "habitually resident" unless the contract was concluded and the goods or services delivered in another country;[143] while a merchant could only sue in the country where the consumer is habitually resident.[144]

While the draft Hague Convention is similar to the E.U. Regulation, it is an evolving document that clearly demonstrates many of the differences between common and civil law approaches to jurisdiction in civil and commercial cases. One of the main points of disagreement[145] has to do with the use of forum selection clauses. One proposed alternative would copy the E.U. Regulation on Jurisdiction word-for-word (that is, a forum selection clause would be ineffective unless it was entered into after a suit was commenced or it granted the consumer additional places in which to sue).[146] A second alternative is identical to this, except that a country, on signing the Convention, could declare that it would enforce forum selection clauses.[147] A third alternative would give effect to forum selection

---

the Brussels Convention in all of the E.U. Member States except for Denmark. *See* discussion *supra* note 120; Dreyfuss, *supra* note 1, at 427.

[141] The Hague Convention on Jurisdiction and Foreign Judgments in Civil and Commercial Matters, art. 6, Oct. 1999 (Draft) [hereinafter Hague Convention 1999].

[142] *Id.* art. 10.

[143] The Hague Convention on Jurisdiction and Foreign Judgements in Civil and Commerical Matters, art. 7(2), June 2001 (Working Revision) [hereinafter Hague Convention 2001]. The June 2001 Working Revision is cited because of the cumbersome and confusing language of the October 1999 Draft.

[144] Hague Convention 1999, *supra* note 141, art. 7(2). The October 1999 Draft is cited because this provision is omitted (apparently unintentionally) from the June 2001 Working Revision.

[145] For additional difficulties the delegations are facing in drafting a "harmonizing" convention, see Dreyfuss, *supra* note 1.

[146] Hague Convention 1999, *supra* note 141, art. 7(3).

[147] Hague Convention 2001, *supra* note 143, art. 7, alternative B, variant 2.

clauses, but allow countries to declare that they would not enforce them.[148]

The goal of the Conference, of course, is to produce a convention that will harmonize national jurisdictional laws. As the negotiations currently stand, however, this may prove to be difficult. Indeed, if either the second or third alternatives—which reflect the reality that there are differing common and civil law views as to the legitimacy of forum selection clauses—is adopted, the Convention will not harmonize international jurisdictional rules, but perpetuate the existing differences.

B. *Jurisdiction over Property*

In rem jurisdiction, which is the second basis on which courts assume civil jurisdiction, gives courts the power to determine the ownership rights of persons with respect to a property located within the territory of the forum. Thus, the ownership of real property (*i.e.*, immovable property, such as land and buildings) is determined in an *in rem* court proceeding. Similarly, if the ownership of personal property (or movable property, such as computers, software, and title to intellectual property) is contested, it can be determined in an *in rem* court proceeding in the state where the property is physically located.

Two German cases show how courts use *in rem* jurisdiction. In *Epson v. Engelke*,[149] a trial court in Düsseldorf held that it had *in rem* jurisdiction to resolve disputes concerning the ownership of a domain name—a property right—ending with ".de". Accordingly, it ordered a cybersquatter who had registered the domain name of "epson.de" to relinquish ownership. Similarly, in Case 659/97,[150] a court in Berlin held that it had *in rem* jurisdiction to resolve a domain name dispute for names ending in ".com" and ".de" even though the defendant was an American company that had registered the disputed names (concertconcept.com and concertconcept.de) in the

---

[148] *Id.* art. 7, alternative B, variant 1. An Alternative A was included in the June 2001 Working Revision as a matter of reference, although it had no support from the participants at the June 2000 meeting.

[149] Amstgericht Düsseldorf, OLGZ, 340 (1997) 191/96. A summary is posted on the Perkins Coie Internet Case Digest at http://www.perkinscoie.com/resource/ecomm/ netcase/Cases-15.htm.

[150] LG Berlin, OLGZ, 97 (1997) 193/96. A summary is posted on the Perkins Coie Internet Case Digest at http://www.perkinscoie.com/resource/ecomm/netcase/Cases-15.htm.

United States. For these courts, the mere fact that a domain name ended in .de (the country code extension for names having an affiliation with Germany[151]) was sufficient for them to assume *in rem* jurisdiction.

C. Refusal to Exercise International Civil Jurisdiction

Although a court may have *in personam* or *in rem* jurisdiction, it may choose not to assume that jurisdiction. The common way that courts do so in international disputes is by invoking the doctrine of *forum non conveniens*. In essence, this allows a court to decline to hear a case that can also be heard elsewhere if it is either inconvenient or unfair for the forum court to do so. In determining this, a court will consider (1) the private interests of the parties (*i.e.*, the ease and cost of access to documents and witnesses) and (2) the public interests of the forum (*i.e.*, the interests of the forum in the outcome of the dispute, the burden on the court to hear the case, and whether another forum has a much greater interest in the outcome of the dispute).[152]

Not all courts, however, recognize the doctrine of *forum non conveniens*. For example, the state of Texas has forbidden its courts from applying this doctrine.[153] When that is the case, a court must hear every dispute brought before it, so long as it has jurisdiction. This may in part explain the decision of the Texas court in *Braintech, Inc. v. Kostiuk*, to hear a dispute involving a Canadian plaintiff and a Canadian defendant. Because the Texas court believed it had jurisdiction, it had to hear the case.[154]

III. JURISDICTION TO ENFORCE

Jurisdiction to enforce is the power of a government "to induce or compel compliance or to punish noncompliance with its laws or regulations, whether through the courts or by use of executive,

---

[151] Following the establishment of the Internet Corporation for Assigned Names and Numbers (ICANN) in 1999, the responsibility for assigning domain names with country codes shifted from Network Solutions, Inc., in the United States to country code managers.

[152] Gulf Oil Corp. v. Gilbert, 330 U.S. 501, 508–09 (1947); *see* AUGUST, *supra* note 14, at 168–71.

[153] *See* Dow Chem. Co. v. Alfaro, 786 S.W.2d 674 (Tex. 1990).

[154] [1999] BCCA 0169 (Can.). *See supra* text accompanying notes 118–19. In Braintech, the British Columbia Court of Appeal found that a Texas court did not have jurisdiction to award a judgment against a Canadian company based solely on the fact that the company had a passive web site accessible in Texas.

administrative, police, or other nonjudicial action."[155] As a practical matter—and in terms of court proceedings—it involves (1) the power to investigate and apprehend; and (2) the power to carry out a judgment. The first is pre-adjudicatory jurisdiction (leading up to a trial) and the second is post-adjudicatory jurisdiction (carrying out the adjudicated judgment).

A government's enforcement jurisdiction, whether pre- or post-adjudicatory, is almost exclusively territorial.[156] That is, the power to investigate and apprehend or to carry out a judgment is generally confined by the territorial boundaries of the forum. One government's law enforcement offices may exercise their functions in the territory of another nation only with the nation's authorization.[157] Absent that authorization, attempts to investigate, apprehend, or impose a judgment in another country are a violation of international law.

A. *Jurisdiction to Investigate and Apprehend*

While it is clear that a law enforcement officer may not travel to another country to investigate a crime without that country's authorization, what if the investigation is conducted remotely? As mentioned earlier, the Federal Bureau of Investigation is developing a tracking program named Magic Lantern to ferret out online terrorists and other criminals.[158] The program works by installing a Trojan Horse virus on a suspect's computer that records and transmits keystrokes typed into the computer. This means that the FBI does not have to physically access the machine and the machine can be anywhere in the world.[159] May the FBI deploy the program outside the United States without violating international law? In the United States the answer is yes; in the rest of the world it is no. This is because, in the United States, the misconduct of a law enforcement

---

[155] RESTATEMENT (THIRD) OF FOREIGN RELATIONS LAW OF THE U.S. § 401(c) (1987).

[156] *Id.* § 432(2).

[157] *Id.*

[158] *See supra* text accompanying note 64.

[159] Elinor Mills Abreu, Reuters *FBI Confirms 'Magic Lantern' Project Exist*, (Dec. 12, 2001), *at* http://dailynews. yahoo.com/htx/nm/ 20011212/tc/tech_magiclantern_dc_1.html.

official in investigating or bringing a suspect to trial is not grounds for dismissing a case,[160] while in the rest of the world it is.[161]

For example, in *United State v. Romano*[162] an informant working for the U.S. Drug Enforcement Agency called an Italian national in Palermo, Italy several times by telephone from New York and convinced him to come to New York to take part in a drug sale. After the Italian arrived in the United States, the government arrested him. The U.S. Second Circuit Court of Appeals rejected the Italian's motion to dismiss the case on the basis of government misconduct, holding that the government's conduct was "not 'the kind of outrageous conduct which would violate the defendant's [U.S.] due process rights.'"[163]

---

[160] The rule, which is known as *male captus bene detentus* (improperly arrested, properly detained), was first adopted in the United States in *Ker v. Illinois*, 119 U.S. 436 (1886). In that case, the U.S. Supreme Court held that a U.S. citizen who was abducted by a U.S. official from a foreign country for trial in a U.S. state court could not challenge his indictment or conviction on grounds that he was improperly brought within the jurisdiction of the court. The *male captus bene detentus* rule was affirmed, most recently, in *United States v. Alvarez-Machain*, 504 U.S. 655 (1992), which was a case involving an abduction by U.S. officials in violation of an international treaty provision prohibiting such conduct. The same rule was followed in Attorney-General of the Government of Israel v. Eichmann, 36 I.L.R. 5 (Jm. D.C. 1961) (Isr.) and stated there to be a rule followed in common law countries.

[161] The United Kingdom's House of Lords, in a decision applicable throughout the British Commonwealth, rejected the rule in *Regina v. Horseferry Road Magistrates' Court (Ex parte Bennett)*, [1994] 1 App. Cas. 42 (H.L. 1993).

A number of commentators have discussed the *male captus bene detentus* rule and its rejection outside the United States as a violation of international human rights law. *See, e.g.*, Abraham Abramovsky, *Extraterritorial Abductions: America's "Catch and Snatch" Policy Run Amok*, 31 VA. J. INT'L L. 151 (1991); Richard Downing, *Recent Development: The Domestic and International Legal Implications of the Abduction of Criminals from Foreign Soil*, 26 STAN. J. INT'L L. 573 (1990); Andrew K. Fletcher, *Pirates and Smugglers: An Analysis of the Use of Abductions to Bring Drug Traffickers to Trial*, 32 VA. J. INT'L L. 233 (1991); Theodore C. Jonas, *International "Fugitive Snatching" in U.S. Law: Two Views From Opposite Ends of the Eighties*, 24 CORNELL INT'L L.J. 521 (1991); F.A. Mann, *Reflections on the Prosecution of Persons Abducted in Breach of International Law*, *in* INTERNATIONAL LAW AT A TIME OF PERPLEXITY: ESSAYS IN HONOUR OF SHABTAI ROSENNE 407 (Yoram Dinstein & M. Tabory eds., 1989); Paul Michell, *English-Speaking Justice: Evolving Responses to Transnational Forcible Abduction After Alvarez-Machain*, 29 CORNELL INT'L. L.J. 383 (1996); Kathryn Selleck, Note, *Jurisdiction After International Kidnapping: A Comparative Study*, 8 B.C. INT'L & COMP L. REV. 237 (1985).

[162] 706 F.2d 370 (2d Cir. 1983).

[163] *Id.* (quoting United States v. Nunez-Rios 622 F.2d 1093, 1097 (2d Cir. 1980)).

Compare this U.S. case with *X v. Swiss Federal Prosecutor's Office*,[164] which involved a German attempt to apprehend X, a Belgium national. A German undercover agent contacted X in Belgium by telephone and induced him to go to the Switzerland for a business deal. When the suspect arrived in Switzerland, Germany requested his extradition.[165] The Swiss Federal Tribunal in Lausanne in 1982 refused to grant Germany's request, stating that Germany had acted improperly in contacting X without the authorization of Belgium, and that it would not condone the misconduct by ordering X's extradition.

While these two cases do not involve disputes concerning the use (or misuse) of the Internet, they do suggest how the courts will resolve such disputes. As the *Romano* case points out, a U.S. law enforcement agent may investigate and apprehend a foreign suspect unless in so doing the agent acts in such reprehensible manner as to "shock the conscience" of civilized society.[166] The question then is: how reprehensible must the manner be in order to shock the conscience of civilized society in the United States? The answer is: "truly egregious." In only one case—*United States v. Toscanino*[167]—has a court's conscience been shocked. In that case, the defendant, an Italian, was kidnapped in Uruguay by American agents, blindfolded, tortured, beaten, and interrogated for several weeks before being brought to the United States for trial. Even in *United States v. Noriega*,[168] the Eleventh Circuit Court of Appeals found nothing to shock its conscience when the U.S. military invaded Panama to apprehend and put on trial for trafficking in drugs the sitting president of the country. This being so, one can only conclude that

---

[164] 10 EuGRZ 435 (Judgment of 15 July 1982) (Swiss Federal Tribunal, Lausanne, P1201/81/fs 1983); *see also* Hans Schultz, *Male Captus, Bene Deditus?* 40 SCHWEIZERISCHES JAHRBUCH FÜR INTERNATIONALES RECHT 93 (1984) (reproducing the legal opinion written by Schultz for X).

[165] Because Belgium, like most countries, will not extradite its own nationals, Germany was unable to seek the defendant's extradition from Belgium and had to resort to the subterfuge of inducing him to travel to Switzerland. *See* Wilske & Schiller, *supra* note 1, at 173 n.327.

[166] 706 F.2d at 372. Additionally, investigations must be conducted "consistent with . . . the law of international human rights." RESTATEMENT (THIRD) OF FOREIGN RELATIONS LAW OF THE U.S. § 433(2)(a) (1987).

[167] 500 F.2d 267 (2d Cir. 1974), *reh'g denied*, 504 F.2d 1380 (2d Cir. 1974).

[168] 117 F.3d 1206 (11th Cir. 1997). The Court cited *Ker v. United States*, 119 U.S. 436 (1886) in affirming that the United States properly exercised jurisdiction. 117 F.3d at 1214.

the use of the FBI's Magic Lantern program, or other equivalent programs, to investigate or even apprehend foreign criminal suspects, will not limit a U.S. court's assertion of jurisdiction.

In no other country, however, will such investigatory conduct be tolerated. As the *X v. Swiss Federal Prosecutor's Office*[169] case makes clear, a foreign state's investigation of a criminal suspect without the consent of the local government will not be condoned anywhere (except in the United States). Moreover, should a suspect be apprehended as a consequence of such misconduct, a court will decline jurisdiction in a proceeding brought against the suspect (except in the United States).[170]

Of course, if a suspect freely enters a country on his or her own accord he or she will be subject to arrest for a criminal or regulatory violation committed abroad, even if he or she was acting lawfully overseas. This was the holding of the German court in the *Töben* case, discussed earlier.[171] It was also the U.S. Justice Department's rationale for arresting Dmitry Sklyarov in June 2001 while he was visiting the United States.[172] Sklyarov, a Russian citizen, helped design a software product for his Russian employer, ElcomSoft,[173] that circumvents the copyright protection measures used on Adobe Systems, Inc.'s e-book. The ElcomSoft product is legal in Russia[174] but violates the U.S. Digital Millennium Copyright Act.[175]

---

[169] *See supra* note 164 and accompanying text.

[170] *See* Regina v. Horseferry Road Magistrates' Court (Ex parte Bennett), [1994] 1 App. Cas. 42 (H.C. 1993); other authorities cited *supra* note 161.

[171] *See supra notes* 39–41 and accompanying text.

[172] *See* Free Dmitry Sklyarov web site, at http://www.freesklyarov.org/ (last visited Dec. 30, 2001). The D.O.J. complaint is *at* http://www.eff.org/IP/DMCA/US_v_Sklyarov/20010707_complaint.html.

[173] The ElcomSoft web site is at http://www.elcomsoft.com (last visited Dec. 30, 2001).

[174] Jennifer Lee, *In Digital Copyright Case, Programmer Can Go Home*, N.Y. TIMES (Dec. 14, 2001), *at* http://www.nytimes.com/2001/12/14/technology/14HACK.html.

[175] 17 U.S.C. § 1201(b)(1)(A) (1998). For a critique of the problems with this provision of the Digital Millennium Copyright Act, see Niels Ferguson, *Censorship in Action: Why I Don't Publish my HDCP Results*, *at* http://www.macfergus.com/niels/dmca/cia.html (last visited Dec. 30, 2001). In December 2001, following intense public opposition as well as abandonment of the case by Adobe, the Justice Department dropped its case against Sklyarov and ElcomSoft and allowed Sklyarov to return to Russia. Lisa Rein, *Dmitry Sets the Record Straight*, O'REILLY NETWORK WEBLOGS (Dec. 21, 2001), *at* http://www.oreillynet.com/cs/weblog/view/wlg/983.

B. *Jurisdiction to Enforce Judgments*

Once a court has handed down a judgment, the judgment is enforceable anywhere within the territory of the forum.[176] Additionally, a judgment is directly enforceable overseas as long as this is not "unreasonable"[177] or contrary to local law.[178] For example, a lien judgment against a defendant's assets in a bank also applies to the defendant's assets in the bank's overseas branches, unless this is forbidden by the law in the countries where the branches are located.[179]

This same rule applies in cyberspace, as the case of *Ligue Contre la Racisme et l'Antisémitisme v. Yahoo*[180] makes clear. As previously mentioned, a French trial court assumed jurisdiction over Yahoo, an American company, for posting Nazi memorabilia on the Internet that was accessible in France contrary to French law. The court's judgment ordered Yahoo to either remove the memorabilia from its American web sites or to make those web sites inaccessible in France.[181] Yahoo argued that it was unable to make its web sites inaccessible to French viewers, so it removed the memorabilia.[182] Yahoo then brought suit in a U.S. court requesting a declaratory judgment that the French court's orders are unenforceable in the United States.[183] The U.S. District Court for the Northern District of California granted Yahoo's request. It did so because the French court's order "chilled Yahoo!'s First Amendment rights" in the

---

[176] RESTATEMENT (THIRD) OF FOREIGN RELATIONS LAW OF THE U.S. § 431(1) (1987).

[177] *Id.* §§ 403(1), 431.

[178] *See* Libyan Arab Foreign Bank v. Bankers Trust Co., 1 Lloyd's Rep. 259 (Q.B. 1988) (Eng.); RAY AUGUST, INTERNATIONAL BUSINESS LAW 349 (3d ed. 2000).

[179] RESTATEMENT (THIRD) OF FOREIGN RELATIONS LAW OF THE U.S. § 431(1) reporter's notes n.4 (1987).

[180] *See* sources cited *supra* note 134.

[181] *See* sources cited *supra* note 134.

[182] George A. Chidi, Jr. & Rick Perera, *Yahoo's Nazi Ban Draws Free Speech Concerns*, PCWORLD.COM, *at* http://www.pcworld.com/news/article/0,aid,37524,00.asp (Jan. 4, 2001).

[183] Yahoo, Inc. v. La Ligue Contre la Racisme et l'Antisémitisme, 169 F. Supp. 2d 1181 (N.D. Cal. 2001).

566 / Vol. 39 / *American Business Law Journal*

United States.[184] To reiterate, a court's judgment is enforceable in the forum's territory and it is enforceable abroad to the extent that it is reasonable and not contrary to local law.

IV. JURISDICTIONAL ISSUES CREATED BY THE ADVENT OF THE INTERNET

The cases we have examined so far (in the context of the jurisdictional bases on which courts assume jurisdiction), also highlight a variety of new jurisdictional issues that have appeared following the creation of the Internet. Among the more important are forum avoidance, retailer entrapment, tax cheating, and the infringement of free speech.

A. Forum Avoidance

Merchants like to avoid the pitfall of defending themselves in every place where they offer a product or service. To do so, they commonly include a forum selection clause in their contracts specifying the particular courts in which they may be sued. Indeed, this is standard practice in the United States[185] and in most countries outside the European Union. Virtually every online, non-European merchant has a forum selection clause that attempts to avoid the liability outside of a chosen forum, Netscape's forum selection clause, quoted earlier,[186] being a case in point.[187]

The rationale for enforcing these clauses was set out by the U.S. Supreme Court in *The Bremen v. Zapata Off-Shore Co.*[188] Overruling the

---

[184] *Id.* at 1194. The two defendants in the case, La Ligue Contre la Racisme et l'Antisémitisme and L'Union des Etudiants Juifs de France, promptly announced that they would appeal the decision. *French Humanitarian Organizations Appeal Yahoo! Decision on Nazi Memorabilia*, (Dec. 5, 2001), at http://globalarchive.ft.com/globalarchive/article.html?id=011205006245.

[185] Section 110 of the Uniform Computer Information Transactions Act of 1999 specifically recognizes the validity of choice-of-forum clauses. The Act, posted at http://www.law.upenn.edu/bll/ulc/ucita/ucita1200.htm, is currently in force only in Maryland and Virginia. *See* National Conference of Commissioners on Uniform State Laws Legislative Fact Sheet, at http://www.nccusl.org/nccusl/uniformact_factsheets/uniformacts -fs-ucita.asp (last visited Dec. 30, 2001). The ABA Section Report similarly advocates the use of choice-of-forum clauses. *See ABA Section Report, supra* note 1, ¶ 1.2.1.

[186] *See supra* note 85 and accompanying text.

[187] Another example is the forum selection clause posted on the Brazilian InterNAU.com. br web site *at* http://www.internau.com.br/dom_contrato.asp (last visited Dec. 30, 2001).

[188] 407 U.S. 1 (1972).

longstanding practice in U.S. courts of holding such clauses to be contrary to public policy,[189] and citing the then-current practice in English courts of enforcing forum selection clauses,[190] the Court said that "in light of present-day commercial realities and expanding international trade we conclude that the forum clause should control absent a strong showing that it should be set aside."[191] Considering that England, as an E.U. Member State, no longer will enforce forum selection clauses in consumer contracts, and considering the current "present day realities" of cyberspace, which puts distant consumers at a decided disadvantage in dealing with both scrupulous and unscrupulous merchants, one has to wonder if the Supreme Court will long continue to uphold its decision in *The Bremen*. It seems to this author—at least with respect to consumer contracts—that it should not.

As mentioned earlier, the E.U. Regulation on Jurisdiction and the Recognition and Enforcement of Judgments in Civil and Commercial Matters[192] makes forum selection clauses ineffective, not only for online transactions, but for all consumer transactions in the European Union.[193] Also, as mentioned earlier, The Hague Conference on Private International Law is attempting to reconcile the differing approaches to forum selection clauses in its Draft Convention on Jurisdiction and Foreign Judgments in Civil and Commercial Matters.[194] Two of the Draft's proposed Alternatives that are now under discussion, however, would allow ratifying countries to choose between giving effect to forum selection clauses or making them ineffective.[195] The matter, clearly, is yet to be decided.

B. Retailer Entrapment

Retailer entrapment involves consumers who attempt to acquire products or services that they are forbidden to purchase. It is not the consumer, however, who is prosecuted, but the retailer. The two most obvious examples of this are minors who want to view adult

---

[189] *Id.* at 9.

[190] *Id.* at 11, n.12.

[191] *Id.* at 15.

[192] Council Regulation 44/2001, *supra* note 120.

[193] *Id.* art. 17; *see supra* note 130 and accompanying text.

[194] *See supra* notes 136–48 and accompanying text.

[195] *See supra* notes 147–48 and accompanying text.

materials and gamblers who want to place bets from territories where gambling is illegal. The usual defense to retailer entrapment is a licensing agreement that requires consumers to certify that they are adults or that they are domiciled in a territory that does not outlaw the product or service they seek to buy. This defense, however, is decidedly inadequate.

For example, in the *New York v. World Interactive Gaming Corp.* case discussed earlier,[196] the defendant required users to enter a home address before they could enter bets, and it refused to deal with customers whose addresses were in a state where gambling was illegal.[197] A New York deputy attorney general, however, was able to use a fictitious Nevada address to gain access to the defendant's site from New York and place bets.[198] Additionally, because he was able to do so through a simple deception, the court held that ordinary consumers were able to do so, too, and that the defendant therefore had not made a good-faith effort to comply with New York's gamblers' laws.[199] In other words, asking individuals to certify that they are legitimate consumers of a product or service is not going to protect retailers from criminal liability because consumers are too likely to cheat.

This being so, is there a way for an online retailer to determine the consumer's domicile? In the *Ligue Contre la Racisme et l'Antisémitisme v. Yahoo, Inc.* case, discussed earlier,[200] the French Court gave Yahoo the option of electronically screening visitors to its Web sites and excluding French residents from viewing pages with Nazi memorabilia.[201] Yahoo claimed that this was impossible to do. The Court then appointed a panel of experts to ascertain whether Yahoo was correct. The experts reported that Yahoo, with technology available in November 2000, could determine the physical location of ninety percent of the users accessing its web site and that it could

---

[196] 714 N.Y.S.2d 844 (N.Y. App. Div. 1999); *see supra* notes 34–37 and accompanying text.

[197] 714 N.Y.S.2d at 855.

[198] *Id.*

[199] *Id.* at 861.

[200] *See supra* notes 134–35, 180–84 and accompanying text.

[201] Summary Order of May 22, 2000 *supra* note 134.

deny access to particular pages to those who were physically located in France.[202]

Is this technology the answer? One has to think so. Since November 2000, the technology for identifying online users—known as geo-location software—has improved dramatically. By the summer of 2001, geo-location software could trace "backwards the connection route established by an on-line user" and locate "down to the city where a person is logging on"[203] and it could do so with ninety-eight to ninety-nine percent accuracy.[204]

As the U.S. court in *World Interactive Gaming Corp.* and the French court in *Yahoo* point out, online merchants can avoid liability for providing products or services in locations where they are illegal by making a "good-faith" effort to keep those products and services from being accessed from places where they are illegal.[205] Indeed, geo-location software seems to be precisely the way that online merchants can demonstrate their good faith and this author has to suspect that court orders mandating its use will become commonplace in the future.[206] In fact, cautious merchants—including Amazon.com,

---

[202] Interim Court Order, No. RG: 00/05308 (Nov. 20, 2000) *at* http://www.cdt.org/speech/international/001120yahoofrance.pdf.

Yahoo, of course, declined to use the technology. Instead it removed the Nazi memorabilia from its web site and then it brought suit in the United States and got a declaration that the French judgment was unenforceable. *See supra* notes 182–84 and accompanying text.

[203] Matthew Leising, *New Software Pinpoints Location of Web Users*, FIN. TIMES, Aug. 1, 2001, *at* http://globalarchive.ft.com/globalarchive/articles.html?id=010801007388.

Companies offering geo-location products include Digital Envoy, at http://www.digitalenvoy.net (last visited Dec. 30, 2001); Quova, at http://www.quova.com (last visited Dec. 30, 2001); NetGeo, at http://www.netgeo.com (last visited Dec. 30, 2001); and InfoSplit, at http://www.infosplit.com (last visited Dec. 30, 2001);

[204] *Geography and the Net: Putting It in Its Place*, THE ECONOMIST, Aug. 9, 2001, *at* http://www.quova.com/article.cfm?ID=97; NetGeo: Features and Benefits, *at* http://www.netgeo.com/technology/features.html (last visited Dec. 30, 2001).

[205] 714 N.Y.S.2d 844, 855 (N.Y. App. Div. 1999); Interim Court Order of Nov. 20, 2001, *supra* note 202.

[206] One author has suggested two alternative solutions to the retailer entrapment problem: (1) user registration of anyone who wants to do business online, including both merchants and consumers, and (2) the establishment of an online international cybercourt. Susan Nauss Exon, *A New Shoe Is Needed to Walk Through Cyberspace Jurisdiction*, 11 ALB. L.J. SCI. & TECH. 1, 49–53 (2000). In light of the fact that the U.S. Congress has traditionally been unwilling to mandate a national identification card for U.S. citizens, it seems highly unlikely that it would warm to an online system that would do the same thing. Similarly, given the U.S.

c|net, net2phone,[207] CCN, the *Financial Times*, Microsoft, Network Associates,[208] and VeroTrust[209]—have already begun to deploy geo-location software.

C. Tax Cheating

Online tax cheating is not a problem at present because of current moratoriums on collecting sales and other kinds of consumption taxes (*e.g.*, value added taxes) on online sales.[210] But when the moratorium expires,[211] it could well be a problem. It will not be a problem for the sale of tangible goods, because the place of shipment and the place of delivery are identifiable and no different from those of off-line sales. It will be a problem for intangible goods, because the place of shipment and the place of delivery are in cyberspace. Either or both of the parties to such a transaction can lie as to their actual physical location. Neither, as things stand now, can ascertain if the other is telling the truth.

No matter whether the consumption tax is collected, in the territory of the buyer or in the territory of the seller (and this is still being debated[212]), the attraction for buyers and sellers to cheat is

---

government's longstanding opposition to international courts, the creation of an online international cybercourt seems to be equally unlikely.

[207] Amazon.com, c|net, and net2phone are Quova customers. *See* http://www.quova .com/customers.htm (last visited Dec. 30, 2001).

[208] CCN, *The Financial Times*, Microsoft, and Network Associates are Digital Envoy customers. *See* http://www.digitalenvoy.net/customers.shtml (last visited Dec. 30, 2001).

[209] VeroTrust is a NetGeo customer. *See* http://www.netgeo.com/aboutus/customers .html (last visited Dec. 30, 2001).

[210] In the United States the moratorium was created by the Internet Tax Freedom Act, Pub. Law 105-277 (Oct. 21, 1998), *at* http://cox.house.gov/nettax/law.html. Internationally, a moratorium was implemented by the World Trade Organization at its 1998 Ministerial Meeting. WTO Ministerial Declaration on Electronic Commerce, WT/Min(98)/DEC/2, *at* http://www.wto.org/english/tratop_e/ecom_e/mindecl_e.htm (last visited Dec. 30, 2001).

[211] The U.S. moratorium is scheduled to expire on Nov. 1, 2003. Pub. Law No. 107-75 , extending expiration date of Internet Tax Freedom Act, Pub. Law 105-277, 112 Stat. 2681–719 (1998). The WTO moratorium expired in November 1999 when the Ministerial Meeting in Seattle failed to issue a new declaration. WTO Ministerial Declaration on Electronic Commerce, WT/Min(98)/DEC/2, *supra* note 210.

[212] *See* Organization for Economic Cooperation and Development Work Program on Taxation of Electronic Commerce, *at* http://www1.oecd.org/daf/fa/e_com/e_com.htm (last visited Dec. 30, 2001). On February 12, 2002, the European Union adopted a regulation requiring that value added taxes be collected in the jurisdiction of the buyer.

strong. For example, if State X has a five percent sales tax and State Y has no sales tax on online transactions, both the consumer and the seller may purport to be from State Y.

So how is this predicament to be avoided? The answer appears to be, as with retailer entrapment, through the use of geo-location software. Using this software, a merchant dealing with a consumer can identify the consumer's location and both merchants in a non-consumer transaction can identify each other's location. The merchants can then direct payment (using online banking) to the appropriate government authority.

D. *Free Speech*

The *Yahoo, Töben,* and *Waddon* cases demonstrate that free speech is not uniformly protected worldwide. In *Yahoo,*[213] as noted earlier, a French court assumed jurisdiction over Yahoo, an American company —even though the company had no business contacts with France— because Yahoo posted online items of Nazi memorabilia that French law regards as defamatory to a substantial segment of the French population.[214] In *Töben,*[215] the German Federal Supreme Court held that an Australian defendant could be criminally prosecuted in Germany for posting materials on the Internet denying the Holocaust, in violation of a German law forbidding the glorification of the Nazi party. And, in *Waddon,*[216] a British court convicted a British defendant who posted materials on a U.S. web site because the materials were obscene according to British, but not U.S., standards.

In *Waddon,* the British court was able to assert its jurisdiction because the defendant was a British national domiciled in Britain.[217] In *Töben,* a German court was able to assert jurisdiction over the defendant, an Australian national, because the defendant chose to

---

Virtual VAT, FIN. TIMES, Feb. 13, 2002, at 12, *at* http://globalarchive.ft.com/globalarchive/article.html?id=020213001851.

[213] *See* sources cited *supra* notes 134–35, 180–84.

[214] Crispian Balmer, Reuters, *Yahoo Ordered to Bar French from Nazi Web Sites,* (Nov. 20, 2000), *at* http://dailynews.yahoo.com/h/nm/20001120/ wr/france_yahoo_dc_2.html.

[215] *See* sources cited *supra* notes 39–41 and accompanying text.

[216] *See* sources cited *supra* note 33 and accompanying text.

[217] *See* sources cited *supra* note 33 and accompanying text.

voluntarily visit Germany.[218] In *Yahoo*, the French court attempted to extend its jurisdiction over a U.S. defendant that was not domiciled in France.[219] The defendant in *Yahoo* responded by getting a judgment from a U.S. court declaring that the French court's order is unenforceable in the United States.[220]

The conclusion to be drawn from these cases seems clear. Individuals and juridical entities may speak out on the Internet to the extent allowed to do so by their country of domicile, even if this violates the censorship laws of other countries. However, if they choose to travel or to establish foreign branches, agencies, or establishments, they will be subject to prosecution abroad.

V. Conclusions

The criteria for courts to assert jurisdiction over crimes and civil actions in cyberspace have begun to take concrete form. In criminal and regulatory cases, the traditional nexuses used by courts to assume jurisdiction over international defendants—the territoriality nationality, protective, and universality nexuses—all apply in cyberspace. At present, however, only the territoriality nexus has been directly invoked by the courts. This is likely to change as the number of cyber cases increases. Treaty drafters, such as those working on the Council of Europe's Convention on Cybercrime,[221] as well as the great majority of commentators writing on cyber crime,[222] are encouraging courts to assume jurisdiction using any of the traditional nexuses. Furthermore, this is so despite the possibility that the exercise of overlapping jurisdiction may adversely impact global trade, global travel, and international human rights.

In civil cases, both the common law world and the European Union are moving to assert *in personam* jurisdiction over merchants and consumers who consummate transactions over the Internet. In the common law world, this requires a showing of a connection between the transaction and the forum. In the European Union, suits in consumer disputes are ordinarily brought in the consumer's state

---

[218] *See supra* note 41.

[219] *See supra* note 135 and accompanying text.

[220] Yahoo, Inc. v. La Ligue Contre la Racisme et l'Antisémitisme, 169 F. Supp. 2d 1181 (N.D. Cal. 2001).

[221] *See supra* note 77 and accompanying text.

[222] *See* sources cited *supra* note 1.

of domicile, while non-consumer disputes are heard in the forum where the contract was to be performed.

Civil *in rem* jurisdiction, which is consistently defined worldwide, is presently being used in German courts to assert jurisdiction over domain names, software, and other kinds of intellectual property. It seems likely that it will be used in the same way in other courts in the future.

While the criteria for courts (both national and international) to assume jurisdiction are quickly taking shape—and the pattern worldwide is reasonably consistent—the decisions that have defined those criteria have created problems, especially with respect to forum avoidance, retailer entrapment, tax cheating, and free speech.

Forum selection clauses are enforceable worldwide for almost all kinds of transactions. The exception is for consumer contracts. In the European Union, the clauses are unenforceable; while in the United States and elsewhere, they are enforceable. These differing approaches are reflected in the Draft Hague Convention on Jurisdiction and Foreign Judgments in Civil and Commercial Matters, where the negotiating parties have yet to agree to a uniform treatment; and it looks as if they will include both approaches in the final convention.

Improved geo-location software looks to be the mechanism that courts and merchants will adopt for dealing with retailer entrapment and tax cheating. As for free speech, individuals and juridical entities may exercise it to the extent they are allowed to do so in their country of domicile provided they do not travel or establish overseas branches, agencies, or establishments. Travelers and overseas investors who choose to speak freely on the Internet are well advised to heed that ancient warning: *caveat peregrinator*,[223] and choose carefully their foreign destinations. If they fail to do so, they may end up arrested, like Dmitry Sklyarov, for conduct that was legal in their home jurisdiction but illegal in the place they visit.

---

[223] Latin for "be wary foreign traveler."

[13]

Cyber Crime and Punishment: Filtering Out Internet Felons

Jessica Habib[*]

INTRODUCTION

On January 21, 2003, Kevin Mitnick once again became a free man.[1] In 1999, the hacker once labeled "the most-wanted computer criminal in U.S. history" by the government[2] pled guilty to "possession of unauthorized access devices with intent to defraud in violation of [18 U.S.C. § 1029(a)(3)]."[3] Mitnick's prison term ended in January 2000, after which he was subjected to a three-year period of supervised release.[4] During this period, he was denied access to "computers, computer-related equipment and certain telecommunications devices, including cellular telephones," without the prior approval of his probation officer.[5] The terms of Mitnick's release prohibited him from using the Internet during this period,[6] a probation condition that has become a controversial issue and has generated disagreement among the

---

[*] J.D. Candidate, Fordham University School of Law, 2004; B.A. Wesleyan University, 1999. The author would like to thank Professor Joel Reidenberg for his comments and encouragement. She also would like to thank her family for its abundant love and support throughout law school and beyond.

[1] See Matt Richtel, *Barring Web Use After Web Crime*, N.Y. TIMES, Jan. 21, 2003, at A1.

[2] *Id.*

[3] United States v. Mitnick, No. 97-50365, 1998 U.S. App. LEXIS 10836, at *1 (9th Cir. May 20, 1998).

[4] See Richtel, *supra* note 1 (noting that Mitnick was released from prison in January 2000 and that he could not use the Internet until January 2003).

[5] *Mitnick*, 1998 U.S. App. LEXIS 10836, at *2.

[6] See Richtel, *supra* note 1.

courts.[7] According to Mitnick, "'[n]ot being allowed to use the Internet is kind of like not being allowed to use a telephone'"[8]—an argument that has been embraced by some courts.[9] On the other hand, proponents of banning Internet access by cyber-criminals focus on the Internet's role in committing the crime and reject the argument that Internet restrictions entail a great hardship.[10]

The abundant data on the extent of Internet use shows that the Internet has become an indispensable tool for a myriad of uses.[11] As such, it has revolutionized information gathering and communication and has transformed the economy.[12] The number of people using online resources has grown rapidly in recent years and continues to proliferate.[13] For these reasons, it seems that supervised release conditions that ban or restrict Internet use would hamper an individual's access to an extremely valuable medium and, thus, should not be permitted. In fact, several felons have challenged such deprivations as unconstitutional, often based on First Amendment guarantees of freedom of association and of the press.[14] Sentencing courts, however, are granted wide discretion in determining supervised release conditions and must balance the protection of the public with the liberty interests of the convicted individual.[15] In so doing, some courts have given greater weight to the former consideration and have upheld the conditions;[16] others have emphasized the latter in rejecting such sentencing conditions.[17] In light of the broad discretion of the courts, they clearly have the authority to impose such conditions. Courts

---

[7] *See id.* (noting that U.S. circuit courts of appeal have reached different conclusions as to the validity of Internet-use restrictions).

[8] Associated Press, *F.C.C. Lets Convicted Hacker Go Back On Air* (Dec. 27, 2002) [hereinafter Associated Press, *Hacker Back On Air*], *available at* 2003 WL 3734116.

[9] *See* discussion *infra* Part II.A.

[10] *See* discussion *infra* Part II.B.

[11] *See* discussion *infra* Part I.B.

[12] *See id.*

[13] *See id.*

[14] *E.g.,* United States v. White, 244 F.3d 1199 (10th Cir. 2001); United States v. Crandon, 173 F.3d 122 (3d Cir. 1999); United States v. Mitnick, No. 97-50365, 1998 U.S. App. LEXIS 10836, at *1 (9th Cir. May 20, 1998); *see also* discussion *infra* Part III.B (discussing First Amendment challenges to probation conditions).

[15] *See* discussion *infra* Part I.A.

[16] *See* discussion *infra* Part II.B.

[17] *See* discussion *infra* Part II.A.

determining the appropriateness of such conditions, however, should focus narrowly on the Internet's role in facilitating the crime and whether the restriction will prevent the underlying criminal conduct.

Part I of this Note will introduce the federal guidelines and goals used to determine supervised release conditions and will discuss the extent to which the Internet has become a routine and necessary feature of society. Part II will address the split among courts that have upheld or overturned Internet-use bans as a part of supervised release. Part III will explore the factors that these courts have employed in making their decisions by distinguishing different types of computer crime and comparing the ban on Internet use to other instances where convicts have been deprived of what are normally considered fundamental rights and liberties. This part will argue that given the pervasiveness of Internet use in modern society and the Internet's fundamental role in facilitating communication, courts should tailor supervised release conditions carefully to reflect how the Internet use related to the criminal act.

I. SENTENCING DISCRETION VERSUS THE NATURE OF THE INTERNET

At the heart of the controversy surrounding supervised release restrictions on Internet use is the tension between the broad discretion courts may exercise in the area of supervised release conditions and the Internet's pervasiveness in modern society.[18] A court must use its discretion to consider its competing obligations to society and to the convict poised to reenter society, with certain statutory criteria to guide its decisions.[19] These decisions become even more complex if the realities of modern life—in this case, the

---

[18] *See generally* Brian W. McKay, Note, *Guardrails on the Information Superhighway: Supervising Computer Use of the Adjudicated Sex Offender*, 106 W. VA. L. REV. 203, 219–33 (2003) (discussing the split among U.S. circuit courts of appeal with respect to Internet bans).

[19] *See* U.S. SENTENCING COMMISSION, GUIDELINES MANUAL §§ 5D1.1–.3 (guidelines on imposing a term of supervised release); *see also* Harold Baer, Jr., *The Alpha & Omega of Supervised Release*, 60 ALB. L. REV. 267, 269–85 (1996) (discussing the requirements for imposing a term of supervised release).

extent to which the Internet has become an essential means of communication—are also considered.

A. Sentencing Guidelines and Goals

In general, courts may exercise considerable discretion in determining whether to sentence an offender to a term of supervised release and what the conditions should be, limited by the class of felony.[20] Under 18 U.S.C. § 3583, a court choosing to include such a term must impose on the defendant certain mandatory restrictions, principally addressing the commission of other crimes as well as the use of controlled substances.[21] In addition, the penultimate sentence of section 3583(d) states that a court may order "any other condition it considers to be appropriate,"[22] thus conferring broad discretion upon courts to establish further conditions.

The judgment of the courts is subject to three limitations, however. First, section 3583(d)(1) states that the condition must be "reasonably related to the factors set forth in section 3553(a)(1), (a)(2)(B), (a)(2)(C), and (a)(2)(D)."[23] These factors are "the nature and circumstances of the offense and the history and characteristics of the defendant"[24] and the need for the sentence, *inter alia*, to deter criminal conduct, protect the public, and provide the

---

[20]   *See generally* 18 U.S.C. § 3583(a) (2000) (inclusion of a term of supervised release after imprisonment); 18 U.S.C. § 3583(b) (listing the authorized time periods of supervised release for each class of felony, the longest of which is five years).

[21]   *See* 18 U.S.C. § 3583(d) (conditions of supervised release).

[22]   *Id.* The section states, in pertinent part:

   The court may order, as a further condition of supervised release, to the extent that such condition—

   (1) is reasonably related to the factors set forth in section 3553(a)(1), (a)(2)(B), (a)(2)(C), and (a)(2)(D);

   (2) involves no greater deprivation of liberty than is reasonably necessary for the purposes set forth in section 3553(a)(2)(B), (a)(2)(C), and (a)(2)(D); and

   (3) is consistent with any pertinent policy statements issued by the Sentencing Commission pursuant to 28 U.S.C. 994(a);

   any condition set forth as a discretionary condition of probation in section 3563(b)(1) through (b)(10) and (b)(12) through (b)(20), and *any other condition it considers to be appropriate.*

   Id. (emphasis added).

[23]   18 U.S.C. § 3583(d)(1).

[24]   18 U.S.C. § 3553(a)(1) (2000).

defendant with educational training or medical care.[25] Several courts have found Internet bans appropriate based on these factors,[26] suggesting that this provision of Section 3583(d) does not significantly limit a sentencing court's discretion.[27]

Second, section 3583(d)(2) sets forth another important limitation, prohibiting the infliction of any "greater deprivation of liberty than reasonably necessary for the purposes set forth in section 3553(a)(2)(B), (a)(2)(C) and (a)(2)(D)."[28] This factor has been critical in the decisions of several appeals courts to reject release conditions prohibiting Internet access, based upon their perception of the role of the Internet with respect to everyday activities.[29] The third limitation is that the condition must be "consistent with any pertinent policy statements issued by the Sentencing Commission pursuant to 28 U.S.C. 994(a)," which generally refers to various provisions and purposes of title 18.[30]

---

[25] *See* 18 U.S.C. § 3553(a)(2).

[26] *See infra* Part II.B.

[27] For example, in *United States v. Crandon*, 173 F.3d 122 (3d Cir. 1999), the U.S. Court of Appeals for the Third Circuit needed only one paragraph to find a district court's Internet restrictions acceptable under the standards of 18 U.S.C. § 3583(d)(1). *See id.* at 127–28. The issue under section 3583(d)(2)—whether the restrictions constituted a greater deprivation of liberty than reasonably necessary—received more extensive analysis. *See id.* at 128.

[28] 18 U.S.C. § 3583(d)(2); *see also supra* notes 24–25 and accompanying text (listing the relevant provisions of 18 U.S.C. § 3553).

[29] *See infra* Part II.A.

[30] 18 U.S.C. § 3583(d)(3). 18 U.S.C. § 994(a) states:

The Commission, by affirmative vote of at least four members of the Commission, and pursuant to its rules and regulations and consistent with all pertinent provisions of any Federal statute shall promulgate and distribute to all courts of the United States and to the United States Probation System—

(1) guidelines, as described in this section, for use of a sentencing court in determining the sentence to be imposed in a criminal case, including—

(A) a determination whether to impose a sentence to probation, a fine, or a term of imprisonment;

(B) a determination as to the appropriate amount of a fine or the appropriate length of a term of probation or a term of imprisonment;

(C) a determination whether a sentence to a term of imprisonment should include a requirement that the defendant be placed on a term of supervised release after imprisonment, and, if so, the appropriate length of such a term;

(D) a determination whether multiple sentences to terms of imprisonment should be ordered to run concurrently or consecutively; and

Clearly, courts have the authority to decide that an offender should be banned from using the Internet, as long as this condition comports with the factors described above. The question remains, however, whether this power should be used to fashion such a condition, given the Internet's prevalence in modern society. The difficulty lies in balancing the sentencing goals of protecting the public and the liberty of the individual, in a context where the Internet has become synonymous with the free flow of information, ideas, and communication.

B. *Internet Use*

Much of the information about Internet use that the courts rely upon seems to be based on anecdotal evidence,[31] but there is a great deal of empirical evidence on the subject as well.[32] Several courts, such as those in *United States v. Sofsky*,[33] *United States v. Peterson*,[34] and *United States v. White*[35] have emphasized the

---

(E) a determination under paragraphs (6) and (11) of section 3563(b) of title 18;

(2) general policy statements regarding application of the guidelines or any other aspect of sentencing or sentence implementation that in the view of the Commission would further the purposes set forth in section 3553(a)(2) of title 18, United States Code, including the appropriate use of—

(A) the sanctions set forth in sections 3554, 3555, and 3556 of title 18;

(B) the conditions of probation and supervised release set forth in sections 3563(b) and 3583(d) of title 18;

(C) the sentence modification provisions set forth in sections 3563(c), 3564, 3573, and 3582(c) of title 18;

(D) the fine imposition provisions set forth in section 3572 of title 18;

(E) the authority granted under rule 11(e)(2) of the Federal Rules of Criminal Procedure to accept or reject a plea agreement entered into pursuant to rule 11(e)(1); and

(F) the temporary release provisions set forth in section 3622 of title 18, and the prerelease custody provisions set forth in section 3624(c) of title 18; and

(3) guidelines or general policy statements regarding the appropriate use of the provisions for revocation of probation set forth in section 3565 of title 18, and the provisions for modification of the term or conditions of supervised release and revocation of supervised release set forth in section 3583(e) of title 18.

[31] *See, e.g., infra* notes 78, 99–101 and accompanying text.

[32] *See infra* notes 39–65.

[33] 287 F.3d 122 (2d Cir. 2002).

[34] 248 F.3d 79 (2d Cir. 2001).

[35] 244 F.3d 1199 (10th Cir. 2001).

ubiquity of the Internet in overturning sentencing conditions that banned Internet use.[36] Courts affirming such restrictions, such as the U.S. Court of Appeals for the Third Circuit in *United States v. Crandon*,[37] have acknowledged the Internet's prevalence, but ultimately justified their rulings on alternative factors.[38]

The Internet's pervasiveness and explosive growth is well described in a 2002 U.S. Commerce Department Report, titled "A Nation Online: How Americans Are Expanding Their Use of the Internet" ("Commerce Department report"): "Few technologies have spread as quickly, or become so widely used, as computers and the Internet. These information technologies are rapidly becoming common fixtures of modern social and economic life, opening opportunities and new avenues for many Americans."[39] Indeed, a significant portion of the population now relies on the Internet to conduct various activities of daily life, as it is a powerful tool with countless practical uses, including communication, education, research, employment, shopping, and entertainment.[40] According to Jeffrey Cole, director of the University of California, Los Angeles ("UCLA") Center for Communication Policy, "The Internet has surpassed all other major information sources in importance after only about eight years as a generally available communications tool."[41] A year-to-year UCLA study found that among Internet users, the Internet ranked above books, newspapers, television, radio, and magazines as a very important or extremely important information source.[42]

---

[36] *See infra* Part II.A.

[37] 173 F.3d 122 (3d Cir. 1999).

[38] *See infra* Part II.B.

[39] DEP'T OF COMMERCE, A NATION ONLINE: HOW AMERICANS ARE EXPANDING THEIR USE OF THE INTERNET 1 (2002), *available at* http://www.ntia.doc.gov/ntiahome/dn (last visited Mar. 24, 2004). The report, generated with U.S. Census Bureau data, was jointly prepared by two Commerce Department agencies: the Economics and Statistics Administration and the National Telecommunications and Information Administration. *See id.*

[40] *See infra* notes 42–65.

[41] Dawn Kawamoto, *Net Ranks as Top Information Source*, ZD Net News, *at* http://zdnet.com.com/2100-1105-982995.html (Jan. 31, 2003).

[42] *See* UCLA CTR. FOR COMMUNICATION POLICY, THE UCLA INTERNET REPORT: SURVEYING THE DIGITAL FUTURE 82 (2003) (noting that nearly three-quarters of Internet users consider the Internet to be a very important or extremely important source of information, a ranking higher than for books, television, radio, newspapers, or

Other studies have focused on the types of information gathered on the Internet, demonstrating that its utility as an information source has many aspects.[43] For example, one study concluded that about two-thirds of all Americans, Internet users and non-users alike, expect to find information about health care, government agencies, news, and commerce on the Internet.[44] Among Internet users alone, the study concluded that about eighty percent expected to find such information online.[45] Furthermore, thirty-nine percent of all Americans said that they would first turn to the Internet for government information, and thirty-one percent would first look online for health-care information.[46] Along with underscoring expectations about the accessibility and dependability of this information, this result also indicates that people are willing to rely on the Internet as their initial source of information about two essential, even personal, issues. Indeed, the court in *United States v. White* compared the Internet to books, based on the instant access to the information it provides.[47]

---

magazines), *available at* http://ccp.ucla.edu/pages/internet-report.asp (last visited Mar. 19, 2004).

[43]   *See* JOHN B. HORRIGAN & LEE RAINIE, PEW INTERNET & AMERICAN LIFE PROJECT, COUNTING ON THE INTERNET 5 (2002) ("The dissemination of the Internet has transformed how many Americans find information and altered how they engage with many institutions, such as government, health care providers, the news media, and commercial enterprises."), *available at* http://www.pewInternet.org/reports/toc.asp?Report=80 (last visited April 8, 2004).

[44]   *See id.* at 2. The study found that sixty-five percent of all Americans expect to find government-agency information or services on the World Wide Web. *Id.* Additionally, sixty-three percent of all Americans expect that a business will have a Web site giving them information about a product they are considering buying; sixty-nine percent expect to find reliable, current news online; and sixty-seven percent expect to find reliable information about health or medical conditions on the Web. *Id.*

[45]   *See id.* The study found that eighty-two percent of Internet users expect to find to find government-agency information or services online; seventy-nine percent expect that a business will have a Web site giving them information about a product they are considering buying; eighty-five percent expect to find reliable, current news online; and eighty-one percent expect to find reliable information about health or medical conditions on the Web. *Id.*

[46]   *Id.* at 8.

[47]   *See* United States v. White, 244 F.3d 1199, 1207 (10th Cir. 2001) ("The communication facilitated by [information technology] may be likened to that of the telephone. Its instant link to information is akin to opening a book.").

With Internet use expanding across the population—regardless of income, education, race, age, ethnicity, or gender[48]—the Internet also is furthering democratic governance by helping local officials and their constituents communicate.[49] A Pew Internet & American Life Project ("Pew") survey of 2,000 mayors and city council members concluded that "local officials have embraced the Internet as part of their official lives and most now use email to communicate with constituents," noting that that eighty-eight percent of local officials use the Internet in the course of their official duties.[50] Among these "online officials," sixty-one percent use e-mail to communicate with citizens at least weekly, and seventy-five percent use the World Wide Web ("Web") at least weekly for research in the course of their official duties.[51] Furthermore, the survey indicated that local officials learn about their constituents' activities and opinions through the Internet, and more local groups are getting recognized or heard in this fashion.[52] Therefore, in addition to learning about government services on the Internet, people are increasingly going online to communicate with their representatives and to participate in civic affairs, while elected officials have turned to the Internet to communicate with their constituents.[53] The Internet is not the exclusive method by which citizens participate in government, but such use will likely

---

[48] *See* DEP'T OF COMMERCE, *supra* note 39, at 1.

[49] *See* Christopher Swope, *E-Gov's New Gear*, GOVERNING, Mar. 2004 (noting that states, cities, and counties are "trying out new modes of interactivity, channeling public participation both over the Internet and in face-to-face high-tech town hall meetings"), *available at* http://www.governing.com/archive/2004/mar/interact.txt (last visited April 9, 2004).

[50] ELENA LARSEN & LEE RAINIE, DIGITAL TOWN HALL 1 (2002) (prepared for the Pew Internet & American Life Project), *available at* http://www.pewinternet.org/reports/-toc.asp?Report=74 (last visited March 25, 2004).

[51] *Id.*

[52] *Id.* The report does caution, however, that "while the use of email adds to the convenience and depth of civic exchanges, its use is not ushering a revolution in municipal affairs or local politics." *Id.*

[53] *See, e.g.*, Charles Bermant, *E-Mails to Officials Can Help You Blow Off Steam*, SEATTLE TIMES, Jan. 10, 2004 (urging residents to write e-mail messages to local officials and stating that letter writers "should expect an individual look-in-the-eye response"), *available at* http://seattletimes.nwsource.com/html/inbox/2001833798_ptinbo10.html (last visited March 25, 2004).

continue to grow, potentially putting those deprived of Internet use at a disadvantage in these essential matters.

Searching for employment is another rapidly growing type of Internet use.[54] Between March 2000 and May 2002, the number of Americans who looked for employment online increased by sixty percent, according to another Pew study.[55] Although percentages of Internet users looking for jobs online vary by sex, race, age, and class, forty-seven percent of all adult Internet users in the United States have looked online for job information.[56] In addition, the study found that fifty-two million Americans have looked on the Web for information about jobs, "and more than [four] million do so on a typical day."[57] Furthermore, this study indicates that many have found the Internet useful in obtaining additional job training.[58] These numbers show that the Internet is now widely used for researching employment opportunities. Some obvious reasons for this growth include the efficiency of using online services, such as Vault.com and Monster.com, to research job opportunities throughout the country and distribute résumés, as well as the facility with which users can search online editions of newspapers from other locales.[59]

The Internet is not only widely used to find employment, but also has become ubiquitous in the workplace as well.[60] Employed

---

[54]   *See infra* notes 55–59; *see also* Lorraine Farquharson, *The Best Way to . . . Find a Job*, WALL ST. J., Sept. 15, 2003 (discussing different ways to use the Internet to find a job).

[55]   ANGIE BOYCE & LEE RAINIE, ONLINE JOB HUNTING 1 (July 2002) (prepared for the Pew Internet & American Life Project), *available at* http://www.pewinternet.org/reports/-toc.asp?Report=65 (last visited March 25, 2004).

[56]   *Id.* at 2.

[57]   *Id.* at 1.

[58]   *See id.* at 2 (stating that of the forty-seven million Internet users who had sought additional career education or training in the preceding two years, twenty-nine percent reported that their use of the Internet played an important role in their securing the training).

[59]   For example, the *New York Times* Web site provides access to job listings at http://www.nytimes.com/pages/jobs/index.html.

[60]   *See* DEP'T OF COMMERCE, *supra* note 39, at 60 ("The workplace provides an important venue for many adults to use computers and the Internet."); DEBORAH FALLOWS, EMAIL AT WORK: FEW FEEL OVERWHELMED AND MOST ARE PLEASED WITH THE WAY EMAIL HELPS THEM DO THEIR JOBS 5 (2002) (prepared for the Pew Internet &

adults ages twenty-five and over use their computer at work more frequently to access the Internet and e-mail than for any other purpose, including word processing, desktop publishing, spreadsheets, databases, and graphics and design, according to the Commerce Department report.[61] About forty-two percent of these workers used the Internet and e-mail at work by September 2001, up from about twenty-six percent in August 2000.[62] These figures demonstrate that Internet use at work has become prevalent and continues to grow, likely due to the ease with which the Internet allows people to communicate. This is an important consideration with respect to Internet use restrictions, especially since such a restriction could last up to five years under the sentencing guidelines, depending on the class of felony.[63]

As yet another Pew study emphasizes, people increasingly turn to the Internet at "major life moments."[64] Of those Internet users who had experienced one of the major life moments identified in the survey over a certain period, the greatest proportion said that the Internet played a crucial role in choosing a school or college (thirty-six percent), followed by starting a new hobby (thirty-three percent), obtaining additional career training (twenty-nine percent), buying a new car (twenty-seven percent), helping another person deal with a major illness (twenty-six percent), and changing jobs (twenty-five percent).[65]

These results, as well as the findings discussed above, illustrate the myriad of Internet applications to daily life, in which the quest for information is the common denominator. The growth of Internet use is both rapid and widespread, and the variety of

---

American Life Project) ("The use of email has become almost mandatory in most U.S. workplaces.").

[61] *See* DEP'T OF COMMERCE, *supra* note 39, at 60.

[62] *Id.* at 57, 60.

[63] *See* 18 U.S.C. § 3583(b) (2000).

[64] *See* NATHAN KOMMERS & LEE RAINIE, USE OF THE INTERNET AT MAJOR LIFE MOMENTS 2 (2002) (prepared for the Pew Internet & American Life Project) (stating that information on the Web is important to significant numbers of Americans when they are making important choices related to education and job training, investments and large purchases, and health care), *available at* http://www.pewInternet.org/reports/toc.asp?-Report=58 (last visited March 21, 2004).

[65] *Id.* at 3. The survey questioned 1,415 Internet users about a total of 15 different major life events. *Id.* at 2.

matters for which people increasingly seek information online—
from mundane personal choices to significant life decisions—
demonstrate a high level of comfort with the information it has to
offer.[66]

The conclusion to the Commerce Department report states in
part:

> The Internet has become a tool that is accessible to and
> adopted by Americans in communities across the
> nation.. . .As a result, we are more and more becoming a
> nation online: a nation that can take advantage of the
> information resources provided by the Internet, as well as a
> nation developing the technical skills to compete in our
> global economy.[67]

In addition to its many social and other practical uses, the
Internet is a necessary tool of economic competition, which begs
the question: to what extent does deprivation of its use put people
at an economic disadvantage?[68] The numerous surveys and studies
regarding Internet usage establish an important backdrop against

---

[66] *See* Toni Fitzgerald, *America's Growing Web Dependence*, MEDIA LIFE (discussing a
Pew Internet & American Life Project study and expressing surprise at "how quickly
Americans have come to trust the information" found on the Internet), *at*
http://www.medialifemagazine.com/news2003/jan03/jan20/5_fri/news1friday.html (Jan.
24, 2003); Press Release, UCLA Ctr. for Communication Policy, First Release of
Findings From the UCLA World Internet Project Shows Significant 'Digital Gender Gap'
in Many Countries (Jan. 14, 2004) (statement of Director Jeffrey Cole) (stating that most
Internet users worldwide "generally trust the information they find online"), *available at*
http://ccp.ucla.edu/pages/NewsTopics.asp?Id=45 (last visited Apr. 9, 2004).
[67] *See* DEP'T OF COMMERCE, *supra* note 39, at 91.
[68] *See, e.g.,* United States v. Peterson, 248 F.3d 79, 83–84 (2d Cir. 2001) (concluding
that restrictions on Internet use and computer ownership constitute "an occupational
restriction" and noting that the items prohibited under the conditions "include technology
that [the defendant] would likely need to hold any computer-related job"); *see also* Doug
Hyne, Note, *Examining the Legal Challenges to the Restriction of Computer Access as a
Term of Probation or Supervised Release*, 28 NEW ENG. J. CRIM. & CIV. CONFINEMENT
215, 216 (2002) ("[O]ne can foresee a future where the majority of occupations will, at
least in some way, necessitate that an employee use the internet. In light of this fact,
restricting the use of the internet as a term of probation may hamper an individual from
gaining employment.").

which to examine supervised release conditions that may limit access to the Internet's abundant uses.[69]

II. CONFLICTING APPROACHES TO INTERNET CRIME SENTENCING

There are several key factors that the federal appeals courts have weighed in their consideration of supervised release conditions that ban Internet access, computer use, or both.[70] Outcomes have often turned on a particular court's view of the role of the Internet and whether its use was incidental or necessary to commit the crime.[71] While such cases require the examination of several criteria, the principal factors may be gleaned from these highly fact-specific cases.[72]

A. *Indispensability of the Internet and the Deprivation of Liberty*

Some courts have concluded that a member of modern society cannot afford to be without Internet or computer access, and, thus, generally have overturned prohibitions on Internet use during the supervised release period.[73] The Second Circuit, for example, developed a position on the Internet to which it has adhered rather strictly in two such decisions.[74] In *United States v. Peterson*,[75] the court struck down an Internet ban imposed on a felon who had pled guilty to bank larceny, was previously convicted of incest, and had

---

[69]   *See* Richtel, *supra* note 1 (statement of Jennifer S. Granick, Director, Stanford Center for Internet and Society) ("The A.T.M. is a computer; the car has a computer; the Palm Pilot is a computer. Without a computer in this day and age, you can't work, you can't communicate, you can't function as people normally do in modern society.").

[70]   *See* discussion *infra* Parts II.A–.B.

[71]   *Compare Peterson*, 248 F.3d at 82 (holding that restrictions on defendant's computer ownership and Internet access are not reasonably related, *inter alia*, to the nature and circumstances of the offense), *with* United States v. Crandon, 173 F.3d 122, 127–28 (3d Cir. 1999) (noting that defendant used the Internet "as a means to develop an illegal sexual relationship with a young girl" and concluding that a restriction on defendant's Internet access is "related to the dual aims of deterring him from recidivism and protecting the public").

[72]   *See* discussion *infra* Parts II.A–.B.

[73]   *E.g.*, United States v. Freeman, 316 F.3d 386, 391–92 (3d Cir. 2003); United States v. Sofsky, 287 F.3d 122, 124 (2d Cir. 2002); *Peterson*, 248 F.3d at 81–84; United States v. White, 244 F.3d 1199, 1206–08 (10th Cir. 2001).

[74]   *See Sofsky*, 287 F.3d 122; *Peterson*, 248 F.3d 79.

[75]   248 F.3d 79.

accessed legal adult pornography on his home computer.[76] The court found that the prohibition was not "'reasonably related'" to Peterson's offense,[77] and clarified its position with respect to the Internet:

> Computers and Internet access have become virtually indispensable in the modern world of communications and information gathering. The fact that a computer with Internet access offers the possibility of abusive use for illegitimate purposes does not, at least in this case, justify so broad a prohibition. Although a defendant might use the telephone to commit fraud, this would not justify a condition of probation that includes an absolute bar on the use of telephones. Nor would defendant's proclivity toward pornography justify a ban on all books, magazines, and newspapers.[78]

In comparing the Internet to commonplace items such as the telephone and newspapers, the court signaled in this instance that the value of the Internet outweighed the potential for abuse.[79] Peterson's Internet restrictions also prohibited the use of "'commercial computer systems/services' for employment purposes without a probation officer's permission,"[80] in addition to a complete ban on all technology (such as a CD-ROM and other storage devices) necessary to connect to the Internet or even to work at a computer-related job, as the Second Circuit noted.[81] The court noted that the defendant "consistently worked in computer-related jobs and, beginning in May 1997, operated his own computer business" and, thus, concluded that the Internet and computer restrictions were not reasonably related to the bank

---

[76]   *Id.* at 81, 84.

[77]   *Id.* at 82 (citing 18 U.S.C. § 3563(b)).

[78]   *Id.* at 83 (computer restriction which "would bar [defendant] from using a computer at a library to do any research, get a weather forecast, or read a newspaper online" was excessively broad) (citing *White*, 244 F.3d at 1206).

[79]   *See id.; see also* Donna A. Gallagher, Comment, *Free Speech on the Line: Modern Technology and the First Amendment*, 3 COMMLAW CONSPECTUS 197, 199 (1995) (arguing that although electronic bulletin board services can facilitate abuse, "the positive impact of the Internet greatly outweighs the negative").

[80]   *Peterson*, 248 F.3d at 83.

[81]   *See id.* at 81, 83–84.

larceny conviction.[82]   The sentencing condition would unnecessarily hamper such employment during the supervised release period, the court found.[83]

Applying the reasoning in *Peterson*, the Second Circuit reversed an Internet ban in another notable case, *United States v. Sofsky*.[84]   Gregory Sofsky pled guilty to receiving child pornography in light of evidence that he downloaded over 1,000 images of child pornography from the Internet and exchanged images with others online.[85] He was sentenced to ten years in prison, to be followed by a term of supervised release during which, *inter alia*, he was not allowed to access the computer or Internet without approval of a probation officer.[86]   Sofsky's conduct was more closely related to the Internet than the offense in *Peterson*,[87] and the conditions allowed Sofsky to obtain approved access.[88] In addition, the court acknowledged that Sofsky's access to computers and the Internet could "facilitate . . . his electronic receipt of child pornography."[89] The court relied on its stance in *Peterson* to vacate the ban and remand the case to the district court for a more restricted condition, however, finding that it "inflict[ed] a greater deprivation on Sofsky's liberty than [was] reasonably necessary,"[90] in the language of the federal supervised release guidelines.[91]

The *Sofsky* court expanded upon the statement in *Peterson* that a defendant's use of the telephone to commit fraud would not justify a complete ban on telephone use:[92] "The same could be said of a prohibition on the use of the mails imposed on a defendant

---

[82] *Id.* at 84.

[83] *See id.*

[84] *See Sofsky*, 287 F.3d 122.

[85] *Id.* at 124.

[86] *Id.*

[87] *See supra* note 76 and accompanying text (noting that defendant in *Peterson* had pled guilty to bank larceny and was previously convicted of incest, and had accessed legal adult pornography on his home computer).

[88] *Sofsky*, 287 F.3d at 124.

[89] *Id.* at 126.

[90] *Id.*

[91] *See supra* note 28 and accompanying text.

[92] *See Sofsky*, 287 F.3d at 126 (citing *Peterson*, 248 F.3d at 83); *see also supra* note 78 and accompanying text.

convicted of mail fraud. A total ban on Internet access prevents use of e-mail, an increasingly widely used form of communication . . . ."[93]   This line of reasoning indicates a reluctance to identify the Internet as the root of the underlying conduct, although in this case the court acknowledged that the Internet could facilitate the continuation of the criminal act for which the defendant was convicted.[94] However, the fact that the Internet was incidental to the commission of the underlying crime—that is, the crime could have been committed without going online—may have made the court less willing to restrict access to the Internet for legitimate purposes.[95] Although Sofsky could seek approval from his probation officer to use the Internet, the court still concluded that the condition was too restrictive, and that the possibility for abuse should not prevent access to such indispensable technology.[96]

Other circuits have relied on similar reasoning. For example, the Tenth Circuit in *United States v. White* was unwilling to uphold an Internet ban in the sentencing of Robert Emerson White, who was caught purchasing child pornography videos online by a government sting operation.[97]   The court took issue with the wording of the condition, which stated that White "'shall not possess a computer with Internet access throughout his period of supervised release.'"[98] The court thought that a restriction on the *possession* of a computer with Internet access "missed the mark" if the district court intended to prevent access to online child pornography, since White could simply access the Internet on a computer he did not own.[99] The court also thought that if

---

[93]   *Sofsky*, 287 F.3d at 126.

[94]   *Id.* at 126, 127.

[95]   The distinction between Internet crime and Internet-related crime is discussed further in Part III.A of this Note.

[96]   *See Sofsky*, 287 F.3d at 126–27. The court suggested that a more focused restriction, limited to pornography sites and images, could be enforced by unannounced inspections of the defendant's premises and examination of material stored on his or her computer and software. *Id.* at 127. In addition, the court noted that the government could conduct a sting operation on the defendant—"surreptitiously inviting him [or her] to respond to Government placed Internet ads for pornography." *Id.*

[97]   United States v. White, 244 F.3d 1199, 1201 (10th Cir. 2001).

[98]   *Id.* at 1205.

[99]   *Id.*

"possess" were to entail "the concept of use," however, then the condition was overbroad:

That reading would bar White from using a computer at a library to do any research, get a weather forecast, or read a newspaper online. Under these circumstances, the special condition is "greater than necessary," and fails to balance the competing interests the sentencing court must consider.[100]

The court clearly views the Internet as an essential tool with many basic uses, and, as in *Peterson* and *Sofsky*, associates it with other fundamental resources: "The communication facilitated by this technology may be likened to that of the telephone. Its instant link to information is akin to opening a book."[101]

In this same vein, the Third Circuit denied an Internet ban where a felon pled guilty to possession and receipt of child pornography,[102] which ostensibly did not involve the Internet.[103] The court relied heavily on *Sofsky* for the proposition that forbidding the felon, Robb Walker Freeman, from possessing a computer or using any online computer service without written permission of his probation officer was too great a deprivation of liberty.[104] Furthermore, the court noted that it was not necessary to prevent "access to email or benign internet usage, when a more focused restriction, limited to pornography sites and images, can be enforced by unannounced inspections of material stored on Freeman's hard drive or removable disks."[105]

Evidently, some courts have focused on the nature of the Internet as an indispensable tool with many practical and commonplace uses in rendering their decisions about conditions of supervised release that ban or severely restrict Internet use.[106] Even in situations where the Internet played a role in the commission of the crime, these courts have deemed a ban on

---

[100] *Id.* at 1206 (citation omitted).
[101] *Id.* at 1207.
[102] United States v. Freeman, 316 F.3d 386, 392 (3d Cir. 2003).
[103] *Id* at 387.
[104] *See id.* at 391–92.
[105] *Id.* at 392.
[106] *E.g., Freeman,* 316 F.3d 386; *Sofsky,* 287 F.3d 122; United States v. Peterson, 248 F.3d 79 (2d Cir. 2001); *White,* 244 F.3d 1199.

Internet use as a greater deprivation of liberty than allowed under the supervised release guidelines.[107] Conversely, other courts have focused on the use of the Internet as essential tool to the commission of the crime in reviewing, and often upholding, Internet use prohibitions instituted by sentencing courts.[108]

B. *The Internet as a Tool of Crime and the Protection of the Public*

When the trial court in *United States v. Mitnick* imposed supervised release conditions on the infamous computer hacker Kevin Mitnick, preventing his use of computers without probation officer approval, he challenged the sentence as restrictive of his First Amendment rights.[109] The U.S. Court of Appeals for the Ninth Circuit upheld the conditions in a terse, unreported opinion, stating simply: "[T]he conditions imposed are reasonably related to legitimate sentencing goals and are no more restrictive than necessary."[110] Mitnick broke into computer networks of large corporations and stole software, acts that necessitated the use of computers and the Internet.[111] The Ninth Circuit relied on the broad sentencing discretion of the district court to dismiss Mitnick's challenge, indicating that it viewed his computer use a threat to the public.[112] This leads to the inference that the court considered the Internet an essential tool of Mitnick's crimes, thus justifying the ban.

In *United States v. Crandon*, another instance of an appellate court upholding an Internet restriction, Richard Crandon pled guilty to one count of receiving child pornography.[113] His crime, however, entailed much more than downloading illicit material; Crandon met a fourteen-year-old girl online, ultimately meeting

---

[107] *E.g.*, *Sofsky*, 287 F.3d 122; *White*, 244 F.3d 1199.

[108] *E.g.*, United States v. Harding, No. 02-2102, 2003 U.S. App. LEXIS 1371 (3d Cir. Jan. 28, 2003); United States v. Paul, 274 F.3d 155 (5th Cir. 2001); United States v. Crandon, 173 F.3d 122 (3d Cir. 1999); United States v. Mitnick, No. 97-50365, 1998 U.S. App. LEXIS 10836 (9th Cir. May 20, 1998).

[109] 1998 U.S. App. LEXIS 10836, at *2.

[110] *Id.*

[111] *See* Richtel, *supra* note 1.

[112] *Mitnick*, 1998 U.S. App. LEXIS 10836, at *2.

[113] *Crandon*, 173 F.3d at 124.

her in person to have sexual relations and take photographs of the encounter.[114] Crandon and the girl repeatedly spoke over the telephone after the visit, discussing the prospect of his return to Minnesota to bring her to his home in New Jersey.[115] Crandon returned to Minnesota the following month, at which time he and the girl departed for New Jersey, although along the way he learned that authorities were looking for them and, thus, he sent her back to Minnesota.[116]

The Third Circuit acknowledged that "computer networks and the Internet will continue to become an omnipresent aspect of American life."[117] The court, however, rejected Crandon's argument that the supervised release condition banning access to the Internet or other computer networks without approval of a probation officer was not logically related to his offense, violating his rights of speech and association.[118] The court also rejected the argument that the restrictions preventing "access to any form of computer network"[119] should be vacated because they hindered Crandon's employment opportunities due to the extent in which businesses have "integrate[d] computers and the Internet into the workplace."[120] Rather, the court concluded that the restrictions on employment and First Amendment freedoms were acceptable because the special condition "[was] narrowly tailored and [was] directly related to deterring Crandon and protecting the public."[121]

The court apparently found a direct relationship between the Internet and the crime, unlike in *Peterson*,[122] and was more influenced by the defendant's use of the Internet to victimize a young girl than by his argument that the restriction would impede his employment opportunities or constitutional rights.[123] Thus, the

---

[114] *Id.* at 125.
[115] *Id.*
[116] *Id.*
[117] *Id.* at 128.
[118] *See id.* at 127–28.
[119] *Id.* at 125.
[120] *See id.* at 127–28.
[121] *Id.* at 128.
[122] *See supra* notes 81–82 and accompanying text.
[123] *See Crandon*, 173 F.3d at 128 (rejecting defendant's argument that "as businesses continue to integrate computers and the Internet into the workplace, the special condition

court emphasized that the Internet was the instrument by which Crandon developed a sexual relationship with the fourteen-year-old girl, from their initial meeting to their continuous communication that resulted in his visit to Minnesota.[124] The fact that the Internet was not merely incidental to the commission of the crime led the court to affirm the sentence as necessary to deter such future conduct and protect the public.[125]

In *United States v. Harding*,[126] the Third Circuit followed its decision in *Crandon* to uphold an Internet ban imposed on Jamie Harding, a man who was found with numerous photographs, computer disks, and videotapes containing pornographic images of children.[127]   The district court imposed supervised release conditions banning him from accessing the Internet without the prior approval of his probation officer.[128] Although Harding was apparently permitted to own a computer, the court required him to consent to unannounced inspections of his computer equipment by a probation officer to ensure that he did not connect to an Internet server.[129]

The opinion did not clarify whether the images found on Harding's computer were retrieved from or distributed to others through the Internet;[130] the court did indicate that he possessed a scanner,[131] though that could simply mean that Harding preferred to store the images digitally. Nonetheless, the court compared this instance to *Crandon* to conclude that the ban was justifiable given

---

may hamper his employment opportunities upon release, as well as limit his freedoms of speech and association").

[124] *See id.* at 125, 127.

[125] *Id.* at 127–28. The court stated:

> In this case, Crandon used the Internet as a means to develop an illegal sexual relationship with a young girl over a period of several months. Given these compelling circumstances, it seems clear that the condition of release limiting Crandon's Internet access is related to the dual aims of deterring him from recidivism and protecting the public.

Id.

[126] No. 02-2102, 2003 U.S. App. LEXIS 1371 (3d Cir. Jan. 28, 2003).

[127] *Id.* at *2.

[128] *Id.* at *2–*3.

[129] *Id.* at *3.

[130] *See id.* at *2.

[131] *Id.*

the interest in protecting the public and deterring future criminal conduct,[132] although in *Crandon* the Internet was used to contact a future victim directly.[133] Based on this distinction, *Harding* does not seem to fall "within the teachings of *Crandon*,"[134] and seems to contradict the Third Circuit's decision in *Freeman* (decided the same month as *Harding*) rejecting a ban on Internet use for a defendant who had been convicted of possessing child pornography that he had loaded into his computer.[135] In fact, the Third Circuit distinguished *Freeman* from *Crandon* since there was no evidence that Freeman had used the Internet to contact young children,[136] which also may have been the case in *Harding*.[137] Furthermore, *Harding* contradicts the Second Circuit's reasoning in *Sofsky*, which the *Freeman* court cited for the proposition that a ban on Internet use would prevent access to "benign internet usage."[138] In any event, there is some inconsistency within the Third Circuit as to what circumstances support Internet use restrictions as a condition of supervised release.

In *United States v. Paul*, Ronald Scott Paul was restricted from using computers or the Internet in the wake of his prison sentence for knowing possession of child pornography after numerous pornographic images of children were found on his personal computer, in addition to the photographs, magazines, books, and videotapes containing similar images that were found in his home.[139] Paul admitted to having downloaded the computer images from the Internet, but argued that the prohibition was too broad and would restrict his ability to use computers and the Internet for legitimate purposes.[140] The court, however, chose instead to focus on Paul's use of the Internet and e-mail "to encourage exploitation of children by seeking out fellow 'boy

---

[132] *See id.* at *4–*5.
[133] *See supra* text accompanying note 114.
[134] *Harding*, 2003 U.S. App. LEXIS 1371, at *5.
[135] United States v. Freeman, 316 F.3d 386, 391–92 (3d Cir. 2003).
[136] *Id.* at 392.
[137] *See supra* text accompanying notes 130–31.
[138] *Freeman*, 316 F.3d at 392.
[139] United States v. Paul, 274 F.3d 155, 158 (5th Cir. 2001).
[140] *Id.* at 168.

lovers' and providing them with advice on how to find and obtain access to 'young friends,'"[141] and to "advise fellow consumers of child pornography how to 'scout' single, dysfunctional parents and gain access to their children and to solicit the participation of like-minded individuals in trips to 'visit' children in Mexico."[142] As in *Crandon*, to which the court in this case analogized, much of Paul's predatory behavior occurred through the Internet, which he used to "'initiate and facilitate a pattern of criminal conduct and victimization.'"[143] Thus, the court reasoned that Paul's crime was, in fact, very closely related to the Internet and affirmed the ban.[144]

The discussion above indicates that the role of the Internet in the commission of the crime is a crucial factor in the determination of whether to uphold a supervised release condition prohibiting its use, although this factor is not necessarily dispositive.[145] For example, the *Sofsky* court overturned the Internet ban for a felon who used the Internet to download child pornography and to exchange it with others, focusing instead on the potential of such a restriction to infringe upon the defendant's liberty.[146] Sofsky's conduct, however, was not as egregious as the use of the Internet to contact potential victims as in *Crandon*,[147] or to teach others how to do the same as in *Paul*.[148] Nonetheless, other factors bearing on whether courts should ban certain offenders from using the Internet altogether must be explored further.

III. CRITERIA FOR DEVELOPING INTERNET USE RESTRICTIONS

Internet bans only should be permitted in circumstances where they are warranted based upon narrow criteria because they have the potential to inhibit access to a number of resources with respect

---

[141] *Id.* at 169.

[142] *Id.* at 168.

[143] *Id.* at 169 (quoting United States v. White, 244 F.3d 1199, 1205 (10th Cir. 2001)). Although the *Paul* court quoted the language of *White*, a case that overturned an Internet ban, it distinguished *White* factually and rejected its reasoning. *See id.* at 169–70.

[144] *Id.* at 168–70.

[145] *See, e.g.*, United States v. Sofsky, 287 F.3d 122, 124 (2d Cir. 2002).

[146] *See supra* notes 84–96.

[147] *See supra* notes 113–25.

[148] *See supra* notes 139–44.

to many different fundamental uses, such as communication, education, governance, and information gathering.[149] While terms of supervised release tend to last only a few years,[150] restrictions on Internet use may prevent people from further developing important skills, such as those required in the workplace.[151] Such commonplace uses of the Internet are rapidly becoming essential and should not so readily be denied.

As such, courts should consider the manner in which the Internet was employed to commit a crime when fashioning supervised release conditions that restrict Internet use. Attempts have been made to create these distinctions, which focus on the nature of the underlying offense as well as the nature of the Internet use.[152] In addition, comparing the deprivation of Internet use to other types of conditions that implicate certain rights, liberties, and commonplace activities is a useful method of analyzing the way in which courts exercise their sentencing discretion.

A. Internet Crime Versus Internet-Related Crime

While beneficial in countless ways, the advent of new technologies over recent decades also has given rise to numerous new types of crimes as well as new methods of committing crime in general.[153] Accordingly, there have been attempts to reform

---

[149] *See* discussion *supra* Part I.B.

[150] *See, e.g.*, WILLIAM J. SABOL ET AL., DEP'T OF JUSTICE, OFFENDERS RETURNING TO FEDERAL PRISON, 1986–97, at 2 (2000) (stating that the average term of supervised release imposed during 1998 was forty-one months), *available at* http://www.ojp.-usdoj.gov/bjs/abstract/orfp97.htm (last revised Sept. 22, 2000).

[151] *See supra* notes 60–63 and accompanying text.

[152] *See* discussion *supra* Part III.A.

[153] *See* Mark D. Rasch, *Criminal Law and the Internet, in* THE INTERNET AND BUSINESS: A LAWYER'S GUIDE TO THE EMERGING LEGAL ISSUES 141, 141 (Joseph F. Ruh, Jr. ed., 1996) ("While computer technology permits business to work more efficiently, communicate more effectively, and become more productive, the computer, as a tool, permits those with less benevolent intention to evade the law. What's worse, with the advent of new information technologies, more information—and more sensitive information—is stored in a manner which makes it more accessible to more individuals—not all of whom have purely wholesome motives.").

criminal laws to sufficiently address computer crime.[154]   In the process, distinctions between "computer crime" and "computer related crime" have arisen.[155]   Similarly, a significant distinction could be drawn between Internet crime and Internet-related crime, based on the respective relationships between the crimes and the Internet.[156]

In attempting to define computer crime, one commentator suggested, "computer crime is a criminal offense for which the knowledge of computers is necessary for the successful commission of the offense."[157]   An analysis of this definition states:

> Such a definition distinguishes true *computer crimes* from *computer related crimes* in which computers are used as tools or targets of the criminal offense, but for which knowledge of the workings of a computer is not essential for the successful commission of the offense. Thus, a chain letter typed on a computer's word processing software and thereafter mailed to victims of a fraudulent solicitation is probably not a computer crime, despite the fact that knowledge of the word processing software facilitated the commission of the offense. A similar chain letter sent out over the Internet, and soliciting electronic funds transfers comes closer to a true computer crime especially if responses are electronically sorted or manipulated.[158]

---

[154] DEP'T OF JUSTICE, COMPUTER CRIME & INTELL. PROP. SECTION, THE NATIONAL INFORMATION INFRASTRUCTURE PROTECTION ACT OF 1996: LEGISLATIVE ANALYSIS (1997) (discussing why new computer crime legislation was needed), *available at* http://www.usdoj.gov/criminal/cybercrime/1030_anal.html (last updated July 31, 2003).

[155] *See* Rasch, *supra* note 153, at 143.

[156] For instance, Kevin Mitnick's use of the Internet to hack into computer networks of large corporations should be categorized as an Internet crime, because the crime itself requires Internet technology. *See infra* notes 162–63 and accompanying text.   By contrast, Gregory Sofsky's crime—the receipt of child pornography—did not specifically require the Internet, although the Internet facilitated the crime's commission. *See* United States v. Sofsky, 287 F.3d 122, 124 (2d Cir. 2002). Thus, such acts should be considered Internet-related crime. *See infra* notes 164–65 and accompanying text.

[157] *See* Rasch, *supra* note 153, at 143 (citing DONN PARKER, FIGHTING COMPUTER CRIME (1983)).

[158] *Id.*

Under these criteria, it would seem as if the simple use of the Internet to download illegal material, such as child pornography, would be considered an Internet-related crime. Conversely, a more elaborate scheme requiring use of Internet technology to carry out the crime, such as hacking into protected servers and databases, would rise to the level of direct Internet crime.

Furthermore, in addressing the need to update criminal laws with respect to computers, the Computer Crime and Intellectual Property Section of the U.S. Department of Justice ("DOJ") has identified the different ways in which computers are connected to crime:

> First, a computer may be used as a target of the offense. In these cases, the criminal's goal is to steal information from, or cause damage to a computer, computer system, or computer network. Second, the computer may be a tool of the offense. This occurs when an individual uses a computer to facilitate some traditional offense such as fraud . . . . Last, computers are sometimes incidental to the offense, but significant to law enforcement because they contain evidence of a crime.[159]

In addition, the DOJ has indicated that "[a]lthough certain computer crimes appear simply to be old crimes committed in new ways (e.g., the bank teller who uses a computer program to steal money is still committing bank fraud), some computer offenses find their genesis in [] new technologies and must be specifically addressed by statute."[160] Thus, some crimes involving computers are illegal due to underlying criminal conduct, but others arise out of specific use of certain technologies and could not be committed otherwise.[161]

The above analysis regarding computers may be applied to the Internet to demonstrate that there are people who use the Internet to commit crimes that do not require online resources, crimes that

---

[159] DEP'T OF JUSTICE, *supra* note 154.

[160] *See id.*; Rasch, *supra* note 153, at 143.

[161] *See* Jo-Ann M. Adams, Comment, *Controlling Cyberspace: Applying the Computer Fraud and Abuse Act to the Internet*, 12 SANTA CLARA COMPUTER & HIGH TECH. L.J. 403, 409–15 (1996) (discussing different categories of crimes committed on the Internet).

they might be predisposed to commit in any case, and there are people who commit crimes that require Internet technology.[162] For example, in Kevin Mitnick's infamous acts of hacking into corporate networks, computers and the Internet would be identified under this analysis as both a target and a tool of the offense.[163] Other cases are less clear on whether the Internet was a necessary tool, or merely incidental to the crime, however. In the Internet child pornography cases such as *Sofsky*, *White*, and *Harding*, in which the defendants used the Internet to download or order illicit materials,[164] computers and the Internet could be viewed either as incidental to the commission of the crime of possessing child pornography, or as tools to facilitate offenses that could have been committed in other ways.[165]

This is a fine distinction, and although courts have broad discretion in imposing supervised release conditions, they should be careful in identifying which type of Internet use has occurred and whether banning Internet use will help deter the conduct underlying the offense, given the Internet's pervasiveness and its many practical functions.[166] For example, the Third Circuit likely would have reached a different result in *Harding*—in which it upheld an Internet ban for a defendant convicted of possessing child pornography on his computer[167]—if it had carefully scrutinized the extent to which the Internet was a required element in the commission of the offense, since child pornography has existed long before the advent of the Internet and surely can be obtained elsewhere.[168] *Crandon* and *Paul* are less clear, but in

---

[162] *Compare* United States v. Harding, No. 02-2102, 2003 U.S. App. LEXIS 1371, at *1 (3d Cir. Jan. 28, 2003) (receiving child pornography), *with* United States v. Mitnick, No. 97-50365, 1998 U.S. App. LEXIS 10836, at *1 (9th Cir. May 20, 1998) (possession of unauthorized access devices with intent to defraud).

[163] *See supra* notes 109–12 and accompanying text.

[164] *Harding* upheld an Internet ban, while *Sofsky* and *White* overturned the restrictions. *See* discussion *supra* Part II.

[165] See *supra* text accompanying notes 85, 97, 127 and accompanying text for descriptions of the offenses in these cases.

[166] *See* discussion *supra* Part I.B.

[167] *See supra* text accompanying notes 126–38.

[168] *See* Devon Ishii Peterson, Comment, *Child Pornography on the Internet: The Effect of Section 230 of the Communications Decency Act of 1996 on Tort Recovery for Victims Against Internet Service Providers*, 24 U. HAW. L. REV. 763, 766–67 (2002) (discussing

those cases the courts perceived the defendants' respective uses of the Internet to solicit contact with future victims (*Crandon*) or to find others with similar tastes willing to teach them how to target potential victims (*Paul*) as serious threats to public safety—threats uniquely furthered by the Internet.[169] Certainly, these cases come closer to actual Internet crime than the crime in *Harding*, though they do not rise to the level of the crime in *Mitnick*, in which the use of Internet technology was essential to the hacker's illegal breach of secure data systems.[170]

A notable consideration in the analysis of Internet crime and Internet-related crime is that the anonymity, or pseudonymity as it were,[171] afforded by the Internet likely emboldens offenders whose shame or fear of getting caught might otherwise make them more reluctant to commit certain offenses.[172] In *Crandon*, the court identified the Internet as an "omnipresent" part of American life,[173] but upheld the Internet ban due to its role in initiating contact with the victim.[174] As the *Peterson* court noted, however, use of the telephone to commit a crime such as fraud would not justify a condition of probation barring use of the telephone altogether,[175] and other courts have agreed.[176] Interestingly, in *Crandon*, in which the defendant used the Internet to develop a rapport and eventually a sexual relationship with a young girl, the defendant and the girl communicated regularly over the telephone after their

---

the history of commercial child pornography); Lesli C. Esposito, Note, *Regulating the Internet: The New Battle Against Child Pornography*, 30 CASE W. RES. J. INT'L L. 541, 542–43 (1998) (naming several child pornographic magazines and noting that child pornography exists in many forms).

[169] *See supra* notes 124–25, 142–44 and accompanying text.

[170] *See* Greg Miller, *Hacking Legend's Sign-Off*, L.A. TIMES, Mar. 18, 1999, at A1 (discussing Mitnick's crimes).

[171] *See* Rasch, *supra* note 153, at 143.

[172] *See id.* at 144 (discussing how the anonymity provided by the Internet can impact a user's behavior).

[173] United States v. Crandon, 173 F.3d 122, 128 (3d Cir. 1999) ("Unquestionably, computer networks and the Internet will continue to become an omnipresent aspect of American life.").

[174] *See supra* notes 117–25 and accompanying text.

[175] *See supra* text accompanying note 78.

[176] *See, e.g.*, United States v. White, 244 F.3d 1199, 1207 (10th Cir. 2001); *supra* text accompanying note 101.

initial encounter.[177] Nevertheless, the fact that Crandon used the telephone to maintain contact with his young victim did not factor into the sentencing determination, though perhaps it should have in light of the court's justification of the Internet ban.[178] The court either viewed the Internet as the principal and more insidious device with which Crandon preyed on the young girl to solicit sexual contact, or it took for granted the essential nature of the telephone.[179] The role of the Internet in the commission of the crime is an important consideration with respect to sentencing conditions, and courts tending to enforce Internet bans seem to have done so based on the ease with which people can communicate and obtain information online.[180]

Whether the Internet facilitated the crime was a crucial part of the conclusions of the courts, particularly for those courts putting less emphasis on the extent of the Internet's role in modern society.[181] As discussed above, however, the Internet has become an indispensable medium, access to which should not readily be denied.[182] For this reason, courts carefully should distinguish Internet crime from Internet-related crime, as the inquiry with the latter relates more to the underlying offense for which the defendant has been convicted, and craft supervised release conditions more narrowly in order to prevent deprivation of technology whose prevalence and usefulness continues to grow exponentially.

---

[177] *See Crandon,* 173 F.3d at 125, 127.

[178] *See id.* at 127–28.

[179] *Cf.* United States v. Peterson, 248 F.3d 79, 83 (2d Cir. 2001) (vacating Internet restrictions and stating that "[a]lthough a defendant might use the telephone to commit fraud, this would not justify a condition of probation that includes an absolute bar on the use of telephones"); United States v. White, 244 F.3d 1199, 1207 (10th Cir. 2001) (vacating Internet restrictions and stating that the communication facilitated by Internet technology "may be likened to that of the telephone").

[180] *See* discussion *supra* Part II.B.

[181] *See, e.g.,* United States v. Paul, 274 F.3d 155, 169–70 (5th Cir. 2001) ("[W]e reject the *White* court's implication that an absolute prohibition on accessing computers or the Internet is per se an unacceptable condition of supervised release, simply because such a prohibition might prevent a defendant from using a computer at the library to 'get a weather forecast' or to 'read a newspaper online' during the supervised release term. (quoting United States v. White, 244 F.3d 1199, 1201 (10th Cir. 2001))).

[182] *See* discussion *supra* Part I.B.

B. Supervised Release Conditions With Respect to Other Rights and Liberties

A great impediment to calling upon sentencing courts to limit the use of Internet bans, regardless of the role of the Internet in the commission of the crime, is that previous arguments against supervised release restrictions as unconstitutional or as intruding on other perceived liberties have been largely rejected.[183] In the decisions discussed above, which overturned Internet bans, none of the courts rejected the restrictions as unconstitutional, but rather cited to the sentencing guidelines standard that the condition must not involve a "greater deprivation of liberty than reasonably necessary."[184] In general, First Amendment challenges to probation conditions, such as those in *Mitnick*[185] and *Crandon*,[186] have been unsuccessful. The *Crandon* court cited the U.S. Court of Appeals for the Sixth Circuit's ruling in *United States v. Ritter* for the proposition that "'even though supervised release conditions may affect constitutional rights such as First Amendment protections, most restrictions are valid if directly related to advancing the individual's rehabilitation and to protecting the public from recidivism.'"[187]

1. Freedom of Association

Several cases have addressed restrictions on freedom of association,[188] a right that specifically relates to the function of the Internet as a communication and information-sharing medium.[189]

---

[183] *See, e.g.*, United States v. Crandon, 173 F.3d 122, 127–28 (3d Cir. 1999); United States v. Mitnick, No. 97-50365, 1998 U.S. App. LEXIS 10836, at *2 (9th Cir. May 20, 1998).

[184] *See supra* note 28 and accompanying text; *see also* discussion *supra* Part II.A.

[185] *Mitnick*, 1998 U.S. App. LEXIS 10836, at *2.

[186] *Crandon*, 173 F.3d at 127–28.

[187] *Id.* at 128 (quoting United States v. Ritter, 118 F.3d 502, 504 (6th Cir. 1997)).

[188] *E.g.*, United States v. Bolinger, 940 F.2d 478 (9th Cir. 1991); United States v. Showalter, 933 F.2d 573, 574 (7th Cir. 1991); Malone v. United States, 502 F.2d 554 (9th Cir. 1974); *see also* Stephen S. Cook, *Selected Constitutional Questions Regarding Federal Offender Supervision*, 23 NEW ENG. J. CRIM. & CIV. CONFINEMENT 1, 3–5 (1997) (discussing First Amendment concerns arising in the federal sentencing and probation process).

[189] *See* Hyne, *supra* note 68, at 239–40 (discussing First Amendment challenges to the restriction of computer access as a condition of probation or supervised release).

Thus, it can be argued that an Internet ban would prevent association with those generally contacted through this medium.[190] The two principal concerns supporting limitations on freedom of association are rehabilitation and public safety.[191] In addition, freedom of association cases relate to supervised release conditions that require filtering Internet use or permitting access subject to probation officer approval, since in both instances the restrictions seek to prevent specific activities or contact related to the offense.[192]

In one case, relied upon by the *Mitnick* court in its rejection of the constitutional challenge presented, a defendant pleaded guilty to "being a convicted felon in possession of a firearm" and was sentenced to a term of imprisonment followed by a period of supervised release during which he could not be involved "in any motorcycle club activities."[193] The Ninth Circuit rejected the defendant's freedom of association challenge, referring to the sentencing court's broad discretion as well as to a judicial articulation of sentencing principles: "Probation conditions may seek to prevent reversion into a former crime-inducing life-style by barring contact with old haunts and associates, even though the activities may be legal."[194] Similarly, another court upheld the restriction preventing a white supremacist leader who pled guilty to possession of an unregistered firearm from associating with skinheads or any neo-Nazi or white supremacist organization.[195] The defendant did not appeal the condition of not associating with white supremacist organizations, but he did appeal the requirement barring association with other skinheads or neo-Nazis.[196] The sentencing court explained the correlation between the restriction and the crime: "'Because those groups embrace violence and the

---

[190]   *Crandon*, 173 F.3d at 128.

[191]   *See Bolinger*, 940 F.2d at 480 (holding that restriction on defendant's association rights is valid if primarily designed to meet the ends of rehabilitation and protection of the public, and reasonably related to such ends) (citing United States v. Terrigno, 838 F.2d 371, 374 (9th Cir. 1988)).

[192]   *See* Hyne, *supra* note 68, at 240 (discussing how Internet use can be considered "associating").

[193]   *Bolinger*, 940 F.2d at 479 (9th Cir. 1991).

[194]   *Id.* at 480 (citing Malone v. United States, 502 F.2d 554, 556–57 (9th Cir. 1974)).

[195]   *See* United States v. Showalter, 933 F.2d 573, 574 (7th Cir. 1991).

[196]   *Id.*

threat of violence as a method of advancing their views, [the court found] that [his] association with them would create a high likelihood that [he] would be drawn into that same behavior.. . .'"[197] Affirming this part of the sentencing court's ruling, the appellate court found that "the district court was correct that [the defendant] need[ed] to be separated from other members of white supremacist groups to have a chance of staying out of trouble."[198]

These cases are relevant in the Internet context because the freedom to use the Internet, while not a constitutional right itself, necessarily implicates freedom of speech and association.[199] These cases make clear, however, that a restriction will be upheld despite a constitutional challenge if it appears likely that a certain forum could lead to future misconduct of the same sort, a consideration underlying the supervised release conditions upheld in *Crandon* and *Paul*.[200] In *Crandon*, for example, the defendant had utilized the Internet in a predatory manner;[201] the *Paul* defendant went online partly to counsel others on victimizing children.[202] Likewise, the *Mitnick* court upheld the restriction on computer-related employment in order to protect the public by preventing the defendant from engaging in his former criminal activities.[203]

Because several of the Internet ban cases discussed above pertain to child pornography, an examination of freedom of association cases of this kind is worthwhile, especially with respect to the public safety element that such cases necessarily

---

[197]   *Id.* at 575.

[198]   *Id.* at 575–76.

[199]   *See* Hyne, *supra* note 68, at 239–40.

[200]   *See supra* notes 113–25, 139–44 and accompanying text.

[201]   United States v. Crandon, 173 F.3d 122, 125 (3d Cir. 1999) (beginning a sexual relationship with a fourteen-year-old girl).

[202]   United States v. Paul, 274 F.3d 155, 158 (5th Cir. 2001).

[203]   *See Mitnick*, 1998 U.S. App. LEXIS 10836, at *3–*4. Mitnick served five years in federal prison for stealing software and altering data at Motorola, Novell, Nokia, Sun Microsystems, and the University of Southern California. Associated Press, *Hacker Back On Air*, *supra* note 8. Prosecutors accused him of causing tens of millions of dollars in damage to corporate computer networks. *Id.*

implicate.[204] The Ninth Circuit in *United States v. Bee*[205] upheld a supervised release condition whereby a child molester (1) could not have contact with any minors without probation officer approval; (2) could not loiter within a certain distance of schools, parks, playgrounds, arcades, or any other places primarily used by children; and (3) could not possess any sexually stimulating material considered inappropriate or patronize any place where such material is available.[206] The facts in cases such *Bee* and *Crandon* make sympathy for the defendant difficult.[207] Although the defendant in *Bee* claimed that the first two conditions were too broad and that the third condition was a First Amendment violation and unrelated to his offense, the court upheld all three restrictions.[208] As to the conditions barring unapproved contact with children and preventing the defendant from loitering in places primarily used by children, the court quoted the defendant's own acknowledgement that he would be expected to "'err on the side of avoiding places that the probation officer or the court might deem unacceptable.'"[209]

The justification for upholding the association restrictions is easier to grasp than the rationale for affirming the restriction on sexually stimulating material, apparently including legal adult pornography.[210] This relates to the argument that the restriction on Internet usage denies access to legitimate, legal material, an argument to which some courts have been more sympathetic than others, depending in part on the relationship of the Internet use to

---

[204] Cook, *supra* note 188, at 4 (stating that restrictions of association rights have been upheld based on the rationale that the association would encourage the individual to repeat criminal conduct).

[205] 162 F.3d 1232 (9th Cir. 1998).

[206] *Id.* at 1234.

[207] In *Crandon*, for example, the defendant initiated a sexual relationship with a fourteen-year-old girl through the Internet. *See supra* notes 113–116 and accompanying text.

[208] *Bee*, 162 F.3d at 1234–36.

[209] *Id.* at 1235–36.

[210] *See* United States v. Paul, 274 F.3d 155, 169–70 (5th Cir. 2001) (rejecting defendant's argument that prohibition on accessing Internet is unacceptable because such a ban might impede legitimate uses of the Internet).

the offense.[211] Furthermore, *Bee* involved overriding public safety concerns, as indicated by the court's expectation that the defendant err on the side of caution by avoiding places that probably would be considered unacceptable, but that had not yet been designated as such.[212] The courts in *Crandon* and *Paul* employed similar reasoning to affirm Internet ban conditions, based on the nature of the defendants' respective Internet uses and the great potential for harm to the public, particularly children, if they were to revert to their former behavior.[213]

The court in *United States v. Loy* reached a different conclusion with respect to legal adult material.[214] In *Loy*, Ray Donald Loy was convicted for possession of child pornography, some of which he had a role in producing, with a sentence that included supervised release conditions prohibiting possession of any pornography and unsupervised contact with minors.[215] The court upheld the contact element of the condition, excluding accidental contact such as in public places from the condition, but overturned the proscription on pornography, holding that it was overbroad.[216] The court condoned a restriction on possession of even legal pornography, as in *Bee*, but it found that the restriction had to be more carefully crafted since, as originally drafted, the policymaking power was granted to the probation officer and the condition failed to put Loy on notice of what material he could or could not access.[217] The court also noted that "[a] probationary condition is not 'narrowly tailored' if it restricts First Amendment freedoms without any resulting benefit to public safety."[218] Thus, while supervised release conditions may restrict fundamental rights

---

[211] *Compare* United States v. Peterson, 248 F.3d 79, 80–81 (2d Cir. 2001) (vacating an Internet ban imposed on a felon who had pled guilty to bank larceny, was previously convicted of incest, and had accessed legal adult pornography on his home computer), *with* United States v. Crandon, 173 F.3d 122, 127–28 (3d Cir. 1999) (upholding Internet restrictions in light of fact that defendant used the Internet to develop an illegal sexual relationship).

[212] *Bee*, 162 F.3d at 1234–36.

[213] *See supra* Part II.B.

[214] United States v. Loy, 237 F.3d 251, 254 (3d Cir. 2001).

[215] *Id.* at 254–55.

[216] *See id.* at 254, 266–67.

[217] *See id.* at 266–67.

[218] *Id.* at 266.

in some instances, they should not do so unnecessarily.[219] Yet, this is the potential result of imposing Internet bans that only permit use with probation officer approval, particularly where such use does not entail a direct threat to the public. At the same time, however, such arrangements may provide less restrictive alternatives to blanket Internet bans.[220]

Filtering Internet content and subjecting otherwise banned Internet use to probation officer approval are analogous to freedom of association limitations, since such conditions prohibit defendants from associating with certain people or accessing certain types of material.[221] In *Mitnick*, the court rejected the defendant's contention that the requirement of probation officer approval for access to computers and computer-related equipment was too broad: "The fact that Mitnick may engage in otherwise prohibited conduct with the probation officer's approval makes the conditions imposed less restrictive [than] an outright ban on such conduct."[222] Yet, several of the courts emphasizing the pervasiveness of Internet use in modern society to reject blanket Internet bans have not been persuaded that allowing access through probation officer discretion is a mitigating factor justifying the condition.[223] For example, the *Sofsky* court stated that "[a]lthough

---

[219] *See id.* at 264 (stating that to avoid First Amendment infirmity, a probation condition must be narrowly tailored and directly related to the goals of protecting the public and promoting a defendant's rehabilitation) (citing *Crandon*, 173 F.3d at 128). The Supreme Court in *Grayned v. City of Rockford*, 408 U.S. 104 (1972), opined on the purpose behind the requirement that laws be reasonably precise:

> First, because we assume that man is free to steer between lawful and unlawful conduct, we insist that laws give the person of ordinary intelligence a reasonable opportunity to know what is prohibited, so that he may act accordingly.... Second, ... [a] vague law impermissibly delegates basic policy matters to policemen, judges, and juries for resolution on an ad hoc and subjective basis.... Third ... where a vague statute abuts upon sensitive areas of basic First Amendment freedoms, it operates to inhibit the exercise of [those] freedoms.

Id. at 108–09, *noted in Loy*, 237 F.3d at 262.

[220] *See* Richtel, *supra* note 1 (discussing technologies allowing a probation officer to remotely monitor an offender's computer activity).

[221] *See supra* note 192 and accompanying text.

[222] United States v. Mitnick, No. 97-50365, 1998 U.S. App. LEXIS 10836, at *3 n.1 (9th Cir. May 20, 1998).

[223] *See supra* notes 96, 104–05 and accompanying text.

the condition prohibiting Sofsky from accessing a computer or the Internet without his probation officer's approval is reasonably related to the purposes of his sentencing, in light of the nature of his offense, we hold that the condition inflicts a greater deprivation on Sofsky's liberty than reasonably necessary."[224] Furthermore, the court concluded that alternative methods, such as government sting operations or unannounced inspections of his computer, were available to enforce narrower Internet restrictions relating to Sofsky's offense of downloading child pornography and would prevent the denial of access to legitimate uses of the Internet.[225] Thus, the courts in *Mitnick* and *Sofsky* reached very different conclusions with respect to permitting otherwise forbidden Internet access on the condition of probation officer approval, stemming from their views about the Internet and about the Internet's relation to the offenses.[226]

In a similar consideration of alternative ways to police Internet use, the U.S. Court of Appeals for the Tenth Circuit, in remanding *White* to determine the meaning of a sentencing court's Internet use restrictions, explored the possibility of Internet filtering.[227] The Tenth Circuit found that the sentencing court's conditions were potentially overbroad or too narrow.[228] As part of this analysis, the court stated that installation of filtering software into a defendant's computer appropriately could focus an Internet use restriction, but that such an approach was limited by the effectiveness of the technology and the possibility of circumvention by either the technologically savvy user or the user who simply decided to use a different computer.[229] After cautioning against a blanket ban on computer use and commenting on the ubiquity of cyberspace, the court concluded that "any

---

[224] United States v. Sofsky, 287 F.3d 122, 126 (2d Cir. 2002); *see also* United States v. Freeman, 316 F.3d 386, 391–92 (3d Cir. 2003) (citing *Sofsky* for the propositions that (1) probation officer approval does not make a ban on Internet usage less restrictive and (2) there are alternative methods of enforcing more limited use restrictions).

[225] *Sofsky*, 287 F.3d at 126–27.

[226] *See supra* notes 84–96, 109–12 and accompanying text

[227] *See supra* notes 97–101 and accompanying text (discussing United States v. White, 244 F.3d 1199 (10th Cir. 2001)).

[228] *See White*, 244 F.3d at 1205–07.

[229] *See id.* at 1206–07.

condition limiting White's use of a computer or access to the Internet must reflect these realities and permit reasonable monitoring by a probation officer,"[230] without indicating how this should be achieved.

Freedom of association restrictions largely have been upheld as long as they comport with the sentencing guidelines and goals, under which preventing criminal conduct and protecting the public are primary concerns and must be balanced against the liberty interests of the defendant.[231] These decisions do not bode well for the constitutional challenge to Internet bans, which involve similar balancing due to both the nature of Internet use and its perception as a fundamental part of modern society.[232] For example, the *White* court did not overturn the Internet ban based on the defendant's First and Fourteenth Amendment arguments, but instead focused on the meaning of the condition and its potential for overbreadth, given the numerous legitimate and commonplace functions of the Internet.[233] And as the court in *Crandon* concluded, "in this case the restrictions on employment and First Amendment freedoms are permissible because the special condition is narrowly tailored and is directly related to deterring Crandon and protecting the public."[234] If courts are to reject Internet use bans, they are not likely to do so based on constitutional challenges, but rather on an evaluation of the competing interests of the defendant and the public.[235]

2. Driving

Another type of sentencing condition that relates to performing commonplace activities is the revocation of the driver's license of a defendant, particularly with respect to driving under the influence ("DUI") cases.[236] As one article on license suspensions observed,

---

[230] *See id.* at 1207.

[231] *See supra* notes 193–213 and accompanying text.

[232] *See* discussion *supra* Part II.A.

[233] *See White*, 244 F.3d at 1207; *see also* discussion *supra* Part II.A.

[234] *Crandon*, 173 F.3d at 128.

[235] *See* discussion *supra* Part II.A.

[236] *See* Carlos F. Ramirez, Note, *Administrative License Suspensions, Criminal Prosecution and the Double Jeopardy Clause*, 23 FORDHAM URB. L.J. 923, 923 n.6 (1996).

"the livelihood of the defendant and his or her family may be dependent on the ability to operate a motor vehicle."[237] The article further states that

> "[i]n this society where public transportation is either non-existent or is, at best, inadequate and entire commercial shopping areas are located in suburbs surrounding our cities, [a driver's license can no longer be viewed] as merely a privilege which is given by the State and which is subject to revocation at any time."[238]

This correlates to the arguments regarding the ever-increasing use of the Internet for employment-related purposes, since it has become essential to conducting many types of businesses, in addition to its value with respect to communications, research, and commerce.[239] Those denied the use of computers and the Internet may be technologically immobilized, which can hurt their ability to compete, or perhaps even participate, in the modern economy.[240] Although filtering out Web sites related to the defendant's offense or allowing partial access with probation officer approval may mitigate this effect, courts otherwise averse to blanket Internet bans have not been receptive to such conditions and have deemed them overbroad in any event.[241]

Driver's license suspensions in DUI cases, however, often have been upheld based on the interests in protecting the public and deference to the power of designated authorities to regulate licensed activities.[242] The first reason for these sanctions, known as Administrative License Suspension ("ALS"),[243] is to protect the

---

[237] *Id.* at 943.

[238] *Id.* at 950 (quoting Ohio v. Gustafson, No. 94 C.A. 232, 1995 WL 387619, at *5 (Ill. App. Ct. June 27, 1995) (affirming the trial court's dismissal of DUI prosecution subsequent to the suspension of the defendant's drivers license on double jeopardy grounds)). Of course, "for the person living in a city with different modes of transportation, the harm may not be so great. But, for the majority of people in this country, who live in suburbs or rural areas, this can cause substantial or total immobilization." *Id.* at 950 n.181.

[239] *See* discussion *supra* Part I.B.

[240] *See, e.g.*, United States v. Sofsky, 287 F.3d 122, 126 (2d Cir. 2002).

[241] *See* discussion *supra* Part II.A.

[242] *See* Ramirez, *supra* note 236, at 930–36, 951–52.

[243] *See id.* at 923.

public by deterring drunk driving, both by prohibiting the defendant from driving and instilling fear that a license could be suspended as a result such an offense.[244] The prohibition can be analogized to Internet restrictions, since it effectively prevents the defendant from using the tool with which he committed the crime. The DUI offense is the crime itself, however, and cannot be separated into distinct, criminal components, since neither driving a car nor drinking alcohol is by itself a crime.[245] It is the combination of these elements that creates the crime.[246] In contrast, the crimes for which many of the defendants in the Internet cases were convicted did not necessitate the use of the Internet, although it arguably facilitated the behavior in certain instances.[247] Thus, unlike with DUI cases, it is possible with Internet-related offenses to separate the means by which the offense was committed from the crime itself. Moreover, the defendants in the Internet cases, with the exception of *Mitnick*, were guilty of separate, underlying conduct for which there are criminal statutes unrelated to Internet technology.[248]

---

[244] *See id.* at 932–33 (noting cases that have concluded that public safety justifies administrative license suspension statutes).

[245] *See, e.g.*, Villarini & Henry, LLP, *So You Have Been Arrested for DWI in New York?*, *at* http://villariniandhenry.lawoffice.com/articles.htm (last visited Apr. 15, 2004) (listing the "critical elements" of a DWI conviction). The above analysis assumes, respectively, that (1) the driver has a valid license and (2) the drinker is over twenty-one years of age.

[246] *See, e.g.*, N.Y. VEH. & TR. LAW § 1192 (McKinney 1996) (operating a motor vehicle while under the influence of alcohol or drugs).

[247] *E.g.*, United States v. Harding, No. 02-2102, 2003 U.S. App. LEXIS 1371 (3d Cir. Jan. 28, 2003); *Sofsky*, 287 F.3d 122; *White*, 244 F.3d 1199; *see also supra* text accompanying notes 163–65.

[248] *See, e.g.*, United States v. Freeman, 316 F.3d 386, 387 (3d Cir. 2003) (receipt and possession of child pornography); *Harding*, 2003 U.S. App. LEXIS 1371, at *1 (receipt of child pornography); *Sofsky*, 287 F.3d 122, 124 (receipt of child pornography); United States v. Paul, 274 F.3d 155, 157 (5th Cir. 2001) (knowing possession of child pornography); United States v. Peterson, 248 F.3d 79, 80–81 (2d Cir. 2001) (bank larceny, with prior conviction for incest); *White*, 244 F.3d at 1201 (receiving child pornography and violation of condition of supervised release); United States v. Crandon, 173 F.3d 122, 124 (3d Cir. 1999) (receiving child pornography); *see also* discussion *supra* Part II.

The second significant reason advanced for the ALS sanction is that a driver's license is considered a privilege and not a right.[249] This argument contends that "the government reserves the power to revoke a license if the licensee fails to act in accordance with set regulations. In an ALS, the government merely exercises the power to revoke the driving privileges it has afforded."[250] Unlike driving, however, Internet use is not a regulated activity or privilege for which state permission is required. It may not rise to the level of a right, but it is also difficult to argue that Internet use is a privilege granted by a certain entity, as it simply entails obtaining a connection from a commercial service provider, or availing oneself of any other connected computer terminal, for example, in a public library or at most educational institutions.[251] In sum, while the similarities between the nature of Internet use and of driving are clear, the reasons for restricting each activity subsequent to a criminal conviction are evidently quite different. Accordingly, it should be more difficult to restrict Internet use as the result of a conviction for an underlying crime that the Internet facilitated than it is to suspend a license due to driving under the influence, although courts apparently possess great discretion in both instances.[252]

The comparison to other activities that have been limited by supervised release conditions offers a different perspective on Internet use restrictions.[253] As demonstrated through the freedom of association challenges to supervised release conditions, the constitutionality of the condition is irrelevant as long as it is consistent with the criteria of the sentencing guidelines, criteria which afford courts broad discretion in determining constraints where the public interest is at stake.[254] The analogy to driver's

---

[249] *See supra* notes 237–38 and accompanying text; *see also* Ramirez, *supra* note 236, at 935–36.

[250] Ramirez, *supra* note 236, at 936 (citing State *ex rel.* Schwartz v. Kennedy, 904 P.2d 1044, 1056 (N.M. 1995) (rejecting double jeopardy challenge to administrative license revocation hearing)).

[251] *See generally* DEP'T OF COMMERCE, *supra* note 39, at 35–56 (discussing how and when Americans access the Internet and Internet use among young people).

[252] *See* discussion *supra* Part I.A; *see generally* Ramirez, *supra* note 236, at 924–43 (discussing conflicting judicial interpretations with respect to ALS proceedings).

[253] *See* discussion *supra* Parts III.B.1–.2.

[254] *See* discussion *supra* Part III.B.1.

license suspensions in the wake of DUI offenses is not persuasive, as key differences exist in the reasoning and authority behind such conditions.[255] Nonetheless, the courts often have been granted the discretion to make their own decisions.[256]

C. The Significance of the Underlying Crime

Fashioning supervised release conditions entails a great tension between the interests of protecting the public and preventing too great a deprivation of liberty of the individual being sentenced.[257] This same tension applies to the Internet, since it has bestowed numerous benefits upon society as a whole, but also has created new crimes and new manners in which to commit existing crimes.[258] The very sentencing guidelines from which this conflict emerges afford the courts a significant amount of discretion in crafting and reviewing the conditions intended to deter such future criminal conduct.[259]   Some courts have used this discretion ostensibly to prevent certain crimes in which the Internet is viewed as essential to their commission, by restricting or altogether forbidding Internet access.[260]   Other courts, however, have approached the issue differently, viewing the Internet as a part of everyday life and concluding that its deprivation risks too great an infringement on an individual's liberty.[261]

Courts should take care to limit Internet restrictions to those cases where the Internet was a necessary tool of the offense, without which the underlying crime could not have been committed. The goal of the supervised release condition should be to deter the underlying conduct, not to restrict one of many methods by which the crime has been realized—especially when that method does not involve a weapon, per se, but a technology with abundant legitimate uses.[262] In many cases, there is a fine line

---

[255] *See supra* notes 246–48, 250–51 and accompanying text.

[256] *See* Ramirez, *supra* note 236, at 930–36.

[257] *See supra* notes 24–25, 28 for a description of the factors enumerated by the sentencing guidelines with respect to supervised release conditions.

[258] *See supra* text accompanying notes 159–60.

[259] *See* discussion *supra* Part I.A.

[260] *See* discussion *supra* Part II.B.

[261] *See* discussion *supra* Part II.A.

[262] *See* discussion *supra* Part I.B.

between the use of the Internet to facilitate the crime and use that is merely incidental to its commission.[263]

The threshold analysis, thus, should be whether the defendant could have committed the crime without going online to do so. For example, with respect to a hacking crime like that in *Mitnick*, the Internet was both a tool and a target of the crime, and could not have occurred otherwise.[264] *Crandon* is a case where the distinction is less clear, as it is not evident that the defendant could have forged a relationship with his young victim without first befriending her anonymously in an online chat room, as such a relationship may have been rebuffed or altogether avoided in the physical world.[265] In cases such as *Sofsky* and *Harding*, in which the crimes involved possession of child pornography, it is clear that while the Internet has certainly made such illicit material easier to come by, the defendants could have obtained it elsewhere. In view of the unique nature and extensive uses of Internet technology, courts should be wary of such distinctions and formulate supervised release conditions accordingly.

CONCLUSION

Sentencing determinations entail a difficult balancing act, as they are highly fact-specific endeavors that often involve unsympathetic defendants whose liberty becomes less of an interest depending on the nature of the crime. The willingness of courts to use their broad discretion to carefully examine the relationship of the underlying criminal conduct to the involvement of the Internet will likely depend on the extent to which they view the Internet as a fundamental resource, although, as demonstrated, public safety concerns often override such considerations.[266] As the Internet's importance to modern society continues to increase in the coming years and its relationship to individual liberty interests deepens, it will be interesting to examine the direction

---

[263] *See supra* text accompanying notes 163–65, 247.

[264] *See supra* text accompanying notes 159, 163.

[265] *See supra* notes 114–16, 124, 169 and accompanying text.

[266] *See* discussion *supra* Part II.B.

courts follow in establishing supervised release conditions that restrict Internet use.

Part IV
Cyber Security

[14]

WHO'S TO PROTECT CYBERSPACE?

Christopher J. Coyne, Ph.D. & Peter T. Leeson, Ph.D.***

ABSTRACT

Until now, the evolution of cyber security has been largely driven by market demand and has developed in the absence of formal governance. However, in the post-9/11 world and with an increase in cyber attacks, government's role in cyber security has become a major policy issue. This paper contends that economic principles have been excluded from the debate about who should provide cyber security. This paper seeks to fill this gap. We postulate that an analysis of cyber security in the absence of economic considerations is incomplete. Toward this end, we employ several economic concepts in order to offer insight to policymakers involved in this debate. In doing so, we hope to shed light on the most effective means of securing the Internet.

1. INTRODUCTION

Over the past decade, the growth of cyberspace has enabled individuals across the world to become increasingly connected. Table 1, which shows Internet access for different languages, highlights the extent of Internet expansion across borders and cultures:

Language	Internet Access (millions)	Percentage World Population Online	2004 (est. millions)
English	262.3	35.6	280
European Languages	257.4	34.9	328
Asian Languages	216.9	29.4	263
Total Non-English	474.3	64.4	680
Total World	679.7		940

Table 1: *Global Internet Statistics by Language (2003)*[1]

* Department of Economics, Hampden-Sydney College. Email: ccoyne@hsc.edu.
** Department of Economics, West Virginia University. Email: pete.leeson@mail.wvu.edu.

The development and expansion of the Internet has created innumerable new opportunities for access to information, personal interaction and entrepreneurial ventures.[2] Not only have the costs of communication fallen considerably but also, perhaps even more importantly, the sphere of potential trading partners has expanded dramatically creating immense new gains from exchange. Consider, for instance, the increase in eCommerce over the last four years, as illustrated in Table 2:

	2000	2001	2002	2003	Estimated 2004
Total $ (B)	$657.0	$1,233.6	$2,231.2	$3,979.7	$6,789.8

Table 2: *Worldwide eCommerce Growth*[3]

This is a tenfold increase over a four-year period. The online banking industry also highlights the increasing reach of cyberspace. The number of individuals using online banking services has increased 80 percent, from 13 million to 23.2 million, in the period from September 2001 to September 2003.[4] These rising trends illustrate the general fact that the lives of average citizens are becoming increasingly connected to cyberspace. This interconnectedness goes beyond direct interaction with cyberspace and extends to indirect interaction as well. Many of the services that the average individual relies on—water, electricity, mass transportation and other "critical infrastructure"—are linked to cyberspace although the end user may never realize it.[5] From direct interactions on personal computers and business networks to indirect interactions through critical infrastructure, the existence and development of cyber security is of the utmost importance for cyberspace to achieve its full potential.

---

[1] Source: Global Reach (http://www.glreach.com/globstats/index.php3). Note that the "Total World" does not equal the sum of "Total English" and "Total Non-English." This discrepancy is due to an overlap between English and non-English figures. Many users access the Internet in two languages twice. The "Total World" row is lower than the sum to correct for this overlap. For more on the methodology see: http://global-reach.biz/globstats/refs.php3#overlap.

[2] Varian et al conclude that the world wide web contains a textual content equivalent to that contained in 10 to twenty million books (McMillan 2002, p. 156).

[3] Source: Global Reach (http://www.glreach.com/eng/ed/art/2004.ecommerce.php3).

[4] *Nashville Business Journal*, September 22, 2003 (http://www.bizjournals.com/nashville/stories/2003/09/22/daily5.html).

[5] The Patriot Act defines critical infrastructure as: "Systems and assets, whether physical or virtual, so vital to the United States that the incapacity or destruction of such systems and assets would have a debilitating impact on security, national economic security, national public health or safety, or any combination of those matters."

Cyber security involves freedom from the risk of danger when interacting in cyberspace. As indicated, we consider participation in cyberspace to encompass a wide-range of activities including both direct and indirect interactions. Security takes on many different forms in cyberspace including encryption techniques, firewalls, virus-scanning software, intrusion detection systems and secure payment systems. In the absence of security, the full potential of information technologies cannot be realized because users will be fearful of malicious activities (Cheswick and Bellovin 1994). From simple searches, downloads and communication on the Internet to more complex transactions, individuals require security for their hardware, software, personal information and online exchanges. In addition to the range of activities that require security, there is also a range of Internet users demanding a secure environment. These users include private individuals, businesses and government.

The increasing interconnectedness discussed above does come with the possibility of significant losses through cyber crime. For instance, in 2003, hacker-created computer viruses alone cost businesses $55 billion. This is nearly double the damage they inflicted in 2002 (SecurityStats.com 2004). In a 2004 survey by the Computer Security Institute (CSI), over half of respondents indicated some form of computer security breach over the past twelve months and 100 percent of respondents indicated a website-related incident over that same period (CSI 2004).

In the post-9/11 world, Internet security has become a major policy issue, specifically in the context of national security. Consider for instance the following from Tom Ridge, the former Director of Homeland Security:

"When people think of critical infrastructure, they have a tendency to think of bricks and mortar . . . . But given the interdependency of just about every physical piece of critical infrastructure, energy, telecommunications, financial institutions and the like with the Internet and the cyber side of their business, we need to be focused on both and will be . . . . We [the government] need to do a national overview of our infrastructure, map vulnerabilities, then set priorities, and then work with the private sector to reduce vulnerabilities based on our priorities" (Quoted in Verton 2003, p. 235).

One of our main aims in this paper is to provide a realistic understanding of how cyber security fits in with national security. Is it our contention that in the context of cyberspace, individual security, as it relates to each and every user, and "national security" are inseparable. Just as security at the personal level involves the absence of risk of danger, so too does national security. Indeed, neatly categorizing national security as its own distinct category, separate from cyber security is a difficult task. This is largely due to the fact that national security is directly dependent upon security at the lowest levels of cyber usage.

We often think of national security as a single good provided by government, national defense being one example. Cyber security, however, is distinctly different than this because at the national level it is simply the

476 JOURNAL OF LAW, ECONOMICS AND POLICY [VOL. 1:2

sum of dispersed decisions of individual users and businesses. Highlighting the role that individual users play, Verton writes, "Millions of home computer users with high-speed Internet connections fail to secure their connections, and become potential 'jumping off' points for terrorists and malicious hackers" (2003, p. x). The very essence of the Internet is interconnectivity. What this means is that national security concerns are directly linked to the most basic security issues that the average user faces.

In light of this, it is easy to see why cyber security is currently one of the main policy topics of discussion. The development of cyber security and growth of cyberspace in general has taken place with little central direction. According to its inventor, Tim Berners-Lee, the Internet grew "by the grassroots effort of thousands."[6] Currently, it is estimated that eighty percent of what is deemed "critical infrastructure" is privately owned (Verton 2003, p. x). Potential problems arise, it is argued, specifically because of the Internet's decentralized nature. In short, no one user will be looking out for the national interest and hence national security. It is increasingly common nowadays to hear that the absence of coordinated efforts to protect cyberspace means vulnerabilities will persist. Given this, the conclusion often drawn is that the government must play an active role in protecting cyberspace against cyber crime and cyber terrorism.[7] The exact role that government is to take is still being debated.

As the title of this paper suggests, we focus on answering the question, "Who's to protect cyberspace?" Our core thesis is as follows: Although economic issues are at the center of cyber security, economic considerations have been largely absent from the policy debate. Economics can contribute to adjudicating between the various courses of action in determining policy toward cyber security. Toward this end we employ several basic economic concepts in order to offer insight to policymakers involved in this debate. In doing so we hope to shed light on the most effective means of securing the Internet.

Those in the legal profession have focused on governance issues related to cyberspace, which are closely linked to the issue of security. For instance, Johnson and Post (1996a, 1996b) postulate that since the Internet is not linked to any geographical polity, governance will take place via privately provided rules that lead to the emergence of common standards. Reidberg (1996) argues that the primary source of governance in cyberspace is technology developers. It is his contention that the hardware and software that allows users to operate in cyberspace imposes a set of default rules. Neither of these works, though, incorporates explicit economic analysis into their work. Our paper can be seen as contributing to this dis-

---

[6] *San Jose Mercury News*, January 30, 2001, books section, p. 2.

[7] Pollit (1997) defines cyber-terrorism as: "The premeditated, politically motivated attack against information, computer systems, computer programs, and data which results in violence against noncombatant targets by subnational groups or clandestine agents."

cussion on governance, its new contribution being a focus on the economic aspects of cyber governance and security. There is also a growing body of literature in the area of the economics of information security (see for instance Anderson 2001; Camp and Lewis 2004). While the insights from this literature are extremely relevant to this debate, they have been largely neglected in both the private and policy realms.[8] Given this, and in light of increasing calls for government involvement in cyber security, it makes sense to highlight what economics can contribute.

This paper proceeds as follows. We first apply the economic concepts of marginal costs, marginal benefits and efficiency to the issue of Internet security. Section 3 discusses and applies the concepts of externalities and market failure to cyberspace. In light of this discussion, Section 4 highlights some ways that the market can overcome problems stemming from externalities. Section 5 considers the concept of government failure and the implications for government regulation of cyberspace. Section 6 discusses the policy implications stemming from our analysis. Section 7 concludes by reiterating the main points of our analysis.

2. MARGINAL COSTS, MARGINAL BENEFITS AND THE EFFICIENT LEVEL OF INTERNET SECURITY

When considering any potential course of action, economists focus on weighing the benefits of the action versus its costs. More specifically, economists are concerned with the costs and benefits of undertaking an additional, or marginal, unit of the activity in question. If there is a net gain, where the marginal benefits outweigh the marginal costs, the activity should be undertaken, the result being an economic improvement. Likewise if the marginal costs outweigh the marginal benefits, the activity in question should not be undertaken. Economists refer to a situation as efficient if all possible improvements have been made such that no further improvements are possible.

The logic of efficiency has clear implications for cyber governance and security. If asked, most people would say that the optimal level of cyber breaches is zero.[9] But economics tells us otherwise. From an economic standpoint, what we want is the *efficient level* of cyber breaches. If the damage done by a breach is greater than the cost of the cheapest means of preventing it, than the breach is inefficient and should be eliminated. Likewise, if the cost of the cheapest means of preventing the breach is

---

8   See for instance, "The New Economics of Information Security," Information Week, March 29, 2004. Available at: http://www.informationweek.com/story/showArticle.jhtml?articleID=18402633 (last accessed 7/12/04).

9   We use the term "breaches" here in the broadest possible sense to include such things as hacking, viruses, fraud, cyber terrorism, etc.

greater than the benefit gained, the breach is efficient. Ultimately, what this means is that the efficient level of cyber breaches is not necessarily zero. For instance, if it costs $1 million to prevent a virus or cyber attack that only causes $500,000 worth of damage, the prevention should not be undertaken. In this example, the costs of prevention outweigh the benefits, and it is an efficient cyber breach.[10] We now have a general economic rule for considering the efficient level of computer security. Security efforts should only be undertaken if the marginal benefits outweigh the marginal costs. In general, the efficient level of cyber breaches is where the marginal costs of prevention exactly offset the marginal benefits of prevention.

In many cases, security efforts will be undertaken to prevent potential attacks, which may or may not in fact occur. For example, many of the current efforts undertaken by the government against cyber terrorism are done to prevent a potential attack from occurring. In such cases one can determine an expected probability that such an attack will in fact occur and calculate the expected cost and expected benefit of undertaking the security measure to prevent that attack from occurring.

The immediate implication of applying the basic concepts of marginal costs, marginal benefits and efficiency to cyber security is that the end goal of policy is not necessarily to reduce the level of cyber breaches to zero. Instead, we should aim for a policy mix that yields the efficient level of breaches. Ultimately, what we want to achieve is a policy that sets the punishment for a breach equal to the cost of damage. If this can be achieved, only efficient breaches will be undertaken. In other words, those engaged in breaches will only commit breaches when the benefit they receive is greater than the cost (i.e., damage). Another implication is that considering only the aggregate number of breaches as a metric of the general cyber environment is not informative from an economic standpoint. The number of breaches tells us nothing about the cost they impose or the benefit of preventing them.[11]

The main difficulty with the cost-benefit approach is obtaining the relevant information to determine actual costs and benefits. This becomes even more difficult when attempting to perform this analysis on breaches that may or may not occur because this involves some degree of speculation, not only regarding the probability of a breach, but also the damage it will cause.[12] As we will discuss below, the market is one means of generat-

---

[10] There have been several attempts at measuring the costs of cyber breaches. See for instance, PricewaterhouseCoopers (2000).

[11] For instance, part of the hacker subculture consists of hackers who breach a system and without doing any damage report the security holes to the system administrator. In this sense, they actually provide a benefit in repairing security holes before malicious hackers can take advantage of them. This benefit is not captured when one considers the total number of breaches and it is not clear that one would want to expend resources in preventing these breaches.

[12] The efficient level of security has been debated by among others Anderson (2002) and Schneier (2002).

ing the knowledge required for cyber security investments. Despite these difficulties, we now have a framework in place to judge the efficiency of security efforts.[13] One thing that is clear is that ignoring costs and benefits leads to an incomplete analysis and can potentially lead to wasted resources.

3. THE THEORY OF EXTERNALITIES AND MARKET FAILURE

The notion of externalities is also extremely relevant to the discussion of cyber security. Economists define an externality as a net cost or benefit that an activity imposes on those outside (i.e., external to) the activity. The problem stemming from externalities is that an individual only considers the costs and benefits directly relevant to him. In other words, an individual's decision excludes the costs and benefits that the activity imposes on others.

Externalities can be either positive or negative depending on whether they yield an external benefit or cost. A common example of a positive externality is a scientific research breakthrough. In this case, the good produces a positive externality that has large spillover benefits to those outside the individuals actually engaged in the scientific research. In the case of positive externalities, the primary actor does not internalize all benefits of his action. Theoretically, positive externalities will be undersupplied on the market due to the free-rider problem stemming from non-excludability and pricing issues related to non-rivalry. One common example of a negative externality is pollution from a factory. In such cases, the primary actor does not internalize all costs of his action. Theoretically, negative externalities will be oversupplied because the producer will internalize all benefits of the activity but not all of the costs.

Externalities are said to lead to market failure because the market fails to efficiently distribute costs and benefits such that they are fully internalized. In other words, the market, left to its own devices, will fail to provide the incentives to produce the socially optimal level of goods with positive or negative externalities. The standard conclusion is that government must either be involved in producing the good or service, or must regulate the activity in question in order to align costs and benefits and to ensure externalities are internalized. In the case of negative externalities, government usually penalizes the behavior, while in the case of positive externalities it usually encourages the behavior through subsidies or other incentives.

Given the above rendering of externalities, we can now place cyber security within this context. First, it must be noted that the Internet pro-

---

[13] It should be noted that there is software, for example CORA, which allows firms to calculate the return on a security investment. The software analyzes the costs of security breaches in terms of recovery time and weighs those costs against the benefits of investing in the prevention activity.

480   JOURNAL OF LAW, ECONOMICS AND POLICY   [VOL. 1:2

duces what economists refer to as a network externality in that the value of each connection increases as the total number of connections increases. For instance, while one Internet connection may allow the user to search for specific information, the value of the connection increases as others begin to use the Internet as well. With more connections, there are more users to interact with, whether the purposes are commerce, information or entertainment.

Given the interconnectedness of cyberspace, the actions taken by users will spill over and affect other users. These spillovers can be either positive or negative depending on how we look at the issue. The failure to undertake security measures can potentially have large negative effects on other users. If two users are connected and one fails to secure their system, he is putting the other user at risk as well. Likewise, security efforts undertaken by some users will provide a positive spillover to other users. To understand why, consider an analogy with vaccines. The prevention of communicable disease yields enormous spillover benefits to all members of a society. In other words, each member of a community benefits (i.e., receives a large positive benefit) if the other members of the community are vaccinated against a disease because they do not have to be concerned that they will catch the disease. A potential problem arises though because there is an incentive to free ride. If each individual believes that all others will be vaccinated, there is no reason for them to be vaccinated as well. The case with cyber security can be seen in a similar light. If everyone else's computer is vaccinated against viruses and protected against breaches, other members of the cyber community benefit as well and don't need to take steps to protect their system. For instance, those interacting with the uninfected user who regularly scans his computer do not have to be concerned with receiving a virus infection from that user.

As such, when individual users or businesses take steps to make their own computer or business more secure, they make the general cyber environment more secure as well, thus benefiting all users. Given this, economic theory predicts that individual decision calculus will yield too little security. The individual undertaking the security precautions does not internalize all the benefits, and will seek to free-ride off of the efforts taken by others. Similarly, when users fail to undertake security measures, they only incur part of the cost of their actions. Therefore, theory predicts that security will be undersupplied on the market and vulnerability, or a lack of security, will be oversupplied on the market.

Although not using the exact terminology specified above, policymakers often view cyber security within this framework. To illustrate this, consider the following quote from former Governor James Gilmore who led the Advisory Panel to Assess Domestic Response Capabilities for Terrorism Involving Weapons of Mass Destruction: "So far, pure public/private partnerships and market forces are not acting . . . to protect the cybercommunity. Relying on the private sector's willingness to do the right thing when it comes to security is simply not an answer." (Quoted in Verton 2003, p. 26). In economic terms, Gilmore is indicating that a market failure exists due to a lack of incentive on the unhampered market to "do the right thing" and provide the optimal level of cyber security. Indeed, the notion of externalities and market failure underlies all claims that the market will underproduce cyber security and that the government must intervene and regulate to makeup for the shortfall. Consider the following from Richard Clarke, the former cyber security czar:

> I went around saying that regulation was a bad thing because the government was stupid and would do it badly . . . . But the thing about regulation is that there was always a footnote—like, unless there's market failure, we don't want regulation. If the market doesn't cause voluntary processes [to change], then government gets involved.[14]

The immediate concern that results from issues of externalities and market failure are how these problem can best be remedied. There are at least two possibilities for dealing with the problem. One involves considering possible ways for the market to privately solve externality problems. The second is for government to intervene via regulation. In the next two sections, we treat each of these potential solutions in turn.

4. PRIVATE SOLUTIONS TO EXTERNALITIES

Given that cyber security measures have large positive spillovers, economic theory predicts that these measures will be undersupplied on the market. The question then becomes whether economic theory's predictions are correct or if there are means through which the market can internalize the related externalities. Typically, there are several avenues through which goods possessing strong externalities can be privately supplied.

The key realization is that not all benefits have to be internalized for a good with externalities to be produced at the optimal level. Indeed, nearly every activity has some related externality. The good can be privately produced provided that there are solutions that allow *enough* of the benefits to be fenced off and internalized by the producer. Similarly, the presence of spillovers is itself not enough to prevent some producers from providing a needed good. Some producers may be motivated by good-will or act for other reasons unconnected to monetary rewards and therefore are willing to incur the cost of providing say, a public good, even though they gain little (or even lose) from a profit and loss perspective. In the following subsections we consider these two avenues through which goods possessing positive externalities are privately supplied in the context of cyber security.

---

[14] Source of quote: "RSA: Can regulation cure security's ills?", available at: http://searchsecurity .techtarget.com/originalContent/0,289142,sid14_gci953148,00.html (last accessed 6/7/04).

4.1 Private Provision via Voluntary Donation

Voluntary donations are one method of funding goods with large positive externalities. Donations of money and artwork to museums, contributions to listener and viewer-supported radio and television stations, and donations to health research all serve as some readily apparent examples. While economic theory would predict free-riding in such situations, we observe many individuals making such donations nonetheless.

There are several instances of the private provision of cyber security by the voluntary donation of time and/or money, completely separate from any government organizations encouraging this behavior. One example of this is CyberAngels, an organization that was founded in 1995 by Curtis Sliwa, head of the Guardian Angels. CyberAngels is a completely voluntary program whose goals include: (1) preventing online crimes through education, (2) assisting victims who have suffered from Internet crimes and (3) monitoring legal issues as they relate to the Internet across borders.[15] In line with these goals, the activities of the CyberAngels include searching for online fraud and scams, finding and reporting sites that use children in sexually provocative ways, monitoring children in child chat rooms, offering online classes and assisting victims of online harassment, stalking, fraud and hacking.[16] CyberAngels is funded through private donations from various donors ranging from individuals to corporations.

Microsoft's bounty program provides another illustration of the private provision of cyber security through private donations. In November of 2003, Microsoft announced that it was creating an anti-virus reward program backed by $5 million of its own cash. Under the program, a reward will be offered for information that leads to the arrest of the writers of computer viruses. The first two bounties announced were two $250,000 rewards for information leading to the arrest of the writers of Blaster worm and SoBig.F email viruses. Even more recently, Microsoft offered a $250,000 bounty on the creator of the MyDoom.B virus.[17]

The cases of CyberAngels and Microsoft's anti-virus reward program illustrate that while the free-rider incentive may indeed be present, it is not necessarily the strongest incentive. Other incentives such as good will, a feeling of civic duty or pride, or some notion of fairness or morality may be present as well. The key insight is that while it is appropriate for economic theory to assume a strict self-interestedness among the agents that populate its models, it is inappropriate to maintain that goods with large positive

---

[15] For more on the mission statement of the CyberAngels, see: http://www.cyberangels.org/mission/index.html.

[16] The main website of the CyberAngels program (http://www.cyberangels.org/index.html) is available in four languages.

[17] For details on this program see: http://www.microsoft.com/presspass/press/2003/nov03/11-05AntiVirusRewardsPR.asp.

spillovers will not be supplied privately in the real world based on this assumption. While theory requires the simplification that reducing motivation to a single element entails, we must keep in mind that the world in which we find ourselves is considerably more complex and involves innumerable motivations that may completely outweigh the countervailing motivation of self-interest.[18] Clearly these donations are not, at their current levels, enough to protect cyberspace in its entirety. The main point though is that, contrary to theory, they do in fact exist. As the Internet continues to grow, there is no reason to expect that these types of voluntary donations will not increase as well.

Yet another example of the private provision of cyber security through voluntary donation is open source code. Open source code has a long history in the development of the Internet. In its early stages, the Internet was a simple protocol for exchanging data. The early versions of this protocol included the file transfer protocol (FTP) and the electronic message protocol (SMTP). The subsequent development of the "Gopher" protocol allowed for directories to be depicted graphically. The hypertext transfer protocol (HTTP) and the hypertext markup language (HTML) were created in 1991 and are the foundation of the Internet as we know it today. These protocols were available to all users (i.e., open) and were used to develop many additional applications. Much of the subsequent software and applications developed were "open"—i.e., the source code and object code were available to all other users.[19] The rapid growth of the Internet has been attributed to this early openness of code (Lessig 1999, p. 103). Users could view the code of others and either improve or build upon it. In this regard, open source code can be seen as a good with significant positive externalities that is privately provided.[20] Individual users "donate" or allow for the code they developed privately to be open for all Internet users to view, copy

---

[18] Also of note is the market for "ethcial hackers" which are hired by companies to hack into their systems before "unethical hackers" can. Gartner Inc., a market research firm in Stamford, Connecticut, estimates this to be a $1.8 billion industry for the year 2002 with expected growth of 28% for the next three years. Some ethical hackers focus on one specific operating system such as eEye Digital Security (http://www. eeye.com/html/) that specializes in Microsoft Windows. In addition to assisting their clients, eEye voluntarily reports any holes in Windows to Microsoft, although they have no formal relationship, and doesn't publicly release the information on the security flaw until Microsoft develops a patch. See, Nick Wingfield, "It Takes a Hacker," *The Wall Street Journal*, March 11, 2002 and Brad Stone, "An eEye on Microsoft," Newsweek, March 22, 2004.

[19] Source code is the code that computer programmers write in. Object code is machine-readable (Lessig 1999, p. 103).

[20] Indeed, open source software would be an example of what economists call a pure public good. Once made public, it both non-excludable—all users can access it—and non-rivalrous—one users consumption of the code does not reduce the amount available for others. The notion of public goods and externalities are closely related. A public good possesses large positive externalities and a public bad large negative externalities. For more on open source code as the private provision of a public good, see James Besson, "Open Source Software: Free Provision of Complex Public Goods" available at: http://www.researchoninnovation.org/opensrc.pdf (last accessed 7/7/04).

484   JOURNAL OF LAW, ECONOMICS AND POLICY   [VOL. 1:2

and improve upon. Today, a mixture of open and closed code exists on the Internet. Nonetheless, open source code still plays a critical role in cyberspace and in Internet security.[21]

Open source code relates to the issue of cyber security on two fronts. On the one hand, there are specific security programs based on open source code that are publicly available for downloading by all users. To a greater extent though, security is an issue with all open source code programs. With open source programs, the underlying code is available to all—both benevolent users as well as criminals. As a result, questions of security arise for open source programs given that all users have access to the code.

There is much debate regarding the viability of open source code from a security standpoint. Critics argue that open source code provides potential criminals with the blueprints of the security system. Advocates counter that the constant peer review actually makes programs based on open source code more stable and reliable as compared to commercial code. For instance, Vincent Rijmen, an award winning developer, believes that the open nature of Linux is preferable from a security standpoint, "not only because more people can look at it, but, more importantly, because the model forces people to write more clear code, and to adhere to standards. This in turn facilitates security review."[22] In any case, clearly all users of open source code receive a large positive spillover. Specifically, they gain a large benefit from the initial availability of the code as well as from improvements made to open source code by other programmers.

Another response to critics of open source security code is that those seeking security can take existing open source security code and make minor adjustments that customize the program specifically for the user. These adjustments can be open or closed code but the foundation is available through the initial open source code that existed from the work of others.[23] Several companies now offer security packages based on open source code including Guardent (http://www.guardent.com/), Covalent (http://www .covalent.net) and Astaro Corporation (www.astaro.com), to name a few.[24]

---

[21] To support this claim, consider that the Apache system, the number-one server on the Internet, is open code as is SENDMAIL, one of the most widely used programs for forwarding email (Lessig 1999, p. 104). During the first three years of Apache system's existence, 388 developers contributed 6,092 enhancements and corrected 695 bugs (Mockus et al. 2000). This rate clearly exceeds that of commercially provided software which relies on closed code (Mockus et al 2000, Table 1).

[22] Interview with Vincent Rijman, available at: http://www.linuxsecurity.com/feature_stories/interview-aes-3.html.

[23] A survey by Franke and von Hippel (2002) found that over 19% of the firms who used the Apache system had modified the code while another 33% customized the system by adding on security modules obtained from third parties. Indeed, it is because of the open source code that add-on modules have been developed. As of January 2004, there were over 300 modules developed. See http://modules.apache.org/.

[24] The U.S. Navy also uses an open source security program, SHADOW. See http://www.techweb.com/wire/story/TWB19981008S0010.

In addition to the benefits discussed above, security based on open source code has the additional benefit of being lower cost, as the user does not have to pay licensing fees.

Open source software is clearly an example of a good with significant spillover effects that is nonetheless privately provided. Once it is written and the contribution is made available or "donated" to the cyber community, all users are able to access it and benefit. Although standard economic theory predicts that such goods will fail to be produced on the unhampered market, we observe the opposite. There are several potential incentives that lead to the provision of open source code. One is that those who make their code public benefit from others who improve on their initial code. There is also the potential for fame within the programming sub-culture.[25] While anyone can contribute by posting code, the reputation or fame mechanism serves as a sorting device for other users. Fame provides enough of a benefit for these programmers to provide code to the rest of the cyber community. Open source code has allowed for the continual innovation and development of new applications and programs. While there are both potential costs and benefits to using open source code, it is a clear example of a private solution to the production of a good with significant spillover effects.

4.2 The Private Provision of Internet Security via By-Product

The free-rider problem can also be overcome if it is possible to tie a by-product to the externality. Television commercials are one example of this mechanism. Financing for commercial television comes mostly from private sponsors who pay for advertising to be aired during television programming. The by-product of the externality—here the television program—is the captive viewing audience. We see many analogous examples in cyberspace.

Many Internet applications offer security features free of charge, but tie in other features allowing providers to earn a profit. For instance, most free email applications (e.g., Hotmail, Yahoo mail, etc.) contain virus scan features that check incoming/outgoing emails and attachments for viruses. In order to benefit from these security features, users must register with the provider. The providers make profits through advertisers who target the users of the application. For instance, Hotmail members receive emails from sellers in their inbox. Yahoo offers a pop-up blocker free of charge, but the user must have an account and a companion bar is placed at the top of the Internet browser, providing links to other Yahoo services connected to advertisers.

In order to increase the number of users and garner profits from advertisers, these providers must make their products attractive. Because part of

---

[25] On the issue of fame, see the *Economist* article, "An Open and Shut Case," May 10, 2001.

486   Journal of Law, Economics and Policy   [Vol. 1:2

the attractiveness is security, producers offer this feature. Once again, security increases the value of cyberspace for all users. In this context, cyber security is privately provided because the captive audience has a value that advertisers are willing to pay for. As with advertisers on television, advertisers on the Internet are willing to pay to reach as many people as possible.

In a similar vein, some providers of security software offer one version of their application free of charge, but charge the user for an upgrade. They provide a basic level of security with no charge but include in the package advertisements for the premium versions of their software. A good example of this is Ad-Aware which is developed and distributed by Lavasoft.[26]

The Ad-Aware software erases spyware from a user's computer. Spyware is programming that is tied into downloads—often the user is unaware that it is associated with the download. Once downloaded, spyware uses the available Internet connection to send information from the user's computer to the spyware company. One form of spyware - commercial spyware - tracks the websites visited by the user. Commercial spyware is often associated with adware, which uses the information to send pop-up advertisements that fit with the information related to the user. A second and more dangerous form of spyware - domestic spyware - tracks and captures the activities of the user via their keystrokes. This form is analogous to a wiretap and sensitive information such as passwords and private email and instant messenger conversations are at risk (Mitnick and Simon 2002, p. 203-8). Ad-Aware scans the user's computer memory, registry and hard drives for commercial spyware components and allows for their safe removal.

While the basic version is free of charge, Lavasoft offers two other versions—Ad-Aware Plus and Ad-Aware Professional for a charge. These versions contain more features than the basic version. In this context, the positive externality is the free security software and the by-product is the captive audience that downloads the free version. The captive audience is enough in terms of potential profitability for Lavasoft to provide the basic version free of charge. There are other examples as well. For instance the basic version of ZoneAlarm, a firewall software product, is free of charge to any user. Similar to Ad-Aware, ZoneAlarm charges customers for more advanced versions of its software.

Internet security provided by most firms also falls into this category. Most businesses that utilize cyberspace invest resources in cyber security. It is in their interest to do so for several reasons. For one, as noted in the Introduction, breaches are costly. In economic terms firms should be willing to invest in cyber security up to the point where the costs are equal to the benefits. Moreover, consumers demand that their information and transactions be protected. In order to attract customers, online businesses

---

[26] For more on Lavasoft see: http://www.lavasoft.de/default.shtml.en.

must offer certain security measures. In the absence of minimal levels of security, we would expect the customer base of online firms to decrease significantly. The by-product of the externality—here cyber security, are the customers that are willing to offer the firm business. The key point is that these customers are willing to do so only if a secure environment is provided. The secure environment has significant spillover effects to parties outside the immediate transaction. Despite the fact that firms do not capture all of the benefits, they offer security because they secure enough monetary benefits through their direct interaction with customers providing them with business.

Consider, for instance, the case of formal online payment mechanisms such as PayPal and BidPay. These services allow buyers to make secure payments, via credit card or through their bank account, to sellers. Given that they are dealing with sensitive information regarding their customers, security is of the utmost importance. Given this, PayPal and BidPay make use of encryption technology to protect the information of their customers—both buyers and sellers.[27] The services offered by these middlemen who provide payment mechanisms do provide significant positive externalities. As discussed earlier, the Internet is a network externality which increases in value the more others are connected and able to participate online. By providing the potential for secure transactions, these services increase the value of the Internet to other users by lowering transaction costs.[28] They provide security despite the fact that there are positive spillovers that they do not capture because it is the only way to maintain and increase their customer base and profitability.

Understanding that private businesses have an incentive to invest in Internet security is critical because the greatest fear for government agencies is that terrorists will breach the networks of critical industries and have significant negative spillovers on the economy as a whole. Given this, the key issue is whether these businesses will under-invest in security given that they don't internalize *all* of the benefits. Granted, they produce some cyber security as the numerous examples above illustrate. But the argument is that because of the externality, they will fail to produce the optimal amount. To remedy the problem, government often intervenes to either produce the good altogether or regulate the private production of the good attempting to overcome the market failure. We now turn to a discussion of the potential limitations of government's ability to effectively do this.

---

[27] Additionally, many of these payment applications offer insurance protection as well. For instance, PayPal has a "Seller Protection Policy," which protects sellers against fraudulent buyers, as well as a "Buyer Protection Program," which provides $500 of insurance coverage against fraud at no additional cost to the buyer.

[28] It is estimated that PayPal has 14 million subscribers. Source: http://www.wilsonweb.com/wct5/paypal_assess.htm.

488   JOURNAL OF LAW, ECONOMICS AND POLICY   [VOL. 1:2

5.   THE THEORY OF GOVERNMENT FAILURE

As discussed in Section 3, the theoretical rendering of externalities concludes that the privately optimal level will fall short of the socially optimal level. Government is often called upon to make up the shortfall through intervention and regulation. Policymakers calling for government to actively play a role in the provision of cyber security illustrates this. Fundamentally, their claims are grounded in the belief that the market will either altogether fail to supply Internet security or, where it does, will undersupply security. In many cases, theoretical academic research also concludes that the market will undersupply key elements of cyber security. For instance, the research of Gordon et al. (2003) concludes that security information sharing between firms will be sub-optimal due to the free-rider problem. One possibility, they conclude, is for government to subsidize the sharing of information between firms (2003, p. 479-80). However, just as economic theory suggests that there is the potential for market failures, it also indicates that there is a potential for government failures as well. Just as it is important to understand why the market may only imperfectly provide cyber security, it is equally important to appreciate why the government may fail to supply the efficient level. Therefore, considering the potential benefits of government involvement along with the related limitations and costs is of the utmost importance for an accurate analysis.

One potential option is for government to produce the good, either in conjunction with the market or instead of the market. The difficulty with this option stems from the issue of calculation. It must be realized that goods with significant externalities, just like all other goods, are not produced in one lump, but rather in marginal units. In the market, the profit and loss mechanism serves as the guide for determining the optimal number of units to produce. Admittedly, it is true that where externalities exist, the profit and loss mechanism may not produce the same level as compared to a situation where externalities are fully internalized.

With government, however, the profit and loss mechanism is not just imperfect in the face of externalities—it is necessarily completely absent. This means that the state will never have any way of effectively determining the optimal supply of the good in question. In short, there is no way for any external party to calculate the optimal social stock of cyber security and, hence, to claim that it is over or undersupplied. To do so would require complete and perfect knowledge that one cannot possibly possess. It may be true that private businesses have difficulties calculating the exact return on investment (ROI) for security-related expenditures, but this will be even more difficult for government agents acting outside the profit and loss mechanism. Given this realization, while it is indeed possible that the government may provide more cyber security as compared to the private market, there is no reason to believe that it will provide the socially optimal amount. From an efficiency standpoint, it is not simply a question of the total dollar value of resources invested, but rather the allocation of those resources to their most highly valued uses. Calculating the optimal level of goods is far simpler using a theoretical model with simplified assumptions than it is in reality.

Yet another option is that government can choose to regulate the market production of the good in the hopes of internalizing the externalities. In the case of cyber security, this may involve regulating the specifications of hardware and software in order to internalize the externalities in the hopes of aligning costs and benefits and achieving the socially optimal outcome. The main problem with this solution is the difficulty in gathering the relevant information necessary to effectively regulate.

For instance, the regulators must know and be able to assign the damage done by insecurities in cyberspace. Given the interconnectedness of cyberspace, these vulnerabilities may be difficult to track and assign to a specific user. Given that the regulator aims to align costs and benefits, in addition to knowing the damage done by vulnerabilities, he must also possess the relevant information regarding the costs of remedying the situation. This information will be difficult to obtain. It is in the interest of each user with vulnerabilities to convince regulators that the damage they are causing is lower than the cheapest means of correcting the problem. In other words, it is in their interest to convince regulators that the costs of prevention are greater than the benefits.

Yet another issue deals with the policy flexibility of regulators in the context of cyberspace, and more specifically with what legal scholar Michael Froomkin refers to as "regulatory arbitrage" (1997). Because cyberspace connects users across national boundaries, Froomkin argues it will become increasingly difficult for any one nation to enforce its domestic rules. In other words, users can engage in regulatory arbitrage and evade domestic laws by engaging with users outside their national borders who are not subject to the same laws.

Admittedly, government can take steps to impede the use and effectiveness of cyberspace. For instance, China has attempted to set up an Internet censorship system known as "The Great Firewall of China." While. this effort has raised the cost of engaging in cyberspace, users have found ways around the barrier largely by using servers outside the firewall. In sum, one potential limitation on the government provision of cyber security deals with constraints on flexibility stemming directly from the very nature and magnitude of cyberspace.

As was illustrated by the quotes from policymakers in earlier sections of this paper, one of the criticisms of the market provision of cyber security is that there is a lack of incentive to consider the national interest. However, it is critical to realize that there are perverse incentives in the political realm as well. As Ranum describes his research on the topic of homeland security: "I came face to face with the realization that there are gigantic bureaucracies that exist primarily for the sole purpose of prolonging their

490   JOURNAL OF LAW, ECONOMICS AND POLICY   [VOL. 1:2

existence, that the very structure of bureaucracy rewards inefficiency and encourages territorialism and turf war" (2004, p. xv). Indeed, as public choice theory informs us, political agents face a set of incentives that are in many times misaligned with the interests of the populace.[29] The implications are clear: the presence of misaligned incentives in the market does not give one license to jump to the conclusion that government intervention is preferable. Instead, a complete consideration of potential government intervention must involve a consideration of the incentives faced by political agents and the implications of those incentives for the provision of cyber security.

A final constraint on government regulation of cyber security is the potential for limited control of the response to policies by the private market. When considering a potential regulation, due to genuine structural ignorance, only some of the potential costs, benefits and impact on incentives can be known *ex ante*. Once a regulation is passed, it creates a new set of incentives for both political and economic agents. In many cases, the outcomes that the new policy generates will not be aligned with the initial aim. This will leave government officials in a situation where they can either retract the original policy or pass additional policies to attempt to solve the unintended outcomes. This limitation may be potentially magnified in the case of cyberspace for the reasons addressed above—namely the continually changing cyber environment.

6.   POLICY IMPLICATIONS: INTERNALIZING EXTERNALITIES

We have discussed the potential limitations in both the market and government spheres in the context of cyber security. Fortunately, in addition to providing insight into the limitations of the market and government, economics also provides specific guidelines for policymakers. From an economic standpoint, the market provision of goods and services is preferable to government provision. This is due to the fact that the profit/loss mechanism inherent in the market setting guides economic actors in allocating resources to their most highly valued uses. In the context of cyber security this means that policies should be aimed at taking advantage of the desirable consequences of the market. It is only through the market process that the "right" amount of cyber security can be produced. More specifically, policy should be focused on internalizing the externalities while maintaining the allocative function of the profit/loss mechanism. Recently, several alternative courses of action have been discussed that potentially serve to internalize externalities. In theory, these potential solutions allow the desirable aspects of the market to function while overcoming the potential pitfalls of direct government regulation.

---

[29]   For more on the public choice research program, see Buchanan (2003).

One potential solution is the assignment of property rights. Well-established property rights result in markets incorporating the presence of externalities. Along these lines, one solution that has been proposed by Camp and Wolfram (2000) is the assignment of property rights to cyber vulnerabilities. This solution is similar to proposals for tradable pollution permits. Camp and Wolfram not only provide a taxonomy of vulnerabilities but also propose a means of assigning property rights. They propose that each machine would receive a certain number of vulnerability credits. Processing power is suggested as a measure of how many machines, and therefore how many credits, are to be received.

The authors suggest three potential governance mechanisms to oversee this process: the federal government, the creation of a corporation similar to The Internet Corporation for the Assignment of Names and Numbers (ICANN), or the licensing of companies in the business of creating processing power who would oversee the creation and distribution of credits. Users with vulnerabilities and no credits would have a specific time period to fix the exposure and would additionally have to make a payment to the entity that discovered the vulnerability. As a result, one could envision entrepreneurial users who are in the business of discovering vulnerabilities and profiting from these payments. By defining property rights, the full cost of these vulnerabilities would fall on the owners of the insecure machines.

Given this proposal, one must recognize that there are some potential information problems on the part of regulators, as discussed in Section 5, regarding the specifics of the permits. For instance, regulators will not know the right amount of vulnerability credits to assign in order to get the optimal level of vulnerability. Further, there is the potential for bureaucratic barriers to establishing and maintaining the credit system, especially if it is governed by a government agency. This may limit the effectiveness of this remedy.

Another potential market solution is the continued growth of the already existing cyber insurance market. In addition to traditional insurance coverage, an increasing number of insurance companies are offering coverage for cyber breaches.[30] These insurance policies include coverage against damage related to hack attacks, viruses, network downtime, identity theft and the misuse of proprietary data and information. Cyber insurance is potentially beneficial on several fronts.

For one, there is an internal pressure on companies to maintain a level of security that minimizes their premiums. Insurance companies will develop standards that firms are required to meet. Given that this is a relatively new market, there is no reason to expect that it will not continue to

---

[30] The Insurance Information Institute estimates that cyber insurance could generate $2.5 billion in annual premiums by 2005. Source: Samuel Greengard, "The Real Cost of Cybersecurity," *Business Finance*, April 2003, pp. 52-55. Available at: http://www.businessfinancemag.com/magazine/archives/article.html?articleID=13957&pg=1 (last accessed 6/8/04).

grow as better actuarial data is collected and insurance companies gain a better understanding of how IT systems operate.

There is currently debate about what role the government should take in the cyber insurance market. Some argue that the market should be left to its own devices with market-determined premiums accurately reflecting the risks. Others argue that the government should guarantee cyber insurance and/or put a cap on the insurance policies.[31] Although we avoid engaging in an analysis of this issue, the economic principles discussed in previous sections, specifically issues of economic calculation, can add much insight into this debate regarding the ability of government to effectively regulate this market.

Closely connected to the subject of cyber insurance, yet another potential means of internalizing externalities is extending liability to software authors and/or system operators. In the absence of being held liable, it is argued that these parties have a weak incentive to provide security because they do not incur the full costs of their failure to do so. Fisk (2002) concludes that it would be more effective to extend product liability to system operators as compared to software developers. One reason for this conclusion is that the existence and importance of open source software poses problems for making developers liable. Those that contribute open source software receive no income to offset potential liabilities. Purchasing cyber insurance would be one way of protecting against liability, but would also raise the cost of contributing open source code, so we would expect a decrease in the amount of open source software produced.

Fisk concludes that holding system owners liable is more reasonable and advocates an insurance system where liability for cyber accidents is "expected and accepted without stigma" (2002, p. 4). Similar to the automobile industry, system operators would be required to carry insurance against unexpected events. Fisk contends that the insurance industry would have similar beneficial effects on cyber security to those discussed above. He also envisions the creation of an Underwriters Laboratory that would certify software as secure and create an environment that encouraged effective cyber security.

We have not provided an exhaustive list of all possible courses of action. Instead, our aim here has been to highlight several potential courses of action for policymakers to consider. It is not our goal to endorse any one of these alternatives as being better than the others. Instead, our purpose is to emphasize that whatever course of action policymakers choose, their focus should be on ensuring that the desirable aspects of the market are able to function effectively.

---

[31] The Terrorism Risk Insurance Act, signed in November of 2002, created a three-year federal program that backs insurance companies in addition to guaranteeing that certain terrorist-related claims will be paid.

7. CONCLUSION

Without a doubt, the issue of cyber security will remain an important policy issue in the future. We have offered some insight into this issue from an economic perspective. In addition to the policy implications discussed above, we can put forth several general guiding principles:

1. Economics is a critical aspect of cyber security—Our main argument is that economics has been neglected in the policy debate regarding the most effective means of securing cyberspace. The basic concepts discussed in this paper can offer key insights into the best course of action. Admittedly, obtaining the necessary information to utilize these concepts will not always be easy. Nonetheless it is clear that neglecting the economic aspects of the issue will lead to incomplete and incorrect analyses.

2. National cyber security must be "demystified"—A key aspect of the cyber security issue is understanding the interconnectedness of the cyber environment. Given the interconnected nature of cyber space, the term "national security," in the context of cyber space, is simply the aggregate of individual Internet users whether for personal or business use. One must be careful not to think of "national security" as something that would fail to exist in the absence of government. As Schneier points out, we need to "demystify" Internet security (2003, p. 271). Security is all around us in our daily lives in a multitude of ways and individuals take steps to secure their property, information and transactions. Cyber space is no different

3. Cyber security policy should rely on the market to the greatest extent possible—Economic analysis provides key insights into limitations in both the market and government settings. Given that the market provision of goods and services is preferable to government provision, from an economic standpoint, policy should aim to internalize externalities while maintaining the effectiveness of the profit/loss mechanism in efficiently allocating resources.

REFERENCES

Anderson, Ross. 2001. Why Information Security is Hard: An Economic Perspective. Proceedings of the 17th Annual Computer Security Applications Conference, 358 - 365.

Anderson, Ross. 2002. Maybe we spend too much? Workshop of Economics and Information Security, University of California, Berkeley, May 16-17. http://www.cl.cam.ac.uk/users/rja14/econws/37.txt.

494   JOURNAL OF LAW, ECONOMICS AND POLICY   [VOL. 1:2

Buchanan, James M. 2003. Public Choice: The Origins and Development of a Research Program. Center for the Study of Public Choice, George Mason University, Fairfax, VA.

Camp, L. Jean, and Stephen Lewis, eds. 2004. *Economics of Information Security*. Kluwer Academic Publishers.

Camp, L. Jean, and Catherine Wolfram. 2000. Pricing Security. *Proceedings of the CERT Information Survivability Workshop*, Boston, MA, 31-39.

Cheswick, William R., and Steven M. Bellowing. 1994. *Firewalls and Internet Security: Repelling the Wily Hacker*. Reading, MA: Addison Wesley.

Computer Security Institute and Federal Bureau of Investigation. 2004. *CSI/FBI Computer Crime and Security Survey*. http://i.cmpnet.com/gocsi/db_area/pdfs/fbi/FBI2004.pdf.

Fisk, Mike. 2002. Causes & Remedies for Social Acceptance of Network Insecurity. Workshop of Economics and Information Security, University of California, Berkeley, May 16-17. http://www.cl.cam.ac.uk/users/rja14/econws/35.pdf.

Froomkin, Michael. 1997. The Internet as a Source of Regulatory Arbitrage. In *Borders in Cyberspace*, edited by Brian Kahin and Charles Nesson. Massachusetts: MIT Press, 129-163.

Gordon, Lawrence A., Martin P. Loeb, and William Lucyshyn. 2003. Sharing Information on computer systems security: An Economic Analysis. *Journal of Accounting and Public Policy* 22: 461-485.

Johnson, David R., and David G. Post. 1996a. And how shall the Net be governed? A meditation on the relative virtues of decentralized, emergent law. http://www.cli.org/emdraft.html.

Johnson, David R., and David G. Post. 1996b. Law and borders—the rise of law in cyberspace. *Stanford Law Review* 48: 1367-1405.

Lessig, Lawrence. 1999. *Code and other laws of cyberspace*. New York: Basic Books.

McMillan, John. 2002. *Reinventing the Bazaar*. New York: W.W. Norton and Company.

Mitnick, Kevin D., and William L. Simon. 2002. *The Art of Deception: Controlling the Human Element of Security*. Indiana: Wiley Publishing, Inc.

Mockus, Audris, Roy T. Fielding, and James Herbsleb. 2000. A Case Study of Open Source Software Development: The Apache Server. *Proceedings of the 22nd international conference on Software engineering (ICSE2000)*, 263-272.

Pollitt, Mark M. 1997. Cyberterrorism: Fact or Fancy? *Proceedings of the 20th National Information Systems Security Conference*. October: 285-89. http://www.cs.georgetown.edu/~denning/infosec/pollitt.html.

PricewaterhouseCoopers. 2000. *Security Benchmarking Service/Informa-tionWeek's 2000 Global Information Security Survey.* Summary available at: http://www.pwcglobal.com/extweb/ncpressrelease.nsf/docid/7ABBA8E73B1E901D8525693500548A34.

Ranum, Marcus J. 2004. *The Myth of Homeland Security.* Indianapolis: Wiley Publishing, Inc.

Reidenberg, Joel R. 1996. Governing networks and cyberspace rule-making. *Emory Law Journal* 45: 911-926.

Schneier, Bruce. 2002. Computer Security: It's the Economics, Stupid. Workshop of Economics and Information Security, University of California, Berkeley, May 16-17. http://www.cl.cam.ac.uk/users/rja14/econws/18.doc.

Schneier, Bruce. 2003. *Beyond Fear: Thinking Sensibly About Security in an Uncertain World.* New York: Copernicus Books.

SecurityStats.com. 2004. *Virus Statistics*, January 16, 2004. http://www.securitystats.com.

Verton, Dan. 2003. *Black Ice: The Invisible Threat of Cyber-Terrorism.* New York: McGraw-Hill.

[15]

HACKING, POACHING, AND COUNTERATTACKING: DIGITAL COUNTERSTRIKES AND THE CONTOURS OF SELF-HELP

*Bruce P. Smith**

For better or worse, self-help is alive and well in the realm of computer security. Of the nearly 500 American corporations, governmental agencies, financial entities, and academic institutions polled in the *2004 CSI/FBI Computer Crime and Security Survey*, virtually all employed anti-virus software (99%) and firewalls (98%). Over 80% conducted security audits to identify network-related vulnerabilities. A substantial number participated in collaborative information-sharing organizations designed to collect and disseminate intelligence relating to online threats. And when these defensive measures failed and computer security incidents occurred, as they frequently did, over 90% of the respondents patched their security holes themselves.[1]

Given the challenges associated with ensuring optimal investment in network security – including "free rider" problems, barriers to information sharing, and sheer indifference – such levels of institutional commitment to network defense might appear, at first blush, to furnish grounds for optimism.[2] Yet a closer examination of the data compiled by the Computer

* Richard W. and Marie L. Corman Fellow; Co-Director, Illinois Legal History Program; Associate Professor of Law, University of Illinois College of Law. I am grateful to the editors of *The Journal of Law, Economics & Policy* for inviting me to participate in the symposium on "Property Rights on the Frontier: The Economics of Self-Help and Self-Defense in Cyberspace," to the *Journal* and the Critical Infrastructure Protection Project (CIPP) for sponsoring the proceedings, and to the symposium's attendees (especially Richard Epstein and Emily Frye) for their valuable comments. I have also benefited from the suggestions of Tom Ginsburg, Pat Keenan, Jay Kesan, Richard McAdams, Elizabeth Robischon, and Dan Vander Ploeg.

[1] *See* LAWRENCE A. GORDON ET AL., COMPUTER SECURITY INSTITUTE, 2004 CSI/FBI COMPUTER CRIME AND SECURITY SURVEY 11 fig.16 (2004), *at* http://i.cmpnet.com/gocsi/db_area/pdfs/fbi/FBI2004.pdf [hereinafter 2004 CSI/FBI SURVEY].

[2] On the problems of computer security in networked environments, see, for example, Ross Anderson, *Why Information Security is Hard – An Economic Perspective, at* www.acsac.org/2001/papers/110.pdf (last visited Jan. 23, 2005) (originally presented at the 17th Annual Computer Security Applications Conference, Dec. 10-14, 2001) (identifying various "incentive failures" in achieving secure network environments); Amitai Aviram & Avishalom Tor, *Information Sharing in Critical Infrastructure Industries: Understanding the Behavioral and Economic Impediments* (George Mason Law & Econ. Research Paper No. 03-30; Fla. St. U. College of Law Public Law Research Paper No. 103), http://papers.ssrn.com/sol3/papers.cfm?abstract_id=427540 (last revised Feb. 23, 2004) (discussing reasons for suboptimal investments in network security); Doug Lichtman & Eric Posner, *Holding Internet Service Providers Accountable* (U. Chicago Law & Econ., Olin Working Paper No. 217 (2d Ser.)), http://papers.ssrn.com/sol3/papers.cfm?abstract_id=573502 (last revised Aug. 10, 2004) (focus-

Security Institute (CSI) and the Federal Bureau of Investigation (FBI) calls for a more sober assessment. Although the respondents reported fewer successful attacks on their computer systems than in previous years, over half of them admitted that they had experienced at least one incident of "unauthorized use" within the past year.[3] The variety of security incidents and the average losses associated with them provide some sense of the gravity of the situation: sabotage ($871,000); system penetration ($901,500); Web site defacement ($958,100); telecom fraud ($3,997,500); financial fraud ($7,670,500); theft of proprietary information ($11,460,000); denial of service attacks ($26,064,050); and, most seriously of all, viruses ($55,053,900).[4]

Even more striking than the frequency, variety, and severity of these incidents was the relatively low rate at which they were reported to law enforcement officials: In four out of five cases, the compromised organizations declined even to *report* such incidents to law enforcement.[5] This disclosure rate of 20% was the lowest since the CSI and FBI began compiling such information in 1999.[6] The rate at which compromised entities reported incidents of computer intrusions compares unfavorably to reporting rates for robbery (60.5%), burglary (54.1%), simple assault (42.1%), and even rape and sexual assault (38.5%).[7] Indeed, similarly low rates of reporting criminal offenses are to be found among the most vulnerable and marginalized members of American society: immigrants on temporary visas who have suffered from domestic violence (20.8%) and battered, undocumented immigrants (18.8%).[8]

What explains the profound reluctance of compromised corporations to report computer security incidents to law enforcement officials? In explaining their unwillingness to report, roughly half of the respondents in the

---

ing on the role of ISP immunity in contributing to network insecurity); and Douglas A. Barnes, Note, *Deworming the Internet*, 83 TEX. L. REV. 279 (2005) (addressing obstacles to producing software resistant to computer "worms").

[3] 2004 CSI/FBI SURVEY, *supra* note 1, at 8 fig.11. In 2003, the CERT Coordination Center, a federally funded research and development institute specializing in Internet security, received reports of over 130,000 incidents – a six-fold increase since 2000. *See* CERT/CC Statistics 1988-2004, http://www.cert.org/stats/cert_stats.html#incidents (last updated Oct. 19, 2004) (reporting 21,756 incidents in 2000 and 137,529 incidents in 2003). Several factors make it difficult to analyze these figures, including the possibility of shifts over time in the willingness of entities to report such events to the organizations conducting the surveys.

[4] 2004 CSI/FBI SURVEY, *supra* note 1, at 10 fig.15.

[5] *Id.* at 13 fig.20.

[6] Rates of reporting to law enforcement for the period 1999-2003 were as follows: 1999 (32%); 2000 (25%); 2001 (36%); 2002 (34%); and 2003 (30%). *Id.*

[7] *See* SHANNAN M. CATALANO, BUREAU OF JUSTICE STATISTICS, U.S. DEP'T OF JUSTICE, CRIMINAL VICTIMIZATION, 2003, at 10 (2004), *available at* http://www.ojp.usdoj.gov/bjs/pub/pdf/cv03.pdf.

[8] *See, e.g.,* Lesley E. Orloff et al., Recent Development, *Battered Immigrant Women's Willingness to Call for Help and Police Response*, 13 UCLA WOMEN'S L.J. 43, 68 (2003).

2004 CSI/FBI Survey cited as a "very important factor" their "perception" that "negative publicity would hurt their organization's stock and/or image."[9] Another 35% expressed concern that competitors would use information reported to law enforcement officials to their advantage. One in five stated that they had determined that civil – rather than criminal – remedies would best serve their interests. And another 18% of the organizations surveyed claimed to be unaware that law enforcement officials would even be interested in the intrusions that they had suffered.[10]

Amidst a continuing onslaught of "viruses," "worms," and other forms of "malware," computer security experts and legal scholars have begun to rethink the traditional bifurcated approach to network security, which has relied predominately on private investment in prevention and public investment in prosecution.[11] On the one hand, experts in computer security have questioned whether the billions of dollars spent by private companies on technologies designed to defend computer networks have been commensurate with the security that has actually been achieved.[12] On the other hand, legal commentators have identified a series of challenges associated with public prosecution of computer crimes, including not only the hesitancy of compromised entities to report security breaches, but also the forensic challenges of determining the originators and propagators of mali-

---

[9] Recent research supports the perception that public disclosure of computer security incidents negatively affects stock price. *See* Katherine Campbell et al., *The Economic Cost of Publicly Announced Security Breaches: Empirical Evidence from the Stock Market*, 11 J. COMPUTER SEC. 431 (2003) (cited in 2004 CSI/FBI SURVEY, *supra* note 1, at 16 n.4).

[10] 2004 CSI/FBI SURVEY, *supra* note 1, at 14 fig.21.

[11] "Viruses" and "worms" are self-replicating computer programs that can be designed to damage the computers that they "infect." *See* Wikipedia.org, *Computer Virus, at* http://en.wikipedia.org/wiki/Computer_virus (last visited Jan. 23, 2005) and *Computer Worm, at* http://en.wikipedia.org/wiki/Computer_worm (last visited Jan. 23, 2005). "Malware" refers "to any software designed to cause damage to a single computer, server, or computer network." Microsoft TechNet, *Defining Malware: FAQ, at* http://www.microsoft.com/technet/security/topics/virus/malware.mspx (last visited Jan. 23, 2005). Following Doug Lichtman and Eric Posner, I use the terms "virus," "worm," and "malware" to refer generally to "any category of malicious computer code that is propagated on the Internet, using or interfering with privately owned computer equipment, and done in a way such that the relevant private party has not given informed consent to that use or interference." Lichtman & Posner, *supra* note 2 (manuscript at 8).

[12] A 2003 study by PricewaterhouseCoopers concluded that, although businesses in North America spent roughly 50% more per capita on information security than companies elsewhere in the world, the investment "didn't make them any safer *per se.*" Scott Berinato, *The State of Information Security 2003*, CSO MAG., Oct. 2003, *available at* http://www.csoonline.com/read/100103/survey.html. For discussions of the "cost-effectiveness" of network security, see, for example, Lawrence A. Gordon & Robert Richardson, *The New Economics of Information Security: Information-Security Managers Must Grasp the Economics of Security to Protect Their Companies*, INFORMATIONWEEK, Mar. 29, 2004, *at* http://www.informationweek.com/story/showArticle.jhtml?articleID=18402633 and Lawrence A. Gordon & Martin P. Loeb, *The Economics of Information Security Investment*, 5 ACM TRANS. ON INFO. & SYS. SEC. 438 (2002).

174   JOURNAL OF LAW, ECONOMICS AND POLICY   [VOL. 1:1

cious code, the difficulties of coordinating enforcement efforts across national boundaries, and the rudimentary nature of laws governing cybercrime in many foreign jurisdictions.[13]

In this climate of online risk, growing concern over the cost-effectiveness of defensive safeguards, and relative lack of interest in criminal prosecution, the recent release of a network security product that offers the capacity to launch "counterstrikes" against digital intruders has caused a considerable stir in the Internet security community. In March 2004, Symbiot, Inc. ("Symbiot"), based in Austin, Texas, announced its development of "the first IT security solution that can both repel hostile attacks . . . and accurately identify the malicious attackers in order to plan and execute appropriate countermeasures" – in the company's words, "effectively fighting fire with fire."[14] Although the precise technical details of Symbiot's various security "solutions" remain unclear, the company has stated that its technology could enable users to "reflect" electronic intrusions back on their originators, to "disable," "destroy," or "seize control" of the "attacking assets," or to launch "asymmetric counterstrikes" against the originators of network attacks and, conceivably, even against third parties that have unintentionally contributed to such attacks.[15]

It is not the intention of this paper to assess the technical capabilities, legality, or desirability of Symbiot's various proprietary technologies, whose precise methods of operation remain unknown and which are in a state of ongoing development.[16] Instead, the paper uses Symbiot's technology as a point of departure from which to assess, in a more general way, the legality and desirability of digital "counterstrikes" against hackers and

---

[13] *See, e.g.*, Orin S. Kerr, Essay, *Digital Evidence and the New Criminal Procedure*, 105 COLUM. L. REV. 279 (2005); Jason V. Chang, *Computer Hacking: Making the Case for a National Reporting Requirement* (Berkman Center for Internet & Society at Harvard Law School, Research Pub. No. 2004-07), http://papers.ssrn.com/sol3/papers.cfm?abstract_id=530825 (last revised June 2, 2004); Curtis E.A. Karnow, Launch on Warning: Aggressive Defense of Computer Systems, http://islandia.law.yale.edu/isp/digital%20cops/papers/karnow_newcops.pdf (last visited Jan. 23, 2005) (unpublished paper presented at the CyberCrime and Digital Law Enforcement Conference sponsored by the Yale Law School Information Society Project, Mar. 26-28, 2004); and Stevan D. Mitchell & Elizabeth A. Banker, *Private Intrusion Response*, 11 HARV. J. L. & TECH. 699, 707-10 (1998), *available at* http://jolt.law.harvard.edu/articles/pdf/v11/11HarvJLTech699.pdf.

[14] *Symbiot Security Announces World's First Solution to Strike Back Against Network-Based Attackers; Aggressive New Rules of Engagement Established in "Information Warfare,"* BUS. WIRE, Mar. 4, 2004, *at* http://www.findarticles.com/p/articles/mi_m0EIN/is_2004_March_4/ai_113905129. *See also Symbiot Announces General Availability of iSIMS*, BUS. WIRE, Apr. 1, 2004, *at* http://www.findarticles.com/p/articles/mi_m0EIN/is_2004_April_1/ai_114800004.

[15] Symbiot, Inc., Graduated Response™, *at* http://symbiot.com/graduatedres.html#CYCLE (last visited Aug. 3, 2004) (on file with author).

[16] The company has products in various stages of development. *See, e.g.*, Symbiot, Inc., Symbiot 7200: Solutions / Symbiot 7200, *at* http://www.symbiot.com/7200riskmetricssolutions.html (last visited Jan. 23, 2005) and Symbiot 9600: Solutions / Symbiot 9600, *at* http://www.symbiot.com/9600riskmetricssolutions.html (last visited Jan. 23, 2005).

third-party intermediaries (or "zombies").[17] As we shall see, the paper rejects both the position that parties should be privileged to engage in digital counterstrikes and the position that digital counterstrikes should be completely prohibited. Instead, the article proposes a middle course: Although proportionate counterstrikes against persons who intentionally propagate malware should be privileged, similar counterstrikes against unwitting third-party "zombies" should be subject to a liability rule by which the counterattacking party would be required, in most instances, to pay damages to the third party.

Part I introduces Symbiot's technology and philosophy as set forth in the company's recent public pronouncements. Broadening its focus beyond Symbiot's proprietary technology, Part II examines the main practical and legal challenges facing digital "counterstrike" technologies. Part III then explores a historical analog to the problem of unauthorized access to computer networks: the debate in early nineteenth-century England about the use of "spring guns" to deter persons seeking unauthorized access to land and game. Finally, Part IV offers some preliminary assessments concerning what type of legal regime might best govern the phenomenon of digital "counterattacks."

I. THE PROSPECTS OF COUNTERSTRIKE TECHNOLOGIES

To be sure, digital self-help – even in its "offensive" guise – did not begin with Symbiot. To the contrary, Symbiot itself has claimed that "[o]ne dirty little secret of information security is that corporations have been using 'tiger teams' for years in order to launch highly aggressive counterstrikes against attackers" and that "[t]he counterstrike capabilities of the U.S. Defense Department are even more advanced than corporate practices."[18] Although parties seldom admit to engaging in such measures,

---

[17] Distributed denial of service (DDoS) attacks typically "involve unauthorized intruders commandeering the computers of unsuspecting users and using these distributed systems, referred to as 'zombies,' to flood a particular website or service provider with junk messages." Jacqueline Lipton, *Mixed Metaphors in Cyberspace: Property in Information and Information Systems*, 35 LOY. U. CHI. L.J. 235, 245 n.41 (2003).

[18] Paco Nathan, *What "Countermeasures" Really Means*, O'REILLY.COM, Aug. 3, 2004, *at* http://www.onlamp.com/pub/a/security/2004/08/03/symbiot.html. In the context of information technology, a "tiger team" traditionally refers to a group of experts hired to expose vulnerabilities in the security of one's own network, not necessarily that of an adversary. *See* Whatis.com, *Tiger Team, at* http://whatis.techtarget.com/definition/0,,sid9_gci213146,00.html (last visited Jan. 23, 2005). For a recent glimpse of military cyberwarfare strategy, *see* Norman R. Howes, Michael Mezzino & John Sarkesain, *On Cyber Warfare Command and Control Systems, at* www.dodccrp.org/events/2004/ICCRTS_Denmark/CD/papers/118.pdf (last visited Jan. 23, 2005) (unpublished paper presented at the 9th International Command and Control Research and Technology Symposium in Copenhagen, Denmark, Sept. 14-16, 2004).

fragmentary evidence suggests that such efforts are not unknown. In December 1999, for example, Conxion, the company providing the Web-hosting service for the World Trade Organization, responded to a denial-of-service attack launched by a group of "electro-hippies" by reflecting the attack onto the e-hippies' server.[19] At times, cruder techniques have proved no less effective: An unnamed "senior security manager" at "one of the country's largest financial institutions" has reported visiting "the physical location" where a series of hacker attacks had originated, breaking in, stealing the offending computers, and leaving a note reading "See how it feels?" for the suspected wrongdoers.[20]

Nonetheless, Symbiot has claimed to offer the first commercially available technology specifically designed to permit its users to "strike back" against network intruders.[21] As such, it provides a particularly useful case study through which to examine both the possibilities and problems of digital counterstrike technologies.

A. *Symbiot's Technology*

As of January 2005, Symbiot offered a range of product "solutions," including the Symbiot 5600, styled by the company as "the most advanced risk detection and mitigation solution available on the market today."[22] Beginning in the first quarter of 2005, customers of Symbiot who purchased the Symbiot 5600 system were also to receive access to Symbiot.NET, a "central repository of attacker profiles based on the cooperative surveillance and reconnaissance gathered by all [of Symbiot's] network participants" that is "used to accurately identify attackers, evaluate their methods and intent, and recommend the appropriate countermeasures."[23]

For our purposes, the most fascinating aspect of Symbiot's portfolio of technologies is what it has described as its "iSIMS" (or "Intelligent Security

---

[19] *See* Pia Landergren, *Hacker Vigilantes Strike Back*, CNN.COM, June 20, 2001, *at* http://www.cnn.com/2001/TECH/internet/06/20/hacker.vigilantes.idg/ (discussing efforts of Conxion, the Department of Defense, and other entities to strike back at hackers). In Fall 1998, the Pentagon reportedly responded to an attack on one of its Web sites by "flood[ing] the browsers used to launch the attack with graphics and messages, causing them to crash." Winn Schwartau, *Striking Back: Corporate Vigilantes Go On the Offensive to Hunt Down Hackers*, NETWORKWORLDFUSION, Jan. 11, 1999, *at* http://www.nwfusion.com/archive/1999/54697_01-11-1999.html.

[20] Schwartau, *supra* note 19, at ¶¶ 6-9. The unnamed source also admitted to having resorted, on one occasion, "to baseball bats" on the theory that "[t]hat's what these punks will understand." *Id.* at ¶ 9.

[21] *Symbiot Security Announces*, *supra* note 14.

[22] Symbiot, Inc., Introducing the Symbiot 5600 – Featuring the Power of Risk Metrics, *at* www.symbiot.com/pdf/5600.pdf (last visited Jan. 23, 2005).

[23] *Id.* *See also* Symbiot, Inc., Symbiot.NET: Solutions / Symbiot.NET, *at* http://www.symbiot.com/symbiotnetriskmetricssolutions.html (last visited Jan. 23, 2005).

Infrastructure Management System") platform. According to informational materials distributed by the company, the iSIMS platform "features an intuitive command and control console that aggregates, correlates, and visualizes security event data in real-time." Symbiot assists its users in characterizing the risk associated with particular computer security incidents by generating a three-digit "standardized measure of threat" similar to the "credit scores" provided by credit reporting companies. The vulnerability of a particular network asset during a particular time period is modeled as a function of the threat, the asset's vulnerability, and the value of the asset at risk.[24]

Most notably, Symbiot has described iSIMS as "the only product . . . to offer customers graduated responses to deploy against network based attackers."[25] In prior public statements, Symbiot has described the iSIMS platform as enabling its users to engage in a series of "graduated countermeasures" depending on "the intensity, duration, and realized effect of hostile acts" and the degree of authorization provided by Symbiot.[26] Although the nature and effectiveness of these countermeasures remain unknown, they have been described in general terms by Symbiot as operating in the following ways: *Blocking Traffic* ("providing a brute-force wall of defense"); *Rate-limiting* ("adjusting the bandwidth available to the attacker"); *Diverting Traffic* ("redirecting traffic to some other target network"); *Simulated Responses* ("providing 'decoy' responses to service requests" that appear "legitimate" but do not "stress . . . critical servers"); *Quarantine* ("accepting the attack, but redirecting it into a special 'containment area'" for analysis of its "characteristics"); *Reflection* ("sending the packet content used in the attack back at the attacker"); *Tagging* ("using a means for marking the attacker with information" for the purpose of identifying "subsequent incidents"); and *Upstream Remediation* ("attempting remediation through an attacker's upstream provider").[27]

In a related portion of its informational materials, under a distinctive heading entitled "For Authorized Deployments Only," Symbiot has also identified three "more aggressive countermeasures" whose availability may be "restricted:" *Invasive Techniques* ("obtaining access privileges on the attacker's system, and then pursuing a strategy of disabling, destroying, or seizing control over the attacking assets"); *Symmetric Counterstrike* ("sending exploits and other attacks which are specific to vulnerabilities on the

---

[24] For details, see Symbiot, Inc., iSIMS Overview, *at* http://internet-security.ws/isims.pdf#CYCLE (last visited Jan. 23, 2005) (in possession of author) [hereinafter iSIMS Overview]; Andy Oram, *Symbiot on the Rules of Engagement*, O'REILLY.COM, Mar. 10, 2004, *at* http://www.onlamp.com/lpt/a/4691 (interview with Symbiot's chief officers); and Paco Nathan & William Hurley, *Non-Equilibrium Risk Models in Enterprise Network Security* (Nov. 28, 2004), *at* www.symbiot.com/pdf/nerm.pdf.

[25] iSIMS Overview, *supra* note 24.

[26] Graduated Response™, *supra* note 15.

[27] *Id.*

attacker's system, in an amount proportional to their current attacks"); and *Asymmetric Counterstrike* ("preemptive measures in response to distributed attacks orchestrated by a known source," with "retaliation" potentially "far in excess of the attack that the aggressor has underway").[28]

Symbiot has explained that "asymmetric counterstrikes" – the last and, apparently, most aggressive type of response – "require executive findings based on multiple attributions and prior failed attempts at resolution through upstream providers and local jurisdictions." In such instances, Symbiot has stated that the company's "operations center" might authorize "escalated multilateral profiling and blacklisting of upstream providers," "distributed denial of service counterstrikes," "special operations experts applying invasive techniques," and "combined operations which apply financial derivatives, publicity disinformation, and other techniques of psychological operations."[29]

B.   *Symbiot's Philosophy*

Although such vague descriptions do little to clarify Symbiot's actual methods and technological capacities, the company's officers have spoken at some length about their philosophy in ways that potentially bear on how the law should respond to the promise and problems of digital counterstrike technologies.

In an article published in August 2004, for example, Paco Nathan (Symbiot's Chief Scientist and Vice President of Research and Development) observed that "[w]hen computer security professionals speak about countermeasures, the implications are more subtle than the general public might imagine."[30] As if to allay concerns about the risks of iSIMS-enabled counterstrikes, Nathan provided the following assurances:

> Does it mean that if your grandmother's PC gets a virus, it could be accidentally "neutralized" and all her special cookie recipes obliterated? No. It *does* mean that if she neglects to clean up a bunch of viruses on her hard drive, she might encounter difficulties shopping online. Furthermore, if your grandmother chooses to go online through a cut-rate ISP with a history of sheltering attacks, she will probably have her bandwidth limited by web sites that take security seriously.[31]

Thus, Nathan draws a potentially important distinction between counterstrikes that result in permanent destruction of data and those that merely result in limiting the bandwidth of individuals who propagate – even

---

[28]   *Id. See also* Lyne Bourque, *Symbiot iSIMS: The Counterattack,* EITPLANET.COM, June 29, 2004, *at* http://www.enterpriseitplanet.com/security/features/article.php/3374971.

[29]   Paco Nathan & Mike Erwin, *On the Rules of Engagement for Information Warfare* 4-5 (Mar. 4, 2004), *at* http://www.symbiot.com/pdf/iwROE.pdf.

[30]   Nathan, *supra* note 18, at ¶ 2.

[31]   *Id.* at ¶ 13 (emphasis added).

result in limiting the bandwidth of individuals who propagate – even unintentionally – viruses, worms, and other forms of malware.

In other public statements, Symbiot has defended the moral and legal legitimacy of digital counterstrikes. The chief vehicle for this campaign is a document entitled "On the Rules of Engagement for Information Warfare," which Symbiot made available online in March 2004 shortly before the release of iSIMS.[32] Drawing upon doctrines of international law, Symbiot's "Rules of Engagement" contend that digital counterstrikes – at least as contemplated by Symbiot – are both principled and legal because they subscribe to "the lawful military doctrine of *necessity and proportionality*." According to Symbiot:

> Necessity is defined by the determination of hostile intent and the subsequent use of force in self-defense, justified in situations that are "instant, overwhelming and leaving no choice of means and no moment for deliberation." Proportionality is defined by the limitation of response by the intensity, duration, and realized effect of each attack.[33]

Purporting to rely on "strategies and tactics . . . refined by thousands of years of warfare, diplomacy, and legal recourse," Symbiot's "Rules of Engagement" seek to provide both moral and legal justification for the company's proprietary technology.[34]

II. THE PITFALLS OF COUNTERSTRIKE TECHNOLOGIES

How well have Symbiot's technical, moral, and legal claims been received? Most commentators who have reacted to Symbiot's iSIMS technology have expressed considerable concern about its possible use.[35] This

---

[32] Nathan & Erwin, *supra* note 29.

[33] *Id.* at 2-3 (internal citation removed). The quotation, as Symbiot notes, is from former U.S. Secretary of State Daniel Webster during the *Caroline* Affair. In 1837, the *Caroline*, an American ship being used to transport supplies from New York to a group of armed rebels preparing to invade Canada, was attacked, burned, and thrown over Niagara Falls by a Canadian naval force. British politicians defended the Canadians' actions as self-defense. Webster, by contrast, argued that the perpetrators had not demonstrated the "necessity" of self-defense because they had not responded to a threat that was "instant, overwhelming, leaving no choice of means, and no moment for deliberation." Enclosure (dated Apr. 24, 1841) in Letter from Daniel Webster to Lord Ashburton (July 27, 1842), *available at* http://www.yale.edu/lawweb/avalon/diplomacy/britian/br-1842d.htm#web2 (last visited Jan. 23, 2005).

[34] Nathan & Erwin, *supra* note 29, at 1.

[35] For responses to Symbiot's announcement of the release of iSIMS, see Munir Kotadia, *Security Product to Strike Back at Hackers*, CNET NEWS.COM, Mar. 10, 2004, *at* http://news.com.com/2102-7349_3-5172032.html; Dana Epps, *Rules of Engagement for Information Warfare*, SilverStr's Blog, Mar. 10, 2004, *at* http://silverstr.ufies.org/blog/archives/000547.html; Mike Fratto, *Fundamentals – Retaliation Is Not the Answer*, SEC. PIPELINE, Apr. 15, 2004, *at* http://www.securitypipeline.com/trends/showArticle.jhtml?articleId=18901411; Matthew Fordahl, *Vigilante Justice In Cyberspace*, CBSNEWS.COM, June 21, 2004, *at*

caution appears consistent with the position taken by most corporate executives, who have been reluctant – at least publicly – to support digital counterstrikes as a means of combating network-related intrusions.[36] The Department of Justice, for its part, has seemingly "taken a position unequivocally opposed to the employment of active defenses," both because of perceived challenges in "controlling" so-called "hack back" technologies and because such measures might themselves violate existing laws prohibiting unauthorized access to protected computers.[37]

Broadening our focus beyond Symbiot's proprietary technology, what are the chief practical and legal pitfalls facing companies that wish to launch digital counterstrikes?

A. *Practical Pitfalls*

Experts in computer security have focused principally on the practical risks associated with the use of so-called "hack back" technologies. Some have suggested that electronic countermeasures could slow networks by taking up valuable bandwidth.[38] Most frequently, however, technical experts have expressed concern that digital counterstrikes might harm "innocent" third parties, especially because persons engaged in unlawful online activities frequently route their attacks through passive intermediaries. Once infected, these so-called "zombie" computers can then be controlled by the originator of a worm or virus (the "zombiemaster") and be instructed to disseminate malicious code at some future time.

In recent years, computers in homes, research universities, and even the United States Senate and Department of Defense have been transformed

---

http://www.cbsnews.com/stories/2004/06/21/tech/main625144.shtml; and *System Attacks Back at Hackers*, BLACKCODE NEWS, June 20, 2004, *at* http://www.blackcode.com/news/view.php?id=487.

[36] *See   (Too)   Risky   Business*,   CSO   MAG.,   Nov.   2003,   *available   at* http://www.csoonline.com/read/110103/digex_sidebar_1898.html and Deborah Radcliff, *Hack Back: Virtual Vigilante or Packet Pacifist? Network Executives Have Mixed Feelings About Whether to Retaliate   Against   an   Attack*,   NETWORKWORLDFUSION,   May   29,   2000,   *at* http://www.nwfusion.com/research/2000/0529feat2.html.

[37] Richard W. Aldrich, *How Do You Know You Are at War in the Information Age?*, 22 HOUS. J. INT'L L. 223, 258 (2000). *Accord*, Emily Frye, Transcript of JLEP/CIPP Symposium on Property Rights on the Frontier: The Economics of Self-Help and Self-Defense in Cyberspace 212 (Sept. 10, 2004) (recounting discussions of counterstrike technology with officials in the Computer Crimes Division of the Department of Justice who, in Frye's words, "are not in favor of it") [hereinafter Symposium Transcript].

[38] *See* Sharon Gaudin, *Plan to Counterattack Hackers Draws More Fire*, INTERNETNEWS.COM, Apr. 5, 2004, *at* http://www.internetnews.com/ent-news/print.php/3335811 (addressing issues of "network traffic" and "corporate bandwidth").

into "zombies" in this manner.[39] A prominent legal practitioner has summarized the dangers as follows:

> [Z]ombies in a DDoS attack, may be operated by hospitals, governmental units, and telecommunications entities such as Internet service providers that provide connectivity to millions of people: counterstrikes which are not *very, very* precisely targeted to the worm or virus could easily create a remedy worse than the disease."[40]

In the worst case, as Orin Kerr has suggested, counterstrikes could resemble a "piñata game" in which the counterattacker "hacks" blindly at an unseen target.[41]

Symbiot, for its part, has publicly addressed such concerns. In an interview granted in March 2004, the company's chief officers noted that, "when there is no positive identification of the attacker (that is, we cannot positively attribute an attack back to its source), deploying defensive countermeasures and reporting intelligence would be most appropriate."[42] But the company has also acknowledged that "[t]here is always the possibility of collateral damage." Indeed, Symbiot makes no apologies for the possibility that counterstrikes might be launched against "zombies." According to Symbiot's officers, "when a zombied host or an infected computer has been clearly identified as the source of an attack, it is our responsibility to empower customers to defend themselves." Put simply, "[a]n infected machine, one no longer under the control of its owner, is no longer an innocent bystander."[43]

---

[39] *See, e.g., Your Computer Could be a "Spam Zombie": New Loophole: Poorly Guarded Home Computers,* CNN.COM, Feb. 18, 2004, *at* http://www.cnn.com/2004/TECH/ptech/02/17/spam.zombies.ap/ (estimating "that between one-third and two-thirds of unwanted messages are relayed unwittingly by PC owners who set up software incorrectly or fail to secure their machines"); John Borland & John Pelline, *Hack Leads Point to California Universities,* CNET NEWS.COM, Feb. 12, 2000, *at* http://news.com.com/2100-1023-236827.html?legacy=cnet (referring to attacks against Yahoo!, eBay, CNN, and other companies unintentionally launched from computers at Stanford, UCLA, and the University of California at Santa Barbara); and Jon Swartz, *Hackers Hijack Federal Computers,* USATODAY.COM, Aug. 30, 2004, *at* http://www.usatoday.com/tech/news/computersecurity/2004-08-30-cyber-crime_x.htm (discussing recent discovery by officials at the Department of Justice of "[h]undreds of powerful computers at the Defense Department and U.S. Senate . . . hijacked by hackers who used them to send spam").

[40] Karnow, *supra* note 13 (manuscript at 4-5) (emphasis added).

[41] "It's . . . like, I think, a piñata game. You know the piñata game, where you blindfold somebody and give them a baseball bat and tell them to hack at the piñata." Orin S. Kerr, Symposium Transcript, *supra* note 37, at 231.

[42] Oram, *supra* note 24.

[43] *Id.*

B. *Legal Pitfalls*

Other critics of digital counterstrike technologies have argued that, even if such attacks could be conducted with technical precision, they are likely to run afoul of existing laws prohibiting unauthorized access to computers.

The most obvious – though by no means the only – challenge in this regard is the federal Computer Fraud and Abuse Act (CFAA), by which persons engaged in various forms of "unauthorized access" to computer systems face exposure to both civil and criminal liability.[44] The broad language of the CFAA prohibits both (1) "knowingly caus[ing] the transmission of a program, information, code, or command, and . . . intentionally caus[ing] damage . . . to a protected computer" and (2) "intentionally access[ing] a protected computer without authorization, and . . . recklessly caus[ing] damage."[45] Given the broad and evolving contours of the CFAA, some commentators have suggested that even the relatively benign attempt to *trace* an originator of a computer-related attack through various intermediaries might run afoul of the statute.[46]

For its part, Symbiot has conceded that "[t]he legal environment surrounding the use, misuse, and operation of a system for active network self-defense has many unexplored issues."[47] Although it is impossible to evaluate such issues thoroughly without more information about a given technology's mode of operation once actually deployed, the types of counterstrikes identified by Symbiot (which include "disabling, destroying, or seizing control" over "attacking assets") could conceivably run afoul of provisions in the CFAA.

To date, no court has considered whether digital counterstrikes of the type described by Symbiot violate the CFAA or, for that matter, any other federal or state law. Accordingly, to better assess the legality and desirability of digital counterstrikes in this unsettled area of the law, we turn to a historical analog: the controversy over the use of "spring guns" to combat illegal poaching in nineteenth-century England.

---

[44]   18 U.S.C. § 1030 (2002). Possible exposure to an action under the CFAA by no means exhausts the sources of potential liability. For an overview, see Karnow, *supra* note 13 (manuscript at 5) (noting that "a host of statutes on their face make it illegal to attack or disable computers").

[45]   18 U.S.C. § 1030(a)(5)(A)(i)-(ii).

[46]   "Insofar as private security experts may lack authorization to enter third-party systems, even for investigative purposes, some of the law's prohibitions may impact attempts by private parties to trace and identify unauthorized intruders." Mitchell & Banker, *supra* note 13, at 711. For discussions of the CFAA's scope, see generally Orin S. Kerr, *Cybercrime's Scope: Interpreting "Access" and "Authorization" in Computer Misuse Statutes*, 78 N.Y.U. L. REV. 1596 (2003) and Robert Ditzion, Elizabeth Geddes & Mary Rhodes, *Computer Crimes*, 40 AM. CRIM. L. REV. 285 (2003).

[47]   Although Symbiot's officers have taken the position that "legal liability is borne by the attacker" [i.e., their customer], they have acknowledged that "[t]he legal implications . . . and liabilities arising from the system's use are presently very important for us all to consider." Oram, *supra* note 24.

III. POACHERS AND SPRING GUNS

Like modern-day network security specialists, the owners of English landed estates in the eighteenth and early-nineteenth centuries resorted to a range of defensive self-help measures designed to protect their property and game from unauthorized intruders. Like today, English landowners sought to protect certain things of value (such as deer and birds) whose status as "property" was contested. Like their modern-day counterparts, owners of land periodically resorted to civil and criminal actions against intruders.[48] Moreover, as with proponents of digital counterstrike technologies, property owners in England engaged in various forms of self-help – most notoriously, the placement of spring guns and other mechanical devices designed to retaliate against unauthorized intruders. And, as in the modern age, such devices generated considerable controversy because of the risks that they posed to innocent third parties. With the modern problem of digital self-help in mind, Part III examines the nineteenth-century English spring gun controversy and its later analysis by twentieth-century scholars of law and economics.

A. *The History of Spring Guns*

As Judge Posner has observed, the use of self-help measures to deter poachers became a *"cause célèbre"* in England in the 1820s, occupying the English judiciary, legislature, and press.[49] The debates focused on the use of three types of devices: "spring guns" (designed to discharge automatically when "sprung" by the entry of an intruder); "man traps" (intended to snap on the legs of intruders – or their dogs); and "dog spears" (fashioned to impale dogs employed in the hunting of game upon sharpened metal stakes).

The highlights of the controversy have been explored elsewhere and need only be broached briefly here.[50] In *Ilott v. Wilkes* (1820), the Court of

---

[48] Civil actions in such cases might be brought for trespass. Criminal prosecutions might occur in summary (i.e., non-jury) proceedings before justices of the peace or before juries under the notorious Black Act, which defined various types of poaching-related acts as felonies punishable by death. *See generally* PETER B. MUNSCHE, GENTLEMEN AND POACHERS: THE ENGLISH GAME LAWS, 1671-1831 (1981) and E.P. THOMPSON, WHIGS AND HUNTERS: THE ORIGIN OF THE BLACK ACT (1975).

[49] Richard A. Posner, *Killing or Wounding to Protect a Property Interest*, 14 J.L. & ECON. 201, 202 (1971).

[50] This is not to say, however, that they have always been chronicled accurately. For example, a leading casebook on American tort law has placed the important case of *Bird v. Holbrook* (decided in 1828) in 1825 and the most important Parliamentary act regulating "spring guns" and "man traps" (adopted in 1827) in 1826. *See* RICHARD A. EPSTEIN ET AL., CASES AND MATERIALS ON TORTS 40-43 (7th ed. 2000). The book also claims that the statute concerning spring guns and man traps adopted in 1827 was "repealed in its entirety in 1861" – which indeed it was – but it fails to note that the main

King's Bench took up the question of whether a trespasser who had been *warned* that spring guns had been placed in a wooded tract could maintain an action against the property owner for injuries sustained by entering the property and activating a gun, one of "nine or ten" that had been placed on the property by the owner.[51] In deciding whether a cause of action by the trespasser could lie, Chief Justice Abbott observed that the judges were "not called upon . . . to decide the *general* question, whether a trespasser sustaining an injury from a latent engine of mischief, placed in a wood or in grounds *where he had no reason to apprehend personal danger*, may or may not maintain an action."[52] But in the case where actual notice did exist, the Court of King's Bench determined that no action for injuries caused by the gun could be maintained.[53]

After the decision in *Ilott*, debate concerning the regulation of spring guns shifted to Parliament. Opponents of spring guns argued that the devices had the tendency to harm innocent victims – including children, persons who entered property "by accident," those who ventured in "with some kind and friendly purpose," and even gamekeepers themselves.[54] Proponents of spring guns claimed that the devices "not only acted as a great discouragement to poaching, but tended to prevent the dreadful evils which resulted from the affrays and fights between bodies of game-keepers and

---

provisions of the 1827 statute were included in a separate consolidated act passed in that same year. *Id.* at 44 n.1. For the consolidating measure, see Offenses Against the Person Act, 1861, 24 & 25 Vict., c. 100, § 31 (Eng.). These infelicities do little to detract from Professor Epstein's influential casebook, which remains a "classic."

[51] 106 Eng. Rep. 674 (K.B. 1820). The defendant in *Ilott* owned a wooded tract of land that contained "a right of way for all the king's subjects on foot." *Id.* at 675. He placed guns on the private portions of the land and displayed several "boards" that contained "notice to the public that such instruments were so placed." *Id.* The plaintiff and a companion "went out in the day time for the purpose of gathering nuts," and the plaintiff "proposed to his companion to enter" the defendant's woods. *Id.* After being warned by his companion, the plaintiff entered, whereupon he received the injury at issue in the suit. *Id.*

[52] *Id.* at 676 (emphasis added). That particular question, as the Chief Justice observed, "ha[d] been the subject of much discussion in the Court of Common Pleas, and great difference of opinion ha[d] prevailed in the minds of the learned judges, whose attention was there called to it." *Id. See* Deane v. Clayton, 129 Eng. Rep. 196, 197 (C.P. 1817) (failing to reach decision on the issue of whether an action could be brought by a plaintiff whose dog had been killed by dog spears).

[53] *Ilott*, 106 Eng. Rep. at 676. Justice Bayley, for his part, agreed, noting that the action was barred by the maxim of *volenti non fit injuria* and concluding that "the cause of the injury" was ultimately the act of the plaintiff, not the defendant. *Id.* at 677-78 (Bayley, J.)

[54] 13 PARL. DEB. (2d. ser.) (1826) 1254-55 (Charles Tennyson). In 1818, the *Bury and Norwich Post* reported a typical accident involving an injured gamekeeper:
On Saturday . . . George Davex, gamekeeper to Miss Wenyeve of Brettenham Hall was in the act of taking up a spring gun set by himself, from touching a wire too roughly, he sprang the lock and the contents of the gun lodged in various parts of his body from head to foot.
Bury and Norwich Post (Mar. 25, 1818), *available at* http://www.foxearth.org.uk/1818-1819BuryNorwichPost.html.

poachers" – in effect, *reducing* interpersonal violence.[55] In May 1827, after several years of intermittent debate, Parliament ultimately enacted a statute that made it a misdemeanor for any person to "set or place or cause to be set or placed, any Spring Gun, Man Trap, or other Engine calculated to destroy human Life, or inflict grievous bodily Harm, . . . upon a Trespasser or other Person coming in contact therewith."[56]

English judges promptly took notice.[57] In *Bird v. Holbrook* (1828), the Court of Common Pleas considered the case of a plaintiff who had been injured by a spring gun after climbing into the defendant's walled garden to retrieve a pea-fowl that had strayed.[58] The owner of the garden, who had recently experienced the theft of flowers, had not only placed a spring gun, but had intentionally declined to post any notice to that effect. After entering the garden to retrieve his bird, the plaintiff was shot in "the knee-joint" and suffered "a severe wound."[59] Noting that the recently adopted Parliamentary act of 1827 prohibited the setting of spring guns "even with *notice*, except in dwelling-houses by night," Chief Justice Best concluded that the action could be maintained by the plaintiff.[60] As the court observed, "he who sets spring guns, without giving notice, is guilty of an inhuman act, and that, if injurious consequences ensue, he is liable to yield redress to the sufferer."[61]

B. *The Law and Economics of Spring Guns*

Although of relatively modest interest to legal historians, the English spring gun debate has been familiar to scholars of law and economics since 1971, when it was first explored by Judge Posner in an incisive article pub-

---

[55] 13 PARL. DEB. (2d ser.) (1826) 1266-67 (Stuart Wortley).

[56] 7 & 8 Geo. IV, c. 18, § 1 (1827) (Eng.). The act also covered those who "knowingly and wil[l]fully" permitted such devices to remain in place after they had been set by others. *Id.* § 3. Notably, the act excluded spring guns, man traps, or other "engines" set "from Sunset to Sunrise" in dwelling houses. *Id.* § 4.

[57] The impact on Anglo-American landowners, however, is more difficult to assess. The American case law certainly suggests that innovative self-help strategies persisted. *See, e.g.*, Johnson v. Patterson, 14 Conn. 1 (1840) (corn laced with arsenic placed by defendant on his land); Grant v. Hass, 75 S.W. 342 (Tex. Civ. App. 1903) (spring gun designed to deter the theft of melons); and Katko v. Briney, 183 N.W. 2d 657 (Iowa 1971) (spring gun designed to protect an unoccupied boarded-up farm house against trespassers and thieves). My maternal grandfather George Smillie employed a spring gun loaded with powder in the shed that adjoined his cottage in southern Quebec to prevent depredations when the premises were unoccupied during winter.

[58] Bird v. Holbrook, 130 Eng. Rep. 911, 913 (C.P. 1828).

[59] *Id.*

[60] *Id.* at 916 (emphasis added).

[61] Id.

lished in the *Journal of Law and Economics*.[62] Reflecting the influence of Coase, Posner styled the dispute in *Bird v. Holbrook* as a simple "conflict between [two] legitimate activities" – tulip growing and peahen keeping. In turn, he characterized the use of spring guns as a rational reaction to the rudimentary policing of nineteenth-century rural England: "In an era of negligible police protection, a spring gun may have been the most cost-effective means of protection for the tulips."[63]

Posner ultimately fashioned the following six-part test to determine whether violence in defense of property should be permitted:

(1) Deadly force should not be privileged where the property owner has an adequate legal remedy or where "the threatened property loss is small;"

(2) There should be no privilege to set spring guns "in heavily built-up residential and business areas" because of the likely presence of police and the increased risk of third-party injury;

(3) The privilege to use deadly force to defend property should be forfeited "if the user fails to take reasonable precautions to minimize the danger of accidental injury;"

(4) With respect to property "not sufficiently enclosed to keep out straying animals, children, and youths, the privilege to set spring guns should be limited to the nighttime;"

(5) In situations where deadly force is permissible, "[a]n adult intruder killed or injured in an attempt to steal or destroy property should not be permitted to recover damages" and "[a]n innocent intruder should be denied recovery if carelessness on his part contributed materially to the accident;" and

(6) In cases where neither the landowner nor the innocent intruder had been "demonstrably careless," losses should be borne by the *property owner* because he or she was likely to be in a better position to assess and monitor the hazards.[64]

Under the multi-part test articulated by Posner, "neither blanket permission nor blanket prohibition of spring guns and other methods of using

---

[62] *See* Posner, *Killing or Wounding, supra* note 49. *See also* RICHARD A. POSNER, ECONOMIC ANALYSIS OF LAW 225 (5th ed. 1998) and EPSTEIN ET AL., *supra* note 50, at 43-44.

[63] POSNER, ECONOMIC ANALYSIS, *supra* note 62, at 225. For a particularly scathing indictment of Posner's analysis of the *Bird* case, see Peter Read Teachout, *Worlds Beyond Theory: Toward the Expression of an Integrative Ethic for Self and Culture*, 83 MICH. L. REV. 849, 882 (1985) (reviewing JAMES BOYD WHITE, WHEN WORDS LOSE THEIR MEANING: CONSTITUTIONS AND RECONSTITUTIONS OF LANGUAGE, CHARACTER, AND COMMUNITY (1984)) ("What is most striking about the vision of the world expressed here is that it leaves out entirely the central fact of individual human suffering. What the case 'involved,' Posner insists without apparent embarrassment, is simply the question of which of two economic activities, tulip raising or peahen keeping, would be advantaged by drawing the liability rules one way or another. In his utter preoccupation with the efficiency question . . . he virtually steps over the body of the seriously maimed young man.").

[64] Posner, *Killing or Wounding, supra* note 49, at 214-16.

deadly force to protect property interests is likely to be the rule of liability that minimizes the relevant costs."[65] Decision-makers, in short, must muddle through as best they can.

IV. TOWARDS A LEGAL REGIME FOR DIGITAL COUNTERSTRIKES

But how should policy makers muddle through the issue of digital countermeasures? And does the law-and-economics analysis of spring guns provide any guidance as to the appropriate contours of digital self-help?

Part A examines the extent to which the things that English landowners sought to protect from unauthorized access (i.e., land and game) can be considered analogous to the things that modern-day computer security specialists seek to protect (i.e., computer systems). Part B takes up the question of whether organizations whose computer systems have been attacked should be permitted to strike back against hackers and third-party "zombies."

A. *Land, Game, and Computer Systems*

Before proceeding further, we would be well served to ask a pair of vexing questions: Can computer systems be analogized profitably to real property or animals? And, if so, do the rights associated with property ownership have any relevance to the problem of unauthorized intrusion to computer systems?

As Richard Epstein has observed, the "equipment and facilities" that comprise the Internet "are not by any stretch of the imagination real property."[66] Nonetheless, as Epstein has argued, networked computers can profitably be viewed as "a new form of chattel."[67] And much like eighteenth-century English Parliamentarians expanded the law of theft to protect certain things of value (such as metal fixtures, crops, or animals) traditionally outside the law of larceny,[68] twenty-first century jurists have "breathed new life into the common law" by rendering an ancient doctrine – trespass to chattels – "viable" in the digital world.[69]

As applied to various types of unauthorized access, the operator of a computer system that alleges a claim of trespass to chattels generally must establish that the defendant intentionally "intermeddled" with the plaintiff's

---

[65] *Id.* at 214.

[66] Richard A. Epstein, *Cybertrespass*, 70 U. CHI. L. REV. 73, 76 (2003).

[67] *Id.*

[68] On these Parliamentary efforts, see Bruce P. Smith, *The Presumption of Guilt and the English Law of Theft, 1750-1850*, 23 LAW & HIST. REV. 133 (2005).

[69] Register.com, Inc. v. Verio, Inc., 356 F.3d 393, 436 (2d Cir. 2004).

chattel – in this case, their computer system.[70] The recent case of *Register.com, Inc. v. Verio, Inc.* (2004), decided by the U.S. Court of Appeals for the Second Circuit, is illustrative.[71] In *Register.com*, the defendant was accused of accessing the plaintiff's database of domain names by means of robotic searches. In considering Register.com's theory of trespass to chattels, the appellate court first determined that the plaintiff's computer systems qualified as chattels. The appellate panel then concluded that Verio had likely committed a trespass to chattels by using its robot "to access Register.com's computer systems without authorization to do so, consuming the computer systems' capacity." In concluding that the district court had not abused its discretion in granting preliminary relief on the plaintiff's trespass to chattels claim, the appellate court observed that Register.com's computer systems were "valuable resources of finite capacity," that "unauthorized use of such systems deplete[d] the capacity available to authorized end-users," that unauthorized use "create[d] risks of congestion and overload that may [have] disrupt[ed] Register.com's operations," and that the district court had concluded that the plaintiff would suffer irreparable harm.[72]

On the whole, decisions that have imported property-related concepts into cases involving unauthorized online intrusions have not sat well with scholars of Internet law, who have contended that the "propertization" of the Internet will stifle expression, create a digital "anti-commons," and curtail the public domain.[73] With that said, other scholars have recognized the appeal of property-related metaphors to judges and even the desirability of extending them further.[74] Even Dan Burk, who, in influential article, has

---

[70] RESTATEMENT (SECOND) OF TORTS § 217 (1965). For representative cases, see, for example, *Register.com*, 356 F.3d 393 (affirming preliminary injunction on trespass to chattels theory based on defendant's use of search robots to access plaintiff's database); eBay, Inc. v. Bidder's Edge, Inc., 100 F. Supp. 2d 1058 (N.D. Cal. 2000) (affirming preliminary injunction based on allegation of trespass to chattels in case involving robotic copying of auction-related information); Oyster Software, Inc. v. Forms Processing, Inc., No. C-00-0724, 2001 U.S. Dist. LEXIS 22520 (N.D. Cal. 2001) (refusing to dismiss claim in case involving copying of metatag information by software robot); AOL, Inc. v. LCGM, Inc., 46 F. Supp. 2d 444 (E.D. Va. 1998) (finding liability on trespass to chattels theory in case of spam); and Thrifty-Tel, Inc. v. Bezenek, 54 Cal. Rptr. 2d 468 (Cal. Ct. App. 1996) (applying trespass to chattels theory in case involving unauthorized "cracking" of telephone access codes).

[71] 356 F.3d 393.

[72] *Id.* at 438.

[73] *See, e.g.,* Dan L. Burk, *The Trouble with Trespass*, 4 J. SMALL & EMERGING BUS. L. 27, 53 (2000); Dan Hunter, *Cyberspace as Place and the Tragedy of the Digital Anticommons*, 91 CALIF. L. REV. 439 (2003); Mark A. Lemley, *Place and Cyberspace*, 91 CALIF. L. REV. 521 (2003); James Boyle, *The Public Domain: The Second Enclosure Movement and the Construction of the Public Domain*, 66 LAW & CONTEMP. PROBS. 33 (2003); and Michael J. Madison, *Rights of Access and the Shape of the Internet*, 44 B.C. L. REV. 433, 468 (2003).

[74] *See, e.g.,* David McGowan, *The Trespass Trouble and the Metaphor Muddle*, 1 J.L. ECON. & POL'Y 109 (2005) (suggesting that property metaphors are more apt for the Internet than critics have suggested) and Adam Mossoff, *Spam – Oy, What a Nuisance!*, 19 BERK. TECH. L.J. 625, 664 (2004)

criticized application of the trespass to chattels doctrine to "exotic" and "dubious" computer-related cases, has acknowledged that "[o]ne could easily envision the application of this tort claim to a variety of computer-related situations in which unauthorized users *impaired* the function of a computer system, perhaps by damaging hardware or software, or even by locking the owner out of important computer files."[75]

Indeed, if one accepts that computer systems are a form of property, the malicious propagation of worms and viruses would appear to satisfy the two key elements of a trespass to chattels claim: first, the acts are likely to harm "the possessor's materially valuable interest in the physical condition, quality, or value of the chattel," to deprive the possessor of "the use of the chattel for a substantial time," or to affect "some other legally protected interest of the possessor;" and, second, persons who disseminate malware with the intent of "crashing" a computer system *intend* to intermeddle.[76] Thus, unlike cases where harm is "indirect"[77] or virtually impossible to discern,[78] cases in which entities have had their computer systems damaged or disabled by malware are likely to be in a strong position to prove intentional, direct, and significant harm.[79]

We linger on the tort of trespass to chattels not to suggest that it is a solution to the problem of unauthorized access or, for that matter, a substitute for self-help. To the contrary, companies who decline to report computer security incidents to law enforcement authorities may find the prospects of a trespass-related *civil* suit no more palatable. Yet while conceptualizing unauthorized access to computer systems as a tortious harm to "property" might appear to matter little to those companies disinterested in civil litigation, thinking about such harms as *property*-related harms may provide such companies with latitude to engage in meaningful forms of self-help.

Consider Section 218 of the *Restatement (Second) of Torts*, which describes the prerequisites for a finding of liability on a claim of trespass to

---

(arguing for extension of nuisance law to problem of spam on the grounds that the common law can both "protect legal entitlements, such as the right to use and enjoy one's property without substantial interference, and . . . redress new forms of injury, such as the harmful effects of spam.").

75 Burk, *supra* note 73, at 28-29 (emphasis added).

76 RESTATEMENT (SECOND) OF TORTS § 218 (1965).

77 *See, e.g.,* Intel Corp. v. Hamidi, 71 P.3d 296, 308 (Cal. 2003) ("Intel's theory would expand the tort of trespass to chattels to cover virtually any unconsented-to communication that, solely because of its content, is unwelcome to the recipient or intermediate transmitter.").

78 *See, e.g.,* Ticketmaster, Corp. v. Tickets.com, Inc., 2003 U.S. Dist. LEXIS 6483, No. CV99-7654-HLH(VBKx) (C.D. Cal. Mar. 7, 2003), at *12 ("Since the spider does not cause physical injury to the chattel, there must be some evidence that the use or utility of the computer (or computer network) being 'spiderized' is adversely affected by the use of the spider. No such evidence is presented here.").

79 *See, e.g.,* Physicians Interactive v. Lathian Sys., 2003 U.S. Dist. LEXIS 22868, No. CA-03-1193-A (E.D. Va. Dec. 5. 2003), at *26 (finding that alleged "attacks" by defendants on file servers "were designed to intermeddle with personal property").

chattels. Viewed from one perspective, Section 218 seems to constrict the options of property owners, since it suggests that a party seeking to establish the defendant's "intermeddling" for purposes of a civil suit must establish more than trivial damage. Yet, as David McGowan has observed, comment e to Section 218 also makes clear that the possessors of chattels retain the "privilege to use reasonable force" to protect their possessions – even against those "harmless" interferences for which a formal legal action would be unavailing.[80] In declaring that property owners are privileged to use "reasonable force" to protect their possessions, comment e also refers its readers to Section 77 of the *Restatement*. Section 77 likewise permits property owners to engage in forceful self-help – provided the intrusion is not "privileged," the property owner "reasonably believes that the intrusion can be prevented or terminated only by the force used," and the property owner "has first requested the other to desist and the other has disregarded the request, or the actor reasonably believes that a request will be useless or that substantial harm will be done before it can be made."[81] And, finally, Section 84 authorizes the use of "mechanical devices not threatening death or serious bodily harm" to protect land or chattels "from intrusion" if the use of the device is "reasonably necessary to protect the . . . chattels from intrusion," the use is "reasonable under the circumstances," and "the device is one customarily used for such a purpose, or reasonable care is taken to make its use known to probable intruders."[82]

Considered together, these provisions would appear to provide considerable latitude to property owners to protect their property through various forms of self-help. But do they provide any guidance concerning the permissible scope of electronic counterstrikes designed to protect computer systems from intrusion?

B. *Counterstrikes Against "Hackers" and "Zombies"*

In working through the relevant issues, we might first envision the possibility of four basic types of legal regimes: (1) a regime that subjects counterstrikers to both criminal and civil liability; (2) one that privileges counterstrikers from criminal and civil liability; (3) one that imposes upon them criminal (but not civil) liability; or (4) one that imposes civil (but not criminal) liability. We might next consider two simplified situations: first, where a party has counterattacked against a "hacker" (a party that has inten-

---

[80] RESTATEMENT (SECOND) OF TORTS § 218 cmt. e (1965). *See also* McGowan, *supra* note 74.

[81] RESTATEMENT (SECOND) OF TORTS § 77 (1965).

[82] *Id.* § 84.

tionally engaged in illegal access); and, second, where a party has counter-attacked against a "zombie" (an unwitting third-party intermediary).[83]

A reasonably strong case can be made that counterstrikes against "hackers" – at least when such measures are proportionate to the threat posed – should be privileged. As we have seen, Section 77 of the *Restatement (Second) of Torts* authorizes persons to use "reasonable force" to protect their property in instances where the intrusion is not "privileged," the property owner "reasonably believes that the intrusion can be prevented or terminated only by the force used," and the property owner "reasonably believes that a request will be useless or that substantial harm will be done before it can be made."[84] And Section 84 permits the use of "devices" to accomplish these ends – merely adding the requirement that "the device [be] one customarily used for such a purpose, or reasonable care [be] taken to make its use known to probable intruders."[85] Although it might well be the case that a party that "hacked back" against a network intruder might fall within the language of the CFAA or other statutes, the party would seem to possess a colorable claim – at least under traditional tort principles – that a proportionate counterstrike against a hacker should not expose the counterattacker to either criminal or civil liability.

But how should the law respond to the more difficult problem of counterstrikes against third-party "zombies," who have not engaged in intentional wrongs? As a normative matter, does it make sense for parties that counterstrike against "zombies" to be subjected to criminal and civil liability? With respect to potential criminal liability, a party engaged in digital counterstrikes might seek to invoke the "choice of evils" defense, which excuses certain apparently criminal acts if they are justified by the avoidance of greater harm – though the doctrine's application outside the realm

---

[83] Although my usage of the term "hacker" to refer to persons engaged in unauthorized access by no means exhausts the term's varied meanings in the Internet context, it conforms with the conventions of the popular press. *See* Wikipedia.org, *Hacker*, *available at* http://en.wikipedia.org/wiki/Hacker (last visited Jan. 23, 2005).

[84] *See supra* note 81 and accompanying text. Similarly, Section 3.06(1) of the Model Penal Code ("Use of Force Justifiable for Protection of Property") states that:

> [T]he use of force upon or toward the person of another is justifiable when the actor believes that such force is immediately necessary: (a) to prevent or terminate an unlawful entry or other trespass upon land or a trespass against or the unlawful carrying away of tangible, movable property, provided that such land or movable property is, or is believed by the actor to be, in his possession or in the possession of another person for whose protection he acts . . .

MODEL PENAL CODE § 3.06(1) (1985).

[85] *See supra* note 82 and accompanying text. In turn, Section 3.06(5) of the Model Penal Code ("Use of Device to Protect Property") states that the section's justification extends to devices only if:

> (a) the device is not designed to cause or known to create a substantial risk of causing death or serious bodily injury; and (b) the use of the particular device to protect the property from entry or trespass is reasonable under the circumstances, as the actor believes them to be; and (c) the device is one customarily used for such a purpose or reasonable care is taken to make known to probable intruders the fact that it is used.

MODEL PENAL CODE § 3.06(5) (1985).

of immediate violence to *persons* remains unclear.[86] With respect to possible civil liability, a counterstriker could seek refuge under the doctrine of necessity – a principle, in the words of Professor Epstein, "as old as the doctrine of exclusive ownership itself."[87] As articulated in Section 197 of the *Restatement (Second) of Torts*, the doctrine of necessity states that "[o]ne is privileged to enter or remain on land in the possession of another if it is or reasonably appears to be necessary to prevent serious harm to . . . the actor, or his land or chattels. . . ."[88] Just as a sailor in peril is permitted to dock at another's wharf during a storm – even if damage to the dock might result – the operator of a computer system under siege might be permitted to "trespass" on the system of a third-party "zombie" even if it "damaged" the "zombie" by limiting or slowing its connection to the network.[89]

When confronted by cases in the "real" world, law-and-economics scholars have generally praised the decision of courts to permit parties to invoke the necessity doctrine in cases of intentional trespass – at least where the value to the trespasser is great, the costs of the trespass are modest, and the transactions costs associated with negotiations with the property owner whose property has been entered are high.[90] In the case of a party experiencing a DDoS attack, at least two of these elements would appear to be present: the cost of the incident to the party attacked is great; and the transaction costs of dealing with third-party "zombies" (given the typical case of a rapidly-propagating worm or virus) are likely to be high. Under this formulation of the rule, as long as the costs associated with the intrusion to the systems of third parties were "modest," counterstrikes against third parties would be permitted.

This does not mean, of course, that the costs of such trespasses should be borne by "zombies." As held in *Vincent v. Lake Erie Transportation Co.* (1910), a party that avails itself of the property of another and causes harm

---

[86] Section 3.02 of the Model Penal Code ("Justification Generally: Choice of Evils") states as follows:

> Conduct that the actor believes to be necessary to avoid a harm or evil to himself or to another is justifiable, provided that: (a) the harm or evil sought to be avoided by such conduct is greater than that sought to be prevented by the law defining the offense charged; and (b) neither the Code nor other law defining the offense provides exceptions or defenses dealing with the specific situation involved; and (c) a legislative purpose to exclude the justification claimed does not otherwise plainly appear.

MODEL PENAL CODE § 3.02 (1985).

[87] Richard A. Epstein, *Property and Necessity*, 13 HARV. J. L. PUB. POL'Y 2, 13 (1990) (demonstrating extent to which absolute property rights are qualified by necessity defense).

[88] RESTATEMENT (SECOND) OF TORTS § 197 (1965).

[89] *See* Ploof v. Putnam, 71 A. 188 (Vt. 1908) (remanding to trial court for determination of whether plaintiff could establish necessity of docking during storm).

[90] As Robert Cooter and Thomas Ulen have summarized, "the private-necessity doctrine allows compensated trespass in an emergency" on the grounds that "transaction costs may preclude bargaining." ROBERT COOTER & THOMAS ULEN, LAW AND ECONOMICS 161 (4th ed. 2002).

should be required to pay the costs of the damage.[91] The rule, in short, requires parties to internalize the costs of their actions. If digital counterstrikers accurately calculate the likely damage to themselves and third parties and rationally compare the estimates – assumptions that, admittedly, may be rather heroic given the uncertainties and time pressures involved in online attacks – the damages caused by digital countermeasures taken against third-party "zombies" will presumably be less than the costs borne by the party if it failed to counterstrike.[92]

How might the legal regime that has been outlined above affect the actual behavior of companies operating computer systems, persons interested in spreading malware, and third-party "zombies"? Predicting behavior in this area is perilous, but the following hypotheses seem plausible. The many companies that are currently reluctant to invoke formal law might be encouraged to take more active measures against hackers.[93] Although a hacker who encountered a computer system protected by a digital counterstrike technology might be diverted to a "softer" target or, alternatively, might be spurred to even more malicious ends, these consequences arguably would not arise if the technology were undetectable to the potential wrongdoer.[94] Indeed, like the LoJack car security system, which uses a series of hidden radio transceivers to permit law enforcement authorities to track and recover stolen automobiles, counterattacks that occurred without prior announcement to the hacker might actually reduce (and not simply displace) criminal wrongdoing.[95]

How, in turn, might potential "zombies" act in a legal regime that permitted, for example, counterattackers to limit their bandwidth or otherwise temporarily impair their "zombied" computer systems? As it currently stands, our legal regime provides virtually no incentives for vulnerable "zombies" to take even the most modest and inexpensive measures to pre-

---

[91] 124 N.W.2d 221 (Minn. 1910) (awarding damages to defendant whose dock was damaged by plaintiff's boat during storm). In the words of Judge Posner, "[s]uch liability is appropriate to assure that the rescue is really cost-justified, to encourage dock owners to cooperate with boats in distress, to get the right amount of investment in docks, . . . and, in short, to simulate the market transaction that would have occurred had transaction costs not been prohibitive." POSNER, ECONOMIC ANALYSIS, *supra* note 62, at 90-91.

[92] This also assumes that parties engaging in counterstrikes can be identified and can pay for the damage they cause.

[93] "[T]argets prefer self-help solutions in order to maintain a greater degree of confidentiality . . . than law enforcement typically allows." Mary M. Calkins, *They Shoot Trojan Horses, Don't They? An Economic Analysis of Anti-Hacking Regulatory Models*, 89 GEO. L.J. 171, 197 (2000).

[94] For a useful overview of the phenomenon of diversion, see Koo Hui-Wen & I.P.L. Png, *Private Security: Deterrent or Diversion?*, 14 INT'L REV. L. & ECON. 87 (1994).

[95] *See* Ian Ayres & Steven D. Levitt, *Measuring Positive Externalities from Unobservable Victim Precaution: An Empirical Analysis of Lojack*, 113 Q. J. ECON. 43 (Feb. 1998). Ayres and Levitt found that car owners who install LoJack devices confer positive externalities by making auto theft "riskier and less profitable" and thus reducing auto theft in the aggregate. I am grateful to Richard McAdams for discussing this literature with me.

194   JOURNAL OF LAW, ECONOMICS AND POLICY   [VOL. 1:1

vent their systems from being compromised.[96] Upon initial examination, we might expect a regime that permitted third-party "zombies" to recover damages caused by counterstrikes to be little better. But just as compensation for dock owners provides them with an incentive to help boats in distress, damages payments to third-party "zombies" might encourage them to cooperate actively in responding to network-based attacks.[97] And just as third parties injured by spring guns might be barred from recovering damages if they had been "demonstrably careless," recovery by "zombies" could be barred or reduced in instances where such companies had failed to take reasonable security measures themselves.[98]

CONCLUSION

As this paper has suggested, self-help is alive and well in the Internet age.[99] In this regard, the area of computer security resembles other areas of American law – ranging from repossession, to bail enforcement, to self-defense against threats of immediate bodily harm – where self-help measures remain important.[100] Indeed, our current legal climate in the area of computer security bears certain resemblances to other contexts in which self-help has historically proved appealing, including "frontier" settings where formal legal systems were underdeveloped or non-existent,[101] instances where formal law proved incapable of providing adequate or af-

---

[96] As a leading English network security expert has noted, although "computer users might be happy to spend $100 on anti-virus software to protect *themselves* against attack, they are unlikely to spend even $1 on software to prevent their machines being used to attack Amazon or Microsoft." Anderson, *supra* note 2 (manuscript at 1).

[97] See supra note 91.

[98] *See supra* note 64 and accompanying text.

[99] *See also* Microsoft Corp., Q&A: *Microsoft Establishes Anti-Virus Reward Program*, Nov. 3, 2003, http://www.microsoft.com/presspass/features/2003/nov03/11-05AntiVirusQA.asp and Robert Lemos, *Mozilla Puts Bounty on Bugs*, CNET NEWS.COM, Aug. 2, 2004, *at* http://zdnet.com.com/2100-1105-5293659.html.

[100] For a useful survey of self-help in American law, see Douglas Ivor Brandon et al., *Self-Help: Extrajudicial Rights, Privileges and Remedies in Contemporary American Society*, 37 VAND. L. REV. 845 (1984) (examining role of self-help in self-defense, recovery of property, summary abatement of nuisance, resisting unlawful arrest and excessive force, liquidating damages, and repossessing property).

[101] On vigilante justice in frontier settings, see ROBERT M. SENKEWICZ, VIGILANTES IN GOLD RUSH SAN FRANCISCO (1985).

fordable remedies,[102] and circumstances where potential offenders have proven to be indifferent to the effects of formal legal sanctions.[103]

This is not to suggest that we should accept uncritically the technological, legal, and moral claims of those who advocate the use of counterattacks against those who seek unauthorized access to property. After all, English jurists and Parliamentarians – who devoted roughly a decade to the subject – certainly had no such illusions. Despite the scourge of poachers, the weaknesses of formal law, the failures of "defensive" measures such as fencing and posting land, and the relative cost-effectiveness of spring guns, England's political leaders ultimately decided that private persons could not be trusted to operate spring guns in a socially responsible and socially optimal manner. Network security experts likewise operate in a world of persistent threats, imperfect policing, inadequate defenses, and high costs. But whereas spring guns proved to be "blind, unreasoning, undistinguishing, remorseless engines, [that] sacrificed every thing within their range,"[104] twenty-first century digital counterstrike technologies at least hold out the prospect of counterattacks that are clear-sighted, calculating, discriminating, and – if not remorseful – at least compensable.

---

[102] For example, American landlords in the nineteenth century availed themselves of their right to evict tenants forcibly because civil actions for ejectment were costly, slow, and uncertain. Once American states adopted summary eviction statutes in the late-nineteenth century, the scope of a landlord's permissible self-help against holdover tenants was diminished. *See* JESSE DUKEMINIER & JAMES KRIER, PROPERTY 507-09 (5th ed. 2002).

[103] Thus, John Lott has argued strenuously on behalf of gun ownership as a means of deterring would-be killers from committing murderous acts on the grounds that certain persons who commit homicidal acts seek to maximize the amount of damage they inflict and are indifferent to being punished themselves. *See* JOHN R. LOTT, JR., MORE GUNS, LESS CRIME: UNDERSTANDING CRIME AND GUN CONTROL LAWS (2d ed. 2000).

[104] 13 PARL. DEB. (2d ser.) 1257 (1826).

[16]

VIRTUAL CRIME, VIRTUAL DETERRENCE: A SKEPTICAL VIEW OF SELF-HELP, ARCHITECTURE, AND CIVIL LIABILITY

*Orin S. Kerr**

Recent scholarship in the field of computer crime law reflects a surprising trend: much of it does not concern criminal law or the criminal justice system. According to many scholars, the problem of computer crime can be best addressed by looking beyond criminal law. Cybercrime demands a new model of law enforcement, the thinking goes; the traditional mechanisms of criminal investigation and prosecution cannot deter computer-related crime effectively.[1] The law must turn to alternative approaches that regulate social norms, code, and civil liability to alter incentives *ex ante* without recourse to the criminal justice system.[2]

This essay critiques three of the most prominent proposals to deter computer crime outside of criminal law. The first proposal, self-help, would allow victims of hacking and denial-of-service attacks to defend

* Associate Professor, George Washington University Law School. Thanks to Dan Hunter, Neal Katyal, Doug Lichtman, Dan Markel, Michael O'Neill, and Daniel Solove for their comments on an earlier draft. This essay was prepared for a symposium "Property Rights on the Frontier: The Economics of Self-Defense and Self-Help in Cyberspace" hosted by the *Journal of Law, Economics and Policy*. Thanks to Noah Falk for excellent research assistance, and to the editors of the *Journal of Law, Economics and Policy* for their gracious invitation to speak at the *Journal*'s first symposium.

[1] *See, e.g.,* Michael L. Rustad, *Private Enforcement of Cybercrime on the Electronic Frontier,* 11 S. CAL. INTERDISC. L. J. 63 (2001) (arguing that "criminal law is an inadequate institution of social control against cybercrime," and that there is a "greater role for private 'cybercops' to punish and control cybercrime to close the enforcement gap"); Stevan D. Mitchell & Elizabeth A. Banker, *Private Intrusion Response,* 11 HARV. J. LAW & TECH. 699, 706-708 & fn. 14, 15 (1998) (discussing the need for public private partnerships in the deterrence of computer crimes); Susan W. Brenner, *Toward A Criminal Law for Cyberspace: Distributed Security,* 10 B.U.J. SCI. & TECH. L. 1 (2004) (arguing that cybercrime demands a new model of law enforcement); Nimrod Kozlovski, *Designing Accountable Online Policing, available at* http://islandia.law.yale.edu/isp/digital%20cops/papers/kozlovski_paper.pdf ("The online crime scene introduces complex challenges to law enforcement that inevitably lead to the emergence of a new policing model . . . derive[d] from employing alternative strategies of law enforcement."); AMITAI AVIRAM, *Network Responses to Network Threats: The Evolution Into Private Cyber-Security Associations,* in THE LAW & ECONOMICS OF CYBER-SECURITY (Cambridge University Press; forthcoming 2005); Brent Wible, Note, *A Site Where Hackers Are Welcome: Using Hack-in Contests to Shape Preferences and Deter Computer Crime,* 112 YALE L.J. 1577, 1577 (2003) ("With the failure of traditional law enforcement methods to deal with [the threat of computer crime], computer crime requires a new approach to thinking about deterrence."). *See also infra* notes 3-5.

[2] *See infra* notes 3-5.

themselves by counterattacking and disabling intruders.[3] The concept animating offensive self-help or "hack back" proposals is that private parties may be able to deter and prevent computer crimes through private action more effectively and efficiently than through government action. The second proposal, architecture regulation, was offered recently in an essay by Professor Neal Katyal.[4] Professor Katyal contends that computer crime can be deterred by redesigning the architecture of cyberspace in ways that mirror how architects design physical spaces to deter traditional crime. The third proposal, civil liability, seeks to impose liability on third-party intermediaries such as ISPs for the cost of criminal activity.[5] Although many variations of this proposal exist, my specific interest is on the use of civil liability to encourage ISPs to monitor and deter crime attempted by their subscribers.

This essay offers a skeptical view of the three proposals. I agree that responses to computer crime must look at least in part beyond criminal law. Criminal law addresses only a small piece of the broader puzzle of how to deter misconduct, and that is just as true online as it is offline.[6] At the same

---

[3] *See* Michael E. O'Neill, *Old Crimes in New Bottles: Sanctioning Cybercrime,* 9 GEO. MASON L. REV. 237 (2000); Curtis E. A. Karnow, *Launch on Warning - Aggressive Defense of Computer Systems, available at* http://islandia.law.yale.edu/isp/digital%20cops/papers/karnow_newcops.pdf; Mary M. Calkins, Note, *They Shoot Trojan Horses, Don't They? An Economic Analysis of Anti-Hacking Regulatory Models,* 89 GEO. L.J. 171 (2000); Bruce Smith, *Hacking, Poaching, and Counterattacking,* 1 J.L. ECON. & POL'Y (forthcoming 2005). *Cf.* Eric Talbot Jensen, *Computer Attacks on Critical National Infrastructure: A Use of Force Invoking the Right of Self-Defense,* 38 STAN. J. INT'L L. 207 (2002) (discussing self-help measures under the rules of war).

[4] Neal Kumar Katyal, Essay, *Digital Architecture as Crime Control,* 112 YALE L.J. 2261 (2003).

[5] *See, e.g.,* Doug Lichtman & Eric Posner, *Holding Internet Service Providers Accountable,* SUP. CT. ECON. REV. (forthcoming 2005); Assaf Hamdani, *Who is Liable for Cyberwrongs?,* 87 CORNELL L. REV. 901 (2002); Stephen E. Henderson & Matthew E. Yarborough, *Suing the Insecure?: A Duty of Care in Cyberspace,* 32 N. M.L. REV. 11 (2002); Rustad, *supra* note 1; Neal Kumar Katyal, *Criminal Law in Cyberspace,* 149 U. PA. L. REV. 1009 (2001); Calkins, *supra* note 3, at 219-224; Robin A. Brooks, Note, *Deterring the Spread of Viruses Online: Can Tort Law Tighten the 'Net'?,* 17 REV. LITIG. 343 (1998); David L. Gripman, Comment, *The Doors Are Locked but the Thieves and Vandals Are Still Getting In: A Proposal in Tort to Alleviate Corporate America's Cyber-Crime Problem,* 16 J. MARSHALL J. COMP. & INFO. L. 167 (1997); Michael Rustad & Lori E. Eisenschmidt, *The Commercial Law of Internet Security,* 10 HIGH TECH. L.J. 213 (1995); Susan C. Lyman, *Civil Remedies for the Victims of Computer Viruses,* 21 SW. U.L. REV. 1169, 1172 (1992); Cheryl S. Massingale & A. Faye Borthick, *Risk Allocation for Computer System Security Breaches: Potential Liability for Providers of Computer Services,* 12 W. NEW ENG. L. REV. 167, 185 (1990); Anne Branscomb, *Rogue Computer Programs and Computer Rogues: Tailoring the Punishment to Fit the Crime,* 16 RUTGERS COMPUTER & TECH. L.J. 1, 30-37 (1990); Agranoff, *Curb on Technology: Liability for Failure to Protect Computerized Data Against Unauthorized Access,* 5 SANTA CLARA COMPUTER & HIGH TECH. L.J. 263, 268 (1989).

[6] In the case of traditional crimes, no one would think to argue that criminal law should be the *only* mechanism to prevent crime. No one keeps their doors unlocked at night in the hope that burglars will break in, get caught, and then be prosecuted so as to deter future burglary attempts. Instead, we lock our doors. Conversely, few would argue seriously that there should be no criminal punishment at

time, the three proposals reflect in varying degrees a common conceptual mistake: over reliance on the metaphor of the Internet as a virtual "place." The proposals tend to envision the Internet as a virtual world of cyberspace with virtual streets and virtual management, and use this virtual model to generate assumptions about what kind of legal rules and practices are likely to generate particular results. These assumptions are valid in some circumstances, but they are not valid in many others. As a result, heavy reliance on virtual metaphors risks incorporating assumptions from the physical world that break down when applied to the Internet. When this occurs, virtual metaphors will obscure rather than illuminate the dynamics of computer crime.

This essay argues that responding to computer crime requires confronting the physical reality of what the Internet is and how it works. Both virtual and physical perspectives of the Internet can offer important lessons, but any strategy to deter computer crime must look viable given the physical reality of the network. Strategies that rely too heavily on the virtual metaphors of cyberspace are likely to rely on assumptions drawn from the physical world that do not apply to the Internet; the process of importing concepts from physical space to the virtual world of cyberspace will introduce errors. Over reliance on virtual metaphors will often misrepresent how online crime occurs and thus how it can be deterred. Where virtual metaphors govern, proposals to deter computer crime through civil liability and social norms will prove less effective in practice than they may first appear in theory.

I begin my argument by exploring the tension within Internet law between modeling the Internet using virtual reality and physical reality, with a special emphasis on what this tension means for developing arguments about deterrence and computer crime. The analysis explains that a physical description of the Internet differs dramatically from a virtual description of Internet applications, and argues that any effective model for deterring computer crime must be rooted in the former rather than the latter. In the remaining parts of the paper, I apply this insight to critique the three proposals. I begin with offensive self-help, focusing on Michael O'Neill's article *Old Crime in New Bottles: Sanctioning Cybercrime*; turn next to architecture regulation, focusing on Neal Katyal's essay *Digital Architecture as Crime Control*; and conclude by studying proposals that would impose civil liability on third-party computer operators. In each case, I identify how over reliance on virtual metaphors can frustrate efforts to deter computer crime.

---

all for burglary. We recognize that the criminal justice system offers a marginal deterrent value against burglary and serves important retributive ends as well. The basic regulatory strategy is to combine criminal law with other mechanisms to best deter crime while minimizing other social costs. I submit that this basic approach will likely prove the most effective strategy to deter and punish computer crime, as well.

I. PHYSICAL AND VIRTUAL APPROACHES TO DETERRING COMPUTER
    CRIME

There are two basic ways to model the Internet: from the perspective of physical reality and the perspective of virtual reality.[7] From a virtual perspective, the Internet can be understood as the home of a virtual world of cyberspace that is roughly analogous to the physical world. A user can utilize his keyboard and mouse to go shopping, participate in online communities, and do anything else that he finds online much like he could in the physical world. The Internet is cyberspace, a virtual world with virtual streets and virtual stores, virtual perils and virtual promise that echo the physical world.[8] The physical perspective of the Internet is very different. From a physical perspective, "the Internet" is a name attached to the sprawling and decentralized international network of networks including millions of computer servers and hundreds of millions of miles of cables. The hardware sends, stores, and receives trillions of digits of data every day using a series of common protocols. Many of the computers connected to this network of networks are located outside the United States, along with the majority of its users. Keyboards provide sources of input to the network, and monitors provide destinations for output. From the standpoint of physical reality, the virtual world of cyberspace is just a convenient metaphor. Internet users may decide to use that metaphor to more easily understand particular software applications available via the Internet. But what matters is the physical reality of the network, the actual bits and bytes, rather than the virtual world a user might imagine.

Understanding the distinction between physical and virtual descriptions of the Internet is critical to understand how law can help deter computer crime. The distinction between physical and virtual leads to two basic approaches to deterring cybercrime. From a virtual perspective, the natural starting point for regulating cyberspace is to translate the ways that the law regulates the physical world. If a problem from the physical world carries over into cyberspace, the solution from physical space should be harnessed, modified as necessary, and then applied to cyberspace. In the specific context of computer crime, the virtual perspective suggests that legislatures should study crime prevention strategies that have worked in physical space, and apply a virtual version of that solution to cyberspace. In a sense, computer crime is nothing new: it's just a cyberspace version of old-fashioned physical crime. The switch from physical to virtual may create

---

[7] *See generally* Orin S. Kerr, *The Problem of Perspective in Internet Law*, 91, GEO. L.J. 357 (2003).

[8] *Cf.* Mark A. Lemley, *Place and Cyberspace*, 91 CAL. L. REV. 521, 524 (2003) ("Even if we understand somewhere in the back of our minds that we are not really going anywhere, perhaps when we access the Internet it seems so much like we are in a different physical space that we accept cyberspace as a "real" or physical place.").

some new wrinkles, but the basic problem can draw from solutions already applied in the physical world.

From a physical perspective, computer crime is a different problem and calls for different solutions than you might see from a virtual perspective. The physical perspective teaches that online crimes involve users sending and receiving data in ways that the law seeks to prohibit. Perhaps the data is contraband, such as an image of child pornography. Perhaps the law prohibits the transmission or use of data because particular data is private and belongs to some one else, such as private files exposed by a hacker. Perhaps the data is copyrighted and cannot be distributed without permission. Or perhaps the transmission of data blocks others from being able to access their computers, such as might occur with a denial of service attack. In all of these cases, computer crime law attempts to regulate the transmission of data to avoid identified social harms. To deter computer crime, solutions either must block the transmission by code-based restrictions or else persuade users not to act in ways the law recognizes as harmful.

The distinction between physical and virtual is critical because solutions that appear promising from a virtual perspective might not appear promising from a physical perspective, and vice versa. Consider the example of "broken windows" policing.[9] In the physical world, individuals considering whether to engage in criminal activity often take clues from their physical environment.[10] Visible disorder can undermine law-abiding norms.[11] Tolerance of low-level criminal activity in a neighborhood can signal tolerance of higher-level activity, and may lead to more serious crime. "Broken windows" policing attempts to reverse that process. The visible enforcement of low-level activity signals to wrongdoers that higher level activity will not be tolerated; the hope is that perception of obedience to the law based on observable enforcement of the law helps generate norms of obedience and discourages crime.[12]

Does broken windows policing teach us anything useful about deterring computer crime? From the virtual perspective, the answer might appear to be "yes." Enforcement policies might place a priority on fixing broken "cyber windows," if you will, encouraging the visible enforcement of the law in one region of cyberspace to help generate norms of obedience to law in that region. Visible signs that the law is enforced in one cy-

---

[9] *See generally* GEORGE L. KELLING & CATHERINE M. COLES, FIXING BROKEN WINDOWS: RESTORING ORDER AND REDUCING CRIME IN OUR COMMUNITIES (1996).

[10] *See generally* Robert J. Sampson & Jacqueline Cohen, *Deterrent Effects of the Police on Crime: A Replication and Theoretical Extension,* 22 LAW & SOC'Y REV. 163 (1988).

[11] Dan M. Kahan, *A Colloquium on Community Policing: Reciprocity, Collective Action, and Community Policing,* 90 CAL. L. REV. 1513, 1527-30 (2002).

[12] *See id. But see* BERNARD E. HARCOURT, ILLUSION OF ORDER: THE FALSE PROMISE OF BROKEN WINDOWS POLICING (2001).

berneighborhood might send signals to cybercriminals that they should look elsewhere. From a virtual perspective, it seems plausible to look for ways to signal to potential cybercriminals that the cyber-community will not tolerate criminal activity in a particular corner of cyberspace.[13]

From a physical perspective, however, the answer appears to be "no." The notion of fixing windows in cyberspace makes little sense. Cyberspace is just a metaphor, not an actual place. Applying real-space approaches to "cyberspace" works only if the way that the approach applies to physical space happens to be replicated within the metaphorical understanding of cyberspace. This does not seem to occur in the case of broken windows policing. In the physical world, broken windows policing may work because there is an observable correlation between the visual appearance of a place and whether crime will be tolerated there. Visual appearance communicates information about law enforcement practices, and a potential wrongdoer can factor that into his decision whether to commit an offense.

The same linkage does not apply online. The visual appearance of a "site" on the Internet is merely a string of zeros and ones that the computer has been programmed to send to the user for reassembly and display. The string of zeros and ones does not reflect the social practices, priorities, or condition of the computer or its users. Whether the police pay attention to low-level criminal activity generally will not change the visual appearance of anything. Even if it did, the appearance of a site is known by wrongdoers to be merely a graphic overlay, not a signal of social norms or law enforcement practices. The homepage of a webserver looks the same regardless of whether the server is secure or is riddled with holes. Online intruders get a sense of the security practices used at a potential victim computer not by viewing the homepage of its webserver, but by remotely scanning the computer to determine its software, open ports, and vulnerabilities.[14] The dynamic underlying "broken windows" policing does not seem to apply to crimes involving the transmission of data from computer to computer. As a result, the strategy has little relevance in the context of computer crimes.

This example points to broader lesson about the role of physical and virtual perspectives in the formulation of cybercrime deterrence strategies. While both virtual and physical perspectives of the Internet can offer important lessons, any strategy to deter computer crime must look viable from a physical perspective. Strategies that rely too heavily on the virtual perspective of the Internet are likely to rely on assumptions drawn from the physical world that do not apply to the Internet. The process of importing

[13] *See* Katyal, *supra* note 5, at 1110 (suggesting that an application of the complementarity of crime underlying broken windows policing should lead to the swift and harsh punishment of computer virus authors to avoid copycat crimes).

[14] *See* Ofir Arkin, *Network Scanning Techniques: Understanding How It Is Done, available at* http://www.totse.com/en/hack/introduction_to_hacking/162026.html.

concepts from physical space to the virtual world of cyberspace risks importing too much. It threatens to let virtual metaphors get the best of us, and may point us in directions that do not actually work given the physical reality of the Internet. To ensure effective deterrence, care must be taken to make sure that no unwarranted assumptions are embedded in those strategies when they are transferred to the Internet.

This does not mean that metaphors are never useful, of course.[15] Metaphors harness existing similarities. When a new problem is similar in a relevant way to an old one, metaphors can illuminate how solutions from the old problem might apply to the new. The difficulty arises when one set of similarities generates a metaphor, and the metaphor is then used in other contexts where no relevant similarities exist. Consider e-mail and traditional postal letters. As a communications mechanism, e-mail is akin to traditional postal mail: e-mail is used to send and receive messages much like postal mail. When evaluating legal rules to regulate postal mail as a communications mechanism, it makes sense to invoke the virtual metaphor and begin by considering the legal rules used to regulate postal mail.

But this doesn't mean that snail mail and e-mail always should be treated alike. The fact that they are similar in some ways does not mean that they are identical in every way. For example, the existence of the United States Postal Service to deliver physical letters does not mean a centralized virtual Postal Service is needed to deliver e-mail. The fact that stamps are required to send postal mail doesn't mean stamps are needed to send e-mail. While postal letters and e-mail are alike in some ways, their delivery mechanisms are quite different. We cannot simply declare e-mail the virtual equivalent of physical mail and assume that every legal regulation of the latter should apply to the former. A more nuanced approach is required that looks carefully at the specific ways in which virtual and physical are similar and different.

The remainder of this essay will apply this critique to three sets of proposals that would attempt to deter computer crime outside of criminal law. I will begin with offensive self-help strategies, turn next to architecture regulation, and finish with civil liability for third-party computer operators. In each case, I argue that over reliance on the cyberspace metaphor weakens the analytical framework of the proposals. Excessive use of virtual metaphors creates unwarranted assumptions, and unwarranted assumptions leads to misunderstandings of how the law can deter computer crime.

---

[15] *See generally* Kerr, *supra* note 7, at 389-405 (offering a normative framework for when law should adopt a virtual versus a physical perspective of computers and the Internet).

II. Offensive Self-Help

Should the law permit victims of computer hacking attacks to counter-attack and disable intruders? A number of scholars have suggested that the answer is yes.[16] Professor Michael O'Neill has developed the most prominent proposal.[17] According to Professor O'Neill, traditional mechanisms of criminal investigation and prosecution do not sufficiently deter crime involving the Internet: there are too few cybercops, cybercriminals are too hard to catch, and jurisdictional hurdles often get in the way.[18] As an alternative, O'Neill proposes a regime of offensive self-help, or cyber-vigilantism. Allow victims of computer crimes to hack-back against those that hacked them. The threat of being hacked back will deter the initial round of hacking, O'Neill contends: potential attackers will know that an attack may lead to them being made the next victims, resulting in deterrence akin to a cyber-version of mutual assured destruction.

Professor O'Neill relies explicitly on virtual metaphors to explain and justify his proposal. He writes: "[J]ust as settlers in the American West could not reliably count on the local sheriff to protect them, and instead kept a weapon handy to stymie potential aggressors, Internet users may need to protect themselves."[19] "[C]yberspace is our new frontier,"[20] he adds, and private companies have the virtual firepower to keep "virtual streets"[21] safe. "Just as a homeowner may defend his house, . . . computer companies ought to not only be permitted, but encouraged, to unleash their considerable talents to launch countermeasures against cyber-criminals."[22] O'Neill appears to envision the Internet as a virtual Wild West, with cyber-settlers carrying virtual guns and mounting cyberdefenses against virtual bandits. Just as packing a weapon in the Wild West might deter wrongdoers, so can the threat of a cyberattack deter wrongdoers in cyberspace.

The image is a memorable one, but note the assumption embedded in the virtual metaphor. Use of the virtual metaphor presumes that victims of an attack can find out easily who is attacking them. This was often true in the Wild West, or at least in movies about the Wild West. If Bad Guy wants to attack Good Guy with a six-shooter, he needs to be close enough to see him and have a good chance of hitting him. At that very short dis-

---

[16]   *See supra* note 3. There is a great deal of commentary on a related question of whether the law should allow similar self-help measures by copyright owners to disable computer-facilitated copyright infringement. For the sake of simplicity, however, I will limit my discussion to self-help designed to prevent and deter unauthorized access to computers.

[17]   *See* O'Neill, *supra* note 3.

[18]   *See id.* at 275-77.

[19]   *Id.* at 277.

[20]   *Id.* at 279.

[21]   *Id.*

[22]   *Id.* at 280.

tance, Good Guy can see Bad Guy, too. If Good Guy has the same gun that Bad Guy has and there is no element of surprise, Good Guy and Bad Guy are on equal footing. My sense is that Professor O'Neill's proposal presupposes such a dynamic. Let's assume that Bad Guy is a rational actor. He will decide to kill Bad Guy if the benefit from attacking good guy exceeds the harm to himself. To throw in some unnecessary math, we can say that Bad Guy will attack when

(Chance initial attack will succeed) * (Benefit to Bad Guy if initial attack succeeds) > (Chance Good guy will attempt a counterattack) * (chance counterattack will succeed) * (harm to Bad Guy if counterattack succeeds)

My sense is that O'Neill assumes that the chance that the counter attack will succeed is on par with the chance that the initial attack will succeed. The deterrence dynamic O'Neill seeks to harness is based on a type of ricochet effect; the likelihood that an attack will lead to a successful counterattack deters the initial attack.

Applying this regime to the Internet creates a significant problem, however. It is very easy to disguise the source of an Internet attack. Internet packets do not indicate their original source. Rather, they indicate the source of their most immediate hop. Imagine I have an account from computer *A*, and that I want to attack computer *D*. I will direct my attack from computer *A* to computer *B*, from *B* to computer *C*, and from *C* to computer *D*. The victim at computer *D* will have no idea that the attack is originating at *A*. He will see an attack coming from computer *C*. Further, the use of a proxy server or anonymizer can easily disguise the actual source of attack. These services route traffic for other computers, and make it appear to a downstream victim as if the attack were coming from a different source.

As a result, the chance that a victim of a cyber attack can quickly and accurately identify where the attack originates is quite small. By corollary, the chance that an initial attacker would be identified by his victim and could be attacked back successfully is also quite small. Further, if the law actually encouraged victims of computer crime to attack back at their attackers, it would create an obvious incentive for attackers to be extra careful to disguise their location or use someone else's computer to launch the attack. In this environment, rules encouraging offensive self-help will not deter online attacks. A reasonably knowledgeable cracker can be confident that he can attack all day with little chance of being hit back. The assumption that an attacker can be identified and targeted may have been true in the Wild West, but tends not to be true for an Internet attack.

Legalizing self-help would also encourage foul play designed to harness the new privileges. One possibility is the bankshot attack: If I want a computer to be attacked, I can route attacks through that one computer towards a series of victims, and then wait for the victims to attack back at that computer because they believe the computer is the source of the attack. By harnessing the ability to disguise the origin of attack, a wrongdoer can get one innocent party to attack another. Indeed, any wrongdoer can act as a catalyst to a chain reaction of hacking back and forth among innocent parties. Imagine that I don't like two businesses, *A* and *B*. I can launch a denial-of-service attack at the computers of *A* disguised to look like it originates from the computers at *B*. The incentives of self-help will do the rest. *A* will defend itself by launching a counterattack at *B*'s computers. *B*, thinking it is under attack from *A*, will then launch an attack back at *A*. *A* will respond back at *B*; *B* back at *A*; and so on. As these examples suggest, basing a self-help strategy on the virtual model of the Wild West does not reflect a realistic picture of the Internet. Self-help in cyberspace would almost certainly lead to more computer misuse, not less.

To be fair, it is possible to generate a self-help proposal that does not rely on virtual metaphors. A proponent of the idea could restate it using physical rather than virtual descriptions of the Internet. In my experience, however, the persuasiveness of the self-help argument draws heavily on the virtual metaphor. The model of an online counterattack as a "virtual punch" or "virtual bullet" situates the proposal in a familiar physical setting, and supports the necessary but false assumption that an online victim can successfully disable his attacker much like a physical victim can disable a physical attacker. The virtual model incorporates assumptions that hold in the physical world but tends to hide the very different dynamics at work in the case of Internet attacks.

III. ARCHITECTURE REGULATION

Over reliance on virtual metaphors also blunts the effectiveness of architectural approaches to computer crime. In an interesting essay entitled *Digital Architecture as Crime Control,* Professor Neal Katyal contends that one answer to the problem of computer crime is to apply realspace notions of architecture regulation to cyberspace.[23] Katyal reasons that the "metaphorical synergy" between physical space and cyberspace justifies "a new generation of work" in which scholars apply "the lessons of realspace study . . . to the cybernetic realm."[24] Professor Katyal notes that in the physical world, architects can help deter crime by designing open and well-lit spaces,[25] by fostering notions of territoriality that signal stewardship of property,[26] and by fostering a sense of community.[27] Katyal proposes "reverse-engineering the realspace analysis of architecture . . . to cyber-

---

[23] Katyal, *supra* note 4.
[24] *Id.* at 2261.
[25] *Id.* at 2264-67.
[26] *See id.* at 2268-72.
[27] *See id.* at 2272-79.

space"[28] to "help develop the types of digital bricks and mortar that can both reduce crime and build community" online.[29] If architecture regulation helps prevent crime in physical space, Katyal suggests, it also can help prevent crime in cyberspace.

Katyal relies heavily on virtual metaphors to frame his proposals. He suggests that the very idea of distinguishing between real space and cyberspace has a limited future: "the divide between realspace and cyberspace [is] erod[ing],"[30] Katyal contends. "With wireless networking, omnipresent cameras, and ubiquitous access to data, these two realms are heading toward merger."[31] According to Professor Katyal, architectural concepts "offer a vantage point from which to view this coming collision"[32] between real space and cyberspace.

But does the architectural approach shed light on deterring computer crime? An important difficulty lurks within Katyal's approach. Architecture can deter crime in physical space because architecture defines the properties of the space. Physical space follows immutable rules of physics; by changing the space, architects can change the likelihood that an attempted criminal act in that space will succeed and communicate that to potential perpetrators of criminal activity *ex ante*. Cyberspace is only a metaphor, however. It offers a way to understand the experience of using some Internet applications, but does not create an environment with a universal set of rules that govern all interactions with particular people or things. Any perception of "cyberspace" generally rests on a superficial visual facade over the real network, and a typical cybercriminal will be focused on the real network rather than the facade.

The fact that cyberspace is only a metaphor makes it difficult for architectural insights to advance the debate over strategies to deter computer crime. Users' impressions of the virtual metaphor play little to no role in their decisions to engage in misconduct. In all but a few cases, a potential perpetrator of a computer crime does not enter a "space" that signals the likelihood that a crime would be detected, or that a crime would succeed.[33] Cybercriminals tend to focus on the physical perspective, not virtual ones. They want to hack the network to get the machine to send and receive the information they want. Their focus is code, not the visual overlay. As a result, efforts to deter crime by influencing users' perceptions of the properties of cyberspace will tend to have little effect on computer crime.

I think we can see these difficulties in Professor Katyal's attempt to explain why architectural insights should trigger a new generation of think-

---

[28] *Id.* at 2288.

[29] Katyal, *supra* note 4, at 2289.

[30] *Id.* at 2262.

[31] *Id.*

[32] *Id.*

[33] Internet chat rooms are one obvious exception.

ing about cybercrime deterrence. Although Katyal's proposals are described as architectural, most have only a tenuous connection to architectural concepts. The inherent difficulty of architecting a metaphor encourages attention to be focused elsewhere. Consider the case of "natural surveillance" design principles. In the physical world, architects can design spaces to be well-lit and open; this raises the chances of detection, raises the cost of crime, and therefore helps deter that crime. Katyal's attempt to apply this to cyberspace leads him to conclude that open source software is preferable to closed source software.[34] More people can see the code underlying open source programs, Katyal notes; the code is "open." According to Katyal, the principles of natural surveillance teach that greater exposure facilitates greater attention, and greater attention to code among computer security experts can lead to the identification and correction of security defects.[35] As a result, open source software should lead to more secure code than closed source software.

While it may be right that open source software tends to have fewer defects than closed source software – the technical community generally believes this, and I have no reason to disagree – this insight is not related to natural surveillance. Natural surveillance can be used to deter crime by fostering a sense among potential offenders that an attempted crime is unlikely to succeed; a space is "open" in the sense that it any conduct can be observed by other people who can report the crime. Natural surveillance increases the chance of detection, raising the cost of crime to the wrongdoer. Debates about open source software concern a different question. In those debates, the issue is how to create incentives for software designers to identify and correct security vulnerabilities. The goal is not to dissuade attempted wrongdoing based on fear of detection, but to make code impervious to attack when wrongdoing occurs. Software is "open" not in the sense of being visible to wrongdoers, but in the sense that programmers can obtain copies to review for defects. Despite the superficial connection between the two, natural surveillance principles do not appear to relate to or shed light on the open source debate.

A similar difficulty exists with Katyal's views of how notions of territoriality should impact Internet design. Katyal explains that real space architects can design space to foster a sense of territoriality and responsibility for enclosed and private regions. The use of archways and open gates can create a sense of ownership and private property that can encourage others to stay away.[36] By controlling how people perceive whether there are welcome in particular spaces, architecture can help determine the likelihood that crime will occur there. Katyal contends that cyberspace architects can apply this principle to the Internet by designing systems that facilitate

---

[34] *See id.* at 2264-65.

[35] *See id.*

[36] *See* Neal Kumar Katyal, *Architecture as Crime Control*, 111 YALE L.J. 1039, 1058-59 (2002).

traceability. He focuses on the strengths and limitations of different privacy rules and practices, ranging from logging IP addresses to allowing content owners to subpoena ISPs for subscriber information.

Whatever the merits of these different rules and practices, however, the connection between them and realspace notions of territoriality is indirect at best. Territoriality rests on the perception that a space is someone's property; traceability rests on the idea that it should be possible to connect an individual's conduct to their person. The former deals with shaping attitudes about ownership and property rights *ex ante*; the latter concerns investigating crime *ex post*. To be fair, the two share a common theme of responsibility. In addition, traceability *ex post* can create disincentives to commit crime *ex ante*. At the same time, the fact that territoriality can be used in realspace design does not appear to shed light on the complex tradeoffs among different privacy rules and practices.[37] The connection is too indirect for the former to generate useful insights about the latter.

Finally, Katyal's proposals on community building appear to suffer from the same difficulty. In physical space, architects can design space to facilitate easy interaction and encourage a sense of community and common identity. They can put houses close together, and use public parks as common meeting places. According to Katyal, applying this insight to the Internet suggests that we should embrace (within limits) the end-to-end principle of network design.[38] The end-to-end argument is that the brains of a network operation should be at the ends of the network, rather than the middle; the network should be open to all types of different traffic and let the applications at the end point figure out what to do with them.

Lawrence Lessig and Mark Lemley have argued powerfully that end-to-end design is an important part of the Internet's architecture, and that facilitating future innovation depends on it.[39] They explain that end-to-end design ensures that the network remains open to technological change because the network does not discriminate among old and new types of communications. Katyal contends that the interest in community building also

---

[37] This is not to say that territoriality is irrelevant. Code-based restrictions can create a sense of territoriality, and I have argued elsewhere that such restrictions should be used to draw the line between legality and illegality in the case of unauthorized access statutes. *See* Orin S. Kerr, *Cybercrime's Scope: Interpreting "Access" and "Authorization" in Computer Misuse Statutes*, 78 N.Y.U. L. REV. 1596 (2003).

[38] The end-to-end principle has been latent in the design of the Internet since its inception but was first explored systematically by Jerome Saltzer, David Reed, and David Clark in 1981. *See* Jerome H. Saltzer, David P. Reed, and David D. Clark, *End-to-End Arguments in System Design*, Second International Conference on Distributed Computing Systems (April 8-10, 1981) pages 509-512.

[39] *See* Mark A. Lemley & Lawrence Lessig, *The End Of End-To-End: Preserving The Architecture Of The Internet In The Broadband Era*, 48 U.C.L.A. L. REV. 925, 930-33 (2001). *See also* LAWRENCE LESSIG, THE FUTURE OF IDEAS: THE FATE OF THE COMMONS IN A CONNECTED WORLD 120-22 (1st ed. 2001).

supports end-to-end design.[40] An architect of the Internet would want easy interaction and reciprocity among computers much like a traditional architect would value easy interaction and reciprocity among people in physical space.[41] Because end-to-end facilitates interoperability among programs, the architectural insights of community building suggest the need for end-to-end design.[42]

The difficulty with this analogy is that computers are not people, and the comparison rests on attributes that humans have but Internet applications don't. Reciprocity and interaction can deter crime in physical space because community building creates a notion of shared responsibility. Shared responsibility fosters a willingness to look out for and respond to criminal activity. Reciprocity and interaction among computers generally is a good thing, but it is not clear how it relates to deterrence. Computers do not feel responsibility; they only look out for crime if they are programmed to do so. If there is a connection between end-to-end design and deterring computer crime, it is left unexplained.

To be clear, I share many of Professor Katyal's instincts on the merits. I share his sense that open source has advantages over closed source software, his interest in accountability, and his general agreement with end-to-end design. But labels matter, I think, and in this context architectural labels appear to hide the key questions rather than expose them. The core difficulty is that if the architectural approach is applied uncritically, any proposal can be justified as the application of one or more architectural theories. Every proposal opens law or code to more scrutiny, less scrutiny, or both. Under the architectural approach, however, any proposal that opens law or code to more scrutiny and interaction can be justified as an application of natural surveillance or community building principles. Conversely, any proposal that leads to law or code being less scrutinized can be justified as an application of territoriality principles. The virtual metaphor of cyberspace architecture is too flexible to be of much help in the design of strategies to deter computer crime.

IV. THIRD-PARTY CIVIL LIABILITY

Over reliance on virtual metaphors also undergirds a number of proposals to impose civil liability on third-parties for the costs of criminal activity. Here my critique is relatively narrow and cautious, in part because the literature is extensive and diverse. Scholarly discussion of third-party civil liability for computer crime dates back to the 1970s, and the relevant

---

[40] *See* Katyal, *Digital Architecture, supra* note 4, at 2272-73.

[41] *See id.* at 2273 ("Generally speaking, both online and offline, open networks for communication and transportation promote growth, opportunity, and interconnectivity.").

[42] *See id.*

body of work includes dozens of different proposals.[43] For the sake of simplicity, I will focus on just one subset of this literature: ISP liability for subscriber misconduct. In recent years, a number of scholars have explored whether Reinier Kraakman's insights about the benefits of third-party enforcement can be applied to ISPs.[44] ISPs may be better equipped to deter crime than public law enforcement, the thinking goes. ISPs can monitor their subscribers for signs that they are engaging in computer hacking or distributing viruses, and then disable the accounts or take other action to block the misconduct.[45] By imposing liability on ISPs for the wrongs of their subscribers, the law may be able to create incentives for ISPs to deter the subscribers' criminal activity.

My interest in these proposals concerns the assumptions they make about the powers and capacities of ISPs. The proposals tend to assume that ISPs can monitor and control their property much like a physical property owner can monitor and control physical property. In effect, each computer is like a small patch of cyberspace: its owner should be able to see what is going on in that area of cyberspace much like an employer can watch what is going on in the workplace. The owner can also control what he sees and take action to address problems and eliminate sources of wrongdoing. ISPs can act like chaperones at a high school dance, ferreting out untoward conduct and requiring the offenders to leave.[46] Or perhaps ISPs can develop hacker profiles of characteristic hacker activity; when an account is used in a way common to what a hacker would do, the ISP can study that account closely for signs of illegal activity.[47] The common theme is that computer owners can know and control what is happening within their networks; civil liability can lead to less crime because computer owners have the power (and, with civil liability, the incentive) to minimize criminal activity.

But is this assumption valid? There are good reasons to think the answer is "no." In the context of physical space, third-party monitoring generally refers to visual observation. Visual observation can provide a remarkably efficient surveillance tool to identify wrongdoing. A chaperone

---

[43] *See supra* note 5. For an early article on the role of civil liability see Susan Nycum, *Liability for Malfunction of a Computer Program*, 7 RUTGERS COMPUTER & TECH. L.J. 1, 1-22 (1979) (considering the prospect of civil liability for creators of software programs).

[44] *See* Reinier Kraakman, *Gatekeepers: The Anatomy of a Third Party Enforcement Strategy*, 2 J.L. ECON. & ORG. 53, 100-101 (1986). For applications of Kraakman's idea to ISP monitoring, *see, e.g.*, Katyal, *supra* note 5, at 1095-97; Hamdani, *supra* note 5, at 910-12; O'Neill, *supra* note 3, at 282-84.

[45] *See* Posner & Lichtman, *supra* note 5, at 18-20; Katyal, *supra* note 4 at 2284-85; O'Neill, *supra* note 3, at 282-84.

[46] *See* O'Neill, *supra* note 3, at 283-84. *See* Katyal, *Criminal Law in Cyberspace*, *supra* note 5, at 1096.

[47] *See* Katyal, *supra* note 5, at 1096 ("ISPs could also develop sophisticated hacker profiles that permit them to survey large numbers of users and pick out those who look suspicious because they repeatedly try to enter certain sites.").

at a high school dance can look at the dancers and easily tell if they are acting inappropriately. Visual observation is powerful; our eyes are trained to identify subtle patterns and reach quick conclusions. When proponents of ISP liability discuss ISP monitoring, they tend to draw from our instinct that computer monitoring must be something like visual monitoring. The word "monitoring" generally is used in an abstract way to suggest a virtual form of visual observation.

The virtual metaphor papers over the technical details, however, and those technical details indicate important limitations on ISP abilities. When you look more carefully at the technical problems, a different picture of ISP abilities emerges. Most obviously, ISPs cannot actually "see" accounts. They can only monitor accounts in ways that computer code allows, and that monitoring typically involves some form of wiretapping. Consider rules of liability that would encourage ISPs to determine when a customer is engaging in wrongdoing. How can an ISP know what a customer is doing? The most obvious approach would be to wiretap the customer's account; the ISP could install a surveillance device that taps into and records the user's line of traffic. As a technical matter, however, it is quite difficult to go from a stream of Internet traffic to a conclusion that a particular person was responsible for particular conduct. The data stream does not tell you who is using the account, or in what context. The ISP may be able to identify whether a user's account sent out a particular piece of malicious code, but it lacks the ready means to identify who sent it, or whether it was sent knowingly or unknowingly.

Unless an ISP wants to devote a full-time employee to following the conduct of a few accounts – quite a costly proposition given that ISPs can have millions of customers – the most viable monitoring tactic is "dumb" monitoring that can only look for particular bits and bytes of known code or trends in usage. Dumb monitoring has a high error rate, however, and is relatively easy to defeat. Consider our experience with spam filters. Spam filters monitor and attempt to identify incoming spam in much the same way that an ISP might try to monitor outgoing communications to identify malicious code. As anyone with an e-mail account will attest, spam filters never work perfectly: they only detect a proportion of spam, and occasionally block mail that is not spam. Ease of circumvention is also critical. If a person knows his ISP is monitoring his outgoing traffic to look for malicious code, he can take simple steps to ensure that his code evades the monitoring. He can encrypt the code, or send it in parts, effectively defeating the ISP's filters. In short, comprehensive ISP monitoring appears to be extremely difficult, even putting aside the very important privacy questions it raises. ISPs can have hundreds of thousands or even millions of customers; it is very difficult and time consuming for an ISP to watch just one or two customers in a comprehensive way; and it is easy for any customer to circumvent or defeat ISP monitoring.

Even proposals not reliant on virtual metaphors can be weakened by lack of attention to technical detail, leading to an unwarranted confidence in ISP monitoring abilities. For example, Doug Lichtman and Eric Posner suggest that ISPs may be able to program their computers to create a profile for each user, and then regularly compare that profile to usage patterns.[48] They write:

> [An] ISP can detect criminal behavior by analyzing patterns of use, much as a bank can detect credit card theft by monitoring a customer's pattern of purchases. Some patterns of use are intrinsically suspicious, for instance a continuous stream of communications from a home user. Other patterns are suspicious because they represent a radical departure from the user's ordinary behavior. If an ISP programs its computers to create a profile for each user, and then regularly compares the user's current patterns with that historic profile, the ISP should be able to detect this genre of unauthorized usage and intervene.[49]

While this may sound promising at first, it is worth pointing out the major differences between credit card account monitoring and the kind of ISP monitoring Lichtman and Posner suggest. Credit cards are used to purchase goods and services, and sellers must be registered and report every purchase immediately. Patterns of misuse are easy to identify; a credit card thief typically will attempt to run up as many purchases as the card will handle before a purchase is rejected. An attempt to max out the card will invite suspicion, and it is easy to program a computer to detect when that attempt occurs.

But what are the similar patterns for detecting criminal behavior in the case of an Internet account? Computers connected to the Internet can be used in an infinite number of ways to do an infinite number of things. The diverse range of Internet applications and uses for them makes it difficult (if not impossible) to identify a reliable marker that correlates with criminal activity. Lichtman and Posner suggest that a continuous stream of communications from a home user could signal criminality. But a continuous stream of communications could mean many things. Perhaps the user is merely uploading a large file; perhaps he is using a peer-to-peer networks to distribute files (whether copyrighted or not); perhaps the user has installed software allowing his computer to host Internet relay chat channels; perhaps he is sending e-mails with very large attachments. The transfer of data from a home user does not correlate sufficiently closely with criminal activity to warrant ISP investigation.

These difficulties do not mean that civil liability on third-party providers is necessarily a bad idea. But I think they provide reason for caution. Before the law adopts such a strategy, care should be taken to ensure that they do not rest in part on assumptions carried over from physical world dynamics that may not apply to the Internet.

---

[48]   *See* Lichtman & Posner, *supra* note 5, at 18.

[49]   *Id.*

CONCLUSION

The cyberspace metaphor is a powerful tool. It provides insights that help us understand our online interactions and their social meaning. At the same time, reliance on the virtual metaphor of cyberspace carries considerable dangers. At its worst, the virtual metaphor blinds us to how the Internet works; it substitutes metaphors from physical space instead of the reality of the Internet's dynamics. Deterring computer crime requires more focus on the reality of the network and less on metaphors of virtual worlds. A focus on the physical perspective of the Internet can ensure that concepts of deterrence that sound plausible in theory are also realistic in practice.

Name Index